BRIEFING and ARGUING
FEDERAL APPEALS

WITH AN APPENDIX OF
LATE AUTHORITIES
INCLUDING REFERENCES
TO THE
SUPREME COURT'S
1967 RULES

FREDERICK BERNAYS WIENER
of the District of Columbia Bar

FOREWORD BY THE LATE MR. JUSTICE MINTON

THE BUREAU OF NATIONAL AFFAIRS, INC.   ●   WASHINGTON, D. C.

Copyright 1967

THE BUREAU OF NATIONAL AFFAIRS, INC.
WASHINGTON, D. C.
Second Printing April 1973

PRINTED IN THE UNITED STATES OF AMERICA

Library of Congress Catalog Card Number: 61-10553

FOR

DORIS

Best friend and most perceptive critic

FOREWORD

To get into court and to maintain your right to be there is the object of all pleading and is as important in an appellate court as in a trial court.

In the courts of the United States with which this book deals, one is seldom thrown out of court because of poor pleading. If the jurisdictional facts are there, the court will consider your case. Nevertheless the lawyer will be well advised to pay careful attention to his pleading, since that is his first introduction to the court. A case well pleaded is a case half argued.

In cases on appellate review there are, in addition to pleading, the problems of briefing and oral argument. A brief should be *brief* and concise, while at the same time it is elaborating in written form the propositions laid out in your pleading. Skill in presentation and in arguing those propositions, first in writing and then on your feet, will challenge and command the attention of the court.

This book is a guide to handling of cases on appeal in the Federal courts by one who is eminently qualified to instruct and direct in this field. The author is a distinguished and able advocate at the bar of the Supreme Court of the United States with wide experience in appellate work, stemming from his position as a former Assistant to the Solicitor General of the United States and then from an extensive private practice.

SHERMAN MINTON

ACKNOWLEDGMENTS

"No man is an island," and therefore even one's most personal, individualistic, and single-handed productions necessarily reflect the impact of others.

This book, now in a revised version, is no exception. In the remarks affixed to the earlier edition—written just eleven years ago this month—I listed the many kind friends to whom I was then indebted, some named, others necessarily nameless. Those acknowledgments assuredly carry over into the present volume.

On this occasion, also, my thanks for help and, above all, for additional insights into the subject-matter, are due many persons. Again there are many members of the bench who should not be more particularly identified, but who have continued to shape my thinking and approaches in the field of appellate practice.

And this time, far more than before, I owe a genuine debt to the many doughty opponents whom I have faced in appellate courts over the last ten years. Not infrequently, as indeed the pages that follow bear witness, I did not fully approve of all of their techniques in particular instances. But their talents and resourcefulness have called forth on my part the best that I could muster, and for that I am truly grateful.

And now it is a particular pleasure to express my deep appreciation to named individuals:

To the Hon. Sherman Minton, Associate Justice of the Supreme Court of the United States, Retired, for his kindness in contributing the Foreword.

To the judges, listed in Chapter II, who were good enough to answer my questions regarding the operating methods of their several courts.

To Saul Gordon, Esq., of the New York Bar, my colleague in some uphill battles, for suggesting many helpful revisions of the earlier text.

To my wife, Doris Merchant Wiener, not for reading the manuscript—that, after all, was a chore she could hardly avoid—but for the unerring critical sense that she brought to bear upon it.

To Charles J. Alexander, Esq., of the District of Columbia Bar, for checking every citation. (He volunteered for that detail; I didn't dare request him to assume such drudgery, however necessary.)

To my secretary, Mrs. Hazel Shadix Whitehead, for typing the manuscript.

To the editors of the *American Bar Association Journal*, for permission to reprint a chapter that first appeared in their pages.

And, not least, to the editorial staff of BNA, Incorporated, for assistance in seeing the book through the press, and for the numerous succulent lunches that they contributed in the process.

F. B. W.

Washington, D. C.,
February 1961

PREFACE TO 1967 REPRINTING

The appendix is limited to an enumeration and discussion of late authorities that contradict, modify, or render obsolete statements now appearing in the text and footnotes. Authorities merely additional to those already cited or presenting slight variants on the instances already adduced have not been included, as this volume is neither a revision nor a new edition of what was published in 1961.

It is suggested that the appendix be considered and used as a pocket supplement to the basic text, i.e., the appendix should be examined as a matter of invariable routine in connection with every portion of the text.

F. B. W.

Washington, D. C.,
August 1967

TABLE OF CONTENTS

SECOND PART. BRIEFING THE APPEAL

CHAPTER III. ESSENTIALS OF AN EFFECTIVE APPELLATE BRIEF   37

THIRD PART. ARGUING THE APPEAL

CHAPTER VI. ESSENTIALS OF AN EFFECTIVE ORAL ARGUMENT 277

CHAPTER VII. SUGGESTIONS FOR PREPARATION FOR ORAL ARGUMENT 303

FIFTH PART. SOME ILLUSTRATIVE EXAMPLES

CHAPTER XII. USE OF THE STATEMENT OF FACTS TO ADVANCE ONE'S CASE: SUCCESSIVE BRIEFS IN THE SAME LAWSUIT 397

CHAPTER XIII. SUCCESSFUL PETITIONS FOR REHEARING 422

FACTORS CONDITIONING THE APPEAL

CHAPTER I

THE IMPORTANCE OF APPELLATE ADVOCACY

Section 1. Scope of the book.—This book tells how to brief and how to argue a Federal case on appeal. Its primary purpose is to explain to the lawyer how he can best persuade a Federal appellate court to decide a case in his favor. It is neither a practice manual nor a text on Federal appellate procedure, being written on the assumption that all the procedural steps necessary to perfect the appeal have been or will be timely taken. Consequently this book deals with problems that are common to appeals in whatever Federal court they may be presented.

Many of the principles defined and discussed herein are applicable also to the argument, oral and written, of questions of fact and law presented and heard in Federal trial courts. The task of presenting facts and law effectively, the psychology of persuasion, the requirements of candor and accuracy—these are matters common to forensic effort in every courtroom, at every stage of a litigated proceeding.[1]

Section 2. Scope of this revision.—The first version of the present work, entitled *Effective Appellate Advocacy*, was published in 1950.[2] The present edition differs from the earlier one in three respects.

---

[1] "Every judge would wish that the foregoing advice [excerpts from Sections 96 (An effective opening) and 97 (Clear statement of facts)] were memorized and carried out by every lawyer, not only in arguing appeals but also in presenting matters at *nisi prius*. In fact a great deal of the book contains material that would be useful to lawyers in arguing matters in trial courts, although the title of the book modestly purports to limit its material to work in the appellate courts." Review of the first edition by Judge Alexander Holtzoff, 39 Geo. L. J. 356, 357.

[2] See reviews by Judge Charles Fahy [U. S. Circuit Judge, D. C. Circuit], 3 J. Legal Educ. 471; Judge Alexander Holtzoff [U. S. District Judge, District of Columbia], 39 Geo. L. J. 356; William D. Mitchell [a former Attorney General and Solicitor General of the U. S.], 64 Harv. L. Rev. 350; Owen Rall [of the Chicago Bar], 36 A.B.A.J. 769; C. Brewster Rhoads [of the Philadelphia Bar], 99 U. of Pa. L. Rev. 261; Chief Justice Arthur T. Vanderbilt [Supreme Court of New Jersey], 25 N.Y.U.L. Rev. 933; Paul Ware [of the Chicago Bar], 45 Ill. L. Rev. 531.

(a) *Expansion and Modernization.* The basic features of
the original version have been preserved, and many, many portions have been repeated verbatim. But every passage has been
carefully studied with a view to revision wherever necessary,
whether by way of modernization in order to supply references to
later decisions and later statutes and to add more recent examples;
or through change of emphasis; or, in a number of significant particulars, by change of substance in the light of further experience.

In the process, the original text has been substantially expanded, and a considerable number of additional topics have been
included, in connection with both briefs and oral arguments.
Moreover, the former section on rehearings has been expanded
into a full chapter, and an entirely new chapter, discussing
whether different counsel should be brought in on appeal, has
been added.

(b) *Limitation to Federal Appeals.* For reasons that seemed
sound to me—and are acceptable to the publisher—this revision
has been limited to appeals in the Federal courts. References to
the practice in the specialized Federal appellate courts have been
added. But of course, as will indeed be obvious, the teachings ex-
pounded below are fully applicable, in every substantial particular, to appeals in State courts.

(c) *Illustrative Examples.* The illustrative materials are
now restricted to three subjects: Comparative examples of a Statement of Facts from successive briefs in the same litigation, to illustrate how such a statement can be framed to advance one's case;
two successful petitions for rehearing, one in the Supreme Court
of the United States and one in a United States Court of Appeals;
and the annotated transcript of an oral argument.

On occasion, there will be references to some of the illustrative materials found in *Effective Appellate Advocacy.* But this
should not occasion undue inconvenience. The earlier version is
available in many libraries, and moreover all of the briefs therein
that are referred to below were filed in the Supreme Court of the
United States. Thus they are widely available for examination.
Those printed briefs are distributed, by order of the Court, to
about 20 bar association libraries and law schools all over the country, while about 40 additional libraries receive, by subscription,
additional copies of such briefs on microfilm and microcards. The
printed records in Supreme Court cases are similarly distributed.

Section 3. Importance of appellate advocacy.—Counsel defeated in the trial court—the licked lawyer—is recognized as having two inalienable rights: (1) he may go down to the inn at the county seat, or to his club in town, and cuss the court and/or jury; [3] and (2) he can take an appeal. The shelves of American law libraries, which groan under the constantly accumulating load of reports of decisions in appealed cases, are living proof that the second right has been exercised times without number.

Appeals are therefore important, whether one lawyer seeks on behalf of the appellant to undo the great injustice done his client at the trial, or whether another lawyer, on behalf of the appellee, strives to support the judgment or decree so justly entered in the court of first instance. And, for the same reason, effective appellate advocacy, which is the technique (or, if one prefers, the art) of effectively persuading appellate courts to decide in one's favor, is likewise important.

Once in the appellate court, the lawyer is addressing a tribunal that, individually and collectively, is seeking to do substantial justice. He will be writing and speaking to judges fired by a desire to reach a just result, who in consequence are sensitive to the equities of the particular case.[4] But they must necessarily rely on the opposing advocates to make them aware of those equities, and to point out the facts of record and the applicable rules of law that compel a just decision.

This book endeavors, among other things, to tell lawyers how to stress the equities of their cases persuasively, to the end that they may win their cases on appeal.

Section 4. Can appellate advocacy be learned?—It may be urged—and some friends have suggested—that it would be just as impossible—quite as unhelpful—to attempt to teach advocacy as

---

[3] "In publicly criticizing this Court's opinion the Secretary merely indulged in a practice familiar in the long history of Anglo-American litigation, whereby unsuccessful litigants and lawyers give vent to their disappointment in tavern or press." *United States* v. *Morgan,* 313 U. S. 409, 421.

[4] "If unblamed I may advert to my own experience, I always felt in the exercise of the judicial office irresistibly drawn to the intrinsic justice of the case, with the inclination, and if possible the determination, to rest the judgment upon the very right of the matter. In the practice of the profession I always feel an abiding confidence that if my case is morally right and just it will succeed, whatever technical difficulties may appear to stand in the way; and the result usually justifies the confidence." Dillon, *The Laws and Jurisprudence of England and America* (1894) 17-18.

to write a learned tome on how to paint a picture or how to write a novel. That stricture may well be true as to some of the finer points of the process; certainly neither the writing of a brief nor the oral presentation of an appeal can qualify as an exact science. Nor is there, as to either activity, any single "approved solution." Mr. Wellman entitled his classic guide for the trial lawyer *The Art of Cross-Examination,* and it may well be that appellate advocacy, at least when it is skillfully and effectively practiced, is also something of an art. Nonetheless, the process in its essentials can be stated in terms of rules, or at least of standards of fairly general application. It can therefore be taught—and learned; learned, too, more quickly and somewhat less painfully than simply through one's own mistakes. For in law, as in other fields of human endeavor, it is only the fool who needs to learn by his own experience: the wise man learns, and profits, from the experience of others.

   Section 5. Should appellate advocacy be taught?—Anyone who has ever spent any length of time in an appellate court, whether for instructional purposes or by way of busman's holiday, or even simply waiting for his own case to be reached, will answer that question with a resounding "Yes." Advocacy needs to be taught, and it needs to be learned. Too many, far too many, lawyers burden appellate courts with poorly prepared, poorly presented, and thoroughly unhelpful arguments—for which they receive, and clients pay, substantial and not infrequently handsome fees. Lawyers, like other professional men, can be divided into the classic three-fold scale of evaluation as able, unable, and lamentable. Nonetheless, and after making due allowance for the frailties of mankind, it is really amazing how few good arguments are presented and heard, quite irrespective of the tribunal concerned. About a dozen years ago, I was told by a Justice of the Supreme Court of the United States that four out of every five arguments to which he is required to listen were "not good." While the present revision was in preparation, I inquired whether he considered that the proportion of good arguments had risen. His reply was in the negative, although he suggested the word "inadequate" to characterize most of the arguments he was required to hear. One of his colleagues, a few years earlier, stated publicly that "in the short time that I have been on the bench one of the things that has astonished me most is the number of disappointing arguments to which courts have to listen." [5] And comments from judges of other appellate courts give me no reason to suppose that the percentage of good arguments elsewhere was or is now perceptibly higher.

It would seem to be, therefore, still time for the subject of appellate advocacy to be given some attention. The present book is a response to the conviction that there is nothing mysterious or esoteric about the business of making an effective written or oral presentation to an appellate court, that the governing principles of the process can be extracted and articulated and therefore taught, and that any competent lawyer has the ability, with study and proper application, to write a brief and make an argument that will likewise be competent—and that will further his client's cause.

Section 6. Why bother with advocacy at all?—A representative cross-section of the graduates of one distinguished law school were once polled by the faculty, and asked to rank "the skills of a lawyer" in the order of their importance in their particular branches of practice. "The lowest rating, by a fairly wide margin, was given to skill in advocacy." [6]

Even if this simply means that most alumni of that particular institution never get to court, but instead devote most of their energies to the office or to conferences or consultations with clients, the rating is amazing—and, it is submitted, amazingly wrong. For whenever a lawyer negotiates, or puts a proposition to a client, or even when he discusses a difference of opinion with an associate, he is engaged in advocacy, viz., the process of trying to convince people of something, the technique of persuasion. It is significant that Sir Winston Churchill, speaking of the thirty most active and fruitful years of his life, referred to them as "years of action and advocacy." [7] And it is likewise significant that the very same group of lawyers, especially the older graduates, gave to "the ability to understand and marshal facts" "the highest rating by a considerable margin." [8] Now the marshalling of facts is not a talent *in*

---

[5] Harlan, *What Part Does the Oral Argument Play in the Conduct of an Appeal?*, 41 Corn. L. Q. 6, 10.

[6] Fuller, *Work on the Curriculum*, Harvard Law School Bulletin, No. 2, July 1948, p. 3.

[7] Churchill, *The Gathering Storm* (1948), p. iv. (Copyright by Messrs. Houghton, Mifflin & Co.)

[8] Note 6, *supra*.

vacuo; it is one of the vital elements of advocacy. And, as will be demonstrated below at length and in some detail, it is frequently the most vital element.

The low rating given to advocacy therefore does more than illumine and underscore the view of my distinguished judicial friend that four out of every five lawyers appearing before him have forensic halitosis (or such other oral ailment as may be suggested) ; it indicates that too many members of the bar fail to understand what advocacy really is. It is not simply haranguing a jury about "this poor boy" or the unwritten law, so-called. It is not simply screaming at an appellate court or being "positive" in the Ambrose Bierce sense, which is to say, wrong in a loud tone of voice. It is, whether in court or out, an exercise in persuasion. And that, after all, is why a lawyer appears before an appellate court: to persuade the tribunal to decide the case in his favor. And since when has skill in persuading a particular group of hearers to decide in his favor become a minor factor in the skill of a lawyer?

But it may be urged, and frequently is, that it should be possible to submit the entire case or controversy to the court without any argument, either written or oral. Why not, so the question goes, why not simply hand up the record and the relevant authorities? After all, the judges are disinterested, they are learned in the law, and many of them have bright young law clerks to assist them in their researches. The judges either make or find and declare the law—depending on one's particular jurisprudential views.[9] Therefore, why not leave the whole matter to them, and avoid the contentiousness and the expense and the artificiality of litigation?

The best answer to these suggestions is to apply a technique borrowed from one of the so-called exact sciences. When doctors wish to learn the function of a particular human gland whose workings are not too clear to them, they remove the corresponding gland from a dog or other animal, and study the effects of the excision. Thereafter, when they have observed the behavior of the poor pooch minus that particular organ, they generally acquire considerable insight into what the X gland really does.

---

[9] See Chafee, *Do Judges Make or Discover Law?*, 91 Proc. Am. Philos. Soc. 405. When rights—especially pecuniary rights—depend on the effect to be given an overruled decision that had earlier been relied upon, this problem ceases to be a merely philosophical one. For two striking examples, see *Harris* v. *Jex,* 55 N. Y. 421; *People ex rel. Rice* v. *Graves,* 242 App. Div. 128, affirmed, 270 N. Y. 498, certiorari denied, 298 U. S. 683.

I propose to apply the same technique to a still somewhat cloudy realm of law, and to answer the question, "Why bother with advocacy at all?" by taking an actual case that was not presented in the true advocate's fashion in the brief, and by then examining the result.

Section 7. What happens when a case is not presented in advocate's fashion?—The guinea pig experiment for present purposes will be *Cramer* v. *United States*,[10] the first case in which the Supreme Court of the United States had ever considered a conviction for treason on the merits.[11] It is now some fifteen years old, but its date is immaterial to the principle about to be considered.

Here are representative excerpts from the Supreme Court's opinion:

[The Treason Act, 25 Edw. III] cut a bench-mark by which the English-speaking world tested the level of its thought on the subject until our own abrupt departure from it in 1789.[12]

* * * necessity as well as desire taught a concept that differed from all historical models in the drafting of our treason clause.[13]

The framers combined all of these known protections and added two of their own which had no precedent. * * * And a venerable safeguard against false testimony was given a novel application by requiring two witnesses to the same overt act.[14]

So [the framers] added what in effect is a command that the overt acts must be established by direct evidence, and the direct testimony must be that of two witnesses instead of one. In this sense the overt act procedural provision adds something, and something important, to the definition.[15]

In the *Cramer* case, the petitioner's conviction was reversed, five to four, and the majority opinion, just quoted, asserts that both the constitutional concept of treason and the two-witness re-

---

[10] 325 U. S. 1.

[11] In *Ex parte Bollman*, 4 Cranch 75, and *Stephan* v. *United States*, 318 U. S. 781, 319 U. S. 423, 319 U. S. 783, the Court did not consider the substantive questions. Following *Cramer*, two other treason cases were determined on the merits: *Haupt* v. *United States*, 330 U. S. 631; *Kawakita* v. *United States*, 343 U. S. 717.

[12] 325 U. S. at 17-18.

[13] 325 U. S. at 20.

[14] 325 U. S. at 24.

[15] 325 U. S. at 30.

quirement were new. Both points are developed at some length in the Court's opinion, which extends to nearly 46 pages in the official reports.

But, as a matter of demonstrable historical fact, the constitutional definition of the crime of treason was taken from the English Statute of 25 Edward III, and the two-witness requirement, which had been in and out of English law since 1547,[16] derived from the English Statute of 7 and 8 William III. This appears clearly from an examination of the text of the three provisions.

(i) Constitution of the United States, Article III, Section 3:

Treason against the United States, shall consist only in levying War against them, or in adhering to their Enemies, giving them Aid and Comfort. No Person shall be convicted of Treason unless on the Testimony of two Witnesses to the same overt Act, or on Confession in open Court.

(ii) St. 25 Edward III, stat. 5, c. 2:

* * * if a man do levy war against our Lord the King in his realm, or be adherent to the King's enemies in his realm, giving to them aid and comfort in the realm, or elsewhere, and thereof be provably attained of open deed by the people of their condition: * * * that ought to be adjudged treason. * * * * [17]

(iii) St. 7 and 8 William III, c. 3, sec. 2:

* * * noe Person or Persons whatsoever shall bee indicted tryed or attainted of High Treason whereby any Corruption of Blood may or shall bee made to any such Offender or Offenders or to any the Heir or Heirs of any such Offender or Offenders or of Misprision of such Treason but by and upon the Oaths and Testimony of Two lawful Witnesses either both of them to the same Overtact or one of them to one and another of them to another Overtact of the same Treason unlesse the party indicted and arraigned or tryed shall willingly without violence in open Court confesse the same or shall stand Mute or refuse to plead or in cases of High Treason shall peremptorily challenge above the number of Thirty five of the Jury Any Law Statute or Usage to the contrary notwithstanding.

---

[16] See 7 Wigmore, *Evidence* (3d ed. 1940) § 2036.
[17] Original text in Norman-French; translation from *Rex* v. *Casement*, [1917] 1 K. B. 98, 99.

So far as an indictment for treason alleging only a single overt act is concerned, the quantitative requirement of the St. 7 & 8 Will. III is, of course, identical with that of the Constitution of the United States.

And Mr. Justice James Wilson of the Supreme Court of the United States, who had been a member of the Constitutional Convention and in that capacity had drafted the treason clause,[18] made this observation in 1790 concerning the constitutional definition of the offense:

> * * * This single sentence comprehends our whole of national treason; and, as I mentioned before, is transcribed from a part of the statute of Edward the third. By those who proposed the national constitution, this was done, that, in a subject so essentially interesting to each and to all, not a single expression should be introduced, but such as could show in its favour, that it was recommended by the mature experience, and ascertained by the legal interpretation, of numerous revolving centuries.[19]

The paradox or, if one will, the mystery of the *Cramer* case is twofold. First, the St. 7 & 8 Will. III, which settled the two-witness rule in the law of treason,[20] was not cited in either opinion; second, the opinion of the Court refers to the treason clause of the Constitution as representing a novel application, a new concept, and an abrupt departure, in the face of Mr. Justice Wilson's statement in 1790—and he had drafted the clause in 1787—that the old language was employed because of a desire to carry over the old interpretations.

How account for this extremely curious result?

Section 8. Explanation of the mystery.—Both the St. 7 & 8 Will. III and Mr. Justice Wilson's statement were before the Court in the *Cramer* case.[21] But the Government did not file an advocate's brief after the Court set the case down for reargument. The Government filed, in an Appendix, a very scholarly historical study

---

[18] See Hurst, *Treason in the United States,* 58 Harv. L. Rev. 395, 404-406.

[19] 3 *Works of James Wilson* (1804), 99-100.

[20] See 7 Wigmore, *Evidence* (3d ed. 1940) § 2036. England repealed the requirement in 1945, see St. 8 & 9 Geo. VI, c. 44 (The Treason Act, 1945), apparently in order to deal with the case of Lord Haw-Haw. *Joyce* v. *Director of Public Prosecutions,* [1946] A. C. 347.

[21] See, for the latter, *Appendices to Brief for the United States on Reargument,* No. 13, Oct. T. 1944, p. 277.

of the law of treason, running to 404 pages. It was not, nor did it purport to be, an argument; it was an impartial discussion.[22] In addition, the Government also filed an 88-page brief that was in the nature of a commentary on the Appendix.

The realm of "might have been" is traditionally an unprofitable source of speculation. Whether the *Cramer* case could have been won, whether a fifth justice might have been persuaded to vote the other way if the Government had filed a real brief, i.e., an argumentative document, a written *argument* instead of a colorless, "dispassionate," impartial, and necessarily discursive treatise, is not a question that can be helpfully discussed. But whatever a fighting, argumentative brief might or might not have accomplished, it would certainly have saved the Court the embarrassment of a whopping historical boner as to the concept of treason.

The dissenting judges expressed the views of Mr. Justice Wilson. They said:

> There is * * * no evidence whatever that the offense of adhering to the enemy giving him aid and comfort was designed to encompass a narrower field than that indicated by its accepted and settled meaning. Nor is there the slightest indication that the kind or character of overt acts required were any different than those which had long been recognized or accepted as adequate.[23]

But they had no documentation to support these assertions; the crucial contemporaneous comments of Wilson, J., had been lost, literally lost, somewhere in the 404 pages of "fair, dispassionate, and informative analysis."

Section 9. The advocate's duty.—The basic premise of common-law jurisprudence is the view that the best and surest way of

---

[22] "The following appendices [App. A, Civil and Canon Law Materials; App. B, Anglo-American Materials] have been prepared at the request of the Solicitor General. The authors of the appendices were requested to avoid argumentative support of any particular position, and to select material for inclusion or exclusion solely on the basis of its reliability and its relevance to the questions under review by the Court. The appendices are submitted to the Court in the belief that they constitute a fair, dispassionate, and informative analysis of the law of treason; but the Government does not in any way assume responsibility for, or necessarily agree with, the inferences drawn or the conclusions expressed by the authors." *Appendices to Brief for the United States on Reargument*, No. 13, Oct. T. 1944, p. iii.

[23] 325 U. S. at 76. Compare the concurring opinion in the next treason case, *Haupt v. United States*, 330 U. S. 631, 644, written by the author of the *Cramer* dissent.

ascertaining the truth and arriving at a just result is to have an impartial tribunal make its decision after first hearing the opposing parties present their conflicting contentions in the strongest and most forceful way.

The corollary of that premise is that when the opposing positions are not strongly or argumentatively presented, the tribunal may well fail to ascertain the truth and reach a sound result, and may be led into egregious error. My own considered view, reached after a good deal of searching cogitation, that the *Cramer* case stands as a living monument to that corollary, has since been confirmed, not only by further reflection and ten additional years of appellate practice, but, preeminently, by the distinction drawn in a subsequent Supreme Court case, *Ellis* v. *United States*.[24]

There, after appointed counsel had advised a Court of Appeals that no substantial issue existed even though there was a "possible" area of error, leave to appeal *in forma pauperis* was denied.[25] On certiorari, the Supreme Court, agreeing with the Solicitor General that the issue was not one that could be characterized as frivolous, reversed; the Court said,

In this case, it appears that the two attorneys appointed by the Court of Appeals performed essentially the role of *amici curiae*. But representation in the role of an advocate is required.[26]

Of course the United States, unlike private litigants, does not need to win every case, and so its counsel are not only under what is virtually an obligation to eschew tactics that savor of "anything-to-win," but are in a position to practice litigation strategy, and thus to await a suitable vehicle for establishing a principle. This unique position permits the United States to express doubts in situations that cannot fairly be presented as being either black or white, and, in proper cases, to confess error. See p. 104, *infra*. But in the *Cramer* case, where the authorities supporting the conviction were, at the very least, far stronger than their presentation made them appear, the demonstrable result was that the Court's holding substantially varied the constitutional content of the crime of treason from that intended and articulated by the Framers. And the basic reason for that result was because counsel for the prose-

---

[24] 356 U. S. 674.
[25] *Ellis* v. *United States*, 249 F. 2d 478 (D. C. Cir.) (5-4 decision).
[26] 356 U. S. at 675.

cution "performed essentially the role of *amici curiae*" and did not furnish "representation in the role of an advocate."

Therefore, it may be safely laid down that any lawyer who fails to brief and argue his case so as to present his position in the most effective manner fails in his duty, not only to his client, but also to the court whose officer he is.

A court must be impartial. An advocate must be fair and accurate, but he has no business being impartial. An impartial advocate not only fails in his duty, he fails in his function as well. He is, actually and inescapably, a contradiction in terms.

Chapter II

HOW FEDERAL APPELLATE COURTS
DEAL WITH APPEALS

Section 10. In general.—It is vital to the appellate lawyer to know at least the essential mechanics of the appellate process as applied by Federal appellate judges, because once the actual functioning of appellate courts is studied and appreciated, the need for effective advocacy becomes even more apparent. Sometimes, as in the *Cramer* case, the impression left by the briefs is the controlling factor. In other instances, the oral argument is more apt to be determinative.

Some lawyers feel that oral argument is unimportant, because "the judges will study the briefs"—and the briefs are written by the bright young lads in the office, who are sometimes very bright indeed. But this assumes that an appellate court functions like a radar-operated fire-control director, which causes the projectile always to hit the target provided only that all the relevant data have been correctly supplied. That assumption, in many instances, is neither a safe nor even a correct one. Because the fact of the matter—the brutal, hard fact of the matter—is that cases frequently are won and lost on oral argument.

This is particularly true of the indifferent cases, in which a court is not much interested as an original proposition. There are some cases, of course, that no one can lose—cases that may safely be entrusted to the office boy. There are other cases that no one can win, regardless of the skill or learning or persuasive powers of the advocate concerned. But there is a large intermediate zone of cases, running in my judgment to perhaps a quarter of the total, that do not present pressing problems or burning issues, and as to which it is perfectly obvious that no one would "suppose that civilization will come to an end whichever way this case is decided," [1] where oral argument plays a very substantial if not a decisive part in determining the issue. This conclusion may shock

---

[1] Holmes, J., dissenting, in *Haddock* v. *Haddock,* 201 U. S. 562, 628.

some persons, and lead others to suggest that its statement is not sufficiently deferential or respectful to the courts. I can only say, in the words of the countryman who was queried as to his belief in baptism, "Good Lord, yes! I've seen it done." I have *seen* cases won and lost on oral argument. And the reason for this phenomenon will appear more clearly when the mechanics of the appellate process are examined.

There are two phases to be examined under this heading—the processes of Federal appellate courts before argument, and their processes after argument.

Section 11. Court's practice before argument: Supreme Court of the United States.—To what extent do appellate judges study the record and briefs before counsel get up?

In the Supreme Court of the United States, the justices know in a general way what a case is about before it is argued on the merits, because they have already examined the jurisdictional statement when the case comes up on appeal as of right, or the petition for certiorari when it comes up for discretionary review. Whether thereafter, before the argument on the merits but after the noting of probable jurisdiction or the granting of the writ of certiorari, they read the briefs on the merits, is something that varies with the individual justice and with the burden of work at any particular moment. It varies also with the same justice.

In the past, so I had heard it said by one who had reason to know, only the late Mr. Justice Cardozo made an invariable practice of reading the briefs in advance. But at the present time it is my impression that more of the justices regularly read the briefs on the merits before argument than at any time in the last two decades or so.[2]

Section 12. Court's practice before argument: United States Courts of Appeals.

(i) *First Circuit.* Judge Magruder, for many years Chief Judge, wrote: "I cannot say that we 'invariably' read the briefs before argument, but I think it is the general practice of all of us to do so."[3]

---

[2] An impression since confirmed by one of the present members of the court. See Brennan, *State Court Decisions and the Supreme Court*, 31 Pa. Bar Ass'n Q. 393, 403 (1960).

[3] Letters from the Hon. Calvert Magruder, then Chief Judge, July 27, 1948, and June 6, 1957.

(ii) *Second Circuit.* Former Chief Judge Clark wrote: "Except for the en banc cases, our practice is in general not to read the briefs before the argument. This is not an invariable or ironclad rule, and any member of the court is at liberty to obtain the briefs and appendices before argument and read them. This may be, and indeed often is, done in an important and specially assigned case which a particular panel of the court can confidently expect to have committed to it. In other cases the practice is less usual, for the practical reason that we sit in panels and, since we normally have a press of cases awaiting argument, rather freely postpone or reassign cases from panel to panel. Of course had we a strong tradition for the need of advance reading of briefs, we undoubtedly would not allow this matter of calendar assignment to control; but since there is not, and indeed no real demand in our court for a change, we follow rather happily this traditional course." [4]

(iii) *Third Circuit.* Chief Judge Biggs writes: "The judges make a point of reading the briefs before argument. They do so in every instance except where some unforeseen event occurs, such as a judge being ill or some other emergency arising which requires another member of the court to take his place on short notice." [5]

(iv) *Fourth Circuit.* The late Chief Judge Parker wrote— and Chief Judge Soboloff has confirmed—that "in our court the judges have the practice of reading the briefs before argument, and this practice is almost invariably followed." [6]

(v) *Fifth Circuit.* Judge Sibley, a former Senior Circuit Judge, wrote in 1948 as follows:

When I came on the appellate bench in 1930 neither briefs nor records were examined in advance of argument, the judges preferring to have perfectly open minds until oral argument was heard, and no expression of opinion was made till briefs and record had been read and we went into conference about the case several weeks later. There was quite a lag in making decisions, and some forgetfulness of details. For the past few years we have usually looked over briefs and records in advance of argument, so as to have a general idea of the points in the case, and at the time of argument frequently so tell coun-

---

[4] Letter from the Hon. Charles E. Clark, then Chief Judge, June 25, 1957.

[5] Letters from the Hon. John Biggs, Jr., Chief Judge, September 11, 1948, and June 11, 1957.

[6] Letters from the Hon. John J. Parker, then Chief Judge, July 27, 1948, and June 10, 1957; confirmed by letter from the Hon. Simon E. Soboloff, Chief Judge, February 3, 1959.

sel, and that they need not expend much time in stating the case, but go at once to the discussion. We are rather given also to asking questions about what seems to us the most pressing points. This has all tended to save time and concentrate the argument, and I believe has not produced much prejudgment of the cases.[7]

The briefs are still read in advance today.[8]

(vi) *Sixth Circuit.* In 1948, each judge pursued his individual preference as to reading briefs before or after oral argument.[9] The same is true today, although possibly most of the judges read briefs beforehand.[10]

(vii) *Seventh Circuit.* Former Chief Judge Duffy wrote that, in general, the judges read the briefs before argument.[11]

(viii) *Eighth Circuit.* Former Chief Judge Gardner wrote: "I read all briefs before the argument, not with a view to determining how the case should be decided, but with a view of determining in advance what the issues are. This practice is, I think, generally followed by all our Judges," although "the practice varies to some extent with the individual Judge." [12]

(ix) *Ninth Circuit.* The late Chief Judge Denman wrote: "It is our practice to read the briefs before argument." [13]

(x) *Tenth Circuit.* In this court the judges do not read the briefs before argument.[14]

(xi) *District of Columbia Circuit.* Judge Fahy writes that while the practice is individual as to the judge, "each as a rule goes over the brief before argument." [15]

Section 13. Court's practice before argument: Specialized Federal Courts.

(i) *United States Court of Claims.* Strictly speaking, of course, the Court of Claims is a court of original jurisdiction, with

---

[7] Letter from the Hon. Samuel H. Sibley, a former Senior Circuit Judge, August 17, 1948.

[8] Letter from the Hon. Joseph C. Hutcheson, Jr., then Chief Judge, September 30, 1957.

[9] Letter from the Hon. Xen Hicks, then Chief Judge, October 28, 1948.

[10] See Institute of Judicial Administration, *Appellate Courts—Internal Operating Procedures—Preliminary Report* (July 5, 1957), p. 13.

[11] Letter from the Hon. F. Ryan Duffy, then Chief Judge, June 27, 1957.

[12] Letters from the Hon. Archibald K. Gardner, then Chief Judge, July 29, 1948, and June 11, 1957.

[13] Letters from the late Hon. William Denman, then Chief Judge, September 20, 1948, and June 28, 1957.

[14] Letters from the Hon. Alfred P. Murrah, Circuit Judge, August 5, 1948, and June 13, 1957.

[15] Letter from the Hon. Charles Fahy, Circuit Judge, June 7, 1957.

a very limited and specialized jurisdiction on appeal.[16] But when the Commissioner to whom the case has been assigned is directed by the Court to file his "recommendation for conclusions of law" —a direction that is being made in an increasing number of instances [17]—he writes an opinion, and the case is then presented and handled precisely like appellate cases everywhere. Indeed, there is very little difference for counsel when, even in the absence of such a direction, exceptions are taken only to the Commissioner's report finding the facts. It is proper to add that the essentially appellate nature of the Court of Claims' work has recently been emphasized by the circumstance that, pursuant to a resolution of the Judicial Conference of the United States, Court of Claims cases now appear in the Federal Reporter rather than in the Federal Supplement. This change became effective after 181 F. Supp., and with 276 F. 2d.

Judge Whitaker of the Court of Claims advises that "The practice of examining briefs before the argument varies with the individual judges on our court." [18]

(ii) *United States Court of Customs and Patent Appeals.* Judge Jackson advises that, while the judges "as a rule" read the briefs before argument, the practice varies with the individual judge.[19]

(iii) *United States Court of Military Appeals.* Judge Latimer writes that the practice varies with each judge.[20]

Section 14. Court's practice after argument: In general.— Here two basic questions arise, the answers to both of which condition the task of the advocate.

First, when is the vote taken? Do the judges study the case first and then vote, or do they vote first and then write an opinion following study of the records and briefs? If the vote is taken first,

---

[16] See 28 U.S.C. §§ 1491-1505. With the consent of all appellees, federal tort claims cases may be appealed from district courts to the Court of Claims, 28 U.S.C. § 1504, although no such appeal has yet been docketed; and the Court of Claims has a general appellate jurisdiction over determinations by the Indian Claims Commission, pursuant to 25 U.S.C. § 70s. See, e.g., *United States* v. *Seminole Nation,* 173 F. Supp. 784.

[17] See Stern and Brenner, *The 1957 Revision of the Rules of the United States Court of Claims,* 21 F.R.D. 259, 266, 268. For a recent example of a Commissioner's opinion adopted by the Court of Claims, see *Griffiths* v. *United States,* 172 F. Supp. 691.

[18] Letter from Judge Samuel E. Whitaker, September 26, 1957.

[19] Letter from Judge Joseph R. Jackson, October 11, 1957.

[20] Letter from Judge George W. Latimer, September 4, 1957.

the opinion is very apt to become, certainly in effect, a brief in support of the majority vote [21]—another factor that emphasizes the importance of the impression left at the close of the oral argument.

Second, do all the judges write a memorandum on the case, or is a draft opinion written by only one judge in the first instance? (No Federal appellate court, so far as is known, follows the practice of many State courts of last resort whereby the writing of opinions is assigned in advance by a system of rotation.) If every judge writes a memorandum, then, plainly, there is less of a tendency to one-man opinions. But, under either method, the more fully draft opinions are discussed, the less likelihood there is of one-man opinions, and the greater the probability that the opinion finally handed down will represent the composite views of the entire court.

Section 15. Court's practice after argument: Supreme Court of the United States.—In the Supreme Court, two weeks of argument are normally followed by two weeks of recess; in each of the first two weeks, Monday through Thursday are devoted to arguments, and Friday to conference. A further conference is also held on the last Friday of the recess. Opinions are announced on Mondays when the Court is in session, including the Monday that precedes a recess, and on all Mondays after arguments for the Term have been suspended.

At the conference, the case is stated by the Chief Justice, and then discussed by each Associate Justice in order of seniority. It is then voted on, in inverse order of seniority, the junior Associate Justice voting first. The writing of the opinion in the case is then assigned by the Chief Justice, or, if he is in dissent, then by the senior Associate Justice of the majority. The draft opinion or opinions are then circulated. Thereafter, depending on the difficulty of the case, the opinions are considered at one or more further conferences. Written comments of considerable length are often made by justices to the writer of the opinion and personal discussions

---

[21] "At Conference he was open-minded. But once he had come to a conclusion neutrality ceased. He then became an indefatigable proponent for the position he had reached, an ardent advocate and a forceful writer for the ground that he deemed solid. The Chief Justice delighted to take on all comers around the conference table and armed with precedent and reason to battle, more often successfully than not, for his views." Address of Mr. Justice Reed on the *Occasion of the Dedication of the Birthplace of Chief Justice Stone,* Chesterfield, N. H., August 25, 1948.

take place in chambers between those on the same side of a legal question. I have been told that frequently the form of the opinion is changed and that in unusual cases as many as ten or fifteen drafts are circulated before final acceptance.

Frequently, the critical factor is thus the length of time between argument and conference. If a case argued on a Wednesday is voted on by Friday, necessarily the impression left by the oral argument will be tremendously significant. To the extent that the vote is postponed to the next Friday or to the conference following that one, the brief or the justices' independent research looms larger in the final determination; the greater the time-lag, the more independent study becomes possible. No definite information on this variable is available; all that can be said is that it depends on the apparent complexity of the case, on the state of the calendar, and, of course, on the writer of the opinion.[22]

Section 16. Court's practice after argument: United States Courts of Appeals.

(i) *First Circuit.* Chief Judge Magruder wrote:

At the conclusion of a given sitting, the members of the court invariably have a conference in which the cases are discussed one by one, a tentative vote is taken, and the assignment for opinion writing is made. It is not our practice for each judge to prepare a memorandum on the case. After a draft opinion is ready, it is circulated by mail. Sometimes this gives rise to extensive correspondence back and forth, when disagreements develop or when suggestions for change are made. Occasionally, a further conference is held, either by special arrangement, or more often when the court is assembled in Boston for a later sitting.[23]

---

[22] This practice has been a matter of public knowledge since former Justice Campbell disclosed it at the memorial services for former Justice Curtis. 20 Wall. x. Other formulations appear in Hughes, *The Supreme Court of the United States* (1928) 58-61; Stone, *Fifty Years' Work of the United States Supreme Court*, 53 A.B.A. Rep. 259, 278-280 (1928); Harlan [the elder], *How the Judges of the Supreme Court of the United States Consult*, 30 Am. L. Rev. 903 (1896); Jackson, *The Supreme Court in the American System of Government* (1955) 14-17. For the most recent expositions, by Justices now sitting, see Clark, *The Supreme Court Conference*, 19 F.R.D. 303 (1956); Brennan, *State Court Decisions and the Supreme Court*, 31 Pa. Bar Ass'n Q. 393, 401-402, 404-405 (1960).

The statements in the text have been further checked by way of precaution, and are believed to set forth accurately the existing practice.

[23] Letters from the Hon. Calvert Magruder, then Chief Judge, July 27, 1948, and June 6, 1957.

(ii) *Second Circuit.* Former Chief Judge Clark wrote:

According to the well settled and quite emphasized custom of this court, every sitting judge (and thus normally the three judges of each panel) prepares a memorandum on every case heard. The panels are assigned for a week's hearing of appeals and thus will normally get from fifteen to twenty such appeals. Each memorandum of each judge gives his reaction to the controlling principles of law and ends with his tentative vote. No conference is held until all memoranda are completed and exchanged, although we try to do this promptly and tentatively aim for our conference on the Wednesday or Thursday after the week of argument. At the conference we discuss all the cases, having the benefit of these memoranda, and of course naturally try to answer or otherwise discuss points found in our colleagues' memoranda. Then we reaffirm our tentative votes or modify them as we wish, after which, and at the end of the day's conference, the senior judge assigns the opinions to be written equally among the three sitting judges, with perhaps a quarter or a third of the number to be disposed of Per Curiam on the opinion below or otherwise peremptorily. The panel then separates, and each judge prepares the opinions assigned to him and circulates them among his colleagues, who normally endorse their concurrence or dissent without further conference.[24]

(iii) *Third Circuit* The judges invariably confer with each other immediately after the argument, according to Chief Judge Biggs,

usually on the afternoon of the same day on which argument is had unless (a rare occasion) the court sits so late that it is impossible to confer conveniently. In this event a conference is held as soon as possible, either the following afternoon or within two or three days. There is no time lag unless a judge has been called in emergency and has had no opportunity to examine the record and briefs in which event the interim will be sufficient to let him make the examination. (Note that we use the appendix system rather than the full record.)

The practice of having each judge prepare a memorandum was abandoned about [1941]. In exceptional cases where there is a difference of opinion one or more judges may prepare memoranda for a second or even a third conference.

There is usually no conference to discuss the draft opinions. These are simply circulated to all members of the court, including those who did not sit in the panel as well as those who did sit. This gives an opportunity for rehearing before the court en banc, a privi-

---

[24] Letter from the Hon. Charles E. Clark, then Chief Judge, June 25, 1957.

lege rarely availed of. If more than one conference is had and there are memoranda, the latter are usually discussed.

The members of the court vote at the conference usually immediately after argument. In some difficult cases some member of the court will be assigned the duty of preparing a draft in the form of an opinion and the vote will be taken by letter after the draft is circulated or at a later conference. The opinions are assigned usually at the end of a week of sittings so that opinion writing can be fairly distributed.[25]

(iv) *Fourth Circuit.* The late Chief Judge Parker described the procedure in his court in these terms:

In the afternoon after the argument a conference is had and the case is discussed in the light of the briefs and argument. Sometimes if the case is a difficult one it is carried over for further conference. After the case has been thoroughly discussed the vote is taken and the [Chief] Judge, either then or at the end of the term, assigns the case for opinion. After the opinion is prepared by the judge to whom it is assigned it is sent to all the judges who sat in the case and to all the Circuit Judges who did not sit. If there is controversy as to the content of the opinion the case is again called into conference.[26]

More recently, Chief Judge Soboloff wrote:

The practice in the Fourth Circuit is still as Judge Parker described it. I might add, however, that in a number of cases, before a decision is reached, elaborate memoranda are prepared and circulated among the Judges, and in this process views are clarified.[27]

(v) *Fifth Circuit.* In 1948, Judge Sibley, a former Senior Circuit Judge, described the practice as follows:

We ordinarily hear argument Monday, Tuesday and Wednesday. On Friday we have a conference touching the cases heard that week, and any others held over from previous weeks. No written memorandum is usually presented then. The discussion is informal, and we will likely agree on the proper decision of over half the cases heard that week, and assign them for the preparation of an opinion. Those in which there is doubt or disagreement are held over for further investigation and discussion. Opinions when written are marked with

---

[25] Letters from the Hon. John Biggs, Jr., Chief Judge, September 11, 1948, and June 11, 1957.

[26] Letters from the Hon. John J. Parker, then Chief Judge, July 27, 1948, and June 10, 1957.

[27] Letter from the Hon. Simon E. Soboloff, Chief Judge, February 3, 1959.

a concurrence separately by each judge if entirely satisfactory. If not, objections are brought under discussion. A separate concurring opinion sometimes results, or a dissent. Our present practice is a great time saver, for we now have opinions filed in a majority of our cases within thirty days after argument, and we have little need to reread anything, since it is promptly acted on. I believe the quality of our work has not suffered. * * *

We vote on a case ordinarily after conference and before opinion is written, but each judge is at liberty to change his vote at any time before the opinion is filed, or to call for further conference.[28]

The practice in the Fifth Circuit at this time is substantially the same, according to Chief Judge Hutcheson, who writes:

I would add only this. On account of the increase of our business, we hear arguments now on the first four days of the week. Because of the practice which has existed now for some years past of more thorough and complete study of the briefs and records before argument by all the members of the court, we have a conference each day on the cases heard the day before and any other cases upon which an agreement has not theretofore been reached.[29]

(vi) *Sixth Circuit.* In 1948, the late Chief Judge Hicks described the practice after argument as follows:

We invariably hold a judicial conference on all cases submitted. This conference is held following the arguments on the day the cases are heard. We do not waste time by having each judge prepare a memorandum but exchange our views by oral discussion at a time we deem proper.

The case is assigned to one of our judges for the preparation of a proposed opinion which he submits for the consideration and action of his colleagues. The proposed opinion is discussed among the judges either in correspondence or when we consider it necessary, further conferences are held. The opinion before promulgation has been *fully* considered by each judge and represents the opinion of all. If there is dissent, a dissenting or separately concurring opinion is of course written.[30]

---

[28] Letter from the Hon. Samuel H. Sibley, a former Senior Circuit Judge, August 17, 1948.

[29] Letter from the Hon. Joseph C. Hutcheson, Jr., then Chief Judge, September 30, 1957.

[30] Letter from the late Hon. Xen Hicks, then Chief Judge, October 26, 1948.

The practice today appears to be substantially the same.[31]

(vii) *Seventh Circuit.* Former Chief Judge Duffy advised that the judges consult after the conclusion of the oral argument, a preliminary vote is taken, and the writing of the opinion is assigned at that time. One proposed opinion is prepared and circularized; quite often subsequent conferences are held. The final vote is taken after circulation of the proposed opinion.[32]

(viii) *Eighth Circuit.* Former Chief Judge Gardner wrote:

> The Judges invariably confer with each other at the close of the arguments submitted each day and before the preparation of a memorandum or opinion. The Judges also confer on all the cases at the close of the term. At these conferences we determine on what cases, if any, we are clear what the decision should be. On these we have no further conference. In all other cases each of the participating Judges prepare memoranda. A later conference is held to discuss the memoranda or conference opinions.
>
> On the cases in which we are very clear, we vote at the conference held at the close of the term; on others we vote after the memoranda have been submitted and discussed at a conference. The cases are not assigned for final opinion until after all conferences have been held.[33]

(ix) *Ninth Circuit.* The late Chief Judge Denman described the practice in his court as follows: "Sometimes we confer immediately; sometimes there is a time lag. * * * Sometimes there is a memorandum and sometimes not prior to the assignment of the opinion. No case is assigned for opinion until after a vote by all the participating judges at conference." [34]

(x) *Tenth Circuit.* Judge Murrah, now Chief Judge, wrote:

> The judges do invariably confer with each other on every case after argument, and before preparation of a memorandum. The conference occurs at the conclusion of the docket, and the judges have usually made a cursory examination of the briefs and record. Each judge prepares a memorandum on every case in which he sits, unless in rare

---

[31] See Institute of Judicial Administration, *Appellate Courts—Internal Operating Procedures—Preliminary Report* (July 5, 1957), p. 13.

[32] Letter from the Hon. F. Ryan Duffy, then Chief Judge, June 27, 1957.

[33] Letters from the Hon. Archibald K. Gardner, then Chief Judge, July 29, 1948, and June 10, 1957.

[34] Letters from the Hon. William Denman, then Chief Judge, September 20, 1948, and June 28, 1957.

instances where a conference leaves no doubt of the conclusion and disposition of the case.

A conference is held usually from two to four weeks (depending upon the number of cases heard) after completion of the docket. At this conference, each case is considered in order, the judges reading their conference memoranda, following which the case is discussed in the light of our study and a conclusion reached. * * * The cases are decided at conference on memoranda, unless our first conference leaves no doubt of the conclusion.

The chief judge or presiding judge assigns the opinions after the cases are finally decided pursuant to argument and conference on memoranda. When a case is assigned to a judge, he prepares a proposed opinion which is circulated among those sitting for approval, suggestions or dissents before it is finally filed as the opinion of the court. As a rule the writer of the opinion has before him the three conference memoranda when he undertakes the preparation of the opinion. Thus there can be no doubt of the views expressed by all the judges in the conference memoranda, supplemented by the discussion in conference on the controverted points involved. Our opinions are very definitely not one judge opinions. They represent the composite views of the majority, expressed of course in the language and style of the writer.[35]

(xi) *District of Columbia Circuit.* Judge Fahy writes:

In our Court one case is argued in the morning and one in the afternoon. The morning argument ordinarily ends about lunchtime. A conference on that case is not likely to be held immediately after argument, though sometimes a conference is then held. The general practice is for both the morning and afternoon cases to be conferred upon after the afternoon argument. The conferences are almost always held before the preparation of a memorandum or opinion. Sometimes one or more of us has not formulated even a tentative position at the conclusion of the argument, and wishes more time before conferring. The practice in that event is to set a definite time for a conference, so as to permit additional examination of the record and briefs and further consideration by the judges. Occasionally, but not usually, a memorandum will be prepared. The usual course of events, however, is that the judge to whom the case is assigned drafts and circulates an opinion. The draft opinions are circulated, and occasionally become the subject of a conference as well. Suggestions are often noted on the draft, and the draft is returned to the author with these suggestions. The members usually vote at the first conference, after argument, and

---

[35] Letters from the Hon. Alfred P. Murrah, Circuit Judge, August 5, 1948, and June 13, 1957.

before the draft opinion is circulated. The opinion is assigned at the conference at which the case is decided.[36]

Section 17. Court's practice after argument: Specialized Federal Courts.

(i) *United States Court of Claims.* Judge Whitaker writes:

The judges of our court invariably do confer with each other after the argument and before the preparation of the opinions. At this conference, however, the discussion of the cases is not extensive. It is merely for the purpose of gaining the first impression of the judges, so that a case may be assigned for the writing of the opinion to a judge who will probably be in the majority. This is done immediately after the recess of the court taken after hearing arguments set for its monthly sessions.

If all the judges are in agreement, ordinarily only one opinion is prepared, although concurring opinions are occasionally written. No other formal opinion is written unless some judge dissents. At least some of our judges write short memoranda for their own use after conclusion of the argument.

After circulation of a draft of the opinion proposed for the opinion of the court, there is always a conference, where the opinion is fully discussed, after which a vote is taken.[37]

(ii) *United States Court of Customs and Patent Appeals.* Judge Jackson, a retired judge of this Court who has been sitting very frequently since his retirement, advises that the judges invariably confer with each other on each day following the day's hearings. A tentative vote is taken, but a memorandum is usually circulated only by the judge who has been assigned the opinion; this assignment is made prior to argument. After the draft opinion is prepared, it is circulated and discussed.[38]

(iii) *United States Court of Military Appeals.* Judge Latimer states that the judges "invariably confer with each other immediately after the argument and before the preparation of a preliminary opinion." The judges express their views, and the cases are then assigned. There is no formal vote. The judge assigned to the case writes a preliminary opinion; this is circulated; and the other judges then act.[39]

---

[36] Letter from the Hon. Charles Fahy, Circuit Judge, June 7, 1957.
[37] Letter from Judge Samuel E. Whitaker, September 26, 1957.
[38] Letter from Judge Joseph R. Jackson, October 11, 1957.
[39] Letter from Judge George W. Latimer, September 4, 1957.

Section 18. Importance to the court of the first impression made by the advocate.—The foregoing detailed review of the mechanics of the Federal appellate process documents, underscores, and above all explains the assertion made earlier in this chapter (*supra,* Section 10) that many, many cases are won or lost on oral argument. Necessarily and inescapably, the impression derived from the oral presentation is vital wherever and whenever the briefs are not read before argument, or when the first vote is taken immediately thereafter. And, whether the decision in a particular case reflects what is basically a joint endeavor, or whether realistically viewed, it is (at least initially) the determination of the single judge to whom the case was assigned, the impression derived from the argument is bound to carry over into the later and detailed study of the record and briefs. This is particularly true when one considers the pressure of court calendars. Mr. Justice Holmes noted, fifty years ago, that "one has to consider this element of time. One has to try to strike the jugular and let the rest go." [40] And, not too many years ago, the bar had occasion to get, from a Supreme Court Justice since deceased, a revealing glimpse of "the few hours that can be given to consideration of this case." [41] Thus the time element interacts with the factor of appellate mechanics to add still further significance to the oral presentation.

Only occasionally do judges steel themselves against the impression obtained from the argument. One distinguished judge, of over twenty years' appellate experience, wrote: "I am reluctant to reach conclusions at the close of the oral argument lest my later consideration of the case be influenced thereby." Another wrote that "because of the thoroughness with which cases are reviewed in conference, * * * we do not attempt to obtain impressions on the argument." Then, too, as another judge indicated, "Personally I take in more through the eyes than through the ears."

The last three quotations are from letters written a decade ago by judges of State courts of last resort. Undoubtedly, however, their views are held by many Federal appellate judges.

More frequently, however, appellate judges endeavor to obtain a full understanding of the case from the argument, and, when the presentation has been clear, they succeed in doing so. It goes

---

[40] Holmes, *Walbridge Abner Field* [1899] in *Speeches* (1913) 75, 77.

[41] Jackson, J., dissenting in *Jungersen* v. *Ostby & Barton Co.*, 335 U. S. 560, 572.

without saying that they are very substantially assisted in their work when the argument enables them to obtain such an understanding.

Section 19. Coincidence between first impression and final vote.—I made inquiry of the judges who were good enough to contribute the data collected in this chapter, and in the corresponding chapter of the earlier edition, regarding the extent to which their impressions at the close of the oral arguments coincided with their final votes, and have set forth below the percentage of such coincidence.

By way of preliminary comment on the figures that follow, it should be noted that, as one judge pointed out, "the case may be such that the same result would follow a mere reading of the briefs."

By way of further preliminary, it should also be noted that an unclear or ineffective argument will leave no impression save one of confusion. Thus, one able and distinguished judge (whose name had better be withheld out of consideration for the sensibilities of the bar of his jurisdiction) wrote in these terms:

It may be heresy to say so, but in my experience, oral argument is not as helpful as it should and could be if the advocates would reach the simple point in the lawsuit and discuss it intelligently. The difficulty with the average advocate is that he succeeds primarily in confusing the court rather than clarifying the issues. Many times the logical answer falls into place with a proper understanding of the facts and the issues. In sum, my answer * * * is that most of the arguments leave me in doubt of the conclusion. I do usually manage to gain a clear-cut understanding of the case, even if it be necessary to pull it out of the lawyers.

Another distinguished and learned jurist, a personal friend of long standing who, for a number of reasons, cannot be identified, went even further:

Once in a while, I may confess, at the close of the oral argument none of us seems to know what the hell the case is about; but I assume you won't quote that literally in your forthcoming book on *Appellate Advocacy.*

Well, I do quote it literally—with his later permission—because every appellate judge will admit privately that, after the worst of arguments, the same thing happens in the best of courts.

Finally, a third preliminary warning: there are many close and difficult cases that no judge will feel ready to decide without further and very close study of the record and of the authorities even after model arguments on both sides.

In the ordinary case, however, good oral argument is very important, far more than even many able lawyers realize. I quote at random from a few letters:

I think all our judges desire to hear oral argument, and that the argument is helpful. When the lawyers appear to know their cases, and to have examined the law well, it helps the judge to feel that he has heard pretty much all that he should hear, and saves him much labor in independent checking.

I am one of the judges whose mind is stimulated by argument. With a prior study of the record and briefs and after the interrogation at argument, which proceeds about as it does in the House of Lords, I have usually reached the conclusion which I bring to the specific conference of the judges, though sometimes intervening further study changes the conclusion reached at the termination of argument.

For those of us who have not read the briefs in advance of oral argument, that is the first information we receive about the case. Quite naturally the argument is material.

For a while I read the briefs prior to argument, but I soon abandoned the practice because I found it more interesting and helpful to read the briefs after the lawyers on oral argument had breathed the breath of life into them. I can read a brief much more profitably after my interest has been aroused. * * * Oral argument is of great importance. As I said in the beginning, it breathes the breath of life into the briefs. Without argument, a brief is a cold and uninviting thing. The argument serves at least the purpose of arousing the interest of the judge. If well done, they frequently create in the judge's mind an impression that is not easy to remove.

It [oral argument] is often the decisive factor, and is fresh in the mind when we vote in conference.

All judges of our courts think that oral argument is of great value to a proper understanding of the case.

All judges consider oral argument of great importance in illuminating the issues.

My own philosophy is that, if a case is worth appealing, it is worth arguing. I think its principal value is in the interest and stimulation which it creates as to the issues and questions, not in the answers which it provides. It adds the only human touch there is to the dull impersonal processes of appellate review. It enables me to see through a lot of strengths and weaknesses which the stultified expression of a brief sometimes disguises or leaves colorless. I enjoy the task of opinion writing much more in an argued case than one submitted on briefs. And frankly, I think most judges will write a better opinion under the direct challenge of an oral argument from its psychological impact than otherwise.

It is almost a commonplace that every trial lawyer senses how there generally comes a particular point in the proceeding where the scales have been irrevocably tipped in favor of the side that ultimately prevails. Indeed, when reviewing the transcript of testimony, it is very frequently possible to pick the very turning-point of the trial, the moment after which the result was never in doubt.

In many appellate arguments, it is similarly possible to pinpoint this same instant. An appellate judge once said to me, "Majorities in our court pile up very rapidly." Consequently the task of the appellate advocate in every instance is to endeavor, while he is on his feet and while he can impress the judges with the impact of his presentation, to persuade the judges that his cause is the better one. To the extent that the legal authorities are balanced, so that the decision could go either way, the impression made at the argument may well be the determinative factor in inducing the court to reach its ultimate decision in accordance with that impression. Accordingly, to document this view, inquiry was made of appellate judges.

Apparently there is a closer coincidence in courts that deal largely with private rather than public law controversies. In the first edition of this work, in which were included data from thirty-eight State and Territorial courts of last resort, in addition to data from Federal appellate courts, the percentage of coincidence was very high; the largest group of judges wrote that their final vote coincided with their impression at the close of the argument in 90 per cent or more of all the cases heard. This figure is in accord with what an outstanding state judge revealed two generations ago to Mr. Charles Evans Hughes, then teaching law at the Cornell Law School.[42]

---

[42] Hughes, *The Supreme Court of the United States* (1928) 61-62:
"I suppose that, aside from cases of exceptional difficulty, the impression

In the present edition, which is limited to Federal Appeals, the reported percentage of concordance is substantially lower, varying from "a large majority" and "usually" to several estimates of about 80%, with only one judge placing the percentage of concordance at 90 per cent or higher.

Probably—for this cannot rise higher than informed conjecture—the difference reflects a difference in subject-matter. Constitutional cases, particularly, require reflection, and cannot always be safely decided on the impression, however persuasive, that is made orally. The same is true of cases turning on the interrelationship of complex statutory provisions. This is not to say either that oral argument can be omitted in constitutional or statutory cases, or that a substantial question can safely be left to an insubstantial argument. In this field, also, "Few cases are won but many are lost."

But, whether the issue is one that lends itself to virtual resolution at the argument, so that further study will vary the judicial impression then formed in only a tenth of the cases, or whether it is one of such complexity that oral argument merely provides suggestive topics for judicial reflection, the brief is vitally important also. There must be a brief, to summarize the evidence, to set out record references, to collect citations, to discuss the authorities— to do all that oral argument cannot do and at the same time to buttress and support and substantiate the impression made by oral argument. The inescapable fact of appellate work is that both brief and argument are necessary, that neither can safely be omitted, and that, for effective appellate work, both must reflect the best work of which the advocate is capable.

Please note that I say "effective" rather than "successful" ap-

---

that a judge has at the close of a full oral argument accords with the conviction which controls his final vote. A Judge of the Court of Appeals of New York told me some years ago that he had kept track for a time of his impressions after the oral arguments and found that in ninety per centum of the cases, although, of course, he reserved his vote until after a thorough study, his final judgment agreed with his view at the end of the oral argument. This is so because the judges are conversant with their special material, that is, the prior decisions of the court, and when they apprehend the precise question to be decided they are generally not slow in reaching a conclusion."

In 1948, the Chief Justice told me that the judge to whom he referred was the Hon. Francis M. Finch, then a member of the New York Court of Appeals, and the Dean—at least nominally—of the Cornell Law School.

pellate work. There is no way to guarantee success on appeal. Indeed, if there were, if such a secret were known to me, I should hardly undertake to share it with others.

All I can fairly or properly assert is that success on appeal is far more likely to follow from effective than from ineffective briefs and arguments, and that the remainder of this book will endeavor to show how to write effective briefs and how to make effective oral arguments.

SECOND PART

BRIEFING THE APPEAL

CHAPTER III

ESSENTIALS OF AN EFFECTIVE
APPELLATE BRIEF

Section 20. Introductory.—An appellate brief is a written argument in support of or in opposition to the order, decree, or judgment below. This part of the book explains how to write a good appellate brief. The subject may seem at first blush to be as dull as last night's dishwater, but it is a very important one indeed. When the appellate court, as frequently happens, reads briefs in advance of argument, your brief is the first step in persuasion. When a court reads briefs only after oral argument, then, if it is persuaded to decide the case your way after hearing the oral presentations, your brief becomes the peg on which it can hang its collective judicial hat. And in a close case, where the issue is uncertain and where the legal materials must be studied at considerable length, the brief becomes the factor on which the entire case will be won or lost.

This chapter covers the essentials of effective brief-writing, the next one considers helpful techniques in writing and research, and the third discusses the finer points and details of the process. It is a process that entails, in my judgment at least, a quest for perfection—a quest pursued under the pressure of deadlines and the demands of other cases, a quest perhaps foredoomed to failure by the eternal fallibility of man.

The name of the practitioner, so the scholars say, is writ in water. Certain it is that he has but few tangible mementos of his labors—his name in the reports (misspelled, likely as not) and some bound volumes of briefs on his shelves, gathering dust. (After all, briefs and the opinions they assisted in shaping and influencing represent the preservation of his professional skill.) For my part, I should like some day to write the dream brief, one wholly free from misprints and from awkward expressions, which, on rereading five years later, I would not want to change by so much as a comma (except possibly to add citations to cases subsequently decided that confirm the contentions made) . To the extent that time and other cases permit, I still strive for that goal—but without success up to now.

Such a standard of perfectionism in a brief is doubtless just that—a dream. But there is nothing dreamy about an effective appellate brief—and it is the effective rather than the impossibly perfect brief that is the subject of this chapter.

For the rest, it is really not profitable to discuss an effective brief in terms of abstractions. Too many otherwise excellent discussions of brief-writing are of very little use except to the expert, simply because they are abstract; and, *ex hypothesi*, the expert does not need them. What follows, therefore, will be concrete and detailed.

Most of the examples discussed in the pages that follow will be taken from my own practice. That choice is dictated by convenience, not by egocentricity. Of course there are plenty of other and, I have no doubt at all, better examples. But the briefs discussed here are the ones that arose out of the cases with which I have wrestled; they are the ones I have personally sweated out, where I had intimate acquaintance with the details of the problems presented and with the processes by which ultimate solutions for those problems were reached. Nevertheless, although the examples chosen are thus limited, I have sought to select, not esoteric specialties, but topics of general interest and techniques of general application.

For extended research, the best sources are the libraries of courts, bar associations, and law schools, many of which preserve the records and briefs in appellate cases. There is no better guide to good brief-writing anywhere than the examination and study of briefs written by leaders of the bar and (by and large) by such Government agencies as handle extensive litigation. Briefs in those categories are highly instructive as to form, substance, and technique.

Section 21. List of the essentials of effective brief-writing.— The really essential features are:

    (a) Compliance with rules of court.

    (b) Effective statement of the facts.

    (c) Good, clear, forceful English.

    (d) Argumentative headings.

    (e) Appealing formulation of the questions presented.

(f) Sound analysis of the legal problems in argument on the law.

(g) Convincing presentation of the evidence in argument on the facts.

(h) Careful attention to all portions of the brief.

(i) Impression of conviction that allays the reader's doubts and satisfies his curiosity.

These essentials are discussed in order below. The details and the finer points, i.e., those that help to make the difference between a really good brief and one that is merely adequate, are considered in Chapter V.

Section 22. Compliance with rules of court.—Compliance with rules of court is stated as the first requirement because, even if you should succeed in writing that dream brief, the clerk would not permit it to be filed if it exceeded the permitted length, or if it violated in other obvious respects the rules of the court to which it is tendered. So—first essential—familiarize yourself with the *current* rules of the court in question, and comply with them. The word "current" is advisedly italicized; failure to heed the obsolescence factor in rules of court can be extremely dangerous.[1]

As has been indicated, this book is not a treatise on federal appellate procedure. It does not discuss the question of what rulings are appealable—and so does not consider the scope of the recent Act of Congress which, by permitting interlocutory appeals in certain cases, alters the "final judgment" rule that had been traditional in the federal judicial system since the beginning.[2] Simi-

---

[1] For instance, the older form of petition for certiorari always contained a separate supporting brief; beginning in 1931, the Solicitor General of the United States abandoned the supporting brief and filed a combined document, but many private practitioners continued to use the older form. In the 1954 revision of the Supreme Court's Rules, the Court prescribed the Government form, and provided in its Rule 23 (3) that "No separate brief in support of a petition for writ of certiorari will be received, and the clerk will refuse to file any petition for writ of certiorari to which is annexed or appended any supporting brief."

For a discussion of the reasons underlying this particular change, see my paper on *The Supreme Court's New Rules,* 68 Harv. L. Rev. 20, at 23 and 57-58; the full article explains in detail the scope and purpose of the 1954 revision.

[2] Act of Sept. 2, 1958, Pub. L. 85-919, 72 Stat. 1770, adding 28 U. S. C. § 1292 (b). See Wright, *The Interlocutory Appeals Act of 1958,* 23 F. R. D. 199; Green and Green, *A New Element in Federal Procedure: Interlocutory Appeals Under the New Statute,* 45 A. B. A. J. 681.

The District of Columbia formerly had a provision for special appeals, by

larly, there will be no discussion of the mechanics of preparing the record on appeal, a process that is subject to constant change as more and more circuits adopt the appendix system and provide for the transmission of original papers to the appellate court.[3]

Moreover, there will be no attempt to discuss in detail the provisions concerning briefs as these appear in the rules of Federal appellate courts. For one thing, there is available the excellent text of Messrs. Stern and Gressman on *Supreme Court Practice,*[4] while the rules of all Federal appellate courts are conveniently collected in the USCA and in the Lawyers Coop. edition of the Supreme Court Digest.[5] For another, all of these rules are subject to frequent and drastic changes, so that what was once proper can become literally unacceptable overnight.[6] Consequently, the only safe procedure, whether you are new at the game or whether, although experienced generally, you are writing a brief for a court in which you have not previously practiced, is (a) to read the

---

permission, from interlocutory decrees. Sec. 17-101, D. C. Code (1940 ed.). But in the process of trying somehow to make the District of Columbia resemble a State of the Union (cf. *National Mut. Ins. Co.* v. *Tidewater Co.,* 337 U. S. 582), so that the courts of the District would be integrated into the federal judicial system as simply an eleventh circuit, this useful provision was repealed. Act of May 24, 1949, c. 139, 63 Stat. 89, 110. Certain differences in criminal procedure still remain, however. See *Carroll* v. *United States,* 354 U. S. 394. For two recent warning cases as to timeliness on appeal and on certiorari, respectively, see *United States* v. *Schaefer Brewing Co.,* 356 U. S. 227, and *Federal Trade Comm.* v. *Minneapolis-Honeywell Co.,* 344 U. S. 206.

[3] Since the first version of the present book was published, the First, Second, and Fifth Circuits have shifted to the Appendix system from the former and traditional print-everything method.

Effective July 1, 1960, the Fifth Circuit joined all the others in treating the original papers as the record on appeal. Fifth Circuit, Rule 23; see Stewart, *Comments on the Original Papers Rule,* 22 F. R. D. 211.

[4] Second edition, 1954, published by BNA, Incorporated. In order to facilitate reference to the third edition, which is now in preparation, the chapter as well as the page citation to the second edition is given in every instance.

[5] The rules of all eleven Courts of Appeals will be found in one of the volumes of 28 USCA and in vol. 18 of the L. ed. Digest.

The rules of the Court of Claims appear in another volume of 28 USCA and in 18 L. ed. Digest. The rules of the Court of Customs and Patent Appeals will be found in 18 L. ed. Digest and in Appendix I to the last volume of 35 USCA. The rules of the Court of Military Appeals appear in 18 L. ed. Digest and in the first volume of 10 USCA, following § 867.

The rules of the Supreme Court appear in 17 L. ed. Digest and in a volume of 28 USCA—but the annotations as they appear in the latter set are incomplete and must be supplemented by independent research.

[6] See note 1, *supra.*

rules; (b) to check with the clerk or a lawyer who is frequently before the particular court; and (c) to examine and follow the form of some briefs that have already passed muster under the rules in force.

Since the rules reflect the preference of your audience, an audience you are seeking to persuade, you will be well advised to adjust your own pet notions to those preferences. The judges adopted those rules in the view, rightly or wrongly, that the provisions in respect of briefs will conserve their time and energy.

Three points that are dealt with in the rules of most Federal appellate courts must be carefully checked:

First. Some courts require a particular and frequently somewhat arbitrary arrangement of briefs, with respect to color of cover,[7] rigidly detailed arrangement of matter,[8] summary of argument and of the principal authorities,[9] and prescribed position for the statement of questions presented.[10]

Second. Most clerks, reflecting the views of their courts, are quite fussy about untimely filings.[11]

Third. An increasing number of Federal appellate courts limit the length of the briefs that may be filed without prior express permission. This is now true of all federal circuits except the Fifth.

There is no limit on the length of briefs in the Supreme Court

---

[7] E.g., D. C. Circuit, Rule 17 (a) ; Seventh Circuit, Rule 16 (h).

[8] E.g., Supreme Court, Rule 40 (1) ; D. C. Circuit, Rule 17; Third Circuit, Rule 24; Fourth Circuit, Rule 10; Sixth Circuit, Rule 16; Eighth Circuit, Rule 11 (b) ; Ninth Circuit, Rule 18 (2) ; Tenth Circuit, Rule 19 (3).

[9] E.g., Supreme Court Rule 40 (1) (f) ; D. C. Circuit, Rule 17 (b) (3) and 17 (b) (8) ; Seventh Circuit, Rule 17 (a) (3) ; Eighth Circuit, Rule 11 (b) (Fourth).

[10] E.g., Supreme Court Rules 15 (1) (c) (1), 23 (1) (c), 40 (1) (d) ; D. C. Circuit, Rule 17 (b) (1) ; Third Circuit, Rule 24 (2) (b) ; Sixth Circuit, Rule 16 (2) (a).

[11] Many circuits have rules to the effect that late filing constitutes a ground for dismissing the appeal, and on occasion such dismissals are noted in the Federal Reporter. In one instance, an appellant filed no brief for three years!

Similarly, these instances have been noted in the course of currently scanning the Federal Reporter: (a) Appeal dismissed, because record not in shape for review. (b) Failure to print any evidence in the appendix. (c) "It may be wondered how appellant could have expected the district court to rule other than it did on the very meager record in this case."

It is believed that no useful purpose would be served by supplying citations in these instances.

of the United States, except in one instance of narrow application.[12] But "The failure of a petitioner [for certiorari] to present
with accuracy, brevity, and clearness whatever is essential to a
ready and adequate understanding of the points requiring consideration will be a sufficient reason for denying his petition." [13]
Under earlier versions of the rule there were dismissals for failure
to file arguments that were "direct and concise." [14] And on one
now well-known occasion, briefs on the merits filed by eminent—
and no doubt well-compensated—counsel were stricken because
they contained "burdensome, irrelevant, and immaterial matter." [15]

One additional but extremely important caution must be
noted here: Bear in mind the limitations on the reviewing powers
of the appellate court that apply to your particular case. A finding
of fact made below is scrutinized by different standards depending
on whether it was made by a jury, or by a judge sitting in what

---

[12] A motion for leave to file a brief *amicus curiae* may not exceed 5 printed
pages in length. Supreme Court Rule 42 (3).

[13] Supreme Court Rule 23 (4).

[14] See *Zap* v. *United States*, 326 U. S. 777: "The petition for writ of certiorari in this case is denied for failure to comply with par. 2 of Rule 38 of the
Rules of this Court. The brief filed in support of the petition is not 'direct
and concise' as required by that rule."

The original supporting brief had been 83 pages long. Thereafter, issuance of the order denying the writ was stayed, 326 U. S. 692, and on rehearing certiorari was granted. 326 U. S. 802. Zap's conviction was affirmed, 328
U. S. 624, and a petition for rehearing was denied. 329 U. S. 824. But, at the
next Term, a second petition for rehearing was granted and the indictment
ordered dismissed, because of the absence of women on the grand jury that had
indicted *Mr.* Zap! 330 U. S. 800.

See also Stern and Gressman, *Supreme Court Practice* (2d ed. 1954)
ch. V (F), pp. 204-205, entitled "Length of the petition"; and note the citations there to other instances of petitions being denied because they were too
long.

[15] See Journal, U. S. Sup. Ct., Oct. T. 1928, p. 101: "It is ordered by the
Court that this case be restored to the docket for reargument on January 14,
1929, with the same limitations as to the time of argument and the number of
counsel as in the original hearing; that complete new briefs be filed, and
that the old briefs heretofore filed shall not be used; that the new briefs shall
conform to the rules of this Court, be compact, logically arranged with proper
headings, concise, and free from burdensome, irrelevant, and immaterial matter; * * *" The record contained 2,023 pages, the briefs first filed extended
to 1,924 pages, and the briefs on the second argument contained only 789
pages. The case was *Gilchrist* v. *Interborough Rapid Transit Co.*, 279 U. S.
159. See Frankfurter and Landis, *The Business of the Supreme Court at
October Term, 1928* (1929) 43 Harv. L. Rev. 22, 57.

traditionally would have been a suit in equity, or by an administrative agency.[16] A fact found by the Court of Claims can be reviewed by the Supreme Court only under stringent limitations—if at all.[17] The Court of Military Appeals has not been granted power to review facts; it can review only questions of law.[18] The Supreme Court of the United States, when determining cases brought to it from State courts, reviews only questions of Federal law; it has no jurisdiction to consider purely state law issues.[19] Other examples will readily come to mind. But the basic admonition is the same: The brief-writer must keep constantly in mind the limitations under which his appeal will be considered.

In all candor it must be added that power and consistency are not synonymous in this field. Thus, the extent to which the Supreme Court will disturb findings of fact when reviewing Federal cases cannot be realistically stated in terms of rules. In some antitrust cases it has expressed a reluctance to review the evidence,[20] in others it has set aside findings that were deemed "clearly erroneous" in the sense of Civil Rule 52 (a),[21] while on occasion it appears pretty much to have brushed aside the findings.[22] Similarly, in denaturalization cases, very little respect is,

---

[16] See Stern, *Review of Findings of Administrators, Judges and Juries: A Comparative Analysis,* 58 Harv. L. Rev. 70. Since the foregoing article was published, in November 1944, the Administrative Procedure Act and the Taft-Hartley Act have "expressed a mood" that requires closer judicial scrutiny of administrative findings. *Universal Camera Corp. v. Labor Board,* 340 U. S. 474, 487.

[17] The older rule, rigid to the point of injustice, was that the Supreme Court's review of Court of Claims cases was limited to questions of law, and did not even extend to mixed questions of law and fact. *United States v. Esnault-Pelterie,* 303 U. S. 26. The decision in that case was followed by the Act of May 22, 1939, c. 140, 53 Stat. 752, which expanded the review to include questions of fact, substantially on the basis of the traditional equity appeal. However, the very specific terms of the remedial statute were omitted in the 1948 revision on the ground that they were "unnecessary"!—with the result that no one now knows whether the Supreme Court has any power to review factual findings by the Court of Claims. See *United States v. Penn Mfg. Co.,* 337 U. S. 198, 207-208, note 4.

[18] Art. 67 (d), Uniform Code of Military Justice, now 10 U. S. C. § 867 (d).

[19] See 28 U.S.C. § 1257; Stern and Gressman, *Supreme Court Practice* (2d ed. 1954) ch. III (G), pp. 94-102; Robertson & Kirkham, *Jurisdiction of the Supreme Court of the United States* (Kurland & Wolfson ed. 1951) Part I, passim.

[20] *United States v. Oregon State Medical Soc.,* 343 U. S. 326.

[21] *United States v. United Gypsum Co.,* 333 U. S. 364.

[22] *United States v. du Pont & Co.,* 353 U. S. 586.

in practice, given even concurrent findings of fact made below,[23] a circumstance which, when that rule was first formulated, called forth the mordant comment that "The finality which attaches to the trial court's determinations of fact from evidence heard in open court and which ordinarily saves them from an appellate court's intermeddling, should not be remembered in every case save this one alone." [24]

Section 23. Effective statement of the facts; why necessary.— In many respects, the Statement of Facts is the most important part of the brief; hence the priority given it in the present discussion. The circumstances that numerous other matters may be required by rule of court to precede the Statement of Facts in the printed brief does not in any sense warrant postponing its consideration.

The greatest mistake any lawyer can make, after he has written a fine brief on the law, is to toss in a dry statement of facts and send the thing off to the printer. When I first came to the bar (now more years ago than I like to recall), my chief—Eugene A. Kingman, Esq., of the Rhode Island Bar—used to insist that that was the common error made by the young men in the office—and everything I have seen since then has served only to confirm the truth of his admonition. I owe it to him to acknowledge that I have profited by his wisdom, and learned the great lesson that, in writing briefs, the facts should first be studied, mastered, sweated over—and written out into an acceptable draft before the rest of the brief is even touched.

For facts are basic raw materials of the legal process, as all great lawyers, from ancient worthies down to the great judges of modern times, have recognized. *Ex facto jus oritur*—the law arises out of the fact—is a well-worn maxim of old, to the point of being hackneyed. But it expresses a fundamental truth that, within the memory of most of us, Mr. Justice Brandeis regularly put into practice. As Professor Freund, one of his former law clerks, has written:

---

[23] *Schneiderman* v. *United States,* 320 U. S. 118; *Baumgartner* v. *United States,* 322 U. S. 665. Notwithstanding *Knauer* v. *United States,* 328 U. S. 654, the *Schneiderman-Baumgartner* rule seems still to be law. *Nowak* v. *United States,* 356 U. S. 660; *Maisenberg* v. *United States,* 356 U. S. 670. The same strict standard is applicable to expatriation cases. *Gonzales* v. *Landon,* 350 U. S. 920.

[24] Stone, C. J., dissenting in *Schneiderman* v. *United States,* 320 U. S. at 170.

His belief in the primacy of facts was apparent even in the process of preparing an opinion. However much he encouraged his law clerks to present the results of their legal research in a form which might be directly useful in drafting an opinion, he took on himself the burden of drafting the statement of facts. This was his private assurance that he would not be seduced by the fascination of legal analysis until he had grounded himself in the realities of the case as they were captured in the record.[25]

While the advocate's task and function differ from those of the judge, in that the advocate must persuade while the judge has only to decide, the foregoing excerpt emphasizes the vital significance of bringing the facts of the case to the judges' attention with a view to shaping their decision.

Remember, courts are not automatons, and judges do not cease to be human beings however much they may—as they very properly should—steel themselves against emotional bias. The constantly repeated demonstration that "hard cases made bad law" is living proof of that proposition. The real importance of facts is that courts want to do substantial justice and that they are sensitive to the "equities." Consequently the first objective of the advocate must be so to write his Statement of Facts that the court will want to decide the case in his favor after reading just that portion of his brief.

Section 24. Effective statement of the facts; how to formulate and write it.—First of all, when you write a Statement of Facts, you must remember that you are endeavoring to reach another person's mind. You must also remember that any person's acquisition of knowledge is a cumulative process. Therefore, you must state the facts of the case in your brief as you yourself would wish to read them—the introductory summary first, the details later—in order to get a clear, consecutive, understandable picture of what the case is really about.

A lawyer stating the facts of his case is telling a story, a story the court should be able to accept and understand as it reads along, without having to supplement your narrative by its own independent efforts. Or, to use a different metaphor, the lawyer stating the facts is painting a picture—and those who look at that picture should not be troubled by the details of how the artist mixed his colors. To the extent that the judicial reader may want to check

---

[25] Freund, *On Understanding the Supreme Court* (1949) 50.

the facts of your story, or the art-lover those of the picture, the record references will supply the necessary assurance that what has been depicted is real and not imaginary. (See Sections 44 and 80, below.)

Therefore, always avoid the lazy kind of summary that says, "The witness Quackenbush testified that ———; that ———; that ———; that ———," and so on *ad infinitum* and *ad nauseam*. Any literate stenographer can do that; most lazy lawyers do it; but, as it isn't very helpful to the court and it doesn't forward the case, the good lawyer will not do it.

Similarly, it is a mistake to assume, as many lawyers apparently do, that it is necessary to set out the testimony in the same order in which it was presented at the trial. The trial lawyer must take one witness at a time, and develop what witnesses X, Y, and Z know about incidents A, B, and C. There is generally no other way in which he can get that evidence into the record. But the appellate lawyer, in writing the statement of facts, should marshal his evidence according to topics, logically developed, and not according to witnesses. True, it takes more work, which is why so often it is not done. But the logical topical arrangement is really the only effective one.

No matter how long or short a Statement of Facts may be, it should always be written in such a way as to advance the cause of the party on whose behalf it is prepared. It must not argue or editorialize; its strength lies in selection and juxtaposition, without of course ever appearing to involve the irrelevant.

In many instances, you can add immeasurably to the effectiveness of your Statement of Facts by simply quoting the opinion below, varying it only by adding appropriate record references inclosed in square brackets. If you represent the appellee, this treatment gives the Statement of Facts the additional and very substantial weight that attaches to findings made by the tribunal that saw and heard the witnesses. If you represent the appellant, the same technique gives you the freedom from distracting minor issues that comes from saying that, accepting fully the facts found below, you pitch your entire case on questions of law. Or, otherwise stated, use the opinion below supplemented by references to the record when you are appellant as to the law or when you are appellee as to the facts.

Frequently a Statement of Facts will necessarily be long, particularly when the record is long. In that event it should not be written as one continuous screed. Instead, it should be divided, through the use of subheadings, so that the judicial reader can more easily grasp the relevance of what he reads.[26]

---

[26] Here are examples of subdivisions of the Statement of Facts in two reasonably recent cases, one criminal, the other civil.

(a) *Elkins* v. *United States,* 364 U. S. 206:

A. The initial seizure and the original State proceedings, through the granting of both motions to suppress.

B. The Federal prosecution and the Federal motion to suppress.

C. State court injunction against State officers.

D. Application to Ninth Circuit for writ of prohibition.

E. Petitioners' trial in United States District Court.

F. State contempt proceedings after conclusion of Federal trial; the Federal injunction.

G. The decision of the court below.

(b) *Swift & Co.* v. *United States,* 343 U. S. 373:

A. The economics of direct shipments of livestock.

B. Means open to appellant for receipt of direct shipments of livestock.

(i) Consignment to Omaha Packing Co. sidetrack—$50,000 annually for additional trucking.

(ii) Consignment to Union Stock Yards—$129,000 annually for services neither appropriate to nor desired for livestock already owned by the consignee.

(iii) Consignment to own sidetrack—$254,000 annually for switching charges.

C. Scope of the switching charge in question.

(i) Inapplicability to livestock consigned to Union Stock Yards.

(ii) Inapplicability to other commodities delivered at Swift's sidetrack.

(iii) Switching charge not dependent on distance between Chicago Junction yards and line-haul carriers' break-up yards.

D. Transportation of livestock to consignees in the stockyards district.

(i) Route followed and switching performed.

(ii) Percentage of mixed trains; incidence of trains composed of one and two cars of livestock.

(iii) Transportation of livestock to Swift's Omaha Packing Co. plant.

E. Congestion on Chicago Junction tracks.

F. Factors other than volume of traffic contributing to congestion on Chicago Junction tracks.

(i) Decline in Chicago Junction's motive power since its lease by appellee New York Central.

(ii) Effect of 1946 labor agreement.

(iii) Operations of line-haul carriers on Chicago Junction tracks.

(iv) Refusal of Chicago Junction to grant additional trackage rights.

(v) Union Stock Yards rules directed at dead freight.

G. Covenant in Chicago Junction lease and its invocation by Union Stock Yards. (*Continued on p. 48*)

When the Statement of Facts is long, it is even more necessary to write it so that the judicial reader's interest will never flag, but will always be held, and will constantly be carried in the direction at which the advocate is aiming. That endeavor must never be permitted to sag, even at the end, when the proceedings in the court below are being discussed.

It is a mistake to write simply, "The court below affirmed (R. 74)," when you could have written, "The court below affirmed on the ground that the evidence amply justified the jury in finding petitioner guilty as charged (R. 74)."

Frequently the Statement of Facts can be, as it were, neatly buttoned up by a juicy quotation from the findings or opinion below. If you are appealing, summarize or quote the opinion below when it seems pretty obviously wrong, or summarize or quote from the dissenting judge, or both. If, on the other hand, you are for the appellee, set out the conclusions or the apt quotation from the majority opinion, or do the same for the dissent when it seems unsound on its face.

In short, write your Statement of Facts from the beginning to end, from the first paragraph to the last, with this one aim always before you: to write your Statement of Facts so that the court will want to decide the case in your favor after it has finished reading just that portion of your brief.

It is doubtless tiresome to reiterate all this. But the simple fact is that the fault most universally found in Statements of Facts is that they are too dry, that they do not make the most of what the record affords, and that in consequence they do not advance the case.

Section 25. Effective statement of the facts; how to use the atmospheric trimmings.—Once the basic arrangement of the Statement of Facts has been blocked out, with proper topical introductions and with the facts arranged in logical order—and generally the chronological order is the most logical one—it is time to consider the next step, which is, succinctly, to incorporate the atmospheric trimmings.

H. Evidence bearing on effect of granting appellant's prayer for relief.
    (i) Effect of appellant's shipments alone.
    (ii) Position of the other packers.
    (iii) Evidence as to congestion and disruption.
I. Proceedings before the Commission and in the court below

Here the task is to present the facts, without the slightest sacrifice of accuracy, but yet in such a way as to squeeze from them the last drop of advantage to your case—and that is a task that in a very literal sense begins with the first sentence of your Statement of Facts and continues through the last one (in which you set forth the opinion or judgment below).

Examples of how to do it and of how not to do it will be considered later; here will be set forth some general admonitions that should be heeded.

(a) First and foremost, you must be accurate. You owe that duty to the court, and, equally, you owe that duty to your client. And, for the same reason, you must be candid. If the court finds that you are inaccurate, either by way of omission or of affirmative misstatement, it will lose faith in you, and your remaining assertions may well fail to persuade. See Section 44, below, for a discussion of the application, in this connection, of the maxim *Falsus in uno, falsus in omnibus.*

A Federal appellate judge recently had occasion to remark that "Skilled advocacy is not a substitute for operative facts though that art may supply emphasis and delicate nuances of evidence clearly established by the record." [27]

That statement marks, about as well as it can be drawn in the abstract, the line between the proper use of atmospheric trimmings and the improper use of imperceptible slanting that results in intentional misstatement. It is just as much the duty of the advocate to present his acts favorably as it is his duty to present the law forcefully. It is not in any sense "cute" to wring every advantageous fact out of your record—just so long as the full Statement of Facts is fair, honest, and accurate. I emphasize both aspects because—as a matter of actual fact—quite a number of appellate judges seem to feel that any advice to stress the favorable facts is tantamount to urging deception as an aid to winning on appeal. Any such reaction is the result either of a failure to understand the office of advocacy, or of a failure to analyze one's own thinking—or of both.

The mark of really able advocacy is the ability to set forth the facts most favorably within the limits of utter and unswerving accuracy.

---

[27] Finnegan, J., concurring in *Lusk v. Commissioner of Internal Revenue,* 250 F. 2d 591, 595 (C.A.7).

(b) Second, grasp your nettles firmly. No matter how unfavorable the facts are, they will hurt you more if the court first learns them from your opponent. Draw the sting of unpleasant facts by presenting them yourself. To gloss over a nasty portion of the record is not only somewhat less than fair to the court, it is definitely harmful to the case.

If you fail to heed this injunction, if you omit salient and significant but unpleasant facts, you may be sure that the opposition will rub your nose in them. Consider, for example, the execution done by the following excerpts from an answering brief on a brief-in-chief that omitted pertinent facts. (Proper names have been changed.)

We have documented the United States Attorney's argument on the defense of extortion with record references, not only in order that it might be considered against the context of the evidence in the case, but also because the Smiths' brief falls considerably short of reflecting all of the pertinent facts.

(1) The Smiths start by saying that Milton Smith and Morris Brown voluntarily enlisted in the Air Corps (Br. 7). They fail to state that Sam Smith had them volunteer for the Air Corps in order to avoid having them drafted and assigned to the infantry (R. 184, 276-277).

(2) The Smiths admit that their concern, the Paris Thread Corporation, paid the Berg Company for the uniforms furnished to Jones and other officers of the First Bomber Command (Br. 9). They fail to state that, at Sam Smith's request, the Berg Company's books were later altered to show that the officers themselves paid for the uniforms (R. 190-195; Govt. Ex. 5, 6, 7, R. 192, 193, 195, 1219, 1221, 1223).

*   *   *   *   *

(5) The Smiths quote Sam Smith as urging Jones to leave the boys at Westover and Bradley Fields with the Airborne Engineers because they were happy there (Br. 13, 15). "I said 'Warren please let's forget all about the kids, they are very happy, they met a nice captain, a nice sergeant.' . . . I said Warren I told you once before please let's forget all about the kids, they are happy and I am happy." (R. 1228, 1229.) The Smiths do not say in their brief, nor did Sam Smith tell the United States Attorney, that in fact he approached Colonel ———, Colonel ———, Major ———, and Captain ——— in his attempts to have the boys transferred out of the Airborne Engineers, and that he fainted when Colonel ——— told him that nothing could or should be done (*supra,* pp. 16-18).

(6) The Smiths place Jones in New York on the morning of November 25, urging Sam Smith to come to a decision on whether he

will pay $5,000 to keep the boys from being sent to the Pacific (Br. 16, 35). But their own motion for new trial, on which they rely to establish error here (Br. 33-36), shows that Jones was in Washington on the night of November 24/25, that he left Washington at 9:30 A.M. November 25 and flew to Connecticut, and that he did not arrive at La Guardia Field, New York, until 4 P.M. on that day (Motion, p. 48; U.S. Br. 82-83).

(7) The Smiths twice state that the order transferring the boys from the Air Commando Group at Goldsboro into the Air Transport Command in Wilmington was dated November 29 (Br. 17, 35). This is literally true (R. 1218). But they fail to state that this transfer was directed by a letter from Headquarters Army Air Forces dated November 25 (R. 123, 1218), and that this letter was written in consequence of Jones' telephone call to Miss Graham on November 24 (R. 256-257). Consequently, even if, as the Smiths now assert (Br. 16), the $5,000 was paid not later than November 27, it is still clear that, when the payment was made, Jones had put it out of his power to take Milton and Morris to the Pacific.

(c) Never argue or editorialize in your Statement of Facts. Always be straightforward; indicate the conflict in the evidence, gain whatever advantage you can out of the order of its presentation, but save your argument for the body of the brief. The temptation to slip in a sly remark is sometimes pretty strong; let it go into an early draft, if you must, and get what fun you can out of it; but be sure it is out of the final product.

In short, present your facts accurately, candidly—but always favorably, and always strive to make the most favorable impression, short of actually arguing, with the facts that you have.[28]

---

[28] The reply brief from which the excerpts below are quoted passed over my desk a dozen years ago, but what was then said still warms the cockles:

"An appellant does not often use much space in a reply brief to praise a brief for the appellee. Here, then, though we think commendation due, a few words may seem enough.

"In general, the appellee's brief recites the evidence fairly. Of course, quite properly, the statement is of that most favorable to the Government, but there is little at which to quibble. * * *

"The argument seems to us to say all that can be said for the Government on the points raised, and to say it with great skill; e.g., how much more effective the connotations of the words in the brief * * * than those in the indictment * * *.

"We do not suggest that the choice of words employed in the brief for the appellee goes beyond the license of an advocate. * * *

"Our praise of the appellee's brief is, therefore, tempered with a note of caution. Its art is in its color, not applied in crude daubs, but with restraint that sometimes requires scrutiny to perceive its fundamental flaws. * * *"

Section 26. Examples of effective and ineffective Statements of Facts.—It remains to illustrate the foregoing generalizations with specific and concrete examples. Full Statements of Facts, from briefs filed in a variety of situations, were set out in Chapters 10-13 of the former version of this work, while those appearing in Chapter XII (below, pp. 397-421) illustrate the problem discussed in the next section. The examples in the present section are shorter excerpts selected to illustrate particular techniques.

(a) Courts dislike to referee ideological contests, or to be asked to umpire disputes that exude even the faintest suggestion of mutual zeal to get a question decided,[29] or to assist the litigant who goes to law to vindicate a principle rather than a substantial legal right, or to take advantage of a situation at the expense of the public. The problem in such cases is to make the court aware of what is going on—which obviously cannot be done by calling one's opponent a strike-suitor or his cause a cooked-up case. Usually, in such a situation, the facts of record speak for themselves, and all the advocate need normally do is to set them out, without comment.

An example that comes to mind is that of a bitterly contested proceeding involving a tract of public land that was of no possible value except as a source of rock for a nearby breakwater. If the claimant had succeeded in obtaining it, the neighboring municipality would of necessity have had to pay handsomely for the stone it wanted. In order to convey the desired impression, the brief for the public official commenced its Statement of Facts as follows:

Whaler Island is a small rocky island in the harbor of Crescent City, California, some 3.65 acres in extent (R. 17-18). It is without value for agricultural purposes, is not adapted to ordinary and private occupation, and is of utility only in connection with the improvement and development of the harbor (R. 31).

This island is the land for which the appellant Lyders seeks a patent (Bill, par. V, XVIII; R. 4, 15-16).[30]

In that case, the matter was dropped with its mere statement, and was not further pursued. There was nothing to argue about,

---

[29] Cf. *United States* v. *C.I.O.*, 335 U. S. 106.

[30] *Lyders* v. *Ickes*, 65 App. D. C. 379, 84 F. 2d 232. For earlier stages in the Whaler Island litigation, see *West* v. *Lyders*, 59 App. D. C. 122, 36 F. 2d 108, and *Wilbur* v. *Lyders*, 61 App. D. C. 202, 59 F. 2d 877; for the sequel, see *Lyders* v. *Del Norte County*, 100 F. 2d 876 (C. A. 9), certiorari denied, 308 U. S. 562.

because the circumstances in question were atmospheric only, and legally irrelevant.

In other cases, however, facts going to the infirmity of a party may become relevant, in which event they are properly taken up in subsequent argument. The problem is to distinguish between the Statement of Facts and the Argument, to keep the first absolutely straightforward, and to put the editorializing and characterization where they belong, namely, in the portion of the brief that is headed "Argument."

Examples of the second category arise in situations where review by a higher court is discretionary,[31] and where accordingly the appellate court must be convinced, not so much that the decision below is correct or incorrect, but rather that the question is important and is one that deserves or requires review. In such a situation any fact tending to show that a litigant is more interested in obtaining an advisory opinion than in vindicating his legal rights becomes not only relevant but important and, it may be, controlling.

A case arising out of a World War II removal order, but coming up sufficiently long after V-J Day to be of essentially academic interest, illustrates the point. The plaintiff had been individually ordered excluded from the sensitive West Coast area after having been convicted of conspiracy to commit sedition.[32] He sued the

---

[31] The prime example of discretionary review in the Federal system is, of course, certiorari in the Supreme Court; but there are others.

(a) An appeal to the Supreme Court, though theoretically taken as of right, is in fact discretionary by reason of the device of dismissal for want of a substantial federal question in cases appealed from state courts, and of affirmance without argument in cases appealed from federal courts. Supreme Court Rule 16 (1) (b) and 16 (1) (c) ; Stern and Gressman, *Supreme Court Practice* (2d ed. 1954) ch. VI (F), pp. 233-238, 243-245; see my paper on *The Supreme Court's New Rules,* 68 Harv. L. Rev. 20, 50-51, and particularly the comments of Chief Justice Warren quoted at p. 51. For a more recent formulation, see the address by Mr. Justice Harlan, *Manning the Dikes,* 13 The Record of the Assn. of the Bar of the City of N. Y. 541, 545-546.

(b) The bulk of the jurisdiction of the Court of Military Appeals is discretionary. Art. 67 (b) (3), Uniform Code of Military Justice, 10 U.S.C. § 867 (b) (3).

(c) The District of Columbia has a discretionary jurisdiction to review decisions of the Municipal Court of Appeals for the District of Columbia. Sec. 11-773, D. C. Code (1951 ed.) ; and see the rules governing such review in the pocket part to the volume in 28 USCA that includes the U. S. Courts of Appeals Rules.

[32] Distinguish the mass exclusion orders considered in *Hirabayashi* v. *United States,* 320 U. S. 81, and *Korematsu* v. *United States,* 323 U. S. 214.

Commanding General for damages, a judgment in his favor was reversed on appeal, and he petitioned for a writ of certiorari to review the result. The Statement of Facts in the Commanding General's brief opposing the petition therefore pointed out:

The complaint asked damages in the sum of $3500, but subsequently petitioner filed a waiver of all damages in excess of $100 (R. 83, 291, 296, 303).

In the portion of the General's brief headed "Argument," he adverted to this fact and argued that

* * * The circumstance that, after bringing suit for $3500 (R. 11), petitioner subsequently stipulated that he would waive all damages over $100 (R. 83, 291, 296), strongly suggests that the object of this proceeding for damages was not so much redress for injuries sustained as the obtaining of abstract pronouncements from the courts as to respondent's authority. This he cannot have * * *.

Certiorari was denied,[33] and the factor just mentioned may well have contributed to that result.

(b) It is a commonplace that a very bad man may have a very good case. But judges are human, they want to do substantial justice, and therefore in close cases they are, more or less unconsciously (depending on the individual judge), bound to be influenced by the character of the litigant, particularly when he appears before them as a crusader.

Without doubt, the Jehovah's Witnesses in the 1940's spearheaded much civil rights litigation, and a good deal of constitutional law was written—and rewritten—around their activities. It is not necessary to collect at this point either the cases or the commentaries thereon or even to set out at length the situation out of which the next example arises. Suffice it to say that two members of the sect, Kulick and Sunal, were separately classified as I-A for the draft. When they failed to report for induction, they were indicted, and at their separate trials neither was permitted to attack his draft classification; each was convicted, neither appealed.

Shortly after their convictions, the Supreme Court held, disagreeing with some 40 circuit judges in the process, that, in criminal prosecutions under the Selective Training and Service Act of 1940, defendants did have a right to attack the correctness of their

---

[33] *Wilcox* v. *Emmons*, 67 F. Supp. 339 (S.D. Cal.), reversed *sub nom. DeWitt* v. *Wilcox*, 161 F. 2d 785 (C.A. 9), certiorari denied, 332 U. S. 763.

draft classifications. *Estep* v. *United States* and *Smith* v. *United States.*[34] Accordingly, Kulick and Sunal separately petitioned for habeas corpus, alleging that they were detained without authority of law—on the ground of denial of the right to defend at their original trials. One circuit held that habeas corpus lay in these circumstances, another that it did not, and both cases came before the Supreme Court.

The facts were that Kulick had originally been classified as I-A, i.e., available for immediate military service, and then had been reclassified as IV-D, viz., minister of religion. Thereafter, to quote from the Statement of Facts in the Government's brief,

Nothing further occurred until August 23, 1944, when the local board was indirectly informed by one of respondent's neighbors, who was identified, that respondent spent most of his time at home, except when working as a professional model, in which capacity he sometimes posed in military uniform. Apparently as a result of this information the local board reclassified respondent I-A. He then requested a hearing * * *. Respondent appeared before the local board on August 30, 1944, and at the conclusion of the hearing the following notation was made as a minute entry in respondent's file:

When registrant appeared it was learned after interrogation that he was an artist model—and has been photographed in military uniform; when further questioned regarding C. O. in military uniform his reply was evasive.

The board continued respondent in I-A * * * .

The other individual, Sunal, had originally claimed exemption as a conscientious objector; in his questionnaire, he had stated that his occupation was "automotive carburetor and electrical mechanic," and that "I am not a minister of religion." He was classified I-A. Five days after that classification was made, Sunal for the first time claimed classification as a minister of religion. Hearings and appeals ensued, and he was finally classified in IV-E as a conscientious objector. Thereafter, failing to report, he was tried and convicted, and served a term of imprisonment. All these facts were set forth in the Government's brief. Then, as has already been noted, Sunal petitioned for habeas corpus, challenging the validity of his conviction for failing to report for induction in respect of a new classification made after his release from confinement, on the

---

[34] 327 U. S. 114.

ground that he had not been permitted to attack his new draft classification at that second trial.

The Supreme Court held that the rulings by the convicting courts in the two cases, though erroneous in the light of the subsequent *Estep-Smith* decision, did not deprive either Kulick or Sunal of their constitutional rights, and that accordingly, since they had failed to appeal, they could not thereafter review their convictions on habeas corpus. *Sunal* v. *Large* and *Alexander* v. *United States ex rel. Kulick.*[35] The Court's opinion did not discuss the particular facts of the two cases; it said:

> The local boards, after proceedings unnecessary to relate here, denied the claimed exemptions and classified these registrants as I-A * * *.

The same chief counsel represented the defendants in the present cases and those in the *Estep* and *Smith* cases. At the time these defendants were convicted the *Estep* and *Smith* cases were pending before the appellate courts. The petition in the *Smith* case was, indeed, filed here about two weeks before Kulick's conviction and about a month after Sunal's conviction. The same road was open to Sunal and Kulick as the one Smith and Estep took. Why the legal strategy counseled taking appeals in the *Smith* and *Estep* cases and not in these we do not know. Perhaps it was based on the facts of these two cases. For the question of law had not been decided by the Court; and counsel was pressing for a decision here * * *.[36]

Can it therefore fairly be said that, in deciding the dry and technical question of the scope of habeas corpus, the Supreme Court was entirely uninfluenced by the circumstance that, at the very least, the *bona fides* of the individuals seeking release from confinement was open to question?

(c) Similarly, the most important function of the Statement of Facts in a brief in a criminal case is to indicate something of the party's guilt or innocence. If you represent the prosecution, your aim must be to convey the impression that the convicted man is just as clearly guilty as he can possibly be; if you represent the defendant, you must strive to show that he has been greatly wronged. This is true in both instances not only when the question concerns the sufficiency of the evidence to support the verdict, but whatever

---

[35] 332 U. S. 174, affirming *Sunal* v. *Large*, 157 F. 2d 165 (C.A.4), and reversing *United States ex rel. Kulick* v. *Kennedy*, 157 F. 2d 811 (C.A.2).

[36] 332 U. S. at 175, 181.

the question is, quite regardless of the formal issues raised on the appeal. "Courts delight to do substantial justice."

A striking instance in which this technique was employed is the sordid Restaurant Longchamps tax fraud case, which arose around the end of World War II. Three of the convicted persons appealed without success and then petitioned for a writ of certiorari. At the trial and again in their petition these defendants indicated that there was no denial of the tax frauds charged, and raised only issues arising out of their alleged disclosures prior to the Treasury investigations, and out of the use of their admissions and of the books of their corporations. Notwithstanding the admissions of the tax frauds thus made in the petition, the Government's Brief in Opposition to the granting of certiorari discussed the facts relating to the fraud as fully as if the issue had been the sufficiency of the evidence in the Circuit Court of Appeals rather than the importance of petitioners' questions for purposes of review of their case by the Supreme Court. Indeed, the Statement of Facts was simply lifted verbatim from the Government's brief in the Circuit Court of Appeals. All the shabby details were set out, the evidence relating to the alleged disclosures was discussed at length, and the facts on the credibility of one of the defendants and on his contradiction were stated *in extenso*. (This lad had made the grave mistake, *inter alia*, of testifying to a meeting with the Collector of Internal Revenue, alleged to have taken place at the precise time when that worthy was in fact meeting with eight very substantial and prominent fellow-citizens in connection with the affairs of the Governor Smith Memorial Fund.) Moreover, the findings of the district court, to the effect that the alleged disclosures were neither full nor frank nor voluntarily made, were not simply summarized, but were quoted in full.

The consequence was, not so much that the Brief in Opposition was able to brush off the questions sought to be raised as never having been reached,[37] but that there was necessarily generated a feeling in the mind of any reader that, whether the questions were reached or not, these petitioners were so clearly guilty of such a

---

[37] "The petition in this case presents arguments resting and depending on an assumption which is entirely hypothetical, viz., that petitioners made a voluntary disclosure amounting to a confession which was induced by a promise of immunity. That assumption is quite without support on the present record, in consequence of which the questions sought to be presented are never reached."

particularly outrageous crime that jail was doubtless much too good for them.[38]

(d) Emotions that sway a jury will frequently backfire in an appellate court, or at least prove notably ineffective. But while most appellate judges cannot be charged with being, in the current idiom, bleeding hearts, they are still human beings, and thus are necessarily shocked by anything in the nature of unjustified cruelty.[39] If, therefore, the facts of your case are such as will cause a revulsion of feeling on the part of a juryman, they are bound to have at least a modicum of similar effect on the members of an appellate court.

The recent case of *Hatahley* v. *United States* [40] involved, on its face, cold jurisdictional and legal problems: Were rights under the Taylor Grazing Act, a federal law,[41] affected by a state statute regulating abandoned horses? [42] Had there in any event been compliance with the state statute's terms? [43] Did the Federal Tort Claims Act [44] cover intentional trespasses within the scope of federal agents' authority? The injuries for which redress were sought were the carrying off of horses and mules belonging to the plaintiffs, who were Navajo Indians.

Actually, the depredations were committed with extreme brutality, so much so that an observer commented, "I didn't know they were still doing that to Indians." Here is how the facts were set forth in petitioners' brief:

The animals were rounded up on the range and were either driven or hauled in trucks to a Government-owned or controlled corral

---

[38] *United States* v. *Lustig,* 163 F. 2d 85 (C.A. 2), certiorari denied, 332 U. S. 775, rehearing denied, 332 U. S. 812. For a sequel that undoubtedly eased the pain somewhat, see *Lustig* v. *United States,* 134 C. Cls. 351, 138 F. Supp. 870.

[39] See *Francis* v. *Resweber,* 329 U. S. 459, holding that neither double jeopardy nor cruel and unusual punishment is involved in executing a death sentence after an accidental failure in equipment had rendered a previous attempt at execution by electrocution ineffective. The dissent was written by a justice who more normally voted the other way in similar constitutional and criminal cases, but who appears to have been sufficiently impressed by the rather grisly facts of the first attempt at execution to set them forth in full. 329 U. S. at 480-481, note 2.

[40] 351 U. S. 173.

[41] Now 43 U.S.C. §§ 315-315r.

[42] Utah Code Ann., 1953, c. 47-2.

[43] The trial judge held that there was no compliance with its terms. Conclusion of Law 2, R. 42-44; oral opinion, R. 413-417; No. 231, Oct. T. 1955.

[44] 28 U.S.C. §§ 1346 (b) , 2671-2680.

45 miles away. Horses which could not be so handled were shot and killed by the Government's agents on the spot. The remainder were accorded brutal treatment: the horses were so jammed together in the trucks that some died as a result, and in one instance, the leg of a horse that inconveniently protruded through the truck body was sawed off by a federal employee, one Dee P. Black. (Fdg. 23, 25; R. 33-35.) Later, the animals were taken in trucks to Provo, Utah, a distance of 350 miles, where they were sold to a glue factory and horse meat plant for about $1,700—at around 3 cents a pound (R. 93, 293)—no part of which was received by petitioners (Fdg. 24; R. 34).

It may well be that the circumstances above detailed made no impression whatever on the members of the Court. But if those facts led any of the judges to the conclusion that, for such a wrong, there must be a remedy, then setting out the facts as quoted necessarily contributed to the holding that "These acts were wrongful trespasses not involving discretion on the part of the agents, and they do give rise to a claim compensable under the Federal Tort Claims Act." [45]

Section 27. Use of the Statement of Facts to advance one's case; illustrative examples.—The application of the foregoing techniques will perhaps be more clearly perceived by examining, not examples from different cases, but comparative instances from successive stages of the same case.

In *Von Moltke* v. *Gillies*,[46] the question raised in a habeas corpus proceeding was whether petitioner had freely, intelligently, and knowingly waived her right to the assistance of counsel, and whether she had freely, intelligently, and knowingly pleaded guilty. Her contention was that she had been induced to plead guilty by an F.B.I. agent who, so she alleged, had, by misinforming her as to the law, convinced her that she would be found guilty if she went to trial. The habeas corpus judge had found against her, the circuit court of appeals had affirmed, and she sought certiorari.

The difficult feature of the case, from the Government's point of view, was the dissenting opinion in the C.C.A., which had espoused and believed the petitioner's story.[47] Moreover, the F.B.I. agent had not been a good witness; his denials left something to be

---

[45] 351 U. S. at 181. For sequels, see *United States* v. *Hatahley*, 257 F. 2d 920 (C.A.10), certiorari denied, 358 U. S. 899; *United States* v. *Ritter*, 273 F. 2d 30 (C.A.10), certiorari denied, 362 U. S. 950.

[46] 332 U. S. 708.

[47] See 161 F. 2d at 116-121.

desired.[48] The strong points of the case, for the Government, were the favorable findings of the habeas corpus judge; the strong indications in the record that petitioner's story had originally germinated in the otherwise unfertile atmosphere of the House of Correction; and the fact that petitioner was, throughout, repeatedly contradicted, by other witnesses as well as by herself.

The Brief in Opposition to the petition for certiorari was written under the pressure of meeting a deadline,[49] and in the rush incident to the end of the particular term of court. The Statement of Facts which that document contained did not, therefore, succeed in dispelling the unfavorable impression produced by the dissenting opinion below, and accordingly certiorari was granted.

Preparation of the Government's brief on the merits, however, could proceed in the comparative leisure of the summer "vacation." In the new Statement of Facts, the relevant facts in the record were first divided into undisputed and conflicting evidence, and the latter heading was broken down into some seven separate incidents.

Those incidents were taken up, witness by witness, and were set out in such a way as to emphasize the innumerable instances wherein petitioner contradicted herself or was contradicted by others. The Statement of Facts, which had covered some 15 pages in the Brief in Opposition, was expanded to 29 pages in the brief on the merits, and almost all the material that had originally been relegated to footnotes was brought up into the text. The result was a far more convincing presentation, and although the Government did not win the case in the Supreme Court, it did not lose it either. Three justices voted to affirm, four to reverse and to set petitioner free, and the other two were of the opinion that they could not recreate the crucial incident from the dead record, and so voted

---

[48] Here was the critical portion of his testimony:

"Q. And did you during that discussion use an illustration about a rum runner?

"A. Well, I heard Mrs. Von Moltke say that, and since she did I have been trying to recall, and I cannot remember such an illustration.

"Q. I see.

"A. But it is quite possible that Mrs. Von Moltke's memory is better than mine, and I may have used such an illustration."

[49] Under the Supreme Court Rule then in effect, only twenty days were allowed, after the service of the Petition, for filing the Brief in Opposition; and at that time it took not less than seven days to get a brief through the Government Printing Office.

to remand to the district court "for further proceedings with a view to a specific finding of fact regarding the conversation between petitioner, and the F.B.I. agent, with as close a recreation of the incident as is now possible." [50]

The Statements of Facts in both briefs must be carefully studied for an adequate appreciation of the techniques involved. Logically, they should both be set out at this juncture. But, since both are rather long, it has seemed more convenient to print them in Chapter XII, below.

Section 28. Matters that must be avoided in a Statement of Facts.—Below, in Section 83, under the heading of "Things You Cannot Afford to Do," are collected four outstanding horribles in brief-writing: inexcusable inaccuracy, unsupported hyperbole, unwarranted screaming, and personalities and scandalous matter.

Most of these unpardonables crop up in portions of the brief other than the Statement of Facts; and, at least in my experience, even the most unprofessionally unprofessional inaccuracy is generally met with in the argument portion of the brief (after the writer's ardor has really been inflamed).

Subject to what is said—and collected—in Section 83, a common fault in many Statements of Facts is the tendency to argue and to editorialize. These are faults, because a court reading a statement wants to feel that it is getting the *facts*, and not the advocate's opinion, comments, or contentions.

Here are some examples of argumentation included in Statements of Facts, taken quite at random, and followed by comments:

(a) It is perfectly apparent from a cursory reading of the decision of the Commission (see particularly pp. 489a-499a) and of the Court (R. 597-601) as against the relevant portions of the testimony (61a-182a) that the decision of both Commission and Court is based upon the social philosophy inherent in the "no profit to affiliates" theory, and not on the record facts which the Commission should have found or at least considered and passed upon in this particular case. In other words, we do not have an administrative finding of relevant facts, but refusal

---

[50] When the case was heard again, the trial judge disbelieved petitioner, and discharged her writ of habeas corpus; and his ruling was affirmed on appeal, the same judge still dissenting. *Von Moltke* v. *United States,* 189 F. 2d 56 (C.A. 6). Once more the Supreme Court granted certiorari, this time affirming the judgment below by an equally divided court. *Von Moltke* v. *Gillies,* 343 U. S. 922.

to consider such facts because of the adoption of standards created *ad hoc* by the Commission itself.

(b) Only three of these customers were called by the Commission to testify and give evidence at the hearings. The other customers did not appear at the hearing and no evidence as to them was adduced except the figures set forth in the appendix, which were taken by the Commission's agent from the petitioner's books and records. Therefore there is no complete picture of the transactions between them and the petitioner and no sufficient basis for determining main issues with respect to their transactions. Apparently the Court below has assumed that the practices employed by registrant in dealing with these other customers were the same as those followed in dealing with the customers who testified.

(c) There was substantial, affirmative and uncontradicted evidence that the actual purpose of the accumulation of profits was wholly other than that of avoidance of surtaxes. There was no affirmative evidence that surtax avoidance was a motivating purpose.

The foregoing examples are perfectly proper argumentation, and, had they been included as part of the Argument in each instance, would have been thoroughly effective. All were, however, found in Statements of Facts—where they have no place.

Here are some examples of editorializing:

(d) It is to be observed that petitioners did not move for a directed verdict in the trial court, but they sought a review by the United States Circuit Court of Appeals for the ———— Circuit of the entire record upon the proposition that there was such a lack of evidence in this cause as to make the convictions of the petitioners a miscarriage of justice. It is also to be observed that the petitioner, Richard Brown, was represented in the trial court by counsel other than those now appearing for said petitioner.

Example (d) is editorialized rather than strictly argumentative, but illustrates a tendency on the part of some appellate practitioners to hold trial counsel responsible for the state of the record. It is a natural enough tendency, for all too often new counsel on appeal is called in to do a pulmotor job on the stretcher case left at his door. But, on appeal, you are bound by the record that has been made, be it good or bad. If it is good, fine; if it isn't, you are stuck with it, wart and all, and you help neither yourself nor your case by intimations, however veiled, to the effect that you would have tried it differently had you been trial counsel.

(e) Petitioner's effort to show the reason for the juggling of his classification and unwarranted denial of his rights by the local and appeal boards, was thwarted by the rulings of the trial court (App. 16) in denying G————'s counsel the right to pursue the inquiry on cross examination of the Secretary of the local board, the Government's witness, upon whom it relied to prove its case against defendant G————.

* * * His testimony proved not only such fact [that the Order was void] but his good-faith action, honest conviction of his stand in the premises, which motivated him in his actions in answering the charge of the indictment; questioning the validity of the Order to Report, want of jurisdiction of the board, and no need to report for induction as a condition precedent to challenge such order.

(f) Frank O. and Andrew E. Wilson, doing business under the trade name of Lone Star Oil Company, a partnership, own and operate a chain of seven retail gasoline filling stations in the City of ————, Texas. And they also own the real estate on prominent business corners of the City of ————, upon which they have erected magnificent structures and equipment to house their business.

Examples (e) and (f) illustrate the fault of editorializing and of using characterizations in the Statement of Facts. In (e) the characterizations would probably have been relevant if included in the Argument, but what difference did it make in (f) whether the structures were magnificent or just hovels? The case involved either taxation or an alleged OPA violation—my own notes on it are unclear—but the nature of the structures was irrelevant in either situation.

Finally, by way of extreme instance, there is an example taken from the Statement of Facts in a brief arguing a draft evasion case; further explanatory comment, other than to point out that the capitalization appeared in the original, is surely unnecessary:

(g) Petitioner has advanced the principle of law of self defense as applicable to the facts of this case. A defendant who fails to co-operate with government BECAUSE HE BELIEVES THAT IT MEANS THE LOSS OF IMMORTALITY, even to the extent of refusing to take human life, should be allowed the legal defense which in all the courts of the land permits the TAKING OF HUMAN LIFE when the defendant is in fear of losing his mortal life. Constitution of the United States, Article I Amendments fully justifies this extension of the law of self defense to such a situation as this, since it guarantees the free exercise of religion. The inherent powers of the courts to re-define all defenses to apply to new situations should also be sufficient authority of the Court herein to so extend the law of self defense.

Section 29. Good, clear, forceful English.—Good English is the next essential, though I shall do little more than state it. I don't pretend to be an expert on syntax or rhetoric, and so far as I am personally concerned, I write, for better or worse, entirely by ear. But the observations that follow may be suggestive, and possibly helpful.

A brief should be well written, but to be effective it must be clearly written. You are endeavoring to reach the minds of others, and therefore what you say must, above all, be clear. Clarity is more important in a brief than literary excellence.

Next, what you write should be grammatical. A lawyer is a professional man, in whom poor English should not be tolerated. I know that a good many brief-writers do not (perhaps because they can not) use good English, but there is really no excuse for any such performance. Offhand I should say that the only justified departure from the rules of grammar for a lawyer is the split infinitive, "to specifically perform." In that instance alone, the English Department is of no help to the equity practitioner.

A lawyer should also be at pains in his briefs, whatever may be the case in pleadings and contracts, to minimize legal formalisms such as "the said," "hereinbefore," "thereinafter," and the like.

Nor is it any longer a sign of learning to encumber a brief with excerpts from the Latin—unless they are very pat indeed. But, with the decline of the classics in the secondary schools and colleges, and a waning of the notion that the citizens won't think a man a lawyer unless he constantly spouts legal jargon in his everyday speech, there is much less of that nowadays than there was at the turn of the century or even before the First World War.

The Statement of Facts, as has already been indicated at length, should be straightforward, without embellishments and with a minimum of adjectives. It is not until the Argument portion of the brief is reached that you change the pace, so to speak, of your prose, and (if I may mix a metaphor by mechanizing it) really turn on the steam. From then on out, you *argue!*

Of course, it is well not to press too hard at your own weak points, for frequently the skill of the advocate consists in skating deftly where the ice is thin (or even where there isn't any ice at all). A good many situations will call for what has been aptly called "walking violently on eggs."

But you can't write an Argument without arguing. Consequently statements that might well be preceded in law review articles with the professorial "it would seem" must be introduced in briefs by "it is therefore abundantly clear," or, at the very least, by "it necessarily follows." [51]

Moreover, when you really get to the heart of the case, don't be afraid to hit hard, and don't hesitate to write a fighting brief. There is nothing in brief-writing quite so fallacious as what, for want of a better term, I like to call the striped-pants complex, namely, the notion that it is somehow undignified to make a strong, hard-hitting argument. That idea is really on a par with the view that an advocate should be impartial, or has any business being so—as to which see Sections 7 and 8, and the example there dissected and displayed. You simply can't write an argument on a la-di-da basis or after the manner of that well-known Milquetoast, the soft-toned shortstop.

Style is of course an individual matter. It may be that the Frenchman was right who said that the style is the man. Certainly there is full opportunity in this field for the exercise of individual and personal judgments, since many different styles of writing may be equally effective. There is a wide range of styles in which good argumentation can be written, a range as broad as the personality spectrum of effective advocacy, and within that range it would be silly dogmatism to insist on any particular manner of expression. Literary style after all is a form of art, and in the latter field we may all disclaim technical competence and yet know what we like. That circumstance alone makes style such a difficult matter to discuss.

Ideally, the raw material for such a discussion in the present field would be a library full of briefs, with representative examples of good, bad, and indifferent extracted and compiled within the covers of a single casebook. But there are no such casebooks, and libraries thus equipped are necessarily inaccessible to many practitioners.

---

[51] It is said in Kalven, *Law School Training in Research and Exposition,* 1 J. Legal Educ. 107, 117, "We believe the law-review note is a more fundamental form of legal exposition than the brief." The answer to this proposition in the present connection is that, whether or not the law review note may constitute more fundamental exposition, it is not argumentation; and a brief must, above all, be argumentative. Compare the example of nonargumentative brief-writing considered in Sections 7 and 8, above.

Therefore, I have selected my examples of good, clear, forceful English from opinions of former members of the Supreme Court, which are of course readily available in the reports. The portions of such opinions that follow the statement of the facts and issues are generally written in a more or less argumentative style, and thus are helpful here; and it may be noted that, since dissenting opinions are normally written with more zeal (if not indeed with somewhat less restraint), dissents are an even more valuable source of good and forceful legal writing.

In terms of familiar opinions, my own view—and I put the matter in terms of personal preference because it very largely comes down to that—my own view is that the most effective argumentative style is one like that of the late Chief Justice Hughes, with possibly a touch of Holmes for the snappers at the ends of significant passages. There is something powerful and inexorable about a Hughes opinion—I cite a few at random in the footnote.[52] Read those opinions, note how their reasoning develops logically step by step, get the feel of the pulsating, rhythmical, irresistible argument rolling on towards its predetermined end, and you will appreciate the force of really argumentative writing. Chief Justice Stone also wrote some good, strong opinions, notably in dissent. Those collected in the footnote seem to me outstanding, and to merit reading and rereading.[53]

Other judges have their admirers also—but, I repeat, these are personal preferences. Cardozo, J., wrote beautiful English, but his opinions are too limpid, too lyrical, and on occasion too discursive to constitute the most effective argumentation. Holmes' opinions are generally too epigrammatic for brief-writing, except as to the snapper sentences; a judge can rest on neatly phrased assertion, but an advocate needs something more. The judge needs only to decide; the advocate must persuade.

Some lawyers and judges urge that a brief should always con-

---

[52] E.g., *Sterling* v. *Constantin*, 287 U. S. 378; *Retirement Board* v. *Alton R. Co.*, 295 U. S. 330, 374 (dissent); *Morehead* v. *N. Y. ex rel. Tipaldo*, 298 U. S. 587, 618 (dissent); *United States* v. *Wood*, 299 U. S. 123; *Labor Board* v. *Jones & Laughlin*, 301 U. S. 1; *Apex Hosiery Co.* v. *Leader*, 310 U. S. 469, 514 (dissent).

[53] E.g., *United States* v. *Butler*, 297 U. S. 1, 78 (dissent); *Morehead* v. *N. Y. ex rel. Tipaldo*, 298 U. S. 587 (dissent); *Helvering* v. *Gerhardt*, 304 U. S. 405; *United States* v. *Darby*, 312 U. S. 100; *United States* v. *Local 807*, 315 U. S. 521, 539 (dissent); *Schneiderman* v. *United States*, 320 U. S. 118, 170 (dissent); *Girouard* v. *United States*, 328 U. S. 61, 70 (dissent).

tain short sentences. It is true that excessively long sentences result in turgidity. The force of Chief Justice White's later opinions was very perceptibly marred by this quality, though assuredly they rolled onward to powerful conclusions.[54] But the constant use of short sentences to the exclusion of longer ones imparts a staccato quality to prose writing that also detracts from the final results. Mr. Justice Brandeis' opinions always seemed to me to fall into that category; they were, however, crystal-clear and wholly devoid of verbal embroidery.[55]

As I say, I'm no English professor, and I don't expect my literary preferences in argumentative writing to coincide with those of others. I can only repeat that good, clear, forceful English is an essential; that in this particular activity one learns by doing (particularly with a more experienced person at hand to edit one's early doings) ; and that there is a lot of pay dirt in the dusty volumes of other folks' briefs on the library shelves.

Section 30. Argumentative headings.—Headings should always be argumentative rather than topical or even assertive. For instance, write "This suit is barred by laches because brought twenty-five years after the issuance of the original certificate" rather than "This suit is barred by laches." The first gives the argument in a nutshell, the second does not—though certainly the second assertive heading is infinitely more effective than the merely topical "The question of laches." Similarly, say "Appellant had notice of the defect and therefore is not a holder in due course" in preference to "Appellant is not a holder in due course" or to "Appellant's contention." Otherwise stated, employ the technique of the American newspaper headline rather than that of the English: our journalists say "Bums Down Braves, 9-2," whereas theirs write "Test Match at Lords."

Perhaps the greatest disservice an appellee's lawyer can do his case is to write, "Replying to Appellant's Point I." This is not even topical, and in consequence is completely blind, giving the judicial reader no clue whatever to the substance of the argument. It follows that the "Replying to" type of heading is completely un-

---

[54] E.g., *Minneapolis & St. Louis R. R.* v. *Bombolis,* 241 U. S. 211; *Selective Draft Law Cases,* 245 U. S. 366.

[55] E.g., *Wan* v. *United States,* 266 U. S. 1; *New State Ice Co.* v. *Liebmann,* 285 U. S. 262, 280 (dissent) ; *Louisville Bank* v. *Radford,* 295 U. S. 555; *Ashwander* v. *Tennessee Valley Authority,* 297 U. S. 288, 341 (concurring opinion) .

helpful—and it is just as bad when used in an appellant's reply brief.

Always set out your contentions affirmatively—and for maximum effectiveness formulate your headings so that they will be argumentative.

Subheadings should likewise be argumentative rather than topical or merely assertive, primarily because all are collected in the index at the beginning of the brief, and are thus frequently read first by any judge who wants to get the argument in abbreviated compass.

You lose a lot, therefore, if your subheadings are not precise and specific. If your headings and subheadings are properly argumentative, your argument starts with the index at page i of the brief, and the court will not need to go beyond that point to grasp the essence of your position.

Collecting all the headings and subheadings in the index has also this important incidental advantage: it discloses whatever lack of uniformity is quite likely to have crept into them in the course of your writing, and so provides a convenient opportunity for strengthening revisions (and, it may well be, for catching misprints and other infelicities).

Perhaps this is as good a place as any for the admonition that a main heading should never be followed by just a single subheading. If a proposition cannot be divided into more than one part, it is merely being restated. Therefore, if you find yourself unable to work out more than one subheading, the difficulty is that your main heading is improperly formulated; you had better rewrite it. (I know that the old books on argumentation used to prescribe something that went like this: "Oscar is entitled to rights and privileges, for: (a) Oscar is a citizen." My point is that effective argumentation in a brief requires that this proposition be rewritten either as "Oscar is a citizen and is therefore entitled to rights and privileges," or as "Oscar is entitled to rights and privileges because he is a citizen." The first is probably preferable, and it certainly is so if Oscar's citizenship is the real issue.)

Here is an example of some argumentative headings and subheadings, taken from the index page of the prevailing brief in what for a while was a fairly celebrated case,[56] that are sufficiently

---

[56] *Harris* v. *United States*, 331 U. S. 145.

detailed and precise to give the reader the very heart of the party's contentions immediately:

I. It has always been held that one of the incidents of a lawful arrest is the right to search the premises under the control of the person arrested for the instrumentalities of the crime of which he is accused, and that such a search is a reasonable one within the Fourth Amendment.

A. The cases in this Court prior to 1927 establish that the right to search premises for instrumentalities of crime is an incident of a lawful arrest therein.

B. There may be an exception permitting search of the premises for evidentiary papers incident to a lawful arrest in cases where a crime is actually being committed in the presence of the arresting officers.

C. The *Go-Bart* and *Lefkowitz* cases have been uniformly understood to hold that a search of premises incident to a lawful arrest has as wide a scope as a search authorized by a search warrant, and is limited to the objects for which such a warrant could issue.

D. The right to search premises under the accused's control for instrumentalities of crime as an incident to his lawful arrest is of ancient origin, and its recognition by the courts represents not an encroachment on constitutional protections but rather a reaffirmation of their original boundaries.

You may read all this and disagree, and certainly a series of later decisions substantially whittled down the propositions established in the particular case [57]—at least for a while.[58] It may well be that it has since been overruled *sub silentio*.[59] No matter; the point made here is not whether the quoted assertions still represent the law, it is that, after reading those detailed, specific, and argumentative headings, you know—at once—precisely the substance and scope of the argument.

Here is another example, likewise taken from a prevailing brief in a case decided some years back,[60] that also sets forth a party's arguments, in this instance in step-by-step progression:

---

[57] See *McDonald* v. *United States*, 335 U. S. 451; *Johnson* v. *United States*, 333 U. S. 10; *Trupiano* v. *United States*, 334 U. S. 699; cf. *United States* v. *Di Re*, 332 U. S. 581.

[58] The *Trupiano* case was specifically overruled by *United States* v. *Rabinowitz*, 339 U. S. 56, just a few years later. See, however, *Jones* v. *United States*, 357 U. S. 493.

[59] See *Kremen* v. *United States*, 353 U. S. 346, the facts in which should be compared with those in *Harris*. But see *Abel* v. *United States*, 362 U. S. 217.

[60] *United States* v. *Baltimore & Ohio R. Co.*, 333 U. S. 169.

I. The railroads' refusal to make direct delivery of livestock to sidings located on their line is a breach of their legal duty to the public as common carriers, which the Commission has power to remedy by its order.

A. If Track 1619 were owned by the New York Central, then clearly the Interstate Commerce Act has been violated, and the Commission's order would be unassailable.

B. In view of Section 1 (3) (a) of the Interstate Commerce Act, the situation is not altered in any respect by the circumstance that Track 1619 is owned by a non-carrier.

C. Nor is the situation altered by reason of the New York Central's contract with the Stock Yards which provides expressly for discrimination against livestock, since common carriers cannot by contract relieve themselves from their duties to the public.

D. The Stock Yards' right, if any, to compensation from the New York Central for the use of its land has no bearing upon the validity of the Commission's order requiring the railroads to perform their duties to the public.

There were additional points, but the foregoing was the nub of the argument. Here again, the reader is left in no possible doubt as to the substance or the progression of the propositions presented.[61]

Here is another example, this time of reasonably argumentative headings, but of only ineffective topical subheadings:

I. Section 266 of the Judicial Code, requiring the hearing and determination by three judges of applications for certain interlocutory injunctions, is not applicable to this case. Therefore the three-judge trial court convened pursuant to section 266 was without jurisdiction to issue the interlocutory injunction and abused its discretion in doing so.
> No state statute involved.
> As to order of administrative board or commission.
> ————— v. ————— discussed and distinguished.
> Section 266 inapplicable where order affects only particular district and is of limited scope.
> Conclusion.

* * * * *

III. This action is a suit against the State of ———, of which the Supreme Court has exclusive jurisdiction awarded in section 233 of

---

[61] I thought that the case just cited, which arose out of a dispute at the Cleveland Stock Yards, should control a similar subsequent controversy at the Chicago Stock Yards; but the Court disagreed. *Swift & Co.* v. *United States,* 343 U. S. 373.

the Judicial Code. Being without jurisdiction for this reason, the trial court abused its discretion in granting the interlocutory injunction.
> Statutes.
> Officers' authority as to state court suit.
> Grounds for state court suit.
> As to agreement discharging liability.
> This is a suit against the State.

Quite apart from any substantive aspects, the main headings are weakened by being divided into two sentences, and of course the force of the subheadings is almost completely lost by being rendered topical; the reader does not and cannot obtain any clue to the party's position from reading them.

Specifically, "———— v. ———— discussed and distinguished" would have been much stronger had it been rendered as, "———— v. ———— is not controlling because * * *," going on to indicate briefly why the case is not controlling.

"This is a suit against the State" is assertive rather than topical, but, since it does not go on to say why the suit is one against the state, it is not argumentative.

"Section 266 is inapplicable where order affects only particular district and is of limited scope" is the best of the lot—but it would have been even better if instead of "where order" there had been written "because the order here." Then the subheading would have read, "Section 266 is inapplicable because the order here affects only a particular district and is of limited scope"—and then it would have been a good, thumping, argumentative sentence.

Perhaps it should be added, with reference to the main heading under III, that if the trial court was really without jurisdiction, its issuance of an interlocutory injunction would have been somewhat worse than an abuse of discretion—the latter expression being one that implies the existence of jurisdiction. It is therefore not a good heading. A heading should, at the very least, be consistent with itself, and should not generate judicial disbelief or resistance on a first reading.

Let me take another example of how not to do it:

II. The Rule of Jurisdiction Invoked by the Court Below Is Not Unconstitutional.
  A. The Intent of Congress.
  B. The Constitutional Considerations.

C. The Application of the Constitutional Considerations to This Case.

D. The Effect of Petitioners' Contentions.

Every one of the subheadings is blind, giving the reader no clue whatever to the substance of the argument; and the principal heading is only assertive. It falls short of being argumentative because it does not explain why the rule being appealed from is not unconstitutional—a matter of more than passing importance, since that was the vital issue in the case.

Possibly there is one situation where merely topical headings are justified, namely, when you are simply analyzing the authorities, and are presenting them in a spirit of sweet reasonableness, i.e., where it doesn't make much difference which of several lines the court takes since they all lead to the same result. But with perhaps that single exception, failure to set off the various stages in the Argument portion of the brief with full and detailed argumentative headings detracts materially from the brief's effectiveness.

One additional comment, suggested by a learned friend, may well be added: The reader should never need to refer back to the heading in order to grasp the full sense and meaning of the opening sentence. As phrased by him:

> The text of an argument ought not to depend upon a heading or subheading for an understanding of its meaning. My theory of a heading or subheading is that it ought to be something that the reader can take or leave alone. (I apply the same rule to footnotes.) In reading a brief, a book, or an article, I am annoyed, after I have got into a sentence, to find that I must refer back to a heading to understand the sentence. I test my own work by asking myself whether the text is complete and is understandable without reading either the headings or the footnotes. If so, then I consider the headings and the footnotes as aids which will assist in the reading of the text, but which will not impede that reading.[62]

Section 31. Appealing formulation of the questions presented.—Another essential of an effective appellate brief is the appealing formulation of the questions presented on the appeal—and "appealing" in this connection means the phraseology that will most effectively impel the reader to answer the question posed in the way the writer wants him to answer it. Consequently this is

---

[62] Letter from Owen Rall, Esq., of the Chicago Bar, May 12, 1949.

an extremely important item, particularly since by stating well the question presented you are really choosing the battleground on which your litigation will be contested.

In a number of circuits, the rules provide that the questions presented must be set forth at the outset of the brief, ahead of any other portion.[63] The Supreme Court similarly requires that the questions presented appear early in briefs, petitions for certiorari, and jurisdictional statements.[64]

The formulation of the question is of particular importance whenever review is discretionary, the most usual example being certiorari in the Supreme Court.[65] There the grant or denial of the writ frequently depends in very large measure on the framing of the question. On behalf of the petitioner you help to induce review by making the question appear important and the result below wrong. Contrariwise, when the object to be obtained is the denial of review, the question should be framed in such a way as to minimize the importance of what is involved.

Two forms will fit almost every case. The first and more usual form is to use a sentence beginning with "whether"; e.g., "Whether post-mortem declarations are admissible." The second, usually appropriate only for the more complicated cases, is to state the salient facts and then to add, "The question presented is whether in these circumstances the later proceeding is barred by the earlier judgment." This second method may also be appropriate whenever the simple statement of the question does not make the case appear to be sufficiently interesting or appealing.

In using the first form, the essential technique, generally, is so to load the question with the facts of the particular case or with the relevant quotations from the statute involved, *fairly stated,* that you can almost win the case on the mere statement of the question it presents.

Rules of court that ask for a statement of the question presented to be "expressed in the terms and circumstances of the case but without unnecessary detail" are not violated by such an inclusion of relevant facts.[66] Other rules appear to require the ques-

---

[63] District of Columbia Circuit, Rule 17 (b) (1) ; Third Circuit, Rule 24 (2) (b) ; Sixth Circuit, Rule 16 (2) (a).

[64] Supreme Court Rules 15 (1) (c) (1), 23 (1) (c), 40 (1) (d) (1).

[65] See note 31, *supra,* p. 53.

[66] Supreme Court Rules cited in note 64, *supra;* District of Columbia Circuit, Rule 17 (b) (1), and see the official note to the latter in the original.

tions to be stated "in the briefest and most general terms, without particulars of any kind." [67] The brief-writer must of course comply, but even a short and generalized formulation can be made thoroughly appealing.

Some judges seem to feel that advice to phrase a question appealingly is tantamount to a suggestion for deceiving the court, so that by slanting the question, or even by twisting it out of shape, a busy tribunal may be led to reach an answer favorable to the party. Here again, this is a view that reflects misapprehension of the purpose and content of advocacy.

Let me repeat the caveat already set forth: *fairly stated*. If an excess of zeal leads you to state the question unfairly or inaccurately, the whole thing will boomerang and explode in your face— or, perhaps more to the point, in your client's case.

Here are some examples.

The first one illustrates the problem of how to phrase an issue appealingly, with minimum mention of the facts.

The case turned on the income tax liability of a very wealthy father in the surtax brackets. Papa owned lots of gilt-edged bonds and stuff; before the coupons matured, he clipped them and gave them to his son as a gift. When the coupons matured, sonny boy cashed them, and returned the proceeds as income on his return. This young lad, as it happened, was a substantial distance from the breadline, but he still wasn't up in Papa's tax range. So the revenuers undertook to tax the old man for the income from the coupons.

How phrase the question? The Commissioner of Internal Revenue could have stated it as "Whether a man is taxable on income that his son received"—but that would hardly have induced any court to say "Yes." So he stated the question as follows (first example is from the petition, second from the brief on the merits):

1

Whether the owner of coupon bonds should include in his gross income the amount of coupons which he detached and gave to his son several months prior to maturity.

2

The taxpayer owned coupon bonds. Several months prior to maturity of the interest coupons he detached them and gave them to his

---

[67] E.g., First Circuit, Rule 24 (3) (b); Third Circuit, Rule 24 (2) (b); cf. Sixth Circuit, Rule 16 (2) (a).

son, retaining the bonds themselves. Is he relieved of income tax with respect to such interest coupons?

Both are well-formulated questions. The second is probably a shade the better because it stresses that the taxpayer retained the bonds and then asks on top of that whether he is relieved from tax. (The Supreme Court, by six to three, held that he was not.) [68] Note also the change in the form of the question presented, from the one-sentence "whether" form to the fact-statement-plus-question form, all in the direction of adding appeal. The significant point is less the result in the case than the way that case illustrates to what extent phrasing the question may be a problem in applied semantics.

The next two examples illustrate the permissible use of the loading-with-facts technique:

The first of these concerned an individual who was drafted in 1918 and ordered to report on November 11, 1918. On that day, of course, all draft calls were cancelled. So, after lunching with his draft board, this lad went home, and, in due course, received a "Discharge from Draft." For some years thereafter he enjoyed the tax exemption accorded by the state legislature to all honorably discharged soldiers of the War with Germany. Subsequently the local tax officials tightened up, decided he was not an honorably discharged soldier, and refused to recognize his exemption. After suit, the Supreme Court of the State decided that he was not within the statute.[69] Nothing daunted, he communicated with the Secretary of War; declared that in 1918 he had been ready, willing, able, and fully qualified, and that his service (such as it was) was honorable; and demanded an Honorable Discharge from the Army. Being refused, he brought suit—and the Court of Appeals held that he was entitled to such a discharge. On its face the thing had all the earmarks of comic opera, if not indeed of an exaggerated farce. Actually, however, the decision was a very serious matter for the Army: there were over 45,000 others in like case and issuing Honorable Discharges to all of these would have involved a very considerable administrative chore, and would in addition have placed a substantial financial burden on the United States (and on the States) in view of the mass of veterans' benefit legislation on the books.

---

[68] *Helvering* v. *Horst,* 311 U. S. 112.
[69] *Lamb* v. *Kroeger,* 233 Iowa 730, 8 N.W. 2d 405.

The Secretary of War, therefore, petitioned for review. Here is how he framed the question presented:

Whether a court may, by mandamus, order the Secretary of War to issue an "Honorable Discharge from the Army" to an individual who received a "Discharge from Draft" in 1918, over 25 years prior to the institution of suit, where such individual simply reported for induction on November 11, 1918, returned to his home on that day because of the cancellation of all draft calls by order of the President, never entrained for travel to a military camp, never wore the uniform, and never was accepted for military service by the Army.

The entire case was thus set forth in the question, whose very phrasing underscores the untenability of the "veteran's" position. In the actual case, certiorari was granted, and the decision below unanimously reversed—a mere thirteen days after oral argument.[70]

The next example—a similar unfounded claim similarly dealt with—was the case of the Week-End Sailor—the member of the Temporary Reserve of the Coast Guard who patrolled the waterfront in his spare time and then insisted that he was entitled to veterans' preference in subsequent federal employment. Here again, the question states the case, and here again certiorari was granted and the decision below, which had held such an individual to be a veteran, was promptly reversed.[71] The question was stated as follows:

Whether members of the Volunteer Port Security Force, a branch of the Temporary Coast Guard Reserve, who were assigned duty periods (here, of less than six hours a week) in order to interfere as little as possible with their hours of regular civilian employment during their enrollment, who could be disenrolled at their own request upon representation that their duty assignments conflicted with such civilian employment, who were not subject while on duty to transfer away from their homes without their consent, and who remained at all times subject to the draft provisions of the Selective Training and Service Act, 1940, are entitled to preference in federal employment as "ex-servicemen * * * who have served on active duty in any branch of the armed forces of the United States, during any war," within the meaning of the Veterans' Preference Act of 1944.[72]

---

[70] *Patterson* v. *Lamb,* 329 U. S. 539.

[71] *Mitchell* v. *Cohen,* 333 U. S. 411.

[72] Since then, it has been held that the recipient of a Discharge from Draft is not entitled to preference under the 1944 Act as an original proposition, *McDougall* v. *United States Civil Service Com'n,* 202 F. 2d 361 (D. C. Cir.),

It should be remembered that these techniques are equally applicable to every kind of case, and are not in any sense limited to the somewhat esoteric public law cases that fall to the lot of Government counsel.

Here is an example involving a real estate title that could well arise in any country lawyer's office at the courthouse square. The question as phrased was:

> Whether a lost grant of a fee simple title may be presumed when there has been only spasmodic possession at long intervals, where the original grant and the first mesne conveyance in a complete chain of title disclose the defect in the claimed title and show that a five-year lease was granted by the sovereign, and where no record of a grant from the sovereign appears although the law required records of such grants to be kept.

There's your chain of title—and your case—in a nutshell. And that is an example of almost universal utility, since a land-title dispute could and does arise anywhere.[73]

Section 32. Examples of helpful and unhelpful formulations of the questions presented.—It goes without saying that not all situations are adapted to the loading-with-facts technique of formulating the question presented. But the question presented in any case can be clearly and appealingly stated—or, contrariwise, unclearly and unappealingly. It will probably be helpful to set out as examples the questions presented in each of four cases. The first statement in each instance is the petitioner's formulation of the question; the second is the respondent's. As it happens, review was denied in each instance, and each of the cases is a dozen or so years old. But nothing turns on either factor for present purposes. The significant point for the student of the process is to inquire which of the rival statements is more effective, and why; and whether in his judgment the parties could have stated the problem

---

but is so entitled if he had earlier been accorded preference rights under other legislation. *Ellsworth* v. *Maher,* 257 F. 2d 221 (D. C. Cir.).

See also *Carmel* v. *U. S. Civil Service Comm.,* 255 F. 2d 190 (D. C. Cir.) (two weeks' summer training with the District of Columbia National Guard in time of peace does not bring employee within the Veterans' Preference Act of 1944).

[73] This particular one arose in the middle of the Pacific Ocean, under the law of Hawaii, and involved the ownership of Palmyra Island. The Ninth Circuit decided it twice, once for one side and then for the other, and the Supreme Court split 5-4. *United States* v. *Fullard-Leo,* 331 U. S. 256.

for their purposes more effectively than they did. (For convenience in reference, the citations to the opinions below are included
in the footnotes.)

(A)

Petitioner: "Did the Circuit Court of Appeals for the Sixth Judicial Circuit err in overruling petitioner's contention that until there
had been an adjudication by the proper military tribunal, that the
soldier involved was guilty of violating the Articles of War relating to
desertion, the District Court was without jurisdiction to try the issue
presented by the indictment?"

Respondent: "Whether petitioner could be prosecuted under Section 42 of the Criminal Code [74] for aiding a deserter from the Army before the soldier had been convicted of desertion by a court-martial." [75]

In the foregoing case, the petitioner's statement is defective
principally because it is unclear; it refers to "the issue presented by
the indictment" without any clue to what that issue is. Consequently it fails to do what the correct formulation of "question
presented" must always do, viz., tell the court what the case is
about. Respondent's statement does just that, though it presents
the matter plainly, without any effort at forensic sex appeal.

(B)

Petitioner: "1. Is the Petitioner a native, citizen, denizen or subject of a 'hostile nation or government' liable as such 'to be apprehended, restrained, secured and removed' as an alien enemy?

"2. Is the Petitioner a citizen of the Third German Reich or the
German Nation or Government?"

Respondent: "Whether an alien, born in Bohemia, then a part of
the Austro-Hungarian Empire, in 1905, who later became a Czechoslo-
vakian citizen when the place of his birth was included in that country
after World War I, and who, after the Munich Pact of 1938, while in
the United States, petitioned to be and was recognized as a German
citizen, is now a citizen or subject of an enemy country within the
meaning of the Alien Enemy Act of 1798,[76] despite the re-occupation
of the territory of his birth and former residence by Czechoslovakia." [77]

---

[74] Now 18 U.S.C. § 1381.
[75] *Beauchamp* v. *United States,* 154 F. 2d 413 (C.A. 6), certiorari denied,
329 U. S. 723.
[76] Now 50 U.S.C. §§ 21-24.
[77] *United States ex rel. Reichel* v. *Carusi,* 157 F. 2d 732 (C.A. 3), certiorari denied, 330 U. S. 842.

Petitioner's questions are too generalized to be informative. Respondent, on the other hand, has set forth the facts in his question, through use of the "loading" technique, and has framed it in such a way that there is left but little doubt of the answer.

(C)

Petitioner: "Whether petitioner, a former reserve officer of the Army (and thousands of other reserve officers, whose rights are vitally affected by this, the first case involving their right to retirement pay) may sue in the District Court under the principles enunciated by this Court in *Dismuke* v. *United States,* 297 U. S. 167, and similar cases, to recover the retirement pay provided by Congress in Section 5 of the Act of April 3, 1939, as amended, when he is deprived of such pay by the arbitrary, discriminatory and capricious acts of those charged with administering that statute, such conduct being aimed at preventing petitioner in particular and reserve officers in general from obtaining the benefits promised them by Congress."

Respondent: "Whether a reserve officer can sue in a district court to establish his right to retirement pay on account of alleged disability incident to his military service, where he has not pursued the administrative remedies made available by statute and executive order for the assertion and review of such claims, and in the face of the Tucker Act's specific denial of jurisdiction over 'claims for pensions.' " [78]

Here petitioner has resorted to the "loading" technique, perhaps to an unwarranted degree; respondent has also loaded his question but without resort to epithetic adjectives. The first makes a good jury speech, the second is a compact plea to the jurisdiction.

(D)

Petitioner A: "The question presented is whether or not a retired United States District Judge is entitled to increased compensation at the rate of $15,000 per year provided for District Judges by the Act of July 31, 1946 (Public Law 567, 79th Congress), in lieu of the salary of $10,000 per year currently being paid."

Petitioner B: "1. Whether the new salary law applies to retired judges of whom petitioner is one; whether it is open to construction and legislative history to impose upon it an implied exception of 'retired' judges and petitioner from it and the increase of salaries granted by it to all district judges.

---

[78] *Randolph* v. *United States.* 158 F. 2d 787 (C.A. 5), certiorari denied, 330 U. S. 839. The provision withholding from district courts any jurisdiction over claims for pensions is now 28 U.S.C. § 1346 (d) (1).

"2. Whether the so-called retirement law is 'a special reference' or 'specific aspect' or consideration of salaries of 'retired' judges and 'fixing' the same; whether exercise of the privileges or options of said law is acceptance of an offer on condition that 'he should continue to draw the salary he was receiving when he retired' and restricting him thereto despite the subsequent new salary law and its increase of salary; whether it operates as an implied exception imposed on the new salary law to exclude 'retired' judges and petitioner from the grant thereof; and whether the 'retirement' law is of any *legal* effect save to conditionally authorize appointment of additional judges without permanent increase in the number thereof, and in all else futile, superfluous verbiage affecting the status and salary right of petitioner not at all."

Respondent: "Whether petitioners, who had retired as United States District Judges prior to July 31, 1946, are entitled to be paid at the rate of $15,000 per year, as provided by the Act of July 31, 1946, for 'each of the judges of the several district courts' when the judges' retirement act provides for payment to a retired judge of 'the salary of which he is * * * in receipt' at the time of retirement, and when the salary received at that time was $10,000 a year." [79]

Petitioner *A* has stated the question clearly and without trimmings; Petitioner *B's* statement is—well, not very helpful; but respondent, by quoting the two statutes in his question, has made it pretty plain that the judges retired prior to 1946 were just out of luck—which is what was held.[80]

Additional examples are legion. But the principle is always the same: The most appealing statement of the question is always the one that most effectively impels the reader to want to answer it as the writer of the question wanted him to.

Section 33. Unappealing formulation of the questions presented in order to defeat review.—When you represent the petitioner, you must dress up your questions appealingly in order to induce the higher court to take your case. But, when you appear for the respondent, you are perfectly satisfied with the *status quo,* and consequently your duty to your client requires that you minimize the questions presented by your adversary, in order to make them appear unimportant, or uninteresting except to the parties

---

[79] *Bourquin* v. *United States,* 108 C. Cls. 700, 72 F. Supp. 76, certiorari denied, 332 U. S. 762.

[80] In the 1948 revision of Title 28, Congress changed the law, so that the retired judge now gets the benefit of salary increases occurring after retirement. 28 U.S.C. § 371 (b).

involved, or as turning on a mere question of fact. Here are some examples of effective depressants, taken from successful Briefs in Opposition.

(a) Whether the evidence is sufficient to support the verdict.

(b) Whether there is substantial evidence in the record to support the finding that * * *.

(c) Whether the concurrent findings of the two lower courts that * * * are correct.

(d) Whether petitioner may now rely on Section ———— of the Act of ————, which it failed to call to the attention of either of the courts below.

(e) Whether, in a prosecution for making sales at over-ceiling prices, where the sole question at issue was whether petitioners demanded and received more than the ceiling price, the judge's omission to charge on wilfulness constituted prejudicial error requiring reversal of the convictions, where petitioners' counsel specifically acquiesced in the charge.

One caution may be in order when, on behalf of the winning side below, you employ the "always belittlin' " technique. There is always a tendency to add, by way of conclusion, that the question presented for review is not an important one. Very often, however, the question is important, but review is not, since the case was rightly decided. Therefore, unless you are prepared to concede that the question would not have been important even if you had lost below, don't yield to the tendency. For example, if a court decides that a valid contract requires consideration, the decision is right but the question is clearly of importance, as will be clear by considering the situation if the ruling had gone the other way. Therefore, in the usual situation, don't urge that the question is unimportant; say rather that the decision does not require further review.

Be careful, also, how far you go in asserting that a case is *"sui generis"*; you may be seeking review of the same kind of question later on, and, if your opponent is alert, he is in a position in a close case to persuade the court to make you eat your words.[81]

———

[81] In the first Palmyra Island case (*United States* v. *Fullard-Leo*, 133 F. 2d 743 (C.A.9), certiorari denied, 319 U. S. 748), the Government argued (Br. Op. 8; No. 883, Oct. T. 1942) that "This case is, in petitioners' words (Pet. 5), *sui generis*. Thus it presents no conflict of decisions and moreover is correct." But the second decision, by the Ninth Circuit sitting *en banc*, went the other way (156 F. 2d 756), and this time the Government had to seek review. No

Section 34. Sound analysis of the legal problem in argument on the law.—We come now to the body of the brief, the Argument proper. If and to the extent that a question of law is to be argued, the essential for an effective brief is that the legal problem involved be carefully and soundly analyzed.

First, the legal problem of the case must be broken down into its component parts, to the end that the underbrush, so to speak, may be cleared away, and the vital issues exposed.

Next, the brief-writer must determine which propositions constitute the principal issues, and which only the subsidiary ones.

Finally, when there are alternative propositions, any one of which is sufficient to prevail, the brief-writer must decide in what order he should present his points.

First. Two recent examples will serve to explain and to illustrate what I mean by the kind of analysis that clears away the underbrush.

(a) In the *Benanti* case,[82] State officers, acting in full accordance with State law, tapped the telephone of one suspected of violating the State narcotics laws. In consequence of the information thus obtained, the defendant's car was stopped; the officers, however, found no narcotics but instead discovered alcohol in cans that lacked the stamps required by Federal law. The appropriate Federal officials were notified, a Federal prosecution followed, but it was not until the cross-examination of one of the State officers at

---

opposition was filed, and certiorari was granted. (329 U. S. 697.) I have often wondered whether the Supreme Court would have agreed to review the case on the second occasion if the claimants had opposed and quoted the former characterization.

Probably, however, the decisive factor in the grant of certiorari was the public importance of determining the ownership of this strategically-located island.

In a somewhat similar situation, certiorari was successfully opposed in a railroad land grant case on the grounds that "The present case is *sui generis,* and the issues which it involves are consequently not of public importance," and that "This is the last railroad land grant case now in litigation, or which, so far as respondents are aware, can possibly come into litigation." *Chapman* v. *Santa Fe Pac. R. Co.,* 198 F. 2d 498 (D. C. Cir.), certiorari denied, 343 U. S. 964. Thereafter, the State in which the lands were located taxed the successful claimant for their value in respect of periods when the United States was still in possession and was actively resisting the claim. Certiorari was sought; the State authorities said nothing about *"sui generis";* but review was denied, no doubt for that reason. *Aztec Land & Cattle Co.* v. *Navajo Realty Co.,* 79 Ariz. 55, 65, 283 P. 2d 227, 234, certiorari denied, 350 U. S. 861.

[82] *Benanti* v. *United States,* 355 U. S. 96.

the trial that the prosecutor learned that there had been a wiretap. Defendant's counsel then made a motion to suppress, which was denied, and defendant was convicted. He urged the denial of his motion as a ground of appeal, but to no avail; the Second Circuit said:

We can find no tenable distinction in principle between the rule of policy governing the admissibility in federal courts of evidence illegally obtained by state officers through an unlawful search and seizure, without participation or collusion by federal officials, and the rule of policy which should govern the admissibility of evidence obtained by state officials under similar circumstances in violation of the federal statute against wiretapping. On the contrary, as Judge Learned Hand, speaking for this Court, observed in United States v. Goldstein, 2 Cir., 120 F. 2d 485, at page 490, "it would be a curious result, if a violation of the section were more sweepingly condemned than a violation of the Constitution." The Supreme Court in affirming, Goldstein v. United States, supra, pointed out the limited scope of the rule requiring the exclusion of unconstitutionally obtained evidence, and said, "We think no broader sanction should be imposed upon the Government in respect of violations of the Communications Act." 316 U. S. at page 121, 62 S.Ct. at page 1004. Apart from this authority, surely it cannot be that the violation of a federal statute calls forth implied sanctions more pervasive than those formulated by the Supreme Court to compel obedience to a constitutional mandate.[83]

The foregoing had a most plausible ring, but was it sound? Was the analogy a correct one? In a reply brief filed in support of his petition for certiorari, petitioner argued that—

the question is not whether, as an original proposition, a violation of a statute is to be more sweepingly condemned than a violation of the Constitution (L. Hand, J., in United States v. Goldstein, 120 F. 2d 485, 490 (C.A.2), affirmed, 316 U. S. 114), it is rather whether the statute has a more comprehensive reach by its clear terms than constitutional provisions of limited (Fourth Amendment) and uncertain (Fourteenth Amendment) application.

After certiorari was granted, petitioner made a one-point argument, with several sub-headings; only those bearing on the foregoing analysis of the question are here set out:

---

[83] United States v. Benanti, 244 F. 2d 389, 393 (C.A.2).
It should be noted that all stages of the Benanti case preceded the demise of the "silver platter" doctrine, as to which see below, pp. 89-90.

Evidence obtained in violation of Section 605 of the Federal Communications Act, by any person whosoever, is inadmissible in a federal prosecution in a federal court.

A. A state officer participating in an illegal search and seizure does not violate federal law, whereas a state officer engaged in wiretapping does.

B. Wiretapping evidence obtained by state officers and turned over to federal officers for use in a federal prosecution is inadmissible in a federal court.

C. The terms of Section 605 of the Federal Communications Act render inapplicable the "silver platter" doctrine.

The Supreme Court adopted the foregoing argument, saying:

Furthermore, confronted as we are by this clear statute, and resting our decision on its provisions, it is neither necessary nor appropriate to discuss by analogy distinctions suggested to be applicable to the Fourth Amendment. Section 605 contains an express, absolute prohibition against the divulgence of intercepted communications. *Nardone* v. *United States*, 302 U. S. 379, 382. * * *[84]

Otherwise stated, the underbrush to be cleared away was the assumption that a constitutional provision necessarily has a broader reach than a statutory one. Once this deceptively facile assumption was placed against the actual terms of each provision, it promptly evaporated. The moral is that the brief-writer should never let himself be beguiled by any phrase, no matter how neatly it may be turned.[85]

(b) Another example of essential preliminary analysis may be found in the second hearing of the first cases dealing with the

---

[84] 355 U. S. at 102.

[85] Mr. Justice Holmes long ago observed that "It is one of the misfortunes of the law that ideas become encysted in phrases and thereafter for a long time cease to provoke further analysis." *Hyde* v. *United States*, 225 U. S. 347, 384, 391.

See also the illuminating comments of the late Judge Frank in *United Shipyards* v. *Hoey*, 131 F. 2d 525, 526-527 (C.A.2) : "* * * some of the greatest errors in thinking have arisen from the mechanical, unreflective, application of old formulations—forgetful of a tacit 'as if'—to new situations which are sufficiently discrepant from the old so that the emphasis on the likenesses is misleading and the neglect of the differences leads to unfortunate or foolish consequences. In governmental or business administration, such neglect, when it occurs, provokes justifiable irritation at 'bureaucracy'; in judicial administration it deserves criticism as unenlightened precedent-mongering."

validity of trials by court-martial of civilian dependents, *Reid v. Covert* and *Kinsella v. Krueger*.[86]

In its original opinion, the Supreme Court had relied heavily on the view that such trials involved a cession of jurisdiction by the foreign nations where the trials had taken place,[87] and had in consequence concluded that there was no need to examine the power of Congress, under Article I, Section 8, Clause 14, of the Constitution "To make Rules for the Government and Regulation of the land and naval Forces." [88] As one of the non-concurring justices remarked, "The plain inference from this is that the Court is not prepared to support the constitutional basis upon which the Covert and Smith courts-martial were instituted and the convictions were secured." [89] Or, more realistically if less politely stated, there were not enough votes to uphold the conviction under Clause 14.

A petition for rehearing was duly filed; it is set forth in Chapter XIII, *infra*, pp. 432-440. But the basic problem of how to focus the Court's attention on the Constitution, on Clause 14, and away from the allurement of international affairs, was not thoroughly thought through until after the rehearing had been granted [90] and a new brief was in course of preparation. The principal point to be made was that "Nothing in the Constitution of the United States authorizes the trial of civilians by court-martial in time of peace and not in occupied territory." But first the jurisdictional underbrush needed to be cleared away. Accordingly, the first point on behalf of the dependent wives was set forth as follows:

I. The consent of England and Japan to the exercise of American military jurisdiction within their territories in respect of offenses committed therein did not and could not invest American courts-martial with jurisdiction to try particular persons.

---

[86] 354 U. S. 1.

[87] "Japan, at the time of the offense, had ceded to the United States 'exclusive jurisdiction over all offenses which may be committed in Japan by members of the United States armed forces, the civilian component, and their dependents. . . .' " *Kinsella v. Krueger*, 351 U. S. 470, 473-474. "Foreign nations have relinquished jurisdiction to American military authorities only pursuant to carefully drawn agreements which presuppose prompt trial by existent authority." *Id.*, at 479.

[88] 351 U. S. at 476.

[89] 351 U. S. at 481.

[90] 352 U. S. 901.

A. The territorial sovereign does not confer jurisdiction on the personal sovereign, but simply consents to the personal sovereign's exercise of jurisdiction; and the scope of the latter's jurisdiction depends, not on the territorial sovereign's consent, but on the personal sovereign's law.

B. The American military jurisdiction asserted in the present case did not purport to be conditional, but was rested on an assumed American power.

C. If, as a matter of American law, including American constitutional law, American courts-martial have no jurisdiction to try particular civilians, such courts-martial cannot by treaty or international agreement be given a wider jurisdiction, for the reason that no treaty can prevail over specific constitutional guarantees, in this instance the right to trial by jury.

The argument under IA was then set out with a series of examples, each derived from an actual case, much as a teacher would expound propositions in a classroom. In the interest of brevity, only the summary of that argument is copied from the brief.

I. A. The territorial sovereign does not confer jurisdiction on the personal sovereign, but simply consents to the personal sovereign's exercise of its own jurisdiction; and the scope of the latter depends, not on the territorial sovereign's consent, but on the personal sovereign's law. Thus, if a ship of Country A is in the territorial waters of Country B, and a homicide is committed on board by a member of the crew, primary jurisdiction belongs to the territorial sovereign, so that the territorial sovereign's claim to trying the offender prevails. *Wildenhus's Case*, 120 U. S. 1. But if the territorial sovereign is content to let the personal sovereign proceed with the trial, the latter can do so, thus establishing that the territorial sovereign's jurisdiction is not exclusive but only primary. *United States* v. *Flores*, 289 U. S. 137. If, however, the personal sovereign's law is insufficient to reach the offense, then the territorial sovereign's consent is ineffective to prevent the offender's going free; that course necessarily follows if the courts of the personal sovereign lack jurisdiction of the offense (*United States* v. *Wiltberger*, 5 Wheat. 76) or if the particular court of the personal sovereign lacks jurisdiction of the person (*Toth* v. *Quarles*, 350 U. S. 11). Thus the assumption underlying last June's opinions, that there was a relinquishment of jurisdiction by England and Japan which automatically empowered the United States to try these civilian women by court-martial, is shown to be wholly untenable.

A majority of the Supreme Court was persuaded by this analysis, and although the justices differed as to the scope of their ruling, the holding of the Court was that dependents could not constitutionally be tried by courts-martial for capital offenses.[91]

Second. In what order should the brief-writer's points be presented? This is not a matter as to which one can profitably be dogmatic, but a good working principle is to put one's best foot forward.

(a) Where there are no alternatives, i.e., where you must prevail on every point in order to win, the only solution is to set forth your points in logical, step-by-step progression. This is subject to the qualification that, if there is no particular logical sequence, the point that goes to the very heart of the matter, the point that strikes the jugular, should always be argued first.

Let me take some examples:

(i) In the *Harris* search-and-seizure case,[92] the officers arrested Harris under a warrant, then searched his apartment for the instrumentalities of the crime for which he was arrested, and in the course of that search found the contraband for the possession of which he was tried and convicted. In order to sustain the conviction, it was first necessary to show that the officers had a right to search, next that this right extended to all of Harris's apartment, and finally that they could retain any contraband discovered in the course of that search. The point first mentioned was basic and hence it was argued first; the others followed logically thereafter. Here was the sequence of points:

I. It has always been held that one of the incidents of a lawful arrest is the right to search the premises under the control of the person arrested for the instrumentalities of the crime of which he is accused, and that such a search is a reasonable one within the Fourth Amendment.[93]

II. The search was not a general exploratory search for evidence of crime.

III. The search was not improper because it extended beyond the precise portion of the premises where petitioner was arrested.

---

[91] *Reid* v. *Covert,* 354 U. S. 1, withdrawing *Kinsella* v. *Krueger,* 351 U. S. 470, and *Reid* v. *Covert,* 351 U. S. 487.

Three years later, the Court in a series of cases held that dependents could not be tried by court-martial for non-capital offenses (*Kinsella* v. *Singleton,* 361 U. S. 234), and that civilian employees could not be so tried either, whether their offenses were capital (*Grisham* v. *Hagan,* 361 U. S. 278) or non-capital (*McElroy* v. *Guagliardo,* 361 U. S. 281).

[92] *Harris* v. *United States,* 331 U. S. 145.

[93] For the subheadings under this point, see p. 69, *supra.*

IV. The seizure of the Selective Service documents and their introduction in evidence were proper.

(ii) In the *Hackfeld* Alien Property case,[94] the facts, briefly, were that Hackfeld's Hawaiian property had been seized during the first World War; that it was returned to him, pursuant to an Executive Allowance signed by the President, on a determination that he was an American citizen; and that thereafter he sought a further recovery, after which the Government brought a cross-action for the return of alleged overpayments, asserting that, as a matter of law, Hackfeld had never been an American citizen, and that he had, through his fraud, induced the determination that he was one. The trial judge directed a verdict in favor of the Government on the sole basis that Hackfeld had always been a German and that the additional payments had in consequence been made without authority of law. Hackfeld's estate appealed.

On the appeal, the Government had to show first, that the court had properly gone behind the Presidential Allowance; next, that a certain tax proceeding was not *res judicata* as to Hackfeld's citizenship; third, that the trial judge was right as a matter of law in ruling as he did; and, finally, that the facts of record as to Hackfeld's fraud were sufficient for alternative support of the judgment. So the brief filed in the Second Circuit presented the main points in that order:

I. The Executive Allowance in No Way Constituted a Bar to this Action.
II. The Federal Estate Tax Proceeding is No Bar to this Action.
III. Hackfeld Never Became An American Citizen.
IV. The District Court Should Have Directed a Verdict in Appellees' Favor on the Ground of Fraud.

It is proper to note, however, that these last headings are assertive and not argumentative, and therefore not to be commended as headings.

(iii) In the *Douglas Chandler* treason case,[95] the defendant raised numerous objections to his conviction—that he had been tried in the wrong district, that Congress had not made specific

---

[94] *United States* v. *Rodiek,* 117 F. 2d 588 (C.A. 2), rehearing denied, 120 F. 2d 760, affirmed by an equally divided court, 315 U. S. 783. See also *Rodiek* v. *United States,* 100 C. Cls. 267.

[95] *Chandler* v. *United States,* 171 F. 2d 921 (C.A.1), certiorari denied, 336 U. S. 918.

provision for the trial of offenses committed abroad, that he had been improperly returned to the United States, that treason could not be committed by adherence to the enemy by an American residing in enemy territory, that the overt acts were insufficient and were insufficiently proved, and that the court made errors in the admission of testimony and in its instructions to the jury.

In order to sustain the conviction, it was just as important for the Government to establish that Chandler was tried in the proper district as it was to prove that his acts amounted to treason. But the heart of the case was the proposition that broadcasting propaganda on behalf of an enemy was treason, and so that point was argued first. The details as to arrangement of the Government's points are set forth below in Section 47 under the heading, "Never Let the Other Side Write Your Brief." That is to say, select your own battleground; do not permit opposing counsel to choose it for you. This is an admonition almost universally applicable.

(iv) Sometimes one arrangement of points will be better in order to get into court but less desirable when the merits are to be argued.

Thus, in *Elkins v. United States*,[96] the recent case that overturned the "silver platter" doctrine,[97] certiorari was sought after the Supreme Court had already agreed to review the related case of *Rios v. United States*.[98] In opposing certiorari in *Rios*, the Government had said that "the State of California in this case has not attempted to restrain its officers from turning over evidence to the federal government or from testifying in a federal court." Now, in *Elkins*, such an order had actually been obtained from an Oregon Circuit Court, only to be thereafter disregarded by the United States District Court. Accordingly, in order to demonstrate that *Elkins* was an *a fortiori* case, the questions presented were arranged in the following order:

1. Whether, after a state court has suppressed evidence that it held to be illegally seized as a matter of state law and has enjoined state and county officials from testifying concerning such evidence, a federal conviction may thereafter be had and affirmed, where the federal court

---

[96] 364 U. S. 206.

[97] *Weeks* v. *United States*, 232 U. S. 383, 398; *Lustig* v. *United States*, 338 U. S. 74, 78-79.

[98] *Rios* v. *United States*, 256 F. 2d 173 (C.A. 9), certiorari granted, 359 U. S. 965.

did not undertake any independent examination of the original state seizure but assumed that it was illegal as a matter of state law, and proceeded on the basis of (a) the testimony of the state officers, who were directed by the federal court to testify notwithstanding the state court injunction, and of (b) the suppressed evidence, which was subsequently taken from the constructive custody of the state court under a federal search warrant, on the footing that *Rea* v. *United States,* 350 U. S. 214, involves an application of the Supremacy Clause rather than a doctrine of reciprocity and of comity between state and federal courts.

2. Whether the evidence used against petitioners in the federal prosecution was obtained in violation of their rights under the Constitution of the United States.

3. Whether, if the evidence was unlawfully obtained, it was admissible in the federal prosecution of petitioners because obtained by state officers without federal participation.

Later, after certiorari was granted in *Elkins,* it appeared to counsel that the first question presented contained difficulties the Supreme Court might want to avoid, and that, if the "silver platter" doctrine were to be abandoned, the converse-of-*Rea* issue need never be reached. Accordingly, in the *Elkins* brief on the merits, the points from the petition were rearranged in this order: 2, 3, 1.

After argument, the "silver platter" rule was discarded, thus making it unnecessary for the Court to consider the scope of the *Rea* doctrine. Curiously enough, the Justices who dissented because they preferred to retain the "silver platter" rule were prepared to affirm the *Elkins* conviction without reference to *Rea.*[99]

(b) When you have alternative grounds, place the most appealing one first—and by "most appealing" in this connection is meant the proposition that evokes the least judicial sales resistance.

(i) In the *Hatahley* Indian depredation case,[100] already mentioned in another connection (*supra,* Section 26), the Federal agents had purported to act under the provisions of a State statute dealing with abandoned horses, which had provisions for notice different from those of the Act of Congress covering grazing on the

---

[99] See both dissenting opinions in the case, 364 U. S. at 233 and 251. This may have been an oversight incident to the pressures of winding up the Term; from June 6 through June 27, 1960, the Court handed down opinions that extended (including dissents and concurrences) to over 800 pages in the official reports.

[100] *Hatahley* v. *United States,* 351 U. S. 173.

public domain. The trial judge found and held that the provisions of the State statute had not been complied with, and the record supported an argument that, in any event, the application of those provisions to the petitioners would have involved denying them Due Process of Law. The publication and posting of notices in English is, after all, hardly a constitutionally effective way of warning illiterate and non-English speaking Indians.[101] But the Supreme Court is normally chary of interpreting a State statute as an original proposition,[102] and of course constitutional questions are to be avoided if the case can be otherwise decided.[103] So the petitioners stressed the inconsistency between the state and federal provisions, and presented their points as follows:

I. The Indians' rights under the Taylor Grazing Act could not be affected by the Utah abandoned horse statute.

A. The Taylor Grazing Act gave the present petitioners affirmative rights with respect to the grazing of their horses and burros that were not contained in the Utah abandoned horse statute.

B. The Taylor Grazing Act and the regulations thereunder provided for personal notice to trespassers on the federal range, whereas the Utah abandoned horse statute provided only for notice by publication.

C. The reservation for state police power in the Taylor Grazing Act did not permit the Utah abandoned horse statute to operate in the very sphere that Congress was regulating, viz., grazing on the public domain.

D. The Government's agents were not authorized to invoke the Utah abandoned horse statute.

II. Even if the Utah abandoned horse statute were applicable, its provisions were not followed, and accordingly, it could not justify the slaughter of the Indians' horses for which compensation is sought here.

---

[101] Cf. *Mullane* v. *Central Hanover Bank & Trust Co.*, 339 U. S. 306.

[102] For the present status of the "abstention doctrine," which had its origin in *Meredith* v. *Winter Haven*, 320 U. S. 228, the reader must be referred to a quartet of cases decided on June 8, 1959: *Louisiana P. & L. Co.* v. *Thibodaux City*, 360 U. S. 25; *Harrison* v. *N.A.A.C.P.*, 360 U. S. 167; *Allegheny County* v. *Mashuda Co.*, 360 U. S. 185; and *Martin* v. *Creasy*, 360 U. S. 219. A manful effort to reconcile these decisions will be found in Kurland, *Toward a Co-Operative Judicial Federalism: The Federal Court Abstention Doctrine*, 24 F.R.D. 481.
See also *Clay* v. *Sun Insurance Office*, 363 U. S. 207.

[103] E.g., *Rescue Army* v. *Municipal Court*, 331 U. S. 549; *Parker* v. *City of Los Angeles*, 338 U. S. 327; *District of Columbia* v. *Little*, 339 U. S. 1; *Peters* v. *Hobby*, 349 U. S. 331.

III. Even if the provisions of the Utah abandoned horse statute should be held to have been complied with to the letter, its application to these petitioners involved a denial of constitutional protections.

The Supreme Court held that there was an inconsistency between the Federal regulation and the State statute, that there was no compliance with the Federal regulation for notice, and that the Utah abandoned horse statute was accordingly not properly invoked.[104] This conclusion made it unnecessary for the Court to consider any questions of State law—and thus justified the order in which the points had been arranged in the brief.

(ii) Another example: In cases involving judicial review of administrative action, when you are appearing for the agency, show that the agency was right before you start to argue that, right or wrong, its determination is not subject to judicial review. The other order may be more logical, but it involves substantially more judicial reluctance; courts don't like to be told that their jurisdiction to review is limited.

Thus, in a case which involved the scope of a railroad's release of lands under the Transportation Act of 1940,[105] the two main headings in support of the administrative action giving that release full effect were as follows:

I. Claims to lands granted by the Acts of 1874 and 1904 in lieu of lands granted by the 1866 Act and thereafter relinquished were extinguished by the release here executed pursuant to the Transportation Act of 1940.

II. Apart from the merits, the Secretary's construction of the interrelationship between the Acts of 1866, 1874, 1904, and 1940 involved the exercise of discretion, was reasonable, has not been shown to be clearly wrong, and thus is impregnable to mandamus.

As it happened, the court went directly to the merits and upheld the Secretary,[106] but the same technique employed in similar cases, now that the Administrative Procedure Act has substantially

---

[104] 351 U. S. at 179-180.

[105] *Krug* v. *Santa Fe P. R. Co.,* 329 U. S. 591.

[106] "We agree with the District Court. We think, as it held, that the Secretary of the Interior's construction of the 1940 Act was clearly right. Therefore, we do not discuss the Government's contention that, since the Secretary's construction was a reasonable one, it was an allowable exercise of his discretion which should not be set aside by injunction or relief in the nature of mandamus. See *Santa Fe P. R. R.* v. *Work,* 267 U. S. 511, 517; cf. *Santa Fe P. R. R.* v. *Lane,* 244 U. S. 492." *Krug* v. *Santa Fe P. R. Co.,* 329 U. S. 591, 597.

broadened the scope of review in those situations where it is applicable,[107] may well lead to decisions sustaining the administrative determination. In any event, courts are much more inclined to withhold their hand after first being convinced that the administrative officer was right—which is simply another illustration of the principle that courts delight to do substantial justice or, at the very least, that they are perceptibly influenced by "the equities."

(iii) Similarly, where one alternative involves distinguishing away a recently decided case while the other has a clear path not thus obstructed, argue the latter alternative first in order to avoid the reluctance that courts always feel when they are asked to reshape their recent precedents. Requesting a court to overrule or modify a case but lately decided, after full consideration and over strong dissent, always involves a heavy uphill pull.

Thus, in the *Knauer* denaturalization case,[108] the argument in support of the judgment below, which had cancelled Knauer's citizenship, rested on two elements: fraud in the oath of allegiance, and fraud in his representation that he was attached to the principles of the Constitution. The latter problem had been before the Supreme Court in *Schneiderman v. United States*,[109] a case that was twice argued, and that had not only narrowed the scope of denaturalization proceedings, but had substantially (and, in the view of the dissenting judges, unduly) narrowed the concept of "attached to the principles of the Constitution." [110] Moreover, in *Baumgartner v. United States*,[111] the Court had held that the facts there presented did not establish "beyond a troubling doubt" that Baumgartner had committed fraud in taking the oath of allegiance.

Each of these decisions placed a heavy burden on the Govern-

---

[107] See Sec. 10, Administrative Procedure Act (5 U.S.C. § 1009) ; *Universal Camera Corp.* v. *Labor Board,* 340 U. S. 474; *O'Leary* v. *Brown-Pacific-Maxon,* 340 U. S. 504. Exceptions to the rule of reviewability are specified in Sec. 2 (a) , 5 U.S.C. § 1001 (a) . Curiously enough, the former "impregnable to mandamus" rule reached its highest flowering under the fostering care of the most conservative judges. See *Riverside Oil Co.* v. *Hitchcock,* 190 U. S. 316 (Peckham, J.) ; *Wilbur* v. *United States,* 281 U. S. 206 (Van Devanter, J.) .

[108] *Knauer* v. *United States,* 328 U. S. 654.

[109] 320 U. S. 118.

[110] See Wiener, *"Freedom for the Thought That We Hate": Is it a Principle of the Constitution?,* 37 A.B.A.J. 177 (1951), which sets forth the historical materials.

[111] 322 U. S. 665.

ment, but the *Schneiderman* case was the more impressive and difficult obstacle, partly because it had been a more hotly contested litigation, but essentially because it involved a fuzzier and more debatable concept, viz., the principles of the Constitution. In consequence, it was decided in *Knauer* to argue fraud in the oath of allegiance first, as follows:

I. The evidence establishes beyond a troubling doubt that in 1937, when petitioner renounced allegiance to the German Reich and took an oath of allegiance to the United States, he committed conscious and deliberate fraud.

II. Fraud in the oath of allegiance is a proper ground for cancellation of a certificate of naturalization.

III. The evidence likewise establishes beyond a troubling doubt that petitioner's representation at the time of his naturalization that he was attached to the principles of the Constitution of the United States was consciously and deliberately false; and this is an additional ground for cancelling his certificate of naturalization.

The case was decided in the government's favor on the ground that Knauer's oath of allegiance had been shown to be fraudulent, and the Court thus did not reach the question of attachment.[112]

Other instances of treating precedents that the brief-writer needs to distinguish, generally because his case would be stronger had they never been decided, are considered below in Sections 35 and 53, *infra*, pp. 111-114, 156-159.

(iv) It may happen on occasion that correct analysis and effective presentation require the broader and more difficult proposition to be argued first. A striking illustration of such an instance was the case that involved the refusal of the Rhode Island courts to enforce treble-damage actions for overcharges in violation of OPA ceilings, on the ground that these were actions for penalties based on the statute of a foreign sovereign![113]

Two questions were involved, one being whether such a proceeding was really an action for a penalty, and the other whether, even if it was, it could be maintained none the less. The argument for the plaintiff (joined by the Price Administrator as intervenor)

---

[112] "Since fraud in the oath of allegiance which Knauer took is sufficient to sustain the judgment below, we do not reach the other questions which have been argued." *Knauer* v. *United States*, 328 U. S. at 674.

[113] *Testa* v. *Katt*, 330 U. S. 386.

was that, under the Federal rule, the action was not one for a penalty, but that, even so, the state courts were bound to enforce it. Which point should be argued first? The quotation is from the first argument paragraph of the prevailing brief:

We assume *arguendo* at the outset that the present action—a consumer's action for treble damages under Section 205 (e) of the Emergency Price Control Act as amended—is an action for a penalty even though the actual recovery here was limited to the amount of the overcharge plus an attorney's fee. We make that assumption in order to bring more sharply into focus our contention that, since the courts of Rhode Island are open to actions for penalties founded upon state law, they cannot consistently with the Supremacy Clause of the Constitution refuse to take jurisdiction of similar actions founded on federal law. Thereafter, once the basic question of discrimination against a federal cause of action is disposed of, we proceed to show that, since the consumer's action under the Emergency Price Control Act is a federal right, its nature must be judged by federal standards, and that, under the decisions of this Court, it is clearly a remedial action and not one for a penalty, even though multiple damages plus an attorney's fee may be recovered. That being so, *a fortiori* the Rhode Island courts cannot refuse to entertain such actions.

The Court followed this approach, assumed without deciding that the section in question was a penal statute, and then held that the State courts were not free under Article VI of the Constitution to refuse enforcement of the claim.[114]

(v) The advocate's problem is underscored by the comparison of example (iv), above, with examples (i) to (iii) : When is it appropriate to argue the easier point first and when the harder

---

[114] "For the purposes of this case, we assume, without deciding, that § 205 (e) is a penal statute in the 'public international,' 'private international,' or any other sense. So far as the question of whether the Rhode Island courts properly declined to try this action, it makes no difference into which of these categories the Rhode Island court chose to place the statute which Congress has passed. For we cannot accept the basic premise on which the Rhode Island Supreme Court held that it has no more obligation to enforce a valid penal law of the United States than it has to enforce a valid penal law of another state or a foreign country. Such a broad assumption flies in the face of the fact that the States of the Union constitute a nation. It disregards the purpose and effect of Article VI of the Constitution which provides: 'This Constitution, and the Laws of the United States which shall be made in Pursuance thereof; and all Treaties made, or which shall be made, under the Authority of the United States, shall be the supreme Law of the Land; and the Judges in every State shall be bound thereby, any Thing in the Constitution or Laws of any State to the Contrary notwithstanding.' " *Testa* v. *Katt, 330 U. S. at 389.*

one? The only honest answer, of course, is "it all depends"—because there just isn't any ironclad rule that will fit every case. Normally it is sound technique to start on the line of least resistance, but occasionally a situation will call for grasping the nettle firmly, for arguing the really difficult point at the outset. The last example discussed illustrates such a situation—and it's simply up to the lawyer handling the case to decide which approach is more likely to succeed. There is no ready-made rule of thumb to save you from the pain of choosing which course to pursue—but once you decide, adhere to the approach you have selected, and don't wobble back and forth as though you still couldn't make up your mind.

Section 35. Legal arguments that had better be avoided.— (a) *Weak propositions.* Perhaps the most important admonition under this heading is to avoid arguing weak questions or any in which you have no faith; their inclusion only serves to weaken the rest of your argument, and may well result in serious prejudice to your case.

Indeed, critics of outstanding competence have emphasized that it is the ability to discern weak points, and the willingness to discard weak points, that constitute the mark of a really able lawyer.

For example, Judge Learned Hand, in his tribute to one of America's greatest patent lawyers, the late Charles Neave, said:

> With the courage which only comes of justified self-confidence, he dared to rest his case upon its strongest point, and so avoided that appearance of weakness and uncertainty which comes of a clutter of arguments. Few lawyers are willing to do this; it is the mark of the most distinguished talent.[115]

And the late William D. Mitchell, one-time Attorney General of the United States, and one of the ablest of Solicitors General, wrote:

> Some lawyers, of course, do not have enough confidence in their own judgment or are not competent to select weak points, but the most effective advocate is one who has the courage to eliminate such arguments.[116]

---

[115] Hand, *In Memory of Charles Neave*, in *The Spirit of Liberty* (Dillard's 2d ed. 1951) 127-128.
[116] Book Review (1950) 64 Harv. L. Rev. 350, 351.

Indeed, it may safely be laid down as a proposition of general application that to include a weak point is virtually certain to dilute every strong one.

I can cite two examples to illustrate the foregoing, both drawn from personal experience.

(i) In the *Di Re* case,[117] a dozen or so years ago, the question, stated most favorably for the prosecution, was, "Whether, when officers have been informed that contraband is to be transferred at a certain place, and their observations reasonably justify the conclusion that a transfer has taken place in an automobile at such place, they are justified in searching and arresting a third person present in the automobile about whom they had no previous information." In the Government's petition for certiorari it was urged that Di Re's search could be justified without regard to the validity of his arrest, first, under the principle that a vehicle may be searched by officers having reasonable cause to believe that it is being used to carry contraband; [118] and, second, on the ground that, in any event, probable cause existed for the arrest.[119]

After the petition was granted, and in the course of writing the brief on the merits, I was beset with doubts as to the soundness of the first proposition, because after all it is quite a step from searching the automobile to searching the people who ride in it. In the end, we reversed the order of the points in the brief, arguing first, that "the search of respondent was justified as incident to a lawful arrest," and second, that "alternatively the search of respondent was justified as incident to the search of a moving vehicle reasonably believed to be carrying contraband." At the oral argument I simply stated the alternative point, and did not in any sense bear down on it. But my real mistake was in leaving it in at all. It was a weak point, I had no faith in it, and yet it colored the entire case. We lost, and the Court's opinion took up and demolished our weak ground first. By the time that was disposed of, the

---

[117] *United States* v. *Di Re,* 332 U. S. 581.

[118] See *Carroll* v. *United States,* 267 U. S. 132; *Husty* v. *United States,* 282 U. S. 694; *Scher* v. *United States,* 305 U. S. 251; compare, for decisions after the *Di Re* case, *Brinegar* v. *United States,* 338 U. S. 160, and *Henry* v. *United States,* 361 U. S. 98.

[119] Judge Clark had said, dissenting below, "Police officers cannot be held unreasonable in declining to view as a mere bystander one who accompanies a criminal to a crime rendezvous." *United States* v. *Di Re,* 159 F. 2d 818, 820 (C.A. 2).

Court was in a fine frame of mind to do execution on our strong point—and it did just that.

The weak point, then, didn't help; it only undermined the good point. I don't mean that we would necessarily have prevailed on the stronger point, but at least it would have been considered and disposed of in a more favorable setting. So I learned, and with the conviction derived of painful experience I urge, avoid arguing questions in which you have no faith.

(ii) The next example is from a case decided two years ago, *Williams* v. *Lee.*[120] There the basic problem was whether the courts of Arizona had jurisdiction to entertain an action brought by an Indian trader—a white man—against Navajo Indians living on the Navajo Reservation in respect of a sale that he had made to them there on credit. If the doctrine of *Worcester* v. *Georgia*[121] still had vitality, then this question required a negative answer. The problem for counsel representing the Indians was whether to go further and to urge that the Arizona sheriff could not even enter upon the reservation to serve process; and/or[122] whether to fall back on narrower ground, viz., an Interior Department regulation governing Indian traders which stated that "A trader may extend credit to Indians, but such credit will be at the trader's own risk,"[123] and arguing that the transaction was rendered unenforceable by virtue of that regulation.

In the Supreme Court of Arizona, counsel for the Indians set forth not only the basic proposition, but added both of the other contentions; that tribunal rejected all three. On the question of service, it held that to accede to the proposition urged would result in making the reservation a refuge for malefactors, and it disposed of the regulation by saying that this went to the merits and not to jurisdiction.[124]

The first problem on certiorari was how far to urge the Indians' jurisdictional immunity. It was plain that the State court's

---

[120] 358 U. S. 217.

[121] 6 Pet. 515.

[122] Despite condemnation of the use of "and/or" by eminent authority (see *An And/Or Symposium,* 18 A.B.A.J. 574), I still think that it expresses accurately the thought it is here employed to express, viz., the alternative between either and both; i.e., between A plus B, and B instead of A.

[123] 25 C.F.R. (1958 ed.) § 252.17, promulgated pursuant to 25 U.S.C. § 262. In earlier versions of Title 25, C.F.R., this regulation was numbered § 277.17.

[124] *Williams* v. *Lee,* 83 Ariz. 241, 319 P. 2d 998.

fears of a privileged sanctuary were unfounded, since under a whole line of cases State process ran on an Indian reservation against non-Indians.[125] Moreover, there were expressions in a number of opinions that such process did not run there in respect of matters outside State cognizance.[126] Since the basic issue in the case was the extent of State jurisdiction, it was deemed wiser to drop the more difficult question of process, because after all, if the Indians' jurisdictional position were well founded, such process would be a nullity.

The regulation, however, appeared to furnish a sound basis for reversal of the judgment below, even though it meant resting the case on a narrower jurisdictional basis. So the petition for certiorari raised both questions, in these terms:

1. Whether the courts of Arizona have jurisdiction of an action brought against members of the Navajo Indian Tribe by a non-Indian in respect of a transaction arising within the boundaries of the Navajo Indian Reservation in Arizona.

2. Whether, where a non-Indian trader enters and trades on an Indian reservation pursuant to federal regulations, which declare that he extends credit to Indians only at his own risk, the courts of Arizona have jurisdiction to determine the claim of such non-Indian trader against Indians in respect of a purchase on credit.

After certiorari was granted, and while preparing the brief on the merits, counsel for the Indians learned that originally the regulation had provided that "Credit to Indians will be at the trader's own risk, as no assistance will be given by Government officials in the collection of debts against Indians;" [127] and that the last clause had been stricken at the request of an association of Indian traders, who had successfully urged that, while the Indian Bureau was not to act as a collection agency, its officials should at least use moral suasion to induce Indians to meet their obligations. In the face of that textual history, counsel for the Indians felt themselves unable to argue that the single phrase, "at the trader's own risk," made the obligation such a nullity that it could not be sued upon in a court of competent jurisdiction. With this explanation, duly set out in

---

[125] E.g., *United States* v. *McBratney*, 104 U. S. 621; *Draper* v. *United States*, 164 U. S. 240; *New York ex rel. Ray* v. *Martin*, 326 U. S. 496.

[126] E.g., *United States* v. *Kagama*, 118 U. S. 375, 383; *Langford* v. *Monteith*, 102 U. S. 145, 147; *Utah & N. R. Co.* v. *Fisher*, 116 U. S. 28, 31.

[127] General Indian Regulations of June 29, 1927, ¶ 22.

the Indians' brief, the second question presented by the petition was formally abandoned.

At this juncture the Government, which had been invited by the Court to state its views,[128] picked up the regulation, and argued that it meant that legal or judicial remedies were unavailable to traders seeking to collect unsecured debts from their Indian customers. This argument made it possible for the United States to avoid taking any position on the jurisdictional question—an issue that involved delicate Federal-State relationships in an area where "Present Federal policy calls for the termination of Federal supervision of affairs of Indian tribes desiring such termination, to the extent practicable and as soon as termination is feasible." [129]

In their reply brief, counsel for the Indians emphasized that the regulation point had been abandoned, not because they were urging the Court to make a broad constitutional pronouncement, but solely and simply because they felt that the regulation was not susceptible of the meaning that the Government professed to find therein. At the argument, the Indians' advocate proved that the regulation did not render a sale on credit unenforceable; he presented a list, by name and docket number, of literally hundreds of suits successfully brought by Indian traders against Indians, in respect of sales on credit, in courts of competent jurisdiction, namely, the Indian Tribal Courts.[130]

The opinion of the Supreme Court took the broad jurisdictional ground, reaffirmed *Worcester* v. *Georgia*,[131] strongly suggested that the sheriff should not have entered the reservation [132]—and did not even mention the regulation that the Government had so strenuously put forward!

The result therefore fully vindicated the course taken, pursuant to the admonition earlier set forth: Avoid arguing questions in which you have no faith; instead, have the courage—and the good sense—to abandon such questions.

---

[128] 356 U. S. 930.

[129] *Federal Indian Law* (1958 ed.) 501. The student may find it interesting to compare the statement of the basic jurisdictional principle as it is set forth in Cohen, *Handbook of Federal Indian Law* (1941) 116, with the later version in *Federal Indian Law* (1958 ed.) 502, and then to inquire whether the change reflects intervening decisions or merely an intervening policy.

[130] See 25 C.F.R. (1958 ed.), part 11.

[131] 6 Pet. 515.

[132] See 358 U. S. at 220-222.

(b) *Hornbook generalizations.* Another sound caution is to avoid emphasizing or relying upon elementary, or hornbook, propositions. Any time, for instance, that a lawyer goes all out on the presumption of constitutionality, he all but indicates that he seriously doubts the validity of the statute on which he is relying. Similarly, any time a brief dealing with a question of statutory construction cites *Holy Trinity Church* v. *United States*,[133] an astute court at once recognizes that it is being asked to rewrite a law in the way the legislature should have done but didn't. (This is not to suggest that the days of judicial tinkering with statutes are over, by any means; but a decent regard to prevailing techniques of the *elegantia juris* as applied to the pretzel-bending of statutory provisions (compare Section 57, below) plainly precludes resort to anything as bald as the *Holy Trinity Church* case—which in consequence had better not be cited.)

(c) *Arguments of last resort.* There are other indicia of last resort arguments also, points that should simply not be made, because to make them amounts to giving the court a signal that your case is hopeless—and that you know it is hopeless. In this category fall most of the equal protection clause contentions in constitutional matters,[134] and, in criminal cases, arguments that the indictment was duplicitous or that the court erred in not granting the motion for a bill of particulars.

Indeed, the advance sheets over the last few years indicate that the frequency with which trifling points are presented on appeal on the view that they are somehow "arguable"[135] is itself so serious an appellate problem that it warrants discussion.

We can put to one side the phenomenon of the "great case," so-called. Centuries ago, Lord Coke noted that "many questions are raised rather out of the weight of the matter than the difficulty of the case."[136] Mr. Justice Holmes made the same point within

---

[133] 143 U. S. 457.

[134] "But, it is said, however it might be if this reasoning were applied generally, it fails when it is confined to the small number who are in the institutions named and is not applied to the multitudes outside. It is the usual last resort of constitutional arguments to point out shortcomings of this sort." *Buck* v. *Bell*, 274 U. S. 200, 208, *per* Holmes, J.

[135] "Some lawyers are willing to take a case, if it presents what they describe as an 'arguable' position, on the theory that every man is entitled to have a lawyer present his case." William D. Mitchell in 64 Harv. L. Rev. at 352.

[136] Preface to 10 Co. Rep. (1826 ed.) xxi.

fairly recent memory, saying, "But cost and importance, while they add to the solemnity of our duty, do not increase the difficulty of decision except as they induce argument upon matters that, with less mighty interests, no one would venture to dispute." [137] The problem here considered is the tendency, in wholly run-of-the-mill cases, to magnify trivia. Judges have characterized this tendency in various ways, all essentially similar, none complimentary. Here are some examples: "piddling quibbling"; [138] "a worship of the inconsequential"; [139] "a contention * * * made for good measure rather than for good reason"; [140] "the remaining miscellany of minor contentions." [141] One court has made the obvious comment that "It is familiar technique for an appellant to seize upon every peccadillo committed by the lower court and magnify it until it becomes a blunder of major proportions"; [142] another the remark, which should be equally obvious, that "We do not clutch at gossamers." [143]

Those quotations are not taken exclusively from criminal cases, nor even from appellate opinions; had they been so restricted, there would at least be this excuse, that some convicted person with the means to retain counsel wants desperately to stay out of jail, and accordingly grasps at any straw that comes to hand —the doctrine of *tabula in naufragio* (or, freely translated, any port in a storm) did, after all, have some currency in English equity for many years.[144] Insofar as counsel in a criminal appeal

---

[137] *Sanitary District* v. *United States,* 266 U. S. 405, 425.

See also Holmes, J., dissenting in *Northern Securities Co.* v. *United States,* 193 U. S. 197, 400-401: "Great cases, like hard cases, make bad law. For great cases are called great, not by reason of their real importance in shaping the law of the future, but because of some accident of immediate overwhelming interest which appeals to the feelings and distorts the judgment. These immediate interests exercise a kind of hydraulic pressure which makes what was previously clear seem doubtful, and before which even well settled principles of law will bend."

[138] Clark, J., in *Republic of Italy* v. *De Angelis,* 206 F. 2d 121, 124 (C.A.2).

[139] Leahy, J., in *Tobacco and Allied Stocks* v. *Transamerica Corp.,* 18 F.R.D. 355, 356 (D.Del.).

[140] Murphy, J., in *Application of House,* 144 F. Supp. 95, 99 (N.D. Calif.).

[141] Medina, J., in *Dictograph Products* v. *Federal Trade Commission,* 217 F. 2d 821, 829 (C.A.2).

[142] Lemmon, J., in *Mitchell* v. *United States,* 213 F. 2d 951, 953 (C.A.9).

[143] *Rotundo* v. *Isthmian Steamship Co.,* 243 F. 2d 581, 584 (C.A.2) (*Per curiam;* L. Hand, J., presiding).

[144] See 3 Scott, *The Law of Trusts* (2d ed. 1956) § 311.1.

has a choice between weak points and strong ones, he owes it to his client to abandon those that are weak lest he dilute those that are strong. Insofar as such counsel has no strong points—and in some criminal trials, even when they extended over many days and even weeks, there will not be a single good point for an appeal, much less for certiorari—then there is ultimately involved a conflict of interest between attorney and client, between the client who risks his liberty, and the lawyer who stands to injure his professional reputation.[145] That conflict, necessarily, is one that every lawyer must resolve for himself. But there is hardly the same dramatic conflict when counsel seizes on and makes picayunish contentions in a civil case at the trial level.

Perhaps it should be added that while Federal appellate courts have the power in Federal cases to consider new points not raised below,[146] any request that they do so has hard sledding; [147] and of course "a memorandum of additional points * * * served after another counsel had been added to the battery" [148] signals the afterthought with all of its infirmities.[149] Nor should it be forgot-

---

[145] See Mr. Mitchell's comment, quoted *supra*, note 135; the passage then continues: "Other lawyers decline cases which they consider are without merit, because they take no professional satisfaction in arguing them; and because the litigant deserves to have his case presented by a lawyer (if one is available) who believes in it and, therefore, can argue it more persuasively. It also is true that a lawyer who becomes known as one who does not make a practice of accepting cases in which he does not believe, has a long start in the confidence of the courts and on the road to victory."

[146] See Supreme Court Rule 40 (1) (d) (2) ; Third Circuit, Rule 24 (2) (b) ; Fourth Circuit, Rule 10 (8) ; D. C. Circuit, Rule 17 (b) (1) ; F.R. Crim. P., Rule 52 (b) ; see Note, *Raising New Issues on Appeal*, 64 Harv. L. Rev. 652; compare F.R. Civ. P., Rule 61, and 28 U.S.C. § 2111.

Of course the statement in the text applies only to cases arising within the Federal system; when the Supreme Court reviews cases arising in State courts, it does not consider Federal questions not timely raised below. See Stern and Gressman, *Supreme Court Practice* (2d ed. 1954) ch. III (F) , pp. 85-91.

[147] E.g., *United States* v. *Spector*, 343 U. S. 169, 172-173; *Bird* v. *United States*, 241 F. 2d 516, 520-521 (C.A.1) ; *Armodoros* v. *Robinson*, 241 F. 2d 713 (C.A.7). Note that it took a rehearing in banc before the Ninth Circuit was convinced that it had the power that is specifically granted by Criminal Rule 52 (b). See *Herzog* v. *United States*, 226 F. 2d 561, 235 F. 2d 664, certiorari denied, 352 U. S. 844. The petition for rehearing filed in that case appears in Chapter XII, *infra*, pp. 423-429.

[148] Fee, J., in *Shibley* v. *United States*, 237 F. 2d 327, 334 (C.A.9).

[149] A classic if somewhat frightening example of how what appears at first blush to be a substantial point can be downgraded into insubstantiality when made too late is *Rosenberg* v. *United States*, 346 U. S. 273. See Section 150 at pp. 376-377, below.

ten that, in the Federal system, a criminal appeal which is frivolous is subject to dismissal.[150]

Just to complete the discussion, two special situations with respect to weak points should be noted: Appointed counsel owe an affirmative duty to present points on appeal, regardless of the prospects of success, just so long as those points are substantial.[151] And Government counsel on occasion are under a duty to confess error. The appellate court is not bound by such action,[152] but if reversal follows the appellate court's acceptance of a confession of error, it is hardly appropriate for the trial judge then to complain that he was "sold short." [153]

(d) *Evasion of issues.* At first blush it would appear not only unnecessary but indeed presumptuous to remind lawyers that their briefs must meet the other side's arguments. But a number of documents which have passed over my desk in the last few years indicate that such an obvious admonition still needs to be emphasized. Unless both the opposition and the court are hopelessly obtuse—an unlikely coincidence—it is never safe for a lawyer to write his brief on the wishful assumption that out-of-sight is equivalent to out-of-mind, or that the difficult points of a case can somehow be disposed of by being swept under the rug, as it were, either by not deigning to mention them at all, or else by relegating them to footnotes.

Here are two actual examples:

(i) In *Williams* v. *Lee*,[154] discussed above (pp. 98-100) in another connection, the petitioning Indians urged that under the

---

[150] F.R. Crim. P., Rule 39 (a) ; *United States* v. *Johnson,* 327 U. S. 106, 113; *United States* v. *Peltz,* 246 F. 2d 537 (C.A.2) ; *United States* v. *Visconti,* 261 F. 2d 215 (C.A. 2) ; *Brown* v. *United States,* 277 F. 2d 204 (C.A. 8) ; *Watson* v. *United States,* 281 F. 2d 619 (D. C. Cir.) ; and see the comments of Lemmon, J., in *Price* v. *United States,* 249 F. 2d 17, 18 (C.A.9) , and *Rystad* v. *Boyd,* 246 F. 2d 246, 249 (C.A.9).

Later instances of appeals dismissed because frivolous are too numerous for citation.

[151] *Ellis* v. *United States,* 356 U. S. 674, reversing 249 F. 2d 478 (D. C. Cir.) ; *Cash* v. *United States,* 357 U. S. 219, reversing 261 F. 2d 731 (D. C. Cir.). See also *Hansford* v. *United States,* 357 U. S. 578, and *Kitchens* v. *United States,* 358 U. S. 42. Earlier cases such as *United States ex rel. Tierney* v. *Richmond,* 245 F. 2d 222, and *United States* v. *Ballentine,* 245 F. 2d 223, both C.A.2, are probably no longer law.

[152] *Young* v. *United States,* 315 U. S. 257; compare *Casey* v. *United States,* 343 U. S. 808; *Orloff* v. *Willoughby,* 345 U. S. 83, 87-88.

[153] See *Petition of Plywacki,* 115 F. Supp. 613, 615 (D. Haw.) .

[154] 358 U. S. 217.

doctrine of *Worcester* v. *Georgia*[155] there was no jurisdiction in the State courts to entertain actions against them in respect of transactions taking place on their Reservation. In respect of that basic doctrine, petitioners relied, as had the State court in a previous decision,[156] on a presidential veto of a bill that had proposed to extend State jurisdiction over this particular tribe and on a repassage by Congress of the same bill minus those jurisdictional features,[157] and also on a subsequent Act which had conditionally conferred jurisdiction over Indians on a number of States on condition that those States would take certain steps[158]—which in fact had not been taken in the instant case.

The Government argued that in the veto "there is no indication that jurisdiction already possessed by the respective states should be withdrawn or that no such preexisting jurisdiction was thought to exist"; and that the subsequent Act "did not deal with the reserved jurisdiction which the states already possessed." Both statements appeared—in a footnote![159]

Petitioners accordingly replied,

What 'reserved jurisdiction'? What 'pre-existing or reserved state power'?

Such expressions have a nostalgic pre-Appomattox flavor, but that is assuredly their only distinction. For under the Constitution, there is no reserved state power or jurisdiction over Indians, and there never has been, as anyone who troubles to read *Worcester* v. *Georgia*, 6 Pet. 515, will soon learn. Indeed, only this year both the court below as well as the Supreme Court of the neighboring State of New Mexico held that state courts had no criminal jurisdiction over Navajo Indians committing within the Navajo Reservation acts which if done by non-Indians would have violated the criminal laws of the states concerned. *Application of Denetclaw*, 83 Ariz. 299, 320 P. 2d 697; *State* v. *Begay*, 63 N. M. 409, 320 P. 2d 1017, certiorari denied, 357 U. S. 918.

The Supreme Court mentioned the veto and the repassage of the bill less its objectionable features, pointed out that the State

---

[155] 6 Pet. 515.

[156] See *Begay* v. *Miller*, 70 Ariz. 380, 385, 222 P. 2d 624, 627-628.

[157] See Sen. Doc. 119, 81st Cong., 1st sess., and 95 Cong. Rec. 14784-14785. The modified bill became the Act of April 19, 1950, c. 92, 64 Stat. 44, 25 U.S.C. §§ 631-640.

[158] Sections 6 and 7 of the Act of August 15, 1953, c. 505, 67 Stat. 588, 590.

[159] Brief for the United States as *Amicus Curiae*, No. 39, Oct. T. 1958, p. 7, note 4.

had not accepted jurisdiction under the later Act—and reaffirmed *Worcester* v. *Georgia* in ringing terms.[160]

The question which the student of advocacy may well ask himself is, How can any lawyer worthy of the name really expect to dispose of the central issue of a case by such glancing (and obviously questionable) references in a footnote? And how can a lawyer expect that a court will pay attention to him when he does?

(ii) *United States* v. *Greenberg*[161] was a case turning on the scope of the Fifth Amendment's protection against self-incrimination, with particular reference to the showing of hazard that the witness was required to make before his claim of privilege would be allowed. Adverse rulings below were followed by a petition for certiorari, which was "held" during the pendency of the very similar case of *Hoffman* v. *United States.*[162] In the opinion thereafter handed down in the latter case, the prerequisites for claiming the privilege were set forth in detail; a week later, the judgment in *Greenberg* was vacated, and the cause remanded for reconsideration in the light of *Hoffman.*[163]

On such reconsideration, the Court of Appeals (which had also decided *Hoffman*),[164] adhered to its prior ruling,[165] and when Greenberg then sought certiorari a second time, his petition was granted.[166]

The Government filed an 80-page brief on the merits, the thrust of which is perhaps best portrayed reflexly[167] by the following excerpt from petitioner's reply:

A. The Government starts its argument (U. S. Br. 21) by quoting that portion of the opinion in *Hoffman* v. *United States, 341 U. S. 479, 486,* which commences by saying that

The privilege afforded not only extends to answers that would

---

[160] 358 U. S. at 222-223.

[161] 187 F. 2d 35 (C.A.3).

[162] 341 U. S. 479.

[163] 341 U. S. 944.

[164] 185 F. 2d 617 (C.A.3).

[165] *United States* v. *Greenberg, 192 F. 2d 201 (C.A.3).*

[166] 342 U. S. 917.

[167] I am indebted to the late Mr. Ernest Knaebel, Reporter of Decisions of the United States Supreme Court for more than 27 years, for this expression. See *Selective Draft Law Cases, 245 U. S. 366, 368: "As it is manifestly impracticable to restate these arguments [against the constitutionality of the Selective Draft Law of 1917] separately, perhaps the best recourse available is to exhibit their leading features reflexly, by summarizing the answers to them contained in the single brief of the United States, viz. * * *."*

in themselves support a conviction under a federal criminal statute but likewise embraces those which would furnish a link in the chain of evidence needed to prosecute the claimant for a federal crime.

But the Government's brief, though it extends over 80 pages, never goes on to quote the last portion of the paragraph in question, viz.,

However, if the witness, upon interposing his claim, were required to prove the hazard in the sense in which a claim is usually required to be established in court, he would be compelled to surrender the very protection which the privilege is designed to guarantee. To sustain the privilege, it need only be evident from the implications of the question, in the setting in which it is asked, that a responsive answer to the question or an explanation of why it cannot be answered *might* be dangerous because injurious disclosure *could* result.

(We have italicized the conditional words to emphasize that certainty of incrimination is not a prerequisite to successful invocation of the constitutional privilege.)

Nor does the Government at any point quote the further portion of the *Hoffman* opinion, *id.* at 488, where the Court said that

Petitioner could reasonably have sensed the peril of prosecution for federal offenses ranging from obstruction to conspiracy.

The omitted portions of the *Hoffman* opinion necessarily undercut all of the Government's obviously labored endeavors (U. S. Br. 14-18, 21-55) to whittle down the privilege against self-incrimination to the point where it would be available only in circumstances where the assertion that an answer would be incriminating would in and of itself incriminate the witness.

Five days after argument, the Supreme Court reversed *per curiam*—on the authority of *Hoffman*.[168]

The case may not have been as open-and-shut as counsel for petitioner ultimately brought themselves to think—two justices dissented—but how could any lawyer have thought for a moment that he could overcome the recently decided *Hoffman* opinion by simply ignoring those portions thereof that were unfavorable to him?[169]

In short, "Grasp your nettles firmly" is an admonition fully as applicable to unfavorable points of law as it is to unfavorable facts *(supra,* Section 25).

---

[168] 343 U. S. 918.

[169] See Chapter XIV, below, for a comprehensive discussion of the origin of and sequel to the *Greenberg* and *Hoffman* cases, and for the complete text of the oral argument in the former.

(e) *Requests to overrule cases.* Another line of argument that it is usually desirable to avoid is the out-and-out request that a governing precedent be squarely overruled. Lower courts can't overrule cases (although, believe it or not, they are on occasion asked to do so),[170] and a court of last resort is reluctant to do so.

The progress of Federal constitutional law from 1937 to 1960 is full of instances where old precedents were overruled,[171] but there have been few overrulings in the Supreme Court in the last ten years. The doctrinal hardening became quite evident in the 1947 Term, when three requests for the overruling of prior precedents failed.[172] Contrariwise, in the 1948 Term, where the

---

[170] This is perhaps subject to the qualification that on occasion lower courts or lower court judges correctly divine that a decision of a court of last resort is about to be overruled. See *Barnette* v. *West Virginia State Board of Ed.*, 47 F. Supp. 251 (S.D.W. Va.), affirmed, 319 U. S. 624, where the court, *per* Parker, J., correctly foretold the impending demise of *Minersville School Dist.* v. *Gobitis*, 310 U. S. 586; *United States* v. *Girouard*, 149 F. 2d 760, 764-767 (C.A. 1), reversed 328 U. S. 61, where Woodbury, J., dissenting, accurately predicted the early end of the *Schwimmer* (279 U. S. 644) and *Macintosh* (283 U. S. 605) cases; *United States* v. *Smith*, 106 F. Supp. 9 (S.D. Calif.), where Yankwich, D. J., relied on the dissent of Cardozo, J., in *United States* v. *Constantine*, 296 U. S. 287, 297, as correctly representing the law, in preference to a decision which followed the majority opinion, and which was promptly reversed in consequence, see *United States* v. *Kahriger*, 105 F. Supp. 322 (E.D.Pa.), reversed, 345 U. S. 22; and *Browder* v. *Gayle*, 142 F. Supp. 707 (M.D.Ala.), affirmed, 352 U. S. 903, where Rives, J., correctly predicted that *Plessy* v. *Ferguson*, 163 U. S. 537, lacked current vitality even in the field of intrastate transportation.

[171] See Blaustein and Field, *"Overruling" Opinions in the Supreme Court*, 57 Mich. L. Rev. 151, which collects the cases through 1958.

That list must however be used with caution for a number of reasons. First, it included as "overruled" cases where affirmance by an equally divided court was followed on rehearing by a reversal. Since an affirmance by an equally divided court does not constitute an authoritative precedent, see *United States* v. *Pink*, 315 U. S. 203, 216, and cases there cited, I should not consider that any overruling was involved in that situation. Second, it treats as "overruled" the earlier decisions in the first court-martial cases, whereas in fact the earlier opinions were, on rehearing, not "overruled" but "withdrawn." See headnote in *Reid* v. *Covert*, 354 U. S. 1. Third, it includes a good many cases that were only overruled by implication—and those are precedents that have a way of coming to life again. See pp. 110-111, *infra*.

[172] (a) In *United States* v. *South Buffalo R. Co.*, 333 U. S. 771, the Government asked that *United States* v. *Elgin, J. & E. R. Co.*, 298 U. S. 492, be overruled, but the Court, by a vote of five to four, declined to do so, on the ground that Congress had specifically refused to overturn the earlier case by legislation.

(b) In *Williams* v. *Fanning*, 332 U. S. 490, which involved the question

offending precedent was sought to be distinguished on the ground of intervening legislation and overruling was not requested, the Court held that the legislation was immaterial, and overruled the earlier case, largely because the prevailing brief had demonstrated the factual unsoundness of the doctrine established by that case.[173] Since then, most of the recent doctrinal changes have been effected by "distinguishing" earlier cases,[174] and many of these changes re-

---

whether, in an action for an injunction against a subordinate public officer, his official superior was an indispensable party, the Government argued that *Gnerich* v. *Rutter*, 265 U. S. 388, and *Webster* v. *Fall*, 266 U. S. 507, were utterly inconsistent with *Colorado* v. *Toll*, 268 U. S. 228; it urged, therefore, that the latter case be squarely overruled. The Court held that the cases were consistent on their facts and that, in the situation presented—an action to restrain a local postmaster's enforcement of a mail fraud order issued by the Postmaster General—the superior officer was not an indispensable party. Nothing was overruled—except, silently, the language and reasoning of *Gnerich* v. *Rutter*. See, in this connection, the discussion in 3 Davis, *Administrative Law Treatise* (1958) § 27.08.

(c) In *United States* v. *Line Material Co.*, 333 U. S. 287, and *United States* v. *U. S. Gypsum Co.*, 333 U. S. 364, the Government urged the Court to overrule *United States* v. *General Electric Co.*, 272 U. S. 476, and its doctrine that price-fixing pursuant to a patent license did not constitute a violation of the Sherman Anti-Trust Act. The Court declined to do so, and decided each of the two cases in favor of the Government on the basis of their particular facts.

[173] *Cosmopolitan Shipping Co.* v. *McAllister*, 337 U. S. 783, overruling *Hust* v. *Moore-McCormack Lines*, 328 U. S. 707.

[174] Neither the listing in this nor the footnote following should be regarded as anything more than illustrative.

Compare the following sets of decisions: *Hoffman* v. *United States*, 341 U. S. 479, with *Mason* v. *United States*, 244 U. S. 362; *Rutkin* v. *United States*, 343 U. S. 130, with *Commissioner* v. *Wilcox*, 327 U. S. 404; *Brown* v. *Board of Education*, 347 U. S. 483, with *Gong Lum* v. *Rice*, 275 U. S. 78, and *Missouri ex rel. Gaines* v. *Canada*, 305 U. S. 337; *La Buy* v. *Howes Leather Co.*, 352 U. S. 249, with *Los Angeles Brush Corp.* v. *James*, 272 U. S. 701; *United States* v. *Union Pacific R. Co.*, 353 U. S. 112, with *Northern Pacific R. Co.* v. *Townsend*, 190 U. S. 267; *United States* v. *duPont & Co.*, 353 U. S. 586, with *Thatcher Mfg. Co.* v. *Federal Trade Comm.*, 272 U. S. 554, and *International Shoe Co.* v. *Federal Trade Comm.*, 280 U. S. 291; *Smith* v. *Sperling*, 354 U. S. 91, with *Doctor* v. *Harrington*, 196 U. S. 579, *Venner* v. *Great Northern R. Co.*, 209 U. S. 24, and *Koster* v. *Lumbermens Mutual Co.*, 330 U. S. 518; *Indian Towing Co.* v. *United States*, 350 U. S. 61, with *Dalehite* v. *United States*, 346 U. S. 15; *Moore* v. *Michigan*, 355 U. S. 155, with *Quicksall* v. *Michigan*, 339 U. S. 660; *Green* v. *United States*, 355 U. S. 184, with *Trono* v. *United States*, 199 U. S. 521; *United States* v. *City of Detroit*, 355 U. S. 466, and related cases, with *United States* v. *Allegheny County*, 322 U. S. 174; *Youngstown Co.* v. *Bowers*, 358 U. S. 534, with *Hooven & Allison Co.* v. *Evatt*, 324 U. S. 652; *United States* v. *Parke, Davis & Co.*, 362 U. S. 29, with *United States* v. *Colgate & Co.*, 250 U. S. 300.

flect the inevitable transition in general outlook that is best characterized as an altered climate of opinion.[175]

I have found but two square overrulings since the end of the 1948 Term.[176] That circumstance deserves to be stressed, for it involves far more than pedantic insistence on accurate terminology. The fact is that, unless a case is squarely overruled, it is still available later on.

---

[175] Compare the following sets of decisions: *Zorach* v. *Clauson*, 343 U. S. 306, with *McCollum* v. *Board of Education*, 333 U. S. 203; *Offutt* v. *United States*, 348 U. S. 11, with *Sacher* v. *United States*, 343 U. S. 1; *Shaughnessy* v. *Pedreiro*, 349 U. S. 48, with *Heikkila* v. *Barber*, 345 U. S. 229; *Quinn* v. *United States*, 349 U. S. 155, *Emspak* v. *United States*, 349 U. S. 190, and *Bart* v *United States*, 349 U. S. 219, with *Rogers* v. *United States*, 340 U. S. 367; *Slochower* v. *Board of Education*, 350 U. S. 551, with *Garner* v. *Los Angeles Board*, 341 U. S. 716, and *Adler* v. *Board of Education*, 342 U. S. 485; *Watkins* v. *United States*, 354 U. S. 178, with, e.g., *United States* v. *Bryan*, 339 U. S. 323, and *United States* v. *Fleischman*, 339 U. S. 349; *Teamsters Union* v. *Vogt, Inc.*, 354 U. S. 284, with *Thornhill* v. *Alabama*, 310 U. S. 88, and *American Fed. of L.* v. *Swing*, 312 U. S. 321; *Rowoldt* v. *Perfetto*, 355 U. S. 115, with *Galvan* v. *Press*, 347 U. S. 522; *Machinists* v. *Gonzales*, 356 U. S. 617, with *Garner* v. *Teamsters, &c. Union*, 346 U. S. 485; *Watkins* v. *United States*, 354 U. S. 178, with *Barenblatt* v. *United States*, 360 U. S. 109; *Sweezy* v. *New Hampshire*, 354 U. S. 234, with *Uphaus* v. *Wyman*, 360 U. S. 72.

[176] *United States* v. *Rabinowitz*, 339 U. S. 56, overruling *Trupiano* v. *United States* 334 U. S. 699; *Burstyn* v. *Wilson*, 343 U. S. 495, overruling *Mutual Film Corp.* v. *Industrial Comm.*, 236 U. S. 230.

Elkins v. *United States*, 364 U. S. 206, refused to follow the state seizure aspect of *Weeks* v. *United States*, 232 U. S. 383, 398, but did not specifically overrule the earlier decision.

Plessy v. *Ferguson*, 163 U. S. 537, is now without vitality—see, e.g., *Gayle* v. *Browder*, 352 U. S. 903, and cases there cited—but it has yet to be specifically overruled. See *Brown* v. *Board of Education*, 347 U. S. 483, 494-495.

The older cases on substantive due process may similarly be regarded as no longer having vitality—cf. *Williamson* v. *Lee Optical Co.*, 348 U. S. 483—whether or not they have been in fact expressly overruled.

In *Ullman* v. *United States*, 350 U. S. 422, the Court refused to overrule *Brown* v. *Walker*, 161 U. S. 591; in *United States* v. *Burnison*, 339 U. S. 87, it similarly refused to overrule *United States* v. *Fox*, 94 U. S. 315.

The notorious "dirty business" wiretapping case—*Olmstead* v. *United States*, 277 U. S. 438—has yet to be overruled. See *Goldman* v. *United States*, 316 U. S. 129, 136; *On Lee* v. *United States*, 343 U. S. 747, 758, 762.

The opinions in *Kinsella* v. *Krueger*, 351 U. S. 470, and *Reid* v. *Covert*, 351 U. S. 487, were not overruled, but, on rehearing, were "withdrawn." See 354 U. S. at 1.

The case of *Federal Baseball Club* v. *National League*, 259 U. S. 200, still stands as to baseball (*Toolson* v. *New York Yankees*, 346 U. S. 356), but not as to theatrical productions (*United States* v. *Shubert*, 348 U. S. 222), boxing (*United States* v. *International Boxing Club*, 348 U. S. 236), or football (*Radovich* v. *National Football League*, 352 U. S. 445).

Thus, after the development of the stream-of-commerce concept in the antitrust field,[177] it might very properly have been assumed that the original antitrust decision, *United States v. E. C. Knight Co.*,[178] was completely devoid of vitality. In the *Sugar Institute* case in 1936,[179] which involved the same industry, the *Knight* case was not even cited by counsel,[180] let alone by the Court. But less than two months later, when the Guffey Coal Act came before the Court in the *Carter Coal* case, the *Knight* decision was not only cited, but was strongly relied upon as authority for invalidating the legislation.[181] Truly, cases that have not been squarely overruled can become "ghosts that slay." [182]

To recur to the basic topic of the present discussion:

There is always a basic reluctance to overturn what was once decided, for a number of reasons. First, no one likes to admit that he was once wrong, particularly in the recent past, and judges who have once decided a point after full consideration are certainly no exception to that very human reaction. Second, even judges who most ardently desire to effect new departures strive to maintain at least the appearance of continuity. Indeed, a distinguished legal historian has pointed out that the way to spot Lord Coke's innovations is to look for a sentence beginning "For it is an ancient maxim of the common law." [183]

Consequently, particularly when the precedent in the way is of fairly recent vintage, it is far easier for the advocate to suggest distinctions and differentiations. Frequently an effective technique is to talk around the offending case and to give it a form of

---

[177] E.g., *Swift and Company v. United States,* 196 U. S. 375.

[178] *United States v. E. C. Knight Co.,* 156 U. S. 1.

[179] *Sugar Institute v. United States,* 297 U. S. 553.

[180] As their briefs are set forth in 80 L. ed. at 860-862.

[181] *Carter v. Carter Coal Co.,* 298 U. S. 238, 300-301.

[182] Frankfurter, *A Note on Advisory Opinions,* 37 Harv. L. Rev. 1002, 1008 (1924).

[183] "As a rule of thumb it is well to remember that sentences beginning 'For it is an ancient maxim of the common law,' followed by one of Coke's spurious Latin maxims, which he could manufacture to fit any occasion and provide with an air of authentic antiquity, are apt to introduce a new departure. Sentences such as 'And by these differences and reasons you will better understand your books,' or 'And so the doubts and diversities in the books well resolved,' likewise indicate new law. If I may formulate a theorem of my own, I advance this—the longer the list of authorities reconciled, the greater the divergence from the cases cited." Thorne, *Sir Edward Coke 1552-1952* (Selden Society Lecture) 7.

silent treatment, by emphasizing the principles that lead to a different conclusion. At the very least, this technique may result in a favorable decision on another ground.

Thus, in the *Knauer* case,[184] the Government's brief dealt with the attachment-to-the-principles-of-the-Constitution point of the *Schneiderman* case [185] largely by rearguing that question *de novo*, as an original proposition. As indicated above, Section 34 (b), the Court decided the *Knauer* case on the other ground, though I had the impression at the oral argument that at least some members of the *Schneiderman* majority were seeing the attachment point in a new light.[186] Similarly, in the *Haupt* treason case,[187] it was necessary to undermine the apparent rationale of the then but recently decided *Cramer* case.[188] Again, the brief dealt with many of the *Cramer* premises *sub silentio* in preference to making an all-out assault upon them.[189] In both instances, questions from the bench emphasized the points of similarity with the earlier decisions, and in both instances the replies to those questions stressed what appeared to be the determinative differences.

The same technique is recommended even when the precedent is old. Thus, in the first of the recent cases involving the power to try civilian dependents by court-martial, the Supreme Court in its original opinion [190] relied very strongly on *In re Ross*,[191] an 1891 decision that had upheld, as against a claim to jury trial, the trial of a seaman on an American ship by an American consular court in Japan.

After the rehearing in the first court-martial cases had been granted, one of the problems confronting counsel for the civilian women was, How deal with *Ross*? As is pointed out in detail below (Section 53), there were easily demonstrable reasons why

---

[184] *Knauer* v. *United States,* 328 U. S. 654.

[185] *Schneiderman* v. *United States,* 320 U. S. 118.

[186] See the paper cited in note 110, p. 93, *supra,* where the argument was more fully developed than was possible in the brief.

[187] *Haupt* v. *United States,* 330 U. S. 631.

[188] *Cramer* v. *United States,* 325 U. S. 1.

[189] See Brief for the United States in *Haupt* v. *United States,* No. 49, Oct. T. 1946. A portion thereof was set forth at pp. 342-370 of the earlier version of this work.

[190] *Kinsella* v. *Krueger,* 351 U. S. 470.

[191] 140 U. S. 453.

a square overruling of the *Ross* case would not have been palatable, even though the decision was 65 years old, even though it rested on a proposition no longer valid, and even though it would probably have been decided differently had it arisen *de novo*.

Accordingly, *Ross* was distinguished on a number of grounds. This proved to be a sound approach; on rehearing in the court-martial cases the Court ruled the other way, in a series of opinions which showed that a majority of the justices would not have been prepared to overrule *In re Ross*.

A somewhat stronger approach was taken in *Elkins* v. *United States*,[192] the very recent case which overturned the "silver platter" doctrine that dated from *Weeks* v. *United States*.[193] Following the conclusion reached by the District of Columbia Circuit in *Hanna* v. *United States*,[194] it was argued on behalf of Elkins, not that the state seizure aspect of *Weeks* should be overruled as an original proposition, but rather that the very basis of that part of *Weeks*, which rested on the unchallenged proposition that the Fourth Amendment did not bind the States,[195] had been undercut by the subsequent holding in *Wolf* v. *Colorado*,[196] to the effect that the basic right of freedom from unreasonable searches was a part of the Due Process of Law protected by the Fourteenth Amendment.[197] That is to say, counsel urged that the earlier cases had already been

---

[192] 364 U. S. 206.

[193] 232 U. S. 383, 398.

[194] *Hanna* v. *United States*, 260 F. 2d 723, overruling *Shelton* v. *United States,* 169 F. 2d 665 (D. C. Cir.), certiorari denied, 335 U. S. 834.

[195] *Weeks* v. *United States*, 232 U. S. at 398: "What remedies the defendant may have against [the State officers] we need not inquire, as the Fourth Amendment is not directed to individual misconduct of such officials. Its limitations reach the Federal government and its agencies."

[196] 338 U. S. 25.

[197] *Wolf* v. *Colorado*, 338 U. S. at 27-28: "The security of one's privacy against arbitrary intrusion by the police—which is at the core of the Fourth Amendment—is basic to a free society. It is therefore implicit in 'the concept of ordered liberty' and as such enforceable against the States through the Due Process Clause. The knock at the door, whether by day or by night, as a prelude to a search, without authority of law but solely on the authority of the police, did not need the commentary of recent history to be condemned as inconsistent with the conception of human rights enshrined in the history and the basic constitutional documents of English-speaking peoples.

"Accordingly, we have no hesitation in saying that were a State affirmatively to sanction such police incursion into privacy it would run counter to the guaranty of the Fourteenth Amendment. * * *"

overruled [198]—and the Supreme Court agreed, but only by a 5-4 vote.[199]

As a matter of advocacy—i.e., persuasion, because it is impossible to stress too much the proposition that advocacy *is* persuasion—the oblique approach undoubtedly contributed to the successful outcome in all of the instances considered above.

My own view, therefore, is that unless we once more reach a fluid period like that of 1937-1947, or unless the obstacle in question is really on its last legs, it is generally better not to ask that a case be overruled. Distinguish it away, ignore it—but leave the final *coup de grace* for the court itself to administer, after you have demonstrated in your brief and argument that this is what logic and consistency require.[200]

By way of conclusion it may be ventured that, in law as in war or football or even love, the direct frontal assault on a prepared and fortified position is only rarely a successful maneuver.

Section 36. Convincing presentation of the evidence in argument on the facts.—The problem of effectively arguing facts boils down to so marshalling your evidence as to make it thoroughly convincing to the judicial reader. Basically, three steps are necessary: assertion, presentation, and conclusion. First you state what you intend to show. Next you set forth the evidence, using pertinent quotations from documents and testimony, stressing any in-

---

[198] "The doctrinal basis of the 'silver platter' doctrine, which was simply the undoubted rule that the Fourth Amendment does not apply *eo nomine* to the States (*Weeks* v. *United States*, 232 U. S. 383, 398), has been completely undercut by the later holding of *Wolf* v. *Colorado*, 338 U. S. 25, to the effect that freedom from unreasonable searches and seizures is protected from State action by the Due Process clause of the Fourteenth Amendment.

*   *   *   *   *

"For all of these reasons, we submit that the State seizure aspect of *Weeks* and all later expressions to the same effect 'can no longer be guiding' (*Rochester Tel. Corp.* v. *United States*, 307 U. S. 125, 143), that 'such vitality, as a precedent, as [the State seizure aspect of *Weeks*] then had has long since been exhausted' (*United States* v. *Darby*, 312 U. S. 100, 117), and that accordingly the 'silver platter' rule should 'be allowed a deserved repose' (Holmes, J., in *Adkins* v. *Children's Hospital*, 261 U. S. 525, 567, 570)." Brief for the Petitioners, pp. 72, 74.

[199] *Elkins* v. *United States*, 364 U. S. 206, and note that Mr. Justice Frankfurter was prepared to reverse on the ground that the evidence in question had actually been suppressed by the State courts concerned. 364 U. S. at 249-251. Note, in this connection, his vote for reversal in the analogous case of *Camara* v. *United States*, 364 U. S. 283.

[200] See pp. 108-109 and the instance cited in note 173, *supra.*

consistencies in the case against you, and making full use of that most deadly of all comparisons, the parallel column technique. Finally you conclude, generally by restating your original assertion.

Whenever the case is at all complicated, it is well to divide up the several points you are making, and to make liberal use of argumentative subheadings, so that the direction of your thought is clear. Remember that what you are aiming at is to leave conviction in the minds of your readers, and remember also that no characterization, however apt, ever has the stark impressiveness of verbatim extracts from damaging testimony or from letters that the writer later wishes he had never written. And I repeat: Stress the inconsistencies in your opponent's documents and testimony, bear down on every self-contradiction in the record. For although of course it is the law that a very bad man may have a very good case, none the less courts are human and nobody loves a liar.

Bear in mind, however, that the technique of *arguing* facts is very different from that appropriate for *stating* facts. In writing the Statement of Facts (see Sections 23 to 28), the aim is to state the facts appealingly but straightforwardly, so that the effect derives from the selection and juxtaposition of the facts. Once the Argument is reached, however, the facts should be frankly argued and commented on. The only limitations are those dictated by good taste and professional standards (see Sections 28 and 83), and by the caution that on occasion a restrained argument may be more effective than one that seems to shout too much.

In the Statement of Facts, you get your color from the facts themselves; in the Argument, you get your effect either from arguing inferences from the undisputed facts or from frankly arguing to a conclusion from disputed facts. You do not add comments of your own in the first instance, you do in the second.

The foregoing principles can perhaps not be profitably illustrated except by taking actual briefs involving questions of fact, and comparing the way the evidence is simply set out in the Statement of Facts with the way that same evidence is later argued in the Argument. Two examples of such briefs appeared in Chapter 13 of the earlier version. One involved a case where summary judgment—plus a finding of fraud—was entered below and sustained on appeal; [201] the other was a denaturalization case where

---

[201] *Isenberg* v. *Biddle,* 125 F. 2d 741 (D. C. Cir.) .

the second appellate court did not consider itself bound by concurrent findings below, so that all the evidence had to be reargued as an original proposition.[202] The briefs are longish, considerably too long for inclusion in the present revision.

Both briefs prevailed, and the decision in each instance rested on the facts. Frequently, however, the carefully prepared factual argument in a brief appears to be love's labor lost, because the case goes off on a point of substantive law or on a question of jurisdiction. Whether one's labor *is* actually lost depends on an intangible of the judicial process that cannot be stated in statistical terms, viz., on how far a court deciding a problem of jurisdiction is really affected or influenced by the circumstance that one of the parties is shown by the record to have been an arrant cheat. Does a good brief arguing facts really help the jurisdictional argument in such a situation? All that can be said with assurance is this—it certainly doesn't do any harm.

It should be added, though perhaps only by way of reminder, that the rule that the Statement of Facts should be free of editorial comments and argumentative matter by no means dispenses with the necessity that it set forth the facts as effectively and appealingly as the record will permit. The examples discussed in Section 27, above, and set out in Chapter XII, below, show how a case frequently turns, not so much on how the facts are argued in the Argument, as on how they are arranged in the Statement of Facts.

Section 37. Careful attention to all portions of the brief.— Just as it is a mistake to toss in a dry statement of facts on top of a good argument on the law, and thus to mar the finished product, perhaps with irreparable injury to the case, so also it is a mistake to neglect any other portion of the brief. The circumstance that these other portions are easier to write or less important still does not warrant giving them so little attention that they depreciate the quality of the whole. Three parts of a brief, too frequently given but little care, are considered here.

(a) *Summary of argument.* The rules of the Supreme Court and of some circuits require that all briefs, or all except the very shortest ones, contain a summary of the argument.[203] A number of

---

[202] *Knauer* v. *United States,* 328 U. S. 654.

[203] Supreme Court Rule 40 (1) (f) (in all briefs on the merits, but not in other briefs where the argument portion does not exceed 20 printed pages; and not in reply briefs, see Rule 40 (4)) ; Ninth Circuit, Rule 18 (2) (e) ; D. C. Circuit, Rule 17 (b) (8) .

courts prescribe in detail just how such a summary is to be constructed, and require that it contain a citation to every authority relied upon in the argument proper.[204] What follows is addressed only to the usual situation, not to the specially prescribed forms.

First of all, consider the importance of the summary. It is required in order that the court may have a bird's-eye view of your argument, in somewhat more elaborate form than that available from the index (which, of course, simply sets forth your headings). And, mark this, the summary is one of the portions of the brief read at the outset.[205] You will in consequence be well advised to make your summary as appealing as possible, rather than dry-as-dust, and, generally, to expand it substantially over a mere repetition of your headings.[206]

Therefore, within the space at your disposal, don't be afraid to make it long enough to be effective. The real secret of a good summary of argument is to go beyond mere assertion, because the further you get beyond that, the more convincing the summary will be to the reader. And, although a summary normally should not cite many cases (except when specifically required by rule of court), it is a very good idea to sprinkle your summary with a few of the leading authorities on which you rely. It is well, too, to set off the paragraphs of the summary of argument with roman numerals and sub-letters corresponding to the divisions of the argument proper.

One caution to be added is that the summary should not deviate from the Argument proper; it should be a synopsis of the Argument, not a novel or different train of thought.

(b) *Conclusion.* Generally the conclusion should be pretty formal, as for example:

---

[204] See Seventh Circuit, Rule 17 (a) (3); Eighth Circuit, Rule 11 (b) (Fourth).

[205] The D. C. Circuit, in a note to its Rule 17 (b) (8), states: "Because the summary of argument if properly prepared is most helpful to the court in following the oral argument and will often render unnecessary the making of inquiries by the court which consume time allowed for argument, counsel are urged to prepare the summary with great care."

[206] Supreme Court Rule 40 (1) (f) says of the summary of argument, "It should not be a mere repetition of the headings under which the argument is arranged." And the D. C. Circuit, in the passage quoted from in the preceding note, says, "The summary of the argument should not be a mere repetition of the statement of points or of the assignments of error. The summary should be a succinct, but accurate and clear, picture of the argument actually made in the brief concerning the points or assignments."

The judgment below should be affirmed.

For the foregoing reasons, the judgment below should be reversed, with directions to dismiss the petition.

Or, in a supplemental brief:

For the foregoing additional reasons, the judgment of the district court should be reversed, with directions to enter a judgment granting appropriate relief to the appellant.

On occasion, it is helpful to expand the conclusion somewhat, and to summarize the nub of the argument. Thus, in the case that involved the refusal of a State court to entertain an action based on a Federal statute,[207] the conclusion of the petitioner's brief read:

The decision below is based upon a misconception of the nature of the federal system. The judgment should therefore be reversed with instructions to enter judgment on the verdict.

And, in the *Haupt* treason case,[208] a long brief was concluded as follows:

Petitioner was convicted of treason after a sober, careful, and eminently fair trial, on the basis of evidence clearly establishing by the required two witnesses a number of legally sufficient overt acts of aid and comfort to the enemy, and clearly showing intent to betray. Reversal of the judgment below can be supported only by artificial refinements and technicalities which find no support in the treason clause of the Constitution. We therefore respectfully submit that the judgment below should be affirmed.

Similarly, in the Cleveland Stock Yards case,[209] the prevailing brief, some points of which have already been set out in Section 30 (*supra*, p. 70), concluded as follows:

The ruling of the district court sanctions the continued enforcement of a private contractual arrangement which obstructs the free flow of interstate commerce by the levy of a discriminatory toll on a single commodity. The judgment of the district court should therefore be reversed, with directions to dismiss the complaints.

It is not generally profitable to extend a conclusion further; it loses its effectiveness if made too long or it is turned into a peroration.

---

[207] *Testa* v. *Katt*, 330 U. S. 386.
[208] *Haupt* v. *United States*, 330 U. S. 631.
[209] *United States* v. *Baltimore & O. R. Co.*, 333 U. S. 169.

One caution: Never fail to indicate just what kind of relief you want in addition to reversal, e.g., reinstatement of the judgment of the trial court, or release of the appellant from custody, or dismissal of the indictment. Be specific so that the court's order will likewise be specific.

Thus, in the prevailing brief on rehearing in the first court-martial-of-dependents cases,[210] counsel for the civilian women were anxious to dispose of the suggestion, made by the Government at the original hearing, that in the event Article 2 (11) of the Uniform Code of Military Justice were held unconstitutional, the case of Mrs. Smith should be remanded for a determination of the scope of Article 2 (10).[211] Accordingly, their conclusion was framed in these terms:

> The military jurisdiction over civilians that is involved in these cases cannot be supported as a proper exertion of constitutional power. Its present exercise not only violates express provisions of the Constitution, it is violative as well of every American tradition since the beginning.
> The judgment in No. 701 should therefore be affirmed; and that in No. 713 should be reversed, with instructions to discharge Mrs. Dorothy Krueger Smith from custody forthwith.

The judgment entered disposed of the latter case accordingly.[212] But where, through inadvertence or otherwise, a party

---

[210] *Reid* v. *Covert* and *Kinsella* v. *Krueger*, 354 U. S. 1.

[211] Article 2 (11), now 10 U.S.C. § 802 (11), purported to confer court-martial jurisdiction over all accompanying civilians overseas at all times; Article 2 (10) covered only the traditional jurisdiction over "In time of war, all persons serving with or accompanying an armed force in the field." See Winthrop, *Military Law & Precedents* (2d ed. 1896) *136-*137; 14 Op. Atty. Gen. 22.

Mrs. Smith had been living in Japan during the period of hostilities in Korea, and one question, not litigated at the original hearing (*United States* v. *Kinsella*, 137 F. Supp. 806 (S.D.W.Va.)), was whether such residence amounted to her having been "in the field." The Government had argued (Reply Brief for Appellant and Petitioner, Nos. 701 and 713, Oct. T. 1955, p. 27, note 20), "There is, in our view, substantial ground for holding Article 2 (10) applicable. In the event of reversal in this case on the ground that Article 2 (11) is invalid, that question should remain open on the remand."

[212] "In No. 713, *Kinsella* v. *Krueger*, the judgment of the District Court is reversed and the case is remanded with instructions to order Mrs. Smith released from custody." 354 U. S. at 41. See 354 U. S. at 34, note 61, for references dealing with the scope of Article 2 (10).

fails to ask for the relief to which he is actually entitled, there are apt to be mistakes—and a lot of very red faces all around.[213]

(c) *Appendix.* The Appendix in this connection is not the so-called Appendix Record now required by the rules of most Federal circuits, pursuant to which counsel print pertinent portions of the record (which is not separately printed), as an appendix to their briefs, but is the Appendix to the brief that contains the collection of statutes involved and similar materials, whenever such matter is too long to be set out in the brief proper.

The basic cautions, so far as statutes are concerned, are to quote from the original statute, and, whenever amendments are pertinent, to show clearly and unmistakably the development of the statute through successive amendments.

---

[213] Thus, in a recent case, a petition for certiorari urged that "the action of the Courts of Appeals must be reviewed and reversed here." The Court did so summarily, without argument. *Union Trust Co.* v. *Eastern Air Lines,* 350 U. S. 907. Respondent petitioned for rehearing, seeking alternatively (a) vacating of the order granting the writ, (b) setting of the case for hearing, and (c) remanding the case to permit the Court of Appeals to pass on the several issues left undecided, see 221 F. 2d 62 (D. C. Cir.). Two and a half months later, the Supreme Court amended its order consistently with the third alternative. *Union Trust Co.* v. *Eastern Air Lines,* 350 U. S. 962.

In that instance, there never had been a hearing on the merits, and the error reflected, certainly in part, the effect of a summary disposition. Compare Brown, *Process of Law,* 72 Harv. L. Rev. 77. But, on occasion, the same kind of mistake follows after full briefing and argument.

Thus, some years back, the Court of Claims entered judgment in favor of the plaintiff in the sum of $3,227.93, and the Government petitioned for certiorari, assigning as error the entry of judgment for $1,877.93 in respect of a particular item, as to which it was contended that the contracting officer's determination was final. *John McShain, Inc.* v. *United States,* 88 C. Cls. 284, certiorari granted, 307 U. S. 619. The single item was the only one in issue, but the Government concluded by saying, "It is respectfully submitted that the judgment of the Court of Claims should be reversed, and the cause remanded with instructions to enter judgment in favor of the United States." Less than three weeks after the argument the Supreme Court entered a memorandum *Per Curiam* in the precise language of the conclusion in the brief, viz., "The judgment is reversed, and the cause is remanded to the Court of Claims with instructions to enter judgment in favor of the United States. [Citing cases.]" *United States* v. *John McShain, Inc.,* 308 U. S. 512. This deprived the respondent of the sums admittedly due, with the result that, four weeks later, the Court had to amend its order to read: "The judgment is reversed to the extent that it includes the $1,877.93 alleged to be due from the United States in paragraphs XIV through XXIV of the petition to the Court of Claims, and the cause is remanded to the Court of Claims with instructions to enter judgment in favor of the United States with regard to this item. [Citing cases.]" *United States* v. *John McShain, Inc.,* 308 U. S. 520.

Remember, with reference to federal statutes, that the United States Code is only *prima facie* evidence of the law, except where particular titles have been enacted into positive law.[214] At this writing, as of the close of the 86th Congress, the following titles had been so enacted: 1 (General Provisions) ; 3 (The President) ; 4 (Flag and Seal, Seat of Government, and the States) ; 6 (Official and Penal Bonds) ; 9 (Arbitration) ; 10 (Armed Forces) ; 13 (Census) ; 14 (Coast Guard) ; 17 (Copyrights) ; 18 (Crimes and Criminal Procedure) ; 23 (Highways) ; 28 (Judiciary and Judicial Procedure) ; 32 (National Guard) ; 35 (Patents) ; 38 (Veterans' Benefits) ; and 39 (The Postal Service).[215] In the absence of such enactment, you will frequently do better to rely on the Statutes at Large.

I know that when I was primarily a State practitioner, I had the notion that the United States Code was all that counted. After coming to Washington, however, I soon found out that the experts in the various Federal specialties never used Code citations except for purposes of parallel reference; they always talked about section so-and-so of the National Defense Act, or of the Mineral Leasing Act, or of the Puerto Rican Organic Act, or of sections thus-and-so of the Revised Statutes. Consequently, I learned, or thought I did, to use the Code primarily as a secondary and parenthetical citation, citing and quoting the statute in the first instance as it appeared in the Statutes at Large.

I say "or thought I did" because in one case I didn't check the Appendix carefully, and the statutes involved were printed there as they appeared in the Code, namely, amended up to date. The case involved the effect of successive amendments to the governing statute, and while I was up on my feet, Chief Justice Stone complained in open court that he didn't like the Appendix because it didn't show him the statute before and after. There are, I can assure you, more comfortable courtroom experiences than that one. So—

(i) Always show the statute before and after, whenever something turns on the amendment.

---

[214] 1 U.S.C. § 204 (a) . For a dramatic instance of the inclusion in the Code of a provision that in fact had been repealed, see *Stephan* v. *United States,* 319 U. S. 423 (no direct appeal to the Supreme Court in capital cases) .

[215] The current list of Titles that have been enacted into positive law will be found in a note following the text of 1 U.S.C. § 204 in the pocket part to the USCA.

(ii) If the statute has been amended from time to time, but the case isn't affected thereby, print the statute as it was at the time in question, e.g., when the offense was committed, and indicate that fact.

(iii) Use any available typographical aid to point up the amendments—italics for the new portions, brackets for the old ones, explanatory footnotes, and so forth. And—

(iv) Check your Appendix carefully; you just can't afford to let it go with a once-over-lightly. (I know!)

Of course, an Appendix to a brief is not necessarily restricted to statutes. In appropriate cases, it should set out executive regulations; texts of administrative rulings; legislative materials, whether excerpts from debates or from committee reports; opinions in cases either unreported or not yet reported; forms of conveyances or of relevant documents; explanations of related proceedings; identification, by way of *dramatis personae,* of the individuals involved in the case (as for instance in complicated antitrust proceedings involving many corporate defendants, each having many individual officers who are referred to in the brief) ; lists of exhibits; and the like. Include whatever is relevant or whatever may be of assistance to the court in understanding the case and its background.

In this connection it is appropriate to point out the advisability, when listing the appendices in the index at the beginning of the brief, to indicate what each contains. "Appendix A, Appendix B, and Appendix C," showing where each may be found, does nothing either to whet a judicial reader's curiosity or to add to his knowledge of the case; whereas setting forth the subject matter on the index page, as "Appendix A—Statutory provisions; Appendix B—Summary of Land Court proceedings; Appendix C—Form of territorial conveyance," does, at the very least, indicate the nature of the Appendix materials.

Section 38. Leaving an impression of conviction with the reader and satisfying his curiosity.—If a case is a close one, even the most experienced and learned judges will be in doubt after having read the briefs on both sides. But no one should be left either in doubt or with curiosity unsatisfied after reading the brief on only one side. If anyone is, then the lawyer representing that particular side hasn't written an effective appellate brief.

I have left this element for the end, not because it is the least important but because it is really the sum-total of what you are seeking to do when you sit down to write a brief. At the very least, the brief must be convincing by itself. At the very least, your brief should be in such shape that, if the other side filed nothing, a judge reading your brief would understand the case and be persuaded that you should prevail.

Of course, there isn't any magic talisman for that. All the other items that have been discussed contribute to it, yes, but every case differs from every other case, and so the techniques that carry conviction to the reader in one situation will fail to do so in another.

Perhaps I can best explain what I am driving at under this heading by recalling the circumstances that gave rise to its formulation:

Government briefs for Supreme Court cases are prepared either by the agency concerned (the Securities and Exchange Commission, the Interstate Commerce Commission, and so forth) or by the appropriate division of the Department of Justice—Tax, Criminal, Civil, Antitrust, Lands, and so forth. Those briefs are then reviewed by an attorney on the staff of the Solicitor General, who makes whatever revisions he deems necessary before submitting them to the Solicitor General for final approval. The revisions are often extensive, and on occasion amount to a complete rewriting. The revising process is frequently a painful one, either to the rough-drafter, whose beloved brain children are ruthlessly carved up and irreparably maimed, or to the reviewing lawyer, who is struggling under pressure to supply the analysis or the research or the literary quality that should have been contributed earlier, or to both. I have been in both positions, so I think I can discuss the business dispassionately.

At the reviewing level, my normal inclination was to pass an adequate job, add a few commas or a citation or two, and then let it go on—not because I was more tolerant of other people's sensibilities, but essentially I suppose because I was more indolent. Yet, every once in a while, I would get a draft brief over my desk that I couldn't pass, that I simply had to rewrite despite my basic disinclination to do so—because it wasn't adequate, i.e., it didn't convince me when I read it through but instead left me with a host of bothersome and unanswered questions. So, with (at least) a sigh, I would dig in, start reading cases, think about the problem, reanalyze it, and, by the time a week or so had elapsed, the brief would have been rewritten and recast.

If it left me, who was sympathetically inclined, unconvinced and curious, you can imagine how a judge lacking such an inclination would have reacted to it. A brief just hasn't done its job when it leaves that kind of impression.

Analytically, here are some of the elements that contribute to such a brief's unsatisfactory character:

(a) Inadequate analysis—problem not thought through.

(b) Discussion of a tangential question, as a main point, which was not really reached on the record.

(c) Extensive discussion of a prior decision, urging that it not be extended, without fully stating its facts or holding.

The last is what I have in mind when I speak of unsatisfied curiosity: in order to understand the discussion, it is necessary to get the volume down from the shelf and read the case. But it shouldn't be; a brief should give the reader enough of any case it discusses at length to enable him to know what that case holds and why it is either applicable or inapplicable, without having to look it up in the library. I don't mean for a moment that a judge can escape reading the case when he sits down to write the opinion, but I do insist that he shouldn't have to do so when he first reads the party's brief.

Any tangential thoughts that a reasonably learned lawyer may have as he reads a particular brief should likewise be satisfactorily answered, *in the brief*, as he reads along—why, for instance, the case isn't governed by *Schmaltz v. Commissioner*, just recently decided, or why it isn't affected by the statute passed last year, or why the claim in question isn't barred by limitations. The brief-writer must be sufficiently aware of all such potential questions, not only to be able to answer them, but also to make sure that they are answered in the brief he is writing.

This is particularly true when he writes a brief for an appellee or a respondent. When judges read the briefs, whether before or after argument, it may be assumed that they will follow the logical course (compare Section 111, *infra*) of reading the appellant's or petitioner's brief first. If, then, appellant or petitioner makes what at first blush appears to be a strong, persuasive, and controlling point, and the brief on the other side was written on the hopeful but wholly mistaken assumption that silence is somehow as effective as on occasion it may be dignified (compare some of the examples noted in Section 35 (d) , *supra*) , then the latter brief will not carry conviction to the judicial reader.

It is highly desirable to ignore any personalities that may have crept into the brief filed first (compare Section 83, *infra*) ; name-calling is a contest no one can win. It is well not to pay too much attention to trifles or to arguments that verge on quibbling. Those can usually be disposed of in a sentence or two at the most. But when the other side makes a real, thumping argument, or digs up a citation that really undercuts the judgment you are engaged in defending, you *must* reply. If you do not, your brief will generate doubts in the judges' minds, doubts that a little reflection will only serve to intensify. On an appeal as in a trial, even a poor answer is frequently better than a studied refusal to answer at all.[216]

Section 39. The final accolade.—The real test of whether a brief has been effective—the ordeal by fire—is whether it wins the appeal. True, there are many good briefs that don't win cases, and assuredly there are poor ones (including some exceptionally poor ones) that do. But a brief that didn't win, however close to perfection it may have come, just wasn't an effective brief; since it didn't persuade the court, it lapses into the realm of "fine try"

---

[216] In the first court-martial-of-dependents cases (*Kinsella* v. *Krueger,* 351 U. S. 470, withdrawn on rehearing, *Reid* v. *Covert,* 354 U. S. 1) , the Government relied heavily on a decision of the United States Court of Military Appeals (*United States* v. *Burney,* 6 USCMA 776, 799, 21 CMR 98, 121) , where that tribunal had said, "Conceding we are not in a state of declared war, our foreign armies may be likened to the Army garrisons in the far west during the days of the Indian Wars."

Counsel for the civilian women in reply cited opinions of The Judge Advocate General of the Army from Indian-fighting days, to the effect that a post-trader—successor to the sutler and predecessor of the post exchange—was not amenable to trial by court-martial unless employed on the actual theater of an Indian War (Dig. Op. JAG, 1901, p. 563; *id.,* 1895, pp. 599-600; *id.* 1880, p. 384) , and hence argued that the analogy put forward by the Court of Military Appeals was actually evidence against the asserted jurisdiction.

In some 220 printed pages of briefs subsequently filed by the Government in those cases, it never once made reference to, much less discussed, those published rulings.

It may be ventured that this silent treatment, far from detracting from the authority of those rulings, substantially emphasized their importance. At any rate, when the Court ultimately decided that civilian employees were not amenable to military jurisdiction in time of peace, it relied on the post-trader opinions. *McElroy* v. *Guagliardo,* 361 U. S. 281, 285, note 4. See also Section 70, *infra,* at pp. 220-222.

and "well played." The lawyer needn't be ashamed of it, but the client lost the case, and fees are normally paid with an eye to the final result. The pat story in this connection concerns the Northern gambler who cleaned out all the local talent in a little Southern town, after which the home town boys gathered around in a somewhat menacing manner and insisted that he tell them whether in his opinion Grant or Lee was the better general. The slick Yankee thoughtfully considered the question, gave even more thoughtful consideration to the group around him, and then answered, "Well, gentlemen—they paid off on Grant." So here: clients don't pay off on good losing briefs.

However, when the winning brief is inadequate, and forces the court to do a lot of independent research, and the opinion relies on cases not discussed or even cited by counsel and flatly rejects the proposition advanced by the prevailing side, then that wasn't a very effective brief either; it didn't persuade.

So I conclude that a really effective brief is one that (a) wins your case, and (b) persuades the court to follow your analysis of the problem and to rely on your authorities.

It may reflect an inadequate or erroneous set of values, but I never get the same pleasure out of winning a case when the court goes off on a tack of its own as when it follows the analysis I have labored over and set out in the brief. And I must confess to feeling the ultimate in forensic satisfaction when the court adopts an analogy that I invoked [217] or incorporates into its opinion one of

---

[217] (a) "The analogy suggested by counsel for the appellant seems apposite: namely, that a defendant who commits a crime in Canada, escapes to the United States, and then returns to Canada; he cannot defend on the ground that between the offense and the trial he was beyond the jurisdiction of the Canadian court." *United States* v. *Malanaphy,* 168 F. 2d 503, 507 (C. A. 2), reversed *sub. nom. United States* v. *Cooke,* 336 U. S. 210.

(b) "The Government makes the reasonable contention, and we so hold, that the district into which the accused is first taken under custody and landed is the district into which the accused is 'first brought' within the meaning of § 41 of the Judicial Code [now 18 U.S.C. § 3238]; and this was the district of Massachusetts in the case at bar." *Chandler* v. *United States,* 171 F. 2d 921, 933 (C.A. 1), certiorari denied, 336 U. S. 918.

(c) "Is a dependent wife in Hawaii so intimately a part of the Air Force there so as to be subject to trial by court-martial? Her relationship is just as close—and just as distant—as appellee's was to the Air Force while in England, or, for that matter, precisely the same as the relationship to the armed forces of any dependent wife on any military, naval, or air installation within the United States." Brief for the Appellee, *Reid* v. *Covert,* pp. 66-67.

"The wives of servicemen are no more members of the 'land and naval

my own pet phrases.[218] Those are the trifles that, rightly or wrongly, I regard as the final accolade for the brief-writer.

Forces' when living at a military post in England or Japan than when living at a base in this country or in Hawaii or Alaska." *Reid* v. *Covert*, 354 U. S. 1, 20.

[218] (a) "Then came *Wolf* v. *Colorado*, 338 U. S. 25, with its holding that the substance of the Fourth Amendment was a part of the Due Process of Law guaranteed by the Fourteenth Amendment against invasion by State action. At this point, the doctrinal underpinning of the State seizure aspect of *Weeks* disappeared, as indeed Judge Hastie pointed out in *Hanna* v. *United States*, 260 F. 2d 723 (D. C. Cir.), *supra*, p. 46, the case in which the District of Columbia Circuit overruled its earlier espousal of the 'silver platter' doctrine in *Shelton* v. *United States*, 169 F. 2d 665 (D. C. Cir.), certiorari denied, 335 U. S. 834. *Cessante ratione legis, cessat ipsa lex; cf. Funk* v. *United States*, 290 U. S. 371, 381-385; Criminal Rule 26." Brief for the Petitioners in *Elkins* v. *United States*, p. 52.

"The foundation upon which the admissibility of state-seized evidence in a federal trial originally rested—that unreasonable state searches did not violate the Federal Constitution—thus disappeared in 1949. This removal of the doctrinal underpinning for the admissibility rule has apparently escaped the attention of most of the federal courts, which have continued to approve the admission of evidence illegally seized by state officers without so much as even discussing the impact of *Wolf*." *Elkins* v. *United States*, 364 U. S. 206, 213-214.

"The Court finds such a significant development, destroying in its view the 'foundations,' the 'doctrinal underpinning' of the express and authoritative limitation of the *Weeks* exclusionary rule to cases of federal violations, in what was said in 1949 in *Wolf* v. *Colorado*, 338 U. S. 25, 27-28, * * *" Frankfurter, Clark, Harlan, and Whittaker, JJ., dissenting, 364 U. S. at 237.

(b) "Congress understood that it was writing finis to a long chapter in the Nation's history, and that conditions had entirely changed from the days when truly imperial grants had been deemed necessary to induce entrepreneurs to build the lines of steel without which the West could not have been opened to settlement. Now it was time to close the books, to balance the accounts, to end the further disposal of public lands in aid of construction to which the United States was obligated." Brief for the Petitioners in *Krug* v. *Santa Fe P. R. Co.*, pp. 37-38.

"We think Congress wrote finis to all these claims for all railroads which accepted the Act by executing releases." *Krug* v. *Santa Fe P. R. Co.*, 329 U. S. 591, 598.

(c) "The necessary consequence would be that the writ of habeas corpus would thereby be perverted into what is simply a delayed motion for a new trial, available long out of time, which will forever keep open the prospect that on some later and, it may be, brighter day, the record of trial can be once more reviewed in a more favorable legal climate, and the defendant released from custody for what is then shown to be an error of law on the part of the trial judge." Brief for the Petitioner in *Alexander* v. *U. S. ex rel. Kulick*, p. 27.

"If in such circumstances, *habeas corpus* could be used to correct the error, the writ would become a delayed motion for a new trial, renewed from time to time as the legal climate changed." *Sunal* v. *Large* (and *Alexander* v.

U. S. ex rel. Kulick) , 332 U. S. 174, 182.

(d) "If the officers here had been searching for an automobile, stolen and transported in violation of the National Motor Vehicle Theft Act, 18 U.S.C. 408, it would obviously have been unreasonable for them to have searched defendant's bureau drawers. The same must be said of a search for an unregistered still, possessed in violation of 26 U.S.C. 2810 (a) ." Brief for the United States in *Harris* v. *United States,* p. 77.

"The same meticulous investigation which would be appropriate in a search for two small cancelled checks could not be considered reasonable where agents are seeking a stolen automobile or an illegal still." *Harris* v. *United States,* 331 U. S. 145, 152.

(e) "The traditional view regarded the court-martial, not as a species of legislative court, but as 'a purely executive agency designed for military uses,' which is 'called into existence by a military order,' such order being 'a direction to certain officers named to assemble at a certain time and place and form a court for the trial of a person or persons specifically or in general terms indicated * * * *.' " [Citing Winthrop, *Military Law & Precedents* (2d ed. 1896) *54-55, *229; *Runkle* v. *United States,* 19 C. Cls. 396, 409, reversed on other grounds, 122 U. S. 543; *Manual for Courts-Martial,* U. S. 1951, ¶ 36*b*.] * * * A court-martial is an *ad hoc* tribunal created by a military order * * *." Supplemental Brief on Rehearing on Behalf of Appellee and Respondent in *Reid* v. *Covert,* pp. 82-83.

"Courts-martial are typically *ad hoc* bodies appointed by a military officer from among his subordinates. * * * In essence, these tribunals are simply executive tribunals whose personnel are in the executive chain of command." *Reid* v. *Covert,* 354 U. S. 1, 36.

Chapter IV

SUGGESTIONS FOR WRITING AND RESEARCH

Section 40. Introductory.—This chapter will include a few suggestions to facilitate the process of writing an appellate brief. I have found them helpful in my own practice—after learning each the hard way. I pass them on here, not with any thought that what follows is either the "approved solution" or the last word on the subject, but solely with the view that what I, as one lawyer, have found helpful over the years, may similarly be of assistance to other lawyers.

Section 41. The basic precepts.—The principal suggestions under the present heading can be very simply stated:

(a) Write the Statement of Facts before you write the Argument.

(b) Finish your analytical thinking and complete your basic research before you start to write the Argument.

(c) Write the Argument consecutively.

(d) Write the Summary of Argument last of all.

(e) Check (or, preferably, have someone else check) every citation and record reference.

Section 42. Write the Statement of Facts first.—The importance of the Statement of Facts (compare Section 23, *supra*) demands that this portion of the brief be written first. At this juncture it will be well for the reader to reexamine the account of Mr. Justice Brandeis' method, set forth at page 45.

A lot of lawyers don't do it that way, preferring to toss in a casual or cursory Statement of Facts after they have labored long and lovingly on the intricate learning of their legal argument. I used to do it that way myself on occasion—when I was new at the game. But, for reasons that would simply repeat what is set out at length in Sections 23 to 28, above, I don't do it that way any more: I invariably write the Statement of Facts first, regardless of the nature of the brief, because experience over the years has convinced me that this is the order that results in the most effective product.

It results in a more effective product for two reasons. First (see Sections 23-27, above), the facts are frequently, perhaps usually, the most important element in every case, and so they deserve and should receive primary attention. Second, once your Statement of Facts is completed, it will help you in the writing of your argument; new legal arguments are bound to suggest themselves to you once your Statement of Facts has been properly done.

Sometimes a Statement of Facts can be very short, reflecting the thinness of the record. On other occasions, when the case has a record running to thousands of printed pages, the Statement of Facts is necessarily more voluminous. But it does not follow that the length of the Statement of Facts should increase in direct proportion to the length of the record—although it is true that the longer the record, the longer the labors of the really able lawyer. The remark, variously attributed to Cicero and to Pascal—"If I had had more time, I would have written you a shorter letter"— is apposite here in full measure.

Section 43. How to go about writing the Statement of Facts. —The painful but inescapable preliminary to writing the Statement of Facts is reading the record; there just isn't any short cut or labor-saving gadget to spare the man who actually pushes the pen. If you are unwilling or simply not in a position to take the time to read the record, you must get someone else to write the Statement of Facts.

Assuming that you are at the rough-drafting level of the working staff (i.e., junior partner or law clerk or GS-11 in the Government service), the best way to start is to take a deep breath and simply plunge in, taking more or less complete notes as you go along. Ideally, if time permits, you should make a complete index of the testimony and of the exhibits, preferably with a carbon copy. In well-regulated law offices, this is done by the young men during the trial, usually at night and over week-ends, while the seniors in charge of the litigation are regaining their strength and, generally, keeping their minds open for the larger aspects of the controversy. At any rate, before the appellate brief is about to be written, someone will have to make a workable guide to the transcript of testimony.

One copy is the consecutive index, the second becomes the cross-index. The latter is thereafter marked to show division into topics, after which the index as to each topic is reassembled, either by pasting or copying; this enables you to compress all the testimony on a particular topic into convenient compass without having to run through the entire index anew each time that you pass to a new topic. If the index is not too bulky, you can get the same effect with marginal notes in colored inks or pencils for each particular topic—i.e., red for the merger negotiations, green for the threat of patent litigation, blue for the accounting system, and so on.

Under ideal conditions, with a maximum of clerical help, the easiest and the best way is to dictate the index directly to a stenographer as you go along. It should look something like this:

OATMEAL—DIRECT
   674-675—Is V.P. of Schmaltz Mfg. Co.; has been for 16 years; knows D intimately, socially as well as in business.
   676   —Was present at June 5 directors' meeting; D made the bond issue proposal; unanimously approved.
   677-679—Also present at July 10 directors' meeting; D made report re progress of loan; no one objected.
   680-683—Also present at August 11 directors' meeting; D made further progress report; details re that report.
   683-687—Long colloquy re admissibility of draft minutes; admitted as DX 43.

With someone to take your dictation it isn't nearly so difficult as pushing a pen late at night. When your dictation has been typed, mark up the carbon by topics in the margin, and let the stenographer collect in a single sequence all the testimony under the particular topic, always indicating whose testimony is referred to. E.g.:

H—JUNE 5 DIRECTORS' MEETING
OATMEAL—DIRECT
   676   —Was present at June 5 directors' meeting; D made the bond issue proposal; unanimously approved.
OATMEAL—CROSS
   732-733—Doesn't recall extent of discussion of bond issue proposal at June 5 meeting; only certain there was no objection.
   734   —Positive that was the first time D mentioned it.
   735-736—Never had had earlier talks with him concerning it, either privately or in the office.
   737   —Pl X 73 doesn't change recollection re that.
   738-740—Long colloquy re Pl X 73.

741   —Adheres to statement, bond issue first broached at June 5 dir. meeting.

OATMEAL—REDIRECT

789   —Pl X 73 referred to Schmaltz Mfg. Co.'s subsidiary.

OVERSHOE—DIRECT

973-974—Remembers June 5 directors' meeting vividly; was his wedding anniversary and Mrs. O. was put out over his attending it.

974   —D made some sort of bond issue suggestion; sounded O.K. and D was financial man.

975   —Possibly D mentioned it before; can't recall.

OVERSHOE—CROSS

1001   —Never saw Pl X 73 before coming to court just now.

And so on, for every witness whose testimony bears on this particular topic. When you are all through, you have a workable key to the record, which will instantly locate for you what everyone said on every point; and you will need to refer to the actual record only for exact quotations and, where your index covers two or more pages (i.e., 973-974), for the precise page reference.

As I say, this is the ideal; with less, or less efficient, stenographic help, you will have to curtail your indexing. And of course the time factor cannot be ignored. But it may be stated with considerable assurance that the better the index, the less the time that is later used up in hunting for an elusive but important bit of testimony not reflected therein. Time spent in constructing an effective index to the record is time well invested.[1]

Section 44. Steps after completing the index of testimony.— Having completed your index of the testimony, you will have a fairly good idea of the scope and extent of the record in your case and of the major topics it involves. The next step, then, is to block out the order in which you will set forth those topics in the Statement of Facts. Having done that, you are ready to write: your outline is your guide, your topical index gives you the key to the materials, and you can fill in the record references as you go along. You will frequently need to refer to the actual transcript, either to get the exact page reference whenever the index notes refer to several consecutive pages lumped together, or whenever you deem it helpful to quote exactly from a witness or a document. But,

---

[1] For suggestions on the preparation of a more elaborate index in protracted cases, see *Current Indexing of the Record,* 13 F.R.D. 85.

given outline and index, you have control of your materials, no matter how bulky they are, and you should therefore be able to make very satisfactory progress.

It is well to pause at this point to stress the absolute necessity for having record references to every portion of the Statement of Facts. That need simply cannot be overemphasized. For one thing, a Statement of Facts buttressed by record references carries a reassuring conviction to the reader. For another, when the reader (i.e., specifically, the judge who is going to pass on your case) turns to the record, his curiosity whetted, and finds that what you have said is true, he gains confidence in the accuracy and veracity of what you have written.

Contrariwise, if long passages of assertive prose are devoid of record references, the sophisticated judge is at once beset by doubts. "Where does this fellow get this stuff from?" "Is this just a free-wheeling opening to a jury, or are we here on appeal?" Doubts are immediately generated by any Statement of Facts not supported by page references to the record. And if a record reference duly included turns out not to support the text—look out! *Falsus in uno, falsus in omnibus* is a standard applied not only to witnesses by lawyers and juries, it is a standard applied to lawyers by appellate judges.

The rules of Federal appellate courts vary as to the degree of specificity in which their requirements for referring to the pages of the record or of the joint appendix are couched. But the admonitions just discussed are applicable to all briefs, even where the rules of the particular court are completely silent on the point.

To resume: Once a fair first draft is ready, you will want to read it over for verbal revisions. When those are made, put your corrected Statement of Facts to one side—on ice, as it were.

(Some folks have the verbal fluency, as well as a sufficient number of competent stenographers, to be able to dictate a brief. I just can't; I have to push the pen, and as each portion is finished and revised I send it off for typing in draft—triple-spaced, in order to leave plenty of room for later corrections and additions.)

This seems as good a place as any to mention the desirability of referring to the parties by some designation that will make for understanding and clarity. To call the parties "appellant" and "appellee" throughout in a civil appellate brief is bound to confuse; mistaken references are inevitable; and the designations simply reflect the happenstance of the outcome below and do not characterize the parties' positions in the context of the controversy on appeal.

The object should be to use a characterization conducive to understanding. In a negligence case, it is perfectly adequate to refer to the parties as they were below, as "plaintiff" and "defendant," because the plaintiff is always the injured party. But in a domestic relations controversy—a common example in the District of Columbia Circuit—the terms "plaintiff" and "defendant" only show who brought suit, which is not very illuminating. Hence, in that situation the parties should be referred to as "husband" and "wife." [1a]

Use shorthand terms that assist understanding: e.g., "the corporation," "the minority stockholders," "the Commission." Similarly, where long corporate names are involved, use a compressed shorthand designation, just as courts do in their opinions; e.g., "Allied Chemical and Reagent Co., Inc., hereinafter called simply 'Allied.'"

There is one apparent exception to the basic precept: in a criminal appeal involving only a single defendant, you are perfectly safe in calling the convicted person "appellant" or "petitioner." In that instance, the docket designation cannot possibly confuse. But where there are several appellants or petitioners, the rule just discussed should once more be followed.

A very simple test will solve your problem. Just ask yourself these questions: Will the terms in which your brief refers to the parties enlighten the judge who reads it? Or will your designations simply confuse him?

[1a] After the foregoing was written and was in process of being published, the Fourth Circuit adopted Rule 10 (9) , as follows:

"9. Counsel will be expected, in their briefs and oral arguments, to keep at a minimum references to the parties by their formal designation appearing in the caption of the case, as appellants or appellees, or petitioners or respondents, as the case may be. Ordinarily, it is preferable to identify them as plaintiff or defendant, as in the proceedings below. It will avoid confusion in the argument and study of the case, and the necessity for back-references, if the parties are not repeatedly called 'petitioner,' 'respondent,' 'appellant,' 'libellant,' 'cross-appellee,' etc. It promotes clarity to use names or descriptive terms such as 'the bus,' 'the employee,' 'the injured person,' 'the driver,' 'the pedestrian,' 'the taxpayer,' 'the ship,' 'the stevedore,' etc."

Section 45. Final revision of the Statement of Facts.—Later, when the rest of the brief is also finished, it is a very good idea to reread the record, taking notes then of only those items of testimony you think you missed earlier. Insert those additional references, or those additional topics, in the revised draft Statement of Facts that you had earlier put to one side.

There are bound to be some you have missed, and you will regret every last one if you permit the brief to go into final print before you catch them. There are bound to be others you may have thought you missed that turn up, duly included in your draft. To the extent that such references were included after all, it shows that your system is working—fine! But when you get to the final showdown, it is those you have missed that annoy and cause pain, and it is for this reason that the rereading should not be omitted.

So much for the working level, for the pencil-pusher echelon. Now suppose that you are somewhat higher in the hierarchy, that you are the senior partner who will argue the case, or the Government lawyer who will actually wear the striped pants and emit the sound effects. In that event you should still read the record before the brief goes into final and irrevocable print. (No lawyer, and I will say it dogmatically, here and now and many times again, should ever risk his reputation by arguing a case on a record he has not read. Sometimes no ill-fortune happens, just as sometimes a car going uphill can pass another car on a blind curve without accident. I would consider both instances parallel risks. And therefore, since you should read the record anyway, the time for that reading is when the process can still influence the brief.)

At the nonwriting level, it is not necessary to take very copious notes, but you should note the bits of testimony that, as you read, seem most significant. If the brief has been well written by an able lawyer, most of those items will have been included. But there will always be a few whose significance the man actually arguing the case will more keenly appreciate, and it is the inclusion of those select and significant few that often makes the difference between a good brief and a very good one. So, I repeat, reading the record at this point, when the results of your own analysis can still be added, is time well spent.

As the late Mr. William D. Mitchell, sometime Solicitor General and Attorney General, wrote:

A busy lawyer may properly rely on assistants to furnish him with material or even with drafts of a proposed brief, but his producing the final draft is well worth while. In this way, since his brief and oral argument follow the same lines and logical sequence, he is aided in oral argument. And when the court comes to prepare its opinion they are helped by a brief which has conformed closely to such argument.[2]

One of the most difficult—and unsatisfactory—situations in which an advocate can find himself is to be retained or assigned to argue a case where the brief is already filed. He can then hardly abandon points whose value he doubts, nor can he effectively add new contentions that he regards as substantially stronger. Even if the lawyer who is to argue the case was for one reason or another unable to follow the wise counsel that he should actually have written the final form of his own brief, at the very least he should have been able to make his own decisions as to the points that it should have included.

Finally—and now I am back at the working level—be sure that every record reference and every quotation you have included in the Statement of Facts has been meticulously checked; see Section 66, below.

Section 46. Think before you write the argument.—The basic admonition to the lawyer who is sitting down to write the Argument is simply this: never start to write until you have thought the case through and have completed your basic research. That doesn't mean every citation or every footnote, but it does include a reading, and, whenever required, a rereading, of all the important cases—because the basic authorities are always full of suggestive leads for further development. And be certain that you have really thought your argument through and outlined it, before you put pen to paper (or lips to dictograph). If it doesn't outline properly, it hasn't been properly analyzed—another point on which one may safely be dogmatic. And even with an apparently satisfactory outline, a brief that hasn't been properly thought through or researched just doesn't turn out well. Frequently, of course, your writing is done under the pressure of deadlines; you must begin, even though you feel unready. But in that event, your original indirection and unreadiness are almost certain to be reflected in your final work.

The question will naturally arise, how does one know when

[2] Review of the first version of this work, 64 Harv. L. Rev. at 351-352.

"the case has been thought through" or when "the basic research has been completed"? The only answer is, you come to sense it. There isn't any gauge or instrument, it is just a feeling. How do you know when you have had enough to eat? It's the same sort of thing, an instinctive reaction that develops after a time. You will recognize it, never fear, and when you do, then you can safely start writing—but not before!

The foregoing is not to be misunderstood as advice to put the proposed brief to one side until the imminent approach of the deadline galvanizes you into belated action. The tendency to postpone and to procrastinate is a very human one; "the relative ease with which men are persuaded to postpone troublesome decisions, all make inertia one of the most decisive powers in determining the course of our affairs * * *." [3] The point here is that, as Mr. Justice Holmes once wrote, "It is impact not dead pull that drives a pile." [4] Concentrate on your problem, turn it over in your mind, think about it in tub or shower, try out your hypotheses on associates, live with the case in every spare waking moment—but don't start to write until the sequence and direction of your points have fallen clearly into place in your mind.

Section 47. Never let the other side write your brief.—Always write your brief in such a way as to set out and make the most of your affirmative case. This admonition is perhaps most to be borne in mind when you are appellee or respondent; don't content yourself, in that situation, with a point-by-point reply to appellant or petitioner. Accentuate the affirmative features of *your* case, don't let the other side write your brief or even shape it.

I can illustrate this approach first with an anecdote and then with actual specific instances. The anecdote concerns one of the ablest of Solicitors General, who was asking when the Government's brief in *Oatmeal* v. *United States* would be ready. He was told that it had not yet been started since the petitioner's brief had not yet come in. "What's the matter?" he asked. "Haven't we got a case?"

So, don't follow the appellant's outline of points, even when you must reply to all of them. Put your own strongest point first, because what may be strongest for him may not be so for you.

---

[3] Jackson, J., concurring in *Duckworth* v. *Arkansas*, 314 U. S. 390, 397, 400.

[4] 1 *Holmes-Laski Letters* (Howe ed. 1953) 684.

Here are some examples illustrating applications of this principle.

(a) One of the most instructive instances for the advocate is found in two of the recent cases that involved the constitutionality of military trials of servicemen's dependents.[5] Both sides arranged their points so as to stress those they considered the strongest, without regard to the opposition's arrangement; and the same principle was followed after the grant of rehearing foreshadowed at least a shift of emphasis in the direction of the Court's thinking.

Here were the major headings in the Government's brief on the first hearing of *Reid* v. *Covert:*

II.[6] Article 2 (11) of the Uniform Code of Military Justice is a valid exercise of the power of Congress to make rules for the government and regulation of the land and naval forces, the war power, and the power to make all laws necessary and proper for carrying into execution the sovereign authority of the United States to maintain relations with other sovereignties.

III. Jurisdiction over appellee under Article 2 (11) was not lost by reason of her transportation to the United States, her imprisonment in the Federal Reformatory for Women, or the reversal of her conviction by the Court of Military Appeals.

Otherwise stated, the Government concentrated on sustaining the constitutionality of the assailed statute. Counsel for the dependent woman urged first the nonconstitutional ground, sufficient for her purposes, that jurisdiction if it ever existed had been lost, and then joined issue on the constitutional argument, as follows:

II. Assuming that appellee could constitutionally have been tried by court-martial in England as a person "accompanying the armed forces of the United States without the continental limits of the

---

[5] *Kinsella* v. *Krueger,* 351 U. S. 470, and *Reid* v. *Covert,* 351 U. S. 487; on rehearing, *Reid* v. *Covert,* 354 U. S. 1.

[6] In *Reid* v. *Covert,* counsel for Mrs. Covert had moved to dismiss the appeal, on the ground that the appellant Reid, Superintendent of the District of Columbia Jail, was an officer of the District of Columbia and not of the United States, and so was not entitled under 28 U.S.C. § 1252 to take a direct appeal from a district court to the Supreme Court. The Court postponed the question of jurisdiction to the hearing on the merits, 350 U. S. 985. Pursuant to Supreme Court Rule 16 (4), Point I in both briefs dealt with the jurisdiction of the Supreme Court to entertain the appeal. That jurisdiction was sustained (*Reid* v. *Covert,* 351 U. S. 487, 489-490), and although the earlier opinion was ultimately withdrawn, see 354 U. S. 1, the question of the Supreme Court's jurisdiction of the direct appeal was not thereafter argued or questioned, either by counsel or by any member of the Court.

United States," she ceased to be subject to the Uniform Code of Military Justice after the Air Force returned her to the United States and placed her in civilian custody, and consequently she could not thereafter be retried by court-martial.

III. Article 2 (11) of the Uniform Code of Military Justice is unconstitutional to the extent that it purports to authorize the trial of civilians by court-martial in time of peace.

IV. The treaty power is completely irrelevant in the present case.

V. To the extent that appellant's invocation of the Necessary and Proper Clause brings the matter into the realm of judgment, examination of the realities of trial by court-martial demonstrates that the principle of "the least possible power adequate to the end proposed" is one preeminently applicable to the scope of military jurisdiction.

The first opinions sustained the jurisdiction.[7] After rehearings were granted, however, it was plain to all concerned that a regrouping, so to speak, of the parties' previous arguments was in order, particularly in view of the questions on which the order granting rehearing had invited discussion.[8] The Government then marshaled its contentions as follows:

I. Court-martial jurisdiction over dependents and civilian employees accompanying the armed forces overseas is a practical necessity both as a matter of international relations and to accomplish the military mission.

---

[7] *Supra* note 5.

[8] 352 U. S. 901: "On reargument counsel are invited to include among the issues to be discussed by them the following matters:

"1. The specific practical necessities in the government and regulation of the land and naval forces which justify court-martial jurisdiction over civilian dependents overseas; the practical alternatives to the exercise of jurisdiction by court-martial.

"2. The historical evidence, so far as such evidence is available and relevant, bearing on the scope of court-martial jurisdiction authorized under Art. I, § 8, cl. 14, and the Necessary and Proper Clause, and bearing on the relations of Article III and the Fifth and Sixth Amendments in interpreting those clauses. In particular, the question whether such historical evidence points to the conclusion that the Art. I, § 8, cl. 14, power was thought to have a fixed and rigid content or rather that this power, as modified by the Necessary and Proper Clause, was considered a broad grant susceptible of expansion under changing circumstances.

"3. The relevance, for purposes of court-martial jurisdiction over civilians overseas in time of peace, of any distinctions between civilians employed by the armed forces and civilian dependents.

"4. The relevance, for purposes of court-martial jurisdiction over civilian dependents overseas in time of peace, of any distinctions between major crimes and petty offenses."

II. No adequate alternatives to the exercise of jurisdiction by court-martial are available.

III. Article I, section 8, clause 14, of the Constitution is properly read in conjunction with the necessary and proper clause to constitute a broad grant susceptible of expansion under changing circumstances.

IV. The constitutional distinction between major crimes and petty offenses is not a relevant distinction for purposes of court-martial jurisdiction over civilians in foreign territory.

Counsel for the civilian women felt that, whatever might be the force of the Government's invocation of "practical necessities," i.e., its arguments on the facts, its contentions on the law were far weaker. Accordingly, following the precept of "never let the other side write your brief," the major points made on behalf of the civilian dependents were framed as follows:

I. The consent of England and Japan to the exercise of American military jurisdiction within their territories in respect of offenses committed therein did not and could not invest American courts-martial with jurisdiction to try particular persons.[9]

II. Nothing in the Constitution of the United States authorizes the trial of civilians by court-martial in time of peace and not in occupied territory.

III. The result reached last June is completely irreconcilable with *Toth* v. *Quarles, 350 U. S. 11.*

IV. As long as the object sought to be attained is punishment of crime rather than military control of civilians, practical alternatives are available.[10]

While, as the opinions on rehearing show, the only ground on which a majority of the Court concurred was that civilian dependents could not be tried by court-martial for capital offenses,[11] thus leaving to later determination the scope—and eventual denial—of military jurisdiction over non-capital offenses and over civilian employees,[12] the outcome fully justified the decision on behalf of

---

[9] The reasons for placing this question first are explained at pp. 84-87, *supra.*

[10] Point V, applicable only to Mrs. Covert, reargued the loss-of-jurisdiction contention on the basis of military rulings and the terms of Art. 2 (7), UCMJ, now 10 U.S.C. § 802 (7).

[11] *Reid* v. *Covert,* 354 U. S. 1.

[12] *Kinsella* v. *Singleton,* 361 U. S. 234 (no military jurisdiction over dependents committing non-capital offenses) ; *Grisham* v. *Hagan,* 361 U. S. 278 (same, over employees committing capital offenses) ; *McElroy* v. *Guagliardo,* 361 U. S. 281 (same, over employees committing non-capital offenses).

the women involved to give primacy to the legal arguments, and hence not to follow the order of points put forward by the Government.

(b) Similarly, in the *Douglas Chandler* radio broadcasting treason case,[13] the appellant opened his written argument with an attack on the jurisdictional basis of the prosecution. Here was his order of points:

I. The Court should not have exercised jurisdiction over the person of the defendant.

II. The court lacked jurisdiction of the crime alleged, for

1. Congress has not by law directed the place of trial of crimes committed within the territorial jurisdiction of a foreign government.

2. If Judicial Code, Section 41,[14] is construed as applicable, the District of Massachusetts was not that into which the defendant was first brought.

III. The indictment is duplicitous.

IV. Treason against the United States is not committed by adherence to the enemy by one residing in enemy territory.

V. The overt acts alleged in the indictment are insufficient to establish the offense of treason, for

1. They do not in themselves and in their setting manifest any criminal intention.

2. They are manifestly merely preparatory parts of acts not treasonable unless completed and not set forth in the indictment.

VI. The proof of the overt acts submitted to the jury was insufficient to establish the offense of treason.

VII. The court erroneously admitted evidence upon the issue of the defendant's intent to betray the United States and erroneously instructed the jury upon that issue.

VIII. The court erroneously instructed the jury with respect to the weight to be given the defendant's motives in determining whether he had a specific intent to betray.

I am not suggesting for a moment that this was not an effective presentation for appellant's purpose, and certainly Chandler's defense, ably conducted by appointed counsel,[15] reflected the finest traditions of the American bar. But the foregoing order of points did not center attention on what the prosecution deemed to be the

---

[13] *Chandler* v. *United States*, 171 F. 2d 921 (C.A. 1), certiorari denied, 336 U. S. 918.

[14] Now 18 U.S.C. § 3238.

[15] Messrs. Claude B. Cross and Edward C. Park of the Boston Bar.

controlling legal questions. Consequently, rather than answering Chandler's contentions seriatim, the Government rearranged the points at issue in an entirely different order, and concentrated on the core of the substantive offense:

I. The indictment charged and the evidence established the crime of treason.

    A. Broadcasting propaganda on behalf of an enemy is a treasonable act.

    B. The overt acts were acts which gave the enemy aid and comfort.

    C. All of the overt acts were supported by the testimony of two witnesses within the meaning of the Constitution.

    D. The judgment below must be sustained so long as there is a single sufficient overt act.

    E. Appellant's treasonable intent was not nullified by his belief that what he did was in the interests of the United States.

    F. The recordings were properly received in evidence on issue of appellant's intent.

    G. The indictment is not duplicitous.

II. Congress has made treason committed abroad an offense and Congress had constitutional power to do so.

III. Appellant was lawfully apprehended and lawfully brought within the jurisdiction of the district court.

IV. The District of Massachusetts was the proper forum for appellant's trial.

    A. Congress has made specific provision for the trial of offenses against the United States committed abroad.

    B. The District of Massachusetts was the district into which appellant was first brought.

Chandler's conviction was sustained. But the real proof of the pudding, so far as the prosecution's order of points was concerned, was this: First, the court had this to say concerning the arguments that did not go to the merits:

Counsel for appellant have not suggested any alternative procedure which in their view properly could have been employed to bring Chandler to trial; in fact, all their arguments involve the conclusion, which we deem unacceptable, that there was no way in which a court of the United States could obtain lawful jurisdiction over Chandler unless he should choose to relinquish his asylum in Germany and voluntarily return to the United States.[16]

---

[16] 171 F. 2d at 936.

Second, the court dealt with the question of the proper district, which the prosecution had relegated to the end of its brief, with the remark, "It would indeed be unfortunate if we were compelled to hold, on such a highly technical ground, that this elaborate trial has gone for naught." [17]

The prosecution's order of points, therefore, was vindicated in the result.[18]

(c) In other cases, it may not even be necessary to join issue with the appellant or petitioner. If his strongest point, legally speaking, is not really raised on the facts, you may safely reject his chosen battleground, and stand on your own strong points. Below (see Section 83, pp. 254-258), there is set forth part of a Brief in Opposition to a Petition for Certiorari where the respondent rested on the facts and relegated to a footnote his reply to petitioner's principal legal contention.

But such a course is only justified when there can be no doubt that your opponent's point is without record support. You are never safe in dropping to a footnote answers to substantial questions; such questions do not lend themselves to cavalier sweeping-under-the-rug techniques (see Section 35 (d), at pp. 104-107, *supra*). And if you have a substantial answer to the other side's contentions, it normally deserves something better than the dilution that is bound to result from a misuse of footnotes (see Section 79 and Chapter XII, *infra*).

So, write your brief affirmatively. Put your own strong points forward. Don't be content with simply a point-by-point denial of what the other side has said, and don't go all out demolishing an issue that the other side vainly hopes will seem to be in the case. Any time you simply follow such a course, you are letting the opposition write your brief.

Section 48. Research; some general considerations.—This chapter is emphatically not a rehash of the several excellent works now in print on "How to Find the Law." It is written for the reader who already knows the use of every bibliographical tool, and who, with the aid of digests, encyclopedias, textbooks, sets of

---

[17] 171 F. 2d at 933.

[18] Counsel for the petitioner were gracious enough to say in their reply brief, "* * * The arrangement of the points discussed, in what may be thought the order of their importance, seems to us impressive and one which we perhaps should have adopted."

annotated cases, citators, collections of judicial definitions, and miscellaneous indices, is able to chart a workable path through the morass of current case law. It seeks rather to assist in the evaluation of decisions and in the handling of noncase material, the proper use of which is becoming increasingly significant in appellate practice.

Section 49. Evaluation of decided cases.—Regardless of how closely the facts in a decided case may resemble those in your case, you must always remember that decisions are not fungible, and that turning up the famous bay horse case in a digest does not necessarily solve the brief-writer's problem.

It is of course unnecessary to belabor the proposition that, while decisions of higher courts govern litigation pending in lower courts, the decisions of lower courts do not control cases above except to the extent that their reasoning is persuasive. The difficulties arise out of the practical qualifications to that indisputable general rule.

First, when can a Supreme Court decision safely be taken at less than its face value by a Court of Appeals? One instance is the unusual situation when the lower court feels that the cited decision is about to be overruled.[19] Another, perhaps too little appreciated, is when there is no opinion in which a majority of the justices sitting have joined; in that event, there is no precedent for the future; "the lack of an agreement by a majority of the Court on the principles of law involved prevents it from being an authoritative determination for other cases." [20]

A fuzzier situation by far is the recurring problem of when an earlier decision is to be considered as being no longer law even when it has not been specifically overruled. Sometimes, as in the recent case invalidating an ordinance that enforced segregated transportation,[21] a lower court is safe in assuming that the earlier decision—there *Plessy* v. *Ferguson* [22]—lacks vitality. It is likewise safe to assume that many of the Supreme Court's holdings from the 1920's and 1930's which, on grounds of due process, held unconstitutional a host of regulatory statutes, are similarly no longer

---

[19] See note 170, *supra*, p. 108.

[20] *United States* v. *Pink,* 315 U. S. 203, 216; *Alaska* v. *Troy,* 258 U. S. 101, 111; *Hertz* v. *Woodman,* 218 U. S. 205, 212-214. See also *Supreme Court No-Clear-Majority Decisions: A Study in* Stare Decisis, 24 U. of Chi. L. Rev. 99.

[21] *Gayle* v. *Browder,* 352 U. S. 903, affirming 142 F. Supp. 707 (M.D. Ala.).

[22] 163 U. S. 537.

authoritative.[23] In recent years, too, we have seen that the broader construction now given the Sherman Act has limited the force of *Federal Baseball Club* v. *National League*,[24] decided in 1922, to baseball alone; [25] that decision no longer protects restraints of trade occurring in other spectator sports or activities.[26]

In part, of course, the problem is to predict how far the Supreme Court will hew to the line of *stare decisis*. But what is perhaps more troublesome to the advocate in a court of appeals is the respect that the lower Federal courts pay to Supreme Court dicta, respect that is certainly greater than that accorded those expressions by the Supreme Court itself.

For instance, in the *Hirshberg* case,[27] the question was whether a career sailor who had reenlisted, after an interval of less than 24 hours after discharge, could be tried by court-martial in the subsequent enlistment for an offense committed in the earlier one. The Supreme Court, reversing the Second Circuit, answered that question in the negative, basing its decision entirely on statutory grounds. Believing therefore that no constitutional question was involved, and with the *Hirshberg* case specifically before it, Congress amended the law to provide that in such a situation the offender's amenability to military jurisdiction would continue.[28] When the new statute was thereafter assailed, the District of Columbia Circuit upheld it in the belief that no constitutional issue was involved.[29] But on certiorari the Supreme Court in *Toth* v. *Quarles* [30] decided that the provision was unconstitutional.

---

[23] See *Lincoln Union* v. *Northwestern Co.,* 335 U. S. 525, 533-537, 542-557; *Daniel* v. *Family Ins. Co.,* 336 U. S. 220, 224-225; *Williamson* v. *Lee Optical Co.,* 348 U. S. 483, 488-489.

[24] 259 U. S. 200.

[25] *Toolson* v. *New York Yankees,* 346 U. S. 356.

[26] *United States* v. *Shubert,* 348 U. S. 222 (theatrical productions) ; *United States* v. *International Boxing Club,* 348 U. S. 236 (boxing) ; *Radovich* v. *National Football League,* 352 U. S. 445 (football) .

[27] *United States* v. *Cooke,* 336 U. S. 210.

[28] Art. 3 (a) , Uniform Code of Military Justice, now 10 U.S.C. § 803 (a) . For references to the *Hirshberg* case in the legislative history, see H.R. Rep. No. 491, 81st Cong., 1st sess., pp. 5, 11; Sen. Rep. No. 486, 81st Cong., 1st sess., pp. 8; *Uniform Code of Military Justice,* Hearings before the House Committee on Armed Services, on H.R. 2498, pp. 617, 800, 882-884.

[29] *Talbott* v. *United States,* 215 F. 2d 22, 27 (D. C. Cir.) . See also *Kronberg* v. *Hale,* 180 F. 2d 128, 131 (C.A.9), certiorari denied, 339 U. S. 969 (*Hirshberg* held to be purely statutory) .

[30] 350 U. S. 11.

Just half a century ago, Mr. Justice Holmes defined law as "a statement of the circumstances in which the public force will be brought to bear upon men through the courts." [31] But, for better or worse, law is not an exact science. A lawyer cannot predict the future course of decision in even a single court with either the assurance or the accuracy of the astronomer forecasting the orbits of distant planets, as indeed hosts of defeated litigants, licked lawyers, and reversed lower court judges have learned to their discomfiture.

And this is why: when a single judge delivers an opinion on behalf of many others, the give-and-take of the judicial process obscures a good many unresolved differences. As Justice Holmes once wrote, in the middle of a Term marked by some bitter dissents, "It is worth an effort and some self-suppression to keep things smooth wherever one is called on to cooperate with others." [32] Somewhat more pithy is the comment attributed to another Justice whose concurrence in a particular decision was questioned: "One can't dissent all the time." Therefore, a judicial pronouncement that to the outsider, be he lawyer or judge, appears like a monolithic facade, may in fact conceal some pretty rough, disjointed, and non-uniform elements. It is, therefore, a mistake for the practicing lawyer to decry concurring opinions. Those give a more accurate clue to the future course of decision than does the tidied-up "Opinion of the Court" with its compromises that so often gloss over important disagreements.

Second, when can lower court opinions usefully be cited to the Supreme Court?

Where a good many lower Federal courts have decided the

---

[31] *American Banana Co.* v. *United Fruit Co.,* 213 U. S. 347, 356.

Mr. Justice Holmes had earlier set forth the same views in a well known address, *The Path of the Law* (1897), in *Collected Legal Papers,* 167, 173: "The object of our study, then, is prediction, the prediction of the incidence of the public force through the instrumentality of the courts. * * * The prophecies of what the courts will do in fact, and nothing more pretentious, are what I mean by the law."

[32] 1 *Holmes-Laski Letters* (Howe ed. 1953) 405 (Feb. 7, 1922). A month earlier, Justice Holmes had commenced a dissent with these words: "There are obvious limits of propriety to the persistent expression of opinions that do not command the agreement of the court. But as this case presents a somewhat new field, * * * I venture a few words to explain my dissent." *Federal Trade Comm.* v. *Beech-Nut Packing Co.,* 257 U. S. 441, 456.

same question of practice or procedure in essentially the same way, the resultant mass of authority is bound to be persuasive. Thus, in *Leiter Minerals, Inc.* v. *United States*,[33] the Supreme Court held that 28 U.S.C. § 2283, a provision with a long history that restricts the power of Federal courts to stay proceedings in State courts,[34] was inapplicable to stays sought by the United States; the opinion was buttressed by decisions of lower courts that had reached the same result.[35] On the other hand, where a constitutional issue is or is thought to be involved, even the most unanimous array of opinions below may fail to carry conviction. In *Estep* v. *United States*,[36] as the dissent was at pains to point out, the result reached was contrary to the prior opinions of more than forty circuit judges.

And where a particular constitutional issue comes to the Supreme Court for ultimate decision as a point of first impression, it verges on the ridiculous to hand up, as though it were a vital bit of newly-discovered evidence at a trial, a district court opinion just written on the precise question. To rely on that as "authority" all but amounts to picketing the courtroom from within (outside picketing having now been forbidden by Congress).[37]

Third, what weight do decisions of State courts of last resort have when cited to any Federal court in connection with federal questions? The answer must be, very little—except in connection with details of procedure on which the Federal Rules are unclear, and on which there is as yet no substantial body of Federal law. State cases on constitutional issues such as due process are particularly unhelpful, especially when they reflect the judicial hostility to legislation that was so prevalent in State courts of last resort prior to about 1920.[38]

---

[33] 352 U. S. 220.
[34] It was first enacted in 1793, and from 1911 to 1948 was § 265 of the Judicial Code. See *Toucey* v. *New York Life Ins. Co.*, 314 U. S. 118, 129-134.
[35] 352 U. S. at 226, note 3.
[36] 327 U. S. 114.
[37] 18 U.S.C. § 1507; 40 U.S.C. §§ 13f-13p.
[38] See Pound, *Liberty of Contract*, 18 Yale L. J. 454. It was the decision in *Ives* v. *South Buffalo Ry. Co.*, 201 N. Y. 271, 93 N.E. 431 (1911), holding that a state workmen's compensation law violated the Federal Constitution, that led Congress in 1914 to grant the Supreme Court power to review state court decisions sustaining a claim of federal right. See Frankfurter and Landis, *The Business of the Supreme Court* (1927) 188-198. The statutory provision is now 28 U.S.C. § 1257 (3).

Section 50. The case in point.—In the Supreme Court, certainly as that august tribunal was constituted in the final stages of its most flexible era, when *stare decisis* was hardly paid lip service,[39] citation of the case in point was by no means the last word.

A shining example from my own experience during that period was *Girouard* v. *United States*,[40] the case which held that a conscientious objector was eligible for citizenship. The petitioner, a Seventh Day Adventist, had expressed himself as willing to serve in the armed forces but unwilling to bear arms. As a matter of precedent, his case was ruled, not by that of Rosika *Schwimmer*,[41] who was a fairly fuzzy-minded, world-brotherhood, there-is-no-sovereignty brand of female pacifist; nor by that of Douglas *Macintosh*,[42] who desired to pass on the justness or unjustness of each particular war as it arose, so that he could determine for himself whether to participate; but by that of Marie *Bland*,[43] (argued and decided together with the last preceding) , the Canadian nurse who did not object to war but only to bearing arms.

But—the authority of the *Bland* case, notwithstanding the then recently decided case that sustained a state court's refusal to admit a conscientious objector to the bar,[44] would not have won a single vote in the *Girouard* case; no justice was willing to support *Schwimmer, Macintosh,* or *Bland* as a matter of judicial decision.[45] The Government had therefore to establish a legislative ratifica-

---

[39] For an exposition of the prevailing philosophy, see [Mr. Justice] Douglas, *Stare Decisis* (1946). See also note 171, *supra,* p. 108.

[40] 328 U. S. 61.

[41] 279 U. S. 644.

[42] 283 U. S. 605.

[43] 283 U. S. 636.

[44] *In re Summers,* 325 U. S. 561.

[45] "With three other Justices of the Court I dissented in the *Macintosh* and *Bland* cases, for reasons which the Court now adopts as ground for overruling them. Since this Court in three considered earlier opinions has rejected the construction of the statute for which the dissenting Justices contended, the question, which for me is decisive of the present case, is whether Congress has likewise rejected that construction by its subsequent legislative action, and has adopted and confirmed the Court's earlier construction of the statutes in question. A study of Congressional action taken with respect to proposals for amendment of the naturalization laws since the decision in the *Schwimmer* case, leads me to conclude that Congress has adopted and confirmed this Court's earlier construction of the naturalization laws. For that reason alone I think that the judgment should be affirmed." Stone, C. J., dissenting, 328 U. S. at 72-73.

tion of the earlier decisions. Even that did not convince a majority of the Court, although it did persuade Chief Justice Stone, who had joined in the *Macintosh* and *Bland* dissents, as well as Mr. Justice Frankfurter, who, while still on the Harvard Law School faculty, had been active in sponsoring a legislative repeal of the earlier cases.[46]

In short, in this particular instance the case in point, without more, did not get a single vote.

Section 51. When there is no case in point.—When there is no case in point, either in the Supreme Court or in some lower Federal court, you must draw on other resources. You must have recourse, first of all, to analysis. If you have nothing but logic and reasoning to support and sustain your analysis, by all means use logic. But usually there is available something more than simply your own process of reasoning. There are almost always analogies to which you can profitably turn. Frequently you can make effective use of legislative materials and legislative history. Not infrequently, you will find helpful noncase materials for the asking. But, above all, you must never let a good argument die for want of a decision in point.

This admonition is fully documented in the sections that follow, which discuss the technique of using analogies, the problems involved in statutory analysis and the ascertainment of legislative history, the complexities of distinguishing cases that at first blush appear to be against you, and the use, citation, and reliance upon noncase materials.

In short, when a lawyer says of his case, "There's no law on it," he reveals not so much the paucity of available materials as the limitations of his own professional capabilities.

Section 52. Use of analogies.—The use of apt analogies, I am coming more and more to believe, is the mark of a really good lawyer. Any clerk can look up cases in the digests, but it takes an active, a trained, and above all a resourceful legal mind to search for and find persuasive analogies.

Two fine lawyerlike examples that remain vividly in mind are Mr. Justice Cardozo's analogies in the Social Security cases,[47]

---

[46] See Hearings before the House Committee on Immigration and Naturalization on H.R. 297, 72d Cong., 1st sess., p. 68; and see 75 Cong. Rec. 15356.

[47] *Steward Machine Co.* v. *Davis,* 301 U. S. 548; *Helvering* v. *Davis,* 301 U. S. 619.

and Alfred Bettman's article on the *Constitutionality of Zoning* [48] (which antedated and forecast the Supreme Court's decision on the question).[49] Examine those, study the technique of comparison there employed, and you will begin to appreciate the essential difference between a lawyer on the one hand and a mere attorney at law on the other.

Of course analogies must be accurate, and they must not be carried too far. Two of our greatest judges have left us warnings on that score. Mr. Justice Holmes said: "As long as the matter to be considered is debated in artificial terms there is a danger of being led by a technical definition to apply a certain name, and then to deduce consequences which have no relation to the grounds on which the name was applied."[50] And thirty years later Mr. Justice Cardozo remarked that "When things are called by the same name it is easy for the mind to slide into an assumption that the verbal identity is accompanied in all its sequences by identity of meaning."[51]

But, more frequently than otherwise, the real difficulty is not that the analogy used is doubtful or that it is sought to be extended too far; the trouble is that the lawyer never invokes any analogy at all. The corpus is now so large that, with the inevitable specialization which follows, the current thinking of many if not most practitioners is marked by too much compartmentalization, and far too little cross-fertilization. Not infrequently, judges are apt to think that their colleagues share the bar's shortcomings in this respect in not paying adequate heed to analogous situations.[52]

All too often, the best analogies occur to the brief-writer after the case is over. Thus, on the loss-of-jurisdiction point in the case of the serviceman's wife whom the Air Force sought to retry by court-martial in the District of Columbia after her first conviction following military trial in England had been set aside,[53] I argued

---

[48] 37 Harv. L. Rev. 834 (May 1924).

[49] *Euclid* v. *Ambler Realty Co.*, 272 U. S. 365 (November 1926).

[50] *Guy* v. *Donald*, 203 U. S. 399, 406.

[51] *Lowden* v. *Northwestern National Bank*, 298 U. S. 160, 165.

[52] Cf. *United States* v. *Atlantic Mut. Ins. Co.*, 343 U. S. 236, 242-243 (Frankfurter and Burton, JJ., dissenting); *Pennsylvania Coal Co.* v. *Mahon*, 260 U. S. 393, 416-422, especially at 422 (Brandeis, J., dissenting).

[53] *United States* v. *Covert*, 6 USCMA 48, 19 CMR 174.

The scope of the thrust of the argument originally made in the district court on the woman's behalf appears from *In re Varney's Petition*, 141 F. Supp. 190, 204 (S.D. Calif.), as follows:

that, under an unbroken line of military rulings, any act of the Government separating an individual from the service terminated military jurisdiction over him,[54] and that accordingly to return Mrs. Covert to the United States, and, above all, to place her in civilian custody, made her no longer amenable to military trial.[55] This point was decided adversely on the first argument,[56] and on the rehearing the Government argued that the Air Force's actions evidenced an intent to continue the jurisdiction. I replied that the question of retaining or losing jurisdiction turned on objective acts.[57] I should also have cited—but did not, because not regularly dealing with the field—the then recent case of *Savorgnan* v. *United States*,[58] which held that Mrs. Savorgnan had expatriated herself by naturalization in Italy followed by residence abroad, and that her intention not to give up her American citizenship when she performed those acts was immaterial.

Similarly, I argued that, whatever might have been Mrs. Covert's amenability to military jurisdiction when she was in England, once she was returned to the United States and her conviction was set aside, she came again within the protection of the Sixth Amendment. I cited Lord Mansfield's famous decision in the

---

"One of the important distinctions between that case and this case is well illustrated by the dramatic and accurate statement made by counsel to open his case on behalf of Mrs. Covert in the District Court:

" 'Mr. Wiener: If the Court please, the question in this case is whether a woman, who all of her life has been a civilian, may be tried by an Air Force court martial in time of peace here in the District of Columbia and literally within the shadow of the Capitol dome.' "

[54] Winthrop, *Military Law and Precedents* (2d ed. 1896) * 116-118; Dig. Op. JAG, 1912, p. 514; Dig. Op. JAG, 1912-1940, pp. 162-163; 5 Bull. JAG 35; *id.* 278; *United States* v. *Sippel*, 4 USCMA 50, 53, 15 CMR 50, 53. Later military rulings may in some respects have changed the earlier rule. *United States* v. *Speller*, 8 USCMA 363, 24 CMR 173; *United States* v. *Robertson*, 8 USCMA 421, 24 CMR 231. See, however, *United States* v. *Scott*, 11 USCMA 646, 29 CMR 462.

[55] While Article of War 2 (e) of 1916 through 1948 (10 U.S.C. [1926 to 1946 eds.] § 1472 (e)) rendered subject to military law "All persons under sentence adjudged by courts-martial," Article 2 (7) of the Uniform Code of Military Justice (now 10 U.S.C. § 802 (7)) limits amenability to "All persons in custody of the armed forces serving a sentence imposed by a court-martial." After her return to the United States following her trial abroad, Mrs. Covert had at all times been in civilian custody.

[56] *Reid* v. *Covert*, 351 U. S. 487.

[57] Authorities cited in note 54, *supra;* also *United States* v. *Cooke*, 336 U. S. 210.

[58] 338 U. S. 491.

case of the slave Somerset, brought by his master from Virginia to England in 1772: once the Negro reached English soil he was free.[59] I should also have cited, but did not because unacquainted with them at the time, the host of early cases, from Northern and Southern courts alike, holding that a slave brought to reside in a free State became free in consequence.[60]

Section 53. Handling authorities apparently against you.— One of the most difficult problems for the brief-writer is how to deal with decisions that appear to be against him—and that quite frequently live fully up to their appearances.

Some approaches to this problem have already been discussed in the preceding chapter; see Sections 34 and 35, above.

One solution is to ignore the offending precedent—always provided, of course, that it is not a square holding—and to deal with it *sub silentio*. In the *Haupt* treason case,[61] we—that is to say, Government counsel—were faced with some very strong and, as we believed, very wrong language from the recently decided *Cramer* treason case.[62] See Section 35 (e), *supra*. We felt that we had a winning case on the facts, that *Haupt* was strong in every respect where *Cramer* had been weak. So we undertook to chart an independent course through the historical and judicial materials, which would show beyond peradventure that the language of the *Cramer* case was wrong—but which carefully avoided saying so directly. For the text of the effort, see Point II of the Government's brief in that case; [63] for the text of the result, see the opinion of the Court, and particularly the concurring opinion of Mr. Justice Douglas, who had earlier written the dissent in *Cramer*.[64]

(I should say parenthetically here that, although I fully appreciate the reluctance of any reader to haul down numerous volumes from library shelves, there is really no way of learning the techniques of advocacy other than by the detailed examination of briefs and opinions, plus—ideally—actually hearing the cases

---

[59] *Somerset* v. *Stewart,* Lofft 1, 21 How. St. Tr. 1.

[60] See Levy, *The Law of the Commonwealth and Chief Justice Shaw* (1957) 61-71, citing cases from many jurisdictions.

[61] *Haupt* v. *United States,* 330 U. S. 631.

[62] *Cramer* v. *United States,* 325 U. S. 1.

[63] No. 49, Oct. T. 1946. It appeared at pp. 350-369 of the earlier version of the present work.

[64] See 330 U. S. at 644; 325 U. S. at 48.

argued. The older reporters knew this, and so set down the points of counsel as well as the opinion of the court.)

Another solution is to attack the offending precedent boldly and frontally. As has been indicated above, Section 35 (e), this is an operation that engenders much resistance. It is really successful only when the precedent is generally acknowledged to be on its last legs.

The third way is to distinguish it, a process that is virtually as old as the common law itself. As early as 1310 and 1314, "The fascinating game of 'distinguishing' is already popular,"[65] and the serjeants even then are recorded in the Year Books as saying *"Non est simile," "N'est pas semblable,"* "Not a like case." They, no less than their successors six and a half centuries later, were asking themselves the question, "How can a lawyer most effectively distinguish a case apparently against him?"

The soundest advice on this score is to distinguish the offending precedent boldly: go on a broad ground, don't get bogged down in finicky details, and don't go in for overrefined analysis.

On this point also I found the *Haupt* case[66] most instructive —in teaching me what not to do in the future.

In that case, twelve overt acts of treason had been submitted to the jury, which returned a general verdict of guilty. We argued first that each of the twelve overt acts was supported by the evidence of the required two witnesses.[67] We then went on to argue that, even if some of the overt acts should be deemed not to have been proved by two sufficient witnesses, the judgment of conviction must still be affirmed.

That argument was primarily based on the proposition that, as a matter of the substantive law of treason, it was sufficient to sustain a conviction if, on review subsequent to trial, one overt act charged had been proved by two witnesses, even though additional overt acts alleged in the indictment were not so proved. Such had been the English law since 1660;[68] the earliest American decision

[65] Allen, *Law in the Making* (6th ed. 1958) 187, giving many references at 187-188.

[66] *Supra* note 61.

[67] See note 63, *supra*.

[68] *Trial of the Regicides,* 5 How. St. Tr. 947, 1033; *Trial of Robert Lowick,* 13 How. St. Tr. 267, 277; *Trial of Christopher Layer,* 16 How. St. Tr. 94, 313-314; s.c., *sub nom. The King* v. *Layer,* 8 Mod. 82, 93; 1 Hale, *History of the Pleas of the Crown* *122; Foster, *Crown Law* (1st ed. 1762) 194; 2 Hawkins, *Pleas of the Crown* (4th ed. 1762) 436.

was the same; [69] and every modern American jury considering a case of treason had uniformly been charged to the same effect. [70] An unbroken rule of law from 1660 to 1943, continuous over a period of 283 years, should have been fairly persuasive. But the point was not briefed in the *Cramer* case, which came to the Supreme Court in 1945. There the Court held that two of the three overt acts submitted to the jury had been insufficient, after which it went on to hold, in a *footnote:*

The verdict in this case was a general one of guilty, without special findings as to the acts on which it rests. Since it is not possible to identify the grounds on which Cramer was convicted, the verdict must be set aside if any of the separable acts submitted was insufficient. *Stromberg* v. *California,* 283 U. S. 359, 368; *Williams* v. *North Carolina,* 317 U. S. 287, 292. * * * [71]

The way that this footnote should have been dealt with in the *Haupt* case was as follows: First, the prosecution should have pointed out that for 283 years the rule of substantive law in treason cases had been just the contrary; that in the then fairly recent *Stephan* case [72] the conviction was sustained on appeal notwithstanding the Sixth Circuit's determination of the insufficiency, as a matter of two-witness proof, of four of the ten overt acts submitted to the jury; and that none of the voluminous briefs filed in the *Cramer* case had brought any of these authorities to the Supreme Court's attention. (In view of the disposition made of the *Cramer* case, the way was probably not open for an argument that the holding, having been contained in a footnote, was not to be regarded as a precedent.) [73]

---

[69] *Case of Fries,* Fed. Case No. 5127, 9 Fed. Cas. at 932 (C.C.D. Pa. 1800).

[70] *United States* v. *Fricke,* 259 Fed. 673, 677 (S.D.N.Y.) ; *Stephan* v. *United States,* 133 F. 2d 87, 92 (C.A. 6), certiorari denied, 318 U. S. 781 (see R. 326, 339-341, No. 792, Oct. T. 1942) ; *United States* v. *Haupt,* 47 F. Supp. 836, 839 (N.D. Ill.), reversed on other grounds, 136 F. 2d 661 (C.A. 7) ; *Cramer* v. *United States,* 325 U. S. 1 (R. 442, 446, No. 13, Oct. T. 1944) ; *Haupt* v. *United States,* 330 U. S. 631 (R. 39, No. 49, Oct. T. 1946).

[71] 325 U. S. at 36, n. 45.

[72] *Stephan* v. *United States,* 133 F. 2d 87 (C.A. 6), certiorari denied, 318 U. S. 781.

[73] There was long current a remark attributed to Chief Justice Hughes to the effect that "I will not be bound by a footnote," but unfortunately it is not to be found in any opinion he wrote. Indeed, the footnote in the first *Carolene* case, to the effect that "There may be narrower scope for operation of the presumption of constitutionality when legislation appears on its face to be within a specific prohibition of the Constitution, such as those of the

Second, and here is the nub of the matter, the *Stromberg* and *Williams* cases, cited in the *Cramer* footnote, should have been distinguished on a broad ground, viz., that they dealt with the Supreme Court's review of Federal questions coming up from State courts, whereas what was here presented was appellate review of the sufficiency of a conviction for treason, which involved a well-settled rule of substantive criminal law.

I say, that is the way the *Cramer* footnote should have been dealt with. Unfortunately, I went into far more detail. After stating the rule in the treason cases, I went on to discuss some analogous general rules, viz., that, in mail fraud and conspiracy cases, a verdict stands if a single overt act has been proved, even though the others may be bad; that, in any kind of criminal case, a general verdict on an indictment containing many counts is supported by a single good count; and, similarly, with a general sentence. I argued that, since special verdicts are not generally employed in criminal cases, a contrary rule would mean that a defendant could never be charged with more than one overt act of treason except at the risk of acquittal if a single additional overt act submitted to the jury failed of proof; "that is to say, the more active the traitor and the more complex his treason, the better his chances of escaping the noose." Then I went on to a detailed analysis of the *Stromberg* and *Williams* cases—without stressing the real distinction mentioned above. Finally, I urged that since the doing of the overt acts was not disputed, the jury could not have been misled by an insufficiency of proof as to any overt act.

The result? A reaffirmance of the rule of the *Cramer* footnote —in another footnote! The Court said:

When, speaking of a general verdict of guilty in *Cramer* v. *United States*, 325 U. S. 1, 36, n. 45, we said "Since it is not possible to identify the grounds on which Cramer was convicted, the verdict must be set aside if any of the separable acts submitted was insufficient," of course we did not hold that one overt act properly proved and submitted

first ten amendments, which are deemed equally specific when held to be embraced within the Fourteenth" (*United States* v. *Carolene Products Co.,* 304 U. S. 144, 152, n. 4), foreshadowed, for better or worse, a good deal of constitutional doctrine of the 1940's. Thereafter it was vigorously questioned (see Frankfurter, J., concurring, in *Kovacs* v. *Cooper*, 336 U. S. 77, 90-92) , and at this writing the *Carolene* footnote is in disfavor; currently no provision of the Constitution enjoys preference over any other. See *Ullmann* v. *United States,* 350 U. S. 422, 428-429.

would not sustain a conviction if the proof of other overt acts was insufficient. One such act may prove treason, and on review the conviction would be sustained, provided the record makes clear that the jury convicted on that overt act. But where several acts are pleaded in a single count and submitted to the jury, under instructions which allow a verdict of guilty on any one or more of such acts, a reviewing court has no way of knowing that any wrongly submitted act was not the one convicted upon. If acts were pleaded in separate counts, or a special verdict were required as to each overt act of a single count, the conviction could be sustained on a single well-proved act.[74]

In consequence, prosecutors in later treason cases always asked for special verdicts on the overt acts submitted to the jury.[75] Possibly the result on this point in *Haupt* might have been the same if the *Stromberg* and *Williams* cases had been properly distinguished on broad grounds.[76] At any rate, I have long been certain that it was poor argumentation and presentation to spin the matter out in such great detail, and that the only effective way to have handled the apparently adverse decisions would have been on the basis of the broad distinction suggested above.

In due course, another opportunity to wrestle with a particularly difficult question of how best to distinguish an unusually troublesome precedent presented itself.

As has already been mentioned (pp. 112-113, *supra*), on the rehearing of the cases involving the constitutionality of military trials of servicemen's dependents, counsel for the civilian women decided not to request a direct overruling of the most pertinent earlier decision. To recall the problem briefly to mind in the present connection, the Supreme Court in its first opinion [77] had relied very strongly on *In re Ross*,[78] a decision from 1891 which

---

[74] *Haupt* v. *United States,* 330 U. S. at 641, n. 1.

[75] See, e.g., *Chandler* v. *United States,* 171 F. 2d 921 (C.A.1), certiorari denied, 336 U. S. 918; *Gillars* v. *United States,* 182 F. 2d 962 (D. C. Cir.) ; *Best* v. *United States,* 184 F. 2d 131 (C.A.1), certiorari denied, 340 U. S. 939; *Burgman* v. *United States,* 188 F. 2d 637 (D. C. Cir.) ; *Kawakita* v. *United States,* 190 F. 2d 506 (C.A.9), affirmed, 343 U. S. 717.

[76] Compare *Terminiello* v. *Chicago,* 337 U. S. 1, for an extreme example of finding a federal question; Vinson, C. J. dissenting, remarked (337 U. S. at 7) that "the offending sentence in the charge to the jury was no part of the case until this Court's independent research ferreted it out of a lengthy and somewhat confused record."

[77] *Kinsella* v. *Krueger,* 351 U. S. 470.

[78] 140 U. S. 453.

had upheld, as against a claim to a jury, the trial by an American consular court in Japan of a seaman who was part of the crew of an American ship.

Had *Ross* come up in the 1950's as an original proposition, it would probably have been decided differently. For while the basis of *Ross*, as stated therein, was that "The Constitution can have no operation in another country," [79] the Supreme Court had subsequently held that "The Constitution of the United States is in force * * * wherever and whenever the sovereign power of that government is exerted." [80] But—American consular jurisdiction had existed since before the adoption of the Constitution,[81] it had been exercised for 170 years, and at least one individual had been hanged pursuant to the sentence of a consular court.[82] Consequently, even though by the time of the grant of the rehearing the consular jurisdiction had been abolished by the President pursuant to congressional authorization,[83] it was felt that a square overruling of *Ross* would hardly be palatable fare for the Court, and so had better not be requested. Accordingly, starting from the suggestive leads in one of the first opinions,[84] the following argument was developed in the attempt to distinguish the *Ross* case persuasively:

Extraterritorial military jurisdiction over military personnel flows from hitherto accepted doctrines of international law,[85] whereas the consular jurisdiction rests on express treaty provisions.[86] The only basis for sustaining the non-jury aspect of the

---

[79] 140 U. S. at 464.

[80] *Balzac* v. *Porto Rico,* 258 U. S. 298, 312.

[81] See Arts. 20 and 21 of the Treaty with the Emperor of Morocco, 8 Stat. 100, 103.

[82] *Diplomatic Correspondence, 1864* (H. Ex. Doc. 1, 38th Cong., 2d sess.), Part III, pp. 400-419.

[83] Act of Aug. 1, 1956, c. 807, 70 Stat. 773; 35 Dept. of State Bull. 844 (Nov. 26, 1956).

[84] See the reservation of Frankfurter, J., 351 U. S. at 481, especially at 482-485.

[85] See *The Schooner Exchange* v. *M'Faddon,* 7 Cranch 116, 139-140; *Coleman* v. *Tennessee,* 97 U. S. 509, 515; *Dow* v. *Johnson,* 100 U. S. 158, 165; *Chung Chi Cheung* v. *The King,* [1939] A.C. 160; cf. *Reference re Exemption of U. S. Forces from Canadian Law,* [1943] 4 D.L.R.11. There is an extensive literature on the subject, but probably the better view is that the doctrine of *Wilson* v. *Girard,* 354 U. S. 524, rests on waiver.

[86] 2 Moore, *Digest of International Law,* 593-727; 2 Hackworth, *Digest of International Law,* 512-534.

consular jurisdiction is that it dated from 1786-1787,[87] that it was thus pre-constitutional, and that it was accordingly impliedly excepted from the Sixth Amendment, just as are trials by court-martial of military personnel,[88] trials of petty offenders by judges of inferior courts,[89] trials by the court alone of contemnors,[90] and trials by military tribunals of offenders against the laws of war.[91] But that is also the reason why these women cannot be tried by court-martial; they had a right to jury trial in 1789 and before.[92]

Those arguments convinced a majority of the Court, in varying degrees. Black, J., for himself and three other Justices said:

The *Ross* approach that the Constitution has no applicability abroad has long since been directly repudiated by numerous cases. That approach is obviously erroneous if the United States Government, which has no power except that granted by the Constitution, can and does try citizens for crimes committed abroad. Thus the *Ross* case rested, at least in substantial part, on a fundamental misconception and the most that can be said in support of the result reached there is that the consular court jurisdiction had a long history antedating the adoption of the Constitution. The Congress has recently buried the consular system of trying Americans. We are not willing to jeopardize the lives and liberties of Americans by disinterring it. At best, the *Ross* case should be left as a relic from a different era.[93]

Frankfurter, J., concurring in the result, examined at length the history of consular courts, and said *inter alia:*

Insofar as the opinion [in *Ross*] expressed a view that the Constitution is not operative outside the United States * * * it expressed a notion that has long since evaporated. * * *

The significance of the *Ross* case and its relevance to the present cases cannot be assessed unless due regard is accorded the historical context in which that case was decided. *Ross* is not rooted in any abstract principle or comprehensive theory touching constitutional power

---

[87] See the Treaty cited in note 81, *supra*, and 32 J. Cont. Cong. 353, 363-364.

[88] *Whelchel* v. *McDonald*, 340 U. S. 122, 126-127.

[89] *District of Columbia* v. *Clawans*, 300 U. S. 617; *District of Columbia* v. *Colts*, 282 U. S. 63.

[90] *In re Debs*, 158 U. S. 564, 594-596; and see *accord*, decided afterwards, *Green* v. *United States*, 356 U. S. 165.

[91] *Ex parte Quirin*, 317 U. S. 1; *In re Yamashita*, 327 U. S. 1.

[92] See 1 Winthrop, *Military Law & Precedents* (2d ed. 1896) *144-146; Dig. Op. JAG, 1912, p. 513.

[93] 354 U. S. at 12 (footnotes omitted).

or its restrictions. It was decided with reference to a very particular practical problem with a long history. * * *

The *Ross* case, therefore, arose out of, and rests on, very special, confined circumstances, and cannot be applied automatically to the present situation * * * [94]

And Harlan, J., also concurring in the result, expressed agreement with what Frankfurter, J., had written about the *Ross* case.[95] Two justices dissented.[96]

Plainly enough, not every phase of the arguments made against *Ross* on the rehearing of the court-martial cases prevailed. But the result was that a majority of the Court no longer relied upon the *Ross* case as a basis for sustaining the military trials, and the several opinions also demonstrated the soundness of not having made an out-and-out request to overrule *Ross:* such a request would not have gained the concurrence of a majority of the Court.

Finally, for detailed study of how a great legal craftsman goes about distinguishing and dealing with authorities that stand in his way, the reader is referred to Professor Bickel's fascinating recent work, *The Unpublished Opinions of Mr. Justice Brandeis.*[97] There he will see, in concrete fashion, the techniques employed in this field by a consummate master of the art.

Section 54. Use of dissenting and concurring opinions.— When you are not counsel in a case, but are above the conflict, writing for a non-judicial audience on what the law should be, you are of course perfectly free to quote from dissenting opinions, and to indicate why you prefer the reasoning these set out. As the old professor put it, "What the court says carries no mandate to the logical faculty."

But when you are counsel seeking to win an appeal for your client, you need the votes of a majority of the court in which the case is pending, and consequently you will not help to persuade the judges by quoting from dissents that failed to persuade them, particularly from recent dissents. If the court in question currently follows *stare decisis,* this point would appear to be almost too obvious to require mention.

---

[94] 354 U. S. at 56, 64.
[95] 354 U. S. at 67, 74-75.
[96] 354 U. S. at 78.
[97] (1957).

We have, however, experienced something of a bloodless constitutional revolution since 1937, in which some notable earlier dissents, by judges of the stature of Holmes, Hughes, Brandeis, Cardozo, and Stone, have become law. See Section 35 (e), above. So there has developed, especially in some law schools, a veritable cult of dissent, to such an extent that the lads in their moot court cases will frequently cite the dissenting opinions of a judge whom they like in preference to the majority opinions written by a judge whom they hold in disesteem.

Some carry that habit with them after admission to the bar—where it can only hurt their client's causes.[98]

Just ask yourself this question: If there was a strong dissent in a 7-2 case, and five of the original seven are still on the bench, do you really think you can persuade any of them by quoting the views with which they disagreed, views that expressed in forceful language their own error? Of course not; your task is to persuade three additional judges, and to rely on the old dissent is just the way to fail in that endeavor.

Much the same principle applies to concurring opinions. Those are very helpful to the advocate in any situation where he needs to pick up votes, because they show how the concurring judges feel about the problem, and thus they enable him to shape his arguments in an effort to persuade those judges in the next case. But don't quote from the concurring opinions in the hope that somehow the passage in the brief will prove more persuasive with the other judges now than it was in conference when it was first considered by them.

Reliance on, and quotations from, concurring opinions in a brief are justified only where a court was so divided that no single opinion expressed the views of a majority. In that currently not at all unusual situation,[99] it is perfectly proper—indeed it is often necessary—to urge the concurring views. But don't quote a single

---

[98] For a useful, because realistically practical, evaluation of dissenting opinions, the reader should examine Mr. Justice Jackson's posthumously published work, *The Supreme Court in the American System of Government* (1955) 17-19.

See also Mr. Justice Jackson's comments on how a judge feels when dissenting opinions or extracurricular works are cited. Jackson, *Advocacy Before the Supreme Court: Suggestions for Effective Case Presentations,* 37 A.B.A.J. 801, 804.

[99] See Note, *Supreme Court No-Clear Majority Decisions: A Study in Stare Decisis,* 24 U. of Chi. L. Rev. 99.

judge's views too obviously; he will think you are just trying to curry favor, even to fawn, while the others, whom he failed to persuade in the first instance, are not likely to be persuaded by you at second hand.

Indeed, it is of the essence of advocacy that one endeavors to avoid stirring up opposition on non-essential or collateral matters. Some judges, once they have been outvoted, put the matter to one side, filing it mentally under "finished business." With others, however, a sharp difference of opinion leaves a mark, so that the feelings it engendered are apt to rankle, and for a much longer time than many outsiders would suppose.

Therefore, skirt around the differences disclosed in the reports, if at all possible, and, when you can, use a formula substantially like this: "The issue that divided the Court in *Doe* v. *United States* is not present here." Narrow the area of disagreement as far as feasible—and don't, *don't,* DON'T cite recent dissenting opinions if your objective is victory on appeal.

Section 55. Briefs filed in earlier cases involving the same or related questions.—Not only does the examination of briefs aid the lawyer who is studying the techniques of advocacy (*supra,* Section 20) , but, if the case in which they were filed is related to the one presently before him, he is bound to find therein, at the very least, a good deal of suggestive material. Any lawyer who has access to collections of briefs is therefore very fortunate. The fact that more and more libraries now have microfilm collections of Supreme Court briefs (Section 2, *supra*) testifies to a growing recognition of the importance of those documents.

First of all, if some other lawyer has written a winning brief on the point on which your case will turn, you may save yourself untold preliminary labor by starting your research there. (I say "may," because on occasion examination discloses that it was the court and not the lawyer whose argument won the case.) Once a brief has been filed, of course, it becomes a public document; there is no copyright and hence no infringement; this is therefore a field, preeminently, for the cynical advice to "plagiarize, plagiarize, plagiarize—but remember, please, always to call it 're-search.' "

But there is a second and frequently even more compelling reason for examining briefs filed in earlier cases that involved questions similar to or identical with those in your own case.

It is written in the Bible, "behold, my desire is, * * * that mine adversary had written a book." [100] Well, if mine adversary had written a brief, the chances are that he wrote something very different the last time, particularly if he represents the Government, which, more frequently than not, takes inconsistent litigating positions, sometimes (as in tax matters) because it must.

Mere inconsistency, of course, proves nothing; you are not going to win any appeal simply by making debating points, and of course it is not necessary to cite authority for the proposition that the United States is not subject to estoppel. But if you can establish, through indisputable references, that the other side has made a complete about-face on an issue of substance, or on any proposition that was never fairly debatable, it puts at least a crimp into that party's arguments, and it may well enable you to advance your own presentation right at the outset.

Here are some recent examples that illustrate the uses—and the limitations—of confronting the other side with its earlier arguments.

(a) In *Swift & Co.* v. *United States*,[101] the basic issue was whether the railroads' refusal to deliver livestock at the Swift siding in Chicago without an extra and designedly prohibitive switching charge, in the face of delivery without this charge at the Union Stock Yards, only a few city blocks away, amounted to an unreasonable discrimination under the Interstate Commerce Act. The intervening railroads, whose charges were in issue, and who were defending far more vigorously than the Government, filed as an appendix to their brief a brief that some of Swift's counsel, on behalf of a Swift subsidiary, had presented to the Interstate Commerce Commission twenty years previously, when transportation conditions in the Chicago stockyards area were vastly different.[102] Plainly, there is no estoppel against the assertion of rights under the Interstate Commerce Act,[103] and it may well be that the

---

[100] Job, xxxi. 35.

[101] 343 U. S. 373.

[102] The earlier case was *Hygrade Food Products Corp.* v. *Atchison, T. & S. F. Ry. Co.*, 195 I.C.C. 553; a decree dismissing a suit to enjoin the enforcement of that order was reversed by the Supreme Court. *Atchison, T. & S. F. Ry. Co.* v. *United States,* 295 U. S. 193. When the earlier brief was written, rail shipments of livestock to the Union Stock Yards in Chicago were nearly four times as much as similar shipments for the latest available year shown in the record of the 1952 case.

[103] *Los Angeles Switching Case,* 234 U. S. 294, 312-313.

reproduction of this document earned the strictures that Swift's reply brief made about it.[104] Swift lost the case, and while no one can say what contribution, if any, the old document made toward that result, one point was clear: it didn't help Swift.

(b) In *Opper* v. *United States*,[105] the issue was whether, where an admission is made to law enforcement officers after the date of the acts charged as crimes, it so far resembles a confession as to make it inadmissible in the absence of corroboration. Petitioner relied on *Warszower* v. *United States*,[106] where the Court had said that admissions made prior to the crime do not require corroboration, because "They contain none of the inherent weaknesses of confessions or admissions after the fact." And petitioner quoted from the Government's brief in that case, to the effect that "It is the Government's contention that independent evidence is required only in the case of confessions, and of admissions made after the event and in the context of conversations, interviews, and proceedings relating to the offense itself. The theory of this position squares with the purpose of the rule requiring corroboration." [107]

The Court in *Opper* accepted petitioner's contention (and the Government reasoning from its *Warszower* brief), and held that all admissions after the fact, even of mere elements of the crime, and even when contained in exculpatory statements such as Opper had made, required corroboration.[108] So far, so good. But then the Court went on to consider the quantum of corroboration that was necessary, and, resolving a conflict of long standing between circuits, held that petitioner's statements were sufficiently corroborated [109]—and affirmed his conviction.

---

[104] "We are at a loss to understand what legitimate purpose is now sought to be served by the reproduction of this twenty-year-old document, or by the repeated references thereto and quotations therefrom which interlard the railroad appellees' brief in this case. * * * We assume, of course, that the brief in question has not been exhumed simply to furnish material for an extended argument *ad hominem*." Appellant's Reply Brief, No. 282, Oct. T. 1951, pp. 29-30.

[105] 348 U. S. 84.

[106] 312 U. S. 342, 347.

[107] Brief for the *United States* in No. 338, Oct. T. 1940, pp. 21-22, quoted in Brief for the Petitioner, No. 49, Oct. T. 1954, p. 13.

[108] 348 U. S. at 90-92.

[109] 348 U. S. at 92-94, adopting the rule of *Daeche* v. *United States,* 250 Fed. 566 (C.A.2), in preference to that of *Forte* v. *United States,* 68 App. D. C. 111, 94 F. 2d 236.

(c) In the first two cases involving the military trials of civilian dependents, one of the issues between the parties concerned the scope of the treaty power. As has been shown above, the Government sought to rest those trials, at least in part, on "the power to make all laws necessary and proper for carrying into execution the sovereign authority of the United States to maintain relations with other sovereignties" (*supra*, p. 138), while the civilian women urged that "The treaty power is completely irrelevant in the present case" (*supra*, p. 139).

In support of the latter contention, the brief for both women quoted from the Government's brief in the then recently decided case of *United States* v. *Capps* [110]—a decision which had carefully avoided the treaty issue that had been discussed and considered below [111]—the following statements:

> The basic axiom is that, as a sovereign state, the United States possesses, in its dealing with other states, all of the normal powers of a fully independent nation, subject to constitutional limitations like the Bill of Rights which govern all exercise of governmental authority in this country.
>
> *   *   *   *   *
>
> Together with statutes and treaties, executive agreements are subject to the Bill of Rights and the other clauses of the Constitution which protect all Americans from the excesses of official authority.

In its first opinion in the court-martial cases, the Court stated that "No questions of the legal relation between treaties and the Constitution is presented." [112]

On rehearing, the Government was at pains to refer, not to the treaty power, but to "the powers of the United States in the conduct of foreign affairs." [113] The women concerned cited a number of cases to the effect that a treaty cannot authorize what the Constitution forbids, and repeated the quotations from the Government's brief in the *Capps* case.

The opinion of Black, J., for himself and three other judges, demolished the notion that a treaty or an executive agreement was somehow not subject to constitutional limitations. [114] Frankfur-

---

[110] 348 U. S. 296.

[111] *United States* v. *Guy W. Capps, Inc.*, 204 F. 2d 655 (C.A.4).

[112] *Kinsella* v. *Krueger*, 351 U. S. 470, 480.

[113] Supplemental Brief for Appellant and Petitioner on Rehearing, Nos. 701 and 713, Oct. T. 1955, p. 3.

[114] *Reid* v. *Covert*, 354 U. S. 1, 15-19.

ter, J., concurring in the result, did not deem the treaty power sufficiently relevant to mention; while Harlan, J., also concurring in the result, commented: "To say that the validity of the statute may be rested upon the inherent 'sovereign powers' of this country in its dealings with foreign nations seems to me to be no more than begging the question." [115]

To what extent did the quotations from the Government brief in *Capps* assist in the reaching of the foregoing views? Again, no outsider can venture any answer beyond this, that those quotations certainly didn't help the Government's "foreign relations" arguments on the rehearing of those cases.

(d) Nor were the quotations from its *Capps* brief the only passages from the past with which the Government was confronted in the first two court-martial cases; but here a few words by way of background are necessary.

In *Madsen* v. *Kinsella*,[116] the issue was whether Mrs. Madsen, who had killed her serviceman husband in occupied Germany, could be tried by an American military government court created and functioning under the authority of the American High Commissioner, a civilian. Actually, the only novelty was that almost all previous American military government courts had been created by a Military Governor who was a soldier in uniform,[117] but the simple answer was that the President as Commander-in-Chief could deal with occupied territory in his discretion, either directly, or through a military department, or through the State Department.

Having been tried and convicted by a civilian-appointed military government court, Mrs. Madsen contended that she could only have been tried by a court-martial under then Article of War 2 (d),[118] the forerunner of Article 2 (11) of the Uniform Code of Military Justice.[119] Mrs. Madsen thus became the first civilian woman in legal history who sought to be tried by court-martial;

---

[115] 354 U. S. at 66.
[116] 343 U. S. 341.
[117] See, e.g., *Santiago* v. *Nogueras*, 214 U. S. 260; *Neely* v. *Henkel*, 180 U. S. 109; *Ex parte Ortiz*, 100 Fed. 955 (C.C.D. Minn.). The court considered in *The Grapeshot*, 9 Wall. 129, was created by an Executive Order of President Lincoln. See *United States* v. *Reiter*, Fed. Case No. 16,146 (La. Prov. Ct.).
[118] 10 U.S.C. [1926 through 1946 eds.] § 1472 (d).
[119] Now 10 U.S.C. § 802 (11).

and in her brief she referred to an instance in 1825 where the "wife or reputed wife" of a British soldier in India had been tried there by court-martial.[120] To this the Government had replied, very properly,

In any event, the status of the wife or alleged wife of an English soldier in 1825 has little bearing as to whether the wife of an American soldier was regarded as subject to court-martial jurisdiction then or later. * * * Neither the petitioner nor the respondent has found any case of a wife or other dependent of a soldier who was tried by an American court-martial prior to the revision of the Articles of War in 1916.[121]

The Court sustained the jurisdiction of the tribunal that tried Mrs. Madsen.[122]

A few years later, when the first cases of the civilian wives tried by court-martial originally came before the Court, the Government resurrected the same East Indian instance, whereupon Mrs. Covert and Mrs. Smith quoted the foregoing excerpt from the Government's *Madsen* brief in reply. Subsequently, when the Government filed its reply brief on the rehearing, it devoted over a page to two trials of soldiers' wives in British India in 1825, and to one instance in the same place in 1831 "in which the court-martial of an officer's wife was considered." [123]

This left it open for Mrs. Covert and Mrs. Smith once more to repeat what the Government had said in *Madsen*, and to add the following mordant comment:

The circumstance that the Government now stresses the 1825 situation in India, which in 1956 it mentioned briefly and in 1952 dismissed as irrelevant, reflects, we think, not the suddenly inflated significance of the British military jurisdiction in the days of the East

---

[120] See Winthrop, *Military Law & Precedents* (2d ed. 1896) *133, citing the English text referred to in note 123, below.

[121] Brief for the Respondent, No. 411, Oct. T. 1951, pp. 44-45.

[122] *Madsen v. Kinsella,* 343 U. S. 341. After the second opinion in the *Covert* and *Krueger* cases, Mrs. Madsen again sought habeas corpus, but again without success. *Madsen v. Overholser,* 251 F. 2d 387 (D. C. Cir.), certiorari denied, 356 U. S. 920. See *Reid v. Covert,* 354 U. S. at 35, note 63, where the difference between the two situations is explained.

[123] Reply Brief for Appellant and Petitioner on Rehearing, Nos. 701 and 713, Oct. T. 1955, pp. 47-48, citing Hough, *Precedents in Military Law* (London 1855) 401, 402, 628, 630. Hough was "many years a Deputy Judge Advocate General" as a Lieutenant Colonel in the East India Company's Service, in the days when "John Company" ruled India.

India Company's viceregal sovereignty, but rather the paucity of authorities from any other source that are available for citation in support of the Government's position in the present cases.[124]

Not one of the four opinions on rehearing referred to the British India cases—thus proving the soundness of the Government's treatment of these instances in its 1952 *Madsen* brief.

One caution, however, should always be observed when citing the other side's prior inconsistencies: If your adversary confesses error in his current brief, either on his own motion or after you have exhibited his contrary earlier views, and explains or at least makes a fair effort to explain why those views are now abandoned, do not mention his earlier position further. To do so again in that situation does not add to your argument, it only detracts therefrom, because then repetition shades into personalities and into the inadmissible argument *ad hominem* (see Section 83, below).

(e) If the reader will bear with me as I continue to refight the *Covert* and *Krueger* cases, one other instance therein of the use of prior inconsistent arguments should really not be passed without comment.

In *Toth* v. *Quarles*,[125] the issue had been whether a discharged serviceman, who had committed an offense while in the service, could thereafter be tried by court-martial, there being no civil tribunal of any description with jurisdiction over him. In their Supreme Court brief, the Government had said, "Indeed, we think the constitutional case is, if anything, clearer for the court-martial of Toth, who was a soldier at the time of his offense, than it is for a civilian accompanying the armed forces."

After the Government lost the *Toth* case, in the very same Term in which the court-martial-of-dependents cases were first argued, that admission was just too pat to be overlooked, and counsel for the civilian women used it several times, not only in the briefs but orally as well.

However, in the face of the adverse opinions handed down subsequent to the first hearing, there was no point in laboring the matter further. When a litigant petitions for rehearing, he must rely on fundamentals, not on contradictions.

---

[124] Further Memorandum on Behalf of Appellee and Respondent, Nos. 701 and 713, Oct. T. 1955, p. 6.
[125] 350 U. S. 11.

On the second determination, however, the prevailing opinion picked up that passage. Speaking for himself and three other justices, Black, J., said: "The Government appropriately argued in *Toth* that the constitutional basis for court-martialing him was clearer than for court-martialing wives who are accompanying their husbands abroad"—and at that juncture quoted the passage from the Government's *Toth* brief in a supporting footnote! [126]

"Behold my desire is, * * * that mine adversary had written a book."

Section 56. Statutory analysis.—Sometimes the answer to a given problem is found, not in judicial decisions, but in painstaking analysis of the controlling statute. In such a situation, a lawyer's normal reaction is to look to see how the statute has been construed, to analyze the decisions construing it, and then to write his brief accordingly. That is always, quite properly, the first approach, but too often the tendency is to stop there and to rely solely on the decided cases.

The difficulty with not going further is that all too frequently the court which first construed the statute did not have all the relevant statutory materials before it; that it proceeded to determine the legislative intent without examining the expressions and materials from which that intent could be ascertained; and that subsequent decisions merely interpreted the first case and ceased to attempt to interpret the statute. The consequence of this technique is a stab at statutory analysis that did not analyze the statute but only undertook to reconcile decisions that had similarly failed to analyze it. Accordingly, the ultimate result has frequently been very far from what Congress really had in mind when it passed the act.

So—when you deal with a problem of statutory analysis, start by analyzing the statute, and by studying your particular provision in its setting. In this connection, it is well to bear in mind that annotated codes may be somewhat of a hindrance in this endeavor, for by their very wealth of annotation they render more difficult your bird's-eye survey of the underlying provisions. Therefore it is often helpful to get the feel of the related sections as they appear consecutively in the official edition of the U. S. Code, in such a way as to understand the statute as a whole, before turning to the an-

---

[126] 354 U. S. at 32, note 58.

notations to the separate sections in the USCA or in similar compilations.

Remember that you are not bound by your provision's present position, either in the U. S. Code or in the earlier Revised Statutes. The *Nye* [127] and *Williams* [128] cases hold that it is proper to go back to the law as originally enacted to ascertain the congressional intent.

The Supreme Court years ago said that "The re-enacted sections are to be given the same meaning they had in the original statute, unless a contrary intention is plainly manifested." [129] But that is a general rule only, and then so sapped of vitality by the qualification as to be virtually meaningless. When is a contrary intent "plainly manifested"?

Sometimes there is no problem whatever, as when Congress in its 1948 revision of Title 28 U.S.C. abolished the *Dobson* [130] rule, and restored to courts of appeals the same scope of review in Tax Court cases as they had traditionally retained in tax cases appealed from district courts. [131] Similarly, the 1952 revision of the patent law, Title 35 U.S.C., was designed to eliminate the Supreme Court's "flash of creative genius" requirement [132] as a condition of patentability. [133]

Other situations present more difficult problems. In *Ex parte Collett*, [134] a divided Court found that Congress in its revision of Title 28 intended to change the law by making the doctrine of *forum non conveniens* henceforward applicable in Federal Employers' Liability Act cases; a few years later, *Fourco Glass Co. v. Transmirra Corp.* [135] resolved, over dissent, a conflict between cir-

---

[127] *Nye* v. *United States,* 313 U. S. 33.

[128] *Williams* v. *United States,* 327 U. S. 711.

[129] *United States* v. *LeBris,* 121 U. S. 278, 280.

[130] *Dobson* v. *Commissioner,* 320 U. S. 489. See Paul, *Dobson* v. *Commissioner: The Strange Ways of Law and Fact,* 57 Harv. L. Rev. 753.

[131] Section 36 of the Act of June 5, 1948, c. 646, 62 Stat. 870, 991, amending § 1141 (a), Internal Revenue Code, 1939 (now § 7482 (a), Internal Revenue Code, 1954).

[132] *Cuno Engineering Corp.* v. *Automatic Devices Corp.,* 314 U. S. 84, 91.

[133] 35 U.S.C. § 103. See the explanation of the section in the committee reports, H. R. Rep. 1923 and Sen. Rep. 1979, both 82d Cong., 2d sess. See also Federico, *Commentary on the New Patent Act,* pp. 19-23, at the front of the first volume of 35 USCA.

[134] 337 U. S. 55, and related cases: *Kilpatrick* v. *Texas & Pacific R. Co.,* 337 U. S. 75; *United States* v. *National City Lines,* 337 U. S. 78.

[135] 353 U. S. 222.

cuits with a holding that the same revision made no change in the venue provision governing patent infringement cases.

"Codification involves the apparent paradox that laws must be changed in form that they may remain unchanged in substance." [136] Where the reenactment includes a provision like that in the 1956 codification of Titles 10 and 32, to the effect that "it is the legislative purpose to restate, without substantive change, the law replaced by those sections on the effective date of this Act," [137] counsel is generally safe in ignoring mere changes in phraseology. Absent such a specific direction, however, every codification raises at least as many questions as it resolves—and thus breeds controversy and litigation.

One final (and perhaps unsettling) word: Don't overlook *Erie R. Co. v. Tompkins,*[138] which stands as authority for the proposition that even long-continued construction of a statutory provision will not be followed when further research shows that construction to be erroneous.

Section 57. Legislative history.—After the statute has been analyzed in its setting, the lawyer should routinely check its legislative history: successive drafts, committee reports, and the debates on the floor of Congress. Such material has now become more generally accessible to the bar through publication in a number of legislative services. In libraries, research is facilitated through reference to the "History of Bills and Resolutions" index of the Congressional Record, and by the fact that the later volumes of the Statutes at Large, beginning with volume 33, show the bill number of each act.

In England, it is still not permissible in ascertaining the meaning of a statute to look to any preliminary legislative materials.[139] The first relaxation of that rule in the United States, which came rather later in the day than most lawyers realize, was sensible

---

[136] H. R. Rep. 970, 84th Cong., 1st sess., p. 8; Sen. Rep. 2484, 84th Cong., 2d sess., p. 19. These were the committee reports on the revision of Titles 10 and 32, U.S.C., that was enacted in 1956.

[137] Sec. 49 (a) of the Act of August 10, 1956, c. 1041, 70A Stat. 640.

[138] 304 U. S. 64.

[139] See Allen, *Law in the Making* (6th ed. 1958) 476-480, 497-501; Holdsworth, *Some Makers of English Law* (1938) 294-296.

For an interesting criticism of the English practice, see Frankfurter, J., dissenting, in *Monia v. United States* 317 U. S. 424, 431-432. Cf. *Commissioner v. Acker,* 361 U. S. 87.

enough: where the language of a statute was doubtful, resort might be had to the committee reports and—but with qualifications—to the debates.[140] There were later clarifications, to the effect that little if any weight would be given to the remarks of members not in charge of the legislation.[141] In a sense, these were conventions, like all rules of statutory construction; the task was to ascertain the "intent" of Congress in a situation that Congress obviously did not have in mind when the act was passed. A court construing the statute was frequently in the position of the English judge in the not so apocryphal probate proceeding: "This will has no meaning but it is my duty to give it one."

Nonetheless, the conventions were observed, so that courts would be aloof from the conflicts of the political arena, and free from the cynical approach of "The purpose of the statute? Why, to gain votes, of course!"

In time, however, the emphasis came to be less and less on the language of the statute, and more and more on the legislative materials, in order to give effect to the "intent" of Congress. "When aid to construction of the meaning of words, as used in the statute, is available, there certainly can be no 'rule of law' which forbids its use, however clear the words may appear on 'superficial examination.' " [142] "The meaning to be ascribed to an Act of Congress can only be derived from a considered weighing of every relevant aid to construction." [143]

It is significant that both quotations are from cases decided on the same day in 1940 by five-to-four votes. With the adoption

---

[140] E.g., among the earlier cases, which consider committee reports, *Holy Trinity Church* v. *United States*, 143 U. S. 457, 464-465; *The Delaware*, 161 U. S. 459, 472; *Buttfield* v. *Stranahan*, 192 U. S. 470, 495; *Binns* v. *United States*, 194 U. S. 486, 495-496. One of the first cases to rely upon proceedings on the floor was *United States* v. *St. Paul, M. & M. Ry. Co.*, 247 U. S. 310, 316-318; but see the qualifications noted at p. 318.

For the prevailing practice in 1939-1949, see the list of "decisions during the past decade in which legislative history was decisive of construction of a particular statutory provision," in the opinion of Frankfurter, J., dissenting, in *Commissioner* v. *Estate of Church,* 335 U. S. 632, 667, 687-689.

See also, for the next epoch, *A Decade of Legislative History in the Supreme Court: 1950-1959,* 46 Va. L. Rev. 1408.

[141] E.g., *McCaughn* v. *Hershey Chocolate Co.,* 283 U. S. 488, 493-494, and cases there cited; *United States* v. *Wrightwood Dairy Co.,* 315 U. S. 110, 125.

[142] *United States* v. *American Trucking Ass'ns,* 310 U. S. 534, 543-544.

[143] *United States* v. *Dickerson,* 310 U. S. 554, 562.

of such a technique, of course, the floodgates were open, for the "considered weighing of every relevant aid" necessarily shifts the emphasis from "construction" to a consideration of desirability and of social and economic values. Preoccupation with legislative history and with the legislative debates inevitably draws courts into an evaluation of legislative, i.e., purely political, factors. For a considerable period, therefore, the conventional rules for ascertaining legislative intent were given less and less weight, and in the earlier version of this work, published in 1950, I wrote: "The dispassionate observer may well doubt whether, for instance, after the decisions in the *Jewell Ridge* portal-to-portal,[144] *Girouard*,[145] *Church*,[146] and *Spiegel*[147] cases, even strong legislative history has any meaning whenever a majority of the Supreme Court finds itself not in accord with that meaning—and a reading of the decisions just cited will show that this is not at all a facetious comment."

Each of those four cases has since been legislatively overruled, at least in part,[148] and probably nothing decided thereafter has been quite as extreme. The late Mr. Justice Jackson did a great deal to clear the atmosphere with characteristically pithy phrases in an endeavor to return the principal emphasis in interpretation to the language of the statute. "It is the business of Congress to sum up its own debates in the legislation. Moreover, it is only the words of the bill that have presidential approval, where that approval is given. It is not to be supposed that in signing a bill the President endorses the whole Congressional Record. For us to undertake to reconstruct an enactment from legislative history is merely to involve the Court in political controversies which are quite proper in the enactment of a bill but should have no place in

---

[144] *Jewell Ridge Corp.* v. *Local*, 325 U. S. 161.

[145] *Girouard* v. *United States*, 328 U. S. 61.

[146] *Commissioner* v. *Estate of Church*, 335 U. S. 632.

[147] *Estate of Spiegel* v. *Commissioner*, 335 U. S. 701.

[148] (a) *Jewell Ridge* was overruled by the Portal-to-Portal Act of [May 14,] 1947, c. 52, 61 Stat. 84, 29 U.S.C. §§ 251-262. (b) *Girouard* was overruled, at least in part, first by Sec. 29 of the Internal Security Act of 1950, c. 1024, 64 Stat. 987, 1017, which amended the oath provision (Sec. 335 (a) of the Nationality Act of 1940), and then again by Sec. 337 (a) of the Immigration and Nationality Act of 1952, c. 477, 66 Stat. 166, 258 (now 8 U.S.C. § 1448 (a)). See *Petition of Saccio*, 131 F. Supp. 154 (N.D. Calif.); *In re Krause's Petition*, 159 F. Supp. 687 (S.D. Ala.). (c) *Church* and *Spiegel* were overruled by Sec. 7 and 8 of the Act of Oct. 25, 1949, c. 720, 63 Stat. 891, 894-896.

its interpretation."[149] And again: "I should concur in this result more readily if the Court could reach it by analysis of the statute instead of by psychoanalysis of Congress."[150] Both excerpts are from concurring opinions, but a few years after his death the Court said, "But this is a case for applying the canon of construction of the wag who said, when the legislative history is doubtful, go to the statute."[151]

Perhaps the most amazing—or, if one prefers, amusing—instance of extreme reliance on interpretative materials in preference to the text sought to be construed occurred some years ago, when the Supreme Court changed one of the Federal Rules of Criminal Procedure, and a Court of Appeals had difficulty in understanding the change because "we have not the aid in interpretation of any history * * * or of any report of an Advisory Committee or other material for enlightenment."[152] This is reminiscent of the old-time British general who felt himself unable to direct his troops because of the absence of any staff officer who could sign the general's order.[153]

Of course there are still cases where some of the Justices feel that the Supreme Court has improperly followed the legislative history in preference to the statutory language, but in those instances the real issue that divided the Court was whether that language was in fact so plain as to preclude resort to legislative materials.[154]

And, needless to say, the days of "freewheeling"[155] in the in-

---

[149] *Schwegmann Bros. v. Calvert Distillers Corp.*, 341 U. S. 384, 395, 396. A few years earlier, Jackson, J., had made substantially similar comments in *Problems of Statutory Interpretation*, 8 F.R.D. 121, 123-126.

[150] *United States v. Public Utilities Comm.*, 345 U. S. 295, 319. See also the opinions of Jackson, J., in *United States v. Five Gambling Devices*, 346 U. S. 441, 450; and in *Adams v. Maryland*, 347 U. S. 179, 183-184. Cf. *A Re-Evaluation of the Use of Legislative History in the Federal Courts*, 52 Col. L. Rev. 125.

[151] *Greenwood v. United States*, 350 U. S. 366, 374.

[152] *United States v. Allied Stevedoring Corporation*, 235 F. 2d 909 (C.A. 2).

[153] This incident appears in one of the Boer War chapters of the memoirs of some British World War I commander. I read the book some twenty or more years ago, and regret that I cannot conveniently locate the reference any more exactly at this time.

[154] E.g., *Massachusetts Bonding Co. v. United States*, 352 U. S. 128; *Railway Labor Exec. Assn. v. United States*, 339 U. S. 142.

[155] Harlan, J., dissenting, in *Sinkler v. Missouri Pacific R. Co.*, 356 U. S. 326, 333.

terpretation of statutes are not over, especially where constitutional issues are involved,[156] where statutes that are penal in substance or effect are being construed,[157] and, probably, where the case turns on the FELA.[158] Every lawyer no doubt has his own list of famous—or infamous—instances where in his view undue liberties have been taken with a statute.[159] But it is a mistake to think that a return to the English rule of never looking at the legislative materials would solve our problems here. While the word "freewheeling" would probably never be found in any English opinion (or, more accurately, "judgment"), the process itself, according to an eminent authority, is one entirely familiar to English judges.[160]

At any rate, the advocate in the Federal courts whose case turns on a statute must, as a matter of invariable routine, check the legislative history. Of course, his technique will necessarily vary from case to case. When the language of the statute is your way and the legislative history is opposed, stress the statute; when the situation is reversed, stress the legislative history; when both are favorable, bear down on both—and when both are against you, talk about the "essential purpose" of the legislation, or stress whatever helpful tidbits you may have found in the hearings on the bill.[161] But don't go to the extent of relying on the courtroom tes-

---

[156] E.g., *Lee* v. *Madigan*, 358 U. S. 228; *Kent* v. *Dulles*, 357 U. S. 116.

[157] E.g., *Ladner* v. *United States*, 358 U. S. 169; *Bonetti* v. *Rogers*, 356 U. S. 691; *Yates* v. *United States*, 354 U. S. 298; *Bell* v. *United States*, 349 U. S. 81.

[158] See *Sinkler* v. *Missouri Pacific R. Co.*, 356 U. S. 326. For the time being, the easiest way to evaluate FELA cases in the Supreme Court is to regard them, for virtually every purpose, as *sui generis*. Cf. *Rogers* v. *Missouri Pacific R. Co.*, 352 U. S. 500; *Ringhiser* v. *Chesapeake & O. R. Co.*, 354 U.S. 901.

[159] My own list of particular pets not elsewhere cited includes, not necessarily in order, *Guessefeldt* v. *McGrath*, 342 U. S. 308; *Vermilya-Brown Co.* v. *Connell*, 335 U. S. 377; *United States* v. *duPont & Co.*, 353 U. S. 586; and *United States* v. *Carbone*, 327 U. S. 633. This listing, it should be understood, is representative rather than rigidly exclusive. I should note that the *Vermilya-Brown Co.* case has since been legislatively overruled by Sec. 1 (1) of the Act of August 30, 1957, Pub. L. 85-231, 71 Stat. 514, now 29 U.S.C. § 213 (f) .

[160] Allen, *Law in the Making* (6th ed. 1958) 489-491, 501-512.
The lawyer dealing with State statutes is similarly unencumbered, although for a different reason: "It's not too great an exaggeration to say that, compared to Federal legislation, available background materials on the intended meaning and proper interpretation of a New York statute are virtually zero." Dana, *Background Materials for Statutory Interpretation in New York*, 14 Record of the Ass'n of the Bar of the City of N. Y. 80.

[161] See Note, *Nonlegislative Intent as an Aid to Statutory Interpretation* (1949) 49 Col. L. Rev. 676. Compare note 164, below. For a striking and

timony of a legislator as to what he meant when he reported the bill—as counsel once tried to do in the Court of Claims.[162] Three additional suggestions may be made for cases susceptible to the more orthodox approach: (a) On particular occasions, the committee reports will be valueless—because later disavowed on the floor of Congress.[163] (b) Sometimes the pay dirt is in the reports that preceded the initiation of the legislation. Thus, some years back, the Ninth Circuit was reversed in its construction of the 1938 Amendments to the Bankruptcy Act, in large measure on the strength of the report of the National Bankruptcy Conference, which had proposed the amendment to Congress.[164] (c) Later legislation may be "considered to throw a cross light" [165] on what has gone before, and thus to confirm the earlier interpretation.[166] It is therefore well not to neglect the end of the story.

Section 58. Administrative materials.—Today's practitioner is far better off with respect to access to Federal regulations and similar administrative materials than was the lawyer of a generation ago. The fiasco of the Hot Oil Case,[167] which involved a prosecution for violation of a non-existent regulation, the provision alleged to have been violated having dropped out through an inadvertence in the process of renumbering an amendment thereto, evoked an outcry [168] that resulted in establishment of the Federal

---

perhaps extreme instance of reliance on matter contained in Congressional hearings, see *Shapiro v. United States*, 335 U. S. 1. Cf. *Galvan v. Press*, 347 U. S. 522.

[162] *National School of Aeronautics. Inc. v. United States*, 135 C. Cls. 343, 351-352, 142 F. Supp. 933, 938-939.

[163] *Chicago etc. R. Co. v. Acme Freight*, 336 U.,S. 465.

[164] *Goggin v. California Labor Div.*, 336 U. S. 118.

[165] L. Hand, J., in *United States v. Aluminum Co. of America*, 148 F. 2d 416, 429 (C.A.2).

[166] See *Cammarano v. United States*, 358 U. S. 498, 510.

[167] *Panama Refining Co. v. Ryan*, 293 U. S. 388.

[168] Griswold, *Government in Ignorance of the Law—A Plea for Better Publication of Executive Legislation*, 48 Harv. L. Rev. 198, written before but published simultaneously with the argument and before the decision in the Hot Oil Case, is the most significant article. Professor Griswold, as he then was, had just left the Solicitor General's Office, where of course the Hot Oil Case was pending.

The British, through the publication of *Statutory Rules and Orders*, had solved the problem of publishing executive legislation, but the mass of their parliamentary legislation is such that, even in recent years, there have been prosecutions for alleged violations of repealed statutes. See Allen, *Law in the Making* (6th ed. 1958) 427, n. 2.

Register.[169] Thereafter, all Federal regulations in force were collected in the Code of Federal Regulations, which has since been kept up to date,[170] and so now there is no danger of further hidden-ball plays; although to be sure, as the essentially emotional dissent in the *Merrill* case [171] teaches, there was for some time reluctance to apply the doctrine that publication of a regulation in the Federal Register binds all concerned quite as automatically as does passage of an Act of Congress.

But that doctrine can now hardly be questioned, and therefore in many Federal fields it is necessary for the practitioner always to check all of the pertinent directives promulgated pursuant to statutory authority, whether rules of court, reorganization plans, regulations, or administrative rulings. It is hardly necessary even to suggest such an obvious proposition to tax practitioners. Members of that segment of the bar have numerous excellent tax services at their disposal to keep them not only reasonably current in this respect but actually up-to-the-minute, and they are moreover thoroughly familiar with "the regulations problem" [172] and with the pain it has caused and is causing them and their clients. It is difficult to resist the conclusion that, to an extraordinary degree, the Supreme Court for the last twenty years or so has sustained the Treasury in almost every contest that turned on the validity of tax regulations,[173] even to the length of approving what can only be characterized as a *post litem motam* flip-flop.[174]

---

[169] Act of July 26, 1935, c. 417, 49 Stat. 500 (44 U.S.C. §§ 301-314).

[170] See Sec. 11 of the Act last cited, as amended and supplemented (44 U.S.C. §§ 311-311a); see also Ex. Order 9930, Feb. 4, 1948, 13 Fed. Reg. 519, set out after 44 USCA § 311.
See, however, p. 179, below.

[171] *Federal Crop Ins. Corp.* v. *Merrill*, 332 U. S. 380.

[172] See Griswold, *A Summary of the Regulations Problem*, 54 Harv. L. Rev. 398, and other articles cited at p. 398, note 1; Feller, *Addendum to the Regulations Problem, id.* at 1311; and Griswold, *Postscriptum, id.* at 1323.

[173] *Bingham's Trust* v. *Commissioner*, 325 U. S. 365, stands as a notable exception; but compare *Lykes* v. *United States*, 343 U. S. 118. The Treasury has also generally been sustained in its interpretations of equivocal regulations; here the taxpayers' few but for that reason well-known successes are *Commissioner* v. *Heininger*, 320 U. S. 467; *Lilly* v. *Commissioner*, 343 U. S. 90; *Commissioner* v. *Sullivan*, 356 U. S. 27; and *Commissioner* v. *Acker*, 361 U.S. 87.

[174] In *Cammarano* v. *United States*, 358 U. S. 498, which held not deductible as ordinary and necessary business expenses sums expended by taxpayers in appealing to the electorate to defeat an initiative measure that would have destroyed the taxpayers' business, petitioner relied heavily on *Luther Ely*

In many other fields, too, there are administrative rulings made by agencies and tribunals that operate in particular fields subject to Federal regulation. Many of these rulings are published in regular series of reports [175] and in numerous unofficial but entirely authoritative services.[176] The specialist concerned must of course refer constantly to all such materials, and indeed cannot afford to neglect any of them. For instance, although a former Chief Judge of the Tax Court wrote that memorandum decisions of that tribunal are not to be considered as precedents,[177] the Supreme Court recently relied on a Tax Court Memorandum to show that the Tax Court had abandoned an earlier and fully reported decision.[178]

Law officers' rulings may likewise be relevant; the most important of these are Opinions of the Attorney General, Decisions of the Comptroller General,[179] General Counsel's Memoranda in

---

Smith, 3 T. C. 696, which had permitted deduction of sums expended to promote adoption of a constitutional amendment that would have helped the taxpayer's business, and on the Commissioner's long acquiescence therein, 1944 Cum. Bull. 26. Fourteen years later—after certiorari was granted in the *Cammarano* case over the Government's opposition, 355 U. S. 952—the Commissioner withdrew his acquiescence in *Luther Ely Smith.* See 1958-1 Cum. Bull. 91, first published in *Int. Rev. Bull.,* No. 1958-21, May 26, 1958 at pp. 9, 16-17. Yet the Supreme Court in *Cammarano* appears to have put some store on this delayed-action somersault. See 358 U. S. at 507, note 10.

[175] The best known of these are the reports of the several regulatory commissions and boards, viz., Civil Aeronautics Board; Federal Communications Comm.; Federal Trade Comm.; Interstate Commerce Comm. (three series of reports) ; National Labor Relations Board; Securities and Exchange Comm.; and Tax Court, successor to the Board of Tax Appeals.

Other well known administrative series are the Official Gazette, U. S. Patent Office; Interior Decisions (following Land Decisions series without change of numbering) ; Treasury Decisions; and the Cumulative Bulletin.

A full listing of administrative reports up to 1950 will be found in Price and Bitner, *Effective Legal Research,* 415-420.

[176] E.g., Labor Relations Reporter (including NLRB decisions, Wage-Hour rulings, and decisions and awards of arbitrators) , and The United States Patents Quarterly. Both these series are published by BNA.

[177] Murdock, *What Has the Tax Court of the United States Been Doing?* 31 A.B.A.J. 297, 298-299.

[178] See *Cammarano v. United States,* 358 U. S. 498, 507, note 10, relying on *Mosby Hotel Co.,* P-H 1954 TC Mem. Dec. ¶ 54,288, to establish a change of view by the Tax Court following its decision in *Luther Ely Smith,* 3 T. C. 696.

[179] The Comptroller General's predecessor was the Comptroller of the Treasury, whose opinions were published in the Comp. Dec. for a number of years prior to 1921. Comparison of the *Comp. Dec.* with the *Comp. Gen.* leaves the distinct impression that the earlier series were better reasoned and far less arbitrary.

the *Treasury Decisions,* and, for any question of military law antedating the creation of the Court of Military Appeals in 1951, the
opinions of the service Judge Advocates General.[180]

Such rulings cannot be ignored by the brief-writer, because
frequently courts cite them in support of the result reached in
their opinions.[181] On other occasions, however, an unbroken series
of many rulings over a long period, even when duly cited and
pressed upon the court, will be completely ignored.[182] A somewhat
different situation is presented in the Court of Claims; there a
great deal of litigation involves the frank challenging, and indeed
the frequent overturning, of prior determinations made by the
Comptroller General on the precise demands that are in issue.[183]
It must always be borne in mind that all law officers' rulings are essentially *ex parte,* and that they are regularly made with an eye to
executive preferences. As a very wise and discerning lawyer of an
earlier day once remarked, every volume of the *Op. Att'y. Gen.*
carries on its title-page the unseen but nonetheless unmistakable
motto, "We strive to please." [184] Accordingly, the lawyer litigating
against the Government will not, realistically speaking, be very far

---

[180] See Mott, Hartnett, and Morton, *A Survey of the Literature of Military
Law—A Selective Bibliography,* 6 Vand. L. Rev. 333; Hartnett, *Survey Extended—The Literature of Military Law Since 1952,* 12 Vand. L. Rev. 361.

The two principal present sources of military rulings below the Court of
Military Appeals are the Court-Martial Reports (CMR), which contain opinions of Boards of Review of the several services, functioning under Art. 66,
UCMJ (10 U.S.C. § 866) ; and the Dig. Op. JAG, containing opinions of the
service Judge Advocates General.

[181] See, e.g., the following cases saying that the opinions of the Judge Advocate General of the Army on questions of military law are entitled to particular weight. *Hiatt* v. *Brown,* 339 U. S. 103, 109; *United States* v. *Cooke,*
336 U. S. 210, 216; cf. *Bowen* v. *Johnston,* 306 U. S. 19, 30.

[182] For nearly a hundred years, the Army had held that, when a military
person against whom charges are pending is separated from the service, not by
expiration of term of service, but by affirmative act of the Government, military jurisdiction ceases. Dig. Op. JAG (1912) 514; Dig. Op. JAG (1912-1940)
162-163; 5 Bull. JAG 35, ¶ 359 (6) ; *id.* 278, ¶ 407 (3) ; cf. *United States* v. *Sippel,* 4 USCMA 50, 53, 15 CMR 50, 53. But in the first opinion in *Reid* v.
Covert, 351 U. S. 487, 492, the Supreme Court held that "military jurisdiction,
once validly attached, continues until final disposition of the case."

[183] E.g., *Hamrick* v. *United States,* 120 C. Cls. 17, 96 F. Supp. 940 (cf. 30
Comp. Gen. 40). Cf. *Miguel* v. *McCarl,* 291 U. S. 442. Indeed, to cite "Court
of Claims Reports, *passim*" as authority for the statement in the text would not
be very wide of the mark.

[184] *Ex rel.* my former chief, Colonel Archibald King, U. S. Army, Retired,
who quoted his father, the late George A. King, Esq., of the District of Columbia Bar, to this effect.

in error if he treats law officers' rulings as being essentially in the nature of admissions against interest.

Where, however, a case turns on long-continued administrative practice that is not reflected in published services, or on a ruling or opinion that for some reason does not appear in the Federal Register,[185] or on any information peculiarly within the knowledge of the agency concerned,[186] the Government undoubtedly has the whip hand. Such materials are not normally available to outsiders, and where the documents in question are so old that they have been transferred to the National Archives, the obvious obstacle is that only a very few litigants are in a position to underwrite inquiry there.

Back in the days of the old Model T, a waggish fellow, seeing the report of a forfeiture case entitled *United States* v. *One Ford Automobile,* commented that this caption reflected a most unequal contest. Well, when a case turns on administrative materials, whether those are regulations or unwritten practice or the files that disclose a long-continued but little publicized course of governmental dealing, anyone litigating with the United States is similarly engaged in an unequal contest. Only in very limited areas have there been improvements and amelioration in the direction of spelling out for all to read matters that formerly rested in tradition.[187] By and large, this is a problem not easy of solution, particularly for the lawyer distant from the seat of government and whose client's means are limited.

Nor can I forbear to add that, on occasion, the use by the Gov-

---

[185] See in this connection Newman, *Government and Ignorance—A Progress Report on Publication of Federal Regulations,* 63 Harv. L. Rev. 929. See also, for a regulation not published in the Federal Register, *Seagrave* v. *United States,* 131 C. Cls. 790, 128 F. Supp. 400.

[186] E.g., material showing the administrative practice to recognize the right of a claimant to maintain an independent action after the President had rejected his claim under the Trading with the Enemy Act, supplied at the Court's request in Supplemental Memo for the Respondents, No. 325, Oct. T. 1941 (*Rodiek* v. *United States,* 315 U. S. 783, affirming by equally divided court 117 F. 2d 588 and 120 F. 2d 760 (C.A.2) (the Hackfeld case). See also note 189, *infra.*

[187] As Chief Justice Warren said to the American Law Institute regarding the 1954 revision of the Supreme Court's Rules, "Another objective was completeness and to that end there are included in the revision a number of subjects not covered by the old rules. If our aim in this regard has been achieved counsel need not resort to textbooks nor be reliant on the clerk's office for guidance to the extent theretofore necessary." Quoted 68 Harv. L. Rev. at 91. For the condition obtaining earlier, see *id.* at 36, and 38.

ernment of materials in its own files reflects—or, on the most charitable evaluation possible, appears to reflect—the triumph of
advocacy over accuracy. I have particular reference to *Reid* v. *Covert*,[188] a hard-fought and indeed bitterly-contested litigation in
which a good many of the Government's assertions concerning the
facts as to civilians accompanying the armed forces abroad proved
susceptible to successful contradiction [189]—but only because of the
happenstance that, by reason of military experience and associations, I was in a position to have knowledge of those facts. Inas-

---

[188] 354 U. S. 1, withdrawing earlier opinions at 351 U. S. 470 and 487.
[189] Here are just a few of the assertions involved.

(a) The Government pointed to the presence abroad of over 23,000
American citizen-employees accompanying the armed forces, and said, "All
these civilians are in foreign countries because the United States needs them
there for military reasons." U. S. Supp. Br. on Rehearing, 23-24.

The fact was that the reason for the presence of so many civilians was
budgetary rather than military, since the annual cost of a civilian employee is
normally considerably less than that of a man in uniform. Citations substan-
tiating the fact: H.R. Rep. 1545, 83d Cong., 2d sess., p. 16; Sec. 720 of the Defense Appropriation Act of June 30, 1954, c. 432, 68 Stat. 337, 354; *Department
of the Army Appropriations for 1956*, Hearings before * * * * Subcommittee of the House Committee on Appropriations, 84th Cong., 1st sess., pp. 4, 74,
296-297, 459-463, 1124-1126; *Army Information Digest*, April 1955, p. 47; *Department of the Army Appropriations for 1957*, Hearings, &c., 84th Cong.,
2d sess., pp. 156, 316-318.

(b) The Government argued (Point IIB, U. S. Supp. Br. 57-61) that "As
to offenses which are not crimes under the law of the foreign state, but are
crimes only under American military law, the alternative to court-martial
jurisdiction is no trial at all."

The fact was that the Department of Defense employed over 76,000 non-
American civilians in foreign countries, and that it contracted with foreign
countries for the services of 275,000 additional non-American civilians. U. S.
Civil Service Comm., Federal Employment Statistics Bull., Oct. 1956, p. 9;
103 Cong. Rec. 667-670. Since these 350,000 foreigners were plainly not subject to trial by American court-martial, why would security and discipline be
safe from them but in jeopardy from the 23,000 Americans if the latter were
not subject to American military law?

(c) The Government argued (U. S. Supp. Br. 25-26) that "All civilians
who accompany the armed forces overseas are so closely identified with those
forces as to be indistinguishable from them for all practical purposes."

The fact was that under the NATO and NATO-like arrangements the
United States had already conceded to the receiving states primary jurisdiction
over all crimes committed by civilian dependents. Art. VII (3) (a) and (b),
NATO Status of Forces Agreement (TIAS 2846). In other words, the Government itself had solemnly recognized a distinction between the several groups
involved. (In its Reply Brief on Rehearing, p. 68, note 47a, the Government
said that its negotiators had sought primary jurisdiction over dependents, but
had failed to obtain it. A more lame excuse for failure to disclose a significant
point would be difficult to duplicate.)

much as my clients ultimately prevailed, the foregoing observations are not subject to the discount normally applicable to post-mortem recriminations made by the licked lawyer. But I shudder to think what the position of a litigant similarly situated would have been, whose counsel, however more talented he may have been in every other respect, still chanced not to have had that specialized knowledge.

Section 59. Use of essentially historical materials.—Mr. Justice Holmes, who more than most judges before or since understood both the value and the limitations of historical learning, remarked on different occasions that "historic continuity with the past is not a duty, it is only a necessity," [190] and that "It is revolting to have no better reason for a rule than that it was so laid down in the time of Henry IV." [191]

Legal history in its purely antiquarian aspects will have but few uses for the lawyer. But since there are so many terms in the Constitution of the United States that would be meaningless without a thorough grounding in the common law,[192] and since constitutional law accordingly presupposes an understanding of the common law,[193] historical materials, including the earliest cases, may sometimes be controlling, will generally be helpful—and will always be suggestive.

A number of instances of the effective use of such materials come to mind. Undoubtedly the classic instance of a change of decision in consequence of more accurate historical knowledge was *Vidal* v. *Girard's Executors,*[194] where the Supreme Court modified its earlier decision in *Baptist Ass'n* v. *Hart's Executors* [195] and up-

---

[190] Holmes, *Learning and Science,* in *Collected Legal Papers,* 138, 139. See also *Law in Science and Science in Law, id.* 210, 211: "* * * continuity with the past is only a necessity and not a duty."

[191] Holmes, *The Path of the Law,* in *Collected Legal Papers,* 187. See *United States* v. *Dege,* 364 U. S. 51, which turned on the applicability of the quotation in the text.

[192] See, in this connection, as required reading, the illuminating comments of Jackson, J., concurring, in *D'Oench, Duhme & Co.* v. *Federal Deposit Ins. Corp.,* 315 U. S. 447, 465, 470-471.

[193] "* * * the provisions of the Constitution are not mathematical formulas having their essence in their form; they are organic living institutions transplanted from English soil. Their significance is vital not formal; it is to be gathered not simply by taking the words and a dictionary, but by considering their origin and the line of their growth." *Gompers* v. *United States,* 233 U. S. 604, 610 *(per* Holmes, J.).

[194] 2 How. 127.

[195] 4 Wheat. 1.

held the charitable trust established by Stephen Girard's will, on the strength of then recent publications of the Record Commissioners of England which demonstrated that the English Court of Chancery had entertained jurisdiction over charitable trusts long before the Statute of 43 Elizabeth I.[196]

But there are modern examples also. In *United States v. Wood* [197] the question was whether Congress could constitutionally provide, consistently with the Sixth Amendment's guaranty of trial "by an impartial jury," that Government employees not shown to be actually biased might sit on juries in criminal cases in the District of Columbia. An earlier case in point apparently barred the way.[198] But the Government's brief, which collected and discussed all the early English authorities on the point, some of them from the era of black-letter folios,[199] demonstrated that King's servants were not ineligible *per se* as a matter of common law. The Supreme Court was persuaded by these authorities, and disapproved its earlier decision.[200]

In the *Haupt* treason case,[201] the basic question was whether the constitutional command that "No Person shall be convicted of Treason unless on the Testimony of two Witnesses to the same overt Act" [202] required that "Testimony" to be eyewitness testi-

---

[196] For an interesting instance of a State decision turning on historical fact, see Dumbauld, *A Manuscript from Monticello: Jefferson's Library in Legal History*, 38 A.B.A.J. 389.

[197] 299 U. S. 123.

[198] *Crawford v. United States,* 212 U. S. 183.

[199] All the matter in law French was, however, duly translated into English in the Government's brief. See Brief for the United States, No. 34, Oct. T. 1936.

For cases where the opinion of a modern court relies upon and quotes from the Year Books in the original black-letter law French, see *Dyson v. Rhode Island Company*, 25 R. I. 600, 57 Atl. 771, and *Stevens v. Union Railroad Company*, 26 R. I. 90, 58 Atl. 492. The Rhode Island reports, according to local tradition, had to have a new font of type set on this occasion; the National Reporter System compromised on plain roman, plus some typographical dashes and flourishes.

See Winfield, *The Chief Sources of English Legal History* (1925) 172, n. 5, for modern English instances of citations from the Year Books.

[200] The *Wood* case is still law, although expressions in later decisions have questioned the soundness—and fairness—of its result. See *Frazier v. United States*, 335 U. S. 497; *Dennis v. United States* 339 U. S. 162; *Morford v. United States*, 339 U. S. 258. See also the comments in Goebel, *Constitutional History and Constitutional Law*, 38 Col. L. Rev. 555, especially at 576-577.

[201] *Haupt v. United States*, 330 U. S. 631.

[202] U. S. Const., Art. III, Sec. 3.

mony, or "direct testimony," or whether, if the latter, it excluded any testimony that as a matter of ordinary speech might be considered circumstantial. In order to resolve this question, the Government's brief traced the two-witnesses requirement in treason cases back to the Statute of 7 & 8 Will. III, c. 3, which settled that requirement in the English law for 250 years,[203] and took up and discussed, from the proceedings set forth in Howell's *State Trials*, the rulings under that statute in English treason trials antedating the American Revolution. It then turned to the earliest American trials on the same point. The Government argued, on the basis of these historical materials, that the constitutional requirement did not render insufficient testimony that required some interpretation;[204] and the Supreme Court agreed.

Resort to the reports in Howell's *State Trials* was likewise had in the *Harris* search and seizure case,[205] to show that a search of premises incident to an arrest represented an existing and widespread practice in England that was unaffected by Lord Camden's ruling in *Entick* v. *Carrington*[206]—and reference was made to reports in the *American State Trials* to show that the practice had never theretofore been deemed affected by American constitutional provisions.[207] The Supreme Court agreed, although, as has already been noted in the preceding chapter (Section 30), later decisions since then may well have undermined the present authority of the *Harris* case. Indeed, there have been later decisions which appear to suggest that the very concept of Due Process of

---

[203] The two witness requirement was repealed by the St. 8 & 9 Geo. VI, c. 44 (The Treason Act, 1945), which seems to have been passed to reach the case of Lord Haw Haw. See J. W. Hall, ed., *Trial of William Joyce*, pp. 12-14, 16. Joyce was brought to England from Germany the day after the Treason Act, 1945, received Royal assent. Cf. *Joyce* v. *Director of Public Prosecutions*, [1946] A.C. 347.

[204] See Brief for the United States, No. 49, Oct. T. 1946, at 57-98, set forth at pp. 350-369 of the earlier version of this work.

[205] *Harris* v. *United States*, 331 U. S. 145.

[206] 19 How. St. Tr. 1029.

[207] *Trial of Patrick Hart*, 26 How. St. Tr. 388, 396; *Trial of Henry and John Sheares*, 27 How. St. Tr. 255, 321; *Trial of Arthur Thistlewood*, 33 How. St. Tr. 682, 811-812; *Trial of James Ings*, 33 How. St. Tr. 957, 1047; *Trial of Levi and Laban Kenniston*, 14 Am. St. Tr. 237, 244 (Mass.); *Trial of Richard P. Robinson*, 12 Am. St. Tr. 426, 446 (N. Y.); *Trial of John C. Colt*, 1 Am. St. Tr. 455, 469 (N. Y.); *Trial of Rev. George W. Carawan*, 6 Am. St. Tr. 514, 533 (N. C.); *Trial of Emma Cunningham*, 5 Am. St. Tr. 90, 123 (N. Y.). For the modern English law on the point, see *Dillon* v. *O'Brien*, 20 L. R. Ir. 300, 16 Cox C. C. 245; *Elias* v. *Pasmore*, [1934] 2 K. B. 164.

Law is now deemed to include a constitutional guaranty of privacy.[208]

However, even when they do not find their way into the decision or even into the *ratio decidendi* of the decision, historical materials are at least suggestive and hence helpful to the advocate. I found this to be so in the case of *Wade* v. *Hunter*,[209] which involved the right of the Army to try a soldier by a second court-martial after the partially tried case had been withdrawn from the first court-martial when the tactical situation—in this instance the final advance into Germany in the spring of 1945—made it impracticable to continue the original trial.

The question was whether the second trial improperly subjected Wade to double jeopardy, and the case turned largely on the difference between the provisions of the Fifth Amendment, "nor shall any person be subject for the same offense to be twice put in jeopardy of life or limb," and those of the then 40th Article of War, "No person shall, without his consent, be tried a second time for the same offense * * * ."[210]

Clearly, under the remaining portions of Article of War 40, Wade had not been "tried"; [211] had he, however, been "put in jeopardy"? The Supreme Court had early ruled that the Fifth Amendment did not preclude a second trial in a criminal case after the first trial had terminated in a disagreement by the jury.[212] But the lower courts in more recent cases had been applying a rather mechanical rule, to the effect that "jeopardy" attached once evidence was heard,[213] or even after the jury had been sworn, in a situation where the prosecutor failed to have his witnesses present.[214] An early case was most helpful in resolving this apparent conflict;

---

[208] See *McDonald* v. *United States*, 335 U. S. 451, 453; *Wolf* v. *Colorado*, 338 U. S. 25, 27-28; cf. Clark, J., concurring in *Irvine* v. *California*, 347 U. S. 128, 138-139. See also *Elkins* v. *United States*, 364 U. S. 206.

[209] 336 U. S. 684, affirming 169 F. 2d 973 (C.A. 10).

[210] 10 U.S.C. [1926-1946 eds.] § 1511. The words quoted in the text were derived from the original formulation in Article of War 87 of 1806, 2 Stat. 369.

[211] "* * * but no proceeding in which an accused has been found guilty by a court-martial upon any charge or specification shall be held to be a trial in the sense of this article until the reviewing and, if there be one, the confirming authority shall have taken final action upon the case."

[212] *United States* v. *Perez*, 9 Wheat. 579.

[213] *Clawans* v. *Rives*, 104 F. 2d 240 (App. D. C.) ; *McCarthy* v. *Zerbst*, 85 F. 2d 640 (C.A. 10). See, however, for a broader view, *Pratt* v. *United States*, 102 F. 2d 275 (App. D. C.).

[214] *Cornero* v. *United States*, 48 F. 2d 69 (C.A.9).

there Mr. Justice Washington, who had been a contemporary of the Framers, had said,

> * * * we are clearly of opinion, that the *jeopardy* spoken of in this article [Fifth Amendment] can be interpreted to mean nothing short of the acquittal or conviction of the prisoner, and the judgment of the court thereupon. This was the meaning affixed to the expression by the common law. * * * the moment it is admitted that in cases of necessity the court is authorized to discharge the jury, the whole argument for applying this article of the constitution to a discharge of the jury before conviction and judgment is abandoned, because the exception of necessity is not to be found in any part of the constitution; and I should consider this court as stepping beyond its duty in interpolating it into that instrument, if the article of the constitution is applicable to a case of this kind. We admit the exception, but we do it because that article does not apply to a jeopardy short of conviction.[215]

The *Wade* case was decided, both in the Tenth Circuit and by the Supreme Court, on the scope of the necessity exception and not on any interpretation of "jeopardy," but I found the early decisions extremely suggestive and helpful when I briefed and argued the case in the intermediate court.[216]

Right here I will digress to draw the attention of brief-writers to the mine of material available in the *Federal Cases*—the old circuit court decisions that antedate the Federal Reporter. Many of them, of course, are of only antiquarian interest today. But others are highly authoritative, for two reasons. First, they reflect the constitutional views of judges whose lives, frequently, were contemporaneous with the framing and ratification of the Constitution. Second, they were in large measure the work of the Supreme Court justices riding circuit, and so are regarded as more authori-

---

[215] *United States* v. *Haskell*, 4 Wash. C. C. 402, 410-411, Fed. Case No. 15321, 26 Fed. Cas. at 212 (C.C.E.D.Pa.) . See also *United States* v. *Watkins*, 2 Cranch C. C. 441, 570, Fed. Case No. 16649, 28 Fed. Cas. at 479 (C.C.D.C.) .

[216] Extensive research since then has disclosed that Presidents Monroe and J. Q. Adams, both of whom witnessed the adoption of the Bill of Rights, considered cases of double jeopardy at military law wholly apart from, and without any reference to, the Fifth Amendment. See my paper on *Courts-Martial and the Bill of Rights: The Original Practice*, 72 Harv. L. Rev. 1, 266, at 272-277.

The present law, Article 44 (c) of the Uniform Code of Military Justice, now 10 U.S.C. § 844 (c) , may or may not involve a legislative overruling of the *Wade* case. Cf. Sen. Rep. 486, 81st Cong., 1st sess., at 20. The provision in the current *Manual for Courts-Martial*, U. S. 1951, ¶ 56*b*, is a magnificent straddle.

tative than the run of what today one finds in F. 2d. To a surprising degree, decisions in the Supreme Court, even today, rely or even turn upon what one of the worthies of old said or decided while circuit riding.[217]

A mass of historical materials was likewise adduced in *Reid* v. *Covert* [218] to throw light on two questions. One of these concerned the origins of the consular jurisdiction, a search that extended into deep antiquity; the problem was the evaluation of the weight of *In re Ross;* [219] see pp. 157-158, *supra*. The other question concerned the extent to which court-martial jurisdiction had in fact been exercised over civilians in England and in the United States in the late Eighteenth Century. That inquiry required resort to unpublished opinions and to records of trial in the National Archives.[220]

History is important and indeed sometimes controlling in constitutional litigation, essentially because, as the Supreme Court has several times said, "We do not write upon a clean slate." [221] But if the advocate's presentation of history is to be of any value to the tribunal, it must be both accurate and reliable. The kind of "history" that passes muster before the ladies of a local genealogical group seeking to be reassured regarding the virtues of their forbears can hardly be expected to overwhelm opposing counsel who has even a modicum of historical appreciation, let alone persuade a sophisticated tribunal. And the lawyer dealing with historical materials must constantly be on guard against the dangers

---

[217] *Mitchell* v. *Trawler Racer, Inc.*, 362 U. S. 539, 543-545, 556; *United States* v. *Isthmian S. S. Co.*, 359 U. S. 314, 320; *Bartkus* v. *Illinois*, 359 U. S. 121, 160; *Abbate* v. *United States*, 359 U. S. 187, 193; *Green* v. *United States*, 356 U. S. 165, 186; *Green* v. *United States*, 355 U. S. 184, 202-204; *Costello* v. *United States*, 350 U. S. 359, 362-363; *Quinn* v. *United States*, 349 U. S. 155, 168; *Bisso* v. *Inland Waterways Corp.*, 349 U. S. 85, 101-103; *National City Bank* v. *Republic of China*, 348 U. S. 356, 358, 365; *United States* v. *Morgan*, 346 U. S. 502, 507, 509-510, 515; *United States* v. *Real Estate Boards*, 339 U. S. 485, 490-491; *Farrell* v. *United States*, 336 U. S. 511, 513, 522, 523; *United States* v. *Summerlin*, 310 U. S. 414, 417-418.

[218] 354 U. S. 1.

[219] 140 U. S. 453.

[220] The briefs for the relators in *Kinsella* v. *Singleton*, 361 U. S. 234, and *Wilson* v. *Bohlender*, 361 U. S. 281, likewise reflected extensive references to and quotations from manuscript materials in the National Archives, in the Library of the U. S. Military Academy at West Point, and in the Library of the Historical Society of Pennsylvania at Philadelphia.

[221] *Green* v. *United States*, 356 U. S. 165, 187; *Lee* v. *Madigan*, 358 U. S. 228, 232; *Abbate* v. *United States*, 359 U. S. 187, 190.

of "aftermindedness," [222] of attributing to the past ideas not formulated until the present.[223]

When a court, particularly the Supreme Court, declares the law, all are bound thereby. But judges have no such authority with respect to history. Mr. Justice Jackson, in one of his most incisive judicial comments said, "We are not final because we are infallible, but we are infallible only because we are final." [224] That observation may well be true as to law (including therein constitutional law), but in the field of history neither the Supreme Court nor any other tribunal has similar authority; in that realm a judicial opinion has neither finality nor infallibility.

The truth of historical assertions depends on facts and on facts alone, as these are evidenced and established by actual documents. And where the advocate in his role of historian finds that historical assumptions in earlier opinions are not well grounded, and he then presents new or additional evidence that requires a contrary conclusion, he is not asking the court to overrule itself on a question of law (compare Sections 35 (e) and 53, *supra*) ; he is urging the tribunal to arrive at a different conclusion on a more complete and hence different record—just as the Supreme Court did in *Vidal v. Girard's Executors*,[225] in *United States v. Wood*,[226] and in *Erie R. Co. v. Tompkins*.[227]

Section 60. Use of noncase materials.—The successful advocate is not limited to decisions and statutes, the latest case turned up in the digests, the most recent regulation spawned by a restless bureaucracy, or the last amendment adopted by the legislature. He is free to seek other materials to buttress his arguments, and will frequently find it helpful to do so. There will be discussed be-

---

[222] Cam, *Introduction*, in *Selected Historical Essays of F. W. Maitland* (1957) xix.

[223] "But if Maitland brought law to bear on history, he brought history to bear on law. Again and again he emphasized the danger of imposing legal concepts of a later date on facts of an earlier date—a common fault, before his time, of the majority of legal historians and of many constitutional historians. We must not read either law or history backwards. We must learn to think the thoughts of a past age—'the common thoughts of our forefathers about common things.' 'We must not attribute precise ideas or well defined law to the German conquerors of Britain.' It is as if 'we armed Hengist and Horsa with machine guns or pictured the Venerable Bede correcting proofs.' " *Id.* at xi.

[224] *Brown* v. *Allen*, 344 U. S. 443, 532, 540 (concurring opinion) .

[225] 2 How. 127.

[226] 299 U. S. 123.

[227] 304 U. S. 64; see Section 62 at p. 199, below.

low, not at all exhaustively, the employment of noncase materials as authorities.

(a) *Economic and sociological materials; the Brandeis brief.* The classic instance of the use of economic and sociological materials in constitutional litigation, half a century ago, was in *Muller* v. *Oregon*,[228] which sustained the validity of a state statute limiting the hours of labor for women. There Mr. Louis D. Brandeis, as he then was, filed a brief in which he collected a list of similar state and foreign statutes; "extracts from over ninety reports of committees, bureaus of statistics, commissioners of hygiene, inspectors of factories, both in this country and in Europe, to the effect that long hours of labor are dangerous for women, primarily because of their special physical organization"; and "extracts from similar reports discussing the general benefits of short hours from an economic aspect of the question," [229] all in support of the proposition that the legislation in question bore a reasonable relationship to the public health and safety—admittedly valid exercises of the police power. His success in that case, and the approbation that the brief received in the unanimous opinion written by that rugged apostle of *laissez faire*, Brewer, J., led to increasing use of the same technique in other cases.[230]

Perhaps the most expert development of what accordingly came to be known as the Brandeis brief was presented in *Adkins* v. *Children's Hospital*[231] and the *Gold Clause*[232] and *AAA*

---

228 208 U. S. 412.

229 208 U. S. 420, note.

230 E.g., *Bunting* v. *Oregon*, 243 U. S. 426; *Stettler* v. *O'Hara*, 243 U. S. 629; *Adkins* v. *Children's Hospital*, 261 U. S. 525; see Biklé, *Judicial Determination of Questions of Facts Affecting the Constitutional Validity of Legislative Action*, 38 Harv. L. Rev. 6; Freund, *On Understanding the Supreme Court*, 86-92.

231 261 U. S. 525. In this instance, the brief was notably unsuccessful. "It is said that great benefits have resulted from the operation of such statutes, not alone in the District of Columbia but in the several States, where they have been in force. A mass of reports, opinions of special observers and students of the subject, and the like, has been brought before us in support of this statement, all of which we have found interesting but only mildly persuasive." 261 U. S. at 560, *per* Sutherland, J. Compare Powell, *The Judiciality of Minimum-Wage Legislation*, 37 Harv. L. Rev. 545.

232 *Norman* v. *Baltimore & O. R. Co.* and *United States* v. *Bankers Trust Co.*, 294 U. S. 240; *Nortz* v. *United States*, 294 U. S. 317; *Perry* v. *United States*, 294 U. S. 330; dissenting opinion, *sub nom. Gold Clause Cases*, 294 U. S. at 361.

The brief for the Government in *United States* v. *Bankers Trust Co.*, Nos.

cases,[233] though it may be that those decisions, equally with the later ones in *West Coast Hotel Co.* v. *Parrish*,[234] and the several decisions upholding the National Labor Relations Act [235] and the Social Security Act,[236] were influenced less by what was collected

---

471-472, Oct. T. 1934, contained some 50 pages of economic materials (pp. 18-68) under these headings:

"2. There was a reasonable basis for Congressional determination that the gold clause is contrary to public policy, inconsistent with our present monetary system, and an obstruction to the exercise by Congress of its monetary and other powers.

*   *   *   *   *

"B. The gold clause is an obstruction to the exercise of the powers of the Congress, as shown by its bearing upon recent legislation designed to cope with the monetary and financial crisis."

[233] *United States* v. *Butler*, 297 U. S. 1.

At pp. 179-227 of the Government's brief (No. 401, Oct. T. 1935) it was argued that "The expenditures authorized by the Agricultural Adjustment Act were soundly designed to promote the general welfare." The Appendix to the brief contained, *inter alia*, statements by Secretaries of Agriculture concerning the problems of agricultural surpluses (pp. 70-76); annual average indexes of "real" pay rolls in specified industries in relation to 1929 (pp. 77-78); and foreign laws (1) limiting production of agricultural commodities, (2) affecting agricultural prices on acquisition of agricultural commodities, (3) imposing taxes upon the processing of agricultural commodities to raise revenue for the aid of agriculture and other purposes, and (4) providing for subsidies or other payments in aid of agriculture (pp. 79-100).

[234] 300 U. S. 379.

[235] *Labor Board* v. *Jones & Laughlin*, 301 U. S. 1; *Labor Board* v. *Fruehauf Co.*, 301 U. S. 49; *Labor Board* v. *Clothing Co.*, 301 U. S. 58; dissenting opinion, *sub nom. Labor Board Cases*, 301 U. S. at 76; *Associated Press* v. *Labor Board*, 301 U. S. 103; *Washington Coach Co.* v. *Labor Board*, 301 U. S. 142.

At pp. 40-69 of the Government's brief in the *Associated Press* case (No. 365, Oct. T. 1936), the contention that "Subsections (1) and (3) of Section 8 of the [National Labor Relations] Act, as applied to interstate enterprises, bear a reasonable and direct relation to the protection of interstate commerce from the burden of industrial strife, and consequently are a valid exercise of the commerce power," was documented by a mass of nonlegal materials, collected by economists of the Labor Board, who were named.

Similar materials, similarly collected, were set out at pp. 21-31 of the Government's brief in the *Jones & Laughlin* case (No. 419, Oct. T. 1936), under the heading, "The burden and injury to interstate commerce resulting from industrial strife."

[236] *Carmichael* v. *Southern Coal Co.*, 301 U. S. 495; *Steward Machine Co.* v. *Davis*, 301 U. S. 548; *Helvering* v. *Davis*, 301 U. S. 619.

In the *Steward Machine Co.* case (No. 837, Oct. T. 1936), which involved the validity of Title IX of the Social Security Act, it was argued that "This taxing statute was enacted because of the drain which unemployment had made, and was likely to make in the future, upon the revenues of the nation." The nonlegal material, with due acknowledgments for research assistance, was collected at pp. 9-29 of the Government's brief, under the heading, "The cir-in the winning briefs than by other less strictly scientific considerations. As one of losing counsel in the 1936 New York minimum wage case [237] remarked in 1937, after the *West Coast Hotel* decision had been announced, "Better a poor argument after election than a good one before it." Nonetheless, the Brandeis brief still has a considerable field for usefulness, even in today's climate of constitutional opinion. Thus, in the cases that refused enforcement to restrictive covenants,[238] the Attorney General and Solicitor General of the United States filed a comprehensive brief that included full references to discussions of the social and economic effects of such covenants. And in the case upholding the constitutionality of the anti-communist affidavit provision of the Taft-Hartley Act,[239] the brief in support of the statute collected a vast mass of nonlegal materials showing the reasonable basis for the view that neither the policies of the National Labor Relations Act nor the security interests of the country would be fostered by extending the benefits of the latter Act to labor organizations whose officers were Communists or supporters of Communist-dominated organizations.

(b) *Defense against improper use of economic and sociological materials.* Most imitations are inferior to the original, and numerous imitators of the Brandeis technique have perverted it to improper uses, using noncase materials in situations where they are irrelevant, and drawing those materials from unreliable sources. In any situation where an advocate is faced with what can only be called a pseudo-Brandeis brief, his best—indeed, his only —defense is to emphasize the limitations that surround the use of sociological and economic authorities.

First of all, the Brandeis brief is properly used only in situa-

---

cumstances which 'furnish the occasion for the exercise of power' conferred upon Congress by Article I, Section 8, Clause 1, of the Constitution." The quotation was from the opinion of the Court, *per* Hughes, C. J., in the Minnesota mortgage moratorium case, *Home Bldg. & L. Assn.* v. *Blaisdell,* 290 U. S. 398, 426. Additional economic statistics were set out at pp. 64-77 of a separately bound Appendix.

In *Helvering* v. *Davis* (No. 910, Oct. T. 1936), in support of the contention that "The old age benefit payments contemplated by Title II will promote the general welfare of the United States," the nonlegal materials, duly acknowledged, were collected at pp. 49-74 of petitioners' brief under the heading, "The problem of old-age dependency."

[237] *Morehead* v. *New York ex rel. Tipaldo,* 298 U. S. 587.

[238] *Shelley* v. *Kraemer,* 334 U. S. 1; *Hurd* v. *Hodge,* 334 U. S. 24.

[239] *American Communications Assn.* v. *Douds,* 339 U. S. 382.

tions where there is wide scope for legislative judgment, where "the guaranty of due process * * * demands only that the law shall not be unreasonable, arbitrary or capricious, and that the means selected shall have a real and substantial relation to the object sought to be attained." [240] In the words of Professor (now Mr. Justice) Frankfurter, written in 1931,

Until [Brandeis'] famous brief in *Muller* v. *Oregon,* social legislation was supported before the courts largely *in vacuo*—as an abstract dialectic between "liberty" and "police power," unrelated to a world of trusts and unions, of large-scale industry and all its implications. In the *Oregon* case, the facts of modern industry which provoke regulatory legislation were, for the first time, adequately marshalled before the Court. It marks an epoch in the disposition of cases presenting the most important present-day constitutional issues.[241]

Otherwise stated, the Brandeis brief is appropriate "where constitutional grants and limitations of power are set forth in general clauses, which afford a broad outline," but not "when the provisions of the Constitution, in grant or restriction, are specific, so particularized as not to admit of construction." [242]

Thus, while general concepts of reasonableness are sufficient to sustain many aspects of State criminal procedure against attack based on the Due Process clause of the Fourteenth Amendment— e.g., substituting information for indictment,[243] providing a jury of less than 12 in criminal cases [244] or providing for a majority verdict in such cases,[245] permitting the prosecution to comment on the defendant's failure to testify,[246] granting the prosecution an appeal in criminal cases,[247] introducing new concepts of double jeopardy,[248] and permitting the use of illegally obtained evidence [249]— no amount of demonstrable reasonableness would sustain similar

---

[240] *Nebbia* v. *New York,* 291 U. S. 502, 525.

[241] Frankfurter, *Mr. Justice Brandeis and the Constitution,* 45 Harv. L. Rev. 33, 37, reprinted in Frankfurter, ed., *Mr. Justice Brandeis,* 49, 52.

[242] Both quotations are from *Home Bldg. & L. Assn.* v. *Blaisdell,* 290 U. S. 398, 426, *per* Hughes, C. J.

[243] *Hurtado* v. *California,* 110 U. S. 516.

[244] *Maxwell* v. *Dow,* 176 U. S. 581.

[245] *Jordan* v. *Massachusetts,* 225 U. S. 167, 176.

[246] *Twining* v. *New Jersey,* 211 U. S. 78; *Adamson* v. *California,* 332 U. S. 46.

[247] *Palko* v. *Connecticut,* 302 U. S. 319.

[248] *Brock* v. *North Carolina,* 344 U. S. 424.

[249] *Wolf* v. *Colorado,* 338 U. S. 25.

Federal action in the face of the specific and explicit limitations of the Bill of Rights. It is for this reason that the existence of foreign legislation, which assists in establishing the reasonableness of domestic legislation challenged on due process grounds,[250] failed completely to persuade in three recent cases of military jurisdiction, which turned on specific constitutional prohibitions.[251] In that field, reasonableness in the abstract is of no help; [252] resort must be had to history and practice.[253]

Second, the Brandeis type of brief perverts the most deeply held convictions of its originator when it is used to assemble data showing or tending to show that the law under consideration is unwise or unsound; such arguments are only appropriate when addressed to the legislature.[254]

----

[250] See notes 229-233, *supra.*

[251] Thus, in *United States* v. *Cooke,* 336 U. S. 210, where the Court held that a discharge followed by reenlistment barred trial by court-martial in the subsequent enlistment for an offense alleged to have been committed in the earlier one, the Government cited English statutes to the contrary (Resp. Br., No. 231, Oct. T. 1948, p. 13, n. 4), but without avail. In *Toth* v. *Quarles,* 350 U. S. 11, which held unconstitutional Art. 3 (a), UCMJ (now 10 U.S.C. § 803 (a)), the provision that purported to make discharged servicemen amenable to military law in respect of serious offenses committed while in service for which they could not be tried in any American court, state or federal, the Government similarly invoked, though persuading only the dissenting justices (350 U. S. at 29-31, note 11), British, Canadian, Australian, and New Zealand statutes similar to Art. 3 (a). See Resp. Br., No. 3, Oct. T. 1955, pp. 29-30, note 13. Likewise, in *Reid* v. *Covert,* 354 U. S. 1, which held unconstitutional the military trials of civilian dependents charged with capital offenses, the majority of the Court was not persuaded by the fact that the British Parliament had recently extended military jurisdiction to civilians accompanying the forces abroad (U. S. Supp. Br. on Rehearing; Nos. 701 and 713, Oct. T. 1955, p. 50). See, however, the opinion of Harlan, J., 354 U. S. at 71, note 9.

[252] Cf. Harlan, J., concurring in *Reid* v. *Covert,* 354 U. S. at 66-67.

[253] See, e.g., *Ex parte Quirin,* 317 U. S. 1 (extensive consideration of the history and practice of trying offenders against the laws of war by military tribunals); *District of Columbia* v. *Colts,* 282 U. S. 63 (what petty offenses fall outside the constitutional guaranty of jury trials?); *District of Columbia* v. *Clawans,* 300 U. S. 617 (same); cf. *United States* v. *Wood,* 299 U. S. 123, discussed above, Section 59, p. 182.

[254] "If the proponents of union-security agreements have confidence in the arguments addressed to the Court in their 'economic brief,' they should address those arguments to the electorate. Its endorsement would be a vindication that the mandate of this Court could never give." Frankfurter, J., concurring, in *A. F. of L.* v. *American Sash Co.,* 335 U. S. 538, 553 (and related cases, see p. 542, note).

Those cases (Nos. 27, 34, and 47, Oct. T. 1948) involved the validity of state statutes outlawing the closed shop, i.e., forbidding agreements to employ only union members. On behalf of the appellants, there was filed a document

Third, the materials adduced must be authoritative, representing matters of general knowledge that are comprehended within the basis on which the Court in *Muller* v. *Oregon* [255] first accepted the Brandeis brief, viz., "the state of the art" in patent law.[256] Consequently *ex parte* statements by officials whose assertions of power are being challenged do not qualify, particularly when formulated *post litem motam*. If counsel feels that the existence of facts justifying challenged action must be established, he should prove those facts at the trial, where the officials can be cross-examined.[257] These fairly obvious considerations were overlooked in *Reid* v. *Covert* [258] when the Government on rehearing attempted to prove "The specific practical necessities * * * which justify court-martial jurisdiction over civilian dependents overseas" [259] by adducing letters from overseas commanders. It should hardly occasion surprise that the showing thus made failed to convince a majority of the Court.[260]

---

entitled on its cover "Economic Brief of Appellants." Inside the cover was a treatise, over a hundred pages in length, prepared by an A. F. of L. economist, entitled "The Closed Shop and Union Security." Appendix E to this treatise, which was thus included as a part of the "Economic Brief" submitted to the Court, was a lengthy law review article on the precise constitutional issues raised!

[255] 208 U. S. 412, 419.

[256] "In patent cases counsel are apt to open the argument with a discussion of the state of the art. It may not be amiss, in the present case, before examining the constitutional question, to notice the course of legislation, as well as expressions of opinion from other than judicial sources. In the brief filed by Mr. Louis D. Brandeis for the defendant in error is a very copious collection of all these matters, an epitome of which is found in the margin."

[257] In the Hawaiian martial law cases (*Duncan* v. *Kahanamoku*, 327 U. S. 304), the Government produced its military witnesses, Adm. Nimitz and Lt. Gen. Richardson, at the habeas corpus hearing in the district court. See No. 14, Oct. T. 1945, R. 1006-1078; No. 15, *id.*, R. 55-56, 341-301.

[258] 354 U. S. 1.

[259] This was one of the points on which the Court requested argument when it granted the rehearing. 352 U. S. 901.

[260] "Unlike the kind of reports that Mr. Louis D. Brandeis brought to the attention of the Court through his famous brief in *Muller* v. *Oregon,* * * * the letters exhibited in these cases represent simply expressions by those whose powers are involved. * * *

"But the letters brought forward in the present case are subject to other infirmities also. They are *ex parte*, and, as will be pointed out below in detail, they bristle with points that are left in doubt or else not covered at all, points on which cross-examination would have elicited pertinent information. * * *

"Moreover, the letters now pressed on the Court as determinative of the contested issue are, all too obviously, *post litem motam;* their approach is keynoted by the first sentence of the first letter printed: 'The news that the United

In all fairness, however, it can hardly be said that the "practical necessities" issue was one that would have occurred to counsel when the proceedings were instituted. Moreover, since the relief sought was habeas corpus, the statutory requirement that "The court shall summarily hear and determine the facts'' [261] made it obviously impracticable to remand the two cases to the respective district courts where each had originated for the purpose of conducting lengthy hearings. In earlier constitutional litigation, where the nature of the background facts necessary to sustain the assailed statute was obvious, the Government had indeed developed those facts through witnesses at each trial.[262]

(c) *Scientific materials.* On occasion there arises a point that is susceptible of effective treatment with the use of strictly scientific, nonlegal materials. The *Anne Johnson* case [263] is an apt illustration.

There narcotic agents, attracted by the smell of burning

States Supreme Court has agreed to reconsider the question of the amenability to military law of dependents accompanying military personnel overseas is most disturbing.' No doubt similar communications could be obtained from lawyers, constitutional scholars, and, for that matter, from dependent wives overseas, to the effect that last June's decisions were even more disturbing. But we hardly think that such a course of counter-picketing the inside of the courthouse * * * would be in any degree helpful." Supp. Br. on Rehearing for Appellee and Resp., Nos. 701 and 713, Oct. T. 1955, pp. 141-142.

[261] 28 U.S.C. § 2243.

[262] "I should add at this point that the practice of the government has by no means been limited to the placing of such data in the briefs. In many of the most important constitutional cases, the material has actually been introduced into the record. Sometimes this has been done by calling expert witnesses—government economists or outside economists—or by introducing into the record publications of responsible authorities. This was done, for example, in the Guffey Coal Act case [*Carter* v. *Carter Coal Co.,* 298 U. S. 238], where voluminous testimony was taken regarding the history of labor disturbances in the coal industry and the effect on the volume of shipments and competitive conditions in the industry. It was done in the PWA cases [*Alabama Power Co.* v. *Ickes,* 302 U. S. 464], where testimony was taken regarding studies made by the Bureau of Labor Statistics on the effectiveness of a public works program in the relief of unemployment. It was done at great length in the omnibus TVA case [*Tennessee Electric Power Co.* v. *TVA,* 306 U. S. 118], where a galaxy of engineers—military, civil and hydraulic—testified on both sides concerning the usefulness of the TVA projects for navigation, flood control, and national defense." Freund, *On Understanding the Supreme Court,* 89-90. Professor Freund was on the staff of the Solicitor General of the United States when each of the cited cases was briefed and argued.

[263] *Johnson* v. *United States,* 333 U. S. 10.

opium, entered petitioner's room without a warrant. She was subsequently indicted and convicted for violations of the narcotic laws. She argued that odors alone, uncorroborated by other information, could not be evidence sufficient to constitute probable ground for any search; and she cited numerous cases in support of that contention.[264] The Government urged that smoking opium had a distinctive and unmistakably identifiable odor, quoting not only from the testimony in the case but also from encyclopedias, pharmacopoeias, and similar disinterested sources of information. The Court held that odors alone might well constitute probable cause,[265] but went on to decide, four justices dissenting, that in the circumstances the officers were not entitled to proceed without a warrant.

Here again, when the case is going to turn on scientific facts, it is preferable—and safer—to lay the foundation at the trial, through live witnesses subject to cross-examination (as was done in *Anne Johnson*), and then to use the materials cited in the brief by way of supplement. This was the course followed in the recent case of *Flemming* v. *Florida Citrus Exch.*,[266] upholding an order of the Secretary of Health, Education and Welfare that removed from the certified list of "harmless and suitable for use in food" a coal-tar color used for many years in coloring oranges. The bulk of the scientific testimony was adduced at the administrative hearing, and the brief supplemented the record thus made with additional citations from pharmaceutical journals that had been before the Congress when the governing statute was enacted.

Similarly, in a recent English case, the question concerned the legitimacy of a child born 340 days after the husband left to go overseas with the Army.[267] The evidence of a distinguished doctor —the President of the Royal College of Obstetricians and Gynaecologists—as to the advances made in the science of gynaecology over the preceding twenty years, convinced the judge that the child

---

[264] *Taylor* v. *United States*, 286 U. S. 1; *United States* v. *Kronenberg*, 134 F. 2d 483 (C.A. 2) ; *Cheng Wai* v. *United States*, 125 F. 2d 915 (C.A. 2) ; *United States* v. *Kaplan*, 89 F. 2d 869 (C.A. 2) ; *United States* v. *Lee*, 83 F. 2d 195 (C.A. 2) ; *United States* v. *Schultz*, 3 F. Supp. 273 (D. Ariz.) ; *United States* v. *Tom Yu*, 1 F. Supp. 357 (D. Ariz.) .

[265] 333 U. S. at 13.

[266] 358 U. S. 153.

[267] *M-T* v. *M-T*, [1949] P. 331.

could not possibly have been legitimate, notwithstanding earlier cases, based on the earlier state of knowledge, to the contrary.[268]

In other words, precedents otherwise binding can lose their force under the impetus of advances in scientific knowledge just as well as under the impetus of advances in historical knowledge.

Section 61. Encyclopedias; collections of annotated cases.—It is not belittling the value of encyclopedias or of the several collections of annotated cases to urge that they should be used primarily to orient the lawyer in unfamiliar fields of law, or to supply him with citations to cases and with leads for further research—but that they should not generally be relied upon or cited as authorities. A proper exception would be in situations where law libraries are limited or generally inaccessible. Normally—and certainly before the Supreme Court of the United States or any other Federal appellate court—the careful advocate will never refer to such publications in his briefs except to write, "The cases are collected in ———."

Whenever or wherever library facilities are limited, the lawyer in the field must follow the soldier in the field: he must do the best he can with what he has. But in the larger cities, or in the vicinity of the larger law school libraries, the situation is different; there the warning above is applicable.

Some readers will ask, Why this insistence on such a limited use, in the face of the undoubted fact that some courts of last resort cite these works in their opinions? The real reason, basically, is this: encyclopedias and annotations are written by lawyers who, though honest and diligent, are neither in practice nor in law teaching. Some are undoubtedly able, others are little better than legal hacks. For myself, I admire their industry, and I value it highly, as witness the price law offices pay for the fruits thereof. But I do not regard their analysis of the cases as *authority,* and certainly a survey of the reports indicates that courts of the highest standing do not do so either. I regard any competent lawyer's signature on a brief as being at least as authoritative as these gentlemen's own frequently anonymous say-so.

Consequently, I profit by their labors, which shorten my own correspondingly. But having been fortunate enough always to have access to excellent library facilities, I do not and never have

---

[268] *Gaskill* v. *Gaskill,* [1921] P. 425; *Hadlum* v. *Hadlum,* [1949] P. 197.

cited these works to any court, save always as a reasonably reliable compilation of the decisions.[269]

Section 62. Use of law review materials.—In 1915, Dean Wigmore, in the preface to the second edition of the then Supplement to his monumental—and immortal—treatise on *Evidence*, deplored the prevailing tendency of courts to overlook the treasures locked in the pages of legal periodicals, and to cite a second- or third-rate textbook in preference to a first-rate article in a law review.[270] Those strictures were not repeated in the second edition of his Treatise, published in 1923; by 1930 or thereabouts "the conspiracy of silence" had pretty well been dissolved; [271] and today, the pendulum has swung far in the opposite direction.[272] Indeed, lawyers who would not dream of citing encyclopedias or annotated reports or third-rate textbooks in their briefs seem to think that they will appear to be pretty learned fellows when they refer to and rely upon expressions of opinion in the law reviews.

Law review materials fall into two groups: the leading articles, invariably signed, and the student notes and comments, which, certainly in the older law reviews, are frequently and perhaps generally unsigned.

So far as the student notes are concerned, the brief-writer will, by and large, be well advised to use them as case-finders and as sources for his own ideas, rather than as expressions of authority to be cited to the courts. A little reflection will show the reason why. After all, your task as an advocate is to persuade a court of more or less learned and more rather than less elderly judges to decide your case in your favor. They are not likely to be persuaded by what some lads on a law review have said. Sometimes the judicial reac-

---

[269] In addition to the usual collections of annotated cases, advocates in the Federal courts should be aware of the wealth of useful annotations on points of Federal constitutional and statutory law available in the Lawyers' Edition series of the United States Reports.

[270] Pp. v, vi.

[271] See Maggs, *Concerning the Extent to Which the Law Review Contributes to the Development of the Law* (1930) 2 So. Cal. L. Rev. 181; Cardozo, *Introduction to Selected Readings on the Law of Contracts* (1930), pp. vii, ix: "Certain, in any event, it is that the old prejudice is vanishing. Within the last ten or fifteen years the conspiracy of silence has been dissolving, with defections every year more numerous and notable."

[272] See, as to the increasing frequency of law review citations by the courts, Judge Goodrich's paper, *Law School and Law Teacher—1952*, 5 J. Legal Educ. 7, 13-14.

tion to a law review citation is essentially one of amusement, as for example the remark (probably not wholly apocryphal) attributed to Mr. Justice Holmes: "I don't mind when the lads on the Law Review say I'm wrong, what I object to is when they say I'm right." Sometimes the reaction is one of impatient annoyance; I have heard just precisely that kind of comment, in open court, from one of the most distinguished of Federal judges (directed, I should hasten to add, at my opposition).[273] And on occasion the matter goes beyond that, as witness the testy comments in one of the late Mr. Justice Butler's last dissents:

> The opinion also cites, footnote 7, selected gainsaying writings of professors,—some are lawyers and some are not—but without specification of or reference to the reasons upon which their views rest. And in addition it cites notes published in law reviews some signed and some not; presumably the latter were prepared by law students.[274]

True, student notes are nowadays frequently cited by the courts,[275] and the views expressed above are not in any sense the consequence of sour grapes. I too have tooted on The Bugle, and one note that I committed while in school, which criticized two Supreme Court decisions,[276] was twice cited by that Court—as it qualified the one [277] and overruled the other.[278] I strongly suspect, however, that, in those instances as in the others, the student note citations were added by the justices' law clerks, by ways of encouragement to their former colleagues still at the school.

At any rate, I would urge that, except in rare instances, student notes should not be cited as authority. They should be used,

---

[273] This is particularly so when a student note questions a firmly settled principle; such a suggestion "is not in our opinion to be seriously weighed against the long established view * * *." *Angilly* v. *United States,* 199 F. 2d 642, 644 (C.A. 2).

[274] *O'Malley* v. *Woodrough,* 307 U. S. 277, 298.

[275] E.g., *United States* v. *Witkovich,* 353 U. S. 194, 201; *Zwack* v. *Kraus Bros. & Co.,* 237 F. 2d 253 (C.A. 2); see note 272 *supra;* cf. Clark, J., dissenting, in *Niles-Bement-Pond Co.* v. *Fitzpatrick,* 213 F. 2d 305, 313 (C.A. 2). These are examples only.

[276] Note, *Aftermath of the Supreme Court's Stop, Look, and Listen Rule* (1930) 43 Harv. L. Rev. 926.

[277] *Pokora* v. *Wabash Ry. Co.,* 292 U. S. 98, 106, n. 4, limiting *Baltimore & O. R. R.* v. *Goodman,* 275 U. S. 66.

[278] *Erie R. Co.* v. *Tompkins,* 304 U. S. 64, 74, n. 7, overruling *Swift* v. *Tyson,* 16 Pet. 1.

however, for the ideas they reflect, and as case-finders.[279] Such use will save the brief-writer much labor at the research stage, since law review notes and comments are very apt to contain references to cases that simply do not turn up in the digests.[280]

Leading articles, on the other hand, stand on a different footing. At worst, they represent the opinions of individual lawyers, and hence should have, for purposes of citation, at least the same value as an ephemeral textbook written by some hack in a law publisher's stable and duly bound in buckram or fabrikoid. And, at best, depending in each instance on the stature and reputation of the author, they may well be authoritative.

Thus, Mr. Charles Warren's article, *New Light on the History of the Federal Judiciary Act of 1789*,[281] undermined the authority of *Swift* v. *Tyson*,[282] and was in large measure responsible for *Erie R. Co.* v. *Tompkins*.[283] Rarely has a single bit of historical research so significantly influenced our law. Another classic example of a bit of original legal thinking, one that opened up an entirely new field of law, was the celebrated Warren and Brandeis article on *The Right to Privacy*.[284] Although published over 70 years ago, it is still being cited by courts today.[285] Those are perhaps the two most striking examples, though there have been other recent instances of substantial judicial reliance placed on the reasoning and the research set forth in law review articles.[286] It is

---

[279] I am not ashamed to acknowledge that, on numerous occasions, referring to law review notes has saved me much work in collecting cases, and has turned up worthwhile ideas that advanced my own arguments.

[280] The American Digest System, even now, does not include "Conflict of Laws" as a digest topic. And the heading "Administrative Law and Procedure," which is included in the Fifth and subsequent *Decennial Digests*, did not appear currently until 1948. See 4 *General Digest* (2d Series).

[281] 37 Harv. L. Rev. 49.

[282] 16 Pet. 1.

[283] 304 U. S. 64.

[284] 4 Harv. L. Rev. 193 (1890). See Nizer, *The Right of Privacy: A Half Century's Developments*, 39 Mich. L. Rev. 526 (1941); Feinberg, *Recent Developments of the Law of Privacy*, 48 Colum. L. Rev. 713 (1948).

[285] E.g., *Leverton* v. *Curtis Pub. Co.*, 192 F. 2d 974 (C.A. 3); *Ettore* v. *Philco Television Broadcasting Corporation*, 229 F. 2d 481 (C.A. 3); *Jenkins* v. *Dell Publishing Company*, 251 F. 2d 447 (C.A. 3).

[286] See, for example, Frankfurter and Landis, *Power of Congress over Procedure in Criminal Contempts in "Inferior" Federal Courts—A Study in Separation of Powers*, 37 Harv. L. Rev. 1010. This article, sharply critical of the decision in *Toledo Newspaper Co.* v. *United States*, 247 U. S. 402, was

proper to add, however, that leading articles in law reviews are more respected as authority when they reflect the results of scholarly researches or the views of members of rule-making committees as to the objects sought to be attained by those rules than when they simply set forth the opinions of individual lawyers, either with a client's axe to grind or else rearguing in professional publications the cases they have lost in the courts.

Section 63. The next step in brief-writing.—I shall assume, at this point, that your basic research has been completed, and that you have made useful notes covering your materials.

I will not undertake to make suggestions for note-taking; that is a matter which depends entirely on individual habits and temperament. The standards that follow, however, are universally applicable.

(a) Be accurate; you will waste a great deal of time and effort if you have to go back to get the exact wording of a title or citation that you took down in sloppy fashion the first time.

(b) Make your notes complete enough to be helpful to you, but don't waste your time in doing mere copywork that a stenographer can do more effectively and more economically.

(c) Don't jot down on the same sheet of paper references to unrelated matters; to do that means an infinite amount of shuffling through papers to find a single citation. Your time is more valuable than scratch-paper, even at today's inflated prices for office supplies.

(d) Don't rely on your notes to the exclusion of the reports, particularly as to the leading cases cited. You will have to read and reread those, no matter how extensive your notes may be.

Next, having gone over your notes, and having already ana-

cited by and certainly influenced the Court in *Nye* v. *United States,* 313 U. S. 33, 47, when it overruled the *Toledo* case.

See also Fairman, *Does the Fourteenth Amendment Incorporate the Bill of Rights? The Original Understanding,* 2 Stanf. L. Rev. 5, which demonstrated the historical soundness of *Adamson* v. *California,* 332 U. S. 46, and has since been cited in support thereof. E.g., *Bartkus* v. *Illinois,* 359 U. S. 121, 124.

See also, for varying degrees of reliance on leading articles in law reviews, the following recent cases: *Machinists* v. *Gonzales,* 356 U. S. 617, 622-623; *Local 140 Security Fund* v. *Hack,* 242 F. 2d 375 (C.A. 2) ; *Sunbeam Corp.* v. *Civil Service Employees' Coop. Assn.,* 187 F. 2d 768 (C.A. 3) ; *Mason City & Clear Lake R. Co.* v. *Imperial Seed Co.,* 152 F. Supp. 145 (N. D. Iowa) .

lyzed your case thoroughly, it is time to outline your argument. This involves, among other things, a resolution of the problem of which points to argue first; see Section 34, above. It involves also a formulation of the argumentative headings for the several points in your argument; see Section 30, above. And it involves also, very definitely, a breaking down of your main points into their supporting subsidiary points.

The only general rule universally applicable at this juncture is the warning that, if the outline is faulty, the thinking is faulty. Consequently, if the draft outline won't wash, your case needs further and clearer analysis, and you will have to labor over it some more. Work over it, slave over it if need be, turn to other matters to clear your head if the deadline allows you that luxury. But keep at it until the outline is sound. Then—and only then—are you ready to write.

Section 64. Write consecutively.—There is always a strong temptation to leave the difficult or the less important point for the end—to toss in the jurisdictional argument later, or to do the easy points first and to reserve the difficult one until you get into the swing of writing. That is the easy way, no doubt about it—and a very natural one; years ago, I frequently succumbed to it. But I found that when I did, my briefs would acquire a lopsided twist that no amount of future editing would ever quite eradicate.

So, having learned this also, again the hard way, I pass it on: always write consecutively. Start with Point One and follow through to the conclusion. Go cross-country, as it were, over the easy terrain as well as the rocky ground. And keep right on going.

I don't mean that it is necessary to stop and interrupt the train of your thought while looking up some largely ornamental citation, or to compose a long but somewhat tangential footnote, or even to fill in a little paragraph of text that is going to involve a lot of additional research. Those are the little fringes and tassels, the buttons and bows of brief-writing, that can safely be postponed. They can wait, provided they are not basic. As to the basic argument, however, you must go straight ahead, and with as much steam as you can muster.

Later, after the basic text has been written, and, after submission to partners or colleagues for comment or criticism, it has been revised and where necessary rewritten, you can relax and proceed to fill in the gaps and supply the additional citations that, had you stopped for them earlier, would have distracted you and disturbed the continuity of your writing.

Inevitably, though, it is just those last little trifles that are bound to—and do—take a disproportionate amount of time. They are the touches that require you to leave your office for the more extensive library facilities of Bar Association or courthouse. It has been my experience that the last few citations and the last few footnotes always keep me running breathlessly around the library, fighting the deadline—and delay my meeting it.

Section 65. Write the Summary of Argument last of all.— After the Argument proper has been written and revised, and not before, is the time to write the Summary of Argument. See Section 37 (a), above, for suggestions as to what the Summary should contain. It is well, also, to cite therein a few of the leading cases discussed and relied upon in the body of your Argument, to serve as shorthand guideposts and landmarks for the court. (It was Mr. Justice Reed, when Solicitor General of the United States, who insisted that the Summary of Argument in Government briefs should do so.) And, I repeat, the Summary should summarize what is said in the Argument; it should not go off on a tack—or a frolic—of its own.

As a practical matter, the normal procedure under the pressure of deadlines is to let the Argument go to the printer, and later, when it comes back in galley proof, to insert the Summary of Argument before the entire brief is returned to the press for paging.

Section 66. Finally, check!—Check every citation, quotation, and record reference. *Check every citation, quotation, and record reference!* CHECK EVERY CITATION, QUOTATION, AND RECORD REFERENCE! Regardless of your own intrinsic accuracy, errors are bound to creep into your manuscript. Sometimes it is your fault and at other times it is your stenographer's, but mistakes will slip in either way. The name of a case will be incorrectly rendered, digits in a citation will become transposed, a word in a quotation will be garbled, a line will be left out of a quotation, a record reference or two or three will be completely wrong. Most usually the final typed manuscript will contain a combination of these common errors.

So—when you get the first set of printer's proofs, whether galley or page, check each citation (and every part of it), every record reference, and every quotation whether from record or from decision, *against the original reports and the original record!* This is a must. It is standard operating procedure in the U. S. Solicitor General's Office and on the better law reviews. (The former employs two full-time checkers who do nothing else.) You, as a private practitioner—or as a lawyer in some other Government law office—cannot afford to do less.

If the cost of proof corrections is a factor that must be watched, it is better to have a copy of your final manuscript checked against the original documents; then to enter the corrections on the master copy that goes to the press; and finally to read back every citation and quotation from the proofs against the master copy of the manuscript. This sequence helps keep down the number of corrections requiring resetting of type; most printers use linotype, with the result that a single misplaced digit in a citation requires an entire line of type to be reset.

It should be noted parenthetically that the most effective checking is that done by someone other than the brief-writer, not because checking is a chore to be passed down the line, but because of the demonstrable psychological fact that the author's eye will see the author's thought rather than what is typed or printed. That is why most people are better proofreaders on the other fellow's stuff. Consequently, the admonition here set down—"check"—means, preferably, "have someone else check."

The same counsel is applicable to cross-references. These cannot be inserted until a complete set of page proofs is available, and, in the first instance, must be supplied either by the actual brief-writer or by his No. 1 assistant. But, like everything else in the brief, these cross-references must be checked, again preferably by some one whose critical eye will not be softened either by wishful thinking or by pride of authorship.

To continue: Whenever there have been corrections made in any set of proofs, be sure to check the next succeeding set of proofs, not only to see whether the first corrections have been made, but also to ascertain whether any additional errors have crept in. (They generally have.)

Finally, when you receive the completed briefs from the printer, all clean and nicely bound, don't rush the required number over to the clerk of court in the same happy mood of creative pride with which you distribute cigars to your friends consequent upon the birth of issue. Curb your impulse; sit down and read one copy consecutively. ("Read" here, pre-eminently, means "have someone else read.")

Why? Because, almost inevitably, in the process of correcting the errors noted on the final proofs, new errors will have been made. A most annoying kind of new error, and unfortunately a not too uncommon one, is the transposition of entire lines of type. The fact of the matter is that typographical errors are an unavoidable form of human fallibility, which simply cannot be entirely stamped out, regardless of the efforts made.[287] That being so, it is incumbent on every lawyer to have his finished briefs read carefully, very carefully, before he files them with the court. On the strength of a long and frequently sad experience, I emphasize this final caution; indeed, I cannot emphasize it too strongly.

And if you find slips? Correct them with pen or pencil, and file as corrected. And, of course, when the final copy is way off, the printer is bound to correct his own slips; the customer pays only for proof changes that he makes himself.

At any rate, after the completed briefs have been checked, corrected if necessary, and finally filed, you can relax. If you have been working really hard on the case, you will undoubtedly feel a tremendous let-down at that point. What you do thereafter, before it is time to prepare for the oral argument, will depend largely on such otherwise irrelevant matters as your temperament, your state of health, your doctor's orders, and the local option situation in the particular Federal district.

---

[287] "The most baffling device of the imp [of the perverse] is to cause a new error in the process of correcting an old one. This residuary misprint is one against which there is no complete protection. When General Pillow returned from Mexico he was hailed by a Southern editor as a 'battle-scarred veteran.' The next day the veteran called upon him to demand an apology for the epithet actually printed, 'battle-scared.' What was the horror of the editor, on the following day, to see the expression reappear in his apology as 'bottle-scarred.' " Koopman, *The Perversities of Type,* in *The Booklover and His Books,* 152, 157.

CHAPTER V

THE FINER POINTS OF BRIEF-WRITING

Section 67. Introductory.—This chapter deals with the minutiae of brief-writing, with those details wherein a good brief differs from one not so good. The discussion of some of these details may appear to pertain to trifles, but, as has aptly been remarked, it is the trifles that make perfection—and perfection is no trifle.

There will also be included in this chapter a discussion of the problems peculiar to reply briefs and to briefs *amicus curiae;* and I shall once more stress, from still another approach, the necessity for absolute accuracy in citations and record references.

Section 68. Citations; number of citations.—One of the best, if not the best, single article on appellate arguments is still the late John W. Davis's *The Argument of an Appeal.*[1] In one of the introductory paragraphs of that paper, there appears the following:

> I assume also that the briefs are not overlarded with long quotations from the reported opinions, no matter how pat they seem; nor over-crowded with citations designed it would seem to certify to the industry of the brief-maker rather than to fortify the argument. A horrible example of this latter fault crossed my desk within the month in a brief which, in addition to many statutes and text-writers, cited by volume and page no less than 304 decided cases, a number calculated to discourage if not to disgust the most industrious judge.

I chanced to be in the audience when the foregoing was first delivered, at the Association of the Bar of the City of New York in 1940—and, as it happened, the "horrible example" referred to was the Government's brief in the *Northern Pacific* reargument,[2] a case I had argued against Mr. Davis just a week or so previously. Together with the late Judge E. E. Danly and some others, I had sweated over that brief all summer long. At any rate, when I saw the speaker immediately after his lecture, he seemed nonplussed, and the following conversation took place:

---

[1] Davis, *The Argument of an Appeal,* 26 A.B.A.J. 895.
[2] *United States* v. *Northern Pacific Ry. Co.,* 311 U. S. 317.

W: I'm sorry you didn't like our brief.

D: Well, I did think you cited too many cases.

W: If I were inclined to be critical of your production, I should say that you cited too few cases.

D: Had it occurred to you that we had too few cases which we could cite?

All of which passed off very pleasantly and amiably. I was never too much concerned about the criticism, because after all—as a friend of mine noted when he first saw the paper in print—the reargument was decided in my favor! And the fact that Mr. Davis wrote the Foreword to the first version of the present work was surely an indication that he was never too seriously upset by my countercriticism.

As a general proposition, of course, it goes almost without saying that it is better to cite and discuss a few leading and controlling decisions than to assemble an encyclopedic collection within the covers of a single brief. This has been recognized for centuries.[3] But there are cases and cases, and what may be an excess of citations in one situation may be far too few in another. The matter is entirely relative, and one cannot safely be dogmatic about absolute numbers.

Consider the *Northern Pacific* case: it involved the final adjustment of the land grant to the Northern Pacific Railway and its predecessors, a grant of some forty million acres of land—almost equal to the aggregate area of the six New England states. The litigation in question had been specifically directed by Congress, after an investigation that had lasted five years.[4] Some nine years more elapsed before the U. S. District Court entered an interlocutory decree. Meanwhile Congress had authorized an appeal from that decree, direct to the Supreme Court,[5] because the litigation was simply too complex for ordinary appellate procedures. The

---

[3] "In those days few cases in law were cited, but very pithy and pertinent to the purpose, and those ever pinch most; and now in so long arguments with such a farrago of authorities, it cannot be but there is much refuse, which ever doth weaken or lessen the weight of the argument." 10 Co. Rep. (1826 ed.) xxi-xxii.

[4] Act of June 25, 1929, c. 41, 46 Stat. 41. The investigation was authorized by the Joint Resolution of June 5, 1924, c. 267, 43 Stat. 461; the report of the Joint Committee of Congress that conducted the investigation appears in S. Rep. 5, 71st Cong., 2d sess.

[5] Act of May 22, 1936, c. 444, 49 Stat. 1369.

case was first argued in the Supreme Court in the spring of 1940, some ten years after the proceeding had been brought. Three hours were allowed on each side for oral argument instead of the usual one hour.[6] After that, the Court set the case down for reargument on its own motion, and asked for argument on questions that had not been taken up and on assignments of error that had not been urged at the original argument.[7]

On reargument, the Government filed a brief extending to 295 pages. That brief argued the questions involved by invoking analogies that seemed apposite, and stressed what Government counsel felt was the disregard of settled rules of law on the part of the master whose opinion had been approved by the district court. It was necessary to buttress the analogies with citations so that they would not appear to be mere assertions, and in order to show the number of decisions which, it was contended, the decree below had ignored. Having regard to all of these factors—the complexity of the issues, the circumstance that the Court was obviously in doubt and frankly seeking guidance, and the number of subsidiary points and principles that needed to be explored and developed—I still think now, as I thought in 1940, that the number of citations was not excessive, and that, notwithstanding the acknowledged eminence of the critic, the stricture quoted above was not justified in the particular instance, especially since the Court ultimately reserved decision on some of the fundamental issues as to which there was an equal division of opinion. (Any reader of the foregoing is, of course, free to disagree with me—provided he will first read the 848 pages of the printed record, the numerous bulky exhibits that were not printed, the 460 pages of briefs filed on the original argument, the appendix of relevant statutes running to 156 pages, the 397 pages of briefs filed at the reargument, and the 53-page opinion at 311 U. S. 317.)

Section 69. More about the number of citations.—The normal or usual case, of course, does not require nearly so detailed a documentation, and the brief-writer should adapt his citations to the problem he is facing.

The following standards will cover the usual situations, but they are standards only, not ironclad rules.

---

[6] Journal, U. S. Sup. Ct., Oct. T. 1939, p. 177.

[7] 310 U. S. 615. Six additional hours were allowed for the reargument. Journal, U. S. Sup. Ct., Oct. T. 1940, p. 29.

(a) It is, by and large, unwise to overload one's brief with citations. In this connection it is well for the brief-writer to keep in mind a question I once heard a Supreme Court Justice ask counsel during argument: "Mr. X, I see that on page *ab* of your brief you cite a lot of cases for that proposition. Give me the two most important ones that you want me to read." [8]

(b) Don't weaken a really pat citation that is on all fours by including a lot that bear only tangentially on the issue; and if you have a square holding, don't add the stray dicta from other cases. Possible exception: when the holding is an old one, it may be helpful to add a modern or fairly recent reaffirmation, even though dictum in the later case—to show that the proposition on which you are relying is still recognized as law.

(c) In Federal appeals, to the extent that you are dealing with Federal law of general application, whether constitutional or statutory, your citations are best restricted to a few leading decisions of the Supreme Court, preferably the most recent, plus possibly a few late decisions in the court where you are actually arguing, to demonstrate that tribunal's application of the governing principles involved.

(d) Always adapt your citations to the court and to the question. Thus, in any Federal court, Supreme Court citations are authoritative (with only a very narrow and infrequent exception, see p. 108, above). And, in any Federal court, its own decisions are likewise authoritative, and will be preferred to those of other Federal courts, even of those of coordinate jurisdiction.

When you are in the Supreme Court, on other than constitutional questions, decisions of the lower Federal courts differ in value. It is of course always helpful to be able to point out that the rule for which you are contending has the support of all or nearly all of the eleven circuits, and in that event it is well to give cita-

---

[8] Compare the Eighth Circuit's Rule 11 (b) Fourth, requiring, in the statement of points to be argued, "the cases which are considered to be most apposite and convincing, not exceeding four in number, to be printed in bold-face type."

The District of Columbia Circuit has just added the following to its Rule 17 (b) (3) :

"Counsel are requested to place in the left margin of the Table of Cases an asterisk or asterisks to mark those cases or authorities on which counsel chiefly rely and to add at the end of the Table:

"*Cases or authorities chiefly relied upon are marked by asterisks."

tions from all of them. Where, however, the case is in the Supreme Court to resolve a conflict between circuits, all that counts is the reasoning of the Supreme Court decisions on which you rely. And when the Supreme Court is called upon to determine a constitutional issue of essentially first impression, then, necessarily, the decisions of the lower Federal courts are virtually valueless as authorities, except possibly when they are expressions of the giants of old riding circuit (see Section 59, above), or, occasionally, when an admired contemporary has spoken under circumstances giving his views peculiar weight.[9]

(e) In Federal appeals, State cases are generally valueless or worse on strictly Federal issues (compare Section 49, above), and are helpful in only a very limited number of situations:

(1) Where a Federal question, whether civil or criminal, is unsettled, and where there has been a uniform treatment of the same point in the State courts.[10]

(2) Where a question of evidence is involved.[11]

(3) Where the case is in the Supreme Court on review from the highest court of the State, and you seek to demonstrate that the same State court had previously given recognition to the federal right that you are asserting.[12]

---

[9] E.g., Judge Learned Hand's opinion in *United States* v. *Aluminum Co. of America,* 148 F. 2d 416 (C.A. 2), an antitrust appeal which came before the Second Circuit by virtue of a special statute (now 28 U.S.C. § 2109; see also *United States* v. *United States District Court,* 334 U. S. 258) because, by reason of disqualifications, the Supreme Court could not muster a quorum. Accordingly, the Supreme Court has said that "That case was decided by the Circuit Court of Appeals for the Second Circuit under unique circumstances which add to its weight as a precedent" (*American Tobacco Co.* v. *United States,* 328 U. S. 781, 811), and has treated it accordingly in later antitrust opinions.

[10] See, e.g., the use of State decisions in *Morissette* v. *United States,* 342 U. S. 246, a case dealing with the quantum and kind of criminal intent requisite to conviction for a taking of Government property.

[11] Under Rule 43 (a), F. R. Civ. P., evidence is admissible in a Federal civil case if admissible in the courts of the State where the Federal court is held. Under Rule 26, F. R. Crim. P., the admissibility of evidence in Federal criminal cases depends on the "principles of the common law as they may be interpreted by the courts of the United States in the light of reason and experience." For recent applications, see *Hawkins* v. *United States,* 358 U. S. 74, and *Wyatt* v. *United States,* 362 U. S. 525.

[12] See Section 35 (d), *supra,* for the use made in *Williams* v. *Lee,* 358 U. S. 217, reversing 83 Ariz. 241, 319 P. 2d 998, of the prior Arizona case of *Begay* v. *Miller,* 70 Ariz. 380, 222 P. 2d 624.

(4) Where the question is secondary or essentially illustrative.[13]

(5) And, of course, in diversity cases where State law now governs.

(f) Where sheer weight of numbers is a point in itself, all that weight should be used. For instance, whenever it is appropriate to emphasize the settled nature of the rule relied upon, it is entirely in order to cite more cases than when the particular settled rule was questioned neither by the court below nor by your adversary.

Thus, in the *Petrillo* case,[14] the Government's brief dealt with the contention that in the absence of a separability clause there would be a presumption of inseparability.[15] The brief pointed out that such a presumption was by no means conclusive— and went on to cite in a footnote no less than 47 cases in which the Supreme Court had held statutes severable despite the absence of a separability clause!

Similarly (see pp. 208-209, above), where it is considered necessary to show not just that the rule in the Federal courts is such-and-such but that, in fact, every circuit so holds, it is well that every one of the eleven circuits be represented.

(g) You will need more citations where the question is one of first impression or where you are undertaking to tidy up a confused field of law or where the court below has disregarded settled law, than in a situation where you are dealing only with the application of an earlier decision or with a variant on a well-established rule.

Thus, in *Williams* v. *Fanning*,[16] where the Supreme Court undertook to settle the question whether, in injunction proceedings against a public officer, the officer's official superior was an indispensable party—a matter that, because of the apparent conflict between *Gnerich* v. *Rutter*[17] and *Webster* v. *Fall*[18] on the one

---

[13] See, e.g., the use made of state cases in *Wolf* v. *Colorado,* 338 U. S. 25, in *Bartkus* v. *Illinois,* 359 U. S. 121, 135-136, and in the dissenting opinion in *Green* v. *United States,* 355 U. S. 184, 198, 216-218.

[14] *United States* v. *Petrillo,* 332 U. S. 1.

[15] E.g., *Williams* v. *Standard Oil Co.,* 278 U. S. 235; *Electric Bond & Share Co.* v. *Securities & Exchange Commission,* 303 U. S. 419.

[16] 332 U. S. 490.

[17] 265 U. S. 388.

[18] 266 U. S. 507.

hand, and *Colorado* v. *Toll*[19] on the other, had been in hopeless confusion in the several circuits[20]—the Government's brief cited and classified all the decisions on the question. And in the *Douglas Chandler* treason case,[21] which came before a court that had never in its history had occasion to consider that particular offense, both sides presented voluminous authorities, the object being—in my judgment properly so—to lay before the tribunal every decision and every bit of historical material that would assist in deciding the case. Thorough research in such a situation lightens the court's labors rather than otherwise.[22]

The question of how many cases to cite is an entirely relative one; it is all a matter of proportion and emphasis. There is no one single "approved solution" that can be laid down to fit every situation. The experienced brief-writer soon senses when to cite many cases and when only a few. Like Grandmother's famous recipe, you take a little of this and a pinch of that and add enough of the other until the mixture seems just right.

In this connection, I should add that I always consider it a reflection on my brief when the court's opinion cites a case in point that I did not cite to them.[23] After all, one purpose of any brief is

---

[19] 268 U. S. 228.

[20] Most of the earlier cases are collected in 158 A.L.R. 1126. As there appears, some circuits with a fine impartiality decided the point both ways.

One perceptive commentator believes that the Supreme Court cases since *Williams* v. *Fanning* still go off in all directions and perpetuate the earlier confusion. 3 Davis, *Administrative Law Treatise* (1958) § 27.08.

[21] *Chandler* v. *United States*, 171 F. 2d 921 (C.A. 1), certiorari denied, 336 U. S. 918.

[22] "We have been much aided by the industry and thoroughness of Government counsel and of court appointed counsel for the defendant in their researches on the case, and by the distinguished ability with which they have marshaled their respective arguments." *Id.*, 171 F. 2d at 924.

And see *Cramer* v. *United States*, 325 U. S. 1, 8, n. 9: "Counsel have lightened our burden of examination of the considerable accumulation of historical materials."

[23] In *Henry* v. *Hodges*, 171 F. 2d 401 (C.A. 2), certiorari denied *sub nom. Henry* v. *Smith*, 336 U. S. 968, I cited three cases for the proposition that a statutory requirement qualified by words such as "if available," "when it can not be avoided," and the like, was to be construed as directory rather than mandatory, so that failure to comply with the requirement did not invalidate the proceedings. *Martin* v. *Mott*, 12 Wheat. 19; *Mullan* v. *United States*, 140 U. S. 240; *Swaim* v. *United States*, 165 U. S. 553. The Second Circuit added two additional citations precisely in point, viz., *Bishop* v. *United States*, 197 U. S. 334, and *Kahn* v. *Anderson*, 255 U. S. 1—which I took, then as now, as bespeaking inadequate research on my part.

to assist the appellate court by pointing out the actual state of the decisional law.[24] On occasion, judges are sufficiently annoyed, when counsel neglect their homework, to make pointed references to controlling decisions "apparently overlooked by counsel," [25] or to the lack of essential allegations that both sides have failed to notice in an indictment.[26] Indeed, one of the most untidy areas in our law today can be directly traced to the failure of counsel on both sides to invoke a controlling decision.[27]

The discussion just above sufficiently demonstrates the vice of overloading a brief with too many citations, but it is surely a more serious criticism of counsel when the appellate court says in its published opinion that "The so-called briefs, of two pages and one page respectively, * * * have been of no help to us at all," [28] or when it remarks that "The defendant's brief is unique in that it does not cite a single authority in support of the contentions made." [29]

Section 70. The ornamental citation.—The temptation to toss in a bit of tangential learning or to button up a train of thought with a pat quotation is frequently a very strong one. I know it is that way in my own case, and I note below some instances of that tendency—simply by way of illustration, and not at all, I should hasten to add, to show what a very learned fellow I can be at times.

To the extent that the inclusion of an ornamental citation (or even a few of them) does not interfere with or detract from the main stream of the argument, indulgence in this particular form

---

[24] See the thoroughly unpleasant comments made in *Thys Company* v. *Anglo California National Bank,* 219 F. 2d 131 (C.A. 9) at 133 and *passim.*

[25] *Yee Si* v. *Boyd,* 243 F. 2d 203, 208 (C.A. 9) ; *Phillips* v. *United States,* 243 F. 2d 1, 7 (C.A. 9).

[26] *United States* v. *Deutsch,* 243 F. 2d 435 (C.A. 3).

[27] After *Johnson* v. *Zerbst,* 304 U. S. 458, had substantially broadened the traditional scope of collateral review by habeas corpus of convictions in civilian courts, the Court in *Hiatt* v. *Brown,* 339 U. S. 103, considered an instance of collateral review of a conviction by court-martial; neither side cited *Johnson* v. *Zerbst.* When the question next arose, *Johnson* v. *Zerbst* was cited but not discussed, and the justices divided—actually, splintered—so that there was no opinion of the Court. *Burns* v. *Wilson,* 346 U. S. 137, and see particularly the opinion of Frankfurter, J., dissenting on denial of the petition for rehearing, 346 U. S. 844, 848-849. I have discussed the present state of the law on this point in *Courts-Martial and the Bill of Rights: The Original Practice,* 72 Harv. L. Rev. 1, 266, at 296-303.

[28] *Boufford* v. *United States,* 239 F. 2d 841, 842 (C.A. 1).

[29] *Bell* v. *United States,* 251 F. 2d 490, 494 (C.A. 8).

of vanity can do no harm; it may even give one's brief an appealing overtone of erudition that a court will respect. The first two examples noted below may qualify as illustrations. Then again, the subject may be such that what might ordinarily be considered merely ornamental citations turn out to be strictly utilitarian; example (c), below, is an instance of such a situation.

On occasion, too, the quest for the ornamental citation may turn up either the winning case in point or at least one that will really harry the opposition; see the two examples noted in (d), below. And finally there is the ornamental citation or ornamental discussion that leads nowhere and adds nothing, and is therefore bad. A few Federal judges, living and dead, were given to this practice; examples appear at large in the reports; further identification would be both invidious and unnecessary.

(a) In the *Girouard* case,[30] already discussed in Sections 50 and 57 above, the Government brief stressed that, in view of the legislative history, adoption of petitioner's view would involve the rewriting of an Act of Congress. By way of sharpening the issue, the brief went on:

> In view of this compelling legislative history, of Congressional action and of highly significant Congressional inaction, the rule of the *Schwimmer, Macintosh,* and *Bland* cases has become a statutory rule, having an independent legislative basis, which, we submit, can be reconsidered only by Congress, and which is not open for reconsideration or reexamination here.
>
> We need not stop now to inquire when and to what extent adherence to the precept of *stare decisis* is either necessary or desirable. There is here no question of common law, requiring resolution of the paradox that "law must be stable and yet it cannot stand still," Pound, *Interpretations of Legal History,* 1; cf. Cardozo, *The Growth of the Law, passim.* There is before this Court no problem of reconciling situations which involve similar factual patterns embroidered with varying niceties of legal expression, such as this Court considered against an equivocal background of legislative history in *Helvering* v. *Hallock,* 309 U. S. 106. The present case does not require a reexamination of constitutional doctrine in the light of legislative reenactments which necessarily question earlier judgments or decisions on constitutional issues. See *Helvering* v. *Griffiths,* 318 U. S. 371, 400–401, discussed in Petitioner's Brief, pp. 33–34. Nor is there here any question of either the power or the propriety of this Court's reexami-

---

[30] *Girouard* v. *United States,* 328 U. S. 61.

nation and reconsideration of its prior constitutional determinations; we have ourselves, *supra*, pp. 39–42, invited a reexamination of the constitutional aspects of the *Macintosh* decision.

The proposition here is broader and bolder: It is that this Court rewrite an Act of Congress. It is that this Court, by reconsidering the steps which led to a result which Congress has since independently adopted, arrive at a new result which Congress advisedly refused to adopt.

In the context, Pound and Cardozo were unquestionably ornamental citations, but their inclusion did serve to add support to one of the steps in the argument.

(b) Some dozen or so years ago, a soldier who had been badly wounded in World War II sued the United States to recover just compensation for the use of his body.[31] The case is set out in the following excerpt from the Government's brief in opposition to the petition for certiorari.

STATEMENT

Petitioner, Edward C. Commers, was inducted into the military service on October 19, 1942, pursuant to the provisions of the Selective Training and Service Act of 1940, c. 720, 54 Stat. 885 (50 U.S.C. App. 301 *et seq.*) (R. 4). Prior to that time he was earning, as a manual laborer, at least $200 per month (R. 8). After receiving his basic training he was assigned to the 6th Infantry Division of the United States Army and served with that Division in various campaigns in New Guinea and the Philippine Islands (R. 4-6). In these campaigns he received severe injuries and was afflicted with malaria and other diseases and tropical maladies (R. 5-7). During his service in the Army, from which he was discharged on August 6, 1945, he was awarded two Silver Stars,* one Bronze Star Medal,† three Purple Hearts,‡ and a Good Conduct Medal § (R. 4, 6, 16).

On March 26, 1946, petitioner filed an amended complaint in the

---

[31] *Commers* v. *United States*, 66 F. Supp. 943 (D. Mont.), affirmed, 159 F. 2d 248 (C. A. 9), certiorari denied, 331 U. S. 807.

* Awarded for gallantry in action. See Army Regulations 600-45, 22 September 1943, par. 13.

† Awarded for gallantry in action, to recognize minor acts of heroism in actual combat. Army Regulations 600-45, 22 September 1943, as changed by Changes No. 3, 25 April 1944, par. 15½.

‡ Awarded for wounds received in action. Army Regulations 600-45, 22 September 1943, as changed by Changes No. 7, 14 July 1945, par. 16.

§ Awarded for exemplary behavior, efficiency, and fidelity. Army Regulations 600-68, May 4, 1943.

District Court of the United States for the District of Montana alleging that because of the injuries and sicknesses which he had suffered during his Army service he is unable to follow any substantial gainful occupation as a manual laborer, and that it is reasonably certain that his disabilities will continue in a totally disabling degree throughout his life (R. 7). He is now receiving from the Veterans' Administration of the United States for his disabilities the sum of $34.50 a month when he is not hospitalized and $20 a month when he is in a hospital (R. 8).

The petitioner prayed for a declaratory judgment holding in substance, (1) that the taking of his body and earning power for use in the military forces of the United States was a taking of private property for a public use; (2) that the United States is obligated not only under the Fifth Amendment, but as a matter of natural right, to make just compensation to petitioner and all other veterans disabled in World War II; (3) that petitioner and all other disabled war veterans are constitutionally entitled to try their claims for bodily impairment in the district courts of the United States and to have the jury trial guaranteed by the Seventh Amendment; (4) that the consent of the United States to be sued upon the claims of its war disabled is implied from the Fifth Amendment (R. 15-16).

The United States filed a motion to dismiss the complaint on the grounds that it did not state a claim upon which relief could be granted and that the court was without jurisdiction as the United States had not consented to be sued in this manner (R. 17). The judgment of the District Court (R. 35) granting the motion to dismiss was affirmed by the court below without opinion (R. 48).

ARGUMENT

Petitioner contends that the admitted power of the United States to raise armies by conscription (Pet. 21) is subject to the provision of the Fifth Amendment that "private property" shall not be taken for public use without just compensation, that any soldier whose "bodily integrity and earning power have been consumed in the common defense" is entitled to compensation therefor, and that such soldier may have the existence and extent of his disabilities determined in the courts of the United States and be "justly compensated therefor as a matter of constitutional right" (Pet. 7, 8).

Petitioner's contentions have a certain philosophical appeal, but that is their only merit. Whatever may be the scope of the Fifth Amendment with respect to property destroyed in the course of actual military operations (*United States* v. *Pacific Railroad*, 120 U. S. 227),[32]

---

[32] Since reaffirmed in *United States* v. *Caltex* (*Philippines*), 344 U. S. 149 (1952). [Footnote not in original.]

the short and conclusive answer to petitioner's argument is that, since the ratification of the Thirteenth Amendment, there has been no property right in a living human body. And, while that Amendment ended slavery and all other forms of involuntary servitude (*Clyatt* v. *United States,* 197 U. S. 207; *Bailey* v. *Alabama,* 219 U. S. 219; *United States* v. *Reynolds,* 235 U. S. 133), it did not terminate the numerous civic duties which require the citizen to devote his labor and if need be, his life, to the service of the community. In those categories are included the duty to render military service (*Selective Draft Law Cases,* 245 U. S. 366), the duty to labor for a reasonable time on public roads near his residence without direct compensation (*Butler* v. *Perry,* 240 U. S. 328), and the duty to assist the police to enforce the justice of the state (*Matter of Babington* v. *Yellow Taxi Corp.,* 250 N. Y. 14, per Cardozo, Ch. J.).

This Court has several times pointed out the nature of the obligation of military service. *Jacobson* v. *Massachusetts,* 197 U. S. 11, 29; *Selective Draft Law Cases,* 245 U. S. 366, 378. In the latter case, Chief Justice White said, in words which have frequently been quoted: "It may not be doubted that the very conception of a just government and its duty to the citizen includes the reciprocal obligation of the citizen to render military service in case of need and the right to compel it."

The same thought is expressed in the Congressional declaration contained in Section 1 (b) of the Selective Training and Service Act of 1940, 54 Stat. 885, 50 U.S.C. App. 301 (b): "that in a free society the obligations and privileges of military training and service should be shared generally in accordance with a fair and just system of selective compulsory military training and service."

The basic fallacy of petitioner's view is that he confounds the nation's right to compel the citizen's obligation to render military service with a taking of property. Once that distinction is recognized, his entire case falls. It may be a distinction which is historical rather than logical, but it is well settled; and, here also, "Upon this point a page of history is worth a volume of logic." *New York Trust Co.* v. *Eisner,* 256 U. S. 345, 349. Consequently we do not deem it necessary to discuss the technical jurisdictional infirmities of the present complaint, which are adequately disposed of in the opinion of the District Court (R. 30-39).

The citations of the Army Regulations governing the awards of the lad's decorations were ornamental in the dragged-in-by-the-ears sense, but the citations to the several instances of legally compelled services were necessary to the argument. As to the final Holmes quotation—well, that was just too pat to be omitted.

(c) An example of the mingling of a few ornamental citations with a good many necessary ones was the portion of the *Haupt* treason brief that was printed in the earlier version of this book.[33]

(d) Perhaps in some of the examples just cited the ornamental citations were merely reflections of the brief-writer's more or less angular personality; I must leave that to more objective judges than I. But every once in a while the search for the ornamental citation pays off, and then it compensates for and outweighs a good deal of what might otherwise be simply a somewhat vulgarly ostentatious display of learning.

(1) One example in my practice was the Hackfeld alien property case,[34] in which a vital question, and, in the end, the controlling one, was whether Hackfeld had acquired citizenship in the then Republic of Hawaii through the receipt of a Certificate of Special Rights of Citizenship issued under Article 17 of the Constitution of that Republic.[35] There were no reported cases on the point, argument based on the constitutional provision itself had ranged far and wide, and the Government was faced with an adverse ruling of the Secretary of State that such a Certificate did confer citizenship.[36]

While in Hawaii taking depositions in the case in 1938, I had

---

[33] *Haupt* v. *United States*, 330 U. S. 631. The portions of the Government's brief in that case (No. 49, Oct. T. 1946) dealing with the elements of the crime of treason and with the scope of the two-witness requirement were set forth at pp. 342-370 of *Effective Appellate Advocacy*.

[34] *United States* v. *Rodiek*, 117 F. 2d 588 (C.A. 2), rehearing denied with opinion, 120 F. 2d 760, affirmed by equally divided court, 315 U. S. 783. See also *Rodiek* v. *United States*, 100 C. Cls. 267.

[35] Art. 17, Sec. 2: "Any person not a Hawaiian citizen, who took active part, or otherwise rendered substantial service in the formation of, and has since supported the Provisional Government of Hawaii, who shall within six months from the promulgation of this Constitution procure from the Minister of the Interior a certificate of such service, as herein set forth; and who shall take an oath to support this Constitution and the laws of the Republic so long as he shall remain domiciled in the Republic, shall be entitled to all the privileges of citizenship without thereby prejudicing his native citizenship or allegiance."

Art. 17, Sec. 5: "Any person to whom such certificate shall be granted shall be admitted, upon application, to naturalization, without showing any further qualifications."

Art. 18, Sec. 1: "The naturalization of aliens shall be exclusively within the jurisdiction of the Justices of the Supreme Court."

[36] See 3 Hackworth, *Digest of International Law*, 125. The State Department has gone astray because it blindly followed the ruling in *Bowler's case*, 2 For. Rel. of the U. S. (1895) 853; see also *Godfrey's case, id.* at 867, without

occasion to discuss the matter with a number of eminent local practitioners, now unfortunately all deceased, who assured me that the Hawaiian bar all considered the Secretary's ruling clearly erroneous. These gentlemen had been contemporaries of the Republic of Hawaii: Judge A. G. M. Robertson was then the sole survivor of the Convention that had framed the Constitution of that Republic, Judge W. L. Stanley had served on the bench shortly thereafter, and Governor W. F. Frear had been a judge under Monarchy, Provisional Government, and Republic alike and had moreover been a member of the Commission that had drafted the Hawaiian Organic Act.[37] Surely the unanimous opinion of men such as these, to the effect that the receipt of a Certificate of Special Rights of Citizenship did not confer Hawaiian nationality, was weighty indeed—but how bring their views before the U. S. District Court for the Southern District of New York?

I worked out a somewhat labored syllogism while in the Islands: (1) A U. S. Court would judicially notice the foreign law of an antecedent sovereignty on U. S. soil. (2) However, judicial notice is not judicial knowledge. *Shapleigh* v. *Mier*.[38] (3) Foreign systems of law are, to us, "like a wall of stone"; one has to be brought up within the system to understand it. *Diaz* v. *Gonzales*.[39] (4) Hawaiian law is for this purpose to be regarded as foreign,

---

observing the complete change in the Hawaiian naturalization laws effected by the Constitution of the Republic. Bowler had been naturalized under the laws of the Monarchy, and although Godfrey had become a denizen under the Republic, the real question before the U. S. State Department was not whether he had acquired Hawaiian nationality but whether he had forfeited American diplomatic protection. The moral of these rulings in the light of the Hackfeld case is, I submit, that when a lawyer deals with foreign law, he is well advised to approach that subject with a high degree of intellectual humility. Cf. note 39, *infra*.

[37] Provided for in the Joint Resolution of Annexation, 30 Stat. 750, 751.

[38] 299 U. S. 468.

[39] 261 U. S. 102, 105-106, *per* Holmes, J.: "This Court has stated many times the deference due to the understanding of the local courts upon matters of purely local concern. * * * This is especially true in dealing with the decisions of a court inheriting and brought up in a different system from that which prevails here. When we contemplate such a system from the outside it seems like a wall of stone, every part even with all the others, except so far as our own local education may lead us to see subordinations to which we are accustomed. But to one brought up within it, varying emphasis, tacit assumptions, unwritten practices, a thousand influences gained only from life, may give to the different parts wholly new values that logic and grammar never could have got from the books."

equally with Puerto Rican law. *Waialua Agricultural Co.* v. *Christian.*[40] Therefore, (5) it is proper to look to the views of those brought up within the system.

Fortified by this laboriously constructed syllogism, I duly asked these witnesses (plus two others), "Were persons who received such special rights of citizenship considered by the bar of Hawaii to be Hawaiian citizens?" My opponent screamed that I was asking for the witnesses' opinions on a point of law, as indeed I was; but I got the expected helpful answers, and then took the depositions back to the mainland and prepared for the trial.

In the course of expanding the foregoing for the trial brief on the law, I looked for a suitable ornamental citation to document the first and undisputed proposition that a United States court would judicially notice the foreign law of an earlier sovereign on American soil. A quick check in the digest turned up *Fremont* v. *United States,*[41] where Chief Justice Taney had said:

And when there are no published reports of judicial decisions which show the received construction of a statute, and the powers exercised under it by the tribunals or officers of the government, it is often necessary to seek information from other authentic sources, such as the records of official acts, and the practice of the different tribunals and public authorities. *And it may sometimes be necessary to seek information from individuals whose official position or pursuits have given them opportunities of acquiring knowledge.* [Italics added.]

This of course made the Hawaiian lawyers' opinions admissible; the quest for the ornamental citation had paid off in jackpot fashion. At the trial, the testimony in question went in with the mere citation of the *Fremont* case, and both the District Court and the Second Circuit placed reliance on that testimony in ruling that receipt of the Certificate of Special Rights had not made Hackfeld (who had been born in Germany) a citizen of the Republic of Hawaii.[42]

---

[40] 305 U. S. 91.
[41] 17 How. 542, 557.
[42] "That the mere acceptance of one of these special rights certificates did not entitle the holder to citizenship in the Republic was further shown by a great mass of evidence introduced by the Government, as follows: * * * (2) Five distinguished Honolulu lawyers testified that it was the general understanding of the bar of Hawaii that the mere acceptance of such a special rights certificate had no such effect as Hackfeld claimed." Oral opinion of

(2) Another instance of a quest for the ornamental citation that turned up something far more valuable occurred in the first two cases dealing with the validity of military trials of civilian dependents in time of peace.[43]

In its endeavor to support the military jurisdiction, the Government quoted the following passage from a then recent decision of the Court of Military Appeals:

> Conceding we are not in a state of declared war, our foreign armies may be likened to the Army garrisons in the far west during the days of the Indian Wars. They must be prepared to fight at the drop of a boot, and their state of readiness depends upon control over those who contribute to the success of their operations. Camp followers in those days were considered a necessary part of a military expedition * * *.[44]

Using this analogy, the Government argued that present day civilian dependents were similarly subject to military law.

In the course of preparing the answering brief on behalf of the civilian women, I questioned in my mind the soundness of the analogy, inasmuch as there was considerable law to the effect that Indian Wars, despite their undeclared status, were to be regarded as involving a time of war rather than of peace;[45] and moreover I recalled having seen, somewhere, a comment to the effect that in strictness there was no such thing as a camp follower except in time of war. Any reference to the latter proposition was essentially ornamental; none the less, I looked for and found it; and, when located, the actual holding proved to be far broader than I had recalled it to be. The Judge Advocate General of the Army had early ruled as follows:

Coxe, D. J., directing a verdict for the United States, C.C.A. record, pp. 745-746; Supreme Court record, pp. 635-636, No. 325, Oct. T. 1941.

"The testimony of five distinguished members of the Hawaiian bar accords with our interpretation of the Hawaiian law." *United States* v. *Rodiek, supra,* 117 F. 2d at 594.

[43] *Reid* v. *Covert,* 354 U. S. 1.

[44] *United States* v. *Burney,* 6 USCMA 776, 799, 21 CMR 98, 121, quoted in Pet. Br., No. 713, Oct. T. 1955, p. 75.

[45] See 13 Op. Atty. Gen. 31, 470, and 472; Dig. Op. JAG, 1912, p. 1055; Winthrop, *Military Law & Precedents* (2d ed. 1896) *136-137, *964, *976. Indians violating the laws of war were held subject to trial like any other unlawful belligerents. *Case of the Modoc Indians,* 14 Op. Atty. Gen. 249. But an Indian killing a soldier in battle was accordingly not guilty of murder. *United States* v. *Plenty Horses* (Dist. So. Dak. 1891), cited in Winthrop, *1224-1225.

A post trader is not, under the Act of 1876, and was not under that of 1867 or 1870, amenable to the jurisdiction of a military court in time of peace. The earlier statutes assimilated him to a camp follower, but, strictly and properly, there can be no such thing as a camp follower in time of peace, and the only military jurisdiction to which a camp follower may become subject is that indicated by the 63d Article of War, viz. one exercisable only "in the field" or on the theatre of war. Nor can the Act of 1876, in providing that post traders shall be "subject to the rules and regulations for the government of the army," render them amenable to trial by court martial in time of peace. * * * If * * * the Articles of War are intended to be included, the amenability imposed is simply that fixed by the particular Article applicable to civilians employed in connection with the Army, viz. Art. 63, which attaches this amenability only in time of war and in the field. Thus, though post traders might perhaps become liable to trial by court martial if employed on the theatre of an Indian war, as persons serving with an Army in the field in the sense of that Article, they cannot be made so liable when not thus situated * * *.[46]

Consequently, accepting fully the Government's contention that the jurisdictional situation of modern civilian dependents abroad was identical with that of the camp followers of our post-Civil War Indian-fighting Army, this ruling, which established that the post trader of old was not triable by court-martial except at a time and in an area of actual hostilities,[47] necessarily and inescapably threw the Government lawyers' analogy right back into their collective faces, and turned their contention into a powerful argument in favor of the civilian women.

Indeed, the greatest compliment paid by the Government to the weight of the post trader ruling was the circumstance that, in the over 200 printed pages of argument it presented to the Court after the filing of the brief containing the ruling, and before final decision on rehearing, it never once mentioned—much less discussed—the status of the post trader. While such an ostrich-like technique is not to be commended (compare Section 35 (d) above

---

[46] Dig. Op. JAG, 1880, p. 384, ¶ 4; id., 1895, pp. 599-600, ¶ 4; id., 1901, p. 563, ¶ 2023.

[47] The post trader was succeeded by the post exchange—see *Dugan* v. *United States*, 34 C. Cls. 458; *Kenny* v. *United States*, 62 C. Cls. 328; and *Standard Oil Co.* v. *Johnson*, 316 U. S. 481, for differing accounts of the emergence of the now familiar PX—and, by the time the 1912 edition of the Dig. Op. JAG was being compiled, had become obsolete, so that the older ruling was not again reprinted.

and Section 83 (b) below), in this instance it once more emphasized, though assuredly in highly unorthodox fashion, the fact that
the brief-writer who starts out to look for a merely ornamental citation may in the process uncover a real blockbuster.

Section 71. Citations; manner of citation; in general.—Legal
citations are abbreviations designed to identify the location, the
source, and hence *prima facie* the weight, of the authorities relied
upon by the brief-writer. Citations must be short enough to save
the reader's time, and yet long enough to preclude the slightest
possibility of confusion by reason of over-compression. Like any
other kind of abbreviation constantly in use, legal citations reflect
the conventions and usages of the profession that employs them.
Consequently, while in many instances there is a wide range of variant citation forms that are equally correct and hence equally acceptable, in other instances there is a sharp, clear line between
correct and incorrect usage, a line that sets off the well-educated
lawyer who is steeped in the traditions of a learned profession
from his less privileged brethren to whom the practice of law is
simply a more or less remunerative trade.

Like all professional conventions, fashions in citation forms
change with the times. It was formerly customary to insert a comma
between the volume and the page of the report being cited, as for
instance, "10 Modern, 138." [48] Similarly, when the Federal Reporter was first published, it was only partially abbreviated; the
usual citation was, e.g., "14 Fed. Rep. 682." [49] And, when the
United States Code was still a novelty, one of the most meticulous of
Supreme Court Justices cited it simply as "C.," followed by title
and section numbers.[50] Other examples of changing citation conventions will readily occur to the reader.

The number of persons doing legal writing and thus employ-
ing citations grew markedly as more and more legal journals came
to be published. In time, the editors of those publications—like
editors everywhere—prescribed style manuals to which all con-
tributors were required to conform. At first such formbooks were
simply drawn from the citation usages met with in the older series
of reports. Later, refinements and innovations were introduced,
such as, in Federal citations, an indication of the court deciding the

---

[48] Wallace, *The Reporters* (Heard's 4th ed. 1882) 274.
[49] E.g., 120 U. S. at 111.
[50] Holmes, J., in *Mitchel* v. *Hampel,* 276 U. S. 299, 302.

case. Inasmuch as the Federal Reporter for its first 50 years or so reported the decisions of all the lower Federal courts—the Circuit Courts as long as they existed, the Circuit Courts of Appeals from the time of their creation, and the District Courts until the Federal Supplement began publication—it was obviously most helpful to a reader to have some indication of the authority of a given "Fed." citation.

But along with such useful additions, which were varied in minor details over the years—so that, in the larger law offices, one could tell from a particular lawyer's citation forms just what volumes of the law review he had helped to edit—the law school journals invented and began to use a virtually cryptographic code to signal the weight to be accorded a particular citation appearing in their pages. Along with *accord* and *semble,* which had the support of legal tradition, they introduced the use of "see," "cf.," "but see" and "but cf." Each of these prefixes had a value—in the minds of the editors—as precise as those attaching to algebraic symbols. At this juncture, the path of the law reviews on the one hand, and that of practitioners and judges on the other, diverged sharply; such "introductory signals" carried as little meaning to the profession as, for example, a localized and topical classroom pleasantry. And, ultimately, with the appearance of the 9th edition of *A Uniform System of Citation,* published in 1954, the law reviews in important respects turned their backs on professional tradition, and marched off in a different direction all their own.

The nature of their more important departures from accepted lawyer usage will be pointed out in the sections that follow. At this juncture it will suffice simply to set forth some general observations to guide the lawyer who undertakes to write briefs for real courts (i.e., other than moot courts) .

First of all, follow a system of citation that is clear, that is simple, and with which the judicial reader will feel comfortable. The practitioner in the Federal courts is in consequence well advised to adopt—at least as a starting point—the citation form employed in the official U. S. Reports.

Second, be consistent—or at least reasonably so. (A former colleague always insisted that the only real essential was to avoid inconsistency on the same page.)

Third, be sufficiently flexible to eliminate even an appearance of pedantry. Thus, while it is generally desirable to add the designation of the court in parentheses, as for instance *Parsons* v. *Smith*, 255 F. 2d 595 (C.A. 3), there is no need to do so when you have already indicated the court in your text—e.g., "as held by the Third Circuit in *Parsons* v. *Smith*, 255 F. 2d 595."

Fourth, use *A Uniform System of Citation* with caution. It is full of useful suggestions, but the practitioner will be well advised not to follow it blindly.

Section 72. Citations; manner of citation; titles of cases.— Very frequently the title of a case is extremely long as it appears at the beginning of the report. Thus, a recent Supreme Court case bears the title *United New York and New Jersey Sandy Hook Pilots Association et al.* v. *Halecki, Administratrix.*[51] How much of the foregoing should go into the brief?

One way is to start with the name of the case as it appears at the beginning of the opinion in the official report, and then to hack away at it to reduce that name to more manageable proportions. Another system is to cite the case as it appears in the running head, i.e., the line on the top of the right-hand page of the report above the opinion, and to expand only if necessary.

The latter method—which I will call the running head rule of thumb—is used by the Reporter of Decisions of the Supreme Court. It is also used by the Office of the Solicitor General of the United States. Apart from the weight of that combined authority, it results in the convenience of short case titles, since the U. S. Reports are published in octavo volumes whose pages are small enough to insure a short running head as the case title. It is therefore the preferable method on every ground. Accordingly, in the instance set out above, where the running head in the official reports is *United Pilots Assn.* v. *Halecki*, the case will be thus cited.

Here are some necessary qualifications to the running head rule of thumb:

(a) Where the first word of either party's name is abbreviated in the running head, it will normally be spelled out in the citation.

Thus, the case of *International Harvester Credit Corp. et al.* v. *Goodrich et al., Constituting the State Tax Commission of New York*[52] has the running head *Int. Harvester Corp.* v. *Goodrich*. The first word of appellant's name is abbreviated, hence the case

---

[51] 358 U. S. 613.
[52] 350 U. S. 537.

would be cited in a brief as *International Harvester Corp. v. Goodrich.* Similarly, *U. S. Gypsum Co. v. Nat. Gypsum Co.*[53] in the running head becomes *United States Gypsum Co. v. National Gypsum Co.* in the brief, while *Pan-Atlantic Corp. v. Atl. Coast Line*[54] in the running head is written as *Pan-Atlantic Corp. v. Atlantic Coast Line* in the brief.

(b) Very frequently one of the parties is an agency sufficiently well known so that it can be unmistakably identified by its initials, which accordingly are simply abbreviated in the running head. E.g., *United States v. I.C.C.*,[55] *S.E.C. v. Louisiana Pub. Serv. Comm'n.*,[56] *F.T.C. v. National Casualty Co.*[57] The official reports in such instances apply qualification (a), above, and spell out the name of the agency in later citations—*Interstate Commerce Comm., Securities & Exch. Comm., Federal Trade Comm.* In cases involving the National Labor Relations Board, the consistent running head rendering has been *Labor Board*—e.g., *Labor Board v. Steelworkers.*[58] There the basic rule of thumb disposes of the question of how to cite.

While a variant form of citation, with initials alone not set off by periods—ICC, SEC, FTC, NLRB—cannot fairly be considered plainly wrong, the lawyer writing briefs for Federal courts will undoubtedly do better to follow the style book of the U. S. Reports.

(c) Where one of the parties is an organization similarly known by initials, the practice appears to vary. Thus, *United States v. C.I.O.*[59] and *N.A.A.C.P. v. Alabama*[60] are cited just as they appear in the running head, initials, periods, and all. On the other hand, *A.F. of L. v. Watson*[61] has later been cited, on consecutive pages, both as *American Federation of Labor v. Watson* and as *A.F. of L. v. Watson.*[62] In this instance, you pays your money and you takes your choice—just try to be consistent, at least in the same brief.

---

[53] 352 U. S. 457.
[54] 353 U. S. 436.
[55] 352 U. S. 158.
[56] 353 U. S. 368.
[57] 357 U. S. 560.
[58] 357 U. S. 357.
[59] 335 U. S. 106.
[60] 357 U. S. 449.
[61] 327 U. S. 582.
[62] The expanded version appears at 345 U. S. 245, the contracted one at 345 U. S. 246.

But, while you may expand a Supreme Court running head abbreviation, don't abbreviate it simply for the sake of abbreviating. Thus, whether you agree or disagree with the Segregation Cases, their citation will read more smoothly as *Brown* v. *Board of Education* than as *Brown* v. *Board of Educ.* The first version is that of the running head,[63] the second the work of the law reviews. Silly, isn't it?

(d) Habeas corpus cases present a problem for any brief-writer who does not follow the running head rule.

Suppose that one, Schmaltz, being detained in an institution presided over by a warden answering to the name of Zilch, brings habeas corpus seeking release from this form of enforced hospitality. The petition filed in the district court will normally be captioned *United States on the relation of Joseph Schmaltz* v. *Oscar J. Zilch, Warden, &c.* On occasion, and in some courts, this cause will, despite such a caption, be docketed simply as *Schmaltz* v. *Zilch.*[64] As the case travels from court to court, the running heads of the reported opinions will appear in any of three possible versions: *U. S. ex rel. Schmaltz* v. *Zilch; United States* v. *Zilch; Schmaltz* v. *Zilch.*

How cite the case? Here again, the brief-writer will be well advised to be consistent in following the reports in their inconsistencies and to follow the running head, whatever it is. True, *United States* v. *Kinsella*, followed by the citation, will not advise the casual reader whether he is reading the opinion of the district court in the case of Mrs. Smith [65] or of Mrs. Dial,[66] but then *Green* v. *United States*, depending on the citation, may be either the recent double jeopardy case [67] or the decision in the succeeding volume on the constitutionality of non-jury trials in contempt pro-

---

[63] 347 U. S. 483 and 349 U. S. 294.

[64] In the *Covert* case, I captioned the petition, *United States of America on the Relation of Clarice B. Covert* v. *Curtis Reid, Superintendent of the District of Columbia Jail.* See R. 1, No. 701, Oct. T. 1955. To no avail; the Clerk docketed the case as *Covert* v. *Reid*, and *ex rel.* never reappeared. *Quaere*, was this an instance of applying the real-party-in-interest principle of Rule 17 (a), F. R. Civ. P., to a habeas corpus proceeding, notwithstanding Rule 81 (a) (2), which makes the Rules of Civil Procedure applicable to habeas corpus only at the appellate stage?

[65] 137 F. Supp. 806 (S. D. W. Va.), ultimately reversed, 354 U. S. 1, *sub nom. Kinsella* v. *Krueger.*

[66] 164 F. Supp. 707 (S. D. W. Va.), affirmed, 361 U. S. 234, *sub nom. Kinsella* v. *Singleton.*

[67] 355 U. S. 184.

ceedings,[68] while *United States* v. *duPont & Co.* may similarly be either the cellophane antitrust case [69] or the General Motors antitrust case.[70]

So—follow the running head. And do likewise in the Miller Act [71] cases, which provide that the action on the contractor's bond is to be brought in the name of the United States for the use of the person suing. E.g., *United States* v. *Carter.*[72]

(e) The National Reporter System, despite its many admirable qualities, is not always characterized by meticulous nicety in collateral editorial matters, particularly with reference to running heads. In the tax field, for instance, the No. 1 revenuer formerly appeared interchangeably as *Commissioner of Internal Revenue, Com'r of Internal Revenue, Commissioner of Internal Rev., Commissioner of Int. Rev.,* and *Commissioner of I. R.* More recently, he is shown in the running head simply as *C.I.R.* In this instance the solution is to require the running head rule to yield to simplification: Just cite as *Commissioner,* neither more nor less. And, inasmuch as all of the Federal volumes have appeared in the larger quarto size for many years, with larger pages accommodating a longer running head, judicious trimming of complicated corporate names on the part of the brief-writer is entirely in order, even for the most devoted followers of the running head rule.

(f) In the reports of the Tax Court and of the Court of Claims, the running head includes only the name of the petitioner and of the plaintiff, respectively. After all, every Tax Court petitioner sues the Commissioner of Internal Revenue, every Court of Claims plaintiff the United States. At this point it is well to invoke the principle (p. 223, *supra*) that the brief-writer should keep the judicial reader comfortable. The Court of Claims cites its cases in the usual way, e.g., *Loth* v. *United States,*[73] notwithstanding that the running head is rendered as *Margaret R. Loth, et al.* The Tax Court, on the other hand, cites its own prior rulings by running head alone: *Nathan Fink.*[74] My own preference, therefore, is to

---

[68] 356 U. S. 165.
[69] 351 U. S. 377.
[70] 353 U. S. 586.
[71] Act of August 24, 1935, c. 642, 49 Stat. 793; 40 U.S.C. §§ 270a and 270b.
[72] 353 U. S. 210. Civil Rule 17 (a) expressly excepts such cases from the real-party-in-interest requirement.
[73] 133 C. Cls. 476.
[74] 29 T. C. 1119.

follow each court's system of citation for my citation of its decisions in other courts.[75]

(g) If the running head in the official report differs from that in an unofficial one, follow the former if it is available. If not, and if you are dealing with U. S. cases, you can be certain that the official running head reads *New York* and not *State of New York*. Therefore, always omit *State of* in such cases if and when it appears in the running head of an unofficial report.

(h) Finally, in the English reports, as well as in many of the earlier American reports, the name of the case is carried, not in a running head, but in a side-note. In those instances, use the side-note for the form of the citation.

Section 73. Citations; manner of citation; reports.—What follows immediately below must be considered in the light of any applicable court rules; some place considerable emphasis on how cases should be cited, and as to whether or when citations to the National Reporter System should be included.

(a) *U. S. reports.* When citing cases from the U. S. reports prior to volume 91 U. S., always cite by the name of the reporter and not by the subsequently assigned consecutive number. Thus, the citation to *Marbury* v. *Madison* is 1 Cranch 137, *not* 5 U. S. 137; to *Luther* v. *Borden*, 7 How. 1, *not* 48 U. S. 1; to *Ex parte Milligan*, 4 Wall. 2, *not* 71 U. S. 2. Citations to such cases other than by the name of the reporter alone mark the brief-writer as a legal illiterate, or, at the very least, as one not very well brought up or educated.[76]

I am aware that, beginning in 1954, the law reviews introduced the thoroughly abominable system of using the numerical numbers plus a parenthetical citation to the reporter: e.g., 5 U. S. (1 Cranch) 137; 48 U. S. (7 How.) 1; 71 U. S. (4 Wall.) 2. It seems sufficient to remark that it is one of youth's inalienable privi-

---

[75] In this particular instance, the lads on the law reviews appear to have the edge on the Solicitor General and his staff.

[76] For convenience of reference, the following is the order of U. S. Reports:

4 of Dallas (Dall.)
9 of Cranch (now not generally abbreviated)
12 of Wheaton (Wheat.)
16 of Peters (Pet.)
24 of Howard (How.)
2 of Black (not generally abbreviated)
23 of Wallace (Wall.)

leges to be not only wrong, but stubbornly wrong to boot. No lawyer worth his salt is going to abandon the Supreme Court's own
consistent usage in favor of this perverse innovation. Interestingly
enough, in order to obtain for their pages a recent article by a Supreme Court Justice, the lads on one law school review were required by the author, as the price of publication in their pages, to
return to the traditional citation form.[77]

Moreover, notwithstanding the estimable concerns that publish the collateral sets of U. S. Supreme Court reports, there is no
need to encumber a brief with parallel citations to S. Ct. or to L.
ed.; the case can always be found, in any library, and in any of the
other reports, with the U. S. citation alone.

In this connection, and to prove that the foregoing is not just
a personal whim, it may be appropriate to quote from a letter received from a prominent member of a large metropolitan bar commenting on a chapter of this book when it first appeared in a legal
periodical:

> My second point is probably one with which you had nothing to
> do: the citation in your article and footnotes of "Sup. Ct." and "L. ed."
> citations along with the official citations to the United States reports.
> Except in the case of U. S. citations (and even there when a case has
> not been officially reported), I list parallel citations to all the reports,
> but I believe that where U. S. cases are officially reported it is burden-
> some, not only to the writer, but—more important—also to the
> reader, to give these unofficial citations in addition to the U. S. cita-
> tion. The practice is not particularly helpful to the reader because
> the unofficial reports are keyed to the official reports on the outside
> label of the appropriate volume. I would like to see someone in your
> position of prominence strike a blow for freedom from this burdensome
> practice which I think is an invention of book publishers not helpful
> to practicing lawyers. While, as my comments earlier in the letter will
> perhaps indicate, I am a believer in consistency and a proper amount
> of symmetry in the writing and in the printing of briefs, I believe that
> the burden of giving and reading parallel citations to U. S. cases far
> outweighs any possible benefit flowing from them.

Moreover, the official advance sheets are now so nearly current that there is much less excuse than formerly for citing the col-

---

[77] See Frankfurter, *John Marshall and the Judicial Function,* 69 Harv.
L. Rev. 217. The statement in the text is supported by the column entitled
With the Editors, at p. vii of the December 1955 issue of the cited publication.

lateral and unofficial reports even for recently decided cases; that may depend, however, on local library facilities. It should also be noted that the quickest service for the text of recent opinions of the Supreme Court is the *U. S. Law Week,* published by BNA, Incorporated, which is generally received in the mail the day after the decisions—two days before the slip opinions.

Recent and hence still unreported cases are cited by number and date of decision. E.g., "*Elkins* v. *United States,* No. 126, this Term, decided June 27, 1960." Where page reference is necessary, simply say "p. 7 of slip opinion." [77a] That form of citation facilitates reference, inasmuch as the slip opinions are circulated to the members of the Supreme Court, to all other Federal judges, and to the Department of Justice, which distributes them to its lawyers both in Washington and in the field. The several sets of slip opinions are constantly referred to, the unofficial advance sheets rarely if at all. If you do not have access to the slip opinions, then by all means use the U. S. Law Week citation.

(b) *Federal reports.* Cite as Fed., F.2d, or F. Supp., as the case may be; for at least twenty years or so it has been customary to omit the parentheses around the "2d." In the Federal Reporter itself, the parentheses dropped out beginning with 93 F. 2d, early in 1938. It is not wrong to cite the first series of the Federal Reporter as "F.," but "Fed." is preferable, because it is less apt to cause confusion in the inevitable situation where the "2d" has somehow dropped out of an "F.2d" citation.

Always add in parentheses, in order to indicate the weight of the citation, an indication of the court deciding the case; e.g., for district courts: (S.D.N.Y.), (E.D.Ill.), (D.Mass.); for the U. S. District Court for the District of Columbia: (D.D.C.); and for the old circuit courts: (C.C.S.D.N.Y.), (C.C.D.Kan.).

The intermediate Federal appellate courts started out as circuit courts of appeals, but in 1948, for no good or ascertainable reason,[78] became courts of appeals for the ——— circuit. Cite either as (C.A. 3) or as (3d Cir.); there is really not much difference; I prefer, and hence use, "C.A. 3."

[77a] See, for example, the citations to the slip opinions in the Petition for Rehearing that is set forth in Section 173, below.

[78] See 28 U.S.C. § 43 (a). For the reasons, or lack of them, see H. R. Rep. 308, 80th Cong., 1st sess., p. 5; Maris, *New Federal Judicial Code,* 34 A.B.A.J. 863, 865.

The appellate court in the District of Columbia is now, by virtue of statute, the United States Court of Appeals for the District of Columbia Circuit [79]—a circuit which extends only through the corridors of a single courthouse! To identify its decisions, some brief-writers add the indication (D. C. Cir.) ; others continue to use the older version (App. D. C.) ; some write (C.A.D.C.) ; while still others use (App. D. C.) if the case was decided before the District of Columbia was constituted a circuit and either (D. C. Cir.) or (C.A.D.C.) for post-1948 cases.[80] Personally I prefer the alternative last mentioned, viz., (App. D. C.) for pre-1948 decisions, and (D. C. Cir.) for cases decided thereafter. However, for briefs filed in that court, the rules require, in every instance, parallel citations to its own App. D. C. and U. S. App. D. C. reports,[81] in which event of course no further indication is necessary.

As to the old Federal Cases, that grand but now unfortunately rare series which reprints the old circuit court reports antedating 1880, the practice varies. Those cases are properly cited by number rather than by volume and page, but ideally the old report should be cited also: e.g., *Despan* v. *Olney*, 1 Curt. 306, Fed. Case No. 3822 (C.C.D.R.I.). A variant is to add the number of the Federal Cases volume, viz., 7 Fed. Cas. No. 3822. For page citations, write *Despan* v. *Olney*, 1 Curt. 306, 309-310, Fed. Case No. 3822, 7 Fed. Cas. at 535.

I won't assert that to cite the old Federal Cases without the name of the original report is on a par with citing the early U. S. cases by the consecutive volume number rather than by the name of the reporter, but I am confident that no real lawyer who has any feeling for the formative years when the Justices of the Supreme Court rode circuit will do so. After all, such a step would be on a par with citing an English decision prior to 1865 simply by its *English Reprint* location, without any reference to the report in which it first appeared and by which it can be recognized.

---

[79] See 28 U.S.C. § § 41, 43 (a) .

[80] Its original name was "Court of Appeals of the District of Columbia." Act of Feb. 9, 1893, c. 74, 27 Stat. 434. Some forty years later, following the Supreme Court's determination of the status of the District of Columbia courts in *O'Donoghue* v. *United States*, 289 U. S. 516, Congress changed the name to "United States Court of Appeals for the District of Columbia." Act of June 7, 1934, c. 426, 48 Stat. 926.

[81] D. C. Circuit, Rule 17 (b) (10) . This series is numbered consecutively; 75 U. S. App. D. C. is the first volume with the longer title.

(c) *Parallel citations to Federal cases.* When the Circuit Courts of Appeals were first established, their opinions were officially reported and were cited as "C.C.A." That series ceased publication in 1919 or thereabouts, most libraries now do not have it, and consequently citations thereto are not only useless but burdensome besides.

The Court of Claims has its own series of reports, which it cites as "C. Cls." Some but not all of its present day decisions appear in F. Supp., and, since 1960, in F.2d. See p. 19, *supra.* For a Court of Claims brief, cite only C. Cls., unless the case is still unreported, in which event you may use either the slip opinion citation or F. Supp. or F.2d. For briefs in other courts, adapt your citations to their and your library facilities; parallel citations, if readily available, will probably be most convenient all around.

The Court of Customs and Patent Appeals prefers a citation without periods, and without any parenthetical designation as to "Pat." or "Cust.," viz., CCPA.[82] The comments regarding parallel citations to F. Supp. and F.2d in the Court of Claims are applicable to parallel F.2d citations in this court.

In citing Court of Military Appeals cases, it is customary to omit periods but to use parallel citations: e.g., *United States* v. *Buck,* 9 USCMA 290, 26 CMR 70. However, when writing a brief just for that court, there is generally no need to add the CMR reference when you cite simply its own decisions.

(d) *Subsequent history.* Spell out "affirmed," "reversed," and "affirmed [or reversed] on other grounds," and, similarly, indicate changes in the title of the case other than mere transpositions: e.g., *In re Title of Kioloku,* 25 Haw. 357, affirmed *sub nom. Territory of Hawaii* v. *Hutchinson Sugar Co.,* 272 Fed. 856 (C.A. 9); *Ex Parte Drainer,* 65 F. Supp. 410 (N.D.Cal.), affirmed *sub nom. Gould* v. *Drainer,* 158 F. 2d 981 (C.A. 9). There is no need to italicize the English words in any of these indications.

Is it necessary or desirable to add a reference to "certiorari denied" when that is the fact? *Brown* v. *Allen* [83] reaffirmed the original understanding that a denial of certiorari is without substantive significance—except that the State prisoner seeking Fed-

---

[82] Notice by the Court, Dec. 15, 1958, which points out that the Customs portion begins with page 1 in each volume, while the Patent section commences at page 700.

[83] 344 U. S. 443.

eral relief by way of habeas corpus must, as a procedural prerequisite, show that he duly sought certiorari to review the State supreme court's affirmance of his conviction! [84] Accordingly, some Supreme Court Justices have complained that "the bar, in briefs, and lower courts, in their opinions, continue to note such denials by way of reinforcing the authority of cited lower court decisions." [85]

My own view is that the "certiorari denied" citation—both words spelled out, please—is a desirable addition, not in any sense because it adds weight to the opinion, but simply to show the travel of the case: e.g., *Chapman* v. *Santa Fe Pac. R. Co.,* 198 F. 2d 498 (D. C. Cir.), certiorari denied, 343 U. S. 964. Where the names of the parties change completely, indicate that, but do not do so simply where the names are reversed as the losing party below becomes a petitioner: e.g., *Blaustein* v. *United States,* 44 F. 2d 163 (C.A. 3), certiorari denied *sub. nom. Sokol* v. *United States,* 283 U. S. 838.

Be sure to indicate, in any event, the grant of certiorari that is later followed by a dismissal of the writ either by stipulation or because the case later became moot. The grant of the writ in such instances is a signal—indeed, a red flag—that the lower court's decision was considered sufficiently doubtful to warrant review.[86]

Citations to denials of rehearing are better omitted, except only when the court has written an opinion in connection with such denial: e.g., *United States* v. *Rodiek,* 117 F. 2d 588 (C.A. 2),

---

[84] *Darr* v. *Burford,* 339 U. S. 200. For an example of the curious result of insisting on the earlier application for certiorari, see *Leyra* v. *Denno,* 347 U. S. 556, a case which may be cited for the proposition that collateral review is apt to be more rewarding than direct review, even on an identical record. More recently, however, there has been an indication that the *Darr* v. *Burford* rule may be becoming more flexible. See *Thomas* v. *Arizona,* 356 U. S. 390, 392, note 1.

[85] Frankfurter and Harlan, JJ., in *Elgin &c. Ry. Co.* v. *Gibson,* 355 U. S. 897.

[86] See, e.g., *Perlstein* v. *United States,* 151 F. 2d 167 (C. A. 3), certiorari granted, 327 U. S. 777, and dismissed because moot, 328 U. S. 822 (court-martial jurisdiction over civilian employees); compare the cases cited in note 91, p. 87, *supra.* See also *United States* v. *Fenno,* 167 F. 2d 593 (C. A. 2), certiorari granted, 334 U. S. 857, and dismissed by stipulation of counsel, 335 U. S. 806 (military jurisdiction over Fleet Reservist); compare *United States* v. *Bledsoe,* 152 F. Supp. 343 (W. D. Wash.), affirmed, 245 F. 2d 955 (C. A. 9) (Fleet Reservists cannot be recalled to active duty simply for trial by court-martial).

rehearing denied, 120 F. 2d 760, affirmed by equally divided court, 315 U. S. 783.

(e) *State cases.* The rules of the Supreme Court now require parallel citations to both the official and unofficial citations of the State court's opinion below,[87] and hence, by inference, similar parallel citations throughout the brief. A number of Courts of Appeals specifically require such parallel citations throughout.[88]

Practitioners who have access to the larger law libraries are undoubtedly spoiled in not realizing the handicaps under which lawyers and judges without such facilities operate. Probably the safest rule of thumb for any court not familiar to you that does not prescribe the form of State citations, or where there is no well-defined local practice, is to include both the official and the Reporter citation whenever both are available.

To the extent that your Federal brief involves the citation of State cases (see Sections 49 and 69, *supra*), follow the practice of the jurisdiction in question as to the method of citing the early reports. In Massachusetts, for example, these are invariably cited by the names of the reporters; in North Carolina, to take an instance of the other tradition, a rule of court requires that they be cited by consecutive number.[89] In Virginia, as the official reports show, the practice is to use parallel citations: e.g., 13 Gratt. (54 Va.) 587.[90]

(f) *English reports.* Cite by the name of the original reporter, using the traditional abbreviation; there are many lists of these available, in numerous law dictionaries and bibliographical manuals. Whether the parallel citation to the English Reprint series should be added depends on the library facilities available, but it is not generally necessary and certainly not required. For the reports from 1865 through 1890, be sure to add the "L.R." prefix, else confusion with abbreviations that are very similar will result. From 1891 on, when the date in square brackets was included at the front of the citation, "L.R." is omitted; e.g., *Cipriani* v. *Burnett,* [1933] A.C. 83. Some brief-writers add " (C.A.) " to

---

[87] Supreme Court Rules 15 (1) (a), 23 (1) (a), 40 (1) (a).

[88] Seventh Circuit, Rule 17 (a) (3); Eighth Circuit, Rule 11 (b) (Second); Ninth Circuit, Rule 18 (2) (a); Tenth Circuit, Rule 19 (3) (Third); D. C. Circuit, Rule 17 (b) (10).

[89] Rule 62; see 247 N. C. ii.

[90] 199 Va. at 355.

indicate a decision of the Court of Appeal in the King's or Queen's Bench, Chancery, and Probate series, and " (H.L.) " or " (P.C.) " to show whether an Appeal Case was decided by the House of Lords or by the Judicial Committee of the Privy Council. In the last twenty-five years or so, the familiar Law Reports have had competition from the All England Law Reports series, cited by date, volume, and page; e.g., *London County Council* v. *Lees,* [1939] 1 All E.R. 191. Since that series does not carry any indication of the court involved, it will be found more convenient to add one—in the case cited, " (K.B.D.) ." It is not for an American practitioner to make a choice between the two series of reports; suffice it to remark that the Law Reports are more generally available in this country, and are more familiar to most judges, being an older series. The point is probably not very vital; few briefs written in connection with Federal appeals in the United States will ever have occasion to cite a single English decision.

(g) *Dates of cases.* Whether to include the dates of decisions is a matter of taste rather than of rule. The law reviews have popularized the notion of including the date of every case they cite. The practice in the U. S. Solicitor General's Office is to include the date as part of the citation only when it seems relevant to the argument, and not otherwise. That course saves the brief-writer infinite trouble, and withholds nothing of significance from the court. It is accordingly the preferable course.

Section 74. Citations; manner of citation; constitutions, statutes, and treaties.— (a) *Constitutions.* Include Article and Section in the citation, and add the clause if necessary: e.g., U. S. Const., Art. I, Sec. 8, Cl. 14. The Amendments may be identified either with the number spelled out or in Roman numerals: Fifth Amendment, XIV Amendment. Capitalization is in order; I do not quarrel with the standard of capitalizing less rather than more, but fail to understand why the law review lads insist on writing "sixth amendment" in lower case when they consistently capitalize some prepositions, as, e.g., Letter From Madison to Jefferson; Treaty With Iran on Commerce and Navigation. Apart from the circumstance that the latter usage violates a fairly universally recognized convention, the former runs contrary to the practice of the Supreme Court, which invariably uses capitals in speaking of the amendments—First Amendment, Tenth Amendment, etc.

When citing State constitutions in Federal briefs, give the

date unless the particular State has had only a single one since its admission, or unless the court in which you are appearing can be in no possible doubt as to your reference.

(b) *Federal statutes.* Remember (see Section 37 (c) , above) that the United States Code is not positive law except as to those titles that have been specifically so enacted. Consequently, when citing a Federal statute prior to 1957, in a situation where full reference thereto is necessary, give date, chapter number, Stat. citation, and U.S.C. citation: e.g., Sec. 2 of the Act of July 9, 1956, c. 525, 70 Stat. 510, 39 U.S.C. § 902 (g) . This full form is required by the rules of some courts.[91] Where the statute in question contains a built-in short title (as distinguished from a mere "popular name"), it is generally permissible, certainly after the original citation, to use only the official short title plus the U.S.C. citation: e.g., Sec. 204 of the War Orphans' Educational Assistance Act of 1956, 38 U.S.C. § 1054.

Beginning with the 85th Congress and vol. 71 Stat., chapter numbers were dropped. Admittedly this innovation has a number of advantages.[92] I may be pardoned, however, if I consider it highhanded to change, without any statutory sanction whatever, a system that had been in effect for 168 years, since the beginning of the Republic—and in direct line of descent from the method of numbering English statutes, used for many centuries before.[93]

At any rate, Federal statutes after 1956 are cited by substituting the public law number for the chapter number: e.g., Sec. 1 of the Act of March 23, 1959, P.L. 86-4, 73 Stat. 13, 50 U.S.C.

---

[91] D. C. Circuit, Rule 17 (a) (10) .

[92] (a) There was no concordance between Chapter numbers and Public Law numbers for two reasons. First, the Chapters included covered both Public and Private Laws, numbering them chronologically, so that c. 124, for instance, would virtually never be Public Law 124. Second, the Chapter numbers started anew for each session, whereas the Public Law numbers ran consecutively through an entire Congress. (b) In the past, government lawyers spoke of "Public Law 810," without more, a shorthand reference that was perfectly clear to the initiated—but not to others. The new method of numbering public laws—e.g., "P. L. 86-3"—identifies the statute for all time, and thus avoids infinite confusion.

[93] I made inquiries in a number of places on this score: there was no statute; there was informal clearance by the Joint Committee on Printing; and the idea to vary a practice of such long standing came from an employee in the General Services Administration, and resulted in an incentive award! It is proper to add that, in the course of those inquiries, many active practitioners admitted not knowing that chapter numbers had been discarded.

App. § 467 (c) . Interestingly enough, when the chapter numbers were dropped, the slip laws as well as the West Publishing Company's *U. S. Code Congressional and Administrative News* began to carry the Stat. citation, though the latter gives only the opening page of the Act.

For more casual references, it will frequently suffice to cite only the U. S. Code, and, whenever the original act has been amended several times and only its present form is relevant, with nothing turning on the changes made by successive amendments, it will be more convenient to do so. (Another way out is to do a partial job, viz., "R.S. § 5252, as amended (33 U.S.C. § 4) .")

Remember that the proper citation of the Code, by statute,[94] is "U.S.C."; "U.S.C.A." refers not to the Code, but to the annotated edition published by West and Edward Thompson.

It is generally annoying to the reader if the U.S.C. citation is constantly encumbered by the date of the edition you are using— 10 U.S.C. (Supp. I to 1958 ed.) § 1552. The solution is to indicate somewhere in your brief—a footnote to the first statutory citation is usually the most appropriate place—that "All citations to the U. S. Code are to the 1958 edition as amended through the close of the 86th Congress, unless otherwise indicated," or that "All citations to Title 38, U.S.C., are to the 1958 revision." [95] Then dates to other editions will be used only where something turns on the changes made in the earlier version.

(c) *State statutes.* With the citation of State statutes as with the citation of State cases, follow the prevailing local practice, whatever that may be. In an unfamiliar jurisdiction, you will soon get the feel of the proper citation by reading a few recent cases (if you are not associated with a local practitioner) .

(d) *Treaties and the like.* Beginning as of January 1, 1950, treaties and other international agreements contracted by the United States have appeared in a separate series, *United States Treaties and Other International Agreements,*[96] and not in the

---

[94] 1 U.S.C. § 204 (e) .

[95] While the revision of the present book was in progress, the 1958 edition of the United States Code, which includes all legislation through the 1st session of the 85th Congress, was being published, and Supp. I thereto has appeared.

[96] Pursuant to 1 U.S.C. § 112a, as added in 1950. The reason for this change was administrative. The then newly created General Services Administration had been given the responsibility, up to then lodged in the State Department, of publishing the Statutes at Large. Since, very plainly, the

Statutes at Large, where they had formerly been published.[97] The new series is most conveniently cited simply as "U. S. Treaties." [98] Inasmuch as the several volumes are paged consecutively through their several parts, the citation need not include any reference to the part of the volume.

Cite by short title, date of signing, TIAS number, and U. S. Treaties volume: e.g., Treaty of Amity and Economic Relations with Ethiopia, Sept. 7, 1951, TIAS 2864, 4 U. S. Treaties 2134. In accordance with diplomatic usage, the date is that of signing rather than of ratification or entry into force,[99] and the TIAS number is added for convenience, since many individuals who have the treaty in slip form do not have access to the bound volumes.

Section 75. Citations; manner of citation; miscellaneous.— (a) *Texts.* Give the name of the author in roman, the title in italics, and include the edition and its date: e.g., 3 Wigmore, *Evidence* (3d ed. 1940) § 995. This is required by some court rules.[100] Volumes are designated by arabic numerals, regardless of what actually appears on the spine of the binding. The form-book boys now insist on putting the edition and date at the end, which is confusing; the edition and date identify the work which is being cited and thus are part of the title.

---

diplomats knew more about treaties than the housekeepers, the two series were separated. See S. Rep. 1923 and H. R. Rep. 2909, both 81st Cong., 2d sess. See also Surrency, *The United States Statutes at Large*, 52 L. Lib. J. 33.

[97] The earliest Indian treaties are in 7 Stat., the earliest foreign treaties in 8 Stat. From 9 Stat. through 64 Stat., all treaties appeared either in the back of the Stat. volume or, where one volume appeared in several parts, in the later parts. A complete list of all treaties in the Statutes at Large will be found at 64 Stat. B1107-B1182. Further Indian treaties were forbidden by the Indian Appropriation Act of March 3, 1871 (R. S. § 2079, now 25 U. S. C. § 71).

The earlier treaties up to 1863 have been republished by the State Department in a new edition under the supervision of Dr. Hunter Miller.

[98] The flyleaf of the first volume suggests "U S T" as the citation form. That will be fine, say ten years hence, when more people learn about the new series; but until bench and bar generally become aware that treaties no longer appear in the Statutes at Large, the "U. S. Treaties" citation seems preferable.

[99] In this instance, the Senate consented and advised to ratification on July 21, 1953; the President signed on August 4; Ethiopia ratified on August 12; ratifications were exchanged on September 8; the President proclaimed the Treaty on November 3; and it entered into force in accordance with its terms on October 8. Following the usage set forth in the text accordingly avoids considerable confusion.

[100] D. C. Circuit, Rule 17 (a) (10).

(b) *Legal periodicals.* Unlike cases, articles are cited by the full title and not by the abbreviated—frequently the substantially abbreviated—running head. In the case of serials consecutively paged, the date is not necessary to the identification, and hence if it is to be included at all, it belongs at the end: Howe, *Oliver Wendell Holmes at Harvard Law School,* 70 Harv. L. Rev. 401 (1957). On the other hand, if the publication is paged anew in each issue, then the date is a part of the identification, and must precede the page: Wiener, *The Uniform Code of Military Justice,* 1 Combat Forces J. (Sept. 1950) 19.[101]

(c) *Legislative materials.* Cite committee reports and congressional documents by number, Congress, and session: e.g., Sen. Rep. No. 492, 69th Cong., 2d sess.; H. Doc. 96, 74th Cong., 1st sess. Cite the bound Congressional Record by volume and page, without date: 40 Cong. Rec. 7040. Remember, however, that the pagination of the daily edition is different, or nearly always so; accordingly, add the date in such cases: 106 Cong. Rec. 13453 (daily ed., June 27, 1960) . The older Congressional Globe was paged anew at each session, hence it must be cited by session and page: Cong. Globe, 37th Cong., 3d sess., p. 1253.

In citing Congressional hearings, use as a title the heading that appears at the top of the cover, and abbreviate liberally thereafter, being careful not to omit the committee, the bill number, or the Congressional session: e.g., *Uniform Code of Military Justice,* Hearings, House Committee on Armed Services, 81st Cong., 1st sess., on H.R. 2498, pp. 784-785.

(d) *Administrative materials.* The late Judge Hough deprecated using the expression "the Federal specialties (as though they were a 'line of goods') ," [102] but it is precisely in those specialized fields—admiralty, patents, trademark and copyright, wages and hours, labor relations, military law—that the brief-writer most frequently cites administrative materials.

By analogy to the principle that technical terms are to be interpreted in their technical sense,[103] specialized citations are most conveniently rendered in the forms familiar to the specialists concerned. For example, before the advent of the Uniform Code of Military Justice, the Army's code was contained in the Articles

---

[101] How else get this particular article into the present book?
[102] Book Review, 36 Harv. L. Rev. 117, 119.
[103] Cf. 7 Wigmore, *Evidence* (3d ed. 1940) § 1955.

of War, that of the Navy in the Articles for the Government of the Navy; military lawyers used the abbreviations "AW" and "AGN," respectively, as prefixes for the particular provision cited; and those accordingly are the preferable citations for use in briefs submitted to courts of general jurisdiction. When many similar specialized abbreviations are used, it is a good idea to provide a glossary, either by way of footnote, or on a page facing page 1 of the brief. Such a course is infinitely more convenient than any attempt to improvise a new system of citations, or to try to torture specialized forms into the Procrustean bed of a formbook.

The same approach is recommended for any other specialty: follow the accepted usage of the informed technicians in the particular field.

(e) Supras *and* infras. Use *supras* and *infras* sparingly; it is very annoying to any reader to be required to hunt for the original citation, and it isn't going to make the judge who reads your brief more receptive to your contentions if he has to backtrack, groping through pages he has already read, when he wants to locate the citation that now for the first time interests him. It is not uncommon, in the process of making revisions under the pressure of a deadline, for the original citation to drop out entirely; in that event, the decision on which you are relying will be utterly lost. Accordingly—in self-defense—some court rules prohibit the use of *supras* altogether.[104]

The best solution in most instances is to use both the *supra* and the original citation; the first indicates that you have already cited the case before, the second makes the citation immediately available. And do the same thing when you are using a page reference later on: e.g., "*Cramer* v. *United States,* 325 U. S. 1, *supra*"; "or, as the Court said in the *Cramer* case, *supra,* 325 U. S. at 35."

There is really nothing more irritating than to read, time and time again, "See *Wilson* v. *United States, supra,* at 743"—and then to have to try to find the volume from somewhere on up the line.

(f) *Accepted typographical conventions.* "Conform in little things" is always sound advice, and particularly so when applied to

---

[104] Seventh Circuit, Rule 17 (a) (3) : "In references to decisions once cited in the brief, the word 'supra' shall not be employed, but the volume and page shall be stated."

typographical forms; if you have an irresistible urge to innovate, and feel that you must blaze a trial, channel that impulse so that it will not carry over into briefs written for Federal appellate courts.

For instance, historians who cite from manuscripts always use the abbreviation "MS.," or, in the plural, "MSS." It may not be any more logical than the symbol "LL.B." to denote the possession of a law degree, but it is universally accepted. Consequently, on those rare occasions when your brief makes reference to manuscript material, cite it according to the convention, and don't lapse into "Ms." or "ms." simply because some schoolboys think differently.

Section 76. Citations; accuracy of citations.—As has been noted (Section 66, above), the only safe way is to check your proof against the original reports—*not* against your original notes! It is very easy indeed for a judge to lose interest in your brief if, because of a mistake in the citation, he can't find the case you cite. He may take a keen interest in *you* after such an experience, i.e., to see what manner of would-be lawyer this is who writes such sloppy briefs, but he probably won't concentrate very hard on your brief after that.

Similarly, misspelling the name of a well-known case marks you as a lawyer distinctly under par. When the case is a leading one in its field, and one of the parties thereto a person of some prominence, as for instance the case of *Philadelphia Co. v. Stimson,* 223 U. S. 605, which was brought against Mr. Henry L. Stimson during his first tour of duty as Secretary of War and which is still a leading authority in the area of suits-against-the-United States,[105] then, if you cite it as *Philadelphia Co. v. Stimpson,* it marks you as distinctly under par professionally. (I should add that this is not an imaginary illustration.)

When you check your citations from the manuscript, it is well to correct any deviations from the running-head standards discussed in Section 72, above. However, if you are already in proof, substantial accuracy alone need be looked for; it is not fair to a

---

[105] See, e.g., *Harmon v. Brucker,* 355 U. S. 579, 582; *Anti-Fascist Committee v. McGrath,* 341 U. S. 123, 141, 156; *Larson v. Domestic & Foreign Corp.,* 337 U. S. 682, 690-691, 699-700, 708, 716; *Williams v. Fanning,* 332 U. S. 490, 493; *Land v. Dollar,* 330 U. S. 731, 736, 737, 742.

client, even a rich client, to make him bear the cost of proof corrections simply for the sake of consistency in the style of running heads in the cases cited.

And, finally, if you fail to use that indispensable tool of legal research, *Shepard's Citations,* you are apt to commit the unpardonable legal sin of citing an overruled case. Your face will then be as red as *Shepard's Citations'* own scarlet covers, any court is bound to mistrust anything you say thereafter, and certainly the incident will not help your case.[106]

So—check citations, check names of cases, and Shepardize everything in the brief. Any time you think these steps aren't necessary, some avoidable mistake will happen along and prove that they are!

Section 77. Use of quotations.—It is a good, sound rule of thumb that quotations from opinions should be included only when they add something, and that, whenever possible, they should be short rather than long. But I cannot at all agree that they should invariably be omitted. (Compare the excerpt from Mr. Davis' paper quoted in Section 68, above.)

After all, a good many judges read briefs while sitting in easy chairs, and it is therefore going to advance your case if you quote enough pat matter to satisfy their curiosity without discommoding them and making them get up—particularly if their reading takes place where they do not have ready access to the law library.

Sometimes limitations of space will automatically curb the number and extent of your quotations. But, even when the length of a brief is unlimited, I think that the question "To quote or not to quote" is essentially a matter of judgment and proportion, not susceptible of being reduced to fixed rules (compare Sections 68 and 69, above, as to number of citations), and that all one can do is to formulate some standards. I venture the following:

(a) Quote only when the quotation adds something. A good standard to follow is to use a quotation whenever a court has said

---

[106] On occasion, judges fail to Shepardize. See *In re Yokoyama,* 170 F. Supp. 467, 473, note 25 (S. D. Calif.; Jan. 28, 1959), citing *Kinsella* v. *Krueger,* 351 U. S. 470, without any apparent realization that this opinion had been withdrawn on rehearing some two and a half years earlier, on June 10, 1957, and that the judgment below, originally affirmed, was then reversed. 354 U. S. 1.

Cf. *Oklahoma Packing Co.* v. *Gas Co.,* 308 U. S. 530, 309 U. S. 4, 7-8, 309 U. S. 703, 705-709.

something as well or better than you are able to do on your own, or, pre-eminently, when some judge of acknowledged authority says what you are trying to say in language more striking or more dramatic than a journeyman lawyer writing a brief would feel free to use. A good illustration, for the first instance, is the quotation from Chief Justice Taney at p. 219, above; and, for the second, the Holmes quotation at p. 216.

(b) Always quote when the mere statement of the case's holding whets but does not satisfy the reader's curiosity.

(c) Never quote hornbook propositions (except in the very rare instance where a lower court has utterly disregarded hornbook law).

(d) Never, *never,* NEVER, quote sentences out of context. To do so is an unpardonable professional sin; besides, it leaves you wide open to being shown up by the opposition.

(e) In at least four instances, or so it seems to me, fairly extensive quotations are justified in any court:

First, when you are relying on temporarily unfamiliar decisions, and you need to recall the exact *ratio decidendi* to the court's mind. Thus, in *Testa* v. *Katt,*[107] the question was whether a State could refuse to enforce in its courts a cause of action arising under a Federal statute where that cause of action was in conflict with the public policy of the State. The point had not arisen for thirty years, and so it was considered helpful to include in the Government's brief rather long quotations from the opinions in the two leading cases, *Second Employers Liability Cases,*[108] and *Minneapolis & St. Louis R. R.* v. *Bombolis.*[109] Those quotations served to bring the reasoning of those decisions to the judges' attention, without unduly taxing either their memories or their comfort. Omission of the quotations, in the circumstances, would have made the brief much harder to follow—and of course Chief Justice White's rolling periods in the *Bombolis* case could not have been either profitably or intelligibly rendered in small compass.

Second, when you are relying on materials not readily accessible. For instance, in the *Haupt* treason case,[110] the Government quoted extensively from Howell's *State Trials;* no library has

---

[107] 330 U. S. 386.
[108] 223 U. S. 1.
[109] 241 U. S. 211.
[110] *Haupt* v. *United States,* 330 U. S. 631.

more than one set, and it was necessary to bring the cases to the attention of nine judges. Similarly, Government briefs in a number of military law cases in the late 1940's quoted extensively from the opinions of Army Boards of Review.[111] In those days, only the Army had such Boards,[112] and their opinions were not printed, only multilithed, and in such limited quantities that they were not available in even the largest law libraries. In order to bring them fairly to the attention of the courts, it was therefore necessary to set them out at length in the briefs. Today, when all the armed forces have Boards of Review,[113] whose opinions are published in the C.M.R. series, similarly extensive quotations would be neither necessary nor justified.

Third, when you are dealing with documents or exhibits in a long record—papers that cannot fairly be summarized. Thus, in the Government's brief in the *Line Material* reargument,[114] the memoranda and documents leading up to the cross-license agreements there considered were very fully set out. It was difficult, perhaps impossible, fairly to characterize all the nuances of the many vital exhibits involved, and the record was so bulky that even the most conscientious of judges would be disinclined to hunt for the originals. Indeed, in that particular brief, which extended to 159 pages, the first 153 pages were devoted exclusively to argument on the facts.

Fourth, when it is necessary to go back to the fundamentals in a situation where a concept originally formulated has been imperceptibly altered in a series of later decisions, and the briefwriter is endeavoring to persuade the court to return to orthodoxy. Thus, in *Parsons* v. *Smith*,[115] which involved the right of a contractor mining coal to a deduction for percentage depletion on the footing that he had an "economic interest" in the enterprise, a lessee as *amicus curiae* undertook to show, illustrating his argument with copious quotations, that the original concept was "eco-

---

[111] E.g., *Humphrey* v. *Smith,* 336 U. S. 695; *Henry* v. *Hodges,* 171 F. 2d 401 (C.A. 2), certiorari denied *sub nom. Henry* v. *Smith,* 336 U. S. 968; *DeWar* v. *Hunter,* 170 F. 2d 993 (C.A. 10), certiorari denied, 337 U. S. 908.

[112] Pursuant to Article of War 50½ of 1920 (10 U.S.C. [1926 through 1946 eds.] § 1522); Article of War 50 of 1948 (10 U.S.C. [Supp. II to 1946 ed.] § 1521).

[113] Art. 66, Uniform Code of Military Justice, now 10 U.S.C. § 866.

[114] *United States* v. *Line Material Co.,* 333 U. S. 287.

[115] 359 U. S. 215.

nomic interest in the mineral in place representing a capital investment," that the contractor could not show that he had made any such investment, and that he was therefore not entitled to any share of the depletion allowance. The Court agreed with *amicus curiae*, from which it may be inferred that it found the quotations useful.[116]

But, as I say, it is all a matter of judgment and proportion, depending on the nature and needs of the particular case.

Section 78. Quotations; accuracy of quotations.—The caution that all citations must be checked is peculiarly applicable to quotations. Unless every quotation is carefully read, each against the original, significant words will become distorted, and, likely as not, whole lines will drop out.

After all, consider how quotations get into a brief. Your stenographer copies them from either the original record or report, or, in many instances, from your copy of the original (in which event you may well have contributed some slips of your own). Even if she is a trained legal stenographer, she is not a lawyer; the context of the quotation, particularly when the subject-matter is dry and uninteresting, will not arouse her most intense absorption; she may be and frequently is thinking about her current boy friend and similar emotional uncertainties; and—notwithstanding the XIX Amendment, mankind still must struggle with the fallibility of female functionaries. So—check against the original. You will kick yourself mentally around the courthouse square any time you neglect to do so—and it won't help your reputation for accuracy either.

Section 79. Footnotes.—Perhaps no single implement of all the vast apparatus of scholarship is so thoroughly misused in the law as the footnote. There may be some justification in the manifold areas of the academic world for that formidable display of learning and industry, the thin stream of text meandering in a vale of footnotes, but such a technique is quite self-defeating in the law: it makes the writer's thoughts more difficult to follow— and hence far less likely to persuade the judicial reader.

The worst offenders on this score are undoubtedly the law reviews, whose student editors have at least the excuse of being still at the apprentice stage, and whose faculty editors may have had but

---

[116] For the details of the problem, see my paper on *"Economic Interest" —The Rise and Fall of a Slogan*, 37 TAXES 777.

insufficient opportunity to gain firsthand acquaintance with judicial psychology. Next in order are the attorneys at law who are not lawyers but who like to make a show of erudition.

It is entirely proper, and indeed helpful, to use footnotes in a brief (a) to indicate qualifications to statements in the text, where such qualifications would interrupt the thought if they remained in the text, and (b) to include citations on points of secondary importance.

On occasion, some lawyers relegate to a footnote their reply to particular arguments made by the opposing party. This is a risky technique, which is proper only in very limited situations.

In the usual instance, yielding to the temptation to minimize the other side's contentions by giving them footnote treatment will lead counsel into the error of dealing inadequately with important issues. In that situation—see the examples discussed in Section 35 (d) , above—the usual result is that the footnote technique backfires.

It is only when a particular argument is totally lacking in factual record support that it is safe to dispose of it in a footnote; see the example set out at pp. 254-256, below, where, with the text emphasizing the facts of record to show that the other side's primary contention was never reached, footnote reply proved entirely adequate.

But unless the opposition's argument is, as in the last cited instance, utterly devoid of support in the record, it deserves reply in the text of your brief, and it is only your case that will be hurt when you drop your own views down to a footnote.

It is similarly improper, and it can similarly be of distinct disservice to your cause, to use footnotes as a means of setting out a parallel line of argument. Whenever you do that, you detract appreciably from the force of your contentions—and you may do serious damage to an important principle.

An unfortunate example of this double-stream-of-argument employment of footnotes appeared in the Government's brief in the *Schneiderman* denaturalization case.[117] The question was the meaning of the expression in the naturalization laws, "attached to the principles of the Constitution of the United States,"

---

[117] *Schneiderman* v. *United States,* 320 U. S. 118.

which has been on the books since 1795.[118] It was sought to show, by presentation of the legislative history, that the phrase meant more than mere law-abiding acceptance of American government by one who did not at heart believe in a republican form of government—and the legislative history in fact showed that very clearly.[119] But by dividing up the legislative history materials between text and footnote, the argument could not easily be followed, was weakened, and in the end failed to persuade the Court.[120] A few years later, in the *Knauer* case,[121] the same materials were set forth, without substantial additions of material but in one consecutive argumentative screed [122]—and the Court chose to decide the case on other grounds.[123]

---

[118] Sec. 1, *Thirdly*, and Sec. 2 of the Act of Jan. 29, 1795, c. 20, 1 Stat. 414, 414-415; Sec. 1, *Thirdly* and *Fourthly*, of the Act of April 14, 1802, c. 28, 2 Stat. 153, 154; R. S. § 2165, *Third* and *Fifth;* Sec. 4, *Fourth,* of the Act of June 29, 1906, c. 3592, 34 Stat. 596, 598; Sec. 332 (a) (17) of the Act of October 14, 1940, c. 876, 54 Stat. 1137, 1155; Sec. 316 (a) of the Act of June 27, 1952, c. 477, 66 Stat. 163, 242 (8 U.S.C. § 1427 (a)).

[119] James Madison had argued against the adoption of this requirement in 1795, saying (4 Annals of Cong. 1023) : "It was hard to make a man swear that he preferred the Constitution of the United States, or to give any general opinion, because he may, in his own private judgment, think Monarchy or Aristocracy better, and yet be honestly determined to support this Government as he finds it." But Congress adopted the requirement over Madison's objections (*id.*) .

[120] See the reference at 320 U. S. 118, 133, n. 12, to "the discursive debates on the 1795 Act."

[121] *Knauer* v. *United States,* 328 U. S. 654.

[122] Brief for the United States, No. 510, Oct. T. 1945. The portions thereof relevant here were set forth at pp. 417-426 of the earlier version of this book; the substance of what was there printed also appears, somewhat expanded, in my paper on *"Freedom for the Thought That We Hate": Is it a Principle of the Constitution?,* 27 A.B.A.J. 177 (1951) .

[123] Judge Learned Hand had said, in *United States* v. *Rossler,* 144 F. 2d 463, 465 (C.A. 2) : "That attachment to the principles of the Constitution which the law exacts at naturalization is not addressed to the heart; it demands no affection for, or even approval of, a democratic system of government; but merely an acceptance of the fundamental political habits and attitudes which here prevail, and a willingness to obey the laws which may result from them." The difficulty with this approach is that it requires the applicant for citizenship merely to be law-abiding—which is of course all that is required of any alien; for every alien dwelling here owes a temporary allegiance to the United States, so much so that, if he fails in that allegiance and extends aid and comfort to the enemy, he commits an act of treason. *Carlisle* v. *United States,* 16 Wall. 147; *Radich* v. *Hutchins,* 95 U. S. 210. Speaking for the First Circuit, therefore, Judge Magruder very properly declined to follow the *Rossler* case. See *Stasiukevich* v. *Nicolls,* 168 F. 2d 474, 477 (C.A. 1) .

A similar weakening of a good case through too great use of footnotes, this time in the Statement of Facts, occurred in *Von Moltke* v. *Gillies*.[124] In Chapter XII, pp. 397-421, below, two versions of the Statement of Facts in that case are set forth, one with much of the relevant testimony appearing in footnotes, the other with all of it brought up into the text, with the use of only a very few tangential footnotes. Study those two examples, and see for yourself how in text there is strength, in footnotes weakness.

Section 80. Record references.—Remember, in connection with citing exhibits, that the rules of some courts require you to state, not only the page at which the exhibit appears in the record, but also the page at which it was offered in evidence.[125] The reason for this requirement is that, when the members of the court read an exhibit in the record—and exhibits are normally printed separately from the testimony—they want to know, without having to search a long record, what was said when that exhibit was offered, and whether it was admitted generally or only for a limited purpose.

At the risk of offensive repetition, I will emphasize again the matter discussed in Section 44, above: the imperative and absolute necessity for backing up every assertion of fact in your Statement of Facts with a record reference to show that what you say is established by the record and is not simply conjured up out of thin air, whole cloth, and similar material of spontaneous generation. It is well, too, to repeat the record references when you repeat the assertion in the Argument, certainly when the point is critical or even of substantial importance. At that latter juncture, when the judicial reader is bound to catch the significance of the asserted fact, his curiosity will be aroused. Don't make him thumb back to try to find the particular reference in a long Statement of Facts, and don't lead him on a species of treasure hunt with a tantalizing " *(supra,* p. 16) ." Have the reference right there so that he can turn to it immediately: " (R. 298) ." Remember also that a Statement of Facts or an Argument richly sprinkled with record references will always have a very reassuring effect on any legal reader.

There are also instances when the use of record references will

---

[124] 332 U. S. 708.
[125] Supreme Court Rule 40 (2) ; Eighth Circuit, Rule 11 (b) (Third) ; Ninth Circuit, Rule 18 (2) (d) .

enable you to adopt, to your advantage, the factual portions of the opinion below as your own Statement of Facts.

(1) Suppose you are the appellee in a non-jury case where, pursuant to Rule 52 (a), F.R. Civ. P., the judge has written an opinion without making additional findings of fact. Since, under the same Rule, those findings will not be set aside unless "clearly erroneous," you can virtually win the case with a Statement of Facts that quotes the opinion and inserts record references in square brackets to support every sentence that the judge wrote.

(2) Or, suppose that you are the appellant in a case turning on a mixed question of law and fact, and you wish to concentrate on the law without cluttering up your argument with minor factual differences. Use the same technique; commence the Statement of Facts in your brief by saying, "For purposes of this appeal we accept the facts as set forth in the opinion of the court below (R. 249-253)," and then just copy that opinion, interpolating bracketed record references in support of every assertion made therein.

And, here again, as in connection with citations and quotations, absolute and unswerving accuracy must be the goal; inaccuracies, particularly inaccuracies of substance, are generally unforgivable and always dangerous. A court particularly dislikes a citation to fact A when all that the citation establishes is fact B, from which you proceed to draw an inference that fact A exists.[126]

So—have all record references checked, preferably by a person other than the one who has written the brief. Such others are

---

[126] See these comments by the late Chief Justice Vanderbilt of New Jersey, who played such an active part in the drafting of the Federal Rules of Civil and Criminal Procedure:

"Even more inexcusable than defective documentation of the facts is the habit indulged in by some counsel of citing page and line for a statement of fact when a reading of the page and line cited does not sustain the point for which it is cited, but only some inference which counsel seeks to draw from the testimony. When counsel is referring to testimony to sustain facts testified to, all he needs to do is cite page and line. But when he is asking the court to make an inference from the testimony thus referred to, he should tell us not only what the inference is, but from what the inference is drawn. There are plenty of words in the English language to express the fact of inference. Nothing is more annoying in studying a brief either as an advocate or a judge than to have citations given which do not directly support the facts for which they are cited." *The New Rules of the Supreme Court on Appellate Procedure,* 2 Rutgers Univ. L. Rev. 1, 27-28.

invariably better proofreaders than the brief-writer—the latter is always unconsciously inclined to see the mental image of what the word or citation should be rather than the strictly visual image of what is actually is. Moreover, having some one else do the checking insures independent scrutiny. It is much better to have your text questioned and doubted by an office associate in the first instance than by a court.

Section 81. Indicating emphasis.—On occasion a court will adopt a rule forbidding the use of italics in briefs; most courts, however, leave such matters to the judgment and good taste of the brief-writer.

A sound general rule is to use italics sparingly. If they are used too freely in the text of a brief, they are apt to be regarded as (what indeed they frequently are in fact) insults to any judicial reader's intelligence. It is perfectly possible to write a strong, forceful, even a fighting brief, without a single word italicized for emphasis.

The most appropriate use for italics, by and large, is to point up a particular passage in a quotation. At the very least, this will catch a reader's eye, because a good many lawyers and judges who read legal matter almost invariably tend to skip quotations at first reading.

In any event, never proceed beyond italics to capitals and worse, whether in quotations or elsewhere in your text. I recall vividly a written comment on a brief, made by a most able lawyer in the U. S. Solicitor General's Office just before World War II: "and for the love of God, no bold face!"

Section 82. Going outside the record.—It is permissible to go outside the record in these instances:

(i) As to anything in the realm of judicial notice—and in some courts that is a broad domain indeed.[127] Remember that judicial notice means that no evidence need be presented; consequently, even on motion to dismiss, counsel may properly hand up, as an exhibit for the convenience of the court, matter that may be

---

[127] See, e.g., 9 Wigmore, *Evidence* (3d ed. 1940) § § 2565-2583; Morgan, *Judicial Notice,* 57 Harv. L. Rev. 269; compare 2 Davis, *Administrative Law Treatise* (1958) chap. 15 (Official Notice).

For some interesting recent examples of the scope of judicial notice, see *Ussery* v. *Anderson-Tully Co.,* 122 F. Supp. 115, 122-123 (E. D. Ark.) ; *Bruni* v. *Dulles,* 121 F. Supp. 601, 603 (D.D.C.) ; *Calmar S. S. Corp.* v. *Scott,* 197 F. 2d 795, 797 (C.A. 2) .

so noticed. This may seem too elementary to be mentioned, nor would it have been, but for the circumstance that the Supreme Court in a very recent case was required to reaffirm the principle.[128]

(ii) In the Supreme Court of the United States, as to administrative practice. That tribunal goes further than most other courts in receiving outside-the-record proof of administrative practice and will give due and careful weight to official letters setting forth such practice [129]—always provided, of course, that they are not simply self-serving assertions of power. Compare Section 60 (b), above.

(iii) As to anything showing or tending to show that the controversy has become moot.[130]

(iv) In some courts, as to almost anything resting in official files.[131]

---

[128] See *Alaska* v. *American Can Co.*, 358 U. S. 224, 226-227, taking judicial notice of the Journals of the then Territorial House and Senate and of a House bill, over respondents' objections that a court cannot judicially notice legislative drafts, and reversing both courts below, which had sustained those objections on various grounds; see 246 F. 2d 493, 499-500 (C.A. 9), and 137 F. Supp. 181, 185 (D. Alaska).

[129] See, e.g., *Vermilya-Brown Co.* v. *Connell*, 335 U. S. 377; *Foley Bros.* v. *Filardo*, 336 U. S. 281.

Frequently the Court asks counsel to submit available materials as to such practice. Thus, in the Hackfeld case, *Rodiek* v. *United States*, 315 U. S. 783, the Court at the oral argument requested the Government to file material supporting its assertion that the administrative practice under the Trading with the Enemy Act was to recognize the right of a claimant to bring suit under Sections 9 (50 U.S.C. App. § 9) even if his claim had been disallowed by the President or by the officer to whom the President had delegated his authority.

For an instance of the Supreme Court's notice of administrative practice on its own motion, see *Fisher Music Co.* v. *Witmark & Sons*, 318 U. S. 643, 657-658.

[130] The Supreme Court allows the greatest latitude in bringing such facts to its attention. For a discussion of available methods, with full citations to cases, see Robertson and Kirkham, *Jurisdiction of the Supreme Court of the United States* (Kurland & Wolfson ed., 1951) § 275.

For a striking recent example, see *Taylor* v. *McElroy*, 360 U. S. 709.

[131] Thus, in *Red Canyon Sheep Co.* v. *Ickes*, 69 App. D. C. 27, 98 F. 2d 308, the court judicially noticed certain proceedings in the Interior Department, including an unpublished Solicitor's opinion. In that case, counsel for the Secretary asked the court to go that far in order to be able to move to dismiss, and to avoid trial. At the present time, the same result can be obtained simply by moving for summary judgment, and by bringing the relevant papers to the attention of the court in a covering affidavit, under Rule 56 or Rule 12 (b), F. R. Civ. P.

(v) As to anything in the particular court's own files.[132]

(vi) Possibly, but sparingly, in other situations. Thus, in the *Trailmobile* case,[133] where a returned veteran was the unfortunate victim of a bitter dispute between rival unions, the Government (representing the veteran) set out in its brief—and at the argument—relevant matters that had occurred since the ruling below.[134] But that is probably the verge of the law; even there the foregoing departures from the record encountered hard going.

Subject to the foregoing, you depart from the record at your peril. The courts will not listen to details resting only in the knowledge of the brief-writer, and generally resent any such efforts to supplement the record, for this very good reason: such efforts turn the advocate into an unsworn witness for his client.

Similarly, once your appellate record is made up, you cannot hope successfully to supplement it by adding documents that would have been relevant and admissible at the trial. Recently, when the Government attempted thus to pretty up a case in the Supreme Court by filing additional documents with the Clerk, the other side moved to strike not only those documents but also the portions of the Government's brief relating thereto—and that motion was granted in full.[135]

Section 83. "Things you cannot afford to do."—The four outstanding faults of brief-writers, in my judgment, are (a) inexcusable inaccuracy; (b) unsupported hyperbole; (c) unwarranted screaming; and (d) personalities and scandalous matter.

They are don'ts, not only from the point of view of one's own

---

[132] E.g., *National F. Ins. Co.* v. *Thompson,* 281 U. S. 331; *United States* v. *Pink,* 315 U. S. 203, 216, and cases there cited.

[133] *Trailmobile Co.* v. *Whirls,* 331 U. S. 40.

[134] E.g., that, after the entry of the C. C. A. decree adverse to the Union, the Union suspended Whirls from membership and requested the Company to suspend him from work; and that the Company, while telling Whirls not to report to work, had none the less kept him on the payroll, on leave of absence with full pay.

[135] See *Lawn* v. *United States,* 355 U. S. 339, 354: "In that connection [the Government] has filed here what is said to be a transcript of a hearing accorded to Lawn at his request on May 12, 1952, which it says contains photostatic copies of the check and check stub in question voluntarily produced by Lawn. Lawn has moved to strike that transcript and the portions of the Government's brief relating thereto. That motion must be sustained as we must look only to the certified record in deciding questions presented. *McClellan* v. *Carland,* 217 U. S. 268."

professional standards and self-respect, but also from the narrow aspect of intelligent self-interest: every one of these faults is bound to backfire in the most unpleasant and costly way.

Below are listed some examples of these faults that I have encountered. In each of the instances I have indicated what the other side was able to do by way of reply; in none of these instances did success rest with the offending party.

(a) *Inexcusable inaccuracy.* In one case of conspiracy, which for a number of reasons need not be more particularly identified, the charge was that two of the defendants, who will be called the Smiths, conspired to defraud the Government of the faithful services of an officer, who shall be called Captain Jones.

At an appellate stage, the Smiths, whose defense was that certain payments by them to Captain Jones had been extorted by him, complained of the trial judge's failure to charge the jury that, if they found the payments had been extorted, there would be no basis for any finding of conspiracy.

The Smiths' handling of this contention is perhaps best shown reflexly, by setting out the answering excerpt from the prosecution's reply brief:

> The Smiths complain at some length that the trial court's charge as to the basic issues concerning them was inadequate (Br. 18-24).
>
> They say (Br. 20) —
>
> As regards the Smiths, the basic issue in the case was whether or not the payments had been extorted by Captain Jones by threats to violate his duty, or had been made pursuant to conspiracy to seduce Jones from fulfilling his duty.
>
> They then go on to quote three sentences from the court's charge (Br. 21, 22, 23), and conclude (Br. 21) —
>
> It will be observed that there was no statement by the Trial Court anywhere in the charge that the jury could find that there would in law be no conspiracy or agreement on the part of the Smiths as charged in the indictment if the jury believed the contention of the defense, namely, that the Smiths were the victims of a shrewd and ruthless plan of extortion.
>
> The difficulty with considering particular isolated sentences of a charge instead of the charge as a whole, or even a portion of the charge, is that important aspects are apt to be overlooked. The Smiths' sampling technique in this instance has produced the very consequences which might have been anticipated; they failed to note that the trial judge did in fact charge on the precise point with which they were

concerned. He added, following the sentence quoted by the Smiths at Br. 22, and preceding the sentence quoted by the Smiths at Br. 23, the following (R. 1134) :

However, as to the payments of money, if you believe that they were coerced by the defendant Jones, that is, that they would not have been made at all in whole or in part except for Jones' threats, then such payments would not be the result of agreement nor any evidence of a crime. And if you so believe, and also are not satisfied beyond a reasonable doubt by other evidence in the case that the conspiracy existed as charged in the indictment, you should find all the defendants not guilty, as Jones is not here charged with extortion.

The foregoing intervening excerpt is nowhere quoted in the Smiths' brief.

Well, the Smiths went to jail. And, apart from any question of professional standards, it was a fact that, had the trial judge's charge been set out in full, without omissions, the omitted sentence would not have appeared to do nearly so full justice to the Smiths' theory as isolating it in the reply brief did.

(b) *Unsupported hyperbole.* Whenever a lawyer exaggerates any substantial distance beyond the record, he is simply asking for trouble—and the greater the exaggeration, the more devastating the impact of the inevitable reply.

I have in mind a criminal case involving tax evasion, where the essential defense was that the petitioners had made a disclosure of their tax discrepancies, so that, they contended, they had obtained immunity from prosecution. In their brief they stated that the court below

wholly failed to consider the important and undisputed facts pertinent to the question whether the Petitioners' confession, unique for frankness and completeness, was induced by the Treasury Department's promise of immunity.

This assertion, that the petitioners' confession was "unique for frankness and completeness," really left the lads wide open. Here are the answering paragraphs from the prosecution's brief:

1. The District Court found as a fact that "at no time between February 28, 1945 and April 25, 1945, was any act of the defendants or of the corporate taxpayers prompted or brought about by any inducement held out to them by any person in authority or any person connected with the government" (Fdg. 19, R. 2176), and that "at no

time" during those dates "were the defendants or the corporate tax-payers coerced or compelled or induced, either with or without proc-ess, to make incriminatory disclosures" (Fdg. 20, R. 2177).

The District Court likewise found as a fact that the March cur-rency redeposits "were prompted by the belief that currency in bills of large denominations might in effect become contraband and not by any desire or intention voluntarily to disclose frauds on the revenue" (Fdg. 19, R. 2176), and that the filing of two additional fraudulent tax returns after substantial redeposits of currency had been made "conclusively establishes that the redeposit of currency was no evidence of any intention on the part of the defendants or the corporate tax-payers to make voluntary disclosure of the frauds theretofore prac-ticed," and "that said redeposits had no connection with or bearing upon crimes against the revenue" (Fdg. 24, R. 2178). The Circuit Court of Appeals characterized the contention that the making of these deposits amounted to a voluntary disclosure in response to a promise of immunity as "fantastic" (R. 2196).

The District Court further found that "Neither the defendants nor the corporate taxpayers at any time prior to April 25, 1945 dis-closed the fraudulent practices of the corporate taxpayers to any gov-ernment official" (Fdg. 18, R. 2176), and also specifically found that statements submitted in affidavits to the effect that "voluntary dis-closure" was discussed between E. Allan X ———— and Collector P ———— on March 26, April 10, 20, and 24, were false (Ibid.). The Circuit Court of Appeals thought it "clear" that "the investigation be-gan at the latest on March 24, 1945" (R. 2197-2198).

The first disclosure was that contained in the letters of April 25, 1945 (R. 2123-2124; see also R. 134), which contained an invitation to examine the corporate taxpayers' books. Those letters, the District Court found, "were not frank and full disclosures, were not volun-tarily made, and were delivered at a time when the defendants well knew that an investigation of their affairs and those of the corporate taxpayers had actually been initiated" (Fdg. 22, R. 2177-2178). "On April 25, 1945, the extent of the frauds practiced by the corporate tax-payers was not disclosed" (Fdg. 14, R. 2175). These "belated and partial revelations" (Fdg. 23, R. 2178) were "prompted solely by the fact that the defendants and the corporate taxpayers knew that an investigation of their affairs had begun and that an Internal Revenue Agent had made an appointment, deferred at the request of the de-fendants and of the corporate taxpayers, to commence an examination of the books of the defendant Henry X ———— on April 23, 1945" (Fdg. 19, R. 2176-2177). The subsequent investigation of the books of the corporate taxpayers, between May and August 1945 "was invited by the defendants and by the corporate taxpayers with full knowledge that an investigation had been commenced which would lead to the discovery of fraudulent entries in the books of the corporate taxpayers, and with full knowledge of the fact that said investigation could be commenced and continued with or without the consent of the defendants or the corporate taxpayers" (Fdg. 21, R. 2177).

The Circuit Court of Appeals likewise noted "that the corporate records were in no sense the result of any promise of immunity. They were furnished long after the government investigation had begun" (R. 2198).

These concurrent findings, accurately reflecting the record (see Statement, *supra,* pp. 13-23), need not be independently reviewed here. *Goldman* v. *United States,* 316 U. S. 129, 135, cf. *United States* v. *Johnson,* 319 U. S. 503, 518; *Delaney* v. *United States,* 263 U. S. 586, 589-590. They made it abundantly clear that the questions suggested by the petition are academic, without actual relationship to the present record. Those questions happen to be without any substantive merit,* though that is now beside the point. But it may be noted in leaving this aspect of the case that, considering all the circumstances, petitioners' reference to their April 25 letters as "confessions, unique for frankness and completeness" (Pet. 27), involves not so much hyperbole as irony.

Review was, of course, denied; and if the lawyers who penned the quotation in question had any sensibilities at all, they must (at least figuratively) have been eating off the mantelpiece for days and days.

So—don't exaggerate or overstate; the farther your departure

---

* Even if petitioners had made full disclosure, it is clear, as charged by the trial court, that prosecution would not be foreclosed. *Whiskey Cases,* 99 U. S. 594; *United States* v. *Blaisdell,* 3 Ben. 132, Fed. Case No. 14,608 (S.D.N.Y.); cf. *Gladstone* v. *United States,* 248 Fed. 117 (C.C.A. 9), certiorari denied, 247 U. S. 521; *United States* v. *McCormick,* 67 F. 2d 867 (C.C.A. 2), certiorari denied, 291 U. S. 662. The most authoritative formulation of the voluntary disclosure policy merely implies a self-imposed administrative limitation by the Treasury Department not to refer cases to the Department of Justice for prosecution. Actually, it would seem that there would be nothing to prevent an indictment without referral. Cf. *United States* v. *Morgan,* 222 U. S. 274. Here there is no suggestion that the Department of Justice effected a compromise after indictment, see Executive Order No. 6166 (*supra,* pp. 3-4), and the suggestion that there was any earlier compromise by the Treasury Department under Section 3761 of the Internal Revenue Code (*supra,* pp. 2-3), was correctly characterized by the court below as "illusory" (R. 2199), on the authority of *Botany Mills* v. *United States,* 278 U. S. 282. [Footnote from the brief, written when the intermediate Federal courts were still Circuit Courts of Appeals.]

from the record, the more painful the return trip will be. Consequently, whenever you are tempted to go all out for hyperbole, remember the classic admonition to "take a pillow along, so that when you get thrown out of court you'll land soft."

(c) *Unwarranted screaming.* Exaggeration comes in both plain and fancy types. The latter model, which can be recognized by its emotional content, is now and doubtless always will be popular with crusaders.

There comes to mind a petition that raised certain questions involved in an expulsion from the West Coast by the military. It raised some difficult questions, too; but petitioner's counsel chose to slop over, as follows:

> It is a fair inference that in regard to the forcible expulsion, as in regard to the denial of a right to hearing (*supra,* pp. 16-20), respondent was chiefly interested in an assertion of the breadth of military power, rather than in a fear of harm to the country by petitioner.

Not only was that passage unnecessary, it was extremely unwise, because on the question of good faith and good motives, respondent was on impregnable ground—as his brief was at pains to point out:

> 3. * * * Respondent's removal of petitioner through the use of military personnel was specifically and expressly authorized by Secretary of War Stimson, by Assistant Secretary of War McCloy, and by General Marshall (R. 265-266). Moreover, he had been advised both by the Attorney General of the United States and by the Judge Advocate General of the Army that he could lawfully exercise such power (R. 248, 254). Respondent did not remove petitioner from California to Nevada until petitioner had prosecuted his injunction proceeding in the district court, seeking to enjoin respondent from "directly or indirectly by any means, method or device whatsoever from executing or causing to be executed" the exclusion order here in question (R. 247). The right to use military personnel in carrying out the order had been asserted before the court in the injunction proceeding (R. 256-257). Not until the district court had denied petitioner's suit for an injunction and had given judgment for respondent did the latter proceed to enforcement. Furthermore, as the district court in the present case concluded, respondent "acted in good faith and with the highest motives, and with an honest belief that Executive Order 9066 and Law 503 empowered him to lawfully do and direct" the acts and things for which it is here attempted to hold him liable (R. 299-300).

Similar findings of good faith and reasonableness were made by the district court in the injunction case (R. 278-279, 281-282) and by the circuit court of appeals here (R. 337-338).

The temptation to indulge in a bit of counterscreaming was strong, but counsel refrained, adding only the following footnote at the end of the second paragraph just quoted.

In view of those findings, and in the face of other findings that the action here was taken pursuant to legal advice and after express approval by General DeWitt's military and civil superiors (*supra*, pp. 7, 11-12), the statement in the petition (Pet. 31) that "respondent was chiefly interested in an assertion of the breadth of military power, rather than in a fear of harm to the country of petitioner" is of course wholly unwarranted.

Review was denied; in other words, petitioner's screaming, shown to have been unsupported by the record, simply backfired. Indeed, it approached and all but entered the realm of angry personalities.

(d) *Personalities and scandalous matter.* The argument *ad hominem* in a brief is always unpardonable, not simply because it is something no decently constituted brief-writer would include, but because, like all the other faults, it fails of its purpose: appellate courts have a hard enough time deciding the merits of the cases presented to them without embarking on collateral inquiries as to the personality or conduct of the lawyers involved. They recoil from any attempt even to ask them to consider such matters, and are always embarrassed by the request. So—granted that your opponent's disbarment is long overdue, granted in any event that his conduct in the particular case was shameful and thoroughly unprofessional, take those matters up with the grievance committee, and don't inject them into either the written or the oral argument of an appeal.[136]

In much the same category, at least in my judgment, is the constant use of the adjective "learned" when referring to the judge or to the court below. A little reflection will show that it is

---

[136] "It should be noted the counsel for both sides in their briefs would have made more effective presentations had they devoted less attention to each other's shortcomings as lawyers. They should know that this is the sort of thing of which a court gets tired." *Tele-King Distributing Co. v. Wyle,* 218 F. 2d 940, 943 (C.A. 9).

always used, or very nearly so, as biting sarcasm. It adds nothing; it had better be omitted.

At the other extreme is the use of "honorable"—"we therefore submit that this Honorable Court should reverse the judgment below." Better leave that to the bailiff, who starts with "Oyez, oyez, oyez"—the last vestigial remnant of Anglo-Norman and Law French in American law—and who concludes, "God save the United States and this Honorable Court." Make it a rule to omit that particular adjective from briefs; judges don't like being fawned upon by members of the bar.

Finally, there are the two ultimate horribles. One is the brief which violates the rule of conduct that written arguments, "though often in sharp controversy, shall be gracious and respectful to both the court and opposing counsel, and be in such words as may be properly addressed by one gentleman to another." [137] The other is the brief that contains scandalous matter, i.e., which imputes improper motives to counsel or to a court. On occasion, such documents have resulted in disciplinary action, although usually they are simply stricken, frequently on the court's own motion.[138]

Probably an example will be in order; here again, the violation will be demonstrated reflexly, by setting forth the motion to strike that was filed promptly after the offending brief was served:

---

[137] *National Surety Co.* v. *Jarvis*, 278 U. S. 610, 611, *per* Taft, C. J. Compare *United States* v. *Miller*, 233 F. 2d 171, 172, note 1 (C.A. 2) : "A brief of a * * * purported 'friend of the court,' being a curious compound of scurrility and irrelevance, the filing of which is not objected to by the United States Attorney, may remain lodged in the files of the court as an example of how lawyers should not act."

[138] See J. Sup. Ct., Oct. T. 1934, pp. 105, 149-150, 79 L. ed. 1714 (six months' suspension and payment of $250 fine) ; J. Sup. Ct., Oct. T. 1935, pp. 77, 159, 80 L. ed. 1411-1412, 1414 (rule to show cause why counsel should not be disbarred; on counsel's apology, brief stricken, and rule discharged) ; *Missouri-K.-T. R. R. Co.* v. *Texas*, 275 U. S. 494 (brief stricken) ; *Knight* v. *Bar Association*, 321 U. S. 803 (brief stricken on Court's own motion) ; *Matter of Fletcher*, 344 U. S. 862 (same) .

This problem seems to be a timelessly recurring one, as witness the following from a case decided by the Third Circuit within the year (citation advisedly omitted) :

"The petition for rehearing filed by the attorneys for the petitioners contains intemperate and gross language. The use of such language by members of the bar in a petition to the court verges upon contemptuous conduct. A repetition of such conduct on the part of counsel will bring disciplinary action. The Clerk will be ordered to strike from the petition the language in question."

Now comes the Solicitor General on behalf of the petitioner herein, and prays that the respondent's Brief in Opposition to the Petition for a Writ of Certiorari be stricken because it contains scandalous matter. *Green* v. *Elbert,* 137 U. S. 615, 624; *Royal Arcanum* v. *Green,* 237 U. S. 531, 546-547. Compare *Cox* v. *Wood,* 247 U. S. 3, 6-7, where, however, the language seems to have been more restrained.

The principal objectionable passages in respondent's Brief in Opposition in the present case are the following:

Petitioner sought to abuse and insult the intelligence of the Court of Appeals by this same type of unsupportable claim which he must of necessity know to be completely false. Yet he persists with this same technique of urging unsupportable arguments which he must know to be completely false in this Court again. It is outrageous that an officer of the U. S. under oath to uphold the laws of the United States and supposedly advised of the rudiments of ethical conduct should advance frivolous argument merely for the purpose of delay and should dare to use so contemptible and obviously dilatory a device which outrages common decency. (P. 13.)

* * * * *

Petitioner then assaults (at p. 20, brief for petitioner) the importance of title, a fundamental legal conception having vital necessity and meaning to all free peoples, and countless consequences in the law of sales. He forgets that *United States* v. *Lee* turned specifically on what he casually terms "technical doctrines of passage of title." He asks this Court to brush aside ownership of property as merely "technical." Many of his predecessors in this immoral doctrine, who have regarded the ownership of another as "technical," are filling our jails. (P. 18.)

* * * * *

Toward the bottom of page 16, petitioner goes on in an attempt to place himself above the law by insinuating that he has some celestial status that removes him personally from the reach of the law to which "a recalcitrant private vendor" would be subjected. This is indicative of petitioner's concept of all law—namely, that he is above it, that he is the law himself, and that he is immune from the enforcement of the law upon him by this or any other Court.

* * * * *

* * * When the day comes that anyone in respondent's position cannot resort to the Courts for protection of his property under law merely because some bureaucrat seeks to hide his incompetence and injustice behind a protecting shield of sovereign immunity, both liberty and reason shall have perished from the land. (P. 15.)

* * * * *

The depths of petitioner's wilful ignorance of these boundaries of sovereign immunity under a free constitution like ours is revealed by his misuse of *Goldberg* v. *Daniels,* 231 U. S. 218. (P. 16.)

The sequel: an apology tendered in person, and a "Motion for Leave to Withdraw" the offending document—which was promptly granted.[139]

The moral of all the foregoing is simply this, that unprofessional conduct in appellate work just does not pay. I could put the matter on a higher plane, of course, but this section is written for those whose minds may still be open on the question.

Section 84. Signatures.—Who shall sign a brief and how is a matter of court rules and—preeminently—of local practice.

In some Federal courts, it is customary to add the firm name; in the Supreme Court and in the District of Columbia Circuit, however, the emphasis is on "individual names" and "individual counsel," [140] which discourages (though it does not forbid) the addition of firm names. Since the latter will not be carried into the reports, there is no advantage in adding them; and it may well be doubted if their appearance enhances in any way the impressiveness—or otherwise—of the brief's contents.

The Supreme Court and two Circuits require that the signature of counsel be followed by his office address.[141] But, in any court, counsel is well advised to add his address, for a very good reason. Suppose that someone reads your masterpiece and wishes to consult you; how will he even know under what city to look in *Martindale-Hubbell* simply from seeing your name? (Of course, you may be so famous that every lawyer throughout the land will know who and where you are, but in that event you won't mind losing the bit of business that the absence of identification may involve.)

Only in the Fifth Circuit is it necessary to add a manuscript signature to one of the required printed copies.[142] Elsewhere there is no such requirement for printed matter except, generally,

---

[139] The Supreme Court's Rules now carry a specific warning that briefs containing scandalous matter "may be disregarded and stricken by the court." Rule 40 (5).

[140] Supreme Court Rule 39 (2) ; D. C. Circuit, Rule 17 (a) (5).

[141] Supreme Court Rule 39 (2) ; Third Circuit, Rule 24 (1) (e) ; D. C. Circuit, Rule 17 (a) (5).

[142] Fifth Circuit, Rule 24 (1).

for the certificate necessary on petitions for rehearing,[143] and, in the Supreme Court, for printed motions other than motions to dismiss or affirm.[144]

In the Second Circuit, following the practice in the New York State courts, the people who sign as "Of Counsel" at the left are those actually handling the case; in other courts, the names designated "Of Counsel" are simply the forwarding lawyers or the lads who go on the brief primarily in a junior capacity.

In the Second Circuit also, again following New York practice, it is customary to print at the right-hand top of the cover of the brief, "To be argued by ———," giving his name. This is obviously convenient for the judges and the clerk alike, but it is a convention not followed anywhere else.

By way of summary: read your court rules, and, when there is no specific provision, ascertain and be guided by the practice followed by the leaders of the bar of the particular court concerned.

Section 85. Reply briefs.—The basic question under this heading is whether any reply brief should be filed at all.

Two circuits forbid the filing of reply briefs except to answer new points; reargument of what already has appeared in the brief-in-chief falls under the ban.[145] The late Mr. William D. Mitchell wrote that "It should be a rare case where * * * a reply brief * * * is justified. In his brief * * * an appellant should be able to cover adequately his own case and anticipate his adversary's." [146] I entirely agree that—subject to the qualifications below—reply briefs should be sparingly used.

(a) Normally, when the issues are clearly drawn, don't file a reply brief; you only discourage the court by burdening it with more matter to read.

(b) When the other side fuzzes up the issues, and you can reclarify the discussion with a short reply brief, it may well be helpful to do so.

(c) When the other side raises an entirely new point, and it is a point of substance, by all means meet that new point in a reply brief.

---

[143] See Section 147, below, at p. 372; and see examples of such certificates appended to the petitions for rehearing that are set out in Sections 170 and 173.

[144] Supreme Court Rule 39 (2).

[145] Seventh Circuit, Rule 17 (e) ; Tenth Circuit, Rule 19 (8).

[146] Book Review, 64 Harv. L. Rev. 350, 351.

(d) When the court (or any member thereof) asks at the argument whether you intend to file a supplemental memorandum on a particular question, you *must* do so. Such an inquiry regardless of its tenor or form, is the equivalent of a command.

If you decide not to file a reply brief, that solves the problem. If, on the other hand, you feel that a last word is imperative, be sure that your reply brief is short, that it is not simply a rehash of the same ground, and that it hits hard. For instance:

The company's brief on reargument, filed October 8, 19— (hereinafter cited as A.B. 2d Br.), fails almost completely to meet the contentions made in the Government's main brief on reargument (cited as U. S. 2d Br.). In addition, the company's brief at a number of places misstates the record.

We shall endeavor to deal, as summarily as possible, with the basic errors contained in that brief, and thereafter with the specific matters in it which seem in most urgent need of correction.

I. THE COMPANY'S BASIC MISCONCEPTIONS

The company's position rests upon three basic errors which reach to the heart of the case.

First.—The Company's brief throughout proceeds on the assumption that the Act of June 25, 19—, declares a common-law forfeiture. Yet, as we have shown at some considerable length (Point I, U. S. 2d Br. 60-79), that assumption is wholly without foundation. Our argument on that point is not met, and the legislative material adduced in support of our construction of the statute is entirely ignored. Indeed, the company in effect ignores everything in the Act except the word "forfeited," and proceeds to impress upon that word its own interpretation of a common-law forfeiture. This basic fallacy underlies the whole of the company's brief, and necessarily removes its arguments a considerable distance from the issues in the case.

* * * * *

The Company asserts (A.B. 2d Br. 43) that the United States took no exception to the finding that the sales were made to the highest and best bidders where the lands were situated. To the contrary, that finding was very specifically objected to before it was made (R. 593, Objection 2).

* * * * *

The Company urges (A.B. 2d Br. 51) that "The United States, with full knowledge, has waived all rights, if any, it ever had." No record references are cited in support of this assertion, and we think that none are available.

* * * * *

An equally bold assertion appears at A. B. 2d Br. 62, where it is said that the statement that second indemnity limits were laid down only at the request of the company is incorrect. Again no record reference is cited; and again the record (R. 805) proves the correctness of the Government's statement.

It is, of course, extremely difficult for any lawyer to know whether, having won his case after filing a reply brief, that document really contributed anything to his ultimate success. The only ground for believing that it may have done so would be in a situation where the court's opinion plainly shows that it did not accept the contentions to which reply was made.

Be sure that the headings of your reply brief, like those of your brief-in-chief, are argumentative; see Section 30, above. There is nothing quite so ineffective as a reply brief with headings that read "Replying to Point III," or "Replying to the Jurisdictional Argument." When appropriate, repeat the headings already used; otherwise fashion new ones that are similarly argumentative, in order to meet the additional contentions; and don't lapse into blind or topical headings simply because you are writing a reply brief.

Finally, and this concerns only Supreme Court cases, is it desirable for the party petitioning for certiorari to reply to the respondent's brief in opposition? A petition for certiorari, preeminently, should anticipate the other side's arguments; more than almost any other argumentative document, it is strictly a one-shot proposition. The rules permit reply briefs at this juncture,[147] but most of them do little to swing the case into the select category of "certiorari granted." In my own practice, I can point to only a single instance where my petition was granted after a reply had been filed. Even on that occasion, I would not for a moment argue *post hoc, propter hoc;* all I can say is that at the time I felt that instant, brief contradiction was necessary. In order that the reader may judge for himself, the full text of that reply, entitled "Petitioner's Supplemental Memorandum," is set forth below:

---

[147] Supreme Court Rule 24 (4).

This Memorandum is impelled by two material misstatements of fact in the Government's Brief in Opposition.

I. A. The Solicitor General says (Br. Op. 7),

* * * so far as we have been able to determine, no basis for claim of privilege with respect to that question [the identification question, "Who?"] was offered.

B. The record shows precisely the opposite.

(1) Petitioner gave a full statement of his reasons for refusing to answer all of the questions which remained unanswered, and that statement was, with the consent of the prosecutor, incorporated into the Grand Jury presentment. See R. 178a, which refers to Question 8, the "Who?" question (R. 5a-6a).

(2) The full statement of petitioner's reasons for standing on his claim of privilege appears at R. 131a-132a and again at R. 174a-176a. A portion—but only a portion—of that statement is reproduced at Br. Op. 4-5. Here is the last paragraph of petitioner's statement, which, as just noted, was applied to the "Who?" question, but which the Solicitor General failed to include in his brief (R. 132a, 176a):

My fear and apprehension that I would tend to incriminate myself is based upon not only that which I have read in the newspapers * but also upon the fact that Morton Witkin, Esq., of my counsel in whom I have great trust and confidence, has advised me that it is his honest and sincere opinion that were I to answer the questions referred to I would be incriminating myself. I believe that his advice is sound and I choose to rely upon it. May I say in conclusion that these two reasons are in addition to and not exclusive of my own inherent belief of self-incrimination due to the fact that I have knowledge of what my answers to the refused questions would be.

(3) Petitioner's comprehensive offer of proof at the trial (R. 48a-53a), which applied to all of the unanswered questions, disclosed additional reasons for his failure to answer.

(4) After petitioner had been found guilty, and before sentence, his counsel said, *inter alia* (R. 66a):

---

* The newspaper accounts (R. 196a-197a), which were received in evidence at the trial (R. 56a), included the following:

Even though there are no Federal laws regarding numbers, slot machines and other rackets, the probers will strike at such rings through the Federal revenue and conspiracy laws, he [Goldschein] said.

*   *   *   *   *

Income tax violations would permit the Government to strike indirectly at racketeers whose activities are not covered by Federal criminal statutes. [Footnote in original.]

* * * in one of the three questions that we failed to answer, the question "Who," my argument *was* he would be giving the names of witnesses against himself * * *

We have italicized the past tense to show that the argument had been made earlier; it is not in the record because the full transcript was not printed.

II. A. The Government's Brief in Opposition continues (Br. Op. 11):

> Moreover, petitioner's apparently full statement of his reasons for refusing to answer the identification question indicates no reason why the disclosure of the names of the numbers writers would endanger him. The reasons stated are all related to the telephone questions. This fact alone would be enough to deny the privilege with respect to this question.

B. The same inaccuracies and omissions already noted under item I permeate this excerpt also: Petitioner's reasons for refusing to answer included an apprehension of self-incrimination based upon the newspaper reports of the prosecutor's plan of reaching numbers operators through the federal tax laws; they included the advice of petitioner's counsel; and they included the fear that if he answered the question "Who?" he would be supplying the prosecutor with the names of witnesses against himself.

As I say, I can't prove that the foregoing did the trick, but since certiorari was granted and the judgment below was reversed five days after oral argument, it is plain that, either by reading the supplemental memorandum or otherwise, the Supreme Court was ultimately convinced that petitioner had adequately established the basis for his claim of privilege.[148]

Section 86. After the reply brief.—Some lawyers, like many women, are uneasy unless they have the last word; and, after brooding over the argument, decide to file still one more written document. Some courts do not permit the filing of anything after the reply brief without special leave,[149] and others similarly limit

---

[148] *United States* v. *Greenberg*, 192 F. 2d 201 (C.A. 3), certiorari granted, 342 U. S. 917, and judgment below reversed, 343 U. S. 918. See Chapter XIV, below, for the full transcript of the oral argument in the Supreme Court in this case. See also Section 35 (d), *supra*, at pp. 106-107.

[149] First Circuit, Rule 24 (8); Second Circuit, Rule 17 (d); Third Circuit, Rule 25 (1); Seventh Circuit, Rule 17 (f); D. C. Circuit, Rule 18 (c). The Supreme Court, however, permits the filing of a supplemental brief contain-

the filing of any document whatever after the argument.[150] What, then, is the lawyer with the last-word-itch to do?

The best advice for this sort of impulse is: don't! Far better to write out what you have in mind, read it aloud to as sympathetic an audience as you can muster—and then relegate it to your file, circular or otherwise.

Post-argument filings are justified in only a rigidly limited class of instances—and their form depends on the rules and practice of the court in question. In the Supreme Court, a letter to the Clerk is acceptable—which is to say, it will not be bounced back for being in letter form. In many Courts of Appeals, on the other hand, a motion for leave to file must be affixed to anything at all submitted after oral argument. Checking with the clerk in advance in this connection may save much embarrassment.

In my view, there are only two instances in which the filing of additional material after the argument is justified:

(a) First, when the court at the argument has asked counsel for additional data of any kind. If a memorandum has been requested orally, then that document should so state. E.g., "Pursuant to the Court's request, etc.," or "Pursuant to permission granted at the argument of this cause, etc." In courts where letters to the clerk are in order, be sure to provide sufficient legible copies for every member of the court, and do not fail to send a copy to opposing counsel.

(b) Second, in the unusual situation where, in a supplemental memorandum filed by your opposition in the situation just mentioned, you find a whopping misstatement. Since there is no other way to reply, a motion for leave to file—or a letter to the clerk—is then in order. Flyspecks or minor errors had better be passed over as one of the unavoidable incidents of litigation; further reply is justified only when the misstatement is both material and significant.

An example of such a communication in the latter situation is set forth in the note below, exactly as it was written to the Clerk

---

ing "intervening matters that were not available in time to have been included" in the brief-in-chief. Supreme Court Rule 41 (5).

[150] Supreme Court Rules 41 (3), 41 (5); Fourth Circuit, Rule 12 (3); Tenth Circuit, Rule 19 (11); D. C. Circuit, Rule 18 (i).

of the Supreme Court.[151] The Clerk later advised that copies were distributed to the Court; there was no reply from the other side. But, in the more usual situation—desist. Normally this kind

-----

[151]   8 March 1957

John T. Fey, Esq.,
Clerk,
Supreme Court of the United States,
Washington 13, D. C.

Re: *Reid* v. *Covert*, No. 701, O.T. 1955.
Kinsella v. *Krueger*, No. 713, O.T. 1955.

Dear Mr. Fey:

A particularly glaring misstatement of fact in the Government's "Supplemental Memorandum * * * Following Reargument" impels this communication.

At page 14 of that document it is stated that I misunderstood the Government's position as to the power of Congress to subject dependents of military personnel to trial by court-martial, and I am correctly quoted from page 70 of the Ward & Paul transcript of the oral argument as having said:

"Then I must confess I was amazed when the Solicitor General said that it is only a question of legislative judgment that any time Congress wants to subject the good ladies at Fort Myer to trial by courts martial, they can do so."

The Government fails to quote, from the same transcript, what the Solicitor General actually said which evoked the foregoing reply. Here are those passages (Ward & Paul transcript, page 14) :

"The Chief Justice: How about the wives and other dependents of military personnel who live on a cantonment in this country; are they camp followers too in the sense that that book describes it?

"Mr. Rankin: I would think they would be under the sense of this book. I think that that is provided for otherwise by the question of whether they are in the field and the fact that Congress has expressly provided that if they are not in the field, they are subject to the jurisdiction of the courts.

"The Chief Justice: Then does Congress say that dependents of military personnel in this country who live on a cantonment are in the military service and would be subject to court martial as these women are?

"Mr. Rankin: I think so far as power is concerned.

"The Chief Justice: Yes, I am talking about power.

"Mr. Rankin: The power is there."

I would not for a moment question the Solicitor General's right to correct what on more mature reflection appears to have been an improvident oral statement. It is doubtless his duty to recede from untenable positions. But I submit that this duty can be fully discharged without the present postargument attempt to attribute error to opposing counsel by less than full disclosure in a printed brief of what the transcript of argument shows to have been actually said in open court.

Respectfully,

/s/ Frederick Bernays Wiener

Counsel for the Appellee in No. 701
and the Respondent in No. 713

cc: Hon. J. Lee Rankin

of final final-word won't be given much attention, and although it may make *you* feel better, it really won't advance your case.

Section 87. Briefs *amicus curiae*; in general.—As long ago as the early years of the Fourteenth Century, counsel were telling the court that "The judgment to be by you now given will hereafter be an authority in every *quare non admisit* in England;"[152] and, a little later, the Chief Justice of the Common Bench observed, "By a decision on this avowry we shall make a law throughout all the land."[153] Even in those distant days, long before any doctrine of precedent had really been formulated,[154] bench and bar thus recognized that a judicial decision affects many more individuals than just the parties to the litigation. And so, over the years, it became customary for those whose rights depended on the outcome of cases pending in courts of last resort to file briefs *amicus curiae*, in order to protect their own interests.

More recently, with the rise of organizations dedicated to the furtherance of particular principles, such briefs were no longer presented only by parties with similar or identical interests or cases, but became vehicles for propaganda efforts. Far from affording assistance to the judges, on occasion they did not even mention the decisive issue on which the case turned, and on which the court ultimately divided.[155] Instead, their emphasis was on the size and importance of the group represented,[156] or on contemporaneous press comment adverse to the ruling of the court.[157] Certainly there were multiplying signs after 1947 that the brief

---

[152] Y. B. 32 & 33 Edw. I (Rolls Series) 32.

[153] Y. B. 3 & 4 Edw. II (Selden Soc., vol. 22) 161.

[154] For the best modern discussions of the growth of the doctrine of precedent, see Allen, *Law in the Making* (6th ed. 1958) 183-230, and Plucknett, *Concise History of the Common Law* (5th ed. 1956) 342-350.

[155] See *Girouard* v. *United States*, 328 U. S. 61, where the decisive issue —whether the reenactment of a statute construed in earlier decisions amounted to Congressional approval of those decisions—was not mentioned in the brief *amicus curiae* filed by the American Civil Liberties Union.

[156] E.g., brief *amicus curiae* of the American Newspaper Publishers Ass'n in *Craig* v. *Harney*, 331 U. S. 367; memorandum *amicus curiae* of the C.I.O. in support of petition for rehearing in *Harris* v. *United States*, 331 U. S. 145. See, in this connection, the mordant comments of the late Mr. Justice Jackson, dissenting in *Craig* v. *Harney*, 331 U. S. at 397.

[157] "The great weight of opinion is that the decision virtually repeals the Fourth Amendment. See Twohey, *Analysis of Newspaper Opinion*, week ending May 10, 1947, p. 4." Memorandum *amicus curiae* of the C.I.O., cited in the preceding note, at 7.

amicus curiae had become essentially a means designed to exercise extrajudicial pressure on judicial decisions, more decorous than but essentially similar to the picketing of courthouses that Congress thereafter prohibited.[158]

Indeed, the presentation of briefs *amicus curiae* became such a problem in the Supreme Court that in 1949 a more restrictive rule as to such briefs was adopted.[159] For a time the then Solicitor General almost automatically refused his consent to motions for leave to file; this threw a greater burden on the Court;[160] now, the policy is more liberal; and the present Government policy and the present Supreme Court rule combine to permit parties with interests more immediate than those of mere propaganda to file briefs *amicus curiae* without undue difficulty.[161]

It must be borne in mind that on this question there exists a sharp difference of judicial opinion. Mr. Justice Black, dissenting from the adoption of the Supreme Court's new rules in 1954, said, "Most of the cases before this Court involve matters that affect far more people than the immediate record parties. I think the public interest and judicial administration would be better served by relaxing rather than tightening the rule against *amicus curiae* briefs."[162]

But the answer to this observation is that it is obviously impracticable to let every affected private person have his say in every Supreme Court lawsuit. Suppose that there is pending a tax case involving the scope of the deduction for "ordinary and necessary" business expenses;[163] could every taxpayer whom that decision might affect be permitted to file a brief? (If the case turns on the scope of a criminal statute, it is of course less likely that those contemplating like misconduct in the future will seek to present their views.)

Similarly, it is not open to any lawyer simply to file a brief or to participate in the argument on the footing that he knows more

---

[158] See 18 U.S.C. § 1507; 40 U.S.C. § § 13f-13p.

[159] Old Supreme Court Rule 27 (9) , 338 U. S. 959.

[160] See the memoranda filed by Frankfurter, J., in *United States* v. *Lance, Inc.,* 342 U. S. 915, and in *On Lee* v. *United States,* 343 U. S. 924.

[161] See Supreme Court Rule 42. See also First Circuit, Rule 24 (10) ; Ninth Circuit, Rule 18 (9) ; D. C. Circuit, Rule 18 (j) .

[162] 346 U. S. 946. Actually, the rule as to briefs *amicus curiae* adopted in 1954 did not effect any substantial changes. See 68 Harv. L. Rev. at 81.

[163] See e.g., *Peurifoy* v. *Commissioner,* 358 U. S. 59, and *Cammarano* v. *United States,* 358 U. S. 498.

about the particular field of law than does counsel for a party, and that he is accordingly better equipped to point out the fallacies in the other side's position. When an outsider did substantially that on one notable occasion, a majority of the Supreme Court joined in saying, "We discountenance this practice." [164]

And, however laudable the motives of many organizations dedicated to fostering their own particular versions of the American-cum-Utopian way of life, it is unfortunately the fact that many briefs filed by such bodies lack the professional qualities that tend to make them most helpful to the tribunal concerned.[165]

Section 88. Briefs *amicus curiae*; position of private counsel. —With briefs *amicus curiae,* as with reply briefs, the basic question is whether to file at all. There is no need here to discuss the problem of those who do not need consent of the parties to file [166]— the Solicitor General, who is frequently constrained to conclude that the United States lacks the burning interest in given private litigation that enthusiastic General Counsels of particular Federal agencies profess to find there; and State Attorneys General, whose duty it is to defend, as *amici curiae,* legislation in their own States that is similar to or identical with legislation from other States actually under challenge.[167] It is similarly unnecessary to discuss the position of the crusading organizations; these have their own standards, their own pet causes, and their own urges, none of which can or will be deflected in any degree by outside arguments. The problem posed by this section is that confronting the private practitioner.

No doubt the soundest view is that the filing of a brief *amicus curiae* on behalf of a client should be seriously considered only when such filing is plainly necessary to protect that client's interest, but not when the only justification for such a course would be the desire to add a "me too," or even a conviction that "anything-you-can-say-I-can-say-better."

A good yardstick for differentiating between the two situations is the Supreme Court rule that sets forth the showing required

[164] *Rosenberg* v. *United States,* 346 U. S. 273, 291-292.

[165] See note 155, *supra.* The example cited in Section 76, above, at p. 241, also appeared in a crusading organization's brief *amicus curiae.*

[166] Supreme Court Rule 42 (4) ; First Circuit, Rule 24 (10) ; Ninth Circuit, Rule 18 (9) (c) ; D. C. Circuit, Rule 18 (j) (1).

[167] For some recent examples, see *New York* v. *O'Neill,* 359 U. S. 1; *Northwestern Cement Co.* v. *Minnesota,* 358 U. S. 450.

to be made in a motion for leave to file a brief *amicus curiae*, namely, "facts or questions of law that have not been, or reasons for believing that they will not adequately be, presented by the parties." [168]

If, for example, a taxpayer is litigating with the Government to establish his right to a deduction that he must share with other parties, in a situation where the Internal Revenue Service is essentially a stakeholder, then another taxpayer who represents a genuinely adverse interest may fairly seek to enter the lists as a friend of the court. An example is the percentage depletion deduction, which in the case of leases must be equitably apportioned.[169] Similarly, in the case which involved the ascertainment of the proper base for the depletion allowance, in that instance fire clay for making burnt clay products, the National Coal Association sought and was granted permission to file a brief *amicus* which pointed out that the statutory provisions governing coal depletion varied materially from all the others.[170] On the other hand, if the taxpayer is claiming a deduction which, if available at all, would inure to the benefit of multitudes of other taxpayers similarly situated, a brief *amicus curiae* should be filed on behalf of one not a party to the litigation only when it can reasonably be demonstrated that the governing considerations have not been, or will not be, adequately presented by the litigants. If no such demonstration can fairly be made, counsel is better advised simply to pass on to the lawyers actually in the case his pet citations bearing on the issues involved.

Suppose, however, that you are the lawyer in the case, and you are approached by outside counsel with a request for your consent to the filing of an *amicus* brief. Should you consent, refuse consent, or, after refusal, file an objection (as the rules of some courts permit you to do)? [171]

This is the kind of predicament that recalls the late Gluyas Williams' cartoon series of "Difficult Decisions"; the competing considerations are, on the one hand, one's natural impulse never

---

[168] Supreme Court Rule 42 (3) ; cf. D. C. Circuit, Rule 18 (j) (2).

[169] See *Commissioner* v. *Southwest Expl. Co.*, 350 U. S. 308; *Parsons* v. *Smith*, 359 U. S. 215; *United States* v. *Stallard*, 273 F. 2d 847 (C.A. 4).

[170] *United States* v. *Cannelton Sewer Pipe Co.*, 364 U. S. 76, motion for leave to file brief *amicus curiae* granted, 363 U. S. 959.

[171] Supreme Court Rule 42 (3) ; Ninth Circuit, Rule 18 (9) (b) ; D. C. Circuit, Rule 18 (j) (2).

to refuse to a fellow lawyer a professional courtesy that one may later want in return, and, on the other, the overriding demands of one's own client's interests (and, usually, the even stronger impulse of not wanting outsiders to mess up one's own case).

Probably the most practical guideline is the old saw, "I can defend myself from my enemies, but Heaven protect me from my friends"; confusion in the enemy ranks is fine, confusion in one's own may be dangerous. So, don't hesitate to consent to the filing of a brief *amicus* against your position, but be very careful indeed about whom you will permit to fight at your side. Unless you can be perfectly sure that your prospective ally's position will be consistent with or complementary to your own, it is safer to refuse consent. Actual objection to his motion for leave to file will rarely be necessary; an intimation that you will probably object generally suffices to head off the unwelcome reinforcement.

The foregoing represents my own considered judgment. There may, however, be exceptions, depending on (a) the nature of the individual or organization seeking to come in with you on your side; (b) the weight the particular court is thought to give the representations of the organization in question; and (c) the extent to which counsel needs, or thinks he needs, reinforcements.

For instance, counsel representing a labor union may feel that he would be helped by a supporting brief from the parent body, the AFL-CIO. Other examples will come readily to mind. But, so far as I am personally concerned, I never consent. "Never? Well, hardly ever."

Section 89. Use of models.—I have earlier suggested (Section 20, above) the utility of studying briefs written by leaders of the bar, so that you may learn how the masters of the business turn it off.

To the extent that the several forms you examine differ, to the extent that several lawyers of equal eminence and learning employ varying styles, use your own judgment, make up your own mind, and, in the words of a now hackneyed but essentially tragic phrase of the Twenties, combine the best features of each.

Be careful, however, not to follow any forms blindly; therein lies the pitfall of the form book, of what one of my former associates used to call the Sears Roebuck catalogue. Use the form of other folks' briefs intelligently and eclectically. And be sure, very sure, that a supervening change in court rules has not rendered obsolete the form you are planning to follow. See Section 22, above.

Section 90. Significance and importance of accuracy.—I will end the discussion of briefs by recurring to that tiresome obsession of mine, the importance of accuracy.

Nothing quite so destroys a court's confidence in a lawyer or in his brief as when it finds that he has made inaccurate statements, either through carelessness or through design. That assertion is true of the entire document.[172] Contrariwise, a court will have complete faith in the briefs of any lawyer who has established his reputation for accuracy. Such a reputation needs to be guarded as carefully as personal honor itself—which in a very real sense it involves.

A brief should be written to persuade; it should pull no punches; but it must be honest, and it must be accurate.

---

[172] See the comments of the First Circuit in *Griffin Wellpoint Corp.* v. *Munro-Langstroth, Inc.,* 269 F. 2d 64, 67, concerning "some of the tricks of advocacy indulged in by counsel for appellant to lend apparent substance to its position," in consequence of which double costs were awarded the appellee.

THIRD PART

ARGUING THE APPEAL

CHAPTER VI
ESSENTIALS OF AN EFFECTIVE
ORAL ARGUMENT

Section 91. Should you argue at all?—At this point it will be assumed that your brief has been filed, that it is in satisfactory shape, and that it contains a minimum of misprints and typographical errors. You must then decide whether to argue the case or to submit it on briefs.

Appellate judges, virtually without exception, say that a case should never be submitted without oral argument, and a good many are on record in print to that effect.[1] According to the late Mr. Justice Jackson, "I think the Justices would answer unanimously that now, as traditionally, they rely heavily on oral presentations."[2] The present Mr. Justice Harlan told an audience, "I should like to leave with you * * * the thought that your oral argument on an appeal is perhaps the most effective weapon you have got if you will give it the time and attention it deserves."[3] A former member of the United States Court of Appeals for the District of Columbia Circuit said, "The longer I sit on the bench the more convinced I become that a lawyer should never submit a case without oral argument."[4] Expressions such as these—and many, many more could be cited—reflect the fact that the task of judgment is infinitely harder when counsel is not present to be questioned regarding his exact position, or to be asked how far the principle he contends for should extend. Just as the trial

---

[1] E.g., Hughes, *Supreme Court of the United States* (1928) 62-63.

[2] Jackson, *Advocacy Before the Supreme Court: Suggestions for Effective Case Presentations*, 37 A.B.A.J. 801 (1951).

[3] Harlan, *What Part Does the Oral Argument Play in the Conduct of an Appeal?*, 41 Corn. L. Q. 6, 11.

[4] Miller, *Oral Argument*, 9 J. of the Bar Ass'n of the D. C. 196.
Similarly, the late Chief Justice Vanderbilt of New Jersey, who while still at the bar played such a prominent part in the drafting and adoption of the Federal Rules of Civil and Criminal Procedure, wrote, "Cases that are not argued are not well decided." Vanderbilt, *A Unified Court System*, 9 F. R. D. 629, 639.

lawyer objects to an offer in evidence of an affidavit by saying, "I can't cross-examine that document," so an appellate judge knows that he cannot cross-examine a brief; he knows that he cannot obtain from a printed document the clarification of issues and positions that the questioning of counsel will afford. More than that, as Mr. Justice Frankfurter once wrote after he had been on the Court upwards of fifteen years, "Oral argument frequently has a force beyond what the written word conveys." [5]

Accordingly, on several occasions in the past, the Supreme Court called for oral argument in cases that counsel had submitted.[6] In an early stage of one of the Segregation Cases, where neither the school authorities nor the State whose statute was under attack filed a brief or indicated a readiness to argue, the Court said, *Per Curiam,* "we request that the State present its views at oral argument. If the State does not desire to appear, we request the Attorney General to advise whether the State's default shall be construed as a concession of invalidity." [7] Thereafter the case was briefed and argued on behalf of that State.[8]

In 1954, the Court adopted Rule 45 (1) , as follows:

The court looks with disfavor on the submission of cases on briefs, without oral argument, and therefore may, notwithstanding such submission, require oral argument by the parties.

In the first instance of a submission after the effective date of that Rule, the Court denied leave to submit the case without oral argument, and, because counsel for the respondent lived at a distance, invited a distinguished law teacher—Dean Griswold of Harvard—to present oral argument in support of the judgment

---

[5] *Rosenberg* v. *Denno,* 346 U. S. 371, 372. Mr. Justice Jackson wrote (*Advocacy Before the Supreme Court: Suggestions for Effective Case Presentations,* 37 A.B.A.J. 801) , "The Bar must make its preparations for oral argument on the principle that it always is of the highest, and often of controlling, importance."

[6] See, e.g., the following items in the *Journal of the Supreme Court:* Oct. T. 1935, p. 126, No. 2; Oct. T. 1936, p. 45, No. 20; Oct. T. 1941, p. 222, No. 782. See also *King* v. *Mullins,* 171 U. S. 404; *Patton* v. *Brady,* 184 U. S. 608. For the circumstances under which the first minimum wage case, *Stettler* v. *O'Hara,* 243 U. S. 629, was set down for argument after it had originally been submitted, see *Felix Frankfurter Reminisces,* 97-101.

[7] *Brown* v. *Board of Education,* 344 U. S. 141, 142.

[8] *Brown* v. *Board of Education,* 347 U. S. 483, 484.

below.[9] Some other federal appellate courts similarly require permission as a prerequisite to submission without argument.[10]

Consequently, quite apart from any question whether refusal on the part of a court or administrative agency to permit oral argument as to particular matters involves a denial of Due Process,[11] counsel should be prepared to argue—because, very plainly, he will hurt his client's case by not doing so.

It may be, of course, that the appellant's case is so completely devoid of merit that you, representing the appellee, will never be called upon, or that you will be told by the presiding judge, as you move toward the lectern, "The Court does not desire to hear further argument." In that event, it is better to accept victory gracefully than to attempt to inflict your eloquence on the tribunal. And there may be instances where it will be desirable, on behalf of the appellee, to say little or nothing.

For example, in one case petitioner's lawyer took such a battering from the court that it was obvious to everyone that the judgment below would be affirmed. Counsel for the respondent arose, bowed, and said, "If the Court please, I must apologize for an error in our brief. At page 39, second line from the bottom, the citation should be to 143 Federal Second and not to 143 Federal." He paused until the members of the court noted the correction, paused again when they looked up, toyed with his watch chain, and proceeded: "Unless there are any questions, I will submit the respondent's case on the brief"—and sat down. I have it on excellent authority that it was one of the most effective arguments ever heard by that court.

But of course, that is the exceptional instance—and a risky technique in the usual case. Normally, it is well to assume that the court desires to hear argument unless it affirmatively indicates the contrary, and normally, also, cavalier belittling of an opposing

---

[9] *Granville-Clark* v. *Granville-Clark*, 349 U. S. 1, 4. The submission appears at J. Sup. Ct., Oct. T. 1954, p. 78, 23 U. S. Law Week 3134, and the order denying leave to submit at 348 U. S. 885.

[10] Fifth Circuit, Rule 20 (4) ; Seventh Circuit, Rule 21 (d) ; U. S. Court of Military Appeals, Rule 47 (b) .

[11] See *Federal Communications Comm.* v. *Station WJR*, 337 U. S. 265, reversing 174 F. 2d 226 (D. C. Cir.) ; cf. *WIBC, Inc.* v. *Federal Communications Comm.*, 259 F. 2d 941 (D. C. Cir.) , certiorari denied *sub nom. Crosley Broadcasting Corp.* v. *WIBC, Inc.*, 358 U. S. 920.

argument is apt to backfire. Certainly, where the appeal is a discretionary one, as on certiorari or—in actual fact—on appeal in the Supreme Court, it is unwise for the respondent or appellee to suggest that, after all, there is nothing in the case to argue about. By granting certiorari or by noting probable jurisdiction, at least four Justices have already indicated the contrary.[12]

At any rate, so far as I personally am concerned, I prefer to get up and talk. That's at least half the fun for me—and, as the materials collected above show, it is certainly safer for the case.

Section 92. List of the essentials of effective oral argument.—The really essential features are:

(a) Appreciation of the purpose of advocacy.
(b) Not reading the argument.
(c) Application of the fundamentals of good public speaking.
(d) An effective opening.
(e) Clear statement of facts.
(f) Complete knowledge of the record.
(g) Thorough preparation.
(h) Attitude of respectful intellectual equality.
(i) Flexibility.

These essentials are discussed in order below. The finer points, i.e., those that make the difference between a first-rate argument and one that is merely run-of-the-mill, are considered in Chapter VIII.

Section 93. Appreciation of the purpose of advocacy.—What is it that a lawyer seeks to do when he argues a case on appeal? Is he there to make a flamboyant speech? Is he there to put on a show for a client? Or is he there to win the case?

The last named, obviously, if only for the mundane reason that higher fees are paid—and, usually, additional retainers become available—to the successful advocate. (Not that the public practice of the law is essentially different; Government or State or County lawyers also all want to win; losing a case is fully as painful to public counsel's psyche as it is to private counsel's pocket.)

---

[12] The divergent views set forth in *Ohio ex rel. Eaton* v. *Price*, 360 U. S. 246, make explicit what formerly was only implicit, viz., that, just as four votes suffice to grant certiorari, four likewise are sufficient to note probable jurisdiction.

Perhaps one of the most penetrating discussions of what a lawyer should strive to do when arguing an appeal appeared in an obituary address written by Mr. Justice Frankfurter some years back on the occasion of the untimely death of one of his former law clerks.

From the first he showed that the stuff of the advocate was in him, and by the time he left the Government, when the Supreme Court adjourned in June, 1952, he had fashioned himself into an accomplished practitioner of the art of persuasion. When he appeared at the lectern, erect and handsome, with an agreeable voice, serene rather than self-confident, tactful but firm, and always master of his case, the Court increasingly was assured of an argument that gave pleasure as well as enlightenment. He respected the traditions of the Supreme Court as a tribunal not designed as a dozing audience for the reading of soliloquies, but as a questioning body, utilizing oral arguments as a means for exposing the difficulties of the case with a view to meeting them. He held up his share of the probing process, and members of the Court were kept alert to observe the responsibilities of the questioner. It is fair to say that in a few short years Stanley Silverberg had attained a stature as an advocate matched by few lawyers coming before the Court, including the most eminent and experienced members of the Bar.[13]

Putting to one side for the moment the quality of the tribute, the significant point in the present connection is the Justice's definition of an advocate: "a practitioner of the art of persuasion." I emphasize that definition because of its importance, and because one would never dream from hearing some appellate arguments that they were being made to persuade a court to agree with the speaker.

The frequency with which counsel will fight a court, either generally or on specific unessential propositions, serves only to underscore the extent to which some lawyers overlook the obvious. One never persuades by antagonizing. You may take a dim view of a particular judge, or of a particular decision, or of a whole series of decisions, or indeed of the prevailing trend of the particular court—but when you appear before that tribunal on behalf of a client—private, corporate, or public—your job is to win your client's case, not to tell off the court, or particular members of the court, or to go all out on any tack not necessary to the case.

---

[13] Frankfurter, *Of Law and Men* (1956) 321-322.

I place first among the essentials, therefore, the truism that advocacy is the process of persuasion.[14]

Section 94. Not reading the argument.—Never read your argument. *Never read your argument.* NEVER READ YOUR ARGUMENT.

Once a lawyer begins to read to the court, whether it is his formal written brief, or the set piece he has written out to constitute his text for the argument, he raises up a curtain between himself and the court. Talk to the court, don't read to them! It is really amazing how many lawyers of ability and reputation will write out an "oral" argument and then get up and read it to the court—and equally amazing how long some courts appeared willing to tolerate the practice.

In its 1954 Rules, the Supreme Court finally put its collective foot down firmly. Rule 44 (1) states,

Oral argument should undertake to emphasize and clarify the written argument appearing in the briefs theretofore filed. *The court looks with disfavor on any argument that is read from a prepared text.*

The italics will not be found in the original; they have been added because of reflections evoked by the emphasized sentence. Had that provision been in effect in the twenty or so years preceding its adoption, it would have hampered not only a large collection of Assistant Attorneys General, whose qualifications for heading a division in the Department of Justice assuredly did not insure their forensic competence, but also a whole host of private practitioners who lacked the facility to argue save by reading what had first been written down, like as not by another hand. And what a commentary Rule 44 (1) is on the number of times the Supreme Court must have been subjected to such performances in

---

[14] Some years back, while lecturing on oral advocacy to the first year students at an Eastern law school, I mentioned, by way of illustrating an answer during the question period, the case of *Erie R. Co.* v. *Tompkins,* 304 U. S. 64. I was aware that the doctrine of that case was regarded with, at the least, considerable reserve on the part of some faculty members at this institution, but I must say I was completely flabbergasted when my citation was greeted with prolonged hisses from the student audience.

Passing the point that most critics of *Erie R. Co.* v. *Tompkins* probably lack any appreciation of the problems raised by *Swift* v. *Tyson,* 16 Pet. 1, which it overruled, the obvious comment in the present connection is that, once law students graduate and get to court—always assuming that they can pass their bar examinations—hissing particular decisions will, in any court, prove to be a most unhelpful technique.

the past! Other federal appellate courts appear not to have been similarly troubled, perhaps because arguments there are not regarded as sufficiently glamorous to be sought after by those whose rank in the legal hierarchy is perceptibly higher than their standing in the scale of advocacy; in any event, the only prohibitions in the Federal courts of appeals are against reading long excerpts from decisions, records, and briefs.[15]

There are not many phases of oral advocacy on which one is warranted in being dogmatic, but this is one of them: Don't read. It is wrong, all wrong. Occasional addresses, i.e., *Remarks on the Dedication of a Memorial to the Former Members of the Society*— something prepared for a particular occasion, where the form of every sentence counts and where there are no interruptions— those can and should be read. (Make sure, however, that even in that instance you read *from* the paper, and not *at* it.)

But in court, when you are engaging in argument, subject to instant, insistent (and frequently fairly constant) interruption, reading just doesn't go over. It raises a veil between the speaker and his auditors. No advocate worthy of the name will ever read his argument to the court—and if the unequivocal character of these statements leaves you unconvinced, just go to court some day and listen to the readers (in courts where reading is still permitted).

Not only that, but an oral argument loses much of its spontaneity if it is written out in advance. It is more natural—and hence more effective—if it is delivered from notes. Below, in the chapter on preparation, are discussed the problems of how extensive those notes should be, and whether and to what extent they may safely be discarded altogether. The point made here is that the advocate should use his notes as a guide, not as a text.

Section 95. Application of the fundamentals of good public speaking.—An effective appellate advocate must have an appreciation of and ability to apply the fundamentals of good public speaking—and that does not mean oratory, because oratory is not necessary. An appellate court is not a jury. It may react like a jury, as witness the timelessness of the observation that hard cases make bad law, but it dislikes to be harangued as though it were in the

---

[15] First Circuit, Rule 28 (3); Third Circuit, Rule 31 (3); Fifth Circuit, Rule 25 (3); Sixth Circuit, Rule 20 (3); Seventh Circuit, Rule 21 (c).

box instead of on the bench. The play on an appellate court's emotions must be subtle and restrained if it is to be effective.

Nonetheless, an argument differs from a dinner-table conversation; and although of course the present chapter does not and cannot purport to be a text on public speaking (any more than Chapter III was a manual on how to write good English), there are certain fundamentals that can be briefly stated.

(a) *You must be heard.* Once you are on your feet, talk is the only medium by which you can communicate your thought to the court, and, unless you can make yourself heard by all of the judges, you are wasting your time and the court's time and are endangering your client's cause. If you are arguing to a bench of five, seven, or nine judges, the end men must be able to hear what you are saying.

It is all very noble to assert (as I have heard some earnest and upright young men say) that honesty precludes resort to any artificialities. The fact of the matter is that a certain degree of artificiality is necessary in order to convey a realistic likeness. Consider, for instance, actors in a play: in order to present to the audience the picture of persons sitting around a table talking quietly, the actors must themselves talk more loudly so that the people in the back of the theater may hear them; and in order that they may be seen, the actors, however manly, must put on grease paint and theatrical lipstick. Artificial? Yes, but without that kind of artifice the audience cannot obtain an impression of realism.

It is the same with a lawyer in an appellate courtroom—most of which have wretched acoustics. He must speak loudly enough so that he can be heard and understood. (Sometimes a public address system is provided, as in the Supreme Court, but that is not usual.)

(b) *You must use proper emphasis.* Here again, emphasis is a species of artifice; but the spoken word without emphasis would be as ineffective—and often as unintelligible—as the written word without punctuation or capitalization. A lawyer worthy of the name cannot afford to use the same tone for "This case comes here on appeal from a decree of the District Court for the Eastern District" as for "This is the gross and shocking fraud that was perpetrated by these respondents."

The matter of proper emphasis can be broken down into not more than four basic admonitions:

(i) *Avoid a monotone.* Perhaps the best way to attempt to reproduce a monotone in print is to set out a paragraph without punctuation: "At this point the shipper called on the railroad to deliver livestock directly to its siding but the railroad refused to do so contending that by reason of its contract with the stockyards it was bound not to deliver such competitive traffic over the track in question without the payment of yardage charges which yardage charges it was no longer willing to absorb and thereupon the shipper instituted its complaint against the railroad before the Commission." That sort of thing is just as difficult to follow by ear as by eye.

(ii) *Avoid the ministerial cadence.* Here the voice goes up and down but without emphasis on particular words, like this:

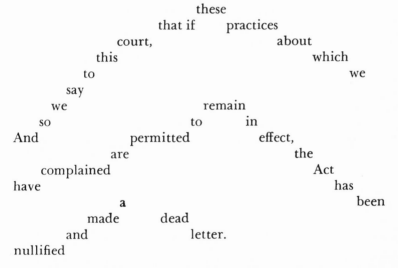

(iii) *Avoid mumbling.* "This—ah—case, turns on the—ah—validity of the—ah—Gadget Restriction Act of—ah—1958. We—that is, the petitioners—ah—contend—ah—that the measure—ah—clearly transcends—ah—the powers vested in the—ah—Congress." And so on, and on, and on.

(iv) *Use the pause.* The only way that an oral statement can be punctuated is by a pause—a short one for a comma (which, after all, is simply a signal for a breath), a longer one at the end of a sentence, and a still longer one when you reach the end of a paragraph. If you want more emphasis, as for instance to mark your taking up an entirely new point, underscore the pause and make it longer by taking a sip of water. Since you cannot wave a red handkerchief to indicate the end of paragraphs or a blue one to signal the completion of points, you must pause in some fashion or other.

The pause is also helpful as a device to regain the court's attention. Sometimes the learned judges just aren't interested. Sometimes that is the fault of the case, more often it is the fault of the lawyer, and sometimes they just aren't paying attention anyway. They are whispering, and passing notes, and reading at the record. Your main proposition is coming up. How make certain that it will have their full attention? Very simple; just use the public speaker's oldest trick: Pause. The sudden silence makes everyone look up, every member of the court eyes the speaker expectantly—and then you give them your big point. It's an ancient ruse, but still one of the most effective.

Section 96. An effective opening.—High on the list of essentials is the admonition to lodge effectively in the court's mind, in the opening minutes, what the case involves, so that interest and understanding will be seized and held. This generally requires the use of a good opening sentence or paragraph. The important point to remember is that the first few minutes are critical, that counsel must catch and hold the court's interest and attention in that time. If he is for the appellant, he must give a thumbnail epitome of "what this case is all about." If he is for the appellee, he must in his opening sentence seize upon the central feature of the case, and, by driving it home, dispel the impression left by his adversary.

The opening should, after the technique of the well-written newspaper account, tell the whole story in the first paragraph, after which it is time to go back and fill in the details. And, like the competent newspaper reporter, the advocate must never keep his audience in suspense; on the contrary, he must give his secret completely away right at the outset.

The process of formulating an effective opening is probably easier when the lawyer is topside, i.e., when he appears for the appellant or petitioner, because then he can work out and polish his opening well in advance. More flexibility is necessary when the advocate is bottomside; then, very frequently, he must improvise in order to be able to tie on to something said by the preceding speaker. In either event, counsel must avoid trivia—and, when he is the second man up, he must, however great the temptation and/or provocation, avoid personalities.

On the whole, I think a good opening is probably more important when the advocate is bottomside, for the appellee or respondent, because then the court is extremely anxious to get, in a nutshell, the gist of the reply to the argument it has been hearing for thirty, forty-five, or sixty minutes. The appellee's case sags perceptibly if counsel, facing this expectant bench, commences with the perfectly immaterial correction that "Petitioner X was not the President of the company, he was only the Vice-President," or when counsel for the appellee, in a case that turns entirely on law, begins by saying, "I would like to review very briefly the facts out of which this case arises."

The court is perhaps not equally alert when appellant rises because at that point there is generally a certain amount of intellectual clearing of the throat, so to speak.

(a) Here are some examples of oral openings, drawn from my own practice and observation, that have held a court's attention:

(i) [For petitioner.]

Respondents were convicted by a jury of conspiring to defraud the United States of the disinterested services of one of its officers. Their judgments of conviction were reversed by the Second Circuit on four separate grounds, and the case is now here on certiorari.

Two of the questions, involving alleged errors on the part of the trial court, concern only the Bayers. Two concern only Radovich—whether a confession of his was admissible, and whether his plea of double jeopardy was a valid one. I shall deal with each of those questions separately in the course of the argument.

The basic facts can be briefly stated. Etc., etc., etc.[16]

Analytically, this opening does two things. First, "convicted by a jury" is pure semantics, resorted to in order to sway sympathy away from the respondents by appealing to that palladium of liberty, the twelve good men and true in the box. Second, it states the issues in a nutshell, so that the court has the bare outline of the case in mind, and will not ask impatient, interrupting questions while the basic facts are being developed.

(ii) [For petitioner.]

---

[16] *United States* v. *Bayer*, 331 U. S. 532.

This case, which is here on certiorari to the Ninth Circuit, involves the protection to be accorded the Government-soldier relationship.[17]

That states the question concisely—and phrases it in such a way as to present the petitioner's contention, i.e., that there is something to be protected, as sympathetically as possible. (If the flag is to be waved effectively in an appellate court, the motion should be languid—as though the flagstaff were a fan.)

(iii) [For respondent.]

Two days after this Court's decision in the *Schwimmer* case, a bill was introduced in Congress to change the rule of naturalization there announced. Hearings were held on the bill, it was discussed on the floor—but it never got out of committee.

And on the first day that Congress was in session following this Court's decision in the *Macintosh* case, a similar bill was introduced in Congress to reverse the result in that case. Hearings were held on that bill, that bill was also discussed on the floor—and that bill never emerged from committee either. Indeed for eleven successive years, through six successive Congresses, the same bill was introduced and reintroduced—and Congress never saw fit to pass it.[18]

That opening focussed attention on the strongest point in the Government's case, i.e., not that the *Schwimmer* and *Macintosh* decisions were right, but that they had subsequently been approved by Congress. That argument, as has been noted (Sections 50, 57, and 70), did not prevail, but the substance of the opening found its way into a strong dissent written by Chief Justice Stone on the last day of his life.[19]

---

[17] *United States* v. *Standard Oil Co.,* 332 U. S. 301.

[18] *Girouard* v. *United States,* 328 U. S. 61.

[19] 328 U. S. at 73-74: "The construction of the naturalization statutes, adopted by this Court in the three cases mentioned, immediately became the target of an active, publicized legislative attack in Congress which persisted for a period of eleven years, until the adoption of the Nationality Act in 1940. Two days after the *Schwimmer* Case was decided, a bill was introduced in the House, H. R. 3547, 71st Cong., 1st Sess., to give the Naturalization Act a construction contrary to that which had been given to it by this Court and which, if adopted, would have made the applicants rejected by this Court in the *Schwimmer, Macintosh* and *Bland* Cases eligible for citizenship. This effort to establish by Congressional action that the construction which this Court had placed on the Naturalization Act was not one which Congress had adopted or intended, was renewed without success after the decision in the *Macintosh* and *Bland* Cases, and was continued for a period of about ten years. All of these measures were of substantially the same pattern as H. R. 297, 72d Cong. 1st Sess., introduced December 8, 1931, at the first session of

(iv) [For respondent.]

The question in this case is whether a good Nazi can be a good American.[20]

This was a denaturalization case, the first to reach the Supreme Court since the process of denaturalization had run afoul of the decisions in *Schneiderman* v. *United States* [21] and *Baumgartner* v. *United States*.[22] It was far stronger for the Government than either of the other two, but I felt that I needed an opening that would really rock the Court on its heels, and make them sit up and take notice. This opening did just that, and the *Knauer* denaturalization was sustained.

(b) It may also be helpful to set down an example or two of how not to do it.

(i) [For petitioner.]

This case comes here on certiorari to review a judgment of the Circuit Court of Appeals for the Eleventh Circuit which reversed an order of the District Court for the Western Caroline Islands that dismissed a bill of complaint for lack of federal jurisdiction.

The facts involve an action for damages brought by a native chieftain of those islands against a medical officer in the Navy. Etc., etc., etc.

The first paragraph is unintelligible orally (and not too easy to understand in writing). The second launches directly into the

---

Congress, after the decision in the *Macintosh* Case. It provided that no person otherwise qualified 'shall be debarred from citizenship by reason of his or her religious views or philosophical opinions with respect to the lawfulness of war as a means of settling international disputes, but every alien admitted to citizenship shall be subject to the same obligations as the native-born citizen.' H. R. 3547, 71st Cong. 1st Sess., introduced immediately after the decision in the *Schwimmer* Case, had contained a like provision, but with the omission of the last clause beginning 'but every alien.' Hearings were had before the House Committee on Immigration and Naturalization on both bills at which their proponents had stated clearly their purpose to set aside the interpretation placed on the oath of allegiance by the *Schwimmer* and *Macintosh* Cases. There was opposition on each occasion. Bills identical with H. R. 297 were introduced in three later Congresses. None of these bills were reported out of Committee. The other proposals, all of which failed of passage * * * *, had the same purpose and differed only in phraseology."

[20] *Knauer* v. *United States*, 328 U. S. 654.
[21] 320 U. S. 118.
[22] 322 U. S. 665.

facts. It will be some time before the court learns what questions are involved. They will either lose interest—or else interrupt. Sometimes judges are reduced to prying the facts out of counsel by a species of cross-examination, which means that counsel isn't doing his job—and isn't helping his case.

In this particular situation, the whole matter could have been very simply and clearly presented as follows:

This case is here on certiorari to the Eleventh Circuit, and involves the question whether an action for damages arising out of an alleged false imprisonment, that is said to be in violation of the constitutional guaranty of due process of law, states a cause of action within federal jurisdiction in the absence of diversity of citizenship. Otherwise stated, the single issue is whether an action seeking damages for a tort involves a federal question whenever the tort is alleged to have been committed in violation of a constitutional provision.

The facts alleged in the complaint and in the affidavits submitted on the motion for summary judgment are as follows: Etc., etc., etc.

When the opening is thus presented, the court knows at the outset just what the question is, and will listen to the facts with some appreciation of their relevance.

(ii) Here is an example of how counsel for a respondent can make or break his case at the outset:

In an action by the United States to recover public money paid out through mistake of law and in reliance on the defendant-appellant's fraudulent representations, appellant's counsel was questioned by the court just before he sat down, as follows:

Judge X: "Are there any facts reflected in the present record which were not before the officers of the government in 1923 and 1924 when the payments were made?"

Appellant's counsel: "No." [He sits down.]

Respondent's counsel: "May it please the Court: This case involves an interesting question regarding the scope of judicial review of the acts of administrative officers. Etc., etc., etc."

And the case sags. What respondent's counsel could have said with the record he had was this:

May it please the Court: I will undertake to answer from the record the question just put to Mr. Y.

There are many facts reflected in this record that were not before the departments concerned when the payments were made.

To begin with, appellant said in 1923 and 1924 that he always believed he had been an American citizen. But this record shows that he swore under oath in 1912 and again in 1914 that he was a subject of Germany, and the record shows that the government officers who passed on his claim were not aware of his earlier inconsistent statements.

And appellant said in 1923 and 1924 that he was an American who was detained in Germany by a sick wife. But appellant swore in 1912 that he was a resident of Germany, and in 1914 that he was a non-resident of America—and here again the officers passing on his claim did not know of his earlier representations to the contrary. Etc., etc., etc.

Such a beginning would electrify the court. First, it effectively undermines appellant's presentation, because it points up the inaccuracy of that presentation. Second, it shows that appellant was a wicked man. (Fraud always sways a court, whether the opinion turns on fraud or not.) So long as it is relevant and not simply dragged in by the ears as an abusive personality, fraud always makes an impression; and a case that analytically may be one of dry-as-dust administrative law very often turns, in fact, on the circumstance that a decision one way would favor the fraudulent party, whereas a decision the other way would strip him of his ill-gotten gains.

Respondent's counsel in fact got three votes out of six— enough for his purposes, since the judgment below was in his favor. But with a proper opening he would have been arguing in an entirely different atmosphere, and might well have got all six.

Section 97. Clear statement of facts.—"The great power at the bar is the power of clear statement!" If that expression standing alone seems unduly sententious—and it hails from the Nineteenth Century, being attributed by Southern lawyers to Judah P. Benjamin, and by Northerners to Rufus Choate—just listen some day to a really able lawyer outlining a complicated fact situation to a court or jury, and compare his exposition with the efforts of some garrulous dowager at the bridge table to explain just what happened to the girls at the last big country club dance. The lawyer states the essentials first, then develops and unfolds the details; the dowager runs on endlessly and repetitiously, expounding whole masses of trivia.

But it is not a matter of sex, or even of lack of training. Everyone knows that there are innumerable lawyers who always start with the dreary details, or who attempt to state a case by carefully embroidering the periphery at the outset.

No matter how complicated the facts may be, they can always be presented in their simple essentials. Mr. Justice Brandeis used to say, "There isn't anything in the world that can't be explained to a jury"—a comment that really stands as a challenge to every lawyer.

Now, how go about this business of explaining a set of facts? First, ask yourself: How would you undertake to learn it? What would you want to know first? What would you want to know next? After that it is simply a matter of explaining the same things in the same order to the court.

Always keep in mind the basic psychological fact that knowledge is cumulative, and work from your essentials outward toward the details. Start with the trunk, take up the branches next, and end with the leaves. Or, in more concrete terms, always headnote your arguments. It is much easier for the court to follow you if you give them an oral outline, not only of the facts, but of the law as well.

Suppose you were retained as counsel for another lawyer: How would you want him to explain his case to you? If you know that, all you need to do is to state the matter to the court in the same way.

Below, in Sections 117, 118, and 120, are discussed certain of the finer points connected with the process, as, for instance, the elimination of unnecessary details and the necessity for sketching the picture in clear, broad strokes after it has been outlined. Here is considered only the immediate essential, namely, will the court —or any listener—know what the case is about when you have finished stating the facts? If the answer is a resounding "Yes!" you are ready to pass on to preparing the legal portion of your argument. If the answer is anything less than that, you had better work over the facts some more.

Bear in mind also that you cannot cross-reference in an oral argument. Specifically, suppose you have a case involving two unrelated points. In the brief, you will set out in your Statement of Facts the facts bearing on point A and follow them with the facts relating to point B. The brief then continues with the law on point A, followed by the law on point B, and if any reader wonders what the facts are as to *B* at that juncture, all he need do is turn back a few pages. In other words, your order in writing is *FA, FB, LA, LB,* where *F* = facts and *L* = law.

But if you argue the case orally in the same way, the court will find such a presentation confusing in the extreme, and this is particularly so if there have been questions regarding *LA.* It is impossible to cross-reference by ear, even for the most acute of men, and if you are facing even a single judge whose mental uptake is on the slow side, his questions born of honest confusion will completely disrupt your presentation. In the case just put, the only sound method of presentation is to state the facts as to *A,* mention that you are deferring the other facts until you reach *B,* and then argue *LA* where it logically belongs, i.e., after the facts out of which it arises. Next you take up *FB,* followed by *LB,* and, once again, everyone is able to follow you.

The same is true in a case involving numerous unrelated points. For instance, in *United States* v. *Bayer* [23] four questions were involved, two of which concerned the Bayers and two Radovich. The first had to do with the admissibility of a confession made by Radovich, and the second with the availability of Radovich's plea of double jeopardy. Point Three was whether the trial judge properly exercised his discretion in refusing to permit the Bayers to introduce additional evidence four hours after the jury had retired, and Point Four, whether the trial judge's concededly accurate charge was so cryptic as to require reversal. Even in the brief, we preceded each point under the argument with a summary of the facts bearing upon it. At the oral argument, the Government's case, after being set out in general outline, was divided up so that the facts bearing on each point immediately preceded the legal argument on that point. Or, using the symbols already employed: General statement, *FA, LA, FB, LB, FC, LC, FD, LD.*

Section 98. Complete knowledge of the record.—If I were asked to name the advocate's secret weapon—a weapon, indeed, that still remains a secret to many—I should say that it is complete knowledge of the record. In this field, pre-eminently, knowledge is power, and in this field, also, forensic reputations painstakingly established can be thrown away by a single lazy lapse. No lawyer, no matter how able he may be, can afford to argue any case in ig-

---

[23] 331 U. S. 532.

norance of the record. It is done, of course, but it is risky, on a par with passing a car on a curving hill; you may pull it off, but the chances are heavily weighted against you. Indeed, whenever any lawyer gets to the point of believing that he can argue cases on the basis of his own past record rather than on the basis of the actual record involved in the appeal being heard, hardening of the forensic arteries has set in, and it is time for him to move over and make room for others.

Of course, experience begets a familiarity with the learning process, and an old hand can pick up—and pick out—the essentials of a record far more easily than a tyro. But the lad who really knows his facts is a far more dangerous opponent even on his first time up than the polished veteran of hundreds of appellate arguments who has given the record a glib once-over-lightly. I have seen lawyers of reputation utterly demolished in a courtroom when they went free-wheeling away from a record they obviously had not read, and were then caught up short by opposing counsel, who knew it inside out. The otherwise gentle visages of appellate judges harden perceptibly when such misstatements are exposed. A lawyer simply has no business getting up to talk about a case he does not thoroughly know.[24]

There are a number of aids to learning a record. First of all, read it. Don't rely on abstracts. Read it yourself. If the case is going to turn on facts, if the other side is going to attack findings in your favor, if the litigation has any complexity at all, there is just no escape from that harsh task. The admonition to read the record may be a counsel of perfection, but no painless substitute for it has yet been invented.

Second, reread the critical portions. Here again, there is no softly padded, anesthetized road to learning.

Third, tab the record with gummed-cloth index tabs, so that you can readily find any material portion without thumbing through it or looking in the index. The details of this process are

---

[24] Lest any reader imagine that the admonitions in the text are addressed to an imaginary situation, let him ponder this passage from an opinion: "The present appeal from a final judgment for the defendant is bottomed upon an erroneous statement of decisive fact in both the brief and the argument of appellant. This error was not pointed out to the court by appellee. The portions of the record which would have revealed the error were not included in the appendix to the brief of either party." *Hartmann* v. *Time*, 180 F. 2d 595 (C.A. 3).

discussed below in Section 105. Tabbing is helpful in itself, just to make you learn the record, to assist you to envisage its scope and in viewing the case in outline.

Fourth, the record will stick in your mind more firmly when you write the brief yourself. When you do that, the case becomes more a part of you than when you simply soak up a brief someone else has written. But very frequently, whether in governmental or private practice, the brief (or at least a finished first draft) will have been written by another hand, so the advice to write the brief yourself may be another counsel of perfection.

Fifth, a good memory helps. Some people are born with what a friend of mine used to call a flypaper mind—everything sticks. It is a distinct advantage to a lawyer to have one, just as it is a distinct advantage to a woman to be born beautiful. But memory can be trained—just as, unless the cosmetics manufacturers are wholly wrong, women can be beautified.

At any rate, when you get up to argue your case, you must know your record better than the court does, because the court relies on counsel to present the facts. You must do the exploratory work; no court is going to plow through thousands of printed pages to find the critical bit of testimony that will win your case. And no court is going to think much of your argument or be impressed by your knowledge of the case if, when a judge asks you a simple question—"Where is the order of the Commission in the record?" "Where is the final contract as agreed upon by the parties?"—you stand there fumbling, unable to put your finger on the vital documents. The judges become impatient, you will feel embarrassment, no one listening in the courtroom is going to think well of you at all—and if opposing counsel stage-whispers, "Page 28," he wasn't moved by just kindness of heart. Rather, he has signaled the court that, if they want to learn about this case, he is the lad they had better ask, not you.

Section 99. Thorough preparation.—No lawyer would dream of filing with the clerk the first rough draft of his brief. Why then present to the court the first draft of your oral argument? [25] Many lawyers, too many of them, do just that—which is why such a lot of

---

[25] One budding barrister in the same audience already mentioned in note 14 to this chapter, *supra,* p. 282, asked, "Just where do you file that first draft of oral argument?" The only answer I could fairly give him was, "Not with the court."

sorry oral arguments are heard in Federal appellate courts through-out the land.

There are, of course, some virtuosos, some people who have a flair for the extemporaneous. If you are one of those fortunate few, the paragraphs that follow are not for you. But if you are a simple, run-of-the-mill fellow, like the rest of us, a carefully re-hearsed and prepared and revised presentation will always be bet-ter than one that is just rolled off the cuff.

Preparation and rehearsal will save you from going off on unprofitable or even untenable side issues, will spare you the waste of precious minutes on nonessentials, and will substantially assist you in eliminating unhappy turns of phrase.

I myself feel that I must go over what I am to say if only for one reason: to time my remarks. There is something inexorable about the ticking of that courtroom clock, particularly when a firm judge is presiding. When your time is up, when the Chief Justice leans over and says, "Your time has expired"—well, you sit down. The stories told of Chief Justice Hughes, "that on one occasion he called time on a leader of the New York Bar in the middle of the word 'if,' " and that "once on being asked by the same gentle-man how much time remained, he replied, with beard bristling, '14 seconds,' " [26] may be apocryphal, but they contain more than a germ of truth. Consequently, you had better know before you start just how much or how little time your direct presentation will take. If you have three points, and can only cover two in your 30 or 45 or 60 minutes, revision is imperative—and you had better make that discovery before you address the court.

But, apart from timing, I feel that repeating what I want to say is helpful in many other respects. In going over the case orally, I generally think of other points to make. Questions arise in my mind that must be checked, questions of fact and of law alike. I progress gradually to a smoother presentation, and can sense what to stress, what to eliminate, where to expand, and where to com-press.

More than that, by practicing the oral argument several times, it becomes fixed in my mind so that when I appear in court I no longer need detailed notes, but can rely with assurance on head-ings and subheadings; I thus avoid the need for elaborate notes

---

[26] McElwain, *The Business of the Supreme Court as Conducted by Chief Justice Hughes,* 63 Harv. L. Rev. 5, 17 (1949).

that tempt one into reading, or nearly reading, the argument. See Section 110, below.

If possible, I plan to go over the argument two or three times. That is often enough to get the context of the contentions in mind, to smooth out the more obvious infelicities, and to learn just precisely how many precious minutes I am using; yet I have not so over-rehearsed as to sound in court as if I had committed my argument to memory.

The result is that, by the time I get up in the courtroom with my striped pants neatly pressed, the court hears, not my first draft, but my third or fourth. Frequently, that draft still leaves a good deal to be desired—but at least it is a much more finished performance than the first.

Section 100. Planning the argument.—Not only must you prepare your argument so that it will fit into the allotted time, you must plan its substance as well. This breaks down into four major aspects.

(a) *Selection of Points.* What points are you going to make? Are you going to repeat what was said by other counsel in the related case just ahead of you? Are you going to stress the points that the other side virtually concedes? Or are you going to argue at length some unimportant issues that are very much in dispute? A lot of lawyers choose some or all of these alternatives—which is another reason for the paucity of good arguments.

Planning in this area involves elimination, but a different kind of elimination than the process of cutting weak points out of your brief (see Section 35 (a), *supra*). When you plan your oral argument, the weak points have already been taken out of your case, and you now must decide which of the points that remain you had better relegate to the briefs, and which you will discuss orally. Never be afraid to say, "The remaining points are not abandoned, but in view of the limited time, we rest those on our brief."

(b) *Avoiding Unnecessary Complexity.* Any argument planned to cover too many points will leave a fuzzy impression. An argument in its essential outline must be kept relatively simple, else it will fail to leave with the court a feeling that the case should be decided in a particular way.

It is far better to cover the really important points orally so as to make a firm impression and then to yield back some of your time, than to use up all of your time to treat all of your points and then leave the court up in the air. As Mr. Justice Jackson wrote, "The impact of oral presentation will be strengthened if it is concentrated on a few points that can be simply and convincingly stated and easily grasped and retained." [27]

(c) *Avoiding Improper Emphasis.* Most cases present a mixture of questions; some are easy, some are difficult—often very difficult. Suppose you have two issues, one in each category. Why stress the hard one when you can win your case on the one that avoids a great many difficulties? Of course, even after arguing some difficult, not to say untenable propositions, you may win in the end. But why go at it the hard way? At any rate, one of the subjects for planning is to select the easier points for the argument, the ones that will generate less opposition from the court.

(d) *Arguing Principles.* Finally, when you are on your feet, argue principles, and argue them broadly. Leave the details of the decisions to your brief, where they can be more helpfully discussed. Effecting that differentiation will be an important feature of your planning.

None of this, of course, means that you can be sure of following your plan. Again to quote Mr. Justice Jackson,

I used to say that, as Solicitor General, I made three arguments of every case. First came the one that I planned—as I thought, logical, coherent, complete. Second was the one actually presented—interrupted, incoherent, disjointed, disappointing. The third was the utterly devastating argument that I thought of after going to bed that night.[28]

This from the man of whom Mr. Justice Brandeis said that he should be Solicitor General for life! [29] But—and here is a question for the rest of us—what chance would an advocate have who had never planned his argument in the first place?

Section 101. Attitude of respectful intellectual equality.— Another essential of an effective argument is a proper mental attitude on the part of the advocate.

---

[27] Jackson, *Advocacy Before the Supreme Court: Suggestions for Effective Case Presentations,* 37 A.B.A.J. 801, 803.

[28] *Ibid.* Compare Rall, *Effective Oral Argument on Appeal,* 48 Ill. Bar J. 572, 588: "Certainly no oral argument is ever as good as the one you make on your way home."

[29] Frankfurter, *Of Life and Men* (1956) 192.

(a) It will not do to say of a court, as one may perhaps say of one's spiritual advisers, "They will show us our errors." If a judge asks, "Where does this power end?" and counsel answers, "That is for this court to say," then, inevitably, the judge will reply, "I am asking for guidance." (I once heard precisely that colloquy in the Supreme Court of the United States.) Moreover, if the lawyer approaches a court with an appreciation that amounts to awe, perhaps verging into fear, he will not be able effectively to stand up to the court's questioning. Counsel simply cannot afford to have a litter of intellectual kittens in the courtroom while he is arguing his case—certainly not if he expects to win it for his client. I have myself witnessed case after case being lost, cases that could have been won, basically because counsel was so terrified of the tribunal and so in awe of its individual members that their questions threw him completely off balance, and, through the mere fact of being asked, quite disabled him from answering. If you set out to argue an appeal, you must be able to engage in give-and-take with the judges. They can point out errors only as errors are pointed out to them.

(b) By the same token, it will not do to talk down to a court, however much the individual advocate may have been more generously endowed with quick perception than some of the judges whom he addresses. Sometimes the lawyer's attitude of superiority rests simply on his own keen sense of self-appreciation. On other occasions, its basis may be a view widely prevalent at the bar that old Judge Overshoe just isn't very bright. And on other occasions, the lawyer may feel that he is such an outstanding expert in the particular field of law involved in his case that he is the professor and the judges simply students—not particularly bright students at that—who are listening to an expository lecture. But, whatever the explanation in any given situation, such an attitude is wrong. It is wrong as a matter of protocol, because the theory is that the judiciary is superior to the bar. And it is particularly wrong as a matter of advocacy, because advocacy is the art of persuasion, and you do not, by talking down to him, ever persuade a man who has the power to decide against you.

(c) The only proper attitude is that of respectful intellectual equality. The respectful part of it is the same quantum and manner of respect and deference that a younger man should show when speaking to an older one, or a junior officer in the military service when engaged in official discussion with a superior much senior to him, or a parishioner talking to a priest, or the law clerk taking up a point of law with the senior partner. Beyond that, however, the argument of an appeal must be undertaken by the advocate on the basis that it is a discussion among equals, whether the argument is made directly or in response to questions from the bench. Counsel must stand up to the judges quite as he would stand up to the senior member of his own firm. If he permits himself to be overawed by comments or questions simply because they emanate from judges, if he proceeds on the footing that a chance offhand remark from the bench is sacrosanct because of its origin and without regard to its intrinsic merits, if he becomes completely unnerved by a judge saying, "Well, now, I don't know about that," then he— and his case—are well on their way to being lost.

Section 102. Flexibility.—An appellate argument is not a set piece. For one thing, it is in most courts far from being a monologue, and for another, it must be adjusted and trimmed according to the reaction it evokes.

Naturally, counsel must make allowance for questions (and, if topside, for rebuttal) when ne plans his argument. If the rules of court permit only 30 or 45 minutes to a side, and judges are prone to ask questions, then, unless the direct presentation is kept to 20 or 30 minutes, counsel will simply not, in the ordinary course, be able to cover all his points.

The time allowed by the rules of most Federal appellate courts varies from one hour to thirty minutes, and only a minority of them allow an hour.[30]

In the Supreme Court of the United States the limit is one

---

[30] Subject to enlargement by special permission upon prior request, the following are the current time limits for oral argument:

One hour: First Circuit, Rule 28 (3) ; Fourth Circuit, Rule 15 (3) ; Fifth Circuit, Rule 25 (3) ("and the court may allow such less time as shall appear to it to be sufficient for a fair presentation of the questions involved in any case") ; Eighth Circuit, Rule 13 (c) ; Court of Customs and Patent Appeals, Rule XXIII.

Forty-five minutes: Second Circuit, Rule 23 (c) ; Third Circuit, Rule 31 (3) ; Sixth Circuit, Rule 20 (3) ; Seventh Circuit, Rule 21 (b) ; Ninth Circuit, Rule 20 (3) ; Tenth Circuit, Rule 20 (3) ; District of Columbia Circuit, Rule 19 (c) (automatically upon request) .

Thirty minutes: Eighth Circuit, Rule 13 (c) (for certain matters) ; Ninth Circuit, Rule 20 (3) , (for certain matters) ; District of Columbia Circuit, Rule 19 (c) (in absence of request) ; Court of Claims (as a matter of practice) ; Court of Military Appeals, Rule 47 (c) .

hour a side,[31] unless the case is on the summary calendar, in which event it is only 30 minutes a side.[32] (Additional time is only very rarely allowed, and never in the ordinary case.)[33] There the Justices ask many, many questions. Consequently, any lawyer who appears for a petitioner or an appellant must plan a direct presentation of not over 40 minutes (20, if the case is on the summary calendar). If he goes beyond that, he has no assurance that he will ever be able to reach everything he needs to say. Moreover, if the questioning takes up a great deal of his time—more than he has made allowance for—he must telescope and thus eliminate subsidiary points. He may, of course, conceivably get an additional allowance of time at the end by reason of the Court's having used up a great deal of his assigned time. That has varied in the past, largely with the individual reaction of Chief Justices; some have sympathized with counsel, others have had more sympathy with the clock. The governing principle has been that counsel is not entitled, as of right, to compensation for time taken by judicial eminent domain.

Therefore, the lawyer must have the essentials of his case so firmly in mind that, whenever his time is in fact cut down, he will know where and what to cut, so that, when he is required to sit down, he will have covered all the vital points. It is not an easy process, particularly when the argument as finally prepared is already a drastically pruned production; and, absent such preliminary trimming and cutting, it is, of course, well-nigh impossible.

Sometimes, in the case of a split argument, counsel can reframe his remarks overnight, or during the recess. But he must be prepared to make his revisions on a substantially extemporaneous basis.

Moreover, and this applies even when there is no pressure as to time, counsel must also be sufficiently flexible to vary his argument on the basis of the reception it receives. If he has planned to spend, say, ten minutes on Proposition A, and finds that his initial statement thereof gets nods of approval from the bench, he need not—indeed, he should not—proceed to elaborate that proposi-

---

[31] Supreme Court Rule 44 (4) .

[32] Supreme Court Rule 44 (3) .

[33] "Any request for additional time * * * shall set forth with specificity and conciseness why the case cannot be presented within the one hour limitation." Supreme Court Rule 44 (4) .

tion further. He should move on to Proposition B. If his statement of that second principle evokes a similar attitude of assent, he should once more move on. If the court does not react, he should proceed to elaborate upon the bare statement. And if he encounters doubts or active opposition, he may have to expand and detail his argument on Proposition B far beyond what he had originally intended.

Sometimes these alternative contingencies can be planned far in advance by setting up one's notes on each point in three parts: the basic proposition, its elaboration, and its further elaboration. Then, depending on the reaction from the court, the lawyer can use one, two, or all three portions.

It is, perhaps, easier, though quite as important, to be similarly flexible when appearing bottomside. If counsel for the appellant has had stormy going on Proposition A, counsel for the appellee is wasting not only his time but the court's as well if he belabors the argument that Proposition A is simply not so. The mere statement should suffice, since the court obviously is on appellee's side. Then more time will be available to argue down Proposition B, as to which the court's reaction appeared favorable to appellant.

It is not easy to attain the necessary flexibility. If, it were, anyone could do it. But it is, I am convinced, essential to effective argument.

Chapter VII

SUGGESTIONS FOR PREPARATION FOR
ORAL ARGUMENT

Section 103. In general.—How should you go about preparing for the oral argument of a case on appeal? Preparation is essential, as anyone will soon find out if he ventures to argue a case without preparation. This chapter will discuss the several aspects of the process, and will set out some approaches and methods that I have found helpful in my own practice. Here, pre-eminently, the question of which is the best method depends upon the personality and personal characteristics of the advocate; methods one lawyer finds helpful may not be so for any other lawyer. The best method is the one that best enables the particular advocate to attain his maximum effectiveness. But the problem can be expressed and discussed in terms applicable to all lawyers and to all cases. For the rest, my justification for discussing particular methods is that the discussion will at least be suggestive; and that, here also, the methods that have helped one lawyer may similarly be of assistance to others.

Section 104. Analysis of the problem of preparation.—The task of preparation involves essentially three phases. The first is attaining mastery of the case, becoming thoroughly familiar with the facts, the applicable law, and the implications of both. Next is the process of compressing that mastery within the confines of the medium, i.e., within the allotted time, so that the essentials can be orally conveyed to the court. Finally, there is the matter of preparing the necessary notes, as an aid to memory while actually up on one's feet. These three aspects of the basic task will be discussed in order.

Section 105. Mastery of the case through tabbing of record and briefs.—One very helpful aid to learning a record, already suggested above in Section 98, is to tab the record with gummed-cloth index tabs, so that any material portion can be found without thumbing through the pages or looking in the index.

Nothing is more awkward or embarrassing in open court than the long and painful pause that takes place when a lawyer is trying to find a critical document in a record. He thumbs through it, and gets flustered and nervous; co-counsel do the same; and the court gets annoyed and impatient. Their time is being wasted by the delay—by this so thoroughly unnecessary delay. With a tabbed record, counsel need not waste a minute of his time or the judges'; he can turn instantly to whatever matter is in question.

At the preparatory stage, tabbing is even more valuable, because it places the elements of the case in their proper perspective. Moreover, it enables the lawyer who first comes into the case on appeal to get the feel and the relative position of the pleadings and of the testimony. Tabbing is therefore particularly important in a case of any length or complexity.

I generally tab all the more important pleadings, all the witnesses (except possibly some of the purely formal ones who can be lumped together under a single heading), and all the more important appellate stages.

Thus, in the *Haupt* treason case,[1] an intricate criminal appeal with a record running to 958 printed pages, the following items were tabbed; they are given here in the order in which they appeared in the record:

Indictment; charge; motion for new trial; sentence; defendant's exceptions; assignment of errors; opening arguments; testimony of two witnesses; colloquy involving a charge of perjury on the part of a witness; testimony of each of about 28 witnesses, some of whom (e.g., several F.B.I. agents testifying to the same point) were lumped together; motion for directed verdict; testimony of each of four defense witnesses; colloquy re overt acts; colloquy re instructions to jury; court's draft of instructions; prosecution's requests for instructions; defendant's requests for instructions; closing arguments; jury's return; rereading of testimony; charge re rereading; verdict; bill of exceptions; evidence on insanity issue; C.C.A. opinion; C.C.A. dissent; petition for rehearing; reply to petition for rehearing; dissenting opinion on denial of rehearing.

All told, including recalled witnesses, this ran to some 64 separate tabs.

In the *Line Material* case,[2] a long and complicated antitrust

---

[1] *Haupt* v. *United States*, 330 U. S. 631.
[2] *United States* v. *Line Material Co.*, 333 U. S. 287.

suit with a record of 2,340 printed pages, the following items were tabbed:

Complaint; answers of each of 11 defendants; interrogatories; three stipulations; testimony of each of 11 witnesses; opinion of the district court; findings; final decree; motion to amend findings; order denying motion; assignment of errors.

There were several hundred exhibits, handled as follows: separate tabs for each 25 Government exhibits, i.e., GX 1, GX 26, GX 51, through GX 476; one tab for the last one (GX 498) and one for GX 400, a large tabulation out of order; a separate tab for each group of defendants' exhibits, marking the larger groups in intervals of 25 exhibits each. In addition, each cross-license agreement involved in the proceeding was separately tabbed. In all, there were some 89 separate tabs for the entire record.

Naturally, no such elaborate apparatus is required with a short record, but even in the very thinnest of records, tabbing is helpful at the argument in facilitating reference—without awkward fumbling—to significant portions or particular pages. And see Section 122, below, for the tabbing of short quotations that are to be read to the court.

Section 106. Mastery of the case through reading and re-reading of pertinent materials.—I have already discussed above, see Section 98, the indispensable if harsh method of learning a record: reading it, and then rereading its critical portions. The problem at the present juncture, however, is the more immediate one of preparation for oral argument. Assuming that you have a fair knowledge of the case already, how can you bring that knowledge into sharper focus for the supreme test of oral argument—the final examination, the time when you *must* know it, the final event to which all else has been building up?

It will generally be most helpful if you start your final preparation by sitting down and reading all the briefs, consecutively and slowly. In that way you acquire a working grasp of the arguments on both sides, soaking up the elements of the case until you become as familiar with them as you were when you wrote your own brief. If someone else wrote the brief, and you contributed little more than your signature, then necessarily this part of your preparation will take longer.

Next, reread the leading decisions on which both parties rely. Here again, if this is your first glance at the briefs, your preparation will take longer. But even if you wrote every word of your side's brief, and looked up all the law singlehandedly, you will still find it helpful to go over the controlling authorities. Frequently a last rereading will be productive of values and emphases that just never occurred to you earlier. And of course, if you are dealing with a brief that someone else wrote, you may be able to get from *your* reading of the decisions thoughts that never suggested themselves even to the able colleagues or juniors who did the research and writing. In either event, however, rereading of the cases as the day of the argument approaches is a must if you are to be properly prepared.

It is not necessary to read every case cited in the brief, at least not after you attain a certain familiarity with the process of advocacy. One's first argument—that is different. The eager-beaver lawyer on his first time up will have read and reread every citation, even the statutory provision under which the appeal was taken, and will probably carry into the courtroom an abstract of every case cited. I am not ashamed to admit that I did just that the first time I had a case to argue in the Supreme Court of the United States. And I knew some Assistant Attorneys General who invariably prepared for argument by setting one or more juniors in their division to preparing such abstracts for their use.

I don't feel that this kind of preparation is really necessary for an advocate of any experience. First of all, with experience one gets the feel of a case and can judge which are the critical authorities, i.e., those on which the case will turn, and those concerning which the court will ask questions. Those are really the ones that need to be thoroughly studied—and if you don't know those when you are on your feet, the abstracts so laboriously prepared by the young men won't help you. As for the others—well, in the unlikely event that some judge should ask, "What were the facts in *Jones* v. *Schmaltz?*," you can always take refuge in, "Well, your Honor, I don't recall them now, but I do know that that case supports the proposition for which we have cited it, namely, that postmortem declarations are inadmissible." It is far more profitable to employ your time in rereading and learning the controlling decisions than in reading and learning the collateral ones.

The critical portions of the record should similarly be reread. You must know the opinion below, or the decree, or the findings, or the commission's order—the points on which your case turns.

You must have mastered those. Similarly, you must be familiar with the crucial portions of the testimony. The rest of it is not so important. And, of course, with experience you will learn which portions are, and which are not, vital in a particular case.

Section 107. Rehearsal; compressing the case into workable compass.—One judge of my acquaintance once told me that in his judgment the art of the advocate lay in a lawyer's mastering the case without letting the case master the lawyer. You must compress your case into workable compass, so that you can present it within the allotted time and still leave a positive impression when you sit down. That process involves not only compression, but also emphasis and elimination—and to be certain that you have succeeded in your endeavor you must go over your presentation. That is, you must rehearse your argument, so that the court will hear a finished oral argument and not simply a first rough draft.

Once more to quote Mr. Justice Jackson,

Do not think it beneath you to rehearse for an argument. Not even Caruso, at the height of his artistic career, felt above rehearsing for a hundredth performance, although he and the whole cast were guided and confined by a libretto and a score.[3]

The principal reasons why rehearsal is necessary have already been indicated (see Section 99, above) : to time one's remarks, to smooth out infelicities, to ascertain where to expand and what to eliminate. The following sections will consider some of the methods of rehearsing.

Section 108. Rehearsal; informal methods.—I always find it extremely helpful to engage in informal rehearsal. Even while the briefs are still in a very formative state, I find it extremely useful to discuss the case with all comers. (Since the record is settled by this time, there is no longer any question of betraying professional confidences.) I discuss the case with anyone who will listen (and probably with some who would prefer not to), at lunch, or in the course of conversation, or while bending the elbow over beer or better—and, by all means, with people who reflect all sorts and shades of opinion, in order to obtain as wide a variety of reactions and to evoke as many objections as possible. If my case involves an antitrust question, I want the big business point of view

---

[3] Jackson, *Advocacy in the Supreme Court: Suggestions for Effective Case Presentations,* 37 A.B.A.J. 801, 861 (1951).

as well as that of the trust-busting crusaders. If it turns on an interpretation of the Bill of Rights, I want the reactions not only of the libertarian Children of the Dawn, but also of those who subscribe to the give-'em-a-fair-trial-and-hang-'em school of thought. Those of my listeners who come up with objections will force me to devise new arguments that I may have overlooked until then. The more shades of opinion I can sample, the slimmer the possibility that I will be caught flat-footed or taken by surprise when I actually argue. In short, to quote Mr. Justice Jackson again, "Use every available anvil on which to hammer out your argument." [4]

This method of informal discussion is also helpful in assisting the advocate to evolve an intelligible and effective statement of facts. Whenever someone asks, "What's this next case of yours really about?," you have an opportunity to rehearse a brief thumbnail exposition. And when you have explained your case to people at lunch in such simple terms that they can follow you between gulps of that day's Blue Plate Special, you are well on your way toward being able to explain it to a court. By the time *they* understand you, any court will.

Section 109. Rehearsal; formal methods.—The foregoing helps you to work out arguments, to formulate effective phrasing, and to block out the essentials of your statement of facts. But the time will come when more formal methods are necessary, if only to ascertain how much time you are using.

There are three or four methods most generally used, and of course no single one works well with every person. Some lawyers prefer to try out their preliminary efforts on The Little Woman. Others inflict it on a moot court of generous friends. Still others undertake the task in decent seclusion, preferably at night, when one is neither disturbed nor disturbing. And a fourth method is to use a sound tape or similar recording device, and then play back one's golden words.

As I say, no particular method will work well for every person, nor am I as positive as I once was that a feminine audience is certain to be too full of admiration to be usefully critical, on the view that, unless she loves you dearly, she wouldn't even listen, and hence is too interested emotionally to be, in fact, your severest critic.

---

[4] *Ibid.*

It all depends on the lady's qualities. If she is either an able lawyer in her own right, or knows enough about law to be able to understand what it is you are talking about, and if—and this is the all important point—and if she has a sure instinct, then her reactions, not only to particular phrases but also to particular arguments, will immeasurably assist you in improving your presentation. If your wife—or current flame, because this is a matter of perception rather than of status—has the necessary if rare attributes just outlined, her attachment and affection will be enlisted in the cause of helping you along the road to improvement; she will avoid the uncritical admiration, even adulation, that is of course completely useless.

The moot court method is considered very helpful by many lawyers, and so it is—provided that the members of the moot court ask questions to develop the critical points in the case, and not simply to inject witticisms. The real difficulty with this method is that the moot court just never thinks of the questions that the real court will ask the next day; it is difficult, if not impossible, to prophesy just what questions will be asked from the bench, even by judges whose general reactions are fairly predictable.

A variant on the moot court method is to find an audience of one, preferably a lawyer with appellate experience, who will listen as you go through your argument. His comments and criticisms will be helpful in polishing up the next draft.

Still another method is to talk into a recording device and to play it back. If you own such a device, this method has many obvious advantages—although its use may be somewhat disconcerting, for it is probably correct to say that the most unsettling experiences anyone can have are the first glimpse of one's own profile and the first time one really hears one's own voice.

For myself, I formerly preferred to go over my notes in decent privacy. Now, however, happily married to a woman with unusually perceptive critical faculties, I rehearse with my wife, all the way from "May it please the Court" down through "Accordingly, the judgment below must be reversed." She records the elapsed time, and makes suggestions—the point about the judge's charge was not clear, the comment about the shifty witness had better be omitted, the crack about the opposition was amusing but should go out, the account of the other victims' entry in the room needs expansion and clarification. Then, in the light of those comments (see Section 111, below) , I revise my presentation, expanding, eliminating, altering, and changing emphasis wherever necessary.

Section 110. Notes for the argument.—When your case is called for argument and you get up, what sort of notes should you place on the lectern before you? Should you have your argument written out, neatly arranged in a loose-leaf binder? Is it better to have informal notes instead, which may be either extensive or fragmentary? Or should you venture to argue without any notes at all?

This is another field where, pre-eminently, individual aptitudes and habitudes govern. Nonetheless, some general observations can usefully be ventured.

(a) *Argument fully written out?* I have no hesitation at all in saying "No," emphatically "No," to the suggestion that an argument be written out in full. If your argument is fully written out, you will read it, and reading one's argument is high on the list of Things Not to Be Done. See Section 94, above. Again, if what is there written fails to convince you, go to court and listen to the readers. After all, if the task of the advocate were the simple one of reading what he (or someone else) had written out in advance, it would save time and anxiety all around to record his sound effects and play them back to the court.

(b) *No notes at all?* I would normally recommend against arguing without any notes at all, for two reasons.

First, any lawyer before an appellate court is under distinct mental pressure: he must be alert, he must have complete control of his materials, he must be able to make immediate response to questions. Why then add a second form of mental pressure, the need to keep in mind the precise order of presentation and every detail of the argument? Notes prevent this second kind of pressure, and free one's mind accordingly. For it is a distinct pressure, even when the advocate is blessed with the famous flypaper memory to which everything sticks. Advocates who are phenomenal mnemonic athletes, whose feats of memory are still talked about years after the event, will nevertheless say that they prefer to argue with notes before them.

Second, arguing a long case without notes is usually so very obvious a stunt that it detracts from the effect the argument should make. It is as though counsel were simultaneously juggling five balls while talking—a wonderful and amazing feat, without question, and one that few individuals can accomplish. But it takes the court's mind off the argument, and so the effort fails of its purpose. The object of an argument, after all, is not to show the court what a wonderful fellow the lawyer is; it is to show the court what a wonderful case the client has. Anything that distracts the court's attention from the merits of the client's case is poor advocacy. Of course, no lawyer should ever be content with less than his best, and there are many instances when a flash of genuine memory pays off, but the obvious and planned effort to show off one's own prodigious powers of memory not only does not contribute anything to a case, it generally detracts therefrom.

The exception, I should say, would be this—a fairly simple case, where the facts are uncomplicated and the issues are narrow. Then a lawyer with a retentive memory who is saturated with the controversy may be justified in arguing without notes. The test is probably a subjective one: Is the lawyer putting on a show? Or is he so full of his case that his talk about it comes forth so readily, so logically, and so effectively that he does not need the help of any auxiliary writing?

(c) *Extensive or fragmentary notes?* The question whether one's notes should be extensive or fragmentary is, of course, the place where the personal equation looms largest. My own preference now is for very fragmentary notes, essentially of headings and catchwords, designed to prevent me from overlooking any points or taking them up in the wrong order. These notes are annotated when necessary, following the practice described in subsection (d), below.

The reason for using fragmentary notes rather than fairly extensive ones is a simple one: I found that, whenever I let myself slip into writing out notes that were too detailed, I became so dependent on them that it was difficult to talk without referring to them, and so was virtually in the rigid and unprofitable position of a speaker with a prepared manuscript before him, unable to meet the judges eye to eye, and hence hampered in establishing rapport with them. So—now I use headings and catchnotes.

And, as has already been indicated above in Section 99, by rehearsing the oral argument several times before actually making it in court, its substance has become sufficiently fixed in my mind that the fragmentary notes, which relieve from the pressure of having to remember the number and the order of points, are entirely sufficient.

(d) *Use of references.* Regardless of how detailed or compressed your notes are, they should contain references to the record and to pertinent cases and statutes, *not for the purpose of citing them during the argument,* but so that you have them ready to meet questions and to avoid the necessity of fumbling through your papers.

Thus, it is well, whenever a case turns on conflicting evidence, to have your notes contain a record reference to every statement of fact you make. Don't, don't, don't read those references to the court as you go along; make your assertions without more; but when a judge leans over and asks, "Where do you find that in the record?," you are instantly prepared with the page in question, because you have it right there before you.

In a sharply contested case, this kind of preparation, involving as it does some fairly extensive documentation, will take a good deal of time. It is, however, well worth while, because it assures you that whenever the court inquires about a challenging or apparently questionable statement, you are prepared to support, with the record itself, what you have just told the court. After a while, the questions will reflect interest and curiosity rather than doubt, and a little later, after you have several arguments under your belt, your statements will have been so regularly backed up by record references that you will have acquired a reputation for accuracy and reliability. The goal to aim for is the stage at which the judges will think—or even say—of you, "When Mr. X tells us that the record shows so-and-so, we know that it does." So—annotating your notes pays.

Similarly, include references to the decree, or to the findings, or to any critical portion of the record about which the court will ask, i.e., which it will want to examine for itself. Do the same with controlling statutes or decisions, and similarly mark any portions of brief or record that are important enough to be quoted verbatim to the court. See Section 122, below.

Needless to say, the habit of marking record references on one's notes is excellent insurance against inadvertent inaccuracy. By checking your proposed statement against the record, you will avoid any distortion into which zeal or wishful thinking might, but for such check, unfortunately lead you.

Contrariwise, the lack of record references may cause serious embarrassment. I once heard an eminent practitioner get up in the Supreme Court of the United States, for a fee that must certainly have run well into five figures, and begin by saying. "Pursuant to the division of the case which the various petitioners have made among themselves, I am going to discuss paragraph X of the decree." Question from the bench: "Where is that in the record, Mr. Y?" And then there ensued an anguished and frantic fumbling, by counsel and by his numerous associates, that lasted for some time.

How much confidence for what was to follow, do you suppose, did a start of this kind generate in the judicial mind?

Section 111. The actual process of preparation.—This will be largely a summary of the foregoing, set out in the order in which I have personally found it helpful to proceed.

After having discussed the case with everyone who would listen, and when the day for argument begins to approach, it is time to prepare in earnest.

I sit down and read the briefs, slowly and consecutively (i.e., appellant's first, regardless of who wrote it). See Section 106, *supra*. If there is then any doubt in my mind as to the precise holding or language of the controlling decisions, I read those too, not neglecting those relied on by the other side. Next, I try to formulate the argument with a view to making the most effective presentation; this may or may not be the order set forth in the brief.

After that, I outline the argument and thereafter make my first draft notes. I have found it most helpful to use a legal size scratchpad, and to scribble notes large enough for me to read easily in court. Then I fill in the necessary record references, and fill in the indications for matters to be read to the court. When I am through, I am ready to rehearse the argument for the first time. See Section 109, above.

Next, I revise wherever revision is necessary, changing emphasis, adding, or eliminating, as the case may be. It will frequently be necessary to check against the record, or to reread a leading case or so, or even to embark on an entirely new bit of research. Then I go over the whole argument again, once more noting the elapsed time, until finally I feel that I am ready to face the court.

If the pressure of other work permits, I find it helpful at

this point to reread portions of the record, or even the entire record if it is a short one. Frequently this last rereading will turn up something I had overlooked, or something that assumes a different significance in the light of the additional research since the first reading. And, in any event, this final rereading of the record always serves to fix it more firmly in mind.

I never put my notes for argument in a binder, because I feel that this interferes with flexibility. If, for example, the court asks a question about a topic I had originally planned to cover later on, so that I must now turn to it earlier than I had planned, it is much easier to have unbound notes that enable me to discuss the topic inquired about by pulling out the appropriate pages, and then to resume where I left off when diverted. Ideally, the notes on each topic can be clipped together. At any rate, notes not clamped into a binder will be easier to handle. More than that, because they are not physically rigid, they will be more conducive to a flexible presentation that adjusts the arguments to the reception they evoke.

Section 112. Peripheral preparation and last minute revisions.—One of the most important finer points of preparation is what may be called peripheral analysis, i.e., a study of the fringe points that are apt to interest an active and well-informed judicial mind. The only safe rule is to familiarize yourself fully on all related details and on the background of the law of your case before you get up to argue. Much of this kind of work turns out to be love's labor lost, because the questions to which you have so painfully worked out answers may not be asked after all. But if the lightning really strikes, the extra effort will have been well worth while, and that which you know down deep to have been just a stroke of luck may to the court and to the listening bar appear a touch of genius.

It is well to bear in mind, also, that neither your notes nor your preparation, however complete and thorough each may be, should ever be regarded as final. When I used to cram for college and law school examinations, I would feel, on the morning of the critical day, "Well, if I don't know it now, I never will." But with arguments it has been brought increasingly home to me that it is a mistake to consider even one's most carefully prepared efforts as set pieces, and that it is always possible, even at the last minute, to effect useful additions and revisions that will add to the persuasiveness and clarity of the ultimate performance. I can think of a good many arguments I have made that were measurably improved by some change I wrote into my notes the morning before going to court. Indeed, in one or two instances, I effected the changes or additions while actually in court, waiting to go on. And, of course, rebuttal arguments (see Sections 133 and 134, below) must be worked out on a substantially extemporaneous basis.

One final caution: Get plenty of sleep the night before. Fatigue slows up the most acute mind, and the lawyer who is physically tired is at a distinct disadvantage both in presenting his case and in replying to questions. And I can add, also with the heartfelt sincerity derived from experience, that the night before an appellate argument had better not be devoted to class reunions or to get-togethers with the lads with whom you fought the war. A courtroom is a mighty uncomfortable place for working off a hangover.

Section 113. All alone.—Once you are up on your feet, you are on your own, and there just isn't anyone who can help you if you aren't prepared. Your colleagues and the young men can pass notes and all that, but those are desperate palliatives for anything but minor details. Unless *you* know your case at this point, it won't be known; the time for planning, for joint endeavor, for cooperative enterprise, has passed; the situation is one for individual initiative, and you are that individual.

Holmes once said:

Only when you have worked alone—when you have felt around you a black gulf of solitude more isolating than that which surrounds the dying man, and in hope and in despair have trusted to your own unshaken will—then only will you have achieved.[5]

Well, once you are up on your feet in a more or less crowded courtroom, it isn't exactly a black gulf of solitude—but you will certainly have to rely on your own unshaken preparation, and unless at that point you are well prepared, you won't achieve.

---

[5] Holmes, *The Profession of the Law*, in *Collected Legal Papers*, 29, 32.

Chapter VIII·

THE FINER POINTS OF ORAL ARGUMENT

Section 114. In general.—Having previously considered and discussed the essentials of an effective oral argument, and the process of preparing to get ready to make one, we are now in a position to take up some of the finer points, namely, wherein a good oral argument differs from one not so good. Here again, trifles make perfection, but perfection is no trifle.

An excellent way to pick up these points by oneself is to go up to court and just listen. If you are about to argue a case before an unfamiliar tribunal, it is a very good idea, time permitting, to get there a day or so in advance, and simply to sit and listen to the cases to get, so to speak, the feel of the court—how the judges react to particular propositions and approaches, to what extent they are willing to let counsel proceed in his own way, to what extent and when they will interrupt with questions, and the like.

Indeed, even in more familiar surroundings, the student of advocacy—and every really able advocate remains a student always, since there is always something to be learned, or relearned—the student of advocacy can invariably pick up useful pointers just by listening to the arguments of other lawyers. In a sense, he is like the interne going on ward rounds. By listening to the really able members of the bar, he will learn what to do, and how the masters of the business turn it off. And, by listening to the not so able members of the bar, he will acquire the equally valuable knowledge of what not to do. Regardless of the quality of the forensic performance, time spent listening to arguments in court is never wasted.

Section 115. Should an argument be divided between two lawyers?—Very frequently, counsel decide among themselves to divide the oral argument, either because they feel that the cause is too complex to be effectively grasped and conveyed by only a single advocate, or else—more frequently—because participation in the argument is viewed as a reward to be shared. It is not un-

316

usual for the lawyer who retains appellate counsel to insist, more or less strongly, upon keeping a part of the argument for himself by way of intangible forwarding fee.

First, if the lawyers concerned make such an arrangment, can it be effectuated?

Some courts prohibit a divided argument. A case on the Supreme Court's summary calendar must be argued by a single lawyer, "except by special permission, which will be granted only upon a showing that parties with differing interests are on the same side." [1] Two circuits permit only a single lawyer to argue in any case except by special permission requested in advance,[2] two more permit only a single lawyer to appear when the adverse party is unrepresented.[3] Other courts restrict the number of counsel to two,[4] sometimes indicating that more may appear by special leave.[5]

In the Supreme Court, in cases on the regular calendar, "Two counsel, and no more, will be heard for each side, except by special permission when there are several parties on the same side." [6] Before the adoption of that rule, there were instances up to quite recently when three counsel were heard; [7] whether similar relaxation would be permitted today must remain a matter of conjecture, although—and this is important—the quoted rule goes on to provide that "Divided arguments are not favored by the court."

The reasons underlying that admonition were adumbrated by Mr. Justice Jackson, a few years before he served on the Committee that drafted the Supreme Court's present rules. He wrote:

If my experiences at the bar and on the bench unite in dictating one imperative, it is: Never divide between two or more counsel the

---

[1] Supreme Court Rule 44 (3) .

[2] Second Circuit, Rule 23 (b) ; Seventh Circuit, Rule 21 (b) .

[3] Eighth Circuit, Rule 13 (b) ; Ninth Circuit, Rule 20 (2) .

[4] First Circuit, Rule 28 (2) ; Third Circuit, Rule 31 (2) ; Fourth Circuit, Rule 15 (2) ; Fifth Circuit, Rule 25 (2) ; Sixth Circuit, Rule 20 (2) ; Eighth Circuit, Rule 13 (b) ; Ninth Circuit, Rule 20 (2) ; Tenth Circuit, Rule 20 (2) ; Court of Customs and Patent Appeals, Rule XXIII.

[5] District of Columbia Circuit, Rule 19 (b) ; Court of Customs and Patent Appeals, Rule XXVII (7) (appeals from the Patent Office) ; Court of Military Appeals, Rule 47 (b) .

[6] Supreme Court Rule 44 (4) .

[7] *In re Yamashita*, 327 U. S. 1 (three counsel heard on behalf of General Yamashita) ; *Dennis* v. *United States*, 341 U. S. 494 (three counsel heard on behalf of petitioners) ; *United Shoe Machinery Corp.* v. *United States*, 347 U. S. 521 (three counsel heard on behalf of appellant) .

argument on behalf of a single interest. Sometimes conflicting interests are joined on one side and division is compelled, but otherwise it should not be risked.

When two lawyers undertake to share a single presentation, their two arguments at best will be somewhat overlapping, repetitious and incomplete and, at worst, contradictory, inconsistent and confusing. I recall one misadventure in division in which I was to open the case and expound the statute involved, while counsel for a government agency was to follow and explain the agency's regulations. This seemed a natural place to sunder the argument. But the Court perversely refused to honor the division. So long as I was on my feet, the Justices were intensely interested in the regulations, which I had not expected to discuss. By the time my associate took over, they had developed a lively interest in the statute, which was not his part of the case. No counsel should be permitted to take the floor in any case who is not willing to master and able to present every aspect of it. If I had my way, the Court rules would permit only one counsel to argue for a single interest. But while my colleagues think such a rule would be too drastic, I think they all agree that an argument almost invariably is less helpful to us for being parceled out to several counsel.[8]

What more is there to say?

Section 116. Appreciating the limitations of the medium.— Perhaps the most illuminating insight into the refinements of oral advocacy is acquired through an appreciation of the limitations of the medium employed. You are speaking, not writing. Your words are received by ear, not by eye. Your impact is evanescent; your audience cannot go back and pick up something they may have missed. There is normally no permanent record of what you have said—unless you hire a stenographer at your own expense to take down your deathless prose, and even then the result is something for your own files, which the court will seldom see.

In the Supreme Court, the public address system that was installed at the beginning of the 1954 Term has tape-recording adjuncts that permit the arguments of counsel to be played back, and, as recent opinions show, concessions and contentions made orally by counsel frequently acquire unexpected permanence as a result. See Section 125, below. None the less, the spoken word is still only

---

[8] Jackson, *Advocacy Before the Supreme Court: Suggestions for Effective Case Presentations,* 37 A.B.A.J. 801-802 (1951).

spoken, no matter how often it is played back. It still conveys only an aural impression.

That salient fact conditions the entire process. Consequently, the basic caution is, don't let your argument get lost in details. Concentrate on the broad strokes. To use a visual metaphor, you are painting a billboard, not constructing a fine-screened half-tone. That admonition carries through everything you say while on your feet, because any oral explanation or exposition that is too detailed simply gets lost. In the paragraphs that follow are set forth some applications of this governing principle.

Section 117. Avoid excessive detail as to dates, facts, and figures.—Never be more detailed on facts, dates, or figures in oral argument than your case requires you to be. Normally, counsel should eliminate months and days in stating dates, and should use good round figures—except only when the more detailed presentation is an essential part of the case.

For instance:

Petitioner was convicted by a jury in Nineteen Hundred and Thirty-Eight. He did not appeal. Thereafter he brought four successive petitions for habeas corpus, in Nineteen Hundred and Forty, Nineteen Hundred and Forty-Two, Nineteen Hundred and Forty-Five, and Nineteen Hundred and Forty-Six. The last petition is the one now before the Court.[9]

Compare the foregoing with the more detailed statement that follows:

Petitioner was convicted by a jury on April twenty-nine, Nineteen Hundred and Thirty-Eight. Thereafter he brought four successive petitions for habeas corpus. The first was filed on June four, Nineteen Hundred and Forty, the second on September twenty-four, Nineteen Hundred and Forty-Two, the third on August six, Nineteen Hundred and Forty-Five, and the fourth on January two, Nineteen Hundred and Forty-Six. It is this fourth petition that is now before the Court.

The latter statement would not be out of place in a brief, but by cluttering up the years, which are the essential dates, with the unessential days and months, the lawyer who has framed his oral statement along the lines of the second example has made it very

---

[9] *Price* v. *Johnston*, 334 U. S. 266.

difficult for the court to follow him by ear. (The figures in the dates have purposely been spelled out to indicate this, but if you still doubt the foregoing comments, have someone read the second statement out loud.)

On the other hand, there are cases where time is of the essence, as for example the case of the Station-Platform Warrior, the lad who reported for the draft on Armistice Day, 1918, and then sought a writ of mandamus in 1945-1946 to compel the Secretary of War to issue him an Honorable Discharge from the Army.[10] There it was vital to the argument for the Court to know that he reported for duty on November 11, 1918, that he was told to go home the same day, that on November 14 he was released from any further obligation to report, and that in January, 1919, he received a Discharge from Draft plus a check for four days' pay.

More generally, however, it is only the framework that is important; if you cover that with too much ornamentation and bric-a-brac, the essentials of your structure tend to get lost.

It is the same with figures; use good, thumping, round numbers in the usual case, and don't go into the odd dollars and the pennies unless the case turns on the little discrepancies—or unless the very coincidence of the odd figures reflects very close action in concert.

Normally, avoid confusing details; use years for dates and round numbers for figures. Paint broad strokes, because the court gets the picture only by ear.

Section 118. Don't attempt to dissect individual cases in open court.—Mr. Justice Cardozo once wrote: "There is, of course, no formula that will fit all situations in appellate courts or elsewhere. If, however, I had to prepare a list of 'Don'ts' for the guidance of the novice, I think I would say that only in the rarest instances is it wise to take up one decision after another for the purpose of dissection. Such autopsies have their value at times, but they are wearisome and gruesome scenes." [11]

You will be well advised, therefore, to state your cases simply as establishing broad propositions, and to leave all the details of the particular decision to your briefs. Unless you do just that, the main thread of your argument will become lost.

Here are two examples of how a case can be stated in court;

---

[10] *Patterson* v. *Lamb*, 329 U. S. 539.
[11] Cardozo, *Law and Literature* (Harcourt, Brace and Co.) p. 37.

the question is whether post-mortem declarations are admissible in evidence.[12]

(A)

Post-mortem declarations have been held to be utterly inadmissible for any purpose, ever since Chief Justice Marshall's justly celebrated opinion in *Schmaltz* against the *Chosen Freeholders* in the 13th of Wheaton.[13] Their inadmissibility has never been questioned since the time of that decision, which has stood as a landmark of the law of evidence, and which has been followed and affirmed and reaffirmed in a whole stack of cases, all of which are collected and discussed in our brief. Indeed, but for the decision below, we should have thought that the proposition was not subject to successful question.

(B)

The question of the admissibility of post-mortem declarations was first passed upon in the case of *Schmaltz* against the *Chosen Freeholders of East Overshoe*, reported at 13 Wheaton 743. That is a leading case, hence it may be helpful to state the facts out of which it arose:

---

[12] Such authority as there is on this point confirms the conclusion set out in the text, viz., that they are inadmissible. See *Mercy* v. *Miller*, 25 Tenn. App. 621, 166 S. W. 2d 628. There the defendant "testified that, after James Mercy died and this suit was brought, he came to her and told her not to worry, he had not given the place to anyone else, and it was hers; but upon objection this was excluded." The Court affirmed a decree adverse to the defendant, saying (25 Tenn. App. at 626), "Another circumstance against her credibility was her attempt to bolster her claim by her unreasonable story that James Mercy had a post-mortem conversation with her confirming her claim."

I am indebted for this reference to my former associate, Alvin O. West, Esq., of the District of Columbia and Tennessee bars.

[13] (a) Of course there are only 12 volumes of Wheaton.

(b) The older lawyers always used to cite reports orally as "the 4th of Wallace," "the 114th Massachusetts," "the 229th United States," and so on. See, for instance, Mr. Justice Holmes' obituary comments on Daniel S. Richardson, Esq., in 1890 (*Speeches,* 47): "His long career is spanned by the reports between the seventh of Metcalf and one of our latest volumes." When I first began to listen to arguments in the United States Supreme Court, the brighter young lawyers (who had picked up the practice from their seniors) used to do so too. It may be a little bit old-fashioned these days, but it adds a little flourish, and so might well be encouraged and preserved.

For two fairly recent examples, see the references in *Williams* v. *United States,* 289 U. S. 553, 564, to "the decision * * * in the 2d of Wallace," and in *United States* v. *Morgan,* 313 U. S. 409, 415, to the "decision in the 307th U. S."

(c) Please note that the page reference is not given orally. It is omitted for the same reason that dates and figures should be simplified (Section 117, above; Section 119, below), viz., to leave a clearer impression of the essentials.

One Oscar Schmaltz claimed a tract of 120 acres in the Township of East Overshoe, as devisee under the will of his uncle, Joseph Schmaltz. New Jersey had a statute at that time—this was in the year 1799—to the effect that the estates of Revolutionary War veterans should be exempt from taxation. If the elder Schmaltz were such a veteran, then the land in question passed to his nephew Oscar, the plaintiff-in-error. But if Joseph Schmaltz were not a veteran, then his estate escheated for nonpayment of taxes to the township, represented by the Chosen Freeholders. Now, Joseph Schmaltz's status as veteran or nonveteran turned on a declaration made, etc., etc., etc.

Question: Which statement more effectively lodges in the court's mind the proposition for which you are contending? Question Two: Didn't Mr. Justice Cardozo hit the nail on the head? So —state your proposition, and don't dissect individual cases in open court. Relegate their details to their proper resting place, viz., your brief.

There is one exception to the foregoing: When the court asks you about a particular case, it is perfectly proper to dissect and distinguish—because then you are talking about details that are familiar to your questioner, rather than cluttering up and confusing a broad proposition which you are presenting to a court that is temporarily unaware of it.

Section 119. **Don't cite too many individual cases in open court.**—In a brief, every proposition of law must be supported by authorities, but this is not only unnecessary in open court, it is generally undesirable to attempt to rest every proposition on a particular case. Argue principles; see Section 100 (d) , *supra.*

The following standards may safely be followed for oral presentation:

Generally, do not cite any cases by name in support of undisputed or hornbook propositions.

Again, do not bother to cite cases by name in support of every subsidiary proposition of your presentation.

Where, however, the immediate subject-matter of a principal heading has not come up recently or involves a somewhat obscure point, it is well to cite a few of the leading, landmark cases as you go along, by way of reassuring the court that you are not just spouting law by ear but have solid authority to support you. Remember —just a few, not the sort of collection you may properly set out and discuss in your brief.

If the field you are discussing is one in which there have been a number of recent decisions, it is generally safe to assume, certainly at the outset, that the judges are acquainted with their own precedents.[14] It should not therefore be necessary to cite many supporting cases orally. Exception One: When it becomes apparent from the reaction you are evoking that the judges are in fact not familiar with the decided cases supporting your proposition, you must of course refresh their recollections. Exception Two: When a court sits in panels of varying composition, it may more frequently be necessary to acquaint the sitting judges with what their brethren have decided.

In any event, do not cite the little cases that simply apply a principle established by a well-known or fairly well-known leading case, except—for these matters cannot be disposed of by rigid rules—except when the satellite or subsidiary case is right on all fours, and except when you are asked about a particular decision. Indeed, there is really nothing like a pat citation for silencing a persistent judicial questioner.[15]

Finally, regardless of the occasion, when you do cite cases orally, content yourself with a simplified citation. For instance: "and that was held by the *Jones* case in the 362nd United States, and again by the *Johnson* case decided earlier this Term." "That

---

[14] "It does not seem to me safe ever to assume that a judge is able to recall exact words of a statute or a document, even if he is known to be familiar with its general terms. * * * But I should make the contrary assumption about the Court's own precedents, particularly its recent precedents. I can think of no more dismal and fruitless use of time than to recite case after case, with explanations why each is, or is not, applicable." Jackson, *Advocacy Before the Supreme Court: Suggestions for Effective Case Presentations*, 37 A.B.A.J. 801, 804 (1951).

[15] When I argued my first case in the Supreme Court, *United States* v. *Summerlin*, 310 U. S. 414, Mr. Justice McReynolds was in his last year of active service. He was the last survivor of the Old Guard, and no doubt his only remaining amusement was the heckling of new Government counsel as they appeared. He began to question me rather intently about "Wasn't there a case a few years back that held—" something to the effect that the United States in commercial transactions is bound by commercial rules. Through dumb good fortune, I had tried in the U. S. District Court for Northern Alabama, the previous Fall, a check case that turned on the decision in *United States* v. *National Exchange Bank*, 270 U. S. 527. It came to mind, luckily enough, and I asked, "Does your Honor mean the case of *United States* against the *National Exchange Bank*, somewhere around the 270th United States?" "That's the case!" exclaimed McReynolds, J. It was easy enough to distinguish, and the old gentleman didn't bother me further during the remainder of the proceedings.

proposition is fully supported by the *Quercia* case, which is discussed at length in both briefs." "There hasn't been any question about that rule of law since *Lilly* against the *Commissioner,* with which your Honors are of course familiar."

Don't, for the reasons set forth in Section 117, above, go into further detail. When you say orally, "There hasn't been any question about that rule of law since *Lilly* v. *Commissioner,* 343 U. S. 90, with which your Honors are of course familiar," you don't add anything helpful to the presentation by adding the page citation. Indeed, you only make your thought more difficult to follow by ear.

Section 120. Other matters that cannot be conveyed by ear. —By the same token, it is generally not very profitable to attempt to state legislative history orally, unless the whole case hinges on it, in which event more detailed treatment is justified. An example of the latter situation was *Girouard* v. *United States,*[16] discussed above in this connection in Section 96. Even for that case, however, it was necessary to state the legislative history in broad and simple terms; compare the statement in open court, *supra,* p. 288, with the details that found their way into the opinion from the brief. See note 19 at pp. 288-289, above.

In general, it is well to rely exclusively on the brief for anything that is so detailed that it sounds fuzzy when you attempt to present it orally. The only test is to try it, i.e., to rehearse it, orally. Regardless of what it is, whether law, or facts, or what not, if it doesn't leave a distinct impression by ear, relegate it to the brief where it can be more leisurely—and more effectively—absorbed by the eye. And never be afraid or ashamed to say, when you are up on your feet, "We have discussed these cases [or that evidence, or the legislative history] fully in our brief, so that I won't take the court's time by discussing the details here." See, for an actual example, pp. 453-454, below.

Section 121. The handling of questions from the bench.—Replying to the questions asked by the judges is without doubt the most difficult aspect of oral argument; certainly it is the most stimulating aspect; and it is unquestionably one of the most important. Yet the basic principles of this particular problem can be broken down into about three admonitions.

---

[16] 328 U. S. 61.

(a) *Learn to think on your feet.* As to this, familiarity with the case helps, and so does thorough preparation, because the more questions you anticipate, the more answers you will have available to supply when the test comes. Undoubtedly a ready wit is of substantial aid; practice helps, and experience helps too, although in large measure quick-wittedness is congenital; you either have it or you haven't.

I have known some lawyers, able and intelligent citizens, too, who were simply struck dumb by questions from the bench, questions which they had anticipated beforehand, and on which they were prepared. The ensuing silences caused those associated with the case to burn their eyes onto the floor, hoping against hope that some trap door would open up through which they could disappear from the horrible scene they were witnessing. If you are one of those forensically weak, silent men—well, the only known cure is to stick to estate planning, brief writing, and office conferences. It's much easier on all concerned.

At the same time, no advocate, however able, will ever be completely satisfied with any answer he has given. A better one will always come to mind in the taxicab back to the office, or, as Jackson, J., said in the passage quoted at p. 298, *supra,* at home after going to bed that night. I once hoped to be able to invent a gadget that would make the taxicab or bedroom answer jump up and hit me while still on my feet in court, but up to now I have still to report utter lack of success. Perhaps the quest for the perfect answer comes under the heading of vain regrets, on a par with that dream brief discussed in Section 20, above. But, like the other, it is probably one of the inescapable pangs of advocacy.[17]

(b) *Never refuse to answer a question.* The precept that counsel should never refuse to answer a question holds good even if the question is not in his case, for the normal reaction of the judge who asked the particular question will be, "Well, I realize

---

[17] That Grand Old Man of American law, Professor Samuel Williston, had this to say of his only argument in the Supreme Court, *Boston & Maine Rd.* v. *Hooker,* 233 U. S. 97: "A defeated counsel often regrets his failure to give the best possible answer to questions put to him from the bench, and I have always regretted a failure to answer to my own satisfaction, at least, an inquiry put to me by Mr. Justice Hughes." But he added, "A man convinced against his will is of the same opinion still, and the decision of the Supreme Court carries no mandate to the logical faculty." Williston, *Life and Law,* p. 283.

that, but I should like to know your position on the point just the same." The judge will insist, so you had better be prepared in advance on the more obvious questions that lie around the edges of your case. If you are not prepared, or if the question comes out of the blue in a case in which you are otherwise prepared up to the hilt, it is better to say, "I should like to consider that question further before venturing an answer," or even to offer to submit a supplemental memorandum, than to refuse pointblank to answer or, what is even worse, obviously to try to evade an answer. As Mr. Justice Harlan has said, "No answer to an embarrassing point is better than an evasive one." [18]

Unreasonable on the part of Judge X to insist? Certainly. But since you are endeavoring to persuade him, you had better cater to his unreasonableness.

Here again, there is an exception: Don't answer in any detail if to do so will take you far away from the thread of the argument, off on an unprofitable tangent, or when there is a possibility that you may be led to discuss an issue that is not, and from your point of view should not be, in the case. In such a situation you must be firm, and you must indicate very respectfully that you will not be drawn into any such peripheral dissertation. See pp. 451-452, below, for an illustration.

How can you tell whether you should or should not answer in full? Here again—it all depends. On the other hand—

(c) *Never postpone your answer.* Almost as bad as refusal, outright or barely concealed, is the all too familiar, "I am coming to that later." Few replies are quite so annoying to a person whom you are endeavoring to persuade; he asks you now because he is interested now, and you dampen his interest in your case if you fail to answer now. Apart from that consideration, which should be fairly obvious to anyone who has thought about the matter, the fact is that promises that "I will take that up later" are left unperformed in appellate courts quite as frequently as promises that "I will connect that up later" are broken in trial courts.

Moreover, and this is another point frequently overlooked, the circumstance that the particular matter inquired about comes at a different place in your own prepared outline is really not an adequate reason for declining to make an immediate reply to a

18 Harlan, *What Part Does the Oral Argument Play in the Conduct of an Appeal?*, 41 Corn. L. Q. 6, 9.

judge who reaches the point somewhat sooner in his own analysis of the case.

Some judges simply refuse to accept a postponement. It is said that once when a question asked by Mr. Justice McReynolds was answered with the too usual "I am coming to that," the Justice snapped back, "You're there now!"

Actually, there is only one solution, namely, to supply a stop-gap answer and move on. When Judge Y asks, "Is it your position that the statute is invalid?," answer, "Yes, that is our position"— and state that you will develop it more fully later, adding a good reason for postponing full discussion, as, for example, that the reason will appear more intelligibly after you have first sketched in your position on points B, C, and D, or after you have outlined the legislative development of the statute, or the like.

Always bear in mind that you must have a better reason for postponement than the happenstance that the point inquired about appears in a different relative position in your own plan of argument.

Section 122. Quotations in open court.—The reason for the basic admonition, "Never read your argument" (Section 94, above), is that reading draws a veil between the advocate and the court. What is true of arguments as a whole is likewise true of lengthy quotations from documents or testimony or opinions. So —never read long quotations to a court. (As is there indicated, see note 15 at p. 283, the rules of some courts prohibit this practice.) Here again, if you are not prepared to take this precept on faith, just go to court and listen to the lawyers who read to the judges copious quotations from decisions or records.

I will not urge, "Never read a quotation"; that would be dogmatic and unsound. I do insist, however, that you should never undertake to read a quotation that is over four sentences or so long, because at about the fourth or fifth sentence the veil begins to form. Therefore, if you do read, the quotation should be short, and above all pat, else departure from the normal standard is not justified.

Moreover, if a particular quotation is so essential to your argument that you feel you *must* read it, tab it specially in the brief or record (as the case may be), so that it is ready for you without fumbling, and so that you can read it smoothly, with perfect transition and without any jerky, jumpy pause. (But remember that if your quotation is at, say, page 83 in the record, and you want to turn to that page when you lift up the tab, you must paste the tab on the leaf that carries pages 81 and 82. If your tab is pasted to page 83, you will turn up pages 84 and 85.)

Two other cautions: First, read *from* the paper, not *at* it; look up at the court while you are reading, don't bury your nose—and your voice—in your text. Second, read slowly, so that you convey the full effect of the passage. There is always a strong tendency, even among the best advocates, to rush the reading. If you want your quotation to be really effective, you must overcome that very natural urge.

Keep your quotations and excerpts short, tab them so that they can be reached without delay, and read them slowly *from* the original—then there is no reason why any veil should come between you and your judicial audience.

Section 123. Use of a striking phrase.—In order to present your contentions in simplified form, it is frequently useful to employ a striking phrase—a dignified slogan, if you please, but a slogan nonetheless.

Perhaps this point will become clearer after a discussion of examples.

(a) The issue turned on the constitutionality of an involved regulatory statute. The entire case was effectively summed up by the statement, "Petitioner is not being denied due process; on the contrary, this statute affords him undue process." [19]

(b) One of the cases involving the military trials of civilian dependents, where it was proposed to retry the relator by court-martial at Bolling Air Force Base in the District of Columbia;

The question in this case is whether a woman, who all of her life has been a civilian, may be tried by an Air Force court-martial in time of peace, here in the District of Columbia and literally within the shadow of the Capitol dome. [20]

---

[19] *Sunshine Coal Co.* v. *Adkins,* 310 U. S. 381. There were two schools of thought on the source of this particular gem; one attributed it to Mr. Justice Jackson, then Attorney General, who argued the case, the other to Chief Justice Hughes, who presided over the Court that heard it. In 1949, Mr. Justice Jackson wrote me that "I would like to claim it but if my title is no better than my memory, it is cloudy."

[20] *Reid* v. *Covert,* 354 U. S. 1, at the original hearing in the District Court. The passage in the text was quoted in *In re Varney's Petition,* 141 F. Supp. 190, 204 (S.D. Calif.) .

(c) A pay case in the Court of Claims: "The question is whether a correction of a military record 'for all purposes' means something less than 'all', so that it is to be interpreted as 'for all purposes except pay and allowances.' " [21]

(d) A denaturalization case: "The issue is whether a good Nazi can be a good American." [22]

(e) Habeas corpus to review a conviction by court-martial, the contention being that the preliminary investigation under old Article of War 70 [23] was inadequate. The issue, as phrased by Government counsel, was "Whether, after a fair trial and painstaking review of the record by the agencies provided by law for that purpose, the convicted person will be set free because of alleged errors occurring *in the hinterland of the proceedings* long prior to the actual commencement of the trial." [24]

If the slogan you have devised is good—really good—it will make an indelible impression, one that will persist in the minds of the judges long after the rest of the argument has evaporated and been forgotten.

There is another kind of slogan that will fit almost any kind of a situation—but that can probably be used only once before any particular bench. One of these is the opening, "This is a most remarkable case." Now, assuredly, that will make any court sit up and take notice, even when it later occurs to the judges that the case is really not so remarkable after all. Another is the expression, to be delivered with all solemnity, "If ever there was a case that"— and then you add whatever may be appropriate, and pause—"*this is that case.*"

---

[21] *Darby* v. *United States,* 173 F. Supp. 619 (C. Cls.).

[22] *Knauer* v. *United States,* 328 U. S. 654.

[23] 10 U.S.C. [1926 to 1946 eds.] § 1542, later A.W. 46 (b), 10 U.S.C. [Supp. II to 1946 ed.] § 1517, now Art. 32, U.C.M.J., 10 U.S.C. [1958 ed.] § 832.

[24] See *Humphrey* v. *Smith,* 336 U. S. 695. The point had been extensively litigated in several circuits. See *Waite* v. *Overlade,* 164 F. 2d 722 (C.A. 7), certiorari denied, 334 U. S. 812; *DeWar* v. *Hunter,* 170 F. 2d 993 (C.A. 10), certiorari denied, 337 U. S. 908; *Henry* v. *Hodges,* 76 F. Supp. 968 (S.D.N.Y.), reversed, 171 F. 2d 401 (C.A. 2), certiorari denied, 336 U. S. 968; *Becker* v. *Webster,* 171 F. 2d 762 (C.A. 2), certiorari denied, 336 U. S. 968; *Hicks* v. *Hiatt,* 64 F. Supp. 238 (M.D. Pa.); *Anthony* v. *Hunter,* 71 F. Supp. 823 (D. Kan.).

I had used the phrase that is italicized in the text in some of my own briefs, but its author was my learned friend, Colonel William J. Hughes, Jr., of the District of Columbia bar.

Both are effective. But, pretty clearly, they can't be usefully repeated, day in and day out, before the same judges.

Section 124. Use of maps and charts.—The need for graphic presentation of matters difficult to describe otherwise—"one picture is worth a thousand words"—justifies inclusion in the brief of maps, charts, or patent drawings. You must have those visual aids in your brief so that the judges can study them at their leisure when the case is under consideration. But it is a great mistake to rely on the map in the brief when arguing the case in open court, and equally a mistake to hand up one set of the applicable exhibits for the use of each member of the court. What you should do is to have an enlarged copy of the map or drawing in the courtroom, on a stand or easel, and sufficiently large so that it can be seen by every member of the bench. (Try it out in the empty courtroom beforehand to make sure it is really big enough for all essential details to be seen by all the judges.) And, when you argue, use a pointer as you explain your exhibit.

Why all this trouble? Because if you hand a map or chart or drawing or what-not to each member of the court, to be looked at while you are talking, you are inviting competition with your argument. You are asking the judges to give you only part of their attention and to donate the balance of it to the papers that you yourself have placed before them. Just as you cannot make much of an impression if your audience is simultaneously listening to another speaker, so you will fail to make an impression if your competition takes the form of a document or a drawing that you have placed in the hands of each member of your audience.

When each judge has a map before him, he will study it and let his mind wander. All sorts of memories will come to mind. "Wallula—oh, yes, there it is. Gosh, I haven't been there since the summer after graduation. Hummmm, I wonder what ever happened to Susie." Or "Peckham. Yes, there was a fellow in my class named Peckham who came from Portland and whose father owned a store. I wonder whether that's the same family." While these reveries go on, while each judge is demonstrating what a wonderful distraction a map can be, the court is listening to counsel with only half an ear. But if there is only a single map up there before the bench, counsel is the center of attraction, particularly when he is using his pointer; all the judges are listening to him, and none is making personal excursions to irrelevant portions of the drawing. In this instance also, if you doubt what I have been saying, just watch what happens in court whenever a lawyer relies on copies of a map he has handed up to each member of the court—then you will certainly agree that it is a great mistake to rest on the map that is in the record or in the briefs *if* you want the court really to understand the case.[25]

There may, of course, be cases that are helped by a lack of understanding on the part of the bench. I once argued, on behalf of the Secretary of the Interior, a motion to dismiss a mandamus case in the former Supreme Court of the District of Columbia. The case turned on whether a certain tract of land had been appropriated and set apart for public use. That question depended on an interpretation of maps and reports contained in Congressional documents. Well, I ran back and forth between counsel table and bench, pointing first to one map and then to another—"Now point *A* on this map, your Honor, is identical with point *G* on this second map"—and so on, until the judge became thoroughly confused and finally said, "Well, this is a very complicated matter, so complicated that I cannot interfere with the discretion of the Secretary, who obviously was not acting arbitrarily. I will grant the motion to dismiss." But, as I say, this technique is only to be recommended when you are setting out to confuse rather than to clarify.

Section 125. Concessions in oral argument.—A concession that you make in oral argument will almost certainly be given effect by the court.[26] If you make such a concession advisedly, fine;

---

[25] I can point to a fairly good batting average in cases where I have used large maps in the courtroom. *United States* v. *Northern Pac. Ry. Co.*, 311 U. S. 317; *United States* v. *Baltimore & O. R. Co.*, 333 U. S. 169; *Hunter* v. *Wade*, 169 F. 2d 973 (C.A. 10), later affirmed, 336 U. S. 684; *Swift & Co.* v. *United States*, 343 U. S. 373.

For an excellent study of this particular problem, see Rall, *Visual Aids in Courts of Review*, 52 N.W. Univ. L. Rev. 90.

[26] See, e.g., *Potts* v. *Dies*, 132 F. 2d 734, 735, note 2 (App. D. C.) ; *Walker* v. *Felmont Oil Corporation*, 262 F. 2d 163, 165 (C.A. 6) ; *In re Wells*, 281 F. 2d 68, 70 (D. C. Cir.). See also *Jefferson Construction Co.* v. *United States*, 283 F. 2d 265, 267 (C.A. 1).

Compare, however, the disclaimer of the defense of qualified privilege in *Barr* v. *Matteo*, 244 F. 2d 767, 769 (D. C. Cir.), after which the case was remanded with instructions to pass on that issue. 355 U. S. 171. The Court of Appeals then sustained the claim of qualified privilege, 256 F. 2d 890, after which the Supreme Court disposed of it on the footing that there was an absolute privilege! *Barr* v. *Matteo*, 360 U. S. 564.

but if you do so inadvertently, on impulse or because of less than complete mastery of the record, you cannot expect the result to be different.

This consequence of being taken at your word is to be distinguished from having your argument misquoted; it is bad enough to lose a case, but infinitely more painful to one's professional pride to have the adverse opinion misstate what one actually said. And the reflection that the three inescapables are death, taxes, and being misquoted serves only partially to ease the hurt.

In the Supreme Court, as has already been indicated (Section 116, *supra*), the arguments of counsel are now taken down on a machine. Many recent opinions of that tribunal, rendered since the installation of the recording equipment, establish the importance that attaches to concessions made in oral argument,[27] and thus emphasize the critical importance of counsel's knowledge of his case.

Hiring a stenographer to take down your argument may be helpful in two respects: If the other side misquotes you, you are then in a position to correct the record; see the example set forth in Section 86, *supra*. Or, if the mistake is your own, whether because of inadvertence, or even because of sheer ignorance, you have an opportunity to address a letter to the clerk—or to move for leave to file a supplemental memorandum—withdrawing or correcting what you said.

Section 126. An appropriate peroration.—An appellate advocate's closing words are important, and they should leave an impression of combined strength and dignity. They must be more than simply a shouted conclusion while the judges are folding up their briefs and turning to the papers in the next case. And, although an appellate court can be moved, it is not a jury; the scope for emotional impact is distinctly limited when the case is on appeal.

Fashioning a proper peroration presents a difficult problem in any circumstances, and a particularly difficult one when counsel's time has been so taken up with questioning that his planned end-

---

[27] See, e.g., *Mesarosh v. United States,* 352 U. S. 1, 7-8, 17-19, 23-24; *Lee Kum Hoy v. Murff,* 355 U. S. 169; *Bartkus v. Illinois,* 359 U. S. 121, 165; *Abbate v. United States,* 359 U. S. 187, 196; *Taylor v. McElroy,* 360 U. S. 709, 710-711; *Breithaupt v. Abram,* 352 U. S. 432, 438, note 5; *Kinsella v. Singleton,* 361 U. S. 234, 243, note 7; *Talley v. California,* 362 U. S. 60, 66-67, note.

ing no longer serves. All that can usefully be ventured are the following considerations:

First, you must have some sort of an ending in order not to leave your argument up in the air, and to avoid tacking on the purely formal "We therefore submit that the judgment below should be reversed." Come up with a conclusion in a nutshell, at the very least. For instance:

> The result is that, without pausing to repeat or even to sum up, the totality of errors in this record, particularly those discussed orally, is such that the conviction now under review simply cannot be permitted to stand.

Next, you should, as a general and all but invariable rule, remain calm and dignified, making your closing as impressive as possible, carefully avoiding anything that is even faintly irrelevant.

Thus, if the question for decision is whether the practices in a particular industry violate the Sherman Antitrust Act, it is a waste of breath and worse for counsel to wind up on a note of how much the industry concerned contributed to the war effort. And if the case turns on the sufficiency of the allegations in a petition for habeas corpus, a peroration built around a letter from the prisoner, which has obviously been censored through the use of shears and which is waved under the eyes of the judges, is simply cheap.

Something more impersonal is necessary in order to close. Perhaps I may be pardoned for including two of my own perorations at this point, the combined batting average of which was .500.

In the *Girouard* case,[28] which turned on legislative ratification *vel non* (see Sections 50, 57, 70, 96, and 120, above) :

> Thus it is clear that the decisions of this Court in the *Schwimmer* and *Macintosh* cases have been legislatively ratified by the Congress. Accordingly, unless this Court is now to sit as a Council of Revision, it must affirm the judgment below.

Well, the judgment was reversed, which prompted Chief Justice Stone to say, concluding his dissent: [29]

> It is not the function of this Court to disregard the will of Congress in the exercise of its constitutional powers.

---

[28] *Girouard* v. *United States,* 328 U. S. 61.
[29] 328 U. S. at 79.

And, announcing that dissent, on the very day he was stricken, with the last coherent words he ever uttered, he had said, "There has been too much of this judicial tinkering with statutes." [30]

Here is another example, from the *Line Material* [31] arguments (which were set out in full in Chapter 17 of the first version of this work):

* * * So we say, overrule the *General Electric* case. But whether you overrule it or simply distinguish and limit it, we submit that it is impossible to justify the sort of thing that was done here, because this sort of thing is a constant menace to the public interest in free competition—and it is nothing new.

It is nothing that has just recently been dreamed up. It goes back many years—not, perhaps, to Adam—but certainly to Adam Smith.

I would like to bring this argument to a close with a single sentence from Adam Smith's *Wealth of Nations,* which is just as timely— and just as timeless—as when it was first written over a century and a half ago. * * *

"People of the same trade seldom meet together, even for merriment and diversion, but the conversation ends in a conspiracy against the public, or in some contrivance to raise prices."

We submit that the judgment below should be reversed.

That one got five votes.

Third, there will be a few—a very few—instances, where genuine, relevant emotion may be very effective. Witness the closing by Senator George Wharton Pepper in the AAA case: [32]

My time is fleeting and I must not pause to sum up the argument I have made. I have come to the point at which a consideration of delegation is the next logical step, and that is to be dealt with effec-

---

[30] The reader may perhaps wonder at my continued preoccupation with the *Girouard* case. I can only say, by way of at least partial extenuation, that it worried a good many other people besides losing counsel (see, e.g., Horack, *Congressional Silence: A Tool of Judicial Supremacy,* 25 Tex. L. Rev. 247; *American Citizenship: Can Applicants Qualify Their Allegiance?,* 33 A.B.A.J. 95; and the several sequels to the article last cited, 33 A.B.A.J. at 323, 540, and 663), and that in 1952 it was legislatively overruled, at least in part. See Section 337 (a) of the Immigration and Naturalization Act of 1952, now 8 U.S.C. § 1448 (a); *Petition of Scaccio,* 131 F. Supp. 154 (N.D. Calif.); *In re Krause's Petition,* 159 F. Supp. 687 (S.D. Ala.). Compare Section 57, *supra,* at p. 172 (note 148).

[31] *United States* v. *Line Material Co.,* 333 U. S. 287.

[32] *United States* v. *Butler,* 297 U. S. 1, 44.

tively by my colleague, Mr. Hale. But I do want to say just one final and somewhat personal word.

I have tried very hard to argue this case calmly and dispassionately, and without vehement attack upon things which I cannot approve, and I have done it thus because it seems to me that this is the best way in which an advocate can discharge his duty to this Court.

But I do not want your Honors to think that my feelings are not involved, and that my emotions are not deeply stirred. Indeed, may it please your Honors, I believe I am standing here today to plead the cause of the America I have loved; and I pray Almighty God that not in my time may "the land of the regimented" be accepted as a worthy substitute for "the land of the free."

All who were present when this peroration was delivered agree that it was most effective—"too effective" was the way one lawyer on the losing side put it—and even today, more than twenty-five years later, it still moves the person who reads it in the cold black-and-white of the reports. Indeed, the passage exemplifies the observation that the advocate "must be something of an actor, not indeed playing a well-learned part before painted scenery, but fighting real battles on other men's behalf." [33]

I will cheerfully confess that I cribbed from and built on that masterpiece from the lips of one who can fairly be characterized as a Nestor of the bar when, greatly wound up, I participated in the reargument of the court-martial cases in 1957 that had gone against me the year before. Here was my closing on that occasion: [34]

If your Honors please, I have tried to argue this case with some degree of objectivity. I have tried to put out of mind as nearly as I can the callous and somewhat obtuse cruelty with which these two women were treated because I felt that I could best discharge my duties to this Court, as well as my duty to them, by dealing with this as a question of constitutional law, which calls for research, reflection and cogitation.

But I cannot conceal my concern over the seriousness of what is involved, because this is about as fundamental an issue as has ever come before this Court, one certainly more vital and fundamental in the constitutional sense than any that has been here for some years.

And it is fundamental and vital because it poses in stark immediacy the question of how far we may properly brace ourselves to with-

[33] Marjoribanks, *For the Defence*, 1-2.
[34] *Reid* v. *Covert*, 354 U. S. 1; excerpt from Ward & Paul transcript of argument on rehearing, pp. 95-97.

stand assault from without, and yet perhaps sow the seeds of our own disintegration from within. Because we have here, I think for the first time, a question involving the impact on the one hand of the supposed needs of the garrison state upon, on the other, the immutable principles of a free nation.

That is a quotation, "The immutable principles of a free nation," not from the writings of some cloistered libertarian philosopher, but from the institution of the Order of the Cincinnati, which was founded in 1783 by the Revolutionary officers who had pledged their lives and shed their blood that this country might be born.

I think we will be aided in the resolution of that problem by considering two sentences from the late Mr. Justice Cardozo's immortal classic, "The Nature of the Judicial Process":

"The great ideals of liberty and equality are preserved against the assaults of opportunism, the expediency of the passing hour, the erosion of small encroachments, the scorn and derision of those who have no patience with general principles, by enshrining them in constitutions, and consecrating to the task of their protection a body of defenders. By conscious or subconscious influence, the presence of this restraining power, aloof in the background, but none the less always in reserve, tends to stabilize and rationalize the legislative judgment, to infuse it with the glow of principle, to hold the standard aloft and visible for those who must run the race and keep the faith."

If your Honors please, I have been enrolled among the body of defenders. I hope this Court will keep the faith.

Effective? That, very obviously, is not for me to judge. But one of the concluding paragraphs of the prevailing opinion may indicate that the concluding paragraphs of the prevailing argument were not wholly wasted. Mr. Justice Black, who announced the judgment of the Court, said on behalf of four of its members:

We should not break faith with this Nation's tradition of keeping military power subservient to civilian authority, a tradition which we believe is firmly embodied in the Constitution. The country has remained true to that faith for almost one hundred seventy years. * * * [35]

Fourth, a word of caution: The Senator Pepper type of appellate peroration will fit but very few cases, and is wholly inappropriate in any case unless the following three prerequisites are first fulfilled:

1. Since an appellate court is not a jury—and this is fundamental, repeated here because so frequently ignored—emotion be-

---

[35] 354 U. S. at 40.

comes effective only when it follows and is rested upon a solid intellectual foundation.

2. The advocate who undertakes to invoke emotion in an appellate court must accordingly be learned in the field he is discussing—or else (which probably amounts to the same thing) have a reputation for learning in that field.[36]

3. Finally—he must be 50 years old or over to carry it off. Genuine emotion resulting from concern over constitutional interpretation is a sentiment not permitted the young.

Section 127. Courtroom manners and mannerisms.—It might seem unnecessary to include pointers on how not to behave, but the list of don'ts that follows has been collected because observation has indicated that violations occur with distressing regularity.

(a) *Never interrupt opposing counsel.* It is an unpardonable breach of manners to interrupt opposing counsel. I add this remark here because I have heard such interruptions even in the United States Supreme Court.

(b) *Don't wander from the lectern.* Judges find most annoying the practice some lawyers have of wandering from the lectern.

(c) *Don't see-saw with glasses.* One of the unhappiest mannerisms, and one of the least pleasant to watch, is the habit some lawyers have of putting their glasses on and then taking them off again, waving them back and forth as though see-sawing. If you need glasses for close reading, but can't see the judges' faces through them, or if you need glasses for distance vision, but can't read with them, then there is only one solution for your next appellate argument: get a pair of bifocals, and wear them while on your feet. Relax and enjoy your maturity; don't annoy your judicial listeners by refusing to admit to membership in the bifocal bracket.

(d) *Avoid unpleasant gestures.* Don't for instance, point an admonitory finger at the bench, or indulge in similar unpleasant gestures.[37]

---

[36] See John Chipman Gray's well-known comment on Story, J.: "* * * he was a man of great learning, and of reputation for learning greater even than the learning itself * * *." *The Nature and Sources of the Law* (2d ed. 1921) 253.

[37] Compare the remarks of the Hon. William D. Mitchell, Solicitor General 1925-1929 and Attorney General 1929-1933, at the *Proceedings in Memory of Mr. Justice Van Devanter*, 316 U. S. v, xvi, xviii-xix: "* * * In the same spirit, he was very kind and helpful to me. During my early experiences as

(e) *Never grimace.* Don't assume a derisive smile while opposing counsel is addressing the court; this is very bad manners. The only safe rule, for counsel's weak points as well as for his good ones, is to keep as set a poker face as you can muster: don't sneer at his poor arguments—and don't look worried at his good ones. There is one exception: when the court laughs, don't hesitate to laugh right along with them—quite regardless of the quality of the humor.

(f) *Desist when your time has expired.* When your time is used up, and the other side has had the last word, don't say anything more—except possibly to ask for permission to file a reply brief. Don't attempt to say anything more; the court will not permit it. And above all, don't argue for the opportunity to be heard. Some of the most painful courtroom scenes in living memory have been the result of lawyers insisting on talking when they had no right to do so and when the court had already indicated that it did not desire to hear them.

Section 128. Courtroom attire.—When in Rome, do as the top-drawer Romans do. This precept is particularly applicable as a guide to what the properly dressed lawyer will wear while arguing a case in an appellate court.

In most appellate courts, it is customary to wear simply a business suit. Where that custom obtains, it would be a mistake to appear in more formal attire. But a decent respect for the bench requires that the lawyer's suit be dark and reasonably conservative, and that his tie be not too strikingly chromatic.

At the same time, the latitude of colors permitted one's garments may well vary with the geographical latitude involved. A white linen suit would probably be regarded differently in Boston than in New Orleans; in any event, make your inquiry in advance so that what you wear conforms to the customs of the bar. On occasion, the practice in the Federal court may be different from that of the local court. Thus, although the advocate in the Supreme Court of Puerto Rico, in accordance with the old Spanish tradition, is required to wear a toga, no such garment is worn when he ap-

---

Solicitor General he found the opportunity, very tactfully, and privately, to suggest ways of improving my court manners. I learned through him how important it is that the Solicitor General, whom the Court must listen to week in and week out for years, should be free from annoying mannerisms. The Court can stand them on occasions, but as a steady diet they become quite unbearable."

pears before the First Circuit when that tribunal sits in San Juan for its February session.[38]

In the Supreme Court of the United States, some years back, counsel would not even be listened to if attired in anything less than a long coat. Consequently, the Clerk used to keep on hand, for the benefit of practitioners hailing from the forks of the creek (up East Overshoe way), three long coats: large, medium, and small. Gradually, however, a relaxation crept in, and the Court began to deign to listen to counsel arguing in business suits.[39]

At the present time, cutaways are worn in the Supreme Court only by Government lawyers and by leaders of the bar from the larger cities. When private practitioners, not previously known to the Court, appear in formal attire, the inevitable judicial reaction is, "Here is a man who respects the highest court." As Mr. Justice Jackson put it, "The lawyer of good taste will not worry about his dress, because instinctively it will be that which is suitable to his station in life—a member of a dignified and responsible profession —and for an important and somewhat formal occasion."[40]

My own view, therefore, is that any private practitioner would be well advised, on any of his appearances before the Supreme Court, to wear formal dress—even if he has to go out and rent it.[41]

I assume, however, that the argument will do the costume justice. There is extant a lovely story concerning one Government lawyer (not now in public life) who on the occasion of his first argument in the Supreme Court, appeared in a new—and obviously wholly-owned—cutaway that was a masterpiece of the tailor's art. He had rough going from the outset, and indeed had not proceeded very far before Mr. Justice X, an acidulous and caustic man, leaned over to Mr. Justice Y, sitting next to him, and stage-whispered all too audibly, "Better dressed than equipped!"

---

[38] Letter from the Hon. Calvert Magruder, for many years Chief Judge, First Circuit, October 2, 1959. The wearing of the toga was described in a letter from the late A. Cecil Snyder, formerly Chief Justice of the Supreme Court of Puerto Rico, quoted at p. 221 of the earlier version of this work.

[39] See Palmer, *What Lawyers Wear—Reverie on a Pink-Shirted Lawyer,* 33 A.B.A.J. 529.

[40] Jackson, *Advocacy Before the Supreme Court: Suggestions for Effective Case Presentations,* 37 A.B.A.J. 801, 862-863.

[41] Not, however, when he is simply being admitted or when he is moving an admission.

A word for the ladies: In any court, on any occasion, wear your best basic black dress or suit with a touch of white at the throat. It is not only eminently appropriate, it is bound to be very becoming.

Section 129. The saving grace.—The saving grace is best used sparingly; intentional, deliberate humor in an appellate court is a dangerous ingredient in untrained hands, and an attempted joke that falls flat chills the atmosphere into a deep freeze. In this field much depends upon the court—some are deadpan, sitting like a collection of wooden Indians, others have a more ebullient temperament. Moreover, much depends on the advocate concerned; it is only the real leaders of the bar who can afford to say things that in other mouths would be inappropriate liberties.

It may be noted, however, that the danger zone for younger practitioners lies in the realm of deliberate, purposeful humor, carefully and often all too obviously planned in advance. Spontaneous wit, so long as it is not lacking in the necessary quantum of deference, is hardly ever resented; to the contrary.

In the view that it may be of interest to examine some examples of permissible light touches, I include a few that have passed muster, or, at least, that have not backfired.

(a) Action by the United States to validate a claim filed in a probate proceeding; the State Supreme Court held the claim void because not filed in time. Government counsel urged that the United States was not bound by state statutes of limitations; counsel for the estate urged that the state enactment was not a statute of limitations, but a statute of nonclaim. On rebuttal:

> The contention seems to be that a rose by some other name— might prove less thorny.[42]

(b) In the *Girouard* naturalization case,[43] already mentioned at some length herein (Sections 50, 57, 70, 96, 120, and 126, *supra*), the basic issue was whether Congress, by refusing to amend the naturalization laws after the *Schwimmer*[44] and *Macintosh*[45] decisions, and by thereafter re-enacting the provisions construed in those cases, had legislatively ratified them. Former Attorney General Cummings, for the petitioner, had argued that the Congres-

---

[42] *United States* v. *Summerlin,* 310 U. S. 414.
[43] *Girouard* v. *United States,* 328 U. S. 61.
[44] *United States* v. *Schwimmer,* 279 U. S. 644.
[45] *United States* v. *Macintosh,* 283 U. S. 605.

sional refusal to amend was inconclusive, because the issue was, as he put it, a "hot potato."

Counsel for the Government urged the significance of the re-enactment of the earlier provisions in the Nationality Act of 1940:

Now this re-enactment, as the legislative history shows, had its origin in the report of a cabinet committee, of which Mr. Cummings, then Attorney General, was a member. And whatever may be the attitude of individual members of Congress, certainly no one could ever fairly accuse my former chief of lack of courage where legislative proposals were concerned, simply because they involved *burning* issues.

The reference was, obviously, to the Court Plan of 1937, and every member of the Court laughed loud and lustily—joined, let it be noted, by the former Attorney General.

(c) The case of the Postprandial Patriot, the man who had lunch with his draft board on Armistice Day, 1918, and then years later attempted to mandamus the Secretary of War to issue him an Honorable Discharge from the Army.[46] (Earlier, in Section 117, above, I referred to this individual as the Station-Platform Warrior, but that may well have been an exaggeration, because the record fails to show that he ever got as far as the railway station.) His counsel had been asked to say in what branch of the service he had been, and counsel had not really satisfied the Court on that point. Government counsel on rebuttal:

I will endeavor to answer that question. Now, he wasn't an infantryman, because he had never been assigned there; nor was he an artilleryman or a cavalryman, because, as we have shown, he wasn't really in the Army. But he did have lunch with his draft board, so I suppose he could be called a trencherman.

(d) In the last round of cases involving the validity of military trials of civilians, Government counsel in response to questions from the bench had contended that court-martial jurisdiction extended not only to the dependents of military personnel and to civilian employees of the armed forces, but also to the dependents of such employees, to employees of contractors, and to the dependents of the contractors' employees as well. On rebuttal, counsel for the civilians said:

Well, this question of how far the asserted military jurisdiction extends raises some strange problems. Indeed, in the committee hearings, which proceeded on the assumption that the jurisdiction was perfectly

---

[46] *Patterson* v. *Lamb*, 329 U. S. 539.

proper, there is an amusing passage—at least I find it amusing—which suggests that while a mother-in-law living with military personnel overseas is subject to military law, this would not be true of one who was simply visiting.

And that would seem to point the way towards a new and painless solution of the mother-in-law problem. [Taking out and looking at watch:] "Of course we want you to stay just as long as you can, Mother dear, but unless we can get you down to the airport promptly, you might become subject to trial by court-martial." [47]

Well, that will give some idea of what can be done, within permissible limits and along wholly relevant lines, to brighten up the proceedings.

Section 130. Avoid personalities.—Never confuse or detract from your argument by dragging in personalities. They are bad enough in briefs (see Section 83, above), but they are infinitely worse in oral argument.

It may well be, of course, that your opponent's disbarment is long overdue, or that the court below is widely referred to as "Old Man Necessity" because (of course) Necessity knows no law. Don't introduce such considerations into argument. The question for decision on appeal is not whether opposing counsel is a Servant of Brotherhood, it is whether his client was. And if you are trying to get Judge Schmaltz reversed, the question isn't whether he is wise or ignorant, it is whether his decision in this particular case was right or wrong. (Besides, if he is really as obtuse as you think he is, the appellate court will be aware of that, too; they are likely to have seen more of his rulings than you have.)

Moreover, counsel on appeal is still a lawyer, and so must maintain the bar's traditional respect for the judiciary, even when the district judge in question is known to every member of the appellate court to be wrong more frequently than he is right. He is still a judge; if the appellate judges think ill of him, they are free to say so privately; you, however, cannot even intimate his shortcomings publicly. As a perceptive friend of mine once put it, "Never forget that there is, after all, a judges' union." Not only

---

[47] *Kinsella* v. *Singleton,* 361 U. S. 234; *Grisham* v. *Hagan,* 361 U. S. 278; *McElroy* v. *Guagliardo,* 361 U. S. 281. The discussion regarding the comparative amenability to military law of a mother-in-law temporarily visiting an officer abroad as compared with that of one living with him there permanently appears in *Uniform Code of Military Justice,* Hearings, House Committee on Armed Services, on H. R. 2498, 81st Cong., 1st sess., at pp. 876-877.

do trial and appellate judges frequently lunch together, in most circuits District Judges in varying degrees of frequency sit as members of the Court of Appeals. Like Lord Nelson's captains, they are, certainly with reference to the bar, a band of brothers. Counsel will be well advised, therefore, to keep his disagreements with their rulings on a purely intellectual basis.

And don't row with counsel, either. Remain calm, dignified, and professional. If the opposition is in fact a disgrace to the profession, you should be at pains not to descend to his level.

Section 131. Sarcasm and bitterness.—Anything in the nature of sarcasm or bitterness is in the nature of a personality, because it injects an emotional element into what should be essentially an intellectual difference of opinion. Hence these also are improper and should be avoided.

On occasion the temptation to indulge in either or both is a strong one. In my own experience, I probably yielded to both emotions in the original argument of the first court-martial cases; [48] some examples—fairly horrible examples, too—are noted in the margin.[49] I will not say that these cases could or would have

---

[48] *Kinsella* v. *Krueger,* 351 U. S. 470; *Reid* v. *Covert,* 351 U. S. 487.

[49] "So that the tradition which the Government invoked in its brief is of only 15 years' standing. And I cannot help being reminded of the freshwater college that was trying to inch into the Ivy League, announcing that 'It is traditional here that freshmen will uncover as they cross the Memorial Quadrangle. This tradition began last Monday.' The tradition of trying civilians by court-martial in the American service is only 15 years old." Ward & Paul transcript, p. 44.

"So I say, I suggest, that it would be much better for the Air Force to devote its very considerable talents to the material and terrific problem of maintaining our air supremacy, in a word, sticking to the wild blue yonder, instead of trying civilian women by court-martial." *Id.,* p. 52.

"But if we can assume that these agreements purported to enlarge the jurisdiction of American courts-martial, then we have this situation—that as applied to the *Covert* case, a woman in the District of Columbia, who normally could claim her double guarantee of jury trial, is, by reason of the act of a foreign parliament, following an executive agreement which does not mention women, deprived of that right to a jury trial here in the District of Columbia. And of that I say, in the language of Mr. Justice Grier, on the last page of the 24th of Howard, *Haud equidem invideo, miror magis*—it is not so much that I am angry, but rather that I marvel at it." *Id.,* p. 55.

"Now, how to deal with them. I have suggested the traditional method for punishing extra-territorially committed crime, namely, by trial in the first district to which the person is brought or is found. That was not deemed too difficult in the post-war treason cases. It is true that there is no power to subpoena witnesses, but the Government had no difficulty last month in flying eighteen Italian subjects, whom it could not subpoena, here for the *Icardi*

been won on the first hearing had a more objective and dispassionate argument then been made, but the items referred to—and there were others of the same nature—did not help my cause, and in the cold, clear, and infinitely painful light of the morning after the original decisions, I became more and more aware of the probable harm that these expressions of personal resentment had done.

Once more to stress the obvious, in an appellate court emotion must have an intellectual foundation on which to rest, and it is far better for the tribunal to be moved to a sense of outrage on its own than for the advocate to expound his personal feelings of chagrin.

If it is permissible to descend to the jargon of Madison Avenue in this connection, the situation is one where the "soft sell" is indicated, where understatement is the most telling weapon. And, lest any reader think this an admonition too quixotic for a realist world, let him ponder the sheer power of restrained statement exemplified by the opinion written by Mr. Justice Brandeis in *Wan* v. *United States*.[50] To quote Professor Felix Frankfurter (as he then was), "in the terrible case of Ziang Sung Wan, his restraint attains austerity." [51] Read that opinion, and ask yourself whether any degree of emotionalism could possibly have been as effective.

Section 132. Should the client be present during the argument of the appeal?—Different considerations apply depending on whether the appeal is from the judgment in a civil or a criminal case, but they all lead to the same conclusion: The client should not (repeat, *not*) be present while his appeal is being argued.

(a) *Criminal cases.* Never let your client be present if the appeal involves a criminal case.

Unless such a case involves simply "a matter of principle," such as a $100 fine for violation of a municipal ordinance the constitutional validity of which is in issue, the appellant of record in a criminal case has a great deal at stake: loss of liberty, loss of reputation, loss frequently of livelihood, loss of property, and, in criminal tax cases, where substantial civil penalties follow upon a successful

---

case. Of course, when that case was thrown out [*United States* v. *Icardi*, 140 F. Supp. 383 (D.D.C.)], it was rather too bad, because those were witnesses that could not have been used over again in other cases." *Id.*, p. 58.

[50] 266 U. S. 1.

[51] Frankfurter, *Mr. Justice Brandeis and the Constitution*, 45 Harv. L. Rev. 33, 105, reprinted in Frankfurter, ed., *Mr. Justice Brandeis* (1931) 49, 124.

prosecution, loss of money in what are frequently very sizeable sums. A man would be somewhat less than human if he were not deeply concerned over these eventualities, and if that concern did not translate itself into an obviously worried look.

Now, courthouses, whether old or new, whether dingy or shiny, are just as much hothouses for rumor and gossip as any dormitory in a girls' finishing school, and therefore the fact that the appellant is making a personal appearance in the courtroom is certain to find its way to the judges. They will, accordingly, be looking for him, first out of sheer curiosity, then as a matter of interest. They will spot him, never fear, and, more likely than not, they will translate his worried look into a consciousness of guilt. "That Schmalzberg fellow looks awfully guilty to me." His presence, accordingly, won't help the appeal, and if you as counsel have rough going with the court, that circumstance won't help the attorney-client relationship—because, inevitably, he will then wish he had retained some other lawyer, on the view that anyone else but the man actually up would have fared differently.

So—insist that your criminal appellant client be not present in person. Have him send an observer, if he is really itchy; after all, the hearing is not *in camera*. But don't let him set foot in the courthouse on the day that you argue his case.

(b) *Civil cases.* Mr. Justice Jackson suggested that the foregoing rule should be generally applied, in all cases. He wrote:

> I doubt whether it is wise to have clients or parties in interest attend the argument if it can be avoided. Clients unfortunately desire, and their presence is apt to encourage, qualities in an argument that are least admired by judges. When I hear counsel launch into personal attacks on the opposition or praise of a client, I instinctively look about to see if I can identify the client in the room—and often succeed. Some counsel have become conspicuous for the gallery that listens to their argument and, when it is finished, ostentatiously departs. The case that is argued to please a client, impress a following in the audience, or attract notice from the press, will not often make a favorable impression on the Bench. An argument is not a spectacle.[52]

---

[52] Jackson, *Advocacy Before the Supreme Court: Suggestions for Effective Case Presentations*, 37 A.B.A.J. 801, 861.

"Every judge knows that a lawyer is very likely to deliver a different oral argument if his client is in the courtroom than if he is not. I am even told that sometimes judges play a little game among themselves called 'Find the Client'!" Rall, *Effective Oral Argument on Appeal*, 48 Ill. Bar J. 572, 574.

The net result is that, regardless of the type of case involved, counsel will be well advised to insist that hís client remain home while it is being argued.

Of course, whatever the nature of the controversy, the forwarding lawyer is not for this purpose to be regarded as a client. The amount or even the fact of his fee may depend on the outcome, but as a professional man he is bound to view the matter with more detachment than the actual client.

Moreover, any appellate argument may be counted on to draw a legal audience, and if the mere thought of fellow lawyers sitting in the courtroom and listening is apt to evoke latent traits of exhibitionism in the advocate who is at the lectern talking, changes in his techniques and attitudes are very much in order. Besides, if the presence of the forwarding lawyer is apt to worry you, how can you fairly expect him to refer more cases to you in the future?

Section 133. Rebuttal.—The first and undoubtedly the most troublesome problem in connection with rebuttal is whether, when you represent the party complaining of the decision below, you should get up at all for a second time. This is a problem—indeed it is frequently a dilemma—that cannot be solved by rote; in the end one's answer boils down to a matter of judgment—tempered by counsel's own temperament.

Advocates of great distinction and ability have suggested that the privilege of the appellant or petitioner to argue in rebuttal should be sparingly exercised. Mr. Justice Jackson wrote:

I would not say that rebuttal is never to be indulged. At times it supplies important and definite corrections. But the most experienced advocates make least use of the privilege. Many inexperienced ones get into trouble by attempting to renew the principal argument. One who returns to his feet exposes himself to an accumulation of questions. Cases have been lost that, before counsel undertook a long rebuttal, appeared to be won.[53]

And the late Mr. William D. Mitchell, who was a distinguished Solicitor General and Attorney General, said in his review of the earlier version of the present work:

---

[53] *Id.,* at 804.

Discussing whether reply briefs or reply arguments are desirable, the author is inclined to resolve doubts by favoring their use. The conclusion might well have been the other way. It should be a rare case where either a reply brief or reply argument is justified. In his brief and oral argument an appellant should be able to cover adequately his case and anticipate his adversary's. Able judges of appellate courts do not wobble back and forth to be captured by the litigant who insists on having the last word.[54]

The considerations governing the filing of reply briefs have been discussed in the light of the foregoing, in Section 85, *supra*. The present section, covering reply arguments, has been rethought with the comments of Justice Jackson and Mr. Mitchell in mind, and has been thoroughly rewritten.

First. If your opponent has been obviously demolished by the court, it is well not to trample on him further by way of a gloating "me too." Not only is it considered poor taste and worse sportsmanship to kick too hard a man who is down, but, more important—because a lawsuit is not a game, it involves serious consequences for the client—more important, such tactics are apt to kindle a feeling of sympathy for your opponent on the part of the court. Rebuttal in such a situation has precisely the opposite effect from what a good closing argument should be designed to accomplish.

Second. Rebuttal is, however, essential, whenever there is a real argument to answer, or whenever the court is obviously in doubt, or whenever there is a palpable misstatement to be corrected or even a residuum of honest confusion to be cleared up. On that score there can be but little disagreement. While I can look back on quite a few rebuttals that added little beyond the satisfaction of having had the last word, I can recall one or two that really advanced the case. It may be helpful to mention them briefly as examples.

(a) In *United States* v. *Summerlin*,[55] already mentioned in Section 129, the question was whether a claim of the United States, tardily presented in a probate proceeding, could be barred by a State statute of limitations that was sugar-coated by being called a statute of nonclaim. In rebuttal, I read from the record that por-

---

[54] Book Review, 64 Harv. L. Rev. 350, 351.
[55] 310 U. S. 414.

tion of the decree of the State court which in terms held the claim "void." [56] Chief Justice Hughes really raised his eyebrows at the sound of that word—and wrote the unanimous opinion reversing the State supreme court.[57]

(b) In another case that will not be otherwise identified, I appeared for the Government, which was seeking to overturn the reversal of a criminal conviction. There were a number of difficult and fuzzy issues in the case, which, quite frankly, could have gone either way. My opponent, a lawyer of reputation, had apparently reached the stage of neglecting preparation; in any event, his argument was rested on a factual foundation that was demonstrably inaccurate. In ten minutes of rebuttal time, I exposed the inaccuracy, the judges' faces hardened noticeably, and the respondents went to jail. In that particular instance, I have no doubt whatever that the outcome of a case that was far from open-and-shut, not only inherently but also throughout most of the argument, ultimately turned on the circumstance that a vital misstatement of fact was exposed by the rebuttal.

Third. Don't get up a second time simply to rehash what has already been fully covered. The court's questions will normally indicate whether any tag ends imperatively require buttoning up. Rebuttal is justified only when it concentrates on the areas of genuine doubt.

In that connection, it is extremely undesirable to come up, ostensibly by way of rebuttal, with newly generated ideas on essentially tangential points that could not possibly have been thought through. Don't risk fuzzing up the final impression your argument left by injecting untested new departures.

Fourth. When you do get up for purposes of contradiction, be sure to go for the essentials. One of the most outstandingly poor rebuttals I have ever heard anywhere began with the announcement that "Petitioner's counsel has been guilty of a mis-

---

[56] "The Court is of the opinion that the United States with respect to filing its claim is in the same position as any other creditor of the estate * * * and that therefore the claim of the United States is void for the reason that it was not filed * * * within * * * months from the time of the first publication of the notice to creditors * * *." R. 12, No. 715, Oct. T. 1939.

[57] "So far as the judgment goes beyond the jurisdiction of the probate court and purports to adjudge that the claim of the United States is void as a claim against the estate of the decedent because of failure to comply with the statute, the judgment is reversed." 310 U. S. at 418.

statement." The courtroom waited expectantly—and then the mountain brought forth this mouse: "He said petitioner was president of the corporation when the record plainly shows that he was simply its vice-president."

Section 134. Preparation of the rebuttal.—Once past the painful question *whether,* the next problem is *how* to prepare an oral rebuttal.

If you are bottomside, representing the appellee or respondent, you can work your reply arguments into your own notes as you listen to opposing counsel, inserting them at the appropriate places. It is generally a good idea to use a red pencil for this purpose, so that you won't overlook the new matter as you come to it.

If you are topside, the process is much more difficult. Indeed, the preparation of an effective rebuttal is really one of the hardest points in the business. And yet it should not be neglected, because, as has already been indicated, it is often preferable to reply when there are unanswered or confused questions still floating around to which decisive answers are available.

Rebuttal argument should hit the jugular and concentrate on the big issues; it should avoid a long list of little things, or a whole lot of minor discrepancies that do not bear on the essentials of the case. Years ago, our debating coaches at college used to distinguish between rebuttals on the hunk system and rebuttals on the birdshot system. I am glad to echo their advice here: eschew birdshot rebuttals.

The process of composing a rebuttal is, necessarily, a continuous one. First, during your opponent's argument you take notes of matters that he is misstating or as to which he is wrong, and that you can usefully reply to and correct. After a while, you can proceed to make tentative formulations of your outline for reply. That tentative outline will generally need to be revised as the argument proceeds, because if you have answer X to your opponent's contention A, and the court picks up X on its own and pretty well tramples A beyond all recognition, then, for reasons already set forth, you can cross out that item—and move to another.

By the time your opponent's argument is drawing to a close, you should have a pretty good idea of the points that are significant enough to warrant mentioning in a reply—and any doubts should be resolved in favor of elimination.

As to the items that you decide to mention, two principles are applicable. First, the opening of your rebuttal should, whenever possible, tie closely on to your opponent's conclusion. Whenever you can do that, you add immeasurably to the effectiveness of your reply. Second, unless you have a great deal of time left over so that you are not pressed by the clock, it is not safe to leave your choicest bit for the very end—because the court's questions may eat up your time and thus prevent your ever reaching that final forensic morsel.

The process of preparing an effective rebuttal, while not easy, is less difficult than the process of deciding whether to reply, and on what issues. In this particular corner of the field, pre-eminently, one can only learn the hard way, viz., by doing—and by reflecting on the rebuttal (or the lack of one) in the light of the result attained. One's hindsight is of course always 20-20, but continuous retrospective introspection on rebuttals is bound to sharpen the advocate's vision for arguments still to come.

CHAPTER IX
THE TASK—AND THE GOAL—
OF THE ADVOCATE

Section 135. The task of presentation.—The basic responsibility of the advocate, after all, is the task of presentation—to present the law and facts of his particular case so that the court will know what the controversy is about, and will want to decide it in his favor.

That task is conditioned by three factors: the length of the record—the facts; the complexity of the questions involved—the law; and the interval allowed for argument—the time.

Each of these three factors varies from case to case. The record may consist of not over ten printed pages, as for example when the appeal involves review of the dismissal of a complaint or of an indictment. The record may run to several hundred or a thousand or even several thousand pages, when the case represents an appeal in a long criminal trial, or in a rate-fixing proceeding, or in the usual antitrust case. Indeed, on occasion, the advocate must deal with what are literally monster records; recent examples are the 15,937 printed pages in the Communist conspiracy case,[1] 12,719 printed pages in the North-South rate case,[2] 16,532 printed pages in the *Hartford-Empire* antitrust case,[3] and 16,832 printed pages in the *Cement Institute* basing-point case.[4] (Curiously enough, the record in the *DuPont-General Motors* antitrust case [5] was a modest one by those standards; it had been so thoroughly compressed by counsel that it extended to only 7510 pages.)

The law factor is similarly a variable. The advocate may have a very narrow legal question to present, one that can be fully and comprehensively briefed in not over 20 pages. He may have a number of very substantial points that will have to be carefully

---

[1] *Dennis* v. *United States,* 341 U. S. 494.
[2] *New York* v. *United States,* 331 U. S. 284.
[3] *Hartford-Empire Co.* v. *United States,* 323 U. S. 386, 324 U. S. 570.
[4] *Federal Trade Commission* v. *Cement Institute,* 333 U. S. 683.
[5] *United States* v. *duPont & Co.,* 353 U. S. 586.

condensed to fit within the limits that many courts currently impose on the length of briefs (see Section 22, *supra*). Or, perhaps, he may be dealing with a very complex series of legal problems or with a novel and highly significant question of constitutional law that cannot be adequately treated except in a brief extending to several hundred printed pages. Thus, in the recent Tidelands Cases,[6] the brief of the United States in support of its motion for judgment on the amended complaint against the five Gulf States concerned—an amended complaint only 19 printed pages long—extended to no less than 425 pages. It was thereafter followed by two reply briefs, of 99 and 34 pages, respectively.

The factor of time is perhaps the least variable of the three; you get just so much time—30, 45, or 60 minutes—and it takes a very considerable showing to get more from any court, what with the pressure of overcrowded dockets everywhere. In the cases that have monster records, generous allowances will be made, but even so the advocate's problem remains, because the enlargement of time is never in direct ratio to the enlargement of the record.[7]

Moreover, if the advocate is to succeed, he must make a favorable impression: his task is to compress the law and the facts of his case into his allotted time—less interruptions—so that the court will obtain not only a clear conception of the case by the time he is through, but a favorable impression of his side as well. This is perhaps the most compelling reason, though assuredly not the only one, why so many experienced lawyers insist that advocacy is essentially an art, which can be mastered only through practice in the application of its governing principles.

Section 136. The task of presentation; a concrete example.— In Chapter 17 of the first version of this work, there was set out the complete stenographic transcript of the arguments in a closely contested antitrust case decided by the Supreme Court about a dozen

---

[6] *United States* v. *Louisiana*, 363 U. S. 1; *United States* v. *Florida*, 363 U. S. 121.

[7] In the cases just cited, eight hours were allowed for argument in *New York* v. *United States;* thirteen hours were allowed for the original argument in the *Hartford-Empire* case, and eight more for the reargument; and eight hours were allowed in the *Cement Institute* case.

In the movie antitrust cases, *United States* v. *Paramount Pictures*, 334 U. S. 131, nine and a half hours were allowed for argument, while in the recent Tidelands Cases, *United States* v. *Louisiana* and *United States* v. *Florida*, thirteen hours were allowed.

These figures include the time for argument on both sides.

years ago—*United States* v. *Line. Material Co.*[8] It was twice argued, and, when finally decided, resulted in three opinions—majority, concurring, and dissent—that alone aggregate 76 printed pages in the reports.

The record in the case extended to 2,340 printed pages, of which all after the first 560 were exhibits—some 500 Government exhibits, and nearly 200 more introduced by the several defendants. By antitrust standards it was perhaps not a very long record, but it was fairly sizeable none the less.

The principal legal question was the scope of the *General Electric*[9] doctrine, i.e., the extent to which price-fixing under patent cross-license agreements was legal notwithstanding the prohibitions of the Sherman Antitrust Act. There were numerous subsidiary questions, some involving the Sherman Act,[10] some turning on the Federal Rules of Civil Procedure,[11] and some concerning the patent law.[12]

That case had to be compressed into a single hour of argument on each side, since requests by both sides for extra time, made for both argument and reargument, had been denied.

Essentially, the task of the lawyers who argued the *Line Material* case was the same as that of lawyers who present any kind of a case in any appellate court: to condense the mass of their materials into an understandable and palatable verbal capsule—to make the case clear to the court, and to persuade the court to decide it in their favor.

How would *you* have tackled that assignment?

If you want to see how four different lawyers went about it, each in his own manner, consult Chapter 17 of the earlier version.

A most eminent critic has suggested, that "whether * * *

---

[8] 333 U. S. 287.

[9] *United States* v. *General Electric Co.*, 272 U. S. 476.

[10] E.g., whether the facts brought the case within the rule of *United States* v. *Masonite Corp.*, 316 U. S. 265; *Interstate Circuit, Inc.* v. *United States*, 306 U. S. 208; and *Standard Sanitary Mfg. Co.* v. *United States*, 226 U. S. 20.

[11] Whether the District Court's findings were "clearly erroneous" within Rule 52 (a), F.R. Civ. P., and whether in any event they were entitled to particular weight, being based primarily on documents.

[12] Particularly whether the combination of the dropout fuse patents with the wet process porcelain box patent fell afoul of the ruling in *Standard Oil Co.* v. *United States*, 283 U. S. 163, 174: "The lawful individual monopolies granted by the patent statutes cannot be unitedly exercised to restrain competition."

examples of oral arguments are of much use may be questioned." [13]
Certainly the printed page "cannot now recreate [the] tone of
voice or the gloss that personality puts upon speech." [14]

None the less, the student of advocacy may find it helpful to
examine recorded arguments, if only to study how other lawyers
have organized their materials. A list of more or less recent arguments in leading cases, all of which are reasonably accessible, is set
forth in the margin.[15]

Section 137. Keying the oral argument to the brief; selection
and arrangement of points for oral argument.—Obviously, all the
manifold details of a case, particularly of a complicated case, cannot be presented in the limited time allotted to oral argument,
even when that time has been enlarged. Some portions, frequently many portions, must be left to the brief. As has already
been pointed out (see Sections 116, 117, 118, and 120, above), the
basic principle is that the essentials should be conveyed orally,
whereas the filling in of the details is best left to the brief. Similarly, because the principal propositions should be covered on oral
argument, the subsidiary points must be relegated to the written
argument. There may well be cases where it is desirable to discuss
only the facts orally, leaving all discussion of law to the brief. No
single rule of thumb, here or elsewhere, will fit every case. But it is
essential to understand fully the advantages and the limitations of

---

[13] The late Mr. William D. Mitchell, former Attorney General and Solicitor General, reviewing the first version of this work, 64 Harv. L. Rev. 350.

[14] Frankfurter and Jackson, JJ., concurring in *Von Moltke* v. *Gillies,*
332 U. S. 708, 727, 730.

[15] Sen. Doc. No. 52, 75th Cong., 1st sess. (the National Labor Relations
Act cases, *Labor Board* v. *Jones & Laughlin,* 301 U. S. 1, and related cases; and
Associated Press v. *Labor Board,* 301 U. S. 103) ;

Sen. Doc. No. 53, 75th Cong., 1st sess. (Social Security tax on employers,
Steward Machine Co. v. *Davis,* 301 U. S. 548) ;

Sen. Doc. No. 71, 75th Cong., 1st sess. (old age benefit provisions of the
Social Security Act, *Helvering* v. *Davis,* 301 U. S. 619) .

Partial transcripts of oral arguments in some other significant modern
cases will be found in the reports:

Norman v. *Baltimore & O. R. Co.,* 294 U. S. 240 (argument of Attorney
General Cummings at pp. 251-272) ;

United States v. *Butler,* 297 U. S. 1 (argument of Solicitor General Reed
at pp. 4-13, 48-52; argument of Senator George Wharton Pepper at pp. 23-44) ;
and

Carter v. *Carter Coal Co.,* 298 U. S. 238 (argument of Frederick H. Wood,
Esq., at pp. 243-255; argument of Assistant Attorney General Dickinson at
pp. 255-269) .

each medium, and to apportion your points between speech and writing in order to achieve the maximum effectiveness in the combined presentation.

A little thought and plenty of preparation will generally suffice to separate those matters that can best be presented orally from those that are better left to the written argument. The more difficult task of selection is to choose the points that can be effectively set forth in the oral argument and to eliminate those that your allotted time will not permit you to cover orally. Suppose you have three major points; each of them is important, but your time will allow you to develop only two of them convincingly. Which two will you pick?

That sort of problem is the elimination test that will separate the cream of the lawyers from the skimmed milk of the mere attorneys at law; because, after all, in the famous last analysis, given brains and learning and a competent grasp of legal techniques, the quality that distinguishes the outstanding lawyer from the lawyer who is simply very good is a highly developed sense of relevance.[16]

And advocacy in open court requires even more: If, as will frequently be the case, the three propositions in the situation just put are equally relevant, to what other test for survival or elimination should they be subjected?

Some advocates will select the two propositions that are most dramatic or arresting, others the two they consider most sympathetic or appealing, still others those propositions they conceive to be the strongest as a matter of logic and hence most satisfying intellectually.

On occasion, the same advocate who would select one set of propositions for presentation to one tribunal would argue the case quite differently if he appeared before another court or before the same court differently constituted. Indeed, there may be instances where the division in a particular court has been so marked that

---

[16] "Mr. Justice Frankfurter compared the lawyer and the scientist. The lawyer, he said, is distinguished as an 'expert in relevance.' Since the law touches life in a wider and perhaps deeper way than any other profession, this ability to ferret out the relevant considerations of any type of problem is a necessary qualification for the lawyer. The scientist, however, though highly trained in what is relevant within the limited area of his field, becomes lost among the maze of conflicting forces that operate outside his particular specialty." *Harvard Law School Record,* vol. 5, no. 9, December 2, 1947.

one or two judges will be the swing men on a particular type of case—and in that event the argument is most effective if addressed essentially to them.

All these techniques, obviously, require more than even the most highly developed sense of relevance: They call for a keen appreciation of the principles of psychology. It may well be, of course, that psychology in its present flowering is neither an exact science nor indeed a science at all. Even so, that circumstance only serves to underscore the view, rather widely held at the bar, that advocacy in its more expert applications is very much an art, because certainly in this instance there is no single answer or formula to solve the problem.

All that can be usefully added here is Mr. Justice Harlan's conclusion: "You will find that thoughtful selection of the issues to be argued orally is a basic technique of every good appellate advocate." [17]

It should be repeated here, also (compare Section 111, above), that the order of presentation of points in the brief is not necessarily the most effective order of presentation for the argument. Frequently it is; often it is not. The written brief can more easily develop the several propositions involved in their strictly logical order, whereas the oral argument may need to depart from that arrangement in order to take up at the outset the crucial issue, or, it may be, the one that appears to be the only one really in dispute.

Where, for example, an appeal involves a jurisdictional question or one of appealability, in addition to issues on the merits, the former issue is almost necessarily the one first reached in the brief. But it can frequently be deferred or omitted in oral argument, depending on the treatment given it by the other side in its brief, or on the court's reaction to it at the outset of the argument.

Contrariwise, in a case involving judicial review of an administrative order, you may prefer to argue the merits in your brief in advance of the issue of reviewability. Compare Section 34, *supra*. Yet, at the argument, it may be more desirable, in the light of the judicial reaction to the appellant's contentions, to mention reviewability first in order to dispose of it, and then to devote the balance of your time to the merits.

---

[17] Harlan, *What Part Does the Oral Argument Play in the Conduct of an Appeal?*, 41 Corn. L. Q. 6, 8.

There is no set formula that will fit every case. The only standard is that of flexibility (Section 102, *supra*) ; the decision in the end must depend on the advocate's judgment of the way the argument is developing.

Section 138. An exercise in persuasion.—The presentation of a case to an appellate court, like any other instance of advocacy, is an exercise in persuasion: You seek to make the judges decide in your favor. Everything must be bent to that end—every sentence in the brief, indeed every footnote; every sentence in the oral argument; every mannerism, every gesture, even the advocate's attire. Every form of oral advocacy involves the impact of one personality on others. In an appellate court, it is the impact of the lawyer on three, five, seven, or nine judges. Though the number on the bench may vary, the advocate's aim remains the same: he must always, persistently, constantly, unflaggingly seek to persuade a majority of his listeners to agree with him.

That being so, he does not help his cause if he antagonizes his judicial audience—or any of them. One never persuades by antagonizing. Flank the difficult forensic obstacles if hitting them head on repels your listeners. The frequency with which counsel will fight a court, either generally or on specific unessential propositions, serves to underscore the extent to which some lawyers overlook the obvious, viz., that advocacy is an exercise in persuasion, and that the advocate is, in Mr. Justice Frankfurter's fine phrase (p. 281, *supra*) , a "practitioner of the art of persuasion."

Section 139. The dangers of crusading.—A crusader, in this connection, is any lawyer who identifies himself too closely or too emotionally with his cause. Once a lawyer starts crusading, he loses the objectivity he needs, he begins to slop over, he rapidly dimishes his effectiveness, and he becomes that stock, hackneyed, and yet constantly reappearing character, the lawyer who represents himself and who in consequence has a fool for a client.

My favorite story on the difference in function between lawyers and crusaders may be apocryphal, though I heard it many years ago from one of high authority who could qualify as "a source believed to be reliable." Here it is:

After the landslide election of 1928, President-elect Hoover was experiencing some indecision regarding the appointment of an Attorney General; consequently, he called upon Chief Justice Taft and besought that eminent statesman's counsel.

The Chief Justice warmly urged the merits of Solicitor General Mitchell, praising that gentleman's learning and competence, and stressing the respect and esteem and confidence with which the Supreme Court regarded him.

Mr. Hoover did not at first warm to the suggestion. Yes, Mr. Mitchell was a fine lawyer, "but he hasn't got an aggressive enough personality. I want someone who will take this issue of Law Enforcement"—this was still in the era of the Experiment Noble in Purpose—"who will take this issue of Law Enforcement to the people, and really go crusading on it."

"Why, Mr. President!" said the Chief Justice, who had himself been Chief Executive, "you don't want a crusader. You've got to do the crusading yourself. What you need is a lawyer!"

I wish it were possible for me to document, with chapter and verse and collection of horrible examples, the timeless truth and the enduring wisdom of Chief Justice Taft's remark. I wish I could cite the numberless instances, since 1933, in court and out, of the ineffectiveness, not to say incompetence, of the attorneys at law who took to crusading, when by remaining detached they could have done an infinitely better, an infinitely more professional, and an infinitely more effective job.

At this juncture I shall have to content myself with a single example, exact identification of which will necessarily be fuzzy.

Some years back a man was convicted under extremely unfair circumstances. Briefly, after the prosecutor's motion to *nolle pros.* was denied, he said he could not conscientiously prosecute, and walked out of the courtroom. The judge thereupon called and examined the witnesses himself, and, after hearing the testimony, found the defendant guilty! A crusading organization became interested in the case, and it retained a well-known, well-advertised, and (financially) completely successful lawyer to perfect the appeal. That appeal was heard by an appellate court of which the less said the better; some of its members later resigned, some were indicted, and its judgments in quite a number of cases were later set aside after extensive litigation because of the corruption with which they had been tainted. This was the court that affirmed the judgment of conviction.

The well-known lawyer thereupon loudly announced that he would petition for a writ of certiorari. Without question, he had a good cert. case, and even the old Court—this was before 1937—

would have reversed.[18] But, even as counsel was talking pretty big about what he would do in the Supreme Court, he failed to move for a stay of mandate, the mandate went down, sentence could not be stayed further—and the great case became moot. "You don't want a crusader, Mr. President; what you need is a lawyer!"

One further caution may not be out of order. When you are opposed by a crusader, avoid the temptation to go countercrusading against him. His emotional instability, his muddy thinking, will all strongly tempt you to have at him in kind. Resist the temptation. Remain detached, lawyerlike, and professional. If you have to operate on him, do so with the calm, impersonal deftness of a surgeon with a scalpel. It may not be as much fun, but it will be more effective—and your crusading opponent will find your technique, if not so immediately painful, certainly more deadly in the end.

Section 140. Inner conviction.—Assuming that the advocate has the technical equipment, assuming that he has mastered not only the principles of advocacy but also the art of applying them, what extra, added feature is there that distinguishes the really outstanding advocate from the run of just able advocates?

In my view, it is an inner conviction of the soundness and correctness of his case. That is not just fervor, and most assuredly it is not crusading, with its screaming and its inevitable concomitant inaccuracies. It is, rather, an abiding conviction that law and justice are both on your side, certainly as to the points you are making.

This inner conviction is often self-induced, frequently by an involved process of rationalization, but it is none the worse for that. The important thing is that you have it, so that you believe what you are saying, or at least believe the reasonableness of what you are saying, and that you are not simply repeating a line of patter, tongue in cheek.

As I review the cases I have argued in appellate courts, it seems to me that, in the present connection, they fall into three groups. Some I believed in wholeheartedly from the start, even passionately, so much so that it took an effort to avoid slopping over. Others were essentially indifferent cases, as to which I had no particular conviction one way or the other at the outset, but where the joy

---

[18] A similar conviction in a British Empire case was reversed by the Privy Council on statutory grounds. *Adan Haji Jama* v. *The King*, [1948] A.C. 225.

of battle, as it were, eventually induced a belief that I was right. (O.K., turn the psychologists loose on that one!) In the third group, I had grave doubts when I started, and I needed to explore the authorities very thoroughly before I found an approach or a theory to which I could really subscribe. Not until then was I able to argue those cases with conviction.

Possibly a concrete example may serve to clarify the sort of mental turmoil that precedes the acquisition of the requisite inner conviction.

In the *Line Material* case,[19] the Government's original argument had hammered at the doctrine of the *General Electric* case,[20] which had held that price-fixing under a patent license did not violate the antitrust laws. That argument rested in part on economic grounds, in part on some strongly held views as to the social values implicit in a patent, and in part (by way of conclusion from the foregoing) on what was conceived to be the proper scope of the patent grant. That argument was nothing more or less than a statement of the credo of the Antitrust Division of the Department of Justice, the Gospel According to Thurman Arnold, and it had been ably presented by the late Assistant Attorney General Wendell Berge.[21] It failed, however, to gain the concurrence of a majority of the Court, and, Mr. Berge having meanwhile resigned from the Department, the *Line Material* case was set down for reargument.[22]

It was then assigned to me, and I had the benefit, not only of the briefs originally filed, but of a stenographic transcript of all the original arguments. I studied record, briefs, and arguments, read a good many decisions, and soaked myself in the atmosphere of the antitrust-patent field. Of course I wanted to win, and, whatever the merits or demerits of the actual case, I viewed it as the leader of the defeated faction in the primary looked on the party's ultimate nominee: "Sure, he's a so-and-so—but he's *our* so-and-so now." But—I could not subscribe to the tenets of the Antitrust Religion. Perhaps salvation lies that way; no matter, I could not with conviction recite the patter of the anti-*General Electric* syllogism. As the

---

[19] *United States v. Line Material Co.*, 333 U. S. 287.
[20] *United States v. General Electric Co.*, 272 U. S. 476.
[21] It was set forth at pp. 509-525 of the earlier version of this work.
[22] Journal, U. S. Sup. Ct., Oct. T. 1946, p. 275.

old preacher said, "And if I do not march in step, it is because I hear a different drummer."

Thereafter, I got busy on the facts, and proceeded to analyze the *General Electric* case as a matter of logic. Eventually I convinced myself that, on the facts, the Government was entitled to a decree without any change in law, and I likewise convinced myself of a logical flaw in the *General Electric* case, viz., that the provision in the agreements in question for the maintenance of the patentee-licensor's own prices did not contribute to the protection of the patent, which was the sole announced justification for the *General Electric* doctrine.[23] After that I had no more inner qualms, and whatever else may be said of my efforts on reargument, they certainly cannot fairly be criticized for reflecting any want of conviction.[24]

To resume: It is, I am convinced, essential to effective advocacy that the advocate have, before he gets up, an abiding inner conviction of the justice of his cause. How he acquires that feeling —whether he starts with it or generates it in the process of preparation—is not really important. But if he is going to carry conviction to his listeners, he must first carry conviction within himself.

Thus, one of his former partners said of Mr. Justice Brandeis,

The prime source of his power was his intense belief in the truth of what he was saying. It carried conviction. Except in capacity to bring about a favorable settlement, he was no good on the wrong side of a case.[25]

And other lawyers of distinction have given expression to the view that, absent a feeling of inner conviction, an advocate will not appear at his best—and will not make as effective a presentation to the court.[26]

---

[23] "If the patentee * * * licenses the selling of the articles, may he limit the selling by limiting the method of sale and the price? We think he may do so, provided the conditions of sale are normally and reasonably adapted to secure pecuniary reward for the patentee's monopoly." *United States* v. *General Electric Co.,* 272 U. S. 476, 490.

[24] See pp. 541-556 and 572-574 of the earlier version of the text.

[25] McClennen, *Louis D. Brandeis as a Lawyer,* 33 Mass. L. Q. (No. 3, Sept. 1948) 3.

[26] Thus, the late Mr. W. D. Mitchell, a former Attorney General and Solicitor General, wrote in his review of the first version of this book (64 Harv. L. Rev. 350, 352) :

"Mr. Wiener points out that appellate advocacy is an effort at persuasion

Section 141. The ultimate tribute.—We have been going upward and onward in this chapter, from the task of presentation as such to the art which, over and above any technical equipment, that task requires; and we have discussed also the advocate's need for possessing a highly developed sense of relevance and an abiding inner conviction of the rightness of his cause.

He must have all those qualities if he is to reach real heights. What, then, is the ultimate to which he may aspire?

I venture to suggest a fitting goal for the advocate, one that may well be unattainable for all but a few, but that is worth striving for none the less. It is this: so to present a case that judges will say to themselves when they hear him, as Chief Judge Cardozo of the New York Court of Appeals used to say when he heard Mr. Charles Evans Hughes, "How can I possibly decide against this man?" [27]

When *your* argument evokes such a reaction, you will have reached the heights!

---

and that a lawyer who believes he is right is the more persuasive because of that. Although this poses a question which may be one of professional standards, it does bear on effectiveness of oral argument. Some lawyers are willing to take a case, if it presents what they describe as an 'arguable' position, on the theory that every man is entitled to have a lawyer present his case. Other lawyers decline cases which they consider are without merit, because they take no professional satisfaction in arguing them; and because the litigant deserves to have his case presented by a lawyer (if one is available) who believes in it and who, therefore, can argue it more persuasively. It also is true that a lawyer who becomes known as one who does not make a practice of accepting cases in which he does not believe, has a long start in the confidence of the courts and on the road to victory."

[27] And see the letter of Mr. Justice Frankfurter in the Washington *Post*, Dec. 16, 1952, quoting Mr. Justice Holmes' comments on Solicitor General Lehmann: "When the full force of Lehmann's moral energy is enlisted in an argument, I hardly dare decide against him."

FOURTH PART

AND IF YOU LOSE—

CHAPTER X

REHEARINGS

Section 142. Petitions for rehearing; in general.—Petitions for rehearing can be more poetically—and more accurately—labeled "Love's Labor Lost": The normal petition for rehearing has about the same chance of success as the proverbial snowball on the far side of the River Styx. This is particularly true when the points raised in such a petition have been fully set forth in a dissent, which is to say that they have already been considered by the court. In that event, to ask for a rehearing by the same judges is an utter waste of time, money, labor, and good white paper. After all, if the dissenting judge or judges were unable to persuade their brethren in the conference room and in chambers—i.e., in oral discussions face to face and without any limitations as to time—it is absurd, indeed it is fatuous, to suppose that losing counsel will meet with more success simply by presenting a necessarily abbreviated written document.

Section 143. Petitions for rehearing; basic reasons for denial.—Charles Evans Hughes, in the interval between his two terms of service on the Supreme Court, wrote that "Petitions for rehearing are an improvement on the tavern [1] as counsel may enjoy the luxury of telling the Court to its face what is thought of its opinion * * *." [2] Later on in the same passage, he quoted Mr. Justice Bradley on the subject, a quotation which goes to the heart of the matter:

It ought to be understood, or at least believed, whether it is true or not, that this Court, being a Court of last resort, gives great consideration to cases of importance and involving consequences like this, and there should be a finality somewhere. This custom of making motions

---

[1] Compare Section 3, p. 5, *supra.* See also Jackson, *Tribute to Country Lawyers: A Review,* 30 A. B. A. J. 136, 139: "* * * this vanishing country lawyer * * * never quit. He could think of motions for every purpose under the sun, and he made them all. He moved for new trials, he appealed; and if he lost out in the end, he joined the client at the tavern in damning the judge —which is the last rite in closing an unsuccessful case, and I have officiated at many."

[2] Hughes, *The Supreme Court of the United States,* 71.

for a rehearing is not a custom to be encouraged. It prevails in some States as a matter of ordinary practice to grant a rehearing on a mere application for it, but that practice we do not consider a legitimate one in this Court. It is possible that in the haste of examining cases before us, we sometimes overlook something, and then we are willing to have that pointed out, but to consider that this Court will reexamine the matter and change its judgment on a case, it seems to me, is not taking a proper view of the functions of this Court. Your application is a proper one to be made, but this matter of motions for rehearing has become—I won't say a nuisance, but very disagreeable to the Court.[3]

Except where something has been overlooked, the routine or indiscriminate granting of rehearings reflects inadequate consideration of the appeal on the original hearing. As Mr. Justice Frankfurter said in his concurring opinion in the *Western Pacific Railroad Case*,[4]

Rehearings are not a healthy step in the judicial process; surely they ought not to be deemed a normal procedure. Yet one who has paged the Federal Reporter for nearly fifty years is struck with what appears to be a growth in the tendency to file petitions for rehearing in the courts of appeals. I have not made a quantitative study of the facts, but one gains the impression that in some circuits these petitions are filed almost as a matter of course. This is an abuse of judicial energy. It results in needless delay. It arouses false hopes in defeated litigants and wastes their money. If petitions for rehearing were justified, except in rare instances, it would bespeak serious defects in the work of the courts of appeals, an assumption which must be rejected.

The other side of the coin appears in an opinion of the same Justice dissenting from the denial of a petition for rehearing:

Because I deem a reargument to be required, I do not mean to imply that it would lead to a different result. The basis of an adjudication may be as important as the decision. The Court has rightly been parsimonious in ordering rehearings, but the occasions on which important and difficult cases have been reargued have, I believe, enhanced the deliberative process.[5]

---

[3] *Ibid.*, 71-72. See also the paragraph which follows:

"Probably the most argued case on record is that of *Pennsylvania* v. *West Virginia* [262 U. S. 553, 623; 263 U. S. 350] with respect to interstate commerce in natural gas, a case that was thrice argued, then decided, and the decision was followed by a rehearing; then three judges dissented from the final decision as they had from the first one, demonstrating that harmony does not always wait on argumentation."

[4] 345 U. S. 247, 268, 270.

[5] *Detroit* v. *Murray Corp.*, 357 U. S. 913, 915.

Section 144. Petitions for rehearing; additional reasons for denial.—In part, of course, the low batting average of petitions for rehearings illustrates a very human trait. Most persons do not like to change their minds once they have made them up—and most judges share that well-nigh universal reaction. There is extant a letter from Mr. Justice Holmes that says, "I guess * * * that the defeated side will apply for a rehearing hinting that we don't understand the patents and that the application will be denied in the belief that we damned well do." [6] Rarely has a prediction been more fully—or more quickly—fulfilled.[7]

It is only on the rarest occasions that a judge can be induced to view the same case differently once he is publicly committed to a particular course of reasoning on the issues that case involves. Confessing error afterwards does not involve the same degree of painful anguish; witness the announcement of three justices that they had changed their views on the flag salute issue,[8] and the comment of another that he would vote differently than he once had on the scope of the Fourth Amendment.[9] Where the earlier view had been expressed in a different capacity, backtracking is of course easier; here the classic instance is the graceful admission by Mr. Justice Jackson that an opinion he had signed as Attorney General on the same issue was, on reflection, completely wrong.[10]

---

[6] Letter Holmes to Laski, Feb. 14, 1930, 2 *Holmes-Laski Letters* (Howe ed. 1953) 1224.

[7] The case was *Minerals Separation Corp.* v. *Magma Copper Co.,* 280 U. S. 400, decided Feb. 24, 1930 (No. 71, Oct. T. 1929). A petition for rehearing, filed March 21, 1930, urged *inter alia* at p. 15 "misunderstanding of the meaning and effect * * * of the direction in" the patent in suit. The files in the case—this was before the denial of petitions for rehearing was noted either in the Journal or in the reports—disclose that the petition was denied on April 14, 1930.

[8] See *Jones* v. *Opelika,* 316 U. S. 584, 623.

[9] See *On Lee* v. *United States,* 343 U. S. 747, 762.

[10] *McGrath* v. *Kristensen,* 340 U. S. 162, 176. The Attorney General's opinion in question was 39 Op. Atty. Gen. 504.

Another example is *Lewis* v. *Manufacturers Nat. Bank,* 364 U. S. 603, 610, where Mr. Justice Harlan disavowed an opinion in which he had joined while one of the Circuit Judges for the Second Circuit.

See also Frankfurter, J., dissenting, in *Henslee* v. *Union Planters Bank,* 335 U. S. 595, 600: "Wisdom too often never comes, and so one ought not to reject it merely because it comes late. Since I now realize that I should have joined the dissenters in the *Merchants Bank* case, 320 U. S. 256, I shall not compound error by pushing that decision still farther. I would affirm the judgment, substantially for the reasons given below. 166 F. 2d 993."

Where, following the first argument, no opinion has been delivered, no one is publicly on record, and many votes in such situations have gone the other way following reargument. The Income Tax Case in the 1890's is the best known instance,[11] though there have been others.[12] But when an opinion has once been announced and subscribed, it requires a rare degree of open-mindedness and intellectual humility for any judge to admit error on the identical issue in the very same case. Mr. Justice Harlan's opinion on rehearing in *Reid* v. *Covert*[13] is an example of this most unusual kind of admission—the only one, to my knowledge, that is to be found in the Supreme Court reports.

Section 145. Rehearings granted in Courts of Appeals.—By way of preliminary, it should be noted that, in this section as well as in those following, "rehearing" is used in its narrow technical sense of a second consideration following a decision. Otherwise stated, "rehearing" does not include a mere "reargument," which follows a court's failure to arrive at or to announce a decision following its original consideration of the cause.[13a]

Petitions for rehearing in Courts of Appeals that succeed not only in being granted but that induce the same three judges to arrive at a different result are, necessarily, infrequent.[14] Occasionally a petition for rehearing, while in form denied, nonetheless broadens the scope of the order remanding the case.[15] In most other in-

---

[11] On the first argument, the question of the constitutional validity of the income tax was reserved, due to an equally divided court, Mr. Justice H. E. Jackson being ill. *Pollock* v. *Farmers' Loan & Trust Co.*, 157 U. S. 429, 586. On rehearing, even though Justice Jackson voted in favor of the validity of the statute, it was invalidated. *Pollock* v. *Farmers' Loan & Trust Co.*, 158 U. S. 601. One judge, very plainly, changed his mind; his identity has never been established.

[12] E.g., *United States* v. *Grimaud*, affirmed by equally divided court, 216 U. S. 614; on rehearing, unanimously reversed, 220 U. S. 506. See Frankfurter and Landis, *The Business of the Supreme Court* (1928) 15-16, note 43.

[13] 354 U. S. 1, 65.

[13a] See *In re Fidelity Tube Corporation*, 278 F. 2d 777 (C.A. 3), which was argued three times before any opinion was handed down. The last reargument (and, in all likelihood, the first reargument) were in banc.

[14] E.g., *Anderson Co.* v. *Trico Products Corp.*, 267 F. 2d 700 (C.A. 2); *Verbeeck* v. *Black Diamond Steamship Corp.*, 273 F. 2d 61 (C.A. 2). See also *Klein* v. *United States*, C.Cls., Jan. 18, 1961, granting a motion for reconsideration and ordering entry of judgment in favor of the plaintiffs.

[15] E.g., *Smith* v. *Flinn*, 264 F. 2d 523 (C.A. 8); *Cross* v. *Pasley*, 270 F. 2d 88 (C.A. 8); cf. *Forman* v. *United States*, 259 F. 2d 128, 261 F. 2d 181, 264 F. 2d 955 (C.A. 9), affirmed, 361 U. S. 416.

stances, the grant of a rehearing reflects a later controlling decision [16] or a later controlling statute or regulation.[17] In any Federal
court, the question of its own jurisdiction is always open, and one
circuit frankly told counsel that he need not apologize for raising a
jurisdictional question only on petition for rehearing.[18]

Normally, then, the only petition for rehearing that is likely
to succeed is one that, in the language of the Eighth Circuit's Rule
15 (a) , is restricted to "directing the attention of the court to some
controlling matter of law or fact which a party claims was overlooked in deciding a case." Unless your petition is thus limited,
you are wasting your time and your client's money.[19]

Section 146. Rehearings in banc in Courts of Appeals.—In
circuits that have five active circuit judges or more—and at present
that means all except the First and Fourth—losing a case by a divided vote is not the end. Losing counsel may petition for a rehearing in banc.[19a]

This practice was first employed in the Third Circuit, and,
being challenged, was sustained by the Supreme Court in the *Textile Mills* case,[20] decided in 1941. The 1948 revision of the Judicial
Code formalized the practice, and provided specifically for hearings in banc, by all the active circuit judges of the circuit.[21] When
the Ninth Circuit struck from its files as unauthorized an unsucces-
ful litigant's petition for a rehearing in banc, the Supreme Court in

---

[16] E.g., *Great Northern Railway Co.* v. *Hyde*, 241 F. 2d 707 (C.A. 8);
Needleman v. *United States*, 261 F. 2d 803 (C.A. 5); cf. *King* v. *Waterman
Steamship Corp.*, 272 F. 2d 823 (C.A. 3).
See also, for a late case, *Manning* v. *United States*, 280 F. 2d 422 (C.A. 5).

[17] E.g., *McGehee* v. *Commissioner*, 260 F. 2d 818 (C.A. 5) (statute);
United States v. *Gibson*, 225 F. 2d 807 (C.A. 9) (regulation).

[18] *Cummings* v. *Redeeriaktieb Transatlantic*, 242 F. 2d 275 (C.A. 3).
See also *United States* v. *New York, New Haven & Hartford R. Co.*, 276 F. 2d
525 (C.A. 2), where a suggestion of lack of jurisdiction was fully considered
on a second petition for rehearing.

[19] For another excellent statement, see *United States* v. *Procter & Gamble
Co.*, 19 F.R.D. 247, 248-249, note 1 (D.N.J.), quoting a District Court rule
that similarly formulates the proper nature of reargument.

[19a] I follow the statute, cited below, in rendering this as "in banc" without
italics. Actually, since the expression is of great antiquity, from the days of
Law French, the correct form is "en banc," and hence preferably italicized.
Would that the only deficiency of the Revisers of Title 28 had been their
ignorance of philology!

[20] *Textile Mills Corp.* v. *Commissioner*, 314 U. S. 326.

[21] 28 U.S.C. § 46 (c). Note that hearings in banc in District Courts have
long been authorized. *FCF Film Corp.* v. *Gourley*, 240 F. 2d 711, 714 (C.A.
3); see *Kovrak* v. *Ginsburg*, 177 F. Supp. 614 (E.D. Pa.).

the *Western Pacific Railroad Case* [22] reversed, pointing out, however, that whether a rehearing in banc should be granted could be determined either by the original panel or by the entire court. The practice accordingly differs from circuit to circuit,[23] but parties are clearly free to request in banc rehearings. Indeed, the Supreme Court has recently indicated that, where an intra-circuit conflict exists, such a conflict must be resolved by an in banc hearing, and can not be submitted to the Supreme Court for decision by means of a certificate.[24] (In the Federal judicial system, as in the Federal military system, the buck never passes up.)

Inasmuch as a rehearing in banc augments the tribunal hearing the cause, it has frequently happened that the court in banc reaches a result just the opposite of that reached by the panel.[25] For, not only will a rehearing in banc add from two to six addi-

---

[22] 345 U. S. 247.

[23] See Second Circuit, Rule 25 (b) ; Maris, *Hearing and Rehearing Cases in Banc*, 14 F.R.D. 91 (practice in Third Circuit) ; *National Latex Products Co.* v. *Sun Rubber Co.*, 276 F. 2d 167 (C.A. 6) (practice in Sixth Circuit) ; Stephens, "In Banc Hearings and Rehearings," in *Shop Talk Concerning the Business of the Court*, 20 J. Bar Assn. of the D. C. 103, 105-109 (practice in District of Columbia Circuit) ; compare *Cafeteria & Restaurant Workers Union* v. *McElroy*, 284 F. 2d 173 (D. C. Cir., 14 Apr. 1960) , certiorari granted, 364 U. S. 81 (same) ; *United States* v. *Gori*, 282 F. 2d 43, 52-53 (C.A. 2) (practice in Second Circuit with respect to whether there shall be new briefs or a reargument—or neither—in connection with in banc consideration) .

In view of the language of the statute, no rehearing in banc can be had when the active circuit judges are equally divided. See *Harmar Drive-In Theatre* v. *Warner Bros. Pictures*, 241 F. 2d 937 (C.A. 2) ; *United States* v. *United Steelworkers of America*, 271 F. 2d 676, 694 (C.A. 3) , affirmed, 361 U. S. 39.

[24] *Wisniewski* v. *United States*, 353 U. S. 901.

[25] E.g., *Howard* v. *United States*, 232 F. 2d 274 (C.A. 5) ; *G. H. Miller & Co.* v. *United States*, 260 F. 2d 286 (C.A. 7) ; *Reardon* v. *California Tanker Co.*, 260 F. 2d 369 (C.A. 2) ; *Noah* v. *Liberty Mutual Ins. Co.*, 267 F. 2d 218 (C.A. 5) ; *Leary* v. *United States*, 268 F. 2d 623 (C.A. 9) .

Compare *Sperry Rand Corp.* v. *Bell Telephone Laboratories*, 272 F. 2d 29 (C.A. 2) (different result as a matter of law, same result in exercise of discretion) .

See also *Strand* v. *Schmittroth*, 233 F. 2d 598 (C.A. 9) (May 3, 1956), rehearing denied, 235 F. 2d 756 (Aug. 2, 1956) , different result after rehearing in banc, 251 F. 2d 590 (June 24, 1957) . On September 18, 1956, in the interval between the last two decisions, Strand filed a petition for certiorari in the Supreme Court (No. 432, Oct. T. 1956) . After the last decision, on December 3, 1957, his motion to dismiss the petition was granted. 355 U. S. 886 (No. 22, Oct. T. 1957) . I am not aware of any other instance where a Court of Appeals reversed itself during the pendency of a petition for certiorari to review its earlier decision.

tional circuit judges to the original bench, depending on the number in the circuit, but, inasmuch as such a rehearing is limited by the statute to "all the active circuit judges of the circuit," [26] it will frequently exclude two of the original panel,[27] and may of course exclude all three, in view of the great statutory flexibility for the composition of a Court of Appeals.[28]

One point long remained open: Suppose one of the active circuit judges hearing the case retires prior to decision; may he participate? In a case where the judge who retired cast the deciding vote, *United States* v. *American-Foreign S. S. Co.*,[29] the Supreme Court, held, only recently, that the act of retirement pending decision terminated his eligibility to participate in the ultimate disposition of the cause.

---

[26] 28 U.S.C. § 46 (c).

[27] E.g., *Reardon* v. *California Tankers Co.*, 260 F. 2d 369 (C.A. 2) (two retired circuit judges on original panel); *Herzog* v. *United States*, 226 F. 2d 561, 235 F. 2d 664 (C.A. 9), certiorari denied, 352 U. S. 844 (district judge and retired circuit judge on original panel).

[28] In addition to "the active circuit judges of the circuit," the following may sit as members of a Court of Appeals:

(a) The Circuit Justice; see 28 U.S.C. § 43 (b); for a recent example, see *Lago Oil & Transport Co.* v. *United States*, 218 F. 2d 631 (C.A. 2) (Mr. Justice Frankfurter).

(b) A retired Justice of the Supreme Court; see 28 U.S.C. § 294 (a); for recent example, see *Lord* v. *Lencshire House, Ltd.*, 272 F. 2d 557 (D. C. Cir.) (Mr. Justice Burton).

(c) A retired circuit judge from the same circuit; 28 U.S.C. § 294 (c); examples are legion.

(d) An active circuit judge from another circuit; 28 U.S.C. § 291 (a); many examples.

(e) A retired circuit judge from another circuit; 28 U.S.C. § 294 (c); see *Presser Royalty Co.* v. *Chase Manhattan Bank*, 272 F. 2d 838 (C.A. 2) (Judge Magruder, Senior Judge, C.A. 1).

(f) A judge of the Court of Claims; 28 U.S.C. § 293 (a); see, e.g., *Anderson Co.* v. *Trico Products Corp.*, 267 F. 2d 700 (C.A. 2) (Judge Madden).

(g) A judge of the Court of Customs and Patent Appeals; see 28 U.S.C. § 293 (a).

(h) A district judge from the same circuit; 28 U.S.C. § 292 (a); daily examples.

(i) A district judge from another circuit; 28 U.S.C. § 292 (c); e.g., *National Latex Products Co.* v. *Sun Rubber Co.*, 274 F. 2d 224, rehearing denied, 276 F. 2d 167 (C.A. 6) (Judge Mathes, District Judge, S.D. Calif.).

(j) A retired district judge from the same or any other circuit; see 28 U.S.C. § 294 (c).

[29] 363 U. S. 685. In the *Herzog* case, *supra* note 27, two of the judges who heard the reargument in banc retired pending decision and then participated therein; but their votes would not have changed the result.

Section 147. Practical details in connection with petitions for rehearing in Courts of Appeals.—While, as has been indicated, the normal petition for rehearing in a Court of Appeals gets fairly short shrift, it does have one undeniable virtue, namely, that the time for certiorari runs, not from the date of the original opinion, but from the date of denial of rehearing.[30] (There are refinements in respect of motions for modification of the judgment and second petitions for rehearing,[31] but the general rule is unquestioned.) Consequently, the filing of a petition for rehearing extends the time for your client to raise additional funds for the next appellate step, and may increase the possibility that some other circuit will rule the other way and so produce a conflict. But these apparent advantages frequently collide with the requirement, imposed by the rules of most courts, that every petition for rehearing must have appended thereto a certificate of counsel that it is filed in good faith and not for purposes of delay.[32]

It has already been noted that in the Eighth Circuit a petition for rehearing is restricted to "directing the attention of the court to some controlling matter of law or fact which a party claims was overlooked in deciding a case." The limitation in the Court of Customs and Patent Appeals is to "points supposed to have been overlooked or misapprehended by the court." [33] (Whether that formulation is really a limitation may well be doubted; every petition for rehearing urges, indeed screams, that the opinion just filed is full of misapprehensions.) At any rate, three courts—the Second, Eighth, and Tenth circuits—impose costs for vexatious petitions for rehearings.[34]

Since this is not a practice manual, there is no occasion in these pages to discuss stay of mandate, supersedeas, or bail pend-

---

[30] See Robertson and Kirkham, *Jurisdiction of the Supreme Court of the United States* (Kurland & Wolfson ed. 1951) § 414 (which incorporates by reference § 384).

[31] See Stern and Gressman, *Supreme Court Practice* (2d ed. 1954) ch. V (A), pp. 163-166, and see particularly *Federal Trade Comm. v. Minneapolis-Honeywell Co.,* 344 U. S. 206.

[32] First Circuit, Rule 31; Second Circuit, Rule 25 (a) ; Third Circuit, Rule 33; Fourth Circuit, Rule 19; Fifth Circuit, Rule 29; Sixth Circuit, Rule 22 (2) ; Eighth Circuit, Rule 15 (a) ; Ninth Circuit, Rule 23; Tenth Circuit, Rule 24 (2) ; District of Columbia Circuit, Rule 26 (a) .

[33] Rule VII.

[34] Second Circuit, Rule 25 (d) ; Eighth Circuit, Rule 15 (d) ; Tenth Circuit, Rule 24 (3) .

ing appeal,[35] nor to warn counsel that failure to make timely substitution of public officers will make the cause abate.[36]

Suppose, however, that you are winning counsel, relaxing in your office while savoring the eternal verities and soothing nuances of the opinion in your favor: Is there anything you should or can do when the opposition, ignorantly refusing to stay licked, files a petition for rehearing? Four circuits do not permit the filing of a response to a petition for rehearing,[37] two plus the Court of Customs and Patent Appeals specifically allow a response,[38] and the rules of the others are silent. In practice, two circuits will ask for a response if they are troubled by the petition.[39]

The soundest advice in this situation is, Sit Tight. You will have ample opportunity to say your say if and when you are called on for a response, or if and when your opponent seeks certiorari. Until then, there is nothing to be gained, financially or spiritually, in rearguing a case you have already won.

Section 148. Rehearings in the Supreme Court of the United States.—How to discourage the unmeritorious petition for rehearing that is filed as a matter of course, and yet to leave the door slightly ajar for that rare instance in which a rehearing should be granted, may well be an insoluble problem. Certainly the Supreme Court's short-lived effort to stem the tide by reducing from 25 to 15 days the time within which to petition for rehearing was unsuccessful;[40] it was accordingly abandoned in the 1954 Rules.[41] There is really only one way to discourage unmeritorious applications for rehearing, and that is to deny them.

In the first five Terms since the 1954 Rules went into effect, about 970 petitions for rehearing were disposed of, and all but 15

---

[35] See Stern and Gressman, *Supreme Court Practice* (2d ed. 1954) ch. V (H) and VI (H), pp. 207-217, 246-249. For a list of opinions of Justices in chambers dealing with these matters, see my paper on *Opinions of Justices Sitting in Chambers,* 49 Law Lib. J. 2 (1956).

[36] *Snyder* v. *Buck,* 340 U. S. 15; *Klaw* v. *Schaffer,* 357 U. S. 346; *Glanzman* v. *Schaffer,* 357 U. S. 347.

[37] Second Circuit, Rule 25 (a) ; Fourth Circuit, Rule 19; Sixth Circuit, Rule 22 (3) ; Eighth Circuit, Rule 15 (c) .

[38] Seventh Circuit, Rule 25 (a) ; District of Columbia Circuit, Rule 26 (b) ; Court of Customs and Patent Appeals, Rule VII.

[39] The Second and Tenth, to my knowledge; but my experience in the former on this point antedates the present version of its Rule 25.

[40] Amended Rule 33, 332 U. S. 857, 875; see 68 Harv. L. Rev. at 83-84.

[41] Rule 58 (1) and (2) .

were denied.[42] Of the 15 granted, only two—*Reid* v. *Covert*[43] and *Flora* v. *United States*[44]—followed opinions on the merits. It may be noted that, in the last 20 years, only five rehearings have been granted following decisions on the merits.[45]

Included in the 15 grants for the quinquennium were six rehearings of affirmances by an equally divided court,[46] although it should be noted that rehearings have been denied even in that situation,[47] and that in the *Sioux City Cemetery* case[48] the grant of rehearing following such an affirmance resulted in dismissal of the petition for certiorari.

Of the other rehearings granted, four were rehearings of earlier denials of certiorari, granted because of intervening decisions;[49] one involved the modification of the judgment earlier entered[50] (in all likelihood by inadvertence, compare Section 37 (b), *supra*) ; while the remaining two were reconsiderations of earlier denials of certiorari, in each instance again denied when reconsidered.[51]

---

[42] The overall figure includes motions to file a petition for rehearing, i.e., petitions out of time, as well as petitions for rehearing filed as of right. The basis for computation was the number of cases. I thumbed the reports and so the final figure is not guaranteed; "E. & O. E.," as the brokers say.

[43] Rehearing granted, 352 U. S. 901, following opinions at 351 U. S. 470 and 351 U. S. 487.

[44] Rehearing granted, 360 U. S. 922, following opinion at 357 U. S. 63.

[45] *Jones* v. *Opelika*, rehearing granted, 318 U. S. 796, following opinion at 316 U. S. 584; *Elgin, J. & E. R. Co.* v. *Burley*, rehearing granted, 326 U. S. 801, following opinion at 325 U. S. 711; *Graver Mfg. Co.* v. *Linde Co.*, rehearing granted, 337 U. S. 910, following opinion at 336 U. S. 271; *Reid* v. *Covert*, *supra* note 43; *Flora* v. *United States*, *supra* note 44.

[46] *Ryan Stevedoring Co.* v. *Pan-Atlantic S.S. Corp.*, rehearing granted, 349 U. S. 926, following affirmance at 349 U. S. 901; *Indian Towing Co.* v. *United States*, rehearing granted, 349 U. S. 926, following affirmance at 349 U. S. 902; *Thompson* v. *Coastal Oil Co.*, rehearing granted, 350 U. S. 985, following affirmance at 350 U. S. 956; *Bartkus* v. *Illinois*, rehearing granted, 356 U. S. 969, following affirmance at 355 U. S. 281; *Ladner* v. *United States*, rehearing granted, 356 U. S. 969, following affirmance at 355 U. S. 282; note 48, *infra*.

[47] E.g., *Giese* v. *Chamberlin*, affirmed by equally divided court, 342 U. S. 845, rehearing denied, 342 U. S. 879.

[48] *Rice* v. *Sioux City Cemetery*, 349 U. S. 70, following affirmance at 348 U. S. 880.

[49] *Remmer* v. *United States*, 348 U. S. 904; *Mitchell* v. *United States*, 348 U. S. 905; *Achilli* v. *United States*, 352 U. S. 1023; *Ohio Power Co.* v. *United States*, 353 U. S. 98.

[50] *Union Trust Co.* v. *Eastern Air Lines*, 350 U. S. 962.

[51] *McNally* v. *Teets*, 352 U. S. 886; *Massengale* v. *United States*, 354 U. S. 936.

In sum, a slim haul; and yet that is par for the course. In the earlier edition of this work it was noted that, at the 1946 through 1948 Terms, the Supreme Court granted 17 petitions for rehearing out of some 600 filed. All except three involved cases considered either on petitions for certiorari or on jurisdictional statements. Of the other three, one turned on an intervening decision; a second was granted after affirmance by an equally divided court and was then reaffirmed after reargument, still by an equally divided court.[52] In the third case, *Graver Mfg. Co.* v. *Linde Co.*,[53] rehearing was granted after opinion, but on rehearing the same result was reached.[54]

In this connection, of the five rehearings granted after opinion in the last twenty years, the result in the end was different in only two cases.[55]

Section 149. Rehearings in the Supreme Court of the United States; mechanics and doubtful areas.—The Supreme Court, like some Courts of Appeals, does not permit responses to a petition for rehearing except at its own request.[56] When such a request is made, the petitioner has every reason to be hopeful,[57] but in at least one recent instance rehearing was denied notwithstanding.[58] Conversely, while Rule 58 (3) states that "No petition for rehearing will be granted in the absence of such a request and an opportunity to submit a reply in response thereto," this limitation has not been adhered to when rehearing is sought following affirmance by an equally divided Court.[59]

It should be noted that, while the filing of a timely petition

---

[52] *Marzani* v. *United States*, 335 U. S. 895, 336 U. S. 910, 336 U. S. 922; see *Effective Appellate Advocacy*, Sec. 82.

[53] 336 U. S. 271.

[54] 337 U. S. 910; 339 U. S. 605. For the successful petition for rehearing in that case, see Chapter 16 of *Effective Appellate Advocacy.*

[55] (a) *Jones* v. *Opelika*, 316 U. S. 584; rehearing granted, 318 U. S. 796; different result, 319 U. S. 103.

(b) *Reid* v. *Covert*, 351 U. S. 487, and *Kinsella* v. *Krueger*, 351 U. S. 470; rehearing granted, 352 U. S. 901; different result and earlier opinions withdrawn, 354 U. S. 1.

[56] Rule 58 (3).

[57] *Reid* v. *Covert*, 352 U. S. 813; *United States* v. *Ohio Power Co.*, 352 U. S. 987; *Flora* v. *United States*, 358 U. S. 871.

[58] *Detroit* v. *Murray Corp.*, 356 U. S. 934 (response requested), 357 U. S. 913 (rehearing denied).

[59] E.g., *Ryan Stevedoring Co.* v. *Pan-Atlantic S. S. Corp.*, 349 U. S. 926; *Indian Towing Co.* v. *United States*, 349 U. S. 926.

for rehearing during the Term stays the mandate until disposition thereof, a separate motion to stay the mandate is necessary if the petition for rehearing is filed while the Court is in vacation.[60]

Finally, there is the vexed question of rehearings out of time. Although Rule 58 (4) categorically states that "Consecutive petitions for rehearings, and petitions for rehearing that are out of time under this rule, will not be received," the mandate will be recalled if in a suitable case it requires correction,[61] and, as *United States* v. *Ohio Power Co.*[62] shows, Rule 58 (4) is not an absolute. The curious are referred to the opinions in that case for a full discussion of the problem. Assuredly, the result in *Ohio Power* will long serve to encourage the persevering and to stimulate the ingenious.

Section 150. Effect of denial of rehearing.—The old saw, that it is better to have loved and lost than never to have loved at all, should not be applied to petitions for rehearing. A "rehearing denied" will frequently weaken a good point when that point later becomes critical.

First, no matter how strong a point may be, it will be far weaker if presented in the last of a long series of requests for reconsideration, because by then the usual judicial attitude recalls General Forrest's turn-down of the lieutenant's renewed application for leave: "Dammit, I told you 'No' twicet!" And, lest any reader deem that comment overly cynical, let him look at the *Rosenberg* case.[63]

There, after six consecutive applications for review had been denied, it was finally contended, on a seventh, that, since the petitioners had been found guilty of a conspiracy alleged in the indictment to have continued from 1944 to 1950, they were not properly sentenced to death by the judge under the Espionage Act of 1917, but could only have been so sentenced upon recommendation of the jury pursuant to the Atomic Energy Act of 1946. Now, whether or not that contention was correct, it would be hard to urge that as an original proposition it was unsubstantial.[64] But it

---

[60] Rule 59 (2).

[61] *Cahill* v. *New York, N.H. & H. R. R. Co.*, 351 U. S. 183.

[62] 353 U. S. 98.

[63] *Rosenberg* v. *United States*, 346 U. S. 273. This opinion, filed after the final ruling in the case, sets out in chronological order all of the applications made on behalf of the petitioners.

[64] See 346 U. S. at 301-310 (opinion of Frankfurter, J.).

was not presented as an original proposition, it was first presented as a renewed, warmed-over, and hence apparently unoriginal seventh proposition, and under unusual circumstances that would have entailed substantial delay in the final disposition of the case.[65] In one of the opinions it was said that "The stay which had been issued promised many more months of litigation in a case which had otherwise run its full course." [66] In another it was said:

> Once the Court conceded, as it did, that the substantiality of the question raised before Mr. Justice Douglas was the sole issue, it became wholly immaterial how many other questions were raised and considered on their merits in the District Court and in the Court of Appeals, or how many times review was sought on these questions and refused by this Court. It was equally immaterial how long a time intervened between the original trial of this case and the present proceeding, and immaterial that this was a last-minute effort almost on the eve of the executions. To allow such irrelevancies to enter the mind not unnaturally tends to bend the judicial judgment in a false direction.[67]

But—the Court by 6-3 held the question unsubstantial, and the Rosenbergs were executed.

Second, lower courts attach far more significance to the Supreme Court's "rehearing denied" than the intrinsic significance of that action probably justifies. Lower courts normally look upon a denial of rehearing as a solemn adjudication on the merits.

Take *Ickes* v. *Fox:* [68] Water-right owners on a federal irrigation project in Washington State brought suit in the District of Columbia to enjoin the Secretary of the Interior from curtailing their supply of water. The defense was that, since the United States owned the water, the proceeding was a suit against the United States, which had not consented to be sued. The District Court granted a motion to dismiss, a divided Court of Appeals reversed, and on certiorari the Supreme Court held adversely to the Secretary. A petition for rehearing was then filed, only to be denied with a slight change in the opinion; [69] and the case went to trial.

---

[65] The stay which the full Court set aside was entered after adjournment for the summer, and was made on the application of a stranger to the cause. As to the latter point, see 346 U. S. at 291-292 (opinion of Jackson, J.).

[66] 346 U. S. at 287, *per* Vinson, C. J.

[67] 346 U. S. at 302, *per* Frankfurter, J.

[68] 300 U. S. 82.

[69] 300 U. S. 640.

Trial resulted in a judgment adverse to the water-right owners, who appealed; the Court of Appeals reversed on the basis of what the Solicitor General had urged in his petition for rehearing six years earlier:

A petition for rehearing filed in the Supreme Court by the Solicitor General makes it apparent that the principal issue in this case was before the Supreme Court on the former appeal. In that petition for rehearing the Solicitor General pointed out to the Court that the decision would lead to serious consequences in the administration of the Reclamation Fund because it gave applicants, on the sole basis of prior deliveries of water, a vested right in a larger amount of water than was stipulated in their contracts. The petition for rehearing pointed out that this amounted to giving them a prescriptive right based on permissive use. The petition also relied on a Washington statute which gave the government the right to appropriate water. We can see no difference between the appellee's position here and his unsuccessful argument before the Supreme Court of the United States.[70]

This second time the Secretary's petition for certiorari was denied.[71]

Let us review these cases: Suppose that, in *Rosenberg*, the question of the legality of the death sentence had been raised after the first denial of certiorari, without the complication of the other five applications that intervened. I suggest that it is unrealistic to suppose that this new point would not have received a more cordial reception had it been made on the second time up rather than on the seventh. Moreover, if, in *Ickes* v. *Fox*, no petition for rehearing had been filed, it would certainly have been more difficult for the Court of Appeals to have reversed the judgment entered after the trial.

I realize that the foregoing comments have the benefit of hindsight, which of course is always 20-20 in each eye. None the less, I strongly urge that, except in the most unusual circumstances, it is the part of wisdom not to ask for a rehearing. It hardly ever helps, but it may do considerable harm. When you're licked, take your shellacking like a little man, and comfort yourself with the thought that you can't lose them all.

Section 151. Examples of successful petitions for rehearing.— What, then, are the circumstances which alone justify a request for

---

[70] *Fox* v. *Ickes*, 137 F. 2d 30, 33 (D. C. Cir.).
[71] 320 U. S. 792.

rehearing? In Chapter XIII, *infra* pp. 422-442, there are set out in full the text of two successful petitions for rehearing, one in a Court of Appeals, the other in the Supreme Court. In that Chapter, also, I endeavor to explain why those two petitions were filed, and why in my view the occasions for filing them fell within the above expressed limitation of "most unusual circumstances."

Chapter XI
NEW COUNSEL ON APPEAL?

Section 152. Professional specialization in England and in the United States.—The English division of the legal profession into barristers and solicitors, each with their respective areas of specialization, has long withstood the test of time, and, so far as we can tell "when we contemplate such a system from the outside," [1] the test of utility as well.

It would of course be vain to hope that in this country we might somehow be persuaded to revert to the English system.[2] However, because of the increasing burdens cast on American lawyers by the mounting complexity of the law, and by their clients' inexorable demands for efficiency and expertise, there exists in this country a considerable degree of specialization within the legal profession, chiefly in urban centers. It is not too difficult, in a given community, to point out the lawyers who hardly ever go to court and those who spend most of their time there. Moreover, particularly in the larger cities, the institution of appellate counsel is constantly gaining in importance.

No single lawyer today can hope to be well versed in every field of legal endeavor that may face him in the course of his practice. Just as in medicine one of the timeworn but timeless jokes concerns the universal expert, the specialist in the skin and its contents, so in law: no one today can even fairly claim to be even reasonably conversant with the entire corpus. Similarly, no lawyer can hope to be expert in all techniques, so as to be able to try a case before a jury or before a judge, or to brief and argue an appeal, with equal facility and skill, and with full and knowl-

---

[1] *Diaz* v. *Gonzales,* 261 U. S. 102, 106. For the heart of the quotation in full, see note 39, Section 70, p. 218, above.

[2] A strong argument to that effect is set forth in Chap. XIII of the late Lloyd Paul Stryker's *The Art of Advocacy* (1954) 251-270, entitled "Barristers and Solicitors—A Plea for a Divided Bar."

edgeable grasp of all the relevant—and different—techniques connected with each activity.

Section 153. Appellate counsel specializes in being a generalist.—The increasing emergence of counsel for appeals reflects a recognition and a growing awareness of the inescapable fact that effective appellate presentation demands the services of a lawyer who is expert, not simply in particular fields of substantive law, but in a particular technique. Otherwise stated, the true appellate counsel specializes in being a generalist. Given a record, properly prepared, he is ready to brief and argue any appeal.

Appellate counsel faces, in an appellate court, a different audience and a different task than those faced in the trial court. It is undoubtedly safe to conclude that appellate counsel who specialize in subtly invoking the predilections of judges of courts of last resort will as a general rule fail to sway with equal success the popular prejudices of jurymen—and jurywomen. By the same token, a top-notch lawyer before a jury may do rather less than well when arguing an appeal.[3] In this connection, I have vividly in mind the comment of the Chief Justice of a State court of last resort, made about an argument presented by counsel in a negligence case: "He made the same jury speech three times—once to the jury at the trial, once to the trial judge on motion for new trial, and the third time to us on appeal."

Section 154. Can anyone argue an appeal?—Yet, to a surprising degree, the view that anyone can argue an appeal is still too prevalent. It certainly obtains among the many able jury lawyers who are rather less than able before an appellate bench, and yet insist on arguing there as well. Curiously enough, the same view also obtains even among the lawyers who are quick to retain specialized trial counsel but would not dream of consulting, much less retaining, specialized appellate counsel. And that view constitutes the inarticulate major premise of every lawyer, high in the hierarchy of his law firm, corporation law department, or government law office, who considers that his position alone supremely qualifies only him to present cases to appellate tribunals.

Indeed, it is fair to say that it is just this view—that anyone

---

[3] "The advocate, who sweeps the jury off their feet with his torrential eloquence, is rarely able to adapt his style to the colder and more judicial atmosphere of the Appeal Courts." Walker-Smith, *Lord Reading and His Cases* (1934) 41-42.

can argue an appeal—which is largely responsible for the generally mediocre level of appellate arguments. Three decades ago, Charles Evans Hughes wrote:

The progress of civilization is but little reflected in the processes of argumentation and a vast amount of time is unavoidably wasted in the Supreme Court in listening to futile discussion; this has the effect of reducing the time for cases which should be fully presented.[4]

If any reader thinks that there has been an improvement in the quality of argumentation in the thirty-three years that have passed since the above was written, let him just sit in the Supreme Court chamber and listen to as few as three consecutive arguments. (If it is inconvenient for him to come to Washington, he can make the same discovery in any courtroom occupied by a United States Court of Appeals.)

Section 155. Appellate argument requires specialization in technique.—The fact of the matter is that appellate argument calls for specialization in technique quite as much as does the trial of a case. As a distinguished member of an eminent State court of last resort recently said, "Nor is the argument of an appeal any less an art, any less a job for the skilled professional, than the conduct of the trial itself." [5] Like the trial lawyer, the appellate lawyer is a specialist in technique rather than in mere subject-matter. He is a generalist who presents his case to a bench of generalists, a bench that is frequently not as versed in the details of the specialty that the particular appeal involves. The specialist who prepared and tried the case is frequently so steeped in the specialty and in all of its assumptions that he finds it difficult to present the details of his controversy to listeners not similarly acquainted with that specialty. The generalist is better able to sort out the significant issues, to bring analogies to bear from related fields, and to evaluate the contentions of the specialist just as the non-specialists on the court are likely to do.

Otherwise stated, the appellate generalist will thus be able to minimize arguments that lack appeal to a non-specialist audience, and, by parity of reasoning, to emphasize contentions that will have greater impact on that audience.

Moreover, quite apart from the differences in technique that stem basically from the character of the respective tribunals, quite

---

[4] Hughes, *The Supreme Court of the United States* (1928) 61.
[5] *People* v. *Breslin*, 4 N. Y. 2d 73, 80, 81, 149 N.E. 2d 85, 89, 90, *per* Fuld, J.

apart also from the comparative emphases on specialization versus generalization, the most vital and significant point is that experience teaches it is better, regardless of the talents of the individual concerned, to entrust the appeal to a lawyer other than the one who tried the case.

Section 156. Appellate specialization in the United States Department of Justice.—In that connection, let us see how the largest and busiest litigant in the land—the United States itself—conducts its appellate business.

At headquarters—which is to say, in the Department of Justice in Washington—all Supreme Court matters are under the direct charge of the Solicitor General. He has a small immediate staff that reviews and revises the draft briefs prepared by the several functional divisions of the Department—Criminal, Civil, Tax, Lands, etc. The Solicitor General decides who will argue the cases that are to be heard on the merits. And he makes the decision for or against appeal in every Government case that is lost below, at every level and in every court.

Only on rarest occasions does a Government lawyer who tried the case or argued it in the Court of Appeals have any significant part in its Supreme Court posture. Probably less than five cases in ten years are thus handled.[6] *Per contra*, the lawyers who have the responsibility for Supreme Court briefs and, preeminently, Supreme Court arguments, have had contact with the case below even more rarely.

This division of labor is not due to any *prima donna* attitude, nor does it reflect the view that a lawyer on the fifth floor of the building is necessarily and inescapably superior in talent to one whose office is on a lower floor. Rather, it represents the

---

[6] The only ones that occur to me at the moment—there may well have been more—are *Fisher* v. *United States*, 328 U. S. 463, argued by Charles B. Murray, Esq., then an Assistant U. S. Attorney for the District of Columbia, and Government counsel in the Court of Appeals, see 149 F. 2d 28; *Dennis* v. *United States*, 341 U. S. 494, argued in part by Irving S. Shapiro, Esq., Special Assistant to the Attorney General, who had participated in the Court of Appeals argument, see 183 F. 2d 201, and had moreover been one of trial counsel; *United States* v. *Fruehauf*, 365 U. S. 146, argued on Jan. 11, 1961, by S. Hazard Gillespie, Jr., Esq., United States Attorney for the Southern District of New York; and *Greenberg* v. *United States*, 343 U. S. 918, argued by Max H. Goldschein, Esq., Special Assistant to the Attorney General, who had twice argued the case in the Court of Appeals, see 187 F. 2d 35 and 192 F. 2d 201, and had also been trial counsel. In connection with the last case, see Chapter XIV, below.

recognition of long experience that a lawyer versed in appeals and therefore able to weigh appellate considerations is better qualified to evaluate cases, particularly where they will be disposed of by a single ultimate tribunal. It is for this reason that the Solicitor General passes on all appeals from District Courts to Courts of Appeals. The United States Attorney may feel, frequently with reason, that "We wuz robbed." But the case may be a poor one to serve as a test; although it can, in all likelihood, be won on appeal, it may have overtones that will make it unappealing or undesirable as a vehicle on certiorari later on; those are considerations that the Solicitor General, with his finger constantly on the pulse of Supreme Court trends, can better appreciate and hence better evaluate. In short, the United States Government, in its appellate work, employs virtually independent appellate counsel.

Interestingly enough, lawyers who enter the Department with doubts about this practice become converted after they have seen it in operation. The following is from a letter by former Assistant Attorney General Rice, then in charge of the Tax Division, who commented on this chapter when it first appeared in a legal periodical:

> As you know, we have long had separate Trial and Appellate Sections in this Division. I was not accustomed to this division of functions when I came here for, although I came from a large New York City firm, the practice there was generally to have the lawyer who tried the case argue the appeal. I am convinced, however, from close association with the work here, that there is merit in the separation of responsibilities, mainly for the reason that the effective trial lawyer is all too often not an effective appellate pleader and *vice versa*. I think there are times when the appellate lawyer, working from a cold record, loses some of the color of the case or tends to isolate issues without sufficient emphasis on the whole factual picture. By and large, however, I believe that the separation of functions is clearly advisable in any activity having volume litigation.[7]

Section 157. Appellate specialization in United States Attorneys' offices.—The same trend is evident in the larger United States Attorneys' offices. In the smaller offices that are located in districts where the work-load is fairly light, the Assistant United States Attorney who tried the Government's case will be expected

---

[7] Letter from the Hon. Charles K. Rice, July 30, 1959.

to handle the case on appeal. However, in the busier districts—
and those include the large centers of population—successive
United States Attorneys have found that they obtain better results
by setting up an appellate bureau or section, whose members brief
and argue on appeal the cases that their colleagues from the civil
and criminal sections have tried.

This division of function, however desirable or useful, is not
rigid. By and large, however, it has been found to be helpful. Assistant United States Attorneys who specialize in appeals find they
enjoy greater ease in participating in colloquies with the appellate
judges than those of their associates who appear only occasionally
in the Court of Appeals. Similarly, the appellate specialists find it
less difficult to meet effectively issues that concern and disturb that
court. And, preeminently in criminal cases, whenever an appellant complains of the conduct of the prosecution, it conduces to a
more objective argument if that conduct is defended by an Assistant United States Attorney who did not participate in the trial.

The Hon. Oliver Gasch, then United States Attorney for the
District of Columbia, kindly furnished a memorandum articu-
lating his reasons for establishing an Appellate Section in his
office; it warrants quotation in full:

It has been my experience as United States Attorney for the District of Columbia that it is most necessary and desirable to establish and
maintain an Appellate Section in this office. Annually, for the past several years, we have been responsible for processing around 300 appeals.
The large majority of these appellate cases are in the United States
Court of Appeals for the District of Columbia Circuit. Approximately
60% of them are criminal cases which in this unique federal district
run the gamut from ordinary common law offenses to prosecutions
based on general federal criminal statutes. On the civil side there is
also great diversity in the subject matter of these cases. Most of them
involve efforts to enjoin the action of the heads of the Executive
Branch of our Government. Quite a few Federal Tort Claims cases
reach the appellate stage.

Assistant United States Attorneys, who by reason of their training,
experience, and scholarly inclinations are assigned to the Appellate
Division of the office, have demonstrated that they can most effectively
represent the Government at this level. Our trial men carry a heavy
load of trial cases. Most of them are in court in connection with trial
matters each day. To expect them to brief and argue appellate matters
in addition to assuming their trial obligations would, in my judgment,

be expecting the impossible. This year, however, we have determined to have each trial man argue at least one appeal. Our reason for doing this is that it seems desirable to have trial men experience some of the difficulties encountered at the appellate level. I think it will cause them to be more concerned about the problem of making a good record.

Generally, however, the objective approach of the appellate advocate is more effective and more efficient. Appellate specialists are more familiar with the appellate rules, procedures, and the many applicable precedents in the appellate courts. Their presentation is more direct and less time consuming. Their ability to answer effectively the questions propounded during oral argument often spells the difference between sustaining one's position and being reversed.

Section 158. Appellate specialization in a large public law office.—The same differentiation between trial and appellate lawyers was similarly found desirable in one of the busiest public law offices in the world, that of the Corporation Counsel of the City of New York. Some years ago, Judge Paxton Blair, who for about a decade was Chief of the Division of Appeals in that office (and who is now Solicitor General of the State of New York), wrote as follows:

> I have always held that the trial man is *not the best man* to handle the appeal, but may even be the worst. * * * In the office of the District Attorney, New York County, a case taken to an appellate court is handed over to what is known as the appeals division or appeals bureau, and briefed and argued by an appeals specialist.
>
> There are, to my mind, overwhelming advantages in this method of handling appeals. The appeals specialist views the case precisely as does the appellate court, through the little square window of the record, so to speak, and not as something viewed from the great outdoors. The trial man's mind cannot free itself of matters which entered in during preparation for trial but which did not get into the record, either because a witness he interviewed failed to respond to a subpoena or was not allowed to testify because of failure to establish qualifications. Or if the witness did testify, some important facts may not have been established because objections to questions were sustained.
>
> Then, too, the style of oratory a trial man develops, through his constant appeal to a jury less learned than himself, is out of place in an appellate court. A calm, conversational style is there appropriate; and

his hearers' learning exceeds his own, or at least he should conduct himself as though it did.[8]

Because of the work load, Judge Blair found it necessary to assign many appeals to the functional divisions of the Corporation Counsel's Office, where the litigation had originated. "Statistics which I kept showed that the men of the appeals division had almost twice as high a batting average as their brethren from other divisions."[9]

Section 159. Appellate specialization in private law offices.— The larger law firms—frequently referred to as law factories (though only by the outsiders) —are generally staffed with enough lawyers of broad appellate experience to permit them to meet, with their own resources, a problem that is essentially one of function and specialization. Yet even there, as will be indicated below in Section 163, the question whether a different lawyer within the office should handle the appellate phase of a case raises problems identical with those faced by an office of moderate size that is considering, in an important cause, the desirability or otherwise of consulting or retaining new counsel on appeal.

Section 160. Advantages of new counsel on appeal.—Apart from the ingrained differences between trial and appellate techniques, and even in a case that does not involve a detailed, self-contained, or esoteric specialty, appellate counsel is frequently able to bring new ideas and a freshness of approach into a case that has already run a long course. No matter how able or talented a particular lawyer may be, after the same individual has prepared a case, presented it to a trial court, and then briefed and argued it on appeal, he will be pretty stale in his thinking if a second briefing and a second argument at another level are required on top of that. Injection of new appellate counsel at that stage is not in any sense a reflection on original counsel; it is a recognition, among other considerations, of the fact that repetition makes for dullness and that a fresh mind may well be able to introduce a new and hence a more effective approach to what has become rather more than a twice-told tale.

---

[8] Blair, *Appellate Briefs and Advocacy*, 18 Ford. L. Rev. 30, 46-47.
[9] *Id.*, note 38, 18 Ford. L. Rev. at 47.

Indeed, even experienced appellate lawyers who have lived rather too long with a particular case are often eager to bring in a colleague for a fresh viewpoint, or to consult with friends on a law faculty for the same reason.

The foregoing considerations are particularly pertinent in connection with Federal litigation. Thus, a case before a regulatory agency starts before the trial examiner, goes to the commission or board, then is reviewed by a Court of Appeals (or a three-judge District Court), then is sought to be reviewed by the Supreme Court on petition for certiorari or jurisdictional statement, and, if review is granted, is finally presented on the merits. And that is the usual, not the unusual, travel of such a controversy, and of many others, as, for instance, civil tax cases. Very, very few lawyers can avoid the dullness, the warmed-over undertones, the effect of stale-sounding canned reasoning that inevitably accompany such a reiteration of arguments.

Section 161. New appellate counsel in the Supreme Court of the United States.—Finally, if the appeal in question—whether the first, or the second, or even the fourth—is taken to a court with whose reactions and current tendencies original counsel is unacquainted, it is generally advisable to retain appellate counsel who is. It is this principle that underlies the centralization of the Government's Supreme Court litigation in the Solicitor General's office. And, even more than in briefs and arguments on the merits, the one-shot written argument made in a petition for certiorari or a jurisdictional statement on appeal requires an intimate knowledge of the Supreme Court's standards for review.

On this subject, a decade's additional experience leads me only to repeat what I wrote in 1950:

I might make the following additional observation about Petitions for Certiorari and similar briefs seeking discretionary review, namely, that they constitute, certainly for the uninitiated, the most difficult form of written argumentation: They must persuade a court, not so much that the ruling below was wrong, but that it warrants review. This view is confirmed, substantially without dissent, by most of my former colleagues in the Department of Justice who deal with Supreme Court briefs, and by my own experience under controlled conditions, viz., returning to the law after nearly five years' service in the Army: I felt able to write a brief on the merits the day I reverted to civilian status, and in fact plunged right into the process of writing one before that day was out; but it took me six months more to get into the swing of composing an acceptable Petition for Certiorari.[10]

The same considerations are of course equally applicable to the writing of Jurisdictional Statements in cases on appeal.[11]

Section 162. Use of appellate counsel at the trial level.— There is one other situation in which it may be helpful to retain appellate counsel, namely, in the important case involving large sums or large principles—and there the retainer should precede the appeal, while the record can still be shaped with the appeal in mind.

This other situation is not that of the "Big Case" exclusively; by no means. For bigness is relative, and the remarks that follow are not addressed to the familiar if happily infrequent instance of the monster antitrust litigation with its galaxy of talent,[12] but to the far more usual and indeed not uncommon case, whose facts can by and large be established without too much difficulty, but whose essential problem is that of shaping a record so as to sustain a carefully formulated proposition of law on appeal—in this instance, on the inevitable appeal, which both sides are prepared to take if the judgment is adverse to either.

Too often—far too often—appellate counsel is called in at the hospital stage, when the case is in the last stages of terminal illness. Similarly, too often appellate counsel finds that an essentially sound case has been seriously weakened by careless handling that did not have the record on appeal in mind.

I am not suggesting for a moment the second-guessing of trial counsel, the hindsight as to that famous just-one-more-last-question on cross-examination. As to these and similar unavoidable risks of a trial, appellate counsel must take the record as Cromwell preferred his portrait—warts and all. Compare Section 28, *supra*. But if, when the litigation starts, it is obvious that there is a great

---

[10] *Effective Appellate Advocacy,* pp. 241-242.

[11] See Stern and Gressman, *Supreme Court Practice* (2d ed. 1954) ch. VI (F), pp. 233-246.

[12] "The court judicially recognizes an array of talent seldom equalled in history." *United States* v. *E. I. du Pont de Nemours & Co.,* 13 F.R.D. 487, 489 (E.D. Ill.) ; for the decision on the merits, see *United States* v. *du Pont & Co.,* 353 U. S. 586; for the final decree, see *United States* v. *E. I. du Pont de Nemours & Co.,* 177 F. Supp. 1 (N.D. Ill.) , probable jurisdiction noted, 362 U. S. 986.

deal at stake; that the case is certain to be appealed, regardless of outcome; and that the ultimate result will turn on questions of law, then the time for appellate counsel to assist is at the outset, when he can consult with trial counsel and work with them with a view to making up the record for the ultimate appeal.

Such work will include research on the law, not the once-over-lightly that all too commonly precedes a trial, but extensive study of the uncharted areas and the factors that may be expected to affect the appellate court in those areas. Before the trial, these labors will also include the preparation of trial briefs, and memoranda on the admissibility of disputed but highly material evidence. During the trial, appellate counsel will advise on the making or withholding of objections and on offers of evidence that will adequately safeguard the client's legal position before the appellate court. Thus appellate counsel assists in shaping the record that he will later defend, and in addition avoids what is so fruitless for the client, the brilliant trial victory doomed to reversal on appeal because of errors in the record.

Here also, the foregoing suggestions have been found helpful in important cases. Once more to quote from Assistant Attorney General Rice's letter,

> I was particularly interested in your remarks as to the use of appellate counsel at the trial stage. You may be interested to know that in a recent, well publicized criminal case, we assigned a lawyer from our Appellate Section to work with the trial lawyers at the outset of the case for the very reasons outlined in your article. This case is now on appeal and we believe that we will derive substantial advantages from the participation of the appellate lawyer at the trial level. As far as I know, this is the first time we have done this and, in view of our manpower shortage, we could not do it often. But if the experiment proves as successful as we hope it will (we feel that we have already received definite benefits at the trial stage), it may be worth repeating in other important cases, particularly where it is evident from the beginning that significant questions of law are present in the case.[13]

Section 163. Considerations underlying retainer of new appellate counsel.—Of course, the run-of-the-mill lawsuit will not support such an elaborate and—necessarily—expensive apparatus. In many, many cases, all too plainly, what is involved will barely

---

[13] Note 7, *supra*.

yield a reasonable fee to a single lawyer. But in a substantial zone of cases on appeal, the question whether to retain new appellate counsel necessarily arises.

First, should someone else be retained at all? That question includes the subsidiary inquiry, in the large law firm of diverse talents, whether a different partner should be entrusted with the appeal, regardless of his personal relationship either to the client or to the subject-matter of the controversy. The entire problem is one that must be carefully pondered, not only in the light of the considerations already outlined above, but also in its bearing on the very heart of the attorney-client relationship. For, if the client can afford first-rate professional assistance at the appellate level, and his trial counsel who lacks appellate experience insists on arguing the case—either on the basis that "This is the first time I have ever had a case in the Supreme Court, and I don't intend to lose that opportunity," or else on the view that "I have fought this all the way and so I propose to see it through"—there is a genuine conflict between the interests of the client and the interests of the lawyer.

Second, if it is decided to retain someone else, who? The "big name" lawyer who will not read the record? Or the lawyer who is somehow supposed "to have the ear of the court"? Both are equally without utility. One Justice of the Supreme Court wrote in an opinion, "Intrinsic professional competence alone matters. The name or fame of counsel plays no part whatever in the attention paid to argument, and is wholly irrelevant to the outcome of a case." [14] Another declared in a published lecture that "it is a grave mistake to choose counsel for some supposed influence or the enchantment of political reputation, and, above all, avoid the lawyer who thinks he is so impressively eminent that he need give no time to preparation except while he is on a plane going to Washington. Believe me when I say that what impresses the Court is a lawyer's argument, not his eminence." [15]

Third, if it is determined to proceed with the lawyers already in the case, is there any advantage to seniority unrelated to professional competence? In other words, does the very real importance of a case mean that it cannot be entrusted to anyone

[14] Dennis v. United States, 340 U. S. 887, per Frankfurter, J.

[15] Jackson, Advocacy Before the Supreme Court: Suggestions for Effective Case Presentations, 37 A.B.A.J. 801, 802.

junior to the senior partner, or the general counsel, or the assistant attorney general?

Here again, a proper answer turns on function and specialization. The person best qualified to conduct an orchestra is not necessarily the most competent soloist; and the talents—or the accidents—that make X the appropriate and indeed logical choice to head a law firm or a government law bureau may be entirely irrelevant to technical appellate competence. Conversely, the ablest advocate may be quite unable to direct or administer even a small group of lawyers or to formulate policies that reach beyond litigation tactics or strategy.

Whatever may be the case as to appellate briefs, where cooperative effort is always helpful, appellate argument is necessarily a solo performance. If counsel is unprepared, if counsel lacks a firm grasp of the controlling issues, if counsel becomes flustered to the point of sputtering silence by questions from the bench, then the little slips his associates hand him—the only help anyone can offer at that juncture—will not rehabilitate either him or his argument. See Section 113, *supra*. In today's complex society, there is wide scope for the talents of the organization man, but appellate argument is not his pigeon; the man on his feet arguing an appeal must be a self-contained individualist.

If the bar gave as much consideration to the selection of appellate counsel as is now generally given to the selection of trial counsel, there would be fewer arguments in appellate courts by lawyers whose talents lie in other directions, and hence far less "not good" arguments than are now heard. The cynical comment that "Many a rich client has a poor lawyer" was uttered by a distinguished appellate judge, since deceased. Considering what is at stake when cases are on appeal, it is indeed surprising why there has not been universal acceptance of the obvious criterion for selecting counsel on appeal, namely, that "Intrinsic professional competence alone matters."

Section 164. Should new appellate counsel be selected on the strength of his percentage of victories?—A baseball manager will —and should—select pitchers on the strength of their won and lost records, other players on the basis of batting averages. But an appellate lawyer's percentage of wins is apt to be irrelevant in any consideration of his qualities.

I once knew a Solicitor General of the United States—not, be it noted, one of the ablest incumbents of the position—who was inordinately proud of his percentage of cases won. But his pride was doubly misplaced. First, the volume of litigation in that Office is such, and the winning cases generally so obvious, that anyone with the right to pick his own vehicles for argument is well nigh certain, quite regardless of his qualities or lack of them, to win at least nine out of ten. Second, this gentleman in fact lost a number of cases that might well have gone the other way, and that advocates more generously endowed with forensic talent in all likelihood would have won.

Moreover, when we consider private litigation, it is at once apparent that the lawyer with a case that will probably be won is not going to retain an appellate specialist; those lads will be retained only in the difficult matters, the uphill fights and the forlorn hopes, areas in which batting averages necessarily tend to be low.

Here is a wry comment on that point from Professor Samuel Williston's delightful autobiography:

> I may add in reference to the frequency with which my aid was unavailing to lawyers who sought my assistance, that it was not generally sought unless the case was one of some desperation. In cases that are easily won, lawyers generally prefer to keep the labor and the compensation entirely to themselves.[16]

To the same effect is a passage from Augustus Garland's musings, written after he had argued *over 130 cases* in the Supreme Court: [17]

> In casting up the account of loss and gain in the foregoing list, the balance is rather against me: I have lost more than I gained. * * *
>
> Upon one occasion, on opinion day, the tide ran so heavily against me, losing about five cases and gaining not one, I was quite ill at ease and moody. Coming out of the court, I got in with Judge Harlan [18] and passing the civilities of the day, he asked me how I felt and I told him

---

[16] Williston, *Life and Law* (1940) 287.

[17] Appropriately enough, he was stricken on January 26, 1899, while arguing *Towson* v. *Moore*, 173 U. S. 17, in the Supreme Court, and died in the Clerk's office the same day. See 172 U. S. 651; 43 L. ed. 598, note; J. Sup. Ct., Oct. T. 1898, pp. 101-102. He was also the protagonist of *Ex parte Garland*, 4 Wall. 333.

[18] The elder.

quite badly, and the reason for it, and that I did not believe I could even get an attorney enrolled in that court any more, and recalled to him my fate on that day. He chided me somewhat, and remarked it was not unusual with the very best lawyers, and told me of his observation here and elsewhere that bad or difficult cases fell to the lot of good lawyers, and they were sought for to deal with just such cases.[19]

It will be appropriate, by way of summary, to conclude with a short sentence from the pen of one who was first an outstanding advocate, and then a great judge, the late Mr. Justice Jackson:

A lawyer's stock in trade is not merely that he always wins his cases, but that he puts up a good fight.[20]

---

[19] Garland, *Experience in the U. S. Supreme Court* (1898) 91-92.
[20] Gerhart, *America's Advocate: Robert H. Jackson* (1958) 44.

FIFTH PART

SOME ILLUSTRATIVE EXAMPLES

CHAPTER XII

USE OF THE STATEMENT OF FACTS TO AD-VANCE ONE'S CASE: SUCCESSIVE BRIEFS IN THE SAME LAWSUIT

Section 165. Comments on the two briefs included herein.— Here are set forth the Statement portions of the briefs discussed in Section 27, above, which illustrate how the Statement of Facts can advance, or fail to advance, a lawyer's case, and which illustrate as well, see Section 79, above, the dangers inherent in the practice of excessive footnoting.

The first Statement of Facts is taken from the Brief in Opposition in *Von Moltke* v. *Gillies,* certiorari granted, 331 U. S. 800, to review 161 F. 2d 113 (C.A. 6). Here the Government's case was lost, literally, because both petitioner's self-contradictions, which were numerous and significant, as well as the denials of her belatedly fashioned story, were all placed in the footnotes. Otherwise stated, all of her allegations were given a preferred billing, while all of the denials were placed in a secondary position.

The second Statement of Facts is from the respondent's briefs on the merits in the same case, which after argument was reversed for further proceedings. 332 U. S. 708. The second State-ment of Facts reflects the identical record, but it is differently organized—and it is the change in organization and arrangement that, without a single word of editorial comment, made evident the Government's strongest affirmative argument, viz., the many discrepancies in, and hence the inherent improbability of, peti-tioner's story.

A caveat should be entered here. If these examples are to be of the slightest use to the student or practitioner of advocacy, he must first steep himself in the facts of the case. At the outset, be-fore turning to the briefs at all, he must read the opinions at 161 F. 2d 113, because those opinions pose the problem that faced the brief-writer. Next, the advocate should turn to the two briefs that follow, and ask himself whether and in what respects one is better than the other. I have already indicated why I think the second superior to the first. Perhaps the reader will disagree; fine, provided he comes up with reasoned grounds for thinking the contrary. (I should add that I have no personal axe to grind in this matter, for while I did argue the case, I did not write either Statement of Facts.)

Of course, if you already consider yourself an accomplished and expert brief-writer, you can skip this entire chapter. But if you feel that you still want to learn something about the process, you will simply have to sit down and soak yourself in the details of this case and in the two ways in which its problems were sought to be met. For it is one of the inescapable facts of the brief-writing business that its principles are meaningful only as they are related to a concrete controversy.

Just a word as to the sequel: When the case was heard again, the trial judge disbelieved petitioner and discharged her writ of habeas corpus. *Re Von Moltke,* Civil No. 5542, E.D. Mich., July 19, 1949. On appeal the Court of Appeals once more affirmed, the same judge still dissenting. *Von Moltke v. United States,* 189 F. 2d 56 (C.A. 6). Again the Supreme Court granted certiorari, but this time there was an affirmance by an equally divided Court. 343 U. S. 922.

So, in the end, Mrs. Von Moltke lost in the courts. But she ultimately had the last word, because on June 11, 1954, the deportation proceedings against her were terminated.* Ironically enough, her co-defendant, Mrs. Behrens, who is mentioned throughout both Statements of Facts, failed to convince even a single judge that she had received the same "advice" as Mrs. Von Moltke. See *Behrens v. Hironimus,* 170 F. 2d 627 (C.A. 4).

Section 166. Statement of Facts from the brief in opposition to the petition for certiorari in *Von Moltke v. Gillies.*

[*2] STATEMENT

On September 17, 1943 (see R. 17), an indictment was filed in the District Court for the Eastern District of Michigan charging that petitioner and others conspired to transmit to the German Reich materials and information relating to the national defense of the United States with the intent that they be used to the injury of the United States, and to collect and publish information in respect of the movement and disposition of the armed forces, ships, aircraft, and war materials of the

---

* Information kindly supplied by the Hon. L. Paul Winings, Chief Counsel, Immigration and Naturalization Service.

United States with intent to communicate such information to the German Reich, in violation of Sections 2 and 4 of the Espionage Act of June 15, 1917, Title I, c. 30, 40 Stat. 217 (50 U.S.C. 32, 34). Forty-seven overt acts were alleged, of which five (Nos. 24, 29-32) concerned petitioner. Four of these five (Nos. 24, 30-32) charged that petitioner met and conferred with one or more of the other defendants on designated dates; the other (No. 29) charged that petitioner introduced one Arndt to another defendant. Each overt act was specifically alleged to have been committed "in pur-[*3]suance of said conspiracy and to effect the object and purpose thereof." (R. 20-34.)

Petitioner was arraigned on September 21, 1943; on the advice of an attorney appointed by the court for the purposes of arraignment only, she stood mute, and a plea of not guilty was entered on her behalf (R. 10-12, 47, 110-113). On October 7, 1943, petitioner signed a waiver of her right to counsel (R. 36), withdrew her plea of not guilty, and entered a plea of guilty (R. 159-160).

On August 7, 1944, petitioner, through counsel, moved for leave to withdraw her plea of guilty on the grounds that it was made without knowledge of her legal rights and understanding of the nature of the offense charged, and that the acceptance of the plea by the court when she was without counsel violated her right to counsel under the Sixth Amendment (R. 37). Following a hearing,[1] the motion was denied by Judge Moinet, who found that petitioner was properly advised of her constitutional rights by the court both prior to and at the time she entered her plea of guilty, that the plea was submitted after due and careful deliberation, that petitioner was advised of and thoroughly understood the nature of the charge contained in the indictment, that the plea was not due to any promises or misrepre-[*4]sentations, and that the motion for leave to withdraw the plea was not filed within the ten-day period prescribed by Rule 2(4) of the Criminal Appeals Rules (18 U.S.C., following § 688), which were then in effect (R. 46-47).

On November 15, 1944, petitioner was convicted on her plea of guilty and sentenced to imprisonment for four years (R. 8-9). So far as the record indicates, no appeal was taken.

On February 7, 1946, petitioner filed in the convicting court a petition for a writ of habeas corpus, alleging that her imprisonment was illegal in that she had been denied the assistance of counsel for her defense and had been coerced, intimidated, and deceived into pleading guilty, in violation of her constitutional rights (R. 1-7). The writ issued (R. 15-16) and a hearing was held (R. 47-170). The district

---

[1] The present record does not contain the proceedings at this hearing. It is stated in the petition for a writ of certiorari that no testimony was taken at the hearing (Pet. 12).

court (Judge O'Brien) found not only that petitioner, "an intelligent, mentally acute woman" (R. 174), who was "obviously of good education and above the average in intelligence" and who had a "fluent and ample" knowledge of English (R. 171), had failed to sustain the allegations of the petition by a preponderance of the evidence, but that the overwhelming weight of the evidence showed that she had freely, intelligently, and knowingly waived her constitutional rights (R. 170-174). The writ was accordingly dismissed, and petitioner was remanded to the respondent's custody (R. 175). On appeal to the Circuit Court of [*5] Appeals for the Sixth Circuit, the judgment of the district court was affirmed (R. 181), one judge dissenting (R. 189-198).

Petitioner testified at the hearing on the writ as follows: She was arrested on August 24, 1943, on a Presidential warrant as a dangerous enemy alien (R. 48, 50). She was living in Detroit at the time with her husband, an instructor in German at Wayne University, and two of her three children, one of whom was suffering from diabetes (R. 48, 59). At some time following her arrest, her husband was suspended from his $4,000-per-annum teaching position and later got a job paying $35 per week (R. 168). In addition to her household duties, petitioner was a member of the Red Cross and a local Parent-Teachers Association, engaged in social work at a Y.W.C.A. International Center, and participated in such voluntary work as gasoline and sugar rationing (R. 89-90). Following her arrest, she was questioned from August 24 to August 27 by two agents of the Federal Bureau of Investigation, both of whom were courteous and friendly to her (R. 49). On September 18, 1943, a copy of the indictment involved herein (see *supra*, p. 2) was handed to her; she read it, but did not understand it (R. 50). On September 21, 1943, she was taken before Judge Moinet to be arraigned; she was advised by the judge that she was entitled to counsel; she stated that she had no money, and the judge said he would appoint counsel for her. A lawyer who [*6] was in the courtroom was appointed as her attorney for the purposes of arraignment only; the lawyer did not see the indictment, but merely asked her how she wished to plead, to which she replied, "Not guilty"; on the lawyer's advice, she stood mute when arraigned, and a plea of not guilty was entered for her.[2] The judge then told her that he "would appoint an attorney

---

[2] Archie Katcher, the attorney appointed by Judge Moinet to represent petitioner at her arraignment, testified that he talked to petitioner in a whispered conversation for a few minutes; that he asked her and a codefendant whom he was also representing, "both at once, whether they understood what this was all about"; that one of them said she did understand, and the other indicated that she too understood; that both indicated they felt they were not guilty; and that he advised them to stand mute when arraigned (R. 110-113).

right away," from which she understood that "the gentlemen was to be expected to come right away"; she was then taken to Wayne County Jail. (R. 51-53.)

Between September 23 and October 7, 1943, the date on which she pleaded guilty, petitioner further testified, agents Kirby, Dunham, Hanaway, and Collard of the F.B.I. came daily to the cell block where she and two female codefendants were incarcerated (R. 53). The agents and the three defendants would engage in "conversations and discussions" concerning "things of interest," such as "hostile publicity, and sentiment, and cost of the trial, and the inquisition of the Federal Judge" (R. 53-54). On one or more of these [*7] occasions, petitioner asked Dunham, "Is it really so bad, that the public is so hostile?"; "* * * if we go to Court, will we be bodily attacked?" Dunham would reply, "It is war time—you have to bear that in mind. Public sentiment grows from war hysteria. You don't need to be afraid; you will be protected." This left her with "the thought that it is terrible to go to court and face a hostile public." (R. 82-83.) [3] On another such occasion, petitioner heard Kirby tell Mrs. Behrens, a codefendant who had pleaded guilty, that "the other defendants" in the case would plead guilty the following week; petitioner asked Kirby whether, if the other defendants pleaded guilty, she would "get a trial for myself"; Kirby replied that he "could not answer this question because he did not know if this would be all right with the prosecuting attorney" (R. 85). [4]

Petitioner also testified that on September 25, 1943, two attorneys conferred with her at the request of her husband for some two and one-half hours (R. 56, 92). One of the attorneys, Okrent, "inquired was I to have counsel," and she [*8] replied that Judge Moinet was going to appoint counsel for her (R. 93). She talked only to Okrent; the other attorney, Berger, "was just sitting there" (R. 92). She at no time asked the attorneys anything about her case (R. 95); the discussion was exclusively concerned with her family affairs (R. 93). [5]

---

[3] Dunham denied that he ever advised or suggested to petitioner that "public feeling was running high" in connection with the case (R. 154).

[4] Kirby testified that when petitioner asked him about her right to a trial in the event the other defendants pleaded guilty, he replied that "the question of the trial would be up to the United States Attorney's office," and might also have stated that he "knew no reason why she should not be tried without the others" (R. 134-135).

[5] Berger testified that, though Okrent "did most of the talking," he also talked to petitioner (R. 114), and, it would appear, quite extensively. He interrogated petitioner as to the charges that had been made against her (R. 114); he would read to petitioner parts of the indictment referring to her, and put her through "a form of cross-examination" (R. 119); the purpose of the interview was to discuss "this case" with her, and not family matters pri-

On or about September 27, 1943 (R. 56), petitioner further testified, she summoned agent Collard for the purpose of obtaining from him "some information as to the indictment. I didn't understand that." Up to that time she had received no advice concerning the indictment. She told Collard that "he has taken my statement and he knew that * * * I didn't do those [*9] things which are called 'Over' Acts." (R. 54-55, 69.) Collard told her that the indictment did not "cover the charge" (R. 55), that it did not "mean much of anything" (R. 76), that "those charges don't mean a thing" (R. 77). He then explained the indictment to her "by an example which he called 'Rum Runners,' " and which she understood as follows: "* * * if there is a group of people in a 'Rum' plan who violate the law, and another person is there and the person doesn't know the people who are planning the violation and doesn't know what is going on, but still * * * this plan is carried out, in the law the man who was present * * * nevertheless is guilty of conspiracy." She then told Collard, "If that is the law in the United States, I don't know how I ever can prove myself innocent, and how will any judge know how am I guilty if this is the law?" Collard then explained about the "Probation Department" and its functions. (R. 55.) Petitioner believed that Collard was qualified to explain the indictment to her because she knew he was a lawyer (R. 56).[6]

[*10] As a result, apparently, of something told her by Mrs. Behrens, the codefendant who pleaded guilty, petitioner began to fear, she further testified, that if she did not "fall in line and plead guilty," her husband would be implicated, as well as herself (R. 60-62). She asked Collard if that was true, and Collard said that "he couldn't an-

---

marily (R. 118); petitioner talked about her family affairs, such as how her husband "was getting along, and whether he would be reinstated," etc. (R. 117), but also talked "About this case, about the indictment, or the conspiracy under the Espionage Act. We wanted to know the whole story, and I presume she told us" (R. 115); the "question of pleading guilty came up" and Berger told her "if you are guilty, plead guilty; and if you are not, do not" (R. 120). The attorneys made it clear, however, that they were not acting as attorneys, but merely as friends of petitioner's husband (R. 116).

[6] Collard, an attorney who had practiced law (R. 140), testified that at petitioner's request, he spent several hours discussing the indictment with her (R. 139-140, 141); that he attempted to explain the nature of a conspiracy to the best of his ability (R. 142); that he could not recall petitioner's asking him to explain the meanings of "feloniously" and "overt act," but that if she did, he probably tried to explain them (R. 143-144); that he was unable to recall his use of any "rum runner" illustration, though he might have used [* 10] such an illustration (R. 142-143); that it was possible that petitioner asked him whether "merely conferring with people who later turned out to be guilty of criminal acts would also make her a criminal" but he could not recall such a question (R. 144).

swer that question" (R. 61). On September 28, 1943, she said to agent Hanaway, "As the matter stands, and as I understand the situation, I am supposed to plead guilty"; she told him she was "willing to cooperate,"[7] but wanted assurance from Assistant United States Attorney Babcock, who was handling the prosecution, of three things—that the publicity concerning the case would be stopped immediately, that she would be incarcerated, if at all, in an institution near Detroit, and that she would never be deported. Hanaway agreed to convey her message to Babcock. Later the same day, petitioner was taken to the marshal's office, where she conferred with Babcock. She told Babcock that she understood "the situation" and knew that he wanted her to plead guilty; that if she pleaded guilty it was [*11] only "to cooperate," and not because she was guilty, which she was not.[8] She then repeated her three "conditions" to Babcock. (R. 58-59.) Because, however, "the answer Mr. Babcock gave me was not fully satisfactory,"[9] and because she was advised by her husband, in a conference with him at about the same time as her visit with Babcock, not to do anything without consulting a lawyer, petitioner decided not to plead guilty that day, and told Babcock that she wanted "to think the whole situation over" (R. 60, 103-104).

Notwithstanding her husband's advice, petitioner further testified, she did not consult a lawyer (R. 65). After further reflection, she finally made up her mind to plead guilty even though she knew she was innocent (R. 64). Accordingly, on October 7, 1943, she talked to Babcock again and told him she was ready to plead guilty. She repeated to him that her plea would be made notwithstanding her knowledge of inno-[*12]cence.[10] Babcock accordingly took her before Judge Lederle

---

[7] Hanaway testified that he had no recollection of petitioner's ever having said that she was pleading guilty because she wanted to cooperate (R. 123, 124).

[8] Babcock testified that petitioner at no time stated to him that she wished to plead guilty in order to cooperate, or that she wanted to plead guilty even though she was not guilty (R. 159).

[9] Babcock testified that he made it very clear to petitioner that he had no control over the publicity connected with the case, her place of incarceration if she pleaded guilty, or the matter of her possible deportation, and could therefore give her no assurance whatever in respect of the three "conditions" she sought to attach to her proffered plea of guilty (R. 158-159, 163-164). Hanaway also testified that Babcock made this clear to petitioner (R. 123, 124-125).

[10] Babcock specifically contradicted this testimony of petitioner (see note 8, *supra*, p. 11). Collard, who was present at this second interview between Babcock and petitioner, testified that he was "absolutely positive" that petitioner did not state, either to Babcock or to himself, that she wanted to plead guilty even though she was not guilty, or in order to cooperate with the Government, but, on the contrary, that she stated she wanted to plead guilty because she was guilty (R. 138).

because Judge Moinet was not in court that day. (R. 65.) Judge Lederle asked her if the indictment had been explained to her, and she replied in the affirmative, though it had not been (R. 67-68). According to her testimony, he also asked her if she was pleading guilty because she felt she was guilty, and she said, "Yes," though this was not true (R. 68). A "note" was handed to her to sign; at first she objected to signing it because it mentioned something about a trial which she did not want; Babcock told her it was all right to sign it, however, so she did (R. 66-67).[11] Judge Lederle then accepted her plea of guilty (R. 72). In a conversation with agents Dunham and Kirby shortly after pleading guilty, [*13] petitioner told them "even then" that she "should not have pled guilty"; that she "had done the wrong thing in pleading guilty" because she was not guilty (R. 72-73).[12]

"Around Christmas," 1943, petitioner further testified, she learned that it was permissible for a defendant to withdraw a plea of guilty (R. 73).[13] Shortly after Christmas, she learned for the first time from Okrent, one of the attorneys who visited her in jail (supra, pp. 7-8), and who eventually represented her in her motion to withdraw her plea of guilty (see R. 37), of a defendant's presumption of innocence and of the fact that, contrary to her prior understanding, a defendant who pleads guilty may not appeal his case (R. 73).

On cross-examination, petitioner testified that after having read the indictment, she definitely felt that she was innocent of the charges contained in it, though she did not know what those charges were (R. 90–91). She admitted that she repeatedly asked the F.B.I. agents for advice as to how to plead, because "There was nobody else I could ask." She denied that the agents ever told her to consult her attorney.[14] She denied that she [*14] ever told the agents that she did not want an attorney.[15] She denied that she ever told the agents that she did not

---

[11] This "note" was a formal waiver of her right to counsel (see R. 36). Babcock testified that Judge Lederle "was extremely careful and meticulous to make sure, as he always does, that [petitioner] understood what she was doing." He further testified that the judge "interrogated her as to whether she wished to have counsel represent her and advised her as to signing a waiver of that right. * * * I wish to say again that I have no distinct recollection now —let me put it this way: if any of our Judges have missed doing that, I would have remembered that very distinctly." (R. 166).

[12] Kirby contradicted this testimony of petitioner (R. 133). Dunham was not questioned concerning this alleged statement of petitioner.

[13] Petitioner's motion for leave to withdraw her plea of guilty was filed August 7, 1944 (supra, p. 3).

[14] Dunham (R. 147, 153), Hanaway (R. 128-129), and Kirby (R. 131-132) all testified that they/advised petitioner to consult counsel about her case.

[15] Kirby testified that when he told petitioner she should consult an attorney, she "jerked her shoulders, and said she was not interested; that she wanted to make up her own mind" (R. 132). Collard testified that on more

want the attorney her husband had sent. (R. 96.)[16] She denied that she ever told the agents that she had had arguments with her husband regarding the matter of retaining an attorney (R. 98).[17] She denied that Babcock ever told her that she should not plead guilty in reliance on any of the three "conditions" she had expressed to him.[18] Asked if she did not know, from the fact that her husband told her she should not plead guilty before consulting an attorney, that she was entitled to a lawyer before pleading [*15] guilty if she wished one, she replied that she did not (R. 103). She denied knowing that she did not have to plead guilty if she did not want to (R. 103, 105-106). She admitted that, after her husband persuaded her, on the occasion of her visit with Babcock, not to plead guilty before seeing a lawyer, she thereafter made the decision to "disregard the advice that your husband had given you" and "plead guilty instead" (R. 103-104). She maintained that she told Babcock that she wished to plead guilty "Though I know I am not guilty," but only "To cooperate, to fall in line, to get it over with," [19] though she admitted that no one had requested her to do that (R. 105).

All four of the F.B.I. agents concerned testified, on behalf of the respondent, that they made no promises of any kind to induce petitioner to plead guilty (R. 122, 124, 131, 137, 147, 151, 153). All testified that petitioner kept trying to induce them to advise her whether to plead guilty or not, but they told her that that was a matter for her or her attorney to decide (R. 121, 128-129, 131-132, 135, 137, 140, 148, 152, 153). Hanaway testified that he told petitioner that "if she felt that she were innocent in her heart she should under no circumstances plead guilty" (R. 122).

[*16] Collard testified that at the time he acceded to petitioner's request that he explain the indictment to her she had a copy of the indictment, had read it, and had the paragraphs pertaining to her circled or otherwise marked (R. 140, 142). He further testified that he be-

---

than one occasion petitioner told him she did not want an attorney (R. 137). Dunham testified that petitioner told him that her husband "was very determined she should have an attorney," but that she felt that the problem of whether to plead guilty or not "was a problem she wanted to decide herself" (R. 148; see also R. 153).

[16] Dunham contradicted this testimony of petitioner (R. 148, 153).

[17] Dunham testified that petitioner told him that her visits with her husband were "unpleasant" because he kept insisting she retain counsel (R. 148).

[18] Babcock testified that he told petitioner that under no circumstances should she plead guilty in reliance on anything he might say concerning the conditions on which she wished to plead guilty, and that she would have to make her decision with respect to her plea "on the basis of whether or not in her own conscience she had to say that she was guilty" (R. 159).

[19] See note 8, *supra*, p. 11.

lieved that petitioner's plea of guilty was made "after due consideration with a full and complete understanding of the charge made
against her" (R. 146; see also R. 147).

Babcock testified that he cautioned petitioner that her decision
whether to plead guilty or not should depend solely on her feeling of
guilt or innocence; that he would never have taken her to court to enter a plea of guilty if she had told him she wished to plead guilty notwithstanding her innocence; that Judge Lederle accepted her plea of
guilty only after proceeding "in the normal way"; that the "normal
way" was for the judge to ask the defendant if it was true that he
wished to plead guilty, if the plea was being tendered by reason of any
promises or threats made to him, if the plea was being made because
the defendant was guilty, and if the defendant had counsel or desired
appointed counsel; and that only upon his receiving satisfactory answers to these questions would the judge accept a plea of guilty (R.
159-160). Other pertinent testimony by Babcock and the F.B.I.
agents is set out in footnotes 3-4, 6-12, 14-18, *supra*.

Section 167. Statement of Facts from the respondent's brief on the merits in *Von Moltke* v. *Gillies*.

[*2] STATEMENT

On September 17, 1943 (see R. 17), an indictment was filed in the
District Court for the Eastern District of Michigan charging that the
petitioner and others conspired to transmit to the German Reich materials and information relating to the national defense of the United
States with the intent that they be used to the injury of the United
States, and to collect and publish information in respect of the movement and disposition of the armed forces, ships, aircraft, and war materials of the United States with intent to communicate such information to the German Reich, in violation of Sections 2 and 4 of the
Espionage Act of June 15, 1917, Title I, c. 30, 40 Stat. 217 (50 U.S.C.
32, 34). Forty-seven overt acts were alleged of which five (Nos. 24,
29-32) concerned petitioner. Four of these five (Nos. 24, 30-32)
charged that petitioner met and conferred with [*3] one or more of
the other defendants on designated dates; the other (No. 29) charged
that petitioner introduced one Arndt to another defendant. Each
overt act was specifically alleged to have been committed "in pursuance of said conspiracy and to effect the object and purpose thereof."
(R. 20-34.)

Petitioner was arraigned on September 21, 1943; on the advice of
an attorney appointed by the court for the purpose of arraignment
only, she stood mute, and a plea of not guilty was entered on her be-

half (R. 10-12, 47, 110-113). On October 7, 1943, petitioner signed a waiver of her right to counsel (R. 36), withdrew her plea of not guilty, and entered a plea of guilty (R. 35).

On August 7, 1944, petitioner, through counsel, filed a motion for leave to withdraw her plea of guilty and enter a plea of not guilty on the grounds that she was not guilty of the crime charged, that her plea of guilty was made "under circumstances of extreme emotional stress and during a time of extreme mental disturbance, without knowledge of her legal rights and without a thorough understanding of the nature of the offense charged," and that the acceptance by the court of her plea of guilty when she was without counsel violated her right to counsel under the Sixth Amendment (R. 37). Petitioner also filed an affidavit in support of this motion (R. 38-45).

[*4] Following a hearing,[1] the motion was denied by Judge Moinet, who found that petitioner was properly advised of her constitutional rights by the court both prior to and at the time she entered her plea of guilty, that the plea was submitted after due and careful deliberation, that petitioner was advised of and thoroughly understood the nature of the charge contained in the indictment, that the plea was not due to any promises or misrepresentations, and that the motion for leave to withdraw the plea was not filed within the ten-day period described by Rule 2 (4) of the Criminal Appeals Rules (18 U.S.C., following § 688), which were then in effect (R. 46-47).

On November 15, 1944, petitioner was convicted on her plea of guilty and sentenced to imprisonment for four years (R. 8-9). No appeal was taken.

Fifteen months later, on February 7, 1946, petitioner filed in the convicting court a petition for a writ of habeas corpus, alleging that her imprisonment was illegal in that she had been denied the assistance of counsel for her defense and had been coerced, intimidated, and deceived into pleading guilty, in violation of her constitutional rights (R. 1-7). The writ issued (R. 15-16) and a hearing was held at which the following testimony was adduced:

[*5] A. *The undisputed evidence.*—Petitioner was the wife of an instructor of German at Wayne University and has lived in the United States since the end of 1926 (R. 2, 48, 70). In addition to her household duties she was a member of the Red Cross and the local Parent-Teachers Association, engaged in social work at the Y.W.C.A. International Center, and participated in such voluntary work as gasoline and sugar rationing (R. 89-90).

---

[1] The present record does not contain the proceedings at this hearing. It is stated in petitioner's brief that no testimony was taken at the hearing (Br. 11). But the judge considered the affidavits on each side (cf. R. 149, 156, 146).

On August 24, 1943, she was arrested on a presidential warrant as a dangerous enemy alien and detained at an Immigration Detention Home (R. 48-50, 126). From August 24 to August 27 she was questioned by two agents of the Federal Bureau of Investigation, Collard and Hanaway (R. 49, 95, 121, 126-127, 143), and she gave them a signed statement (R. 55, 143). She was not thereafter questioned about the case (R. 95, 143). Both of the agents were courteous and friendly (R. 49).

On September 18, 1943, a copy of the indictment involved in the present proceeding was handed to petitioner, and she read it (R. 50). On September 21 she and another woman defendant were brought before Judge Moinet for arraignment. The Judge informed them that they were entitled to counsel, and when they said they had no money for counsel, he stated that he would appoint counsel for them (R. 51). The Court [*6] designated an attorney in the court room to represent them, but, when the attorney stated that he did not wish to be in the case, the judge appointed him for the purpose of arraignment only (R. 51, 110-111). The attorney engaged in a whispered conversation with the women and advised them that it would be to their advantage to stand mute rather than plead not guilty (R. 51-52, 111-112). On his advice, they stood mute and the court entered a plea of not guilty in their behalf (R. 52-53, 112).

Petitioner was then taken to the Wayne County jail (R. 53). Two other women named as defendants in the indictment occupied the same cell block (R. 53). Two other agents of the F.B.I., Kirby and Dunham, came regularly to the cell block to interrogate one of the other women, Mrs. Behrens, and Hanaway also came there occasionally. Petitioner frequently engaged in conversation with these agents. (R. 53-54, 122, 134, 147.)

On September 25, Okrent, an attorney who had been a pupil of petitioner's husband, and Okrent's partner, Berger, called on petitioner. They told her they had come at her husband's request and would let her husband know whether they would take the case. They conversed with petitioner for about 2½ hours. (R. 56-57, 91-93, 114-118.)

Either on September 27 or Octber 2, petitioner asked Collard, one of the F.B.I. agents, who had taken her statement, to call on her, and Collard did so (R. 54, 56, 140). She questioned him about [*7] the indictment and he attempted to explain it to her (R. 55, 75, 140).

On September 28 petitioner, on her own initiative, told Hanaway, another F.B.I. agent, that she would plead guilty if she would receive assurances that there would be no more publicity, that she would not be sent far away from Detroit, and that she would not be deported

(R. 58, 99-100). Hanaway said that he would relay her message to the Assistant United States Attorney, Babcock, who was in charge of the case (R. 58, 100, 123). Petitioner saw Babcock on September 28 in the Marshal's office and repeated those conditions to him (R. 58, 101, 124, 158-159). Babcock stated that he had no control over the matters presented by petitioner but that he would recommend that she be incarcerated near Detroit (R. 58-59, 101, 159). Babcock told her that the question whether to plead guilty or not rested with herself alone and that he was not permitted to influence her (R. 101, 159). She told Babcock that she was not ready to plead guilty that day (R. 60, 125). At her request she had conferred with her husband in the marshal's office, and her husband had asked her not to do anything before she saw a lawyer (R. 60, 103, 148).[2]

[*8] On October 7, petitioner decided to plead guilty (R. 63, 65). She was brought before Judge Lederle (R. 65, 138-139). The Judge at first demurred at accepting her plea because there had been an appearance of counsel in the case, but according to petitioner Babcock assured him that he could accept the plea (R. 66). Petitioner then signed a written waiver of counsel (R. 66-67) reading as follows (R. 36):

> I, Marianna von Moltke, being the defendant in the above entitled cause, having been advised by the Court of my right to be represented by counsel, and having been asked by the Court whether I desire counsel to be assigned by the Court, do hereby, in open court, voluntarily waive and relinquish my right to be represented by counsel at the trial of this cause.

The Judge asked her whether the indictment had been explained to her and she said "Yes" (R. 67-68, 107, 139). The judge asked her whether she was pleading guilty because she felt she was guilty and she replied in the affirmative (R. 68, 107-108, 139).

Petitioner admitted that the agents never threatened her or made promises to her to induce her plea of guilty (R. 99) and the agents testified that they made no threats or promises of any kind to induce her to plead guilty (R. 121, 131, 133, 136, 147).

[*9] B. *The conflicting testimony.*—The circumstances surrounding the succession of events set forth above were the subject of sharply conflicting testimony.

1. Petitioner's understanding of the indictment

Petitioner testified that she read the indictment when it was handed to her but did not understand it (R. 50).

---

[2] After first denying that her husband had received any education in law, petitioner admitted that he had received "a certain amount of education in German law before the first World War" (R. 97).

The attorney who represented her at the time of arraignment testified that he talked to petitioner and the other defendant for a few minutes, that he asked them both "whether they understood what this was all about." One of the women said "yes, they did understand, and the other indicated that she, too, understood" (R. 111).

On cross-examination of petitioner the following occurred (R. 90-91):

Q. Mrs. von Moltke, when you were served with the indictment in this case, did you read it?

A. I read it.

Q. And after you had read the indictment, did you feel you were innocent of the charges that were stated in the indictment?

A. Yes, sir, definitely so.

Q. You did not feel you were guilty of those charges that you read in the indictment?

A. I did not feel guilty of those charges in the indictment.

[*10] Q. Then you knew what the charges were in the indictment.

A. Oh, no, and so far I might explain that to you, I knew—

Q. Just answer my question.

The Court. Answer the question.

A. Yes, I knew, not what the charges were, but I knew as I said before that I saw I was accused of something of which I was not guilty. That was how I understood that.

Q. Well, you read the indictment? Isn't that right?

A. I read the indictment.

Q. And you felt you were innocent of the charges that were described in the indictment?

A. And the overt acts.

Q. And the overt acts?

A. Yes.

2. The visit of attorneys Okrent and Berger.

Petitioner testified that when Okrent and Berger called on her on September 25 at her husband's request, she discussed only family affairs with them, that she talked only to Okrent, and that Berger "was just sitting there" (R. 92-95). She said that Okrent asked her if she was to have counsel and that she replied that Judge Moinet was going to appoint counsel for her (R. 93).

Berger took the stand on petitioner's behalf. He testified that he and Okrent, an associate in [*11] his law firm, went to see petitioner at the request of her husband (R. 114). While Okrent "did most of the talking," Berger also talked to petitioner (R. 114). He interrogated petitioner as to the charges that had been made against her (R.

114), and examined her insofar as the indictment affected her (R. 119). He would read to petitioner parts of the indictment referring to her, and put her through a "a form of cross-examination" (R. 119). The purpose of the interview was to discuss "this case" with her, and not family matters primarily (R. 118). Petitioner talked about her family affairs, such as how her husband "was getting along, and whether he would be reinstated," etc. (R. 117), but also talked "About this case, about the indictment, or the conspiracy under the Espionage Act. We wanted to know the whole story, and I presume she told us" (R. 115). The discussion "was all around the case, and the incidental phases of the case" (R. 119). The "question of pleading guilty came up" and Berger told her "if you are guilty, plead guilty; and if you are not, do not" (R. 120). The attorneys made it clear, however, that they were not acting as attorneys, but merely as friends of petitioner's husband (R. 116).

3. The discussions with the F.B.I. agents

Petitioner testified that between September 23 and the time of her plea of guilty the F.B.I. agents visited her cell block daily, and that after ques-[*12]tioning Mrs. Behrens, a codefendant, they would engage in conversations with the women concerning "things of interest" such as the "hostile publicity, and sentiment, and cost of the trial, and the inquisition of the Federal Judge, and the—oh things which were in the interest of the trial, and our present state" (R. 53-54). On one of these occasions, petitioner testified, she asked Dunham, "Is it really so bad, that the public is so hostile?"; "* * * if we go to Court, will we be bodily attacked?" Dunham replied "It is war time—you have to bear that in mind. Public sentiment grows from war hysteria. You don't need to be afraid; you will be protected." This left her with "the thought that it is terrible to go to court and face a hostile public." (R. 82-83.) On another occasion, petitioner said, she heard Kirby tell Mrs. Behrens, who had pleaded guilty, that "the other defendants" in the case would plead guilty the following week; petitioner asked Kirby whether, if the other defendants pleaded guilty, she would "get a trial for myself"; Kirby replied that he "could not answer this question because he did not know if this would be all right with the prosecuting attorney" (R. 85).

Dunham, Kirby and Hanaway testified that they did engage in conversation with the three women defendants (R. 122, 134, 147). Hanaway testified that he was present in petitioner's cell block on only a few occasions and that at such times there was "general discussion among the [*13] three ladies" which "centered about whether they were going to plead guilty, or they were going to trial, or what was going to happen." "They were all trying to make up their minds."

Hanaway told petitioner that "if she felt that she were innocent in her heart she should under no circumstances plead guilty." (R. 122.) On one occasion petitioner asked him to explain the indictment to her, and he refused, saying, "Mrs. von Moltke, I am not a criminal attorney, and I do not want to attempt to explain this indictment to you." He further told her that "she should either have her attorney, or the United States Attorney explain it to her." (R. 121, 129.)

Dunham testified that petitioner kept "endeavoring to get advice or information from me, or opinions," but that he declined to advise her (R. 151). She avidly read newspaper items concerning her case and "made many insinuations" on the basis of them (R. 151-152). She asked him "what her chances were in case she went to trial," and he told her he could not answer. She "went so far as to ask me if I could cite a similar case and advise her what the outcome was and I told her I could not." (R. 152.) She asked him if he knew whether Dr. Thomas, a codefendant, would plead guilty or not, and he told her he did not know. He finally "came out and told her she should discuss this with an attorney." (R. 153.)

[*14] On one occasion, Dunham testified, petitioner inquired of him as to the nature of the charge against her, and he told her that he "couldn't explain the indictment to her or talk to her about it," and that he "would advise her to discuss the matter with an attorney" (R. 147). Dunham testified that he never advised or suggested to petitioner that public feeling was running high in connection with the cases in which she was involved (R. 154).

Kirby testified that when petitioner asked him whether she would have the right to a trial if the other defendants pleaded guilty he told her that "the question of the trial would be up to the United States Attorney's Office," and that he might have told her that he "knew of no reason why she should not be tried without the others" (R. 134-135).

4. Collard's advice

In regard to her conference with Agent Collard, petitioner testified that about September 27, she asked to see him because she wanted "some information as to the indictment. I didn't understand that" (R. 55, 56). She said she believed Collard was qualified to explain the indictment to her because she knew he was a lawyer (R. 56). She said she told Collard that he had taken her statement and knew that "I didn't do those things which are called 'Over' Acts." (R. 55.) Collard told her [*15] that the indictment did not "cover the charge" (R. 55), that it did not "mean much of anything" (R. 76), that "those charges don't mean a thing" (R. 77). According to her testimony, he then explained the indictment to her "by an example which he called the 'Rum Runners,'" and which she understood as follows: "* * * if there is a group of people in a 'Rum' plan who violate the law, and another person is there and the person doesn't know the people who are planning the violation and doesn't know what is going on, but still * * * this plan is carried out, in the law the man who was present * * * nevertheless is guilty of conspiracy." She then told Collard, "If that is the law in the United States, I don't know how I ever can prove myself innocent, and how will any judge know how am I guilty if this is the law? Collard, petitioner testified, then explained about the "Probation Department" and its functions (R. 55). At another point, petitioner testified that she told Collard that since he had taken her statement he knew that she was never in Grosse Pointe where one of the overt acts naming her was alleged to have occurred, and that she had "nothing to do with all the people named here" (R. 64-65, 75-76). It was after these statements, she testified, that he gave her the rum runners' illustration (R. 76).

Collard testified that on October 2 he received a message that petitioner wanted to talk to him. [*16] When he visited petitioner she had a copy of the indictment that had circled the various "counts" that mentioned her (R. 140, 142). He talked with her for several hours and explained the nature of conspiracy to the best of his ability (R. 141-143). The following occurred on Collard's cross-examination (R. 142-144):

Q. And did you during that discussion use an illustration about a rum runner?

A. Well, I heard Mrs. von Moltke say that, and since she did I have been trying to recall, and I cannot remember such an illustration.

Q. I see.

A. But it is quite possible that Mrs. von Moltke's memory is better than mine, and I may have used such an illustration.

* * * * *

Q. (By Mr. Field): Did Mrs. von Moltke ask you the difference, or to define the difference between a combination, a conspiracy, and a confederation?

A. I am sure I don't know whether she asked me such a question or not.

Q. You don't recall that?

A. No, I don't believe I do.

Q. Did you discuss with Mrs. von Moltke whether she introduced one Edward Arndt to Grace Buchanan Deneen?

A. This is on the occasion of October 2?

Q. October 2, 1943.

A. I will have to answer that by saying that if that is one of the Overt acts in-[*17]volving Mrs. von Moltke, then I did discuss it with her.

Q. And did you explain to Mrs. von Moltke the nature of an Overt act?

A. Well, if she asked me, I probably tried to, but whether she asked me or not I just don't remember.

Q. And did Mrs. von Moltke ask you whether merely conferring with people who later turned out to be guilty of criminal acts would also make her a criminal, and guilty of criminal acts?

A. I do not just recall that particular question. It is quite possible.

Collard testified that he did not indicate to petitioner the course she should pursue (R. 144). He testified that he told her that the question of whether she should plead guilty "was a matter strictly for her, and for nobody else" (R. 137). He reaffirmed the statement he had made in opposition to petitioner's motion to withdraw her plea that the plea was "her free and voluntary act made after due consideration with a full and complete understanding of the charge made against her in the indictment in the instant case" (R. 146). He said on the stand that "As far as I knew and could understand, she understood thoroughly what the whole thing was all about" (R. 147).

On cross-examination petitioner testified as follows (R. 91):

[*18] Q. Now, after you talked to Mr. Collard, did you still feel you were innocent of those charges?

A. Yes, sir, because I told Mr. Collard so.

Q. After Mr. Collard had explained the indictment to you, did you still feel you were innocent of the charges described in the indictment?

A. I told Mr. Collard so, and I could not go outside of the fact of the rum runners—

Q. Regardless of what Mr. Collard told you, you still felt you were innocent of the charges in the indictment?

A. Yes, sir.

In response to a question from the bench, petitioner admitted (R. 75) that no government official told her that she had to prove her innocence.

5. The September 28th conference with Assistant U. S. Attorney Babcock

Petitioner testified that on September 28, when she first said she was going to plead guilty, she told Hanaway, "As the matter stands, and as I understand the situation, I am supposed to plead guilty." She told him she was "willing to cooperate" but wanted her conditions met (R. 58). On cross-examination she admitted that she initiated the discussion of her plea of guilty (R. 99-101). She further testified that she told Babcock that she understood the situation and [*19] knew that he wanted her to plead guilty, but that if she pleaded guilty it was only "to cooperate" and not because she was guilty (R. 58). She also testified that while Babcock gave her no guarantees, he told her he did not believe she would be deported and that they were "human" (R. 58-59, 102-103). She testified that she did not plead guilty on September 28 because "The answer Mr. Babcock gave me was not fully satisfactory" (R. 103), and because her husband, whom she had seen that day, asked her not to do anything without consulting a lawyer (R. 60, 103-104). She therefore told Babcock she wanted "to think the whole situation over" (R. 60).

Hanaway testified that he could not recall petitioner saying that she was pleading guilty because she wanted to cooperate (R. 123-124). All he recalled were the three conditions upon which she wished to predicate her plea (R. 123). He testified that he conveyed petitioner's conditions to Babcock, and that Babcock told him he had no control over those matters but that he would recommend that petitioner be sentenced to an institution near Detroit since her child was ill, emphasizing, however, that his recommendation would not be binding on the Bureau of Prisons (R. 123). Hanaway testified that he conveyed Babcock's message to petitioner (R. 123-124), and that subsequently Babcock repeated the same statements to petitioner in stronger form, pointing out that he did [*20] not know how long he would be an Assistant United States Attorney (R. 124-125). Babcock made it very clear that petitioner's plea of guilty would have to be independent of any of the conditions which she expressed to him (R. 124, 125). Babcock also told petitioner she should not plead guilty unless she was guilty (R. 125).

Babcock testified that he told petitioner that he had no control over the newspapers, that he could do nothing about deportation, since that was a question for the Immigration and Naturalization Service to determine, and that, although he could not control the place of incarceration, he would recommend that she be imprisoned near Detroit where her family might see her (R. 159). He told her that "under any circumstances anything I might reply to her questions must not have any bearing whatsoever upon her decision to plead guilty or not plead guilty; that she would have to decide that for herself, on the basis of whether or not in her own conscience she had to say that she was guilty" (R. 158-159). He vigorously denied that petitioner had at any time told him she was pleading guilty in order to cooperate, or that she was pleading guilty even though she was not guilty (R. 159).

6. The period between the September 28th conference and petitioner's plea on October 7th

Petitioner testified that between September 28 and October 7, as a result of something said by [*21] Mrs. Behrens, she began to fear that if she did not "fall in line and plead guilty" her husband would be implicated. She asked Collard if that was true and Collard said that he couldn't answer that question (R. 60-61).[3] She further testified:

I asked Mr. Collard, "Do you think that in my statement, I told the truth? Mr. Collard said, "Mrs. von Moltke, I know—we know— you told the truth." And I asked Mr. Collard what does the FBI think—is my husband telling the truth? And she said, "Yes, we know that he is telling the truth." Later on I talked to Mr. Dunham, and he said they know my husband would tell the truth whether he hurts himself, or me, or anybody else. But as to this question, I felt that there was some proof in it.

Petitioner also testified that while the F.B.I. agents asked her whether she had seen an attorney (R. 84, 104), none of them ever told her that she should get advice from an attorney (R. 85, 96).

Kirby testified that when the subject of whether she should plead guilty or not came up on one occasion following her conference with Babcock [*22] on September 28, he told her that "that would be a question for her to decide, or her attorney, as we had understood from Mrs. von Moltke that Mr. von Moltke was interested in obtaining an attorney for her." At this suggestion, petitioner "jerked her shoulders and said she was not interested; that she wanted to make up her own mind." (R. 131-132.) On another occasion petitioner inquired of Kirby whether a plea of guilty on her part would bar her husband from being reemployed. He replied that "that was a matter * * * between the University and himself, and the question of her plea was one that she had to decide, based upon her own feeling of guilt or in-nocence." (R. 135.)

Hanaway testified that on one occasion, when petitioner asked him to explain the indictment to her, he told her that she should have either her attorney or the United States Attorney explain it to her (R. 121, 129).

Collard testified that he told her she "could see an attorney at any

---

[3] In her affidavit in support of her motion of August 7, 1944, for leave to withdraw her plea of guilty (see p. 3, *supra*), petitioner stated that "she asked Mr. Collard whether her husband was in any way involved in the matter, and Mr. Collard replied to her that he was sorry but that he could give her no in-formation concerning that fact, and that although at present she realizes that that was a perfectly proper and normal answer, at the time it was given to her, because of her state of mind, this was confirmation of the statement made to her by Mrs. Behrens" (R. 40-41).

time, that that was her privilege" (R. 140) and that she told him that she did not want an attorney (R. 137). He testified that "In all the conversations that I had with Mrs. von Moltke concerning the attorney, it was her idea that she did not want an attorney, and that she wanted to just go ahead without an attorney, and do whatever she was going to do without one" (R. 137).

[*23] Dunham testified that when petitioner questioned him about the indictment and about whether Dr. Thomas, a codefendant, would plead guilty he "finally came out and told her she should discuss this with an attorney" (R. 153). She told him that her husband was determined that she have an attorney but that she didn't want to discuss the matter with an attorney, that "it was a problem she wanted to decide herself." She said she didn't feel an attorney would be of much assistance to her "because her consideration was not only for herself, but for her husband and family" (R. 147-148). Petitioner said that her visits with her husband were unpleasant because he wanted her to have an attorney but she was determined to make up her own mind (R. 148).

On cross-examination petitioner was questioned about her decision not to plead guilty on September 28. The record reveals the following (R. 103-104):

Q. And your husband told you not to plead guilty?

A. He did.

Q. He told you to get a lawyer?

A. Yes; he said I should not before I have seen an attorney; on such a question I should talk to an attorney first about the whole thing.

Q. Then you knew at that time that you were entitled to a lawyer before you pled guilty, if you wanted one?

[*24] A. I did not. I just was wondering about the lawyer who never came.

Q. Well, you knew at that time, did you not, that you did not have to plead guilty if you did not want to? Yes or no?

A. No.

Q. Your husband told you to get a lawyer, didn't he?

A. My husband said to wait until a lawyer comes out.

Q. And you decided not to plead guilty because of that?

A. Because of that, yes.

Q. And you went back to the County Jail?

A. And the answer Mr. Babcock gave me was not fully satisfactory.

Q. At any rate, you decided not to plead guilty because of what your husband told you?

A. Yes.

Q. Did you see your husband about getting a lawyer before you pled guilty?

A. No, sir, I pled guilty, and my husband even did not know it.

7. The events of October 7th, when petitioner waived counsel and pleaded guilty

On October 7, petitioner decided to plead guilty (R. 63). She testified that Collard "came in just to see how I felt about it, and whether I had seen a lawyer, because I said I wouldn't decide before I had seen a lawyer" (R. 65). She told Col-[*25]lard and Hanaway, who was with him, that she wished to "go with them to plead guilty." They asked her "whether I had seen my lawyer, and whether I had thought about what I was going to do." She stated that she replied, "I wish I would know whether that is the right thing, if I go and plead guilty." One of the agents—she could not remember which— then remarked, "At least it might be the wisest thing." (R. 63, 64.) She was then taken to Babcock and again told him she was ready to plead guilty. She testified that she repeated to him that her plea would be made even though she still felt she was not guilty (R. 65). Babcock accordingly took her before Judge Lederle because Judge Moinet was not in court that day (R. 65).

Petitioner testified as follows relative to the proceedings before Judge Lederle: "Mr. Babcock handed the judge what I would call a folder, and Judge Lederle looked into that and said he could not accept the change of plea because there was something about an attorney— * * * I understood that he said there was to be appointed an attorney in this case, or there was appointed an attorney in this case, or there was to be present an attorney—but I knew distinctly the judge said he could not accept the change of the plead, and Mr. Babcock explained to him that this was different, and that he could accept the change of the plead" (R. 66). Judge Lederle asked her if the [*26] indictment had been explained to her, and she replied in the affirmative though according to her testimony it "had not been fully explained" to her (R. 67-68). He also asked her if she was pleading guilty because she felt she was guilty, and she said, "Yes," though according to her testimony this was not true (R. 68). A "note" was handed her to sign and according to her testimony she objected because it mentioned something about a trial, but Babcock told her it was all right to sign it and she did so (R. 66-67). On cross-examination, petitioner testified that (R. 106) "I was so confused, and so nervous I did not hear what the judge said."

Hanaway denied that he told petitioner that it would be wiser to plead guilty (R. 124-125).[4] Babcock denied that petitioner ever stated

---

[4] Collard was not questioned about this incident.

to him that she wanted to plead guilty although she was not guilty (R. 159), and Collard, who was present at the interview with Babcock on October 7, stated that he was "absolutely positive" that petitioner did not make such a statement to Babcock (R. 138). Furthermore, Collard testified, petitioner did not state that she wanted to plead guilty in order to cooperate; she said she wanted to plead guilty because she was guilty (R. 138). Babcock told petitioner that Judge Moinet, the judge who was handling her case, was not available on that day and that it would be much more convenient to wait [*27] until another time, but petitioner said she wanted to enter her plea "right then" (R. 138).

Babcock testified that after petitioner announced to him her decision to plead guilty, he "recounted to her the normal procedure in the court room, telling her that when you appear before one of the United States District Judges, the Judge would ask if she was tendering her plea as a result of any promise made to her, whether it was a result of any threats upon her or whether it was because she was guilty. That he would also ask her if she desired to have counsel appointed to advise her." She reaffirmed her decision to plead guilty (R. 159).

Babcock further testified that after taking petitioner before Judge Lederle (R. 159), he informed the judge that petitioner wished him to make a motion to change her plea from that of not guilty to guilty (R. 160).

* * * Thereupon I recall the Court proceeded in the normal way. Now, the normal procedure is for the Court to ask the Defendant if the information given to the Court is correct, if the Defendant desires to plead guilty, and ask the Defendant if such plea of guilty is tendered by reason of any promises made to the Defendant, if such plea of guilty is made by reason of any threats made upon the Defendant, if such plea of guilty is their voluntary plea and made because the Defendant is guilty and if the Defendant de-[*28]sires to have counsel appointed by the Court. First of all, if the Defendant has counsel of his or her choosing, and if not, if the Defendant desires counsel appointed by the Court to advise the Defendant in connection with the matter. Upon being satisfied that the action tendered by the Defendant is free and voluntary, without promises or threats of any kind and because the Defendant is guilty, the Court will then accept the plea of guilty and proceed with further disposition of the case. (Ibid.)

Babcock denied that petitioner told him, when she signed the waiver, that the reason she was appearing there was because she did not want to go to trial; he testified that he observed petitioner reading the waiver and that she made no statement whatsoever to him regarding it (R. 162-163). He further testified relative to petitioner's understanding of the waiver (R. 166):

* * * Judge Lederle was extremely careful and meticulous to make sure, as he always does, that she understood what she was doing.

* * * * *

He interrogated her as to whether she wished to have counsel represent her and advised her as to signing a waiver of that right. Again, Mr. Field, I hope you understand, and I wish to say again that I have no distinct recollection now—let me put [*29] it this way: if any of the Judges have missed doing that, I would have remembered that very distinctly.

Kirby testified (R. 133) that "the judge inquired whether or not the plea of guilty was upon the suggestion of any Government agent," and petitioner said no.

Collard testified that he was in the court room and that Judge Lederle asked petitioner a number of questions but that he could not recall them all. He said that the judge "went to considerable pains to ask her the questions that he should have to guarantee the rights that she had, and to convince himself * * *" (R. 139).

Petitioner testified that, after leaving the court room, she told agents Kirby and Dunham that she should not have pleaded guilty, that she had done the wrong thing because she was not guilty (R. 72-73). Kirby denied that she made such a statement after leaving the court room, although he testified that much later, in January 1944, she made such a statement (R. 133). Dunham was not questioned about the matter. Collard testified that petitioner made no such remark either to him or to anyone else in his presence as she left the court room and returned to jail (R. 139).

At the conclusion of the testimony, the district judge found that petitioner had failed to sustain [*30] the allegations of the petition by a preponderance of the evidence. He said (R. 170-171, 174):

In the petition filed in this cause the petitioner directly or by implication charges that the District Attorney having the case in charge and agents of the Federal Bureau of Investigation misled her or made promises to her that, which at least some degree, influenced her action in pleading guilty to the charge. I am of the opinion that these charges have now been abandoned by the petitioner but for the purpose of the record I wish to state most vigorously that there was absolutely nothing in the testimony sustaining such charges or implications. The conduct of both the officials of the District Attorney's office and the agents of the Federal Bureau of Investigation were meticulous in safeguarding the rights of the petitioner and that the record is utterly bare of any support of petitioner's contentions.

The petitioner is a woman obviously of good education and above the average in intelligence. Her knowledge of English was fluent and ample.

*   *   *   *   *

The only substantial question in this case is whether the petitioner intelligently and knowingly waived her constitutional rights. It was her obligation to sustain the allegations of her petition by a preponderance of evidence. Not only has she failed in this but I believe that the evidence [*31] is overwhelming against her contentions. The petitioner is an intelligent, mentally acute woman. She understood the charge and the proceedings. She freely, intelligently and knowingly waived her constitutional rights. I conclude, therefore, that there is no merit in her petition and that it shall be dismissed together with the writ.

On appeal, the judgment of the district court was affirmed (R. 181), one judge dissenting (R. 189-198).

CHAPTER XIII
SUCCESSFUL PETITIONS FOR REHEARING

Section 168. Essentials of a successful petition for rehearing. —As has already been pointed out, see Sections 143 and 147 above, if a petition for rehearing is to be more than a futile exercise in articulated frustration, it must concentrate on what the court's opinion has overlooked.

In Attorney General Garland's rugged phrases,

Petitions for rehearing, or motions for new trials, are supposed to gather up the whole case and present it compactly and broadly. This is the great sphere where lawyers are really to show their strength and power and knowledge, and where the courts are at last brought face to face with the very kernel of the case, and after all, where upon consultation with counsel, after each has spoken and been heard, they are to examine profoundly and see what the case does really call for.[1]

Or, to employ a mid-Twentieth Century metaphor, when a lawyer sets out to draft a petition for rehearing, he is facing the moment of truth.

Section 169. Example of a successful petition for rehearing in a Court of Appeals.—In considering the document that is reproduced in the section which follows, the reader should have these dates in mind:

Appellant's reply brief in the *Herzog* case—the one now in question—was filed on April 12, 1955. On the day before, April 11, a division of the Ninth Circuit had decided *Bloch* v. *United States*, 221 F. 2d 786, which reversed a conviction on the strength of an erroneous charge to which no objection had been made at the trial. An identical instruction, similarly not objected to, appeared in the *Herzog* record. When the *Herzog* case was argued, on April 19, counsel for the appellant relied on the *Bloch* decision as an additional ground for reversal; the court requested that this ground be

---

[1] Garland, *Experience in the U. S. Supreme Court,* 53-54.

set forth in a supplemental memorandum, and such a document was duly filed the next day, on April 20.

Six months later, on October 11, 1955, the Ninth Circuit decided the *Herzog* case. 226 F. 2d 561. It held that *Bloch* had been overruled *sub silentio* by *Brown* v. *United States*, 222 F. 2d 293, decided three days later by still a third division of the Ninth Circuit, and that under Criminal Rule 52 (b) a Court of Appeals had no power to consider any error in a charge to which no objection had been made at the trial pursuant to Criminal Rule 30.

Appellant considered this a literally fantastic holding, not only because no other court had ever construed Rule 52 (b) so restrictively, but primarily because, if *Bloch* had been overruled *sub silentio* three days later by *Brown,* then by parity of reasoning *Brown* was similarly overruled *sub silentio* when the Government's petition for rehearing in *Bloch* was denied with opinion two months after that, on June 14, 1955. 223 F. 2d 297.

What should be the next step? If only the misconstruction of Rule 52 (b) had been in question, a petition for certiorari was clearly indicated. But with the Ninth Circuit going off in all directions at once, its several panels apparently unaware of what they were concurrently deciding, it was not at all clear that the Supreme Court would, in the first instance, undertake to resolve this intra-circuit conflict.[2]

Accordingly, counsel for the appellant determined to seek a rehearing in banc in the Court of Appeals.

The basic issue, the scope of Criminal Rule 52 (b) in the light of *Bloch* and *Brown,* assuredly qualified (see Sections 143 and 147 above) as something that the court had overlooked. The other two issues, which were the strongest of those remaining, were added more as an act of faith than by reason of any genuine hope that they would be reconsidered.

Before going on to examine the actual petition for rehearing, the reader should first consult the opinion (*Herzog* v. *United States,* 226 F. 2d 561) concerning which that petition complained.

Section 170. The successful petition for rehearing in *Herzog* v. *United States.*—Below is set out, verbatim, the petition for rehearing filed in the *Herzog* case; the cover, index, and the motion to stay the mandate (in the event of denial) have been omitted.

---

[2] See *Civil Aeronautics Board* v. *American Air Transport,* 344 U. S. 4, 5; *In re Burwell,* 350 U. S. 521, 522.

No. 14,611

In the

UNITED STATES COURT OF APPEALS

For the Ninth Circuit

J. A. HERZOG

Appellant,

vs.

UNITED STATES OF AMERICA

Appellee.

APPELLANT'S PETITION FOR A REHEARING

To the Honorable Clifton Mathews, Richard H. Chambers and William M. Byrne, Judges of the United States Court of Appeals for the Ninth Circuit:

Comes now the appellant in the above-entitled case, and respectfully prays the Court to grant a rehearing.

I. The principal question in the present posture of the case is whether the trial judge's charge to the jury on willfulness was correct, and whether, not having been objected to under Criminal Rule 30 at the trial, this Court on appeal may consider the alleged error under Criminal Rule 52 (b).

In *Bloch* v. *United States,* 221 F. 2d 786, a division of this Court (Bone and Pope, Circuit Judges; Mur-[*2]ray, District Judge), held an identical instruction to be erroneous, held that it could be considered in the absence of objection below, and reversed the conviction.

In *Brown* v. *United States,* 222 F. 2d 293, another division of this Court (Stephens and Fee, Circuit Judges; Wiig, District Judge) held that there was no power to consider errors not objected to below.

In the instant case, still a third division of this Court (Mathews and Chambers, Circuit Judges; Byrne, District Judge), disagreed with the *Bloch* case and agreed with the *Brown* case, "which was decided three days after and overrules *sub silentio* the *Bloch* case" (p. 7 of slip opinion). Judge Chambers concurred, saying (p. 11 of slip opinion), "Although I disagree with the decision in the Bloch case, I would be reluctant to go against it were it not for my belief that Brown v. United States, 9 Cir., 222 F. 2d 293, already has overruled Bloch sub silentio."

II. *Bloch* was decided on April 11, 1955, *Brown* on April 14, 1955. The Government petitioned for a rehearing in the *Bloch* case. If *Brown* had overruled *Bloch,* then, obviously, that petition for rehearing should have been granted. In fact, it was denied on June 14, 1955, in an opinion reported at 223 F. 2d 297.

If therefore it can properly be said that *Brown* overruled *Bloch* *sub silentio* when rendered by a different division of this Court three days later, then it can be contended with equal force that *Brown* was in [*3] turn overruled *sub silentio* by the denial of the Government's petition for rehearing in *Bloch* two months after that.

III. There can be no disagreement with what was said in the prevailing opinion in this case (p. 7 of slip opinion): "The *Brown* case and the *Bloch* case cannot both be right."

In our view, the *Bloch* case, which held that failure to object under Rule 30 was no bar to the invocation of Rule 52 (b) by the Appellate Court, is correct. That view has the support of no less than six other circuits.

First Circuit: Daigle v. *United States,* 181 F. 2d 311, 313 (instruction not objected to below considered by the Appellate Court); *Lash* v. *United States,* 221 F. 2d 237, 240, certiorari denied, 350 U. S. 826 (no conflict between Rules 30 and 52 (b); they are to be construed together).

Third Circuit: United States v. *Cumberland,* 200 F. 2d 609 (judgment reversed for errors in instructions not objected to at the trial); *United States* v. *Ward,* 168 F. 2d 226, 228 (plain error in instructions can be noticed though not called to Court's attention at the trial).

Sixth Circuit: Lazarov v. *United States,* 225 F. 2d 319, 329 ("No exception was taken to the instruction but, of course, an appellate court will consider an error in the charge which is seriously prejudicial or amounts to a grave miscarriage of justice even though no objection was made in the trial court.")

[*4] *Seventh Circuit: United States* v. *Vasen,* 222 F. 2d 3, 5-6, certiorari denied, 350 U. S. 834 (Rules 30 and 52 (b) to be construed together in cases of glaring errors); *United States* v. *Raub,* 177 F. 2d 312, 315 (erroneous instruction may be noticed under Rule 52 (b) notwithstanding failure to comply with Rule 30).

Tenth Circuit: Apodaca v. *United States,* 188 F. 2d 932, 937 (Rules 30 and 52 (b) to be construed together).

District of Columbia Circuit: *Robertson* v. *United States,* 171 F. 2d 345 (plain error in instructions will be noticed though not called to Court's attention at the trial).

There are indications in other decisions of this Circuit that support the *Bloch* rule. See *Remmer* v. *United States,* 205 F. 2d 277, 290, note 16: [1] "Plain error in instructions should of course be noticed re-

---

[1] Judgment vacated on other grounds, 347 U. S. 227; reaffirmed, 222 F. 2d 720 (C.A. 9); certiorari granted, Oct. 10, 1955 (350 U. S. 820), and now pending in the Supreme Court as No. 156, Oct. T. 1955.

gardless of whether the matter was properly brought to the attention of the trial Court." (Mathews, Stephens, and Orr, Circuit Judges.) Compare *Jones* v. *United States*, 175 F. 2d 544 (plain error noticed; no showing of compliance with Rule 30) (Mathews, Healy, and Pope, Circuit Judges).

And, in a case decided shortly after the adoption of the Federal Rules of Criminal Procedure, the Supreme Court cited Rule 52 (b) to reach and reverse [*5] for an erroneous instruction to which no exception had been taken at the trial. *United Brotherhood* v. *United States*, 330 U. S. 395, 411-412.

Finally, the Rules Committee's notes show that the interpretation placed on Rule 52 (b) by most of the circuits and by the *Bloch* ruling in this Circuit, viz., that the rule enlarges the power of the appellate tribunal, was precisely the one intended: "The concept of plain error has served to relieve the harshness of the general rule that an appellate court will not consider alleged errors to which objection and exception were not interposed at the trial." *Preliminary Draft, Federal Rules of Criminal Procedure* (May 1943), p. 198; *Second Draft, Federal Rules of Criminal Procedure* (February 1944), p. 186. In the light of this expressed purpose, we submit that it is not open to conclude that an Appellate Court lacks power to consider an erroneous instruction not objected to at the trial.

We think, therefore, that both the *Brown* case and the prevailing opinion in this case read Criminal Rule 52 (b) too restrictively.

IV. What seems to us particularly disturbing about the affirmance in this case is that it applies one rule to *Bloch* in April and June and another to this appellant in October in substantially identical circumstances; for every element present in the *Bloch* case was present in this case also.

1. The charge condemned in the *Bloch* case was as follows (221 F. 2d at 789):

[*6] "Wilfully in the statute, which makes a willful attempt to evade taxes a crime, refers to the state of mind in which the act of evasion was done. *It includes several states of mind, any one of which may be the willfulness to make up the crime.*

"Willfulness includes doing an act with a bad purpose. It includes doing an act without a justifiable excuse. It includes doing an act without ground for believing that the act is lawful. It also includes doing an act with a careless disregard for whether or not one has the right so to act." (Italics in original.)

The corresponding charge in this case was as follows (R. 1703-1704):

"Now, when we use the term 'Wilful' in speaking of a violation of this statute, as used in this criminal statute and as used in most criminal statutes, we mean an act done with a bad purpose without justifiable excuse, or stubbornly or obstinately or perversely. It may be used to characterize an act done without grounds for believing it is lawful, or conduct marked with completely careless disregard of whether one has a right to do that or not."

The two passages are almost *in haec verba,* without any difference whatever in substance.

2. Appellant in *Bloch* raised no objection to the passage just quoted; appellant here, similarly, raised no objection to the quoted portion of the charge in this case.

Appellant in *Bloch* requested another instruction on willfulness, duly excepted to the failure to give it, [*7] and briefed the issue on appeal; this Court held that the requested instruction was erroneous. (*Bloch* opinion, 221 F. 2d at 787.)

Appellant here requested other instructions on willfulness (Nos. 18 and 19, R. 25-26), excepted to the failure to give them (R. 1711), assigned the failure as error (Point 12 (c), R. 1727-1728), but did not brief it further.

3. The question of intent was of critical importance in both cases. Appellant here conceded that the profit on eleven sales of "executive" or "house" cars in 1948 was not reported but contended that the omission grew out of Smith's manipulation of these particular automobiles in the course of his embezzlement rather than from any intent to evade taxes. (See Appellant's Opening Brief, p. 5.) The Government, for its part, similarly stresses the importance of this item in the alleged "pattern" of evasion. (See U. S. Br., pp. 9-10, 30-34.) The jury might well have thought that the failure to trace the disposition of these eleven cars after Smith was discharged was a "careless disregard" of appellant's obligations, which, under the Court's instruction, would be tantamount to willful evasion.

4. The factual setting in this case is identical with that in *Bloch:* the same instruction, the same lack of objection, the same kind of case. The question is not whether the appellant here would have had standing as an original proposition to assail the instruction in this case after having failed to object to it at the trial. Nor is the question whether, as an [*8] original proposition, the instruction was so glaringly wrong as to call for an exercise of this Court's power under Rule 52 (b) to notice "plain error." Rather the question is whether, after reversing for fundamental error as to the instruction on willfulness in the *Bloch* case, and after denying the Government's petition for rehearing there, this Court can now affirm in this case on the same instruction in the identical factual setting. We submit that affirmance of the present judgment in these circumstances would amount to a discrimination so

unjustifiable as to infringe the Due Process clause of the Fifth Amendment. *Bolling* v. *Sharpe,* 347 U. S. 497, 499.

V. We therefore respectfully suggest, pursuant to the third paragraph of Rule 23 of this Court, that it would be eminently appropriate for this case to be heard in banc, to the end that the important questions of federal criminal law which are left in doubt by conflicting decisions of different divisions of this Court may be authoritatively resolved.

VI. In the event that a rehearing is granted, appellant desires to reargue two additional questions, which are here summarily stated in order not further to lengthen this petition:

1. *The admissibility of the Kelley Blue Books* (Specifications of Error Nos. 2 and 6). Very briefly, the opinion of the Court (slip opinion, pp. 2-3) proceeds on grounds which suggest that an insufficient foundation was laid for the admission of these books, whereas the trial judge, in explicit and unequivoval fashion, based his ruling entirely on materiality. (R. 1521.)

[*9] We believe that, in their setting, the Blue Books had substantial probative value. For 1948, the conviction year, almost all of the used car sales were made to Joe Angel; the Blue Book valuations for the cars sold to him in that year aggregated $35,785, as against $39,245 which Angel claims he paid, and the $34,720 shown on appellant's invoices and records. (Def. Ex. AB for id., p. 4, R. 1789.) [2]

It follows that the exclusion of the Blue Books on the ground of materiality alone amounted to prejudicial error. Moreover, we submit, when a trial judge states (R. 1521), "I will protect the record on that and state that the basis of the ruling has nothing to do with the laying of a foundation as to any document whatsoever," it is not open to an Appellate Court to sustain his ruling on any ground going to a lack of foundation.

2. *The request for examination of the Grand Jury minutes* (Specifications of Error Nos. 8 and 9). The Court's opinion on this point (slip opinion, pp. 4-6) proceeds on two grounds, neither of which we submit is tenable on closer analysis.

Insofar as the opinion suggests that the trial judge was not required to inspect the minutes himself in the absence of a specific request that he do so, the ruling is contrary to what appears to be settled practice elsewhere. See *United States* v. *Cotter,* 60 F. 2d 689, 692 (C.C.A. 2), where, although the request was [*10] for a general inspection of grand jury minutes by counsel, which was refused, the

---

[2] The Blue Book calls for reduction of the price by the estimate of reconditioning cost, but appellant sold used cars at wholesale as is, without reconditioning. (R. 1367-1369.)

judge "went over them himself, decided what parts were relevant, and laid so much open." [2a]

Insofar as this Court's opinion holds that a defendant may neither see nor request the trial judge to examine grand jury minutes for purposes of impeachment until he can first show that those minutes will be impeaching, it establishes a prerequisite for examination utterly impossible of attainment; for, plainly, such a requirement cannot reasonably be imposed in respect of an unknown document. *United States* v. *Krulewitch,* 145 F. 2d 76, 79; *United States* v. *Cohen,* 145 F. 2d 82, 92; both C.C.A. 2.

VII. Rehearing is not sought in respect of any other questions.

Dated, Oakland, California,
November 9, 1955.

Respectfully submitted,

FREDERICK BERNAYS WIENER,
SPURGEON AVAKIAN,
J. RICHARD JOHNSTON,
*Attorneys for Appellant
and Petitioner.*

[*11] CERTIFICATE OF COUNSEL

I, SPURGEON AVAKIAN, one of the attorneys for the appellant, certify that this petition is presented in good faith, that it is not interposed for delay, and that in my judgment it is well founded.

Dated, Oakland, California,

November 9, 1955.

SPURGEON AVAKIAN.

Section 171. Sequel to the rehearing in the *Herzog* case.— The consequence of the foregoing document was a rehearing in banc, limited to the "conflict or apparent conflict" with *Bloch* on the Rule 52 (b) issue.[3] But, while a majority of the Ninth Circuit after reargument repudiated the division's original reading of that

---

[2a] A recent Second Circuit case approved the application of the same practice to F.B.I. reports. *United States* v. *Lebron,* 222 F. 2d 531, 536-537, certiorari denied, 350 U. S. [876] (Oct. 24. 1955; No. 139, Misc.)

[3] Both the division and the full Court limited the reargument to "questions pertinent to the conflict or apparent conflict between the decision herein rendered on October 11, 1955, and the decision of this Court in *Bloch* v. *United States,* 221 F. 2d 786, rehearing denied 223 F. 2d 297."

Rule, thus lining up with every other circuit that had ever considered the point, the holding was that there would be a different result in *Herzog* than in *Bloch*. Judge Stephens dissented on the ground that there was no power to limit the rehearing in banc to a particular issue. The reader is invited to, and should, read the opinions on rehearing, which are reported at 235 F. 2d 664.

Certiorari was sought, but denied, Mr. Justice Douglas dissenting.[4] He had earlier, as Circuit Justice, granted bail pending appeal.[5] Thus the result of the case was, that whereas the Ninth Circuit had originally denied bail pending appeal, which at that time meant that no substantial question was involved,[6] it had the case under consideration for over 13 months, in the course of which it repudiated the basis on which its original affirmance of the judgment had been rested. Moreover, when the substantive issue involved—the definition of wilfulness in tax cases—again arose, the Ninth Circuit concluded that the *Herzog* instruction was wrong, and reversed.[7] It should not therefore occasion surprise that even after four years some residual bitterness still remains whenever the *Herzog* case comes to mind.

The law as to some of the other issues raised and involved is still nebulous. Just what rights there are to inspection of Grand Jury minutes in anyone apart from the United States Attorney and his assistants has not yet been completely clarified by the Supreme Court's later pronouncements in this area.[8] All that can be said is that the Second Circuit still insists that trial judges must themselves make the very kind of personal inspection of those minutes that the trial judge in the *Herzog* case refused to make, a refusal in which he was sustained by the Ninth Circuit.[9]

---

[4] 352 U. S. 844.

[5] 99 L. ed. 1299, 75 S. Ct. 349.

[6] As originally adopted, Rule 46 (a) (2), F. R. Crim. P., permitted bail pending appeal or certiorari "only if it appears that the case involves a substantial question which should be determined by the appellate court." It was in effect in that form when bail was granted on February 11, 1955 (*supra*, note 5).

On April 9, 1956, the Rule was changed to substitute for the quoted clause the words "unless it appears that the appeal is frivolous or taken for delay."

[7] *Forster v. United States*, 237 F. 2d 617 (C.A. 9). *Accord, United States v. Palermo*, 259 F. 2d 872 (C.A. 3).

[8] *United States v. Procter & Gamble*, 356 U. S. 677; *Pittsburgh Plate Glass Co. v. United States*, 360 U. S. 395.

[9] *United States v. Zborowski*, 271 F. 2d 661 (C.A. 2); *United States v. McKeever*, 271 F. 2d 669 (C.A. 2); *United States v. Spangelet*, 258 F. 2d 338

Two of the judges who heard the *Herzog* case reargued in banc retired before the decision was announced, but participated therein. Of course counsel were aware of the additional issue thus presented, which the Supreme Court did not decide for another four years in *United States* v. *American-Foreign S.S. Co.*[10] But there the judge who retired *pendente lite* cast the deciding vote, whereas in *Herzog* there were ample votes to sustain the judgment without the votes of the judges who retired. Hence it was not deemed worthwhile to include the point in the petition for certiorari.

The same was true of the question raised in Judge Stephens' opinion, viz., whether an in banc rehearing could properly narrow the issues, or whether the court on such rehearing was obliged to hear the entire case. It may well be that, since a rehearing of any kind by a Court of Appeals is, like review by certiorari in the Supreme Court, a matter of grace—which the original appeal to the Court of Appeals of course is not—the questions to be heard on rehearing may properly be limited. But, since even reversal on that issue would not have given any assurance whatever of a different result—and there was much soul-searching on the question, with full articulation of the factors involved—that question was not included in the petition for certiorari.

Section 172. Example of a successful petition for rehearing in the Supreme Court of the United States.—As in the example of the Court of Appeals petition for rehearing just discussed, the document set forth in the next section addresses itself to "the very kernel of the case," and in particular, to the ground on which the original decisions rested, viz., that there was no need, in two cases involving the right to try civilian women by court-martial in time of peace, to consider the scope of the clause which gives Congress the power "To make Rules for the Government and Regulation of the land and naval Forces."[11]

That omission drew a sharp comment from the Justice who reserved his vote: "The plain inference from this is that the Court is not prepared to support the constitutional basis upon which the

---

(C.A. 2). Compare the Ninth Circuit's wholly different concept in the first *Herzog* opinion, 226 F. 2d at 566-567.

[10] 363 U. S. 685.

[11] *Kinsella* v. *Krueger*, 351 U. S. 470, 476; Clause 14 of Section 8 of Article I of the Constitution is quoted in the text.

Covert and Smith courts-martial were instituted and the convictions were secured." [12] Or, less elegantly put, there were lacking five votes to hold that civilian dependents could be included within "land and naval Forces."

In counsel's view, there was room for a difference of opinion as to whether the quoted portion of the Constitution—Clause 14 of Section 8, Article I—could embrace persons without any military status, particularly since there had never been any doubt of the power to try by court-martial civilians who in time of war were with the armies "in the field." [13] But whatever the scope of Clause 14, there was in counsel's view no doubt that Clause 14 could not thus be brushed aside as irrelevant and unnecessary to be considered.

Which, stripping away every vestige of anything-less-than-utterly-essential, counsel proceeded to do.

As before, the reader is requested to examine the opinions concerned—*Kinsella* v. *Krueger*, 351 U. S. 470, and *Reid* v. *Covert*, 351 U. S. 487—as indispensable background for an understanding of the document which follows.

Section 173. The successful petition for rehearing in *Reid* v. *Covert*.—Only the cover and the index have been omitted from the *Covert-Krueger* petition for rehearing that is here set out.

IN THE

SUPREME COURT OF THE UNITED STATES

October Term, 1955

No. 701

CURTIS REID, Superintendent of the District
of Columbia Jail, *Appellant,*

v.

CLARICE B. COVERT

On Appeal from the United States District Court for the
District of Columbia

---

[12] *Kinsella* v. *Krueger*, 351 U. S. at 481, *per* Frankfurter, J.

[13] Article 2 (10) of the Uniform Code of Military Justice, now 10 U.S.C. § 802 (10) ; Winthrop, *Military Law and Precedents* (2d ed. 1896) *134-*137 (pp. 99-101, 1920 reprint) ; and see references cited in note 18, below, p. 442.

No. 713

NINA KINSELLA, Warden of the Federal Reformatory for Women, Alderson, West Virginia, *Petitioner,*

v.

WALTER KRUEGER

On Writ of Certiorari to the United States Court of Appeals for the Fourth Circuit

PETITION FOR REHEARING

Now come CLARICE B. COVERT, Appellee in No. 701, and WALTER KRUEGER, Respondent in No. 713, and respectfully pray the Court to grant rehearings in these causes.

[*2] Mrs. Covert and Mrs. Smith, the two civilian women whose fate is here in issue, were tried by *court-martial,* pursuant to Article ? (11) of the Uniform Code of *Military* Justice, and had their convictions successively reviewed by Boards of Review in the Offices of the *Judge Advocate General of the Air Force* and *of the Army,* respectively, and then by the Court of *Military* Appeals. The latter tribunal held, while the present cases were under advisement here, that "Article 2 (11) of the Code is a valid exercise of Congressional power granted by the Constitution 'to make Rules for the Government and Regulation of the land and naval Forces.'" *United States* v. *St. Clair,* 7 USCMA 82, 83, 21 CMR 208, 209, decided May 25, 1956. But this Court declares (slip opinion, No. 713, pp. 6-7) that there is no need to examine the power of Congress under that clause of the Constitution.

The concept of presenting Hamlet without the Prince of Denmark doubtless has fascination. But just as the Melancholy Dane cannot, despite heroic efforts, be completely exorcised from the play, just as he constantly flits back and forth into the action regardless of nomenclature, so in these cases, where the results were reached after ostensible rejection of whatever powers the Constitution has conferred upon Congress to govern the armed forces, a reading of the Court's opinions makes obvious that military considerations were necessarily relied upon to uphold the court-martial proceedings here under review.

A. Thus it is said (slip opinion, No. 713, pp. 7-8) that the United

States must maintain American forces in many foreign countries; that "the lives of military [*3] and civilian personnel alike are geared to the local military organization"; and that by enacting Article 2 (11) "Congress has provided that all shall be subject to the same system of justice and that *the military commander who bears full responsibility for the care and safety of those civilians attached to his command shall also have authority to regulate their conduct.*" [Italics added.] These, without question, are purely military considerations relevant to—and relevant only to—the power "To make Rules for the Government and Regulation of the land and naval Forces."

B. It is said (slip opinion, No. 713, pp. 10-11) that "this case presents no problem of * * * the power of Congress to provide for trial of Americans sojourning, touring, or temporarily residing abroad." But *In re Ross*, 140 U. S. 453, on which the jurisdiction in the present cases is rested, involved the trial by an American consular court of a British subject who was temporarily in Japan only while the American ship in whose crew he served was lying at anchor in Yokohama harbor. See 140 U. S. at 456-457, 470-475. The difference between Ross's situation and that of the two women involved here is that they were abroad for a far less temporary stay, the exact length of which was dependent on their respective husbands' tours of military duty, and that their American links were far less tenuous than those of Ross. Again, the governing consideration is their relationship to the American armed force of which their husbands were members.

C. In No. 701, the Court's opinion (pp. 4-5) speaks of "military jurisdiction," of "military prisoners," and cites decisions of "military courts" in considering whether Mrs. Covert may be retried by a court-martial within the District of Columbia.

[*4] Thus, the Court sustains, in these two cases, an obvious exercise of the power "To make Rules for the Government and Regulation of the land and naval Forces" while disclaiming all inquiry into the extent of that power. And for the first time in the Court's history, it approves the trial of civilian women by court-martial in time of peace.

II

The Court says (slip opinion, No. 713, p. 8) that "The choice among different types of legislative tribunals is peculiarly within the power of Congress," citing *Ex parte Bakelite Corp.*, 279 U. S. 438, 451. But to deal with these cases in terms of legislative choice is to rest on a demonstrable fiction, for it is the incontrovertible fact that Congress never considered that it was being faced with any "choice among different types of legislative tribunals."

The legislative materials reflect no awareness whatever of any constitutional problem. They show without question that, in 1916 when it first extended court-martial jurisdiction over civilians accompanying the armies in time of peace in AW 2 (d), in 1920 when it reenacted that provision, in 1948 when it permitted AW 2 (d) to survive the amendment to the other Articles of War passed in that year, and again in 1949-1950, when it extended the same provision to all of the armed forces as Article 2 (11), UCMJ, Congress never considered the constitutionality of that jurisdiction under any clause of the Constitution,[1] much [*5] less that it made a deliberate selection among classes of available tribunals. The same legislative materials also show that, in 1916, in 1920, in 1948, and again in 1949 and 1950, there was simply no mention of courts other than courts-martial for the trial of accompanying civilians; that at no time in the hearings or on the floor of either house was there even a whisper about consular courts; and that *In re Ross,* 140 U. S. 453, was not cited by anyone, anywhere, at any time. These omissions, it is proper to add, should hardly occasion surprise, inasmuch as the traditional view regarded a court-martial, not as a species of legislative court, but as "a purely executive agency designed for military uses." Winthrop, *Military Law and Precedents* (2d ed. 1896) *54 [1920 reprint, p. 49].

The Court's reference to Congressional choice in connection with Article 2 (11) is the more unreal when it is borne in mind that the Uniform Code of Military Justice in the House was under the unchallenged control of that body's Committee on Armed Services; that extensive hearings were had thereon by the Senate Committee on Armed Services; that a proposal thereafter to take the Code from the calendar for reference to the Senate Committee on the Judiciary was opposed by the Chairman of the Armed Forces Committee on the ground that the Code was essentially a reincorporation of existing law and that it was "an extremely important step toward unification [of the armed services] and provides for reforms in the court-martial [*6] system which should be enacted as soon as possible" (96 Cong. Rec. 1366-1368) ; and that the motion for change of reference was defeated (96 Cong. Rec. 1412-1417) .

To the extent, therefore, that there was any expression of preference, the choice was to consider the Code under the aegis of the Com-

---

[1] "The Code is a uniform system of legal procedure, applicable beyond any constitutional question to all servicemen stationed abroad. It was adopted by Congress only after an exhaustive study of several years duration and the consultation of acknowledged authorities in the fields of constitutional and military law." Slip opinion, No. 713, pp. 8-9, citing the 1949 Hearings before a Subcommittee of the House Committee on Armed Services.

No reference to any specific discussion of the constitutionality of Article 2 (11) is made in the Court's opinion—and none, it is submitted, can be made: There was no such discussion.

mittee most conversant with military problems, which dealt with the matter on the footing of continuing a military policy already on the statute book, and which in consequence would hardly be expected to weigh competing considerations.

In short, insofar as one can properly attribute to Congress any intent with respect to a problem of which it was not really aware, that intent was to proceed under its power to govern the armed forces and not under such powers as it may have had to create a particular type of legislative court from among those available. The latter choice it did not choose to make.

III

Nowhere in the Court's opinions is there any mention of the specific source of constitutional power on which the present extraordinary court-martial jurisdiction over civilians is rested.

Inquiry into the scope of the power to govern and regulate the armed forces is expressly avoided (slip opinion, No. 713, pp. 6-7). The war power—Article I, Section 8, Clause 11—is not mentioned. The now exploded notion that the "cases arising in the land or naval forces" clause of the Fifth Amendment is in itself a source of military jurisdiction (*Toth* v. *Quarles,* 350 U. S. 11, 14) is not sought to be revived. The treaty power is not relied on; the Court says [*7] (*id.,* p. 11) that "No question of the legal relation between treaties and the Constitution is presented." And while there is a reference (*id.,* p. 5) to legislative courts and the line of cases beginning with *American Ins. Co.* v. *Canter,* 1 Pet. 511, the power considered in those cases was that granted by Article IV, Section 3, to "make all needful Rules and Regulations respecting the Territory * * * belonging to the United States," a power that is obviously irrelevant when the United States is on foreign soil with the consent of the foreign sovereign—the situation in both cases here.

The Court does not point to any clause or phrase of the Constitution that confers on the Congress power to withdraw from American citizens seeking protection against the acts of American officials not only the guarantee of trial by jury (Article III, Section 2; Sixth Amendment) and of indictment by grand jury (Fifth Amendment), but also the Sixth Amendment's guarantee of confrontation (*United States* v. *Sutton,* 3 USCMA 220, 11 CMR 220) and the Eighth Amendment's guarantee of the right to bail (Dig. Op. JAG, 1912, p. 481, ¶IC)—and this under a system of procedure formulated by the President pursuant to authority delegated to him in his capacity as Commander-in-Chief. Article 36, UCMJ (50 U.S.C. § 611); *Manual for Courts-Martial, US, 1951* (Ex. Order 10214, 16 Fed. Reg. 1303). It is one matter to draw on the President's inherent power as Commander-in-Chief to discipline the armed forces (*Swaim* v. *United States*, 165 U. S. 553, 555-558) ; it is quite another to rest on that source when dealing with the rights of American civilians. Yet it is the *Manual* prescribed by the President by which the criminal liability of both women has been or will be determined, as the military opinions in their [*8] cases clearly show (No. 701, R. 12-121; No. 713, R. 23-94). Otherwise stated, the test of whether their respective mental states negatived legal responsibility—the sole contested issue before the military authorities in both cases—has been laid down by the President— and only by the President.

What is there in the Constitution that endows the Chief Executive with such untrammelled power over the liberty of two civilians?

To say that the Court's opinions raise more constitutional questions than they resolve is therefore not in any sense hyperbole.

IV

In No. 713, the Court could say (slip opinion, p. 10), "We note that this case presents no problem of the jurisdiction of a military court-martial sitting within the territorial limits of the United States * * *". But that precise problem is squarely presented in No. 701, the case of Mrs. Covert, who was being held for retrial by a general court-martial of the Air Force at Bolling Air Force Base within the District of Columbia.

In her case, the Court holds that a jurisdiction carefully circumscribed to persons accompanying the armed forces "without the continental limits of the United States" (Art. 2(11), UCMJ) is nonetheless applicable to Mrs. Covert within those limits, because (slip opinion, No. 701, p. 5) "military jurisdiction, once validly attached, continues until final disposition of the case." Mrs. Covert has never questioned, at any stage of the present case, the proposition that a rehearing is a continuation of the original proceeding. [*9] But the quoted holding makes the Court more militarist than the military, without a single military precedent to support its conclusion; for the military rulings, from the Civil War down through the Korean conflict, are uniformly to the effect that any separation of the individual from military status by affirmative act of Government, at any stage of the proceedings, terminates military jurisdiction over him.[2] Since discharge, muster out, or release to inactive duty has that effect on a soldier, because it changes him from soldier back to civilian, then surely the Government's act of removing a serviceman's dependent wife from without back to within

---

[2] Dig. Op. JAG, 1912, p. 514, ¶ VIII I 1 (rulings from 1862 on); *United States* v. *Sippel*, 4 USCMA 50, 53, 15 CMR 50, 53 (1954); and see the rulings collected and discussed in appellee's brief at pp. 23-27.

the continental limits of the United States should similarly terminate an amenability to trial by court-martial that is geographically restricted by the Code to civilians overseas.

Mrs. Covert's military status under the Code was dependent on her accompanying the armed forces overseas. When the Government brought her back to the United States it terminated that military status. And certainly her trial by court-martial within the United States is not even sought to be constitutionally justified by any of the considerations set forth in the Court's opinion in No. 713. Nowhere there is it suggested that Ross could have been tried in this country by the consul before whom he was haled in Japan.

If, however, the Court's ruling on this point stands, then some time this fall or winter—because the Air Force is determined to retry Mrs. Covert, almost as [*10] though its military honor were somehow involved [3]—there will be presented the spectacle, frightening in its forebodings for the future, of a civilian woman on trial before a military tribunal in the District of Columbia. This will be the first such trial since that of Mrs. Surratt—which is hardly a pretty precedent, or one of which any American can be proud. See, e.g., Moore, *The Case of Mrs. Surratt* (1954).

V

But there is an issue now presented by these cases that far transcends the future of the two women immediately involved, and which is infinitely more disturbing in its implications than any of the serious constitutional questions already canvassed.

That issue concerns the Court's adjudicatory procedures in these cases.

Both cases were placed on the summary calendar (J. Sup. Ct., Oct. T. 1955, p. 173), and, as the references in the margin show, both were prepared for argument on an accelerated schedule that cut nearly in half the time for briefs allowed under the new Rules.[4]

[*11] The argument itself came late in the Term. Indeed, not only was that argument the last on the calendar, on May 3 (J. Sup.

---

[3] The Solicitor General opposed her motion to stay the mandate pending the Court's disposition of the present Petition for Rehearing unless she would consent to subject herself to further psychiatric probing at St. Elizabeth's during the summer. Otherwise stated, the Government offered her a choice between confinement in jail and confinement in an asylum. On June 18, 1956, however, Mr. Justice Clark granted her motion and stayed the mandate.

[4] There was no printed record below in either case. The Clerk's files show that he transmitted the printed records to counsel for the parties on March 21 and 22. Under Rules 41 (1), 41 (2), and 43 (1), argument should therefore normally have been held some 75 days later. In fact, it took place on May 3, an interval of only 42 days.

Ct., Oct. T. 1955, pp. 230-231) —but it took place very late on that day, concluding long after the usual adjournment hour.[5] The question whether military jurisdiction over Mrs. Covert continued so as to subject her to retrial by court-martial in the United States was not discussed orally by either side, and on the basic issue that is considered by the Court in Mrs. Smith's case, losing counsel was asked only three questions, one of which inquired as to the location of a treaty provision that had been mentioned orally.[6] To the extent, therefore, that there is "a tradition of the Supreme Court as a tribunal not designed as a dozing audience for the reading of soliloquies, but as a questioning body, utilizing oral arguments as a means for exposing the difficulties of a case with a view to meeting them," the lateness of the hour perceptibly impaired the probing process.

Most serious of all, however, is the circumstance that the Court's opinions were announced before the three dissenting Justices had had time to formulate their views, and before another Justice had even been able to reach a decision. It cannot be said that a further period of waiting would have been without effect. Only recently, a Justice whose experience spanned twelve full Terms declared, in his posthumous declaration of constitutional faith, that "not infrequently the detailed study required to write an opinion, or the persuasiveness of an opinion or dissent, will lead to a [*12] change of a vote or even to a change of result." Jackson, *The Supreme Court in the American System of Government*, p. 15.

These petitioners for rehearing, therefore, may justly complain that their contentions did not receive as full consideration as if their causes had been argued a few months earlier. And they cannot forbear to remark that there appears to be no compelling reason of judicial administration why all of the Term's cases must be disposed of within the Term, or why the Court cannot return to its former practice of holding argued cases over the summer for disposition at the following Term.[7] Otherwise there is added to the inherent hazards of litigation the further danger of an inequality of treatment as among liti-

---

[5] The argument ended at 5:40 P.M. (Ward & Paul Transcript, p. 64), whereas the traditional time for adjournment, now codified in Rule 4 (1), is of course 4:30 P.M.

[6] Ward & Paul Transcript, pp. 52, 54.

[7] As late as the 1929 Term, the Court decided eight cases that had been argued during the 1928 Term. *Gonzales* v. *Roman Catholic Archbishop*, 280 U. S. 1; *FTC* v. *Klesner*, 280 U. S. 19; *Sanitary Refrig. Co.* v. *Winters*, 280 U. S. 30; *Williams* v. *Riley*, 280 U. S. 78; *Bekins Van Lines* v. *Riley*, 280 U. S. 80; *Grant* v. *Leach & Co.*, 280 U. S. 351; *Surplus Trading Co.* v. *Cook*, 281 U. S. 647; *Wheeler Lumber Co.* v. *United States*, 281 U. S. 572 (argued April 25, 1929; certificate dismissed May 27, 1929; restored to docket for reconsideration June 3, 1929; decided May 26, 1930).

gants that rests only on the happenstance of the position of the case on the calendar for the particular Term.

But, if the present practice is to be continued, then, assuredly, reargument is called for in these cases. True, "Rehearings are not a healthy step in the judicial process; surely they ought not to be deemed normal procedure." *Western Pacific Railroad Case*, 345 U. S. 247, 270. But certainly the issues that are involved in the present causes would seem to have far more public importance than those that were under consideration in the last two instances wherein this [*13] Court granted a rehearing after opinions had already been published. *Elgin, J. & E. R. Co.* v. *Burley*, 325 U. S. 711, rehearing granted, 326 U. S. 801, second opinions, 327 U. S. 661; *Graver Mfg. Co.* v. *Linde Co.*, 336 U. S. 271, rehearing granted, 337 U. S. 910, second opinions, 339 U. S. 605.

Least of all in the present cases, which will have such far-reaching consequences for so many individuals, and which plainly concern grave national policies as well, can the Court afford to substitute for the patient maturing of the judicial process a method of disposing of causes that all too obviously involves decision by deadline.

VI

This Petition for Rehearing should be granted, and both cases should be set down for reargument on the regular calendar.

Respectfully submitted.

FREDERICK BERNAYS WIENER,
Suite 815 Stoneleigh Court,
1025 Connecticut Avenue, N.W.,
Washington 6, D. C.,

*Counsel for the Appellee in No. 701 and
for the Respondent in No. 713*

CERTIFICATE OF COUNSEL

I certify that this petition is presented in good faith and not for delay.

FREDERICK BERNAYS WIENER

JULY 1956.

Section 174. Sequel to the rehearing in the *Covert* and *Krueger* cases.—Supreme Court Rule 58 (1) states that "A petition for rehearing * * * will not be granted, except at the instance of a justice who concurred in the judgment or decision and with the concurrence of a majority of the court."

Inasmuch as there were five votes against the petitioners, and new members of the Court, as a matter of settled practice, do not vote on petitions to rehear cases in which they did not originally participate, success for this particular petition depended on at least one of the former majority voting to rehear.

Well, the petition for rehearing was granted, Mr. Justice Harlan having moved over, for reasons which he subsequently set forth in the reports, 354 U. S. at 65-67. The student of the judicial process should examine those comments in the light of the petition for rehearing, bearing in mind always that what is urged in chambers and in the conference by other judges may well be more persuasive ultimately than the contentions a licked lawyer has assembled in print in a petition for rehearing.

The sequel of the rehearing in *Covert-Krueger* was happier than the sequel in *Herzog*. Almost a full year after the first opinions—364 days to be exact—those opinions were "withdrawn," and new ones filed. A majority of the Court agreed in holding that a court-martial could not constitutionally try civilian dependents for capital offenses in time of peace; thus both women went free. *Reid* v. *Covert*, 354 U. S. 1.

There was no opinion of the Court, so there was left open for future determination the question of court-martial jurisdiction over civilian dependents committing non-capital offenses, and over civilian employees, whether committing capital or non-capital offenses.

Those subsidiary questions were decided two and a half years later. In *Kinsella* v. *Singleton*,[14] the Court held that there was no military jurisdiction over civilian dependents committing non-capital offenses; in *Grisham* v. *Hagan* [15] that there was similarly no military jurisdiction over civilian employees committing capital offenses; and in *McElroy* v. *Guagliardo* [16] that civilian employees committing non-capital offenses were likewise triable only in civil courts.

"It was a long, hard fight, Mom, but we won."

Paradoxically enough, these holdings involved no new de-

[14] 361 U. S. 234.
[15] 361 U. S. 278.
[16] 361 U. S. 281.

parture, but instead marked a return to the classic views of an older generation of military lawyers. Colonel William Winthrop had laid it down in 1896, in italics, that *"a statute cannot be framed by which a civilian can lawfully be made amenable to the military jurisdiction in time of peace."* [17] And as late as 1912, The Judge Advocate General of the Army had proclaimed the same views "for the information of the Army and Organized Militia of the United States." [18]

---

[17] Winthrop, *Military Law and Precedents* (2d ed. 1896) *146 (p. 107, 1920 reprint).

[18] See *Digest of Opinions of The Judge Advocate General of the Army* (1912) pp. 151-152, 513; *id.* (1901) 56-58; *id.* (1895) pp. 75-77; *id.* (1880) pp. 48-49.

The quotation in the text is from p. 3 of the 1912 edition.

CHAPTER XIV

ANNOTATED CRITIQUE OF AN
ORAL ARGUMENT

Section 175. Purpose of this chapter.—In order to relate some
of the admonitions in the Third Part of the book to an actual
argument in a specific case, I have selected the transcript of the
oral remarks in a reasonably uncomplicated but still interesting
controversy. By way of preliminary, there is set forth the background out of which the case arose, with full citations to the
opinions rendered—and if the reader is to obtain any benefit from
this chapter, he had better read those opinions before he turns to
the transcript. Next comes the argument itself, to which the only
additions are footnote references to the matters cited or quoted
by counsel. That is followed by an analysis of the forensic problems each counsel faced, and how each one solved or attempted to
solve them. Finally, to complete the story, the result of the argument is given, and the subsequent decisions on the point are
briefly discussed.

Section 176. Background out of which case arose.—In the late
1940's and early 1950's, the Department of Justice embarked on a
series of intensive Grand Jury investigations. During the early
1950's, also, the Kefauver Committee was extremely active. Many
witnesses called in both of those investigations claimed their
privilege against self-incrimination. When they thereafter were
ordered to testify and refused, contempt proceedings were instituted against them, and, in the course of defending those proceedings, a good deal of law was made, as the citations in the note
indicate.[1]

---

[1] See, in addition to the cases cited elsewhere in this chapter, *Poretto* v.
United States, 196 F. 2d 392 (C.A. 5) ; *Marcello* v. *United States*, 196 F. 2d 437
(C.A. 5) ; *United States* v. *Costello*, 198 F. 2d 200 (C.A. 2), certiorari denied,
344 U. S. 874; *Aiuppa* v. *United States*, 201 F. 2d 287 (C.A. 6) ; and *United
States* v. *Doto*, 205 F. 2d 416 (C.A. 2), all of which arose out of the Kefauver
Committee's activities; *United States* v. *Girgenti*, 197 F. 2d 218 (C.A. 3), and
United States v. *Coffey*, 198 F. 2d 438 (C.A. 3), which grew out of the same

For present purposes, the first important Supreme Court decision was (*Patricia*) *Blau* v. *United States*,[2] which held that a witness was entitled to claim the privilege in respect of answers to questions which, while innocuous on their face, might none the less supply needed links in the case against the witness. And Patricia Blau's case was followed by *Hoffman* v. *United States*[3] wherein the Court spelled out the governing principles in detail, reversing the Third Circuit in the process.

Greenberg v. *United States* is the subject of this chapter. It was decided by the Third Circuit subsequent to, and on the same reasoning as, its *Hoffman* decision.[4] After certiorari had been granted in *Hoffman*,[5] Greenberg likewise sought review, but his petition was "held" pending the determination of the earlier case.[6] A week after *Hoffman* was decided, the Court granted certiorari in *Greenberg* with this notation: "The judgment of the Court of Appeals is vacated and the case is remanded to that court for reconsideration in the light of *Hoffman* v. *United States*, * * * decided May 28, 1951."[7]

On such reconsideration, the Third Circuit again sustained Greenberg's conviction, holding that his case differed perceptibly from that of *Hoffman*, wherein it had just been reversed.[8] (It is a wholly accurate paraphrase to say that "A court convinced against its will is of the same opinion still.") Again Greenberg petitioned for certiorari—see Section 85 for a memorandum filed in that connection—and again his petition was granted;[9] this time it

---

Grand Jury investigation as the principal case discussed in the present chapter; and *United States* v. *Rosen*, 174 F. 2d 187 (C.A. 2), certiorari denied, 338 U. S. 851; *Alexander* v. *United States*, 181 F. 2d 632 (C.A. 9), certiorari denied, 340 U. S. 920; and *Estes* v. *Potter*, 183 F. 3d 865 (C.A. 5), certiorari denied, 340 U. S. 920; *Brunner* v. *United States*, 343 U. S. 918, reversing 190 F. 2d 167 (C.A. 9), a group of cases arising out of Grand Jury inquiries into Communist activity.

District Court decisions have not been listed.

[2] 340 U. S. 159.
[3] 341 U. S. 479.
[4] 187 F. 2d 35.
[5] 340 U. S. 946.
[6] For the Supreme Court's practice of deferring consideration of petitions for certiorari, see Stern and Gressman, *Supreme Court Practice* (2d ed. 1954) ch. IV (C), p. 154; Robertson and Kirkham, *Jurisdiction of the Supreme Court of the United States* (Kurland and Wolfson ed. 1951) § 319, pp. 621-624.
[7] 341 U. S. 944.
[8] 192 F. 2d 201.
[9] 342 U. S. 917.

was set for argument on the summary docket, with an allowance of thirty minutes for each side.[10]

That argument follows. It is suggested that, by way of preliminary, the following opinions be first read in the order named: (1) *Patricia Blau,* 340 U. S. 159; (2) *Hoffman* below, 185 F. 2d 617; (3) *Hoffman* in the Supreme Court, 341 U. S. 479; (4) first *Greenberg* below, 187 F. 2d 35; (5) second *Greenberg* below, 192 F. 2d 201.

Section 177. The oral argument in *Greenberg* v. *United States.*

IN THE SUPREME COURT OF THE UNITED STATES

October Term, 1951

No. 461

IRVING GREENBERG, *Petitioner,*

v.

THE UNITED STATES OF AMERICA

Washington, D. C.,
Wednesday, April 2, 1952.

The above-entitled cause came on for oral argument at 1:05 P.M.

PRESENT: Chief Justice Vinson and Associates Justices Reed, Black, Douglas, Jackson, Burton, Clark, and Minton.

APPEARANCES: On behalf of the United States of America, M. H. Goldschein, Esq., Special Assistant to the Attorney General; on behalf of Petitioner, Frederick Bernays Wiener, Esq.

PROCEEDINGS

THE CHIEF JUSTICE: Argument in No. 461, *Greenberg* against *The United States of America.*

ARGUMENT ON BEHALF OF THE PETITIONER

By Mr. Wiener

MR. WIENER: If the Court please, this is the second writ of certiorari which your Honors have granted in this case. Three questions are involved.

---

[10] Now, since the effective date of the 1954 Rules, the summary calendar. Supreme Court Rule 44 (3).

The first is a continuing conflict of decision between the court below and this Court as to the proper scope of the constitutional privilege against self-incrimination.[11]

The second question is whether the Government may properly prosecute an individual while at the same time denying him the ability to defend—whether, when the Government prosecutes an individual for the contempt involved in refusing to answer questions claimed by him to be self-incriminating and he seeks to prove their incriminating nature through papers in the possession of the Government and normally privileged, the Government may continue to assert its privilege while continuing the prosecution.

The third question concerns the, we think, material variances between what happened at the trial and what is recited in the formal judgment of conviction.

If the Court please, this case involved the same Grand Jury and the same prosecutor as were involved in the *Hoffman* case decided at the last Term.[12] The background of the case is the prosecutor's announcements of his purpose in the public press. That becomes material because the petitioner stated, in claiming his privilege, that he feared the questions to be incriminating in part because of what he read in the papers. These newspaper accounts were introduced at the trial, and not afterward as in the *Hoffman* case.[13]

This is what the prosecutor was reported as saying: "Even though there are no Federal laws regarding numbers, slot machines and other rackets, the probers will strike at such rings through the Federal revenue and conspiracy laws."

Mr. Goldschein, who is now here representing the Government, was the prosecutor in charge of the investigation. He "stressed the importance of 'conspiracy.'" Further, "A Justice Department spokesman said that as each witness is called, agents of the Bureau of Internal Revenue are prepared to produce income tax reports so that the jury can check his testimony.

"Income tax violations would permit the Government to strike indirectly at racketeers whose activities are not covered by Federal criminal statutes."[14]

During the pendency of this investigation the petitioner refused to answer certain questions before the Grand Jury, and the basic question as to which he claimed his privilege was, "Are you in the num-

---

[11] This was a somewhat sarcastic reference to the rule that a conflict of decision between circuits justifies the granting of certiorari. Supreme Court Rule 19 (1) (b).

[12] 341 U. S. 479.

[13] See 185 F. 2d at 621 and 341 U. S. at 483 and 489.

[14] Record, pp. 196a, 197a.

bers business now?" After I have stated the questions, I will expound the claim of privilege that was made.

The second question revolves around the use of his telephone. He was asked, "What business do you use your telephone for?" He said, "Not for my lawful business."

"Do you use it in your real estate business?" "No."

"Do you use it in any other business?" "Yes."

"What other business do you use it for?" "Not for my lawful business," he said, and he refused to answer further, claiming his privilege.

The third question involved is the identification question. He was asked, "Do you know any numbers writers, people in the numbers business, around your place of business?" He said, "Yes."

Question: "Who?" And as to that he claimed his privilege.

When he persisted in refusal, the Grand Jury presented him for contempt and he was tried.

If the Court please, the claim of privilege was very specific. He claimed that if he answered these questions, he would be incriminating himself under the Federal criminal law, and he cited the statutes; and he also stated that his fear of self-incrimination was based on the advice of counsel, on his own knowledge of what the answers would be, and on what he had read in the newspapers. His claim was very specific. It fills a number of complete pages of the record.

MR. JUSTICE REED: Do you claim the numbers racket is a Federal Crime?

MR. WIENER: No. We do not claim that for a minute. I will explain in a minute why the admission that he is in the numbers business is incriminating under Federal law.

MR. JUSTICE REED: Some of these questions go beyond the numbers business.

MR. WIENER: The "Who" question did. The telephone question didn't go beyond that.

After he was presented by the Grand Jury he was tried for contempt. At the trial he offered to prove that he, himself, was under investigation, that there was a definite plan on the part of the Government to show that he and other witnesses were guilty of violating the Federal tax law, and that it was a part of the plan of the prosecutor, once he answered these questions, to prosecute him or recommend prosecution for violation of Federal law.

He introduced the newspapers and in further substantiation of his contention that these answers would be incriminating under Federal law, he subpoenaed the prosecutor's papers, and he moved to examine the Grand Jury minutes in order to show that these questions in their setting were incriminating and that, if he answered them, Mr. Goldschein would initiate prosecution.

The District Judge sustained the objection to the offer of proof. He refused the subpoena of the prosecutor's files and he denied the motion for the inspection of the Grand Jury minutes.

With his defense withheld the petitioner was found guilty and was sentenced to five months imprisonment and held, pending appeal, in the rather high bail of $10,000.

The conviction was affirmed by the Third Circuit.[15] Your Honors granted certiorari last June, vacated the judgment, and remanded the case for reconsideration in the light of the *Hoffman* decision.[16] The court below reconsidered, reaffirmed,[17] and a second writ of certiorari brings the case here.[18]

As to the first question, whether the petitioner properly showed that the answers to these questions would incriminate him, we say he did under the *Hoffman* case [19] and the *Patricia Blau* [20] decision.

The basis of the difference between the petitioner and the Government on this argument is based on the circumstance that the Government in its rather voluminous brief here never goes on to quote that portion of the *Hoffman* opinion which says that in order to establish the privilege it isn't necessary to prove the incriminating nature of the question beyond a mathematical doubt, otherwise the privilege would be lost in asserting it. All that is necessary is to show a reasonable apprehension in the setting that these questions would incriminate,[21] and I think he made that showing, and this is why: He showed that the prosecutor had announced a plan to strike at the numbers people who were not violating Federal law in the numbers business, to strike at them through the Federal revenue and conspiracy laws. How does one strike at a person for tax evasion? That is the wilful understatement of income under Section 145 (b) of the Internal Revenue Code.[22] The first requirement is to show that the defendant has an income-producing business. Then you go on from there. That is the first requirement. You have to show that he is in an income-producing business if you are trying to establish an understatement of income by circumstantial evidence. That appears from the writings of

---

[15] 187 F. 2d 35.
[16] 341 U. S. 944.
[17] 192 F. 2d 201.
[18] 342 U. S. 917.
[19] 341 U. S. 479.
[20] 340 U. S. 159.
[21] See Section 35 (d), *supra*, at pp. 106-107.
[22] Now § 7201, I.R.C. 1954.

the Government's own tax experts, which we have set forth in the Appendix to our reply brief.[23]

There is no difference of opinion on it. Non-government authorities in the same field say the same thing.[24] The cases establish it. When you are setting out to prove tax evasion—that is, wilful understatement of income in violation of 145 (b) —the first thing you show is that the man had an income-producing business. That is why this question was important. That is why this petitioner specifically claimed his privilege under Section 145 (b) , and he cited it.

MR. JUSTICE REED: How definite was the Government's threat of criminal prosecution?

MR. WIENER: The prosecutor said, "Even though there are Federal laws against numbers, we will get them through the tax laws." He announced, "We have the tax returns as each witness is called before the Grand Jury."

As a matter of fact, people have been indicted and tried under the tax laws arising out of this very investigation. It was a threat to do it under the tax and conspiracy laws.

MR. JUSTICE REED: The criminal laws?

MR. WIENER: Yes, the criminal Federal tax laws.

MR. JUSTICE REED: Did they use the word "criminal"?

MR. WIENER: It was the Grand Jury. It wasn't the Civil Division of the United States Attorney's office. The Grand Jury returns indictments. It doesn't draw complaints for civil actions. I think it was a definite threat and under the *Hoffman* case he proved all he could possibly show without actually incriminating himself.

MR. JUSTICE JACKSON: I suppose the threat was not necessary to the privilege in any event.

MR. WIENER: It makes it an *a fortiori* case, that is all.

MR. JUSTICE JACKSON: If the witness knows that what he will reveal would form the basis of a prosecution, it is enough without a threat.

MR. WIENER: I entirely agree.

MR. JUSTICE JACKSON: I suppose he can assume that the Federal prosecutors will prosecute him if he discloses the facts which show that he ought to be prosecuted.

MR. WIENER: I agree that the threat simply makes it an *a fortiori* case.

---

[23] Rothwacks, *Criminal Tax Prosecutions,* in 1 *Current Issues in Federal Taxation* 269, 282, 283; Rothwacks, *Problems in Criminal Tax Prosecutions,* in 3 *id.* 297, 310-311.

[24] Balter, *Fraud Under Federal Tax Law,* 280, 281.

Under the Federal tax laws, if you have employees, you have to make withholding returns.[25] This petitioner showed that in the numbers business there are employees. He showed he had filed no withholding returns. He was forced to make that showing when the Court sustained the Internal Revenue's representative's claim of privilege in respect to answering. So, if he had said, "Yes, I am in the numbers business," that would have been the link in the chain. If you are in a business which has employees and you did not file withholding returns, and this man had not filed any, then this man would have revealed that a crime had been committed. It is the link in the chain. What more could he possibly have shown other than actually incriminating himself?

These same considerations apply to the question, "Who?" If he had answered who they were, not only would he be supplying witnesses against him, but Mr. Goldschein had stressed the importance of conspiracy and Mr. Goldschein had asked the petitioner the questions, "Do you know Willy Weisberg? Do you know 'Cappy' Hoffman?"

Willy Weisberg is the William Weisberg who was considered in the *Hoffman* case.[26] Cappy Hoffman, the Hoffman record shows, was the Hoffman of *Hoffman* v. *The United States*.[27]

I think the *Patricia Blau* case [28] covers it completely, because here you have a prosecutor saying, "I am going to get you through the conspiracy laws, and I want to know the names of your co-conspirators."

Mr. Justice Burton: This argument as to the danger to himself of a prosecution for violation of the tax laws, that would apply to the operation of a legitimate business as much as it would to the operation of illegitimate business.

Mr. Wiener: Yes, that is correct.

Mr. Justice Burton: He refused to answer because it was an illegitimate business?

Mr. Wiener: That is right. As far as the Federal law is concerned, there is nothing wrong with the numbers business, subject only possibly to the new tax law,[29] which I haven't studied.

Mr. Justice Burton: So, if he is asked what business he is in, he knows he is in a business.

Mr. Wiener: Yes.

---

[25] Sections 1430, 1622, 1627, and 2707, I.R.C. 1939; now Sections 3402 (a), 6672, and 7203, I.R.C. 1954.

[26] See 185 F. 2d at 619, 620; 341 U. S. at 481, 484, 488.

[27] See R. 11-14, No. 513, Oct. T. 1950.

[28] 340 U. S. 159.

[29] Section 471 of the Revenue Act of 1951, 26 U.S.C. [1952 ed.] §§ 3285-3298; now §§ 4401-4423, I.R.C. 1954 (Taxes on Wagering) ; see *United States* v. *Kahriger,* 345 U. S. 22.

If I am in the law business and I have not filed a proper tax return and they ask, "What do you do?," I may incriminate myself if I make the admission.

Certainly, if the prosecutor's announcement says that he is going to get at the numbers people through the revenue laws, I do not think any further showing is necessary.

I come to the second question. The petitioner here said, "I can show that the answers to these questions are incriminating and I will show, if you will let me have Mr. Goldschein's brief case, his papers, his file and let me inspect the Grand Jury's minutes, then I will prove to a mathematical certainty that these are the missing links in the chain."

The judge said, "You first make a showing of incrimination, then I may let you see the papers."

THE CHIEF JUSTICE: Mr. Wiener, I would like to hear you in regard to the state offense angle.

MR. WIENER: Under the *Murdock* case [30] an individual cannot claim privilege before a Federal tribunal because the answer may incriminate him of a State offense. We are not required to reexamine that. We are not required to examine either the possible *Lustig* v. *United States* [31] application; in other words, if there is a preconceived plan, a cooperative effort, between the Federal prosecutor and the State prosecutor that, after the Federal prosecutor obtains the answers which are non-incriminating under Federal law but incriminating under State law, he then turns them over to the State prosecutor, whether the State prosecutor may proceed with the prosecution or not—we do not have that problem. We only have the problem here of an activity proscribed by State law as to which the petitioner, the witness, claims no privilege under State law but says that, "If I answer, if I admit being in this activity, I have incriminated myself under Federal law."

THE CHIEF JUSTICE: What authority is there in back of the Government's position in regard to that?

MR. WIENER: The only authority I can find for the Government's position on the question of self-incrimination is the first portion of the *Hoffman* case, leaving out the rest of the paragraph. [32]

THE CHIEF JUSTICE: I mean as to a State offense, not a Federal offense.

MR. WIENER: It has been assumed all along there is a Pennsylvania statute on it. I don't know.

THE CHIEF JUSTICE: How would a Pennsylvania statute affect this?

---

[30] *United States* v. *Murdock*, 284 U. S. 141.
[31] 338 U. S. 74.
[32] 341 U. S. at 486-487.

MR. WIENER: I don't think it would. We don't think it would.

THE CHIEF JUSTICE: Basically, what is your view as to that issue? He says, "I refuse to answer on the ground of incrimination. It isn't a Federal offense on which I would be incriminated, but a State offense."

MR. WIENER: Under the *Murdock* case,[33] that is not a sufficient claim of privilege.

MR. JUSTICE REED: You are not attacking that case?

MR. WIENER: I am not attacking the *Murdock* case, nor do I have to say the *Murdock* case should be modified by the *Lustig*[34] application. I do not have to go into that at all because the petitioner here made a specific contention of incrimination under Federal law and he cited the Federal statutes.

MR. JUSTICE BLACK: Suppose you are wrong on that, what happens then?

MR. WIENER: Then he goes to jail for five months.

MR. JUSTICE BLACK: You would still not ask the Court to consider whether they can send him to jail for refusing to answer, if he might be convicted in a numbers case?

MR. WIENER: That would require a reexamination of *Murdock*.

MR. JUSTICE BLACK: You are waiving that point?

MR. WIENER: Yes. I do not think we reach it. Under the *Hoffman* and *Patricia Blau* cases we have made a sufficient showing. We do not have that question here. It hasn't been raised at any stage. It hasn't been briefed by either side. I accept it. There may come a time when we will have to—

THE CHIEF JUSTICE: What about this fellow's time? If you waive it, his time is past.

MR. WIENER: I feel, Mr. Chief Justice, as long as the Court applies the doctrine laid down at the last term in the *Patricia Blau* and *Hoffman* cases, the petitioner is not in jeopardy, because those decisions require reversal.

There is another reason. That is what the Government has done here. He claimed his privilege. He said, "I can prove this is incriminating. Let me have the prosecutor's file, let me have the Grand Jury minutes. I will then prove it is the link."

The Government says, "These documents are privileged."

We say, as long as they want to prosecute, they have to waive their privilege. They cannot simultaneously prosecute and assert their privilege in respect to papers which the accused needs for his defense, just as a matter of fairness. If we need authority, there is a whole line of cases in the Second Circuit saying that the Government has its choice,

---

[33] *Supra* note 30.
[34] *Supra* note 31.

either it asserts its privilege or it prosecutes.[35] It cannot do both. As a matter of fairness, it cannot deprive an accused of the documents he needs for his defense. As to that, we also have the authority of the Third Circuit, the court below, in the *Singleton* case,[36] decided after this case. There was a similar question there. I suppose they got the idea from this case. The Court of Appeals examined those documents and the court below said the trial judge should have examined them.

Mr. Justice Jackson: Do you think he has to show any danger in the sense of any evidence of a prosecution? Suppose the prosecutor doesn't have the slightest idea that he is guilty of a crime and his answer, in his opinion, might reveal that he was?

Mr. Wiener: I think that is enough.

Mr. Justice Jackson: You wanted to gild the lily?

Mr. Wiener: I had to, your Honor, because we have lost this case twice below. I think he made a sufficient showing in the District Court the first time.

Mr. Justice Jackson: That is a pretty good reason for doing it.

Mr. Wiener: The court below has twice disagreed with us. We have to go into it at great length.

As your Honor says, that should be sufficient if he makes it in good faith, and he certainly made it in good faith here. When he wanted to get the tax returns, as a matter of fact, got the tax official to testify whether he had filed withholding tax returns, the Government was permitted to assert its privilege and the judge said, "Let Greenberg take the stand if he didn't file. I won't compel the Government to do that."[37]

What he has been forced to do there is all but establish his privilege by incriminating himself.

That leaves only one other point—

Mr. Justice Reed: Would good faith alone be a defense?

Mr. Wiener: Not necessarily. That would go only to mitigation. I think he has done what this Court in the *Hoffman* case said wasn't necessary. As a matter of fact, the Government goes so far that they come perilously close to commenting on his claim of privilege by saying, "Well, everybody knows he is in the numbers business."[38]

There is a third point in the case, but it is too detailed for oral

---

[35] *United States* v. *Zwillman,* 108 F. 2d 802; *United States* v. *Andolschek,* 142 F. 2d 580; *United States* v. *Beekman,* 155 F. 2d 580; *United States* v. *Grayson,* 166 F. 2d 863 (all C.A. 2).

[36] 193 F. 2d 464 (later reversed, 343 U. S. 944).

[37] Record, p. 35a.

[38] "It would be difficult to read the record here and not realize that everybody knows that petitioner is in the numbers business." U. S. Br. 48, No. 461, Oct. T. 1951.

discussion. That has reference to the facts and the consequences of the variance between the record of the trial and the judgment of commitment. That is fully covered in the briefs, and I rely on the briefs for that.

Mr. Justice Clark: What is your position in the event some of the questions are proper and some improper?

Mr. Wiener: I should think that the normal rule would apply, that it would be sufficient to sustain conviction and it would be appropriate to remand for resentencing, but I think all the questions are improper. There are only three unanswered. One is: "Are you in the numbers business now?" The second is: "What other business do you use it for?" The third is: "Who are the numbers people around your place of business?"

Mr. Justice Clark: If you are not correct that all the questions were improper, you think it should be remanded for resentencing?

Mr. Wiener: Yes, because there are fewer. But I think they are all improper. I think the rule is fairly well settled. Of course, there may be a question whether this should be treated as one indictment or whether each question should be treated as a separate count. Perhaps I have conceded too much, treating each as a separate count.

Actually, I think that under the *Hoffman* and *Patricia Blau* cases all of the unanswered questions were improper, so we never really get to that.

ARGUMENT ON BEHALF OF THE UNITED STATES
OF AMERICA
By Mr. Goldschein.

Mr. Goldschein: May it please the Court, the three questions here were asked of Mr. Greenberg at the tail end of many that were asked him before, some of which are repeated here in the brief. This case is different from the *Hoffman* case in that the *Hoffman* case the background of Hoffman was such, as stated by this Court, that it was not perfectly clear that, if he answered the question, he would not incriminate himself for some Federal crime. Here it is limited, his crime is limited. He sets out specifically just what he is fearful of and he says it in this way:

"If I admit that in that business I had employees, then I know that my answer will tend to incriminate me in violation of Sections 1625 (a), 1626 (a), (b) and (c), as well as Section 145 (a), (b) and (c) above referred to."

May it please the Court, the questions asked—or the first one asked him was: "Are you in the numbers business now?"

It was the year 1950. No income tax return was required to be filed until March of 1951. So there can be no incrimination under the income tax laws for failure to file an accurate return. It wasn't due. That question was discussed considerably in the court, and we pointed out to the court that the question had reference to 1950. We went back before the Grand Jury and rephrased the questions. So that there could be no doubt that referred to the year 1950, and took it out of any tax claims.

Then he says:

"Were I to admit that I had no records and kept no account of my other business, lawful or unlawful, other than the business testified to, I would be incriminating myself in violation of the federal income tax laws. I know if I admitted being in any other business, lawful or unlawful, and had employees in the operation of that business and/or if I admitted that, I did not withhold the taxes due to the United States Government, I would be incriminating myself, not only in violation of the income tax laws, which I have enumerated above, but that I may tend to incriminate myself with regard to the conspiracy charges in connection therewith."

He is limiting himself to what he is fearful of and, when we asked him what business he was in or what business he used the telephone for, we didn't have the problem we had in the *Hoffman* case. He might incriminate himself for some statute because of his general background, because the nature of the individual or his past experience was such. Here we have a specific limitation. If he answers the question, it may show that he is in a business and, if he is in a business, he may be asked whether or not he has some employees. Then the question will arise whether or not he paid any withholding taxes for these said employees, and whether or not he paid any social security taxes on these employees, if he had any employees, and if the questions were asked.

There is a great deal of difference between the *Greenberg* case and the *Hoffman* case or the *Patricia Blau* case. In the *Blau* case it is apparent that, if they answered the question, the answer would be a link in the chain of evidence that would correct them with the Smith Act violation. It was a link in the chain of evidence. But here, if he answered that he was in the numbers business, would that be a link in the chain to the violation of any of the statutes here referred to?

Mr. Justice Black: What would be the object in asking that?

Mr. Goldschein: To determine whether or not he knew "Nig" Rosen, who was supposed to be a numbers baron or numbers banker in that area.

Mr. Justice Black: What did that have to do with the Federal statutes? Why was he asked those questions? Was it in connection with some crime?

MR. GOLDSCHEIN: No. These connections were questions that would lead to other questions and other people to determine whether or not the criminal laws were there being violated.

MR. JUSTICE BLACK: Federal criminal laws?

MR. GOLDSCHEIN: Federal criminal laws.

MR. JUSTICE BLACK: What Federal criminal laws?

MR. GOLDSCHEIN: Any.

The letter of authority authorized counsel for the Grand Jury to assist the Grand Jury in making inquiry with reference to the internal revenue, liquor laws, narcotic laws, postal violations, Mann Act laws, or conspiracies to commit violations of those laws, or other violations of the Federal statutes.

MR. JUSTICE BLACK: What did this have to do with that, whether or not he was engaged in the numbers racket?

MR. GOLDSCHEIN: May it please the Court, it is one of the questions that would possibly lead to other questions.

MR. JUSTICE BLACK: Other questions of what kind?

MR. GOLDSCHEIN: Violations of the Federal statutes, may it please the Court.

MR. JUSTICE BLACK: Did his being in the numbers business have anything to do with it?

MR. GOLDSCHEIN: No, sir.

MR. JUSTICE BLACK: Does it have anything to do with the White Slave Law which you mentioned? What was its relevancy? I am just trying to find out what you were asking him about and what for.

MR. GOLDSCHEIN: We were asking about all the people in that area who were engaged in the violation of any law, whether it be State or Federal, to determine whether or not there was any connection between the State and Federal law.

MR. JUSTICE BLACK: You were trying to make him admit he was violating the State law?

MR. GOLDSCHEIN: No, sir. We weren't trying to make him admit anything. All we were trying to do was to find out what the facts were in that community to determine whether or not the Federal laws were being violated. That wasn't a case where the investigators had gone out and made an investigation and turned the information over to the Grand Jury for the purpose of presenting an indictment.

MR. JUSTICE BLACK: So what you convicted him for was for refusing to tell whether he was engaged in numbers; is that right?

MR. GOLDSCHEIN: No, sir. What he was convicted for was refusing to obey the order of the Court to answer the question, "Who were the numbers writers around the area of 1133 West Diamond Street?"

Mr. Justice Black: What did the Federal Government have to do with that?

Mr. Goldschein: They were preliminary questions, may it please the Court.

Mr. Justice Black: Were you up there to enforce the gambling and numbers laws?

Mr. Goldschein: No, sir. We have nothing to do with the numbers laws, the bookmaking laws or any of the other laws.

Mr. Justice Black: You have nothing to do with these laws which you asked him whether he violated?

Mr. Goldschein: No, sir. We weren't concerned with the violation of any State laws, at all.

Mr. Justice Black: Why did you ask him, then?

Mr. Goldschein: May it please the Court, the only way you can find out whether there are any laws violated in a community is by calling everybody in whom you are advised has any connection—

Mr. Justice Black:—with violating any other laws?

Mr. Goldschein: Yes, sir. That is the way it is done, from my experience. I have learned that this is the only way it can possibly be done. You cannot call the doctor in, you cannot call the preacher in, you cannot call the lawyer in, because they have no connection with it, and generally do not know. But you have to call the underworld in, generally. Of course, you, in the course of an inquiry like that, do call bankers in, you call in everbody who—may give you a lead toward any Federal crime, whatever that may be—railroad officials, airplane company officials—wherever the scent leads, you follow.

In so far as the revenue agents were concerned, in connection with that investigation or statements I made to the newspapers, that just didn't happen. We had no revenue agents at the time that Greenberg was called. We had no revenue agents of any kind making any kind of an investigation at the time that Mr. Greenberg came before the Grand Jury.

Mr. Justice Black: I gathered from what you said that this had no relevance to the possible violation of the Federal revenue laws and had no relevance to the possible violation of any other Federal laws.

Mr. Goldschein: May the Court please, let me explain. The presentment charged these men with obstructing the business of the Grand Jury and wilful disobedience of the order of the court, but did not find them guilty under the obstruction of the business of the Grand Jury phase.

If the Grand Jury is limited to asking questions, each question of which must be pertinent to the issue, may it please the Court, then you destroy the inquisitiorial functions of the Grand Jury.

MR. JUSTICE BLACK: Is there any limit to the power of the Grand Jury?

MR. GOLDSCHEIN: No. Under the *Blair* case,[39] there is no limit. The Grand Jury has a right to make inquiry to determine that there is no violation of the Federal statutes.

MR. JUSTICE BLACK: What about violations of local laws?

MR. GOLDSCHEIN: We were not investigating local laws, if your Honor please. It is very often necessary, when you call a man in—

MR. JUSTICE BLACK: That is all you asked him about, a local law?

MR. GOLDSCHEIN: That is all we got to.

MR. JUSTICE BLACK: You just said you weren't interested in that.

MR. GOLDSCHEIN: We are not interested in violations of local laws. In calling a man in, if he is a banker, you want to know what his business is. If he is a lawyer, you ask him what his business is. Always for the record you attempt to identify the individual so that the record will show who it is that is testifying before the Grand Jury.

MR. JUSTICE BLACK: Was that the purpose of this, to try to identify this man?

MR. GOLDSCHEIN: No. We wanted to know about the criminal situation, the crime situation, in Philadelphia. That was the purpose of the Grand Jury.

MR. JUSTICE JACKSON: You hadn't gotten to that?

MR. GOLDSCHEIN: No, sir. We hadn't gotten to that. He refused to answer.

MR. JUSTICE CLARK: He had previously said he was in the real estate business.

MR. GOLDSCHEIN: Yes, sir. He said the Amtol Corporation was a real estate corporation and he was employed by the Amtol Corporation, but he didn't claim any privilege on that because he probably didn't have any employees in that business and/or employees weren't an essential part of that business in his mind, and therefore he didn't claim any privilege on that question. He volunteered that. There wasn't any trouble on that.

MR. JUSTICE CLARK: Mr. Goldschein, on that point of "now" which you emphasized a moment ago, "Are you in the numbers business now," when do you file social security reports?

MR. GOLDSCHEIN: You file them at the end of the year. Withholding tax returns are filed quarterly.

MR. JUSTICE BLACK: That is employee withholding?

MR. GOLDSCHEIN: Yes, sir.

MR. JUSTICE CLARK: Would that be required if he was in the numbers business and had employees?

---

[39] *Blair* v. *United States,* 250 U. S. 273.

Mr. Goldschein: Sir?

Mr. Justice Clark: Would withholding taxes apply if he had employees?

Mr. Goldschein: Withholding taxes would apply if he had employees, but, may it please the Court, it is common knowledge in that area that in the numbers business there are no employees as such that come under the particular statute. He didn't identify himself as being either a banker, a pick-up man or a numbers writer. He testified and said that in the numbers business there are three types of individuals. There is a writer, there is the pick-up man, and there is the banker.

The way it operates is that the numbers writer goes around. He said those keep the records. The writer writes the numbers and takes the bets. He takes out his cut of 25 per cent and turns it over to the pick-up man. The pick-up man collects from all the numbers writers, takes out his 10 per cent, his cut of 10 per cent, and gives the balance to the banker.

That was discussed in the courts below, but it does not appear in the printed record here.

All he was interested in was that, if he disclosed that he was a numbers banker, the next question would be whether he had any employees. The next question after that would be whether he kept any records. Those questions weren't asked. They came squarely within the *Mason* case,[40] and the *Ward* case [41] cited in the *Mason* case. Both were cited with approval in the *Hoffman* case.

In the *Mason* case the Court will recall that a man was asked whether there was a game of cards going on at the table at which he was sitting. The Court in that case held that there was no direct danger of incrimination simply because of a card game going on at a table at which he was sitting or at the next table.

The *Mason* case cites the *Ward* case, a Missouri case, in which a man was asked whether he knew any faro players in that community. He refused to answer that question. The Missouri court, relying on the *Burr* case,[42] said there was absolutely no connection of direct danger of incrimination under those circumstances and held him in contempt.

May it please the Court, the next question that was stressed here was the Government refusing to turn over any records. We say unequivocally that a defendant in any criminal case has a right to call on the Government or anybody to produce any specific document or

---

[40] *Mason* v. *United States,* 244 U. S. 362.

[41] *Ward* v. *State,* 2 Mo. 120.

[42] *United States* v. *Burr* (*In re Willie*), Fed. Case No. 14,692e (C.C.D. Va.).

thing that would tend to prove or disprove any issue in his defense. But we say that there was no request for that in this case. We say in this case it was purely a fishing expedition to see what the Government had in its file. If there was anything that they could use that was in the Government's file for any purpose, it was that much gained.

Here is what the request was:

"Subpoena to bring all records concerned with investigation of Irving Greenberg and used in connection with the examination of Irving Greenberg as a witness before the Grand Jury and with the examination of other witnesses who have appeared before the Grand Jury and have testified about Irving Greenberg."

I cannot imagine a more extensive fishing expedition that this was.

Had there been a request, may it please the Court, to bring in the Grand Jury testimony of Bill Smith who testified against Irving Greenberg, then there might be some basis for that, Bill Smith having been a revenue agent who was making an investigation on Irving Greenberg or making an investigation on a partner of Irving Greenberg or an associate of Irving Greenberg.

Yes, I can see that. But to bring in all the Grand Jury testimony of everybody, without naming them, anybody who mentioned the name of Irving Greenberg, is something that the Court couldn't understand and the Government couldn't understand as being pertinent to any issue or would tend to prove any issue in this case.

Asking for the Government's file, they didn't ask for the statement of any one particular individual that the Government had in its file which would tend to prove or disprove any issue or fact in that case. That wasn't the issue. The issue was: Bring it in and let's look it over and we will be governed by any other further offer of proof after we see what is in the records. That is not the *Zwillman* case[43] or any of the other cases—the *Beekman* case[44] cited in those cases.

May it please the Court, there was a request made in those cases for specific documents.

In the *Andolschek* case,[45] if the Court recalls, there they asked for specific reports that they filed in that case showing their dealings with other people. They didn't make a blanket request for records.

Now, may it please the Court, of course, the courts have held that the formal order of the court is that which is binding, and what the court may say orally at the conclusion of the hearing must give way to the written order. The only difference is that in the presentment the Grand Jury charged that he refused to answer the question, "Are you

[43] *United States* v. *Zwillman*, 108 F. 2d 802 (C.A. 2).
[44] *United States* v. *Beekman*, 155 F. 2d 580 (C.A. 2).
[45] *United States* v. *Andolschek*, 142 F. 2d 580 (C.A. 2).

in the numbers business now," and also in the presentment with the violation of two sections of 401, obstruction of business of the Grand Jury and wilful disobedience of the order of the Court.[46]

May it please the Court, we say that the court incidentally found him guilty of the latter; that is, wilful disobedience of the order of the court, and didn't find him guilty of contempt in refusing to answer the first question. That isn't a variance. If anything, it inured to the benefit of Greenberg.

THE CHIEF JUSTICE: Is that to say that the court didn't find him guilty—

MR. GOLDSCHEIN:—of obstructing—

THE CHIEF JUSTICE:—of declining to answer the question, "Are you in the numbers business now?"

MR. GOLDSCHEIN: Yes, sir, but did find him guilty of refusing to answer the other three questions: "Who," referring to the numbers writers around 1133 West Diamond Street—and "What business do you use it for," referring to the telephone at that address—and "Do you use it for any other business," referring to that same telephone.

MR. JUSTICE BLACK: Is that question number six, seven A, on page 3-A?

MR. GOLDSCHEIN: Page 4 of the Government's brief.

MR. JUSTICE BLACK: I was looking at the record. You brought in 13 questions. How many of those were involved?

MR. GOLDSCHEIN: May it please the Court, that is the presentment. The presentment sets out the questions that he first was asked before the Grand Jury, which he refused to answer. Then he went back before the Grand Jury and answered most of those questions, all except: "Are you in the numbers business now?" Then he subsequently went back before the Grand Jury and refused to answer the question on 6-A and 7, three-quarters of the way down on page 7-A: "Do you use it for any other business?" That is in the record and on page 4 of the brief it also appears.

THE CHIEF JUSTICE: That was asking about the telephone. You say it was a preliminary question.

MR. GOLDSCHEIN: Yes, sir.

---

[46] "§ 401. Power of court

"A court of the United States shall have power to punish by fine or imprisonment, at its discretion, such contempt of its authority, and none other, as—

"(1) Misbehavior of any person in its presence or so near thereto as to obstruct the administration of justice;

"(2) Misbehavior of any of its officers in their official transactions;

"(3) Disobedience or resistance to its lawful writ, process, order, rule, decree, or command."

THE CHIEF JUSTICE: What would have been your follow-up question on it that would have been pertinent to a federal offense?

MR. GOLDSCHEIN: Whether he takes bets over that telephone on horses.

THE CHIEF JUSTICE: That is not a Federal presentment.

MR. GOLDSCHEIN: No, sir, but we know, then, who the bookmakers are, whether he lays off bets with anyone and who the people are that he lays off these bets with. There is the higher up in the bookmaking business. May it please the Court, the *Claiborne* case [47] from Missouri is just such a case.

In that case they questioned the right of the Grand Jury to investigate State offenses. The question referred to some pistols that one Gargotta had in his possession that were used in a murder case in Kansas City prior to that, and Claiborne, a detective, switched pistols—

MR. JUSTICE BLACK: What case is that?

MR. GOLDSCHEIN: *Claiborne.*

MR. JUSTICE BLACK: Is that cited in the brief?

MR. GOLDSCHEIN: I do not think it is cited in the brief. In response to the question asked by the Chief Justice, I was citing a case on that. It is a Fed. 2d case.

MR. JUSTICE BLACK: It didn't come up here?

MR. GOLDSCHEIN: No, sir. It is 77 Fed. 2d 682.

May it please the Court, that apparently was a question of whether or not a policeman committed perjury in the State court or whether or not Gargotta was carrying pistols, apparently a State law violation, but it developed in that case, may it please the Court, that those two pistols that Gargotta used in these murders were stolen from a Federal armory and were Government property.

So, while apparently they were going into matters that were purely within the jurisdiction of the State Court, it developed that it was a Federal violation that Claiborne was indicted on, perjury.

MR. JUSTICE BLACK: But I do not understand when you said there was no possible indictment on which you could come here.

MR. GOLDSCHEIN: No. This investigation, may it please the Court, was not directed at him.

MR. JUSTICE BLACK: Was it directed against anybody else as far as a federal offense was concerned?

MR. GOLDSCHEIN: There was no Federal indictment presented.

MR. JUSTICE BLACK: I am not talking about the indictment.

MR. GOLDSCHEIN: No, sir. This was purely the beginning of an investigation to determine whether or not any Federal laws were being violated. The law enforcement agencies of the Government have

---

[47] *Claiborne* v. *United States,* 77 F. 2d 682 (C.A. 8).

often, may it please the Court, called upon the courts and asked for their assistance in the enforcement of the laws, when it comes to their attention that lawlessness prevails.

Mr. Justice Black: By lawlessness you mean violations of Federal laws?

Mr. Goldschein: That is what we are interested in primarily.

Mr. Justice Black: What other interests do you have?

Mr. Goldschein: We do not have any other. That is our objective. But we only know whether or not there is a violation of the Federal law after we make the investigation, may it please the Court.

Mr. Justice Clark: After you make the investigation to see whether the State laws have been violated?

Mr. Goldschein: No, sir. After we make the investigation we determine whether or not there are any Federal laws being violated and, may it please the Court, that is the only way any inquisitorial power of the Grand Jury is ever invoked or has ever been invoked, just as was done in the *Burr* case,[48] may it please the Court.

A Grand Jury had to be convened to determine whether or not Aaron Burr did violate the sedition laws of the United States. The investigative or law enforcement agencies evidently were not able to make that case without the assistance of the inquisitorial power of the courts, and they called upon the courts to convene a Grand Jury to assist them in making this inquiry.

May it please the Court, that is done regularly, and it must be done in order to enforce the laws.

Mr. Justice Black: Maybe I am wrong, but I understood you to say that this had no materiality. This man was brought in for failing to answer something that had no possible relevancy to a Federal crime. It was the duty of the judge to send him to jail, if he didn't answer it, according to your theory, and there is no limit to the questions that the Federal prosecutor can ask before a Grand Jury.

Mr. Goldschein: That is what the *Blair* case [49] holds, may it please the Court, because, unless you spell out a Federal crime to begin with, no question that you ask the witness before the Grand Jury will have any materiality because it doesn't lead specifically to a Federal crime and, as said in the *Blair* case, the Grand Jury has a right to make inquiry to determine that no Federal law has been violated. The only way you know whether a Federal statute has been violated is after you make the investigation and not before.

Mr. Justice Black: To see if a Federal crime has been committed?

---

[48] *United States* v. *Burr* (*In re Willie*), Fed. Case No. 14,692e (C.C.D. Va.).

[49] *Blair* v. *United States,* 250 U. S. 273.

MR. GOLDSCHEIN: Yes, sir.

MR. JUSTICE JACKSON: Any State crime that yields income to the criminal may be a violation of the Federal law if he doesn't share his proceeds with the Government.

MR. GOLDSCHEIN: There is no doubt about that.

MR. JUSTICE JACKSON: So if you can show him to be mixed in with a lawless enterprise, then you check his income tax returns.

MR. GOLDSCHEIN: Yes, sir.

MR. JUSTICE JACKSON: That is what he was afraid of.

MR. GOLDSCHEIN: I assume that. But he wasn't afraid of it for that year.

MR. JUSTICE JACKSON: It seems to me you get pretty close to it when you make him confess that he is in a lawless enterprise when he knows he hasn't made appropriate tax returns and we know, sitting here—we cannot be so dumb as not to know—that that is really the way the Federal Government gets those people.

MR. GOLDSCHEIN: Yes, but in this instance, in the Greenberg case specifically, his counsel showed the court that he wasn't fearful of violating the income tax laws. He offered to show the income tax returns, to show what he reported from his real estate business. He didn't report any gambling, but he did report miscellaneous. He should have reported gambling instead of miscellaneous.

MR. JUSTICE JACKSON: Then you just said, "Where are the books of the miscellaneous business?"

MR. GOLDSCHEIN: Yes. When we get to that point, there is no doubt, if he violated the income tax law, he can say, "I refuse to answer the question."

MR. JUSTICE JACKSON: I think the hook is enough to catch him if he admits he is in the numbers business.

MR. GOLDSCHEIN: When the chase gets hot, as the Court said.

THE CHIEF JUSTICE: Your time has expired.

REBUTTAL ARGUMENT ON BEHALF OF PETITIONER
By Mr. Wiener.

MR. WIENER: If the Court please, I am amazed at the inconsistencies in the Government's position.

Mr. Goldschein said here, in response to inquiries, that these questions which petitioner refused to answer were not relevant to any Federal crime. The Grand Jury says—record, page 8—"that each of said questions was proper and material to the Grand Jurors' inquiry."

Mr. Goldschein said, in response to inquiries, as to why he was asking these questions, well, it would lead to something else. But he denies that the answers could be a link in the chain in the sense in which it has been used in the self-incrimination cases.

Mr. Goldschein says that he was only asked, "Are you in the numbers business now," but the tax cases say that, if you admit being in the business now, that is competent proof that you were in the business some time back, and that is what got *Johnson* in the 318th U. S.[50] The Court held that it was competent proof to prove it farther back.

In the same way the tax lawyers say in the legal periodicals, first prove he has an income-producing business.[51] My brother Goldschein says on that, that it had nothing to do with it. The District Judge here said, just before sentencing this petitioner, "I don't see much difference between this and the *Hoffman* case." [52]

If the Court please, neither do we, although Hoffman was shown to have been a somewhat more unsavory character, but just as this Court has reminded us many times that the Constitution protects the guilty as well as the innocent, I submit that, when a man claims his privilege against self-incrimination, he doesn't have to show he is a moral monstrosity before he can be allowed that privilege.

(Whereupon at 2:00 P.M., argument in the above-entitled matter was concluded.)

Section 178. Petitioner's problems in the foregoing argument.
—It would be stretching matters quite a bit to urge that, after the decision in the *Hoffman* case just the year before, petitioner's counsel in *Greenberg* was facing an uphill fight. The circumstance that the Court would not allow full time for argument demonstrated the judicial belief that the question was a narrow one, and the *per curiam* reversal that followed the argument by a mere five days [53] was further proof that the case was not one of outstanding complexity or difficulty, even though petitioner lost one vote that Hoffman had had.[54] But the argument does illustrate three points that have been discussed above.

(a) *Don't let yourself be diverted.* Back in *United States* v. *Murdock*,[55] decided in 1931, the Court had held that a witness in

---

[50] See *Johnson* v. *United States*, 318 U. S. 189, 195-196.

[51] See notes 23 and 24, *supra*.

[52] Record, p. 71a.

[53] See 343 U. S. 918: "Argued April 2, 1952. Decided April 7, 1952. *Per Curiam:* Judgment reversed. *Hoffman* v. *United States*, 341 U. S. 479. Mr. Justice Reed and Mr. Justice Burton dissent. Mr. Justice Frankfurter took no part in the consideration or decision of this case."

[54] Mr. Justice Burton, who had been with the majority in *Hoffman*, dissented in *Greenberg*. (Mr. Justice Frankfurter, also with the majority in *Hoffman*, did not hear the argument in *Greenberg* because of illness, and so did not participate in the decision.)

[55] 284 U. S. 141. The conviction was thereafter reversed because the requisite willfulness was found wanting. *United States* v. *Murdock*, 290 U. S. 389.

a Federal court could not successfully refuse to answer a question when its only tendency was to incriminate him under State law. This doctrine was reaffirmed some 13 years later in *Feldman* v. *United States*,[56] over strong and articulated dissent by three Justices.

As the transcript of argument shows, petitioner's counsel steadfastly refused to be drawn into requesting a reexamination of the *Murdock-Feldman* doctrine. Why? Because I felt that if that issue were ever squarely raised, there might result a Donnybrook such as could well endanger the decision. I felt I was on sound ground by reason of *Hoffman* and *Patricia Blau*; why risk a sure thing for a very doubtful, very chancy bet? See Section 121, and reread the second full paragraph at p. 326.

(b) *Don't attempt to cover complex details orally.* The *Greenberg* record showed—I am abbreviating and simplifying substantially—that the Grand Jury's presentment charged both a refusal to answer four questions before the Grand Jury in violation of 18 U.S.C. § 401 (1) and a deliberate disobedience of the order of the District Court to answer those questions, contrary to U.S.C. § 401 (3) ; [57] that, after the trial, the District Judge made a general finding of guilty; but that the judge later signed a formal judgment and commitment which varied the general finding in two respects: First, it found petitioner guilty of only refusing to answer three questions. Second, it found him guilty only of deliberate disobedience of the lawful order of the court, omitting all reference to obstruction of justice by reason of failure to answer questions before the Grand Jury.

On the first appeal, the Court of Appeals dealt with the case on the basis of the recitals in the judgment, and thus passed over the allegedly incriminating character of the fourth question, "Are you in the numbers business now?" [58] But, in its second opinion, it considered that question and held it non-incriminating.[59]

The argument for petitioner was, first, that the judgment pronounced in court controls, and prevails over the later formal commitment; [60] and, second, that the record showed no disobedi-

---

[56] 322 U. S. 487.

[57] See note 46, *supra*, for the text of the statute.

[58] See 187 F. 2d at 37.

[59] See 192 F. 2d at 203.

[60] *Hill* v. *United States*, 298 U. S. 460; *Watkins* v. *Merry*, 106 F. 2d 360 (C.A. 10) .

ence of a direct order by the District Judge, but only that the petitioner declined an opportunity to purge himself of the contempt involved in refusing to answer questions before the Grand Jury. That is to say, petitioner argued that he stood convicted of something he was not shown to have done.[61]

Now, very clearly, the foregoing is extremely complex even as condensed above. To have explained it so that any listener could understand it would have been a difficult task at best, even without time limits. But to have attempted such an explanation within the 30 minutes allowed, when other and controlling issues imperatively required discussion, would have been literally impossible. Hence, following the precepts laid down in Sections 116, 117, 120, and 137, above, the entire question of variance was relegated to the discussion in the brief.

(c) *Don't be afraid to say you don't know.* As the transcript has shown, the petitioner Greenberg had refused to answer several questions. Mr. Justice Clark asked, "What is your position in the event some of the questions are proper and some improper?" My replies were, quite plainly, less than positive; as indicated above, see Section 121, one should never hesitate to admit ignorance, even though I was probably not too far off in my qualified answers.[62] In any event, the Court by reversing the conviction sustained my contention that all of the unanswered questions were improper.

Section 179. Respondent's problems in the foregoing argument.—After the Supreme Court's decision in the *Hoffman* case, the Government was in a most difficult position, a difficulty more than apparent from its written argument. Thus, as was indicated

---

[61] Cf. *Cole* v. *Arkansas,* 333 U. S. 196; *Schooner Hoppet* v. *United States,* 7 Cranch 389, 394; *Carlson* v. *United States,* 209 F. 2d (C.A. 1), and related cases. But cf. *Enrichi* v. *United States,* 212 F. 2d 702 (C.A. 10).

See, however, *Levine* v. *United States,* 362 U. S. 610, where, after the petitioner refused to answer questions put to him by a Grand Jury, and subsequently refused to obey the judge's order directing him to do so, he was punished for a contempt "committed in the actual presence of the court" pursuant to Criminal Rule 42 (a). The issue that divided the Court was whether exclusion of the public from the courtroom violated his constitutional rights, or whether he was simply "a party who * * * raises an abstract claim only as an afterthought on appeal." As in the related case of *Brown* v. *United States,* 359 U. S. 41, the question whether petitioner's refusal to obey the judge's order to answer was simply a continuation of his contumacy before the Grand Jury rather than a new offense was not raised.

[62] See *Nilva* v. *United States,* 352 U. S. 385, 396.

at the argument, the Government in the course of an 88-page brief, of which 35 pages were devoted to the proposition that "There was no real danger that the questions which petitioner refused to answer would have incriminated him," [63] never once saw fit to quote the portions of the *Hoffman* opinion which read as follows:

"However, if the witness, upon interposing his claim, were required to prove the hazard in the sense in which a claim is usually required to be established in court, he would be compelled to surrender the very protection which the privilege is designed to guarantee. To sustain the privilege, it need only be evident from the implications of the question, in the setting in which it is asked, that a responsive answer to the question or an explanation of why it cannot be answered might be dangerous because injurious disclosure could result.

* * * * *

"Petitioner could reasonably have sensed the peril of prosecution for federal offenses ranging from obstruction to conspiracy." [64]

Government counsel was therefore on the horns of a dilemma: On the one hand, he was obliged to urge that his questions were non-incriminating in order to justify petitioner's conviction for refusing to answer them. On the other, he was bound to urge their relevance for purposes of the Federal Grand Jury's functions. All of this dilemma was neatly summed up by (a) the admission by counsel (p. 464, *supra*), "when we get to that point [viz., "where are the books of the miscellaneous business?"], there is no doubt, if he violated the income tax law, he can say, 'I refuse to answer the question' "—followed by (b) the trenchant comment of Jackson, J., "I think the hook is enough to catch him if he admits he is in the numbers business."

The nub of the matter was that the *Patricia Blau* and *Hoffman* cases had, in effect though not expressly, overruled the earlier *Mason* case.[65] And, since the questions had been asked, doubtless

---

[63] U. S. Br., No. 461, Oct. T. 1951, pp. 21-56 (Point I).

[64] 341 U. S. at 486-487, 488. See also, generally, Section 35 (d), *supra*, at pp. 106-107.

[65] "The decision in the Mason case would not be followed today." *United States* v. *Coffey*, 198 F. 2d 438, 440 (C.A. 3). True; see particularly the cases cited in note 71, *infra*. But since the *Mason* case has never been specifically overruled, it is still being cited. See, e.g., Lumbard, J., dissenting in *United States* v. *Courtney*, 236 F. 2d 921, 924, 926 (C.A. 2). Compare Section 35 (e), *supra*, at pp. 110-111.

with *Mason* in mind, before either of the two later cases had been decided, what was left proved difficult to defend.

Section 180. Sequel to *Greenberg* v. *United States*.—As has been indicated above, the argument in *Greenberg* was followed within five days by a *per curiam* reversal.[66] A similar but perhaps even more drastic fate was visited on the Third Circuit's *Singleton* decision [67] five weeks later; that conviction was reversed simply on the strength of the petition, without argument.[68] In due course, these emphatic actions were noticed by Courts of Appeals,[69] with the consequence that for a number of years most convictions in similar circumstances were reversed before reaching the Supreme Court.[70] A few later lapses joined *Singleton* in the ignominy of *per curiam* reversal without argument.[71] It may therefore now be deemed settled law that a witness may properly claim his privilege if to answer *"might* be dangerous because injurious disclosure *could* result." [72]

By and large, almost every one of the contempt convictions was overturned, particularly those arising from refusals to answer questions propounded by the Kefauver Committee.[73] The prin-

---

[66] 343 U. S. 918.

[67] 193 F. 2d 464.

[68] 343 U. S. 944.

[69] See *United States* v. *Coffey*, 198 F. 2d 438 (C.A. 3); *Aiuppa* v. *United States*, 201 F. 2d 287 (C.A. 6); *United States* v. *Doto*, 205 F. 2d 416 (C.A. 2).

[70] See, in addition to the cases cited in note 1, *supra*, *Kiewel* v. *United States*, 204 F. 2d 1 (C.A. 8); *In re Neff*, 206 F. 2d 149 (C.A. 3); *Maffie* v. *United States*, 209 F. 2d 225 (C.A. 1); *Daly* v. *United States*, 209 F. 2d 232 (C.A. 1); *Carroll* v. *Savoretti*, 220 F. 2d 910 (C.A. 5); *United States* v. *Courtney*, 236 F. 2d 921 (C.A. 2); *Ballantyne* v. *United States*, 237 F. 2d 657 (C.A. 5; *In re Portell*, 245 F. 2d 183 (C.A. 7); *United States* v. *Miranti*, 253 F. 2d 135 (C.A. 2); *United States* v. *Triglio*, 255 F. 2d 385 (C.A. 2); *Isaacs* v. *United States*, 256 F. 2d 654 (C.A. 8).

[71] *Trock* v. *United States*, 351 U. S. 976, reversing 232 F. 2d 839 (C.A. 2); *Simpson et al.* v. *United States*, 355 U. S. 7, reversing *Simpson* v. *United States*, 241 F. 2d 222; *Wollam* v. *United States*, 244 F. 2d 212; and *McKenzie* v. *United States*, 244 F. 2d 712, all C.A. 9.

Since then, the Ninth Circuit has—in Navy terminology—"got the word." *Hashagen* v. *United States*, 283 F. 2d 345; and see particularly its comments in *Shane* v. *United States*, 283 F. 2d 355, on the summary reversals cited in the preceding paragraph of this note.

[72] *Hoffman* v. *United States*, 341 U. S. at 487 (italics added).

[73] See *Aiuppa* v. *United States*, 201 F. 2d 287, 300 (C.A. 6):

"Despite the enjoyment by millions of spectators and auditors of the exhibition by television of the confusion and writhings of widely known malefactors and criminals, when sharply questioned as to their nefarious activities, we are unable to give judicial sanction, in the teeth of the Fifth Amendment,

cipal exception was *Rogers* v. *United States*,[74] which turned on waiver, and evoked a vigorous dissent. It seems safe to say that the authority of the *Rogers* case has since been markedly impaired by subsequent decisions narrowing any waiver of the privilege against self-incrimination.[75]

At any rate, before the scope of the privilege to refuse to answer apparently innocuous questions was settled, it presented some fascinating legal inquiries—and, as the present chapter indicates, some challenging problems in advocacy as well.

---

to the employment by a committee of the United States Senate of methods of examination of witnesses constituting a triple threat: answer truly and you have given evidence leading to your conviction for a violation of federal law; answer falsely and you will be convicted of perjury; refuse to answer and you will be found guilty of criminal contempt and punished by fine and imprisonment. In our humble judgment, to place a person not even on trial for a specified crime in such predicament is not only not a manifestation of fair play, but is in direct violation of the Fifth Amendment to our national Constitution."

[74] 340 U. S. 367.

[75] *Quinn* v. *United States*, 349 U. S. 155; *Emspak* v. *United States*, 349 U. S. 190.

APPENDIX OF LATE AUTHORITIES

As the Preface to the present reprinting indicates, the listing below is limited to late authorities that contradict, modify, or render obsolete statements now appearing in the basic text, including the footnotes thereto.

Cut-off dates for authorities examined are as follows: Statutes, through the end of the 89th Congress; Supreme Court decisions, through the end of the 1966 Term in June 1967; Supreme Court Rules, to include the new Rules adopted on June 12, 1967, effective October 2, 1967; other Federal decisions, through 375 F. 2d and 265 F. Supp.

Page 19, note 17, powers of Commissioners of the Court of Claims.—Rule 52(a) of the present Rules of the Court of Claims (revised April 1, 1964) states that

The commissioners shall serve as the trial judges of the court to the extent of the authority therefor prescribed by statute and these rules. As such, they shall have the power to do and perform any acts which may be necessary or proper, under the court's orders of reference and these rules, for the efficient performance of their duties and the regulation of proceedings before them.

Recommendation by commissioners for conclusions of law are contemplated by Rules 52 (b), 54 (b) , 55 (b) , 57 (a) , and 99. The rule last cited became effective on June 1, 1967.

Many current opinions of the Court of Claims accordingly consist of *per curiam* orders adopting and setting forth opinions prepared by commissioners.

Page 20, Section 15, first paragraph, announcement of opinions by the Supreme Court.—On April 5, 1965, the Chief Justice said (J. Sup. Ct., Oct. T. 1964, p. 248):

The Court announces that commencing the week of Monday, April 26, 1965, it will no longer adhere to the practice of reporting its decisions only at Monday sessions, and that in the future they will be reported as they become ready for decision at any session of the Court. As in the past, no announcement of decisions to be reported will be made prior to their rendition in open Court.

The first non-Monday opinions announced under the new practice were delivered on Tuesday, April 27, 1965. *Harman* v. *Forssenius,* 380 U. S. 528; *Armstrong* v. *Manzo,* 380 U. S. 545; *General Motors* v. *District of Columbia,* 380 U. S. 553; *Commissioner* v. *Brown,* 380 U. S. 563.

Page 39, Section 22, certificate of compliance with rules of court.—The Ninth Circuit requires "an attorney responsible for the preparation of the brief" to certify that the brief as filed complies with the court's rules. Rule 18 (2) (g).

Page 40, notes 3 and 4, appendix method in the Supreme Court, and fourth edition of Stern and Gressman, Supreme Court Practice.—Effective October 2, 1967, the parties in Supreme Court litigation will print their own records in an Appendix, preferably a Joint Appendix; there will be no more printing under supervision of the Clerk. And the parties will then file the entire original record when they docket the case. See Sup. Ct. 1967 Rules 17, 26, 29 (3) , 36, and, preeminently, the fourth edition of Stern and Gressman's *Supreme Court Practice,* now in preparation, where the details of the new procedure will be fully explained.

For a briefer summary of the changes made, see Boskey and Gressman, *The 1967 changes in the Supreme Court's Rules,* 42 F. R. D. 139.

Page 41, note 10, changes in and renumbering of Supreme Court rules.—Supreme Court Rule 15(1)(c)(1), now cited, has been slightly changed and is now Supreme Court 1967 Rule 15 (1) (c). The other Supreme Court rules cited remain unchanged.

Page 41, paragraph Third, length of briefs in Federal appellate courts.—The Fifth Circuit has now joined all of the other circuits in limiting the lengths of appellate briefs. Rule 24(e)(2), C.A. 5, adopted in 1964.

Page 53, note 31(a), appeal to the Supreme Court as discretionary.—The discretionary feature of the appeal to the Supreme Court, cited in the text, is further emphasized by Supreme Court 1967 Rule 16(1)(d): "The court will receive a motion to dismiss or affirm on any other grounds which the appellee wishes to present as reasons why the court should not set the case for argument."

Page 53, note 31(c), name of the appellate court in the District of Columbia.—The name of the local appellate court in the District of Columbia was, by Section 6 of the Act of October 23, 1962, Pub. L. 87-873, 76 Stat. 1171, 1172, changed from "The Municipal Court of Appeals for the District of Columbia" to "District of Columbia Court of Appeals." The same act changed the name of the former "The Municipal Court for the District of Columbia" to "District of Columbia Court of General Sessions." But the discretionary jurisdiction of the United States Court of Appeals for the District of Columbia to review decisions of the District of Columbia Court of Appeals still continues; it is now to be found in Sec. 11-321, D. C. Code (Supp. V to 1961 ed.).

Page 73, note 64, statement of questions presented in Supreme Court.—Supreme Court Rule 15(1)(c)(1), now cited, has been slightly changed and is now Supreme Court 1967 Rule 15(1)(c). The other Supreme Court rules cited remain unchanged.

Page 73, note 66, formulation of questions presented.—The First Circuit has adopted a similar rule. Rules 23(3)(b), 23(4)(b).

Page 110, note 176, square overrulings of prior decisions by the Supreme Court.—By square overrulings in this connection are meant instances where the headnote, which is submitted for approval by the Reporter of Decisions to the Justice writing the opinion of the Court, specifically says that a particular decision has been overruled. The text asserts that there have been two such overrulings since the end of the 1948 Term; at this writing there have been quite a few more. *United States* v. *Raines, 362 U. S. 17,* overruling *United States* v. *Reese, 92 U. S. 214,* and *Barney* v. *City of New York, 193 U. S. 430; Mapp* v. *Ohio, 367 U. S. 643,* overruling *Wolf* v. *Colorado, 338 U. S. 25; James* v. *United States, 366 U. S. 213,* overruling *Commissioner* v. *Wilcox, 327 U. S. 404; Construction Laborers* v. *Curry, 371 U. S. 542,* overruling *Montgomery Council* v. *Ledbetter Co., 344 U. S. 178; Gideon* v. *Wainwright, 372 U. S. 335,* overruling *Betts* v. *Brady, 316 U. S. 455; Fay* v. *Noia, 372 U. S. 391,* overruling *Darr* v. *Burford, 339 U. S. 200; Murphy* v. *Waterfront Commission, 378 U. S. 52,* overruling *Feldman* v. *United States, 322 U. S. 487; Jackson* v. *Denno, 378 U. S. 368,* overruling *Stein* v. *New York, 346 U. S. 156; Swift & Co.* v. *Wickham, 382 U. S. 111,* overruling *Kesler* v. *Department of Public Safety, 369 U. S. 153; Harris* v. *United States, 382 U. S. 162,* overruling *Brown* v. *United States, 359 U. S. 41; Spevack* v. *Klein, 385 U. S. 511,* overruling *Cohen* v.

Hurley, 366 U. S. 117; *Afroyim* v. *Rusk,* 387 U. S. 253, overruling *Perez* v. *Brownell,* 356 U. S. 44; *Camara* v. *Municipal Court,* 387 U. S. 523, overruling *Frank* v. *Maryland,* 359 U. S. 360.

But the problem of when and to what extent a prior decision has been drained of vitality cannot be determined solely by resort to the official headnotes. For example, the "silver platter" doctrine of *Lustig* v. *United States,* 338 U. S. 74, was plainly disapproved by *Elkins* v. *United States,* 364 U. S. 206, which refused to follow it, and with the demise of the "silver platter" doctrine the State seizure aspect of *Weeks* v. *United States,* 232 U. S. 383, joined *Lustig* in limbo. Yet the headnotes are silent as to overrulings. Similarly, *Malloy* v. *Hogan,* 378 U. S. 1, very plainly sounded the death knell of both *Twining* v. *New Jersey,* 211 U. S. 78, and *Adamson* v. *California,* 332 U. S. 46, though there may have been delicate distinctions between it and the earlier cases. Here again, the headnote does not mention any prior decision as having been explicitly disapproved. Other examples could easily be supplied.

In this area there remains considerable scope for differences of opinion, as will be seen from the table of "Supreme Court Decisions Overruled by Subsequent Decision" in *The Constitution of the United States,* Sen. Doc. No. 39, 88th Cong., 1st sess., p. 1541, and particularly from the list there (p. 1549) of instances where only the dissenting or concurring justices were of opinion that an overruling had resulted. Those instances may perhaps be subject to some discount, since dissents infrequently tend to understatement, but they cannot be ignored by any advocate desirous of grasping firmly the nettles of a difficult case.

Two concrete examples will serve to illustrate the problem of assaying the present weight of cases not yet specifically overruled—and perhaps assist somewhat in resolving it. In *Adams* v. *Tanner,* 244 U. S. 590, the Supreme Court in 1917 struck down a statute of Washington State making it criminal for employment agencies to collect fees from workers for furnishing them with employment or information leading to such employment, on the ground that it was an unconstitutional interference with an individual's right to engage in a useful and lawful business; McKenna, Holmes, Brandeis, and Clarke, JJ., dissented. Similarly, in 1927, the Supreme Court in *Tyson & Bro.* v. *Banton,* 273 U. S. 418, held unconstitutional the New York "anti-scalper" legislation—a statute limiting the resale premium chargeable on theater tickets—on the ground that places of amusement or entertainment were neither public utilities nor so affected with a public interest as to justify legislative regulation of their charges; Holmes, Brandeis, Stone, and Sanford, JJ., dissented.

More than 30 years later, in 1961, Kansas adopted a debt adjustment act, making criminal the business of debt adjustment except incidentally in the course of law practice. Two members of a three-judge Federal district court held the law unconstitutional, on the ground that it was an unreasonable and unwarranted regulation of lawful business in violation of the Fourteenth Amendment. *Skrupa v. Sanborn,* 210 F. Supp. 200 (D. Kan.). The majority of the court relied primarily on a Pennsylvania decision, *Commonwealth v. Stone,* 191 Pa. Super. 117, 155 A. 2d 453, which in turn had relied heavily on the still unoverruled case of *Adams v. Tanner,* 244 U. S. 590.

On appeal, the Kansas statute was upheld and the judgment below reversed; the Supreme Court, emphasizing that *Adams v. Tanner* was dead, cited extensively from Mr. Justice Holmes' dissent in *Tyson & Bro. v. Banton.* It said (*Ferguson v. Skrupa,* 372 U. S. 726, 731-732 [footnotes omitted]):

> In the face of our abandonment of the use of the "vague contours" of the Due Process Clause to nullify laws which a majority of the Court believed to be economically unwise, reliance on *Adams v. Tanner* is as mistaken as would be adherence to *Adkins v. Children's Hospital,* overruled by *West Coast Hotel Co. v. Parrish,* 300 U.S. 379 (1937). Not only has the philosophy of *Adams* been abandoned, but also this Court almost 15 years ago expressly pointed to another opinion of this Court as having "clearly undermined" *Adams.* We conclude that the Kansas Legislature was free to decide for itself that legislation was needed to deal with the business of debt adjusting. Unquestionably, there are arguments showing that the business of debt adjusting has social utility, but such arguments are properly addressed to the legislature, not to us. We refuse to sit as a "superlegislature to weigh the wisdom of legislation," and we emphatically refuse to go back to the time when courts used the Due Process Clause "to strike down state laws, regulatory of business and industrial conditions, because they may be unwise, improvident, or out of harmony with a particular school of thought." Nor are we able or willing to draw lines by calling a law "prohibitory" or "regulatory." Whether the legislature takes for its textbook Adam Smith, Herbert Spencer, Lord

Keynes, or some other is no concern of ours. The Kansas debt adjusting statute may be wise or unwise. But relief, if any be needed, lies not with us but with the body constituted to pass laws for the State of Kansas.

Shortly thereafter, New York ticket brokers sued to enjoin enforcement of the modified "anti-scalper" legislation of that State, under which the permissible resale advance for each ticket was $1.50 (35 years earlier it had been 50 cents), on the ground that *Tyson & Bro.* v. *Banton* had never been overruled. But the three-judge Federal district court, in the face of *Ferguson* v. *Skrupa,* was not impressed. "We would be abdicating our judicial responsibility if we waited for the Supreme Court to use the express words 'We hereby overrule Tyson,' as the plaintiffs contend we should, before recognizing that the case is no longer binding precedent but simply a relic for the constitutional historians." Accordingly the complaint was dismissed. *Gold* v. *DiCarlo,* 235 F. Supp. 817 (S.D.N.Y.).

Then—and this is the nub of the matter in the present connection—when the plaintiffs stubbornly took an appeal, the Supreme Court affirmed the judgment below on motion, without argument. 380 U. S. 520.

Plainly, then, *Tyson & Bro.* v. *Banton* is not law today. But when was it overruled? By the reasoning of *Olsen* v. *Nebraska,* 313 U. S. 236, decided in 1941? By the language of disapproval in *Skrupa* v. *Ferguson* in 1963? Or by the notation in *Gold* v. *DiCarlo,* 380 U. S. 520, which simply said on April 26, 1965, "The motions to affirm are granted and the judgment is affirmed"?

The short of this rather lengthy discussion—which is still much less extensive than it could easily have been made—is that in all except the most simple situations, any effort to set forth what "the law" is necessarily involves prediction in greater or less degree. Or, as Mr. Justice Holmes put it in a much quoted sentence, "Law is a statement of the circumstances in which the public force will be brought to bear upon men through the courts." *American Banana Co.* v. *United Fruit Co.,* 213 U. S. 347, 356.

The lesson of the present observations is that the formulation of such a statement requires a far more substantial as well as a far more perceptive foundation than simply a list of cases shown by the official headnotes to have been overruled.

Page 121, first paragraph, additional titles of the United States Code enacted into positive law.—The following additional titles of the United States Code have now been enacted into positive law: 5 (Government Organization and Employees); 37 (Pay and Allowances of the Uniformed Services).

Pages 144-147, section 49, evaluation of decided cases.—See also discussion above, pp. 473-476, appendix matter in connection with p. 110 of the basic text.

Page 177, note 177, precedential value of Tax Court memorandum opinions.—The Tax Court's Memorandum Opinions remain unreported because they are not considered as precedents when formulated, but they may well turn out to have precedential value.

What Judge Murdock wrote was (31 A.B.A.J. at 299):

Memorandum Opinions, that is, the ones that are not printed, are supposed to be limited to those having no value as a precedent. . . . If counsel finds in a Memorandum Opinion some precedent of value, he may cite it effectively in his brief, even though the opinion does not appear in the bound volumes of the reports of the court.

Dean Griswold had earlier summed up the situation in these terms (*The Need for a Court of Tax Appeals,* 57 Harv. L. Rev. 1153, 1172):

Memorandum decisions are not cited by the court in its published opinions, and they are not regarded as having much binding effect under the general rule of stare decisis. But they do represent more than two-thirds of the total number of cases decided by the Tax Court.

The key word in the foregoing quotation is "much."

Page 199, note 280, topics included and omitted in the American Digest System.—The American Digest System, which at the time of going to press had reached, in bound form, 2 General Digest (4th Series) for 1967, still does not include "Conflict of Laws." But during the years 1956 to 1966, while the General Digest (3rd Series) was being published, Secured Transactions, Trade Regulation, and Zoning were added as new digest topics.

Pages 210-211, paragraph (g), venue for suits against Government officers.—The addition of Sec. 1391(e) to Title 28 U.S.C. now permits the public officer to be sued (1) where the defendant resides, or (2) where the cause of action arose, or (3) where any real property involved in the action is situated, or (4) where the plaintiff resides if no real property is involved. Therefore the superior officer is suable in the field, and the question discussed in the text can no longer arise.

Page 227, note 70, a further General Motors antitrust case.— Following *United States* v. *du Pont & Co.,* 353 U. S. 586, the General Motors antitrust case, there was a further proceeding in the same litigation involving the scope of the relief to be granted. *United States* v. *du Pont & Co.,* 366 U. S. 316.

P. 231, identification of District of Columbia cases appearing in the Federal Reporter.—As has been pointed out above, pp. 472-473, see p. 53 of the original text, the name of the local appellate court in the District of Columbia is now "District of Columbia Court of Appeals." Sec. 6 of the Act of Oct. 23, 1962, Pub. L. 87-873, 76 Stat. 1171, 1172. But prior to 1934, the name of what is now the United States Court of Appeals for the District of Columbia Circuit was "Court of Appeals of the District of Columbia."

Consequently it might well be confusing if, as suggested in the 1961 text of this book, pre-1948 decisions, before the District of Columbia was a Federal circuit, were to be identified as "(App. D. C.)." True, the decisions of the present (and intermediate) District of Columbia Court of Appeals appear only in the Atlantic Reporter, while the decisions of the earlier (and higher) Court of Appeals of the District of Columbia appeared in the Federal Reporter from 1919. But not every judge reading a brief should be assumed to have at his fingertips an encyclopedic knowledge of legal bibliography.

At the present time, therefore, the brief-writer using Fed. and F. 2d citations without more will be well advised to identify the decisions of the higher court as "(D. C. Cir.)" even when those decisions antedate 1948; e.g., *Wann* v. *Ickes,* 92 F. 2d 215 (D. C. Cir.). If, however, parallel citations are used, there is no parenthetical indicator, and the citation would be *Wann* v. *Ickes,* 67 App. D. C. 291, 92 F. 2d 215.

Page 232, parallel citations to Federal cases.—(a) The "C.C.A." reports, extending to 171 volumes, ceased publication in 1920— which is a little more exact than the "1919 or thereabouts" of the text.

(b) At present there will of course be no Court of Claims cases as yet unreported in C. Cls. that will be found in F. Supp.; they must all be looked for in F. 2d.

Pages 232-233, note 84, requirement of seeking certiorari as prerequisite for collateral Federal attack on State court judgment. —*Darr* v. *Burford,* 339 U. S. 200, cited in the note to support the text, has now been overruled by *Fay* v. *Noia,* 372 U. S. 391.

Page 234, note 88, citation of State cases.—The following States no longer report the decisions of their courts of last resort officially, but rely either on publication in the appropriate series of the National Reporter System or else on publication in an unofficial compilation: Alaska, Florida, Kentucky, Maine, Missouri (and Mo. App.), North Dakota, Oklahoma (and Okla. Crim.), Texas (and Tex. Crim. App.), and Wyoming. In respect of recent decisions in those States, there can accordingly be no further parallel citations.

Page 237, note 95, current edition of the United States Code.—When this Appendix went to press, the 1964 edition of the United States Code was the current one, and Supplement II for 1966 had appeared.

Pages 244-245, note 115-116, entitlement to depletion allowance in coal depletion cases.—The problem of the contractor's entitlement to the depletion allowance in coal mining cases continued long after it was thought to have been placed at rest by *Parsons* v. *Smith,* 359 U. S. 215. The Fourth Circuit, whose approach had there been disapproved *sub silentio,* reverted to its original line of decision by means of distinctions that ultimately all but overruled *Parsons* v. *Smith,* after which it was squarely reversed in *Paragon Coal Co.* v. *Commissioner,* 380 U. S. 624. At the present time the Fourth Circuit appears to have got the message. *Lawson* v. *Commissioner,* 350 F. 2d 396 (C.A. 4).

Page 248, note 125, record references in Supreme Court briefs.—The substance and all of the operative language of Supreme Court Rule 40(2), cited at this point, were left unchanged in the 1967 revision, but to conform to the new appendix system, the introductory sentence now speaks of references "to the appendix or the record."

Page 261, notes 140 and 141, names and addresses of individual counsel on Supreme Court briefs.—Once again, the substance and operative language of Supreme Court Rule 39(2) remain the same, but the exception, formerly expressed as "other than records," now reads, "other than appendices."

Page 262, note 144, requirement of manuscript signature in

printed motions filed with Supreme Court.—This requirement, from Supreme Court Rule 39(2), is continued unchanged in the 1967 rules revision.

Page 264, last paragraph, reply briefs on petition for certiorari.—The 1967 revision of the Supreme Court's rules has sharpened and narrowed the practice at this juncture, distinguishing between reply and supplemental briefs filed by a petitioner for certiorari while his petition is pending.

First, the privilege of filing a reply brief in connection with the petition for certiorari and prior to its consideration is now narrowed to those "addressed to arguments first raised in the briefs in opposition." Supreme Court 1967 Rule 24(4). For this step the Supreme Court now follows the practice of some circuits that forbid the filing of reply briefs except to answer new points. Text, p. 262, note 145.

But, second, Supreme Court 1967 Rule 24(5) specifically states that "Any party may file a supplemental brief at any time while a petition for a writ of certiorari is pending calling attention to new cases or legislation or other intervening matter not available at the time of his last filing."

It is therefore appropriate to emphasize the admonition set forth in the original text (p. 264), that "A petition for certiorari, pre-eminently, should anticipate the other side's argument; more than almost any other argumentative document, it is strictly a one-shot proposition."

Pages 266-267, notes 149 and 150, reply and supplemental briefs on the merits in the Supreme Court.—The Supreme Court in its 1967 rules revision made a distinction between reply briefs and supplemental briefs in cases being heard on the merits.

1. Reply briefs, which formerly would be received "up to the time the case is called for hearing" (Rule 41(3)), will now be received only "up to three days before the case is called for hearing" (1967 Rule 41(3)). This eliminates what formerly was annoying at best, but more generally was highly unfair, viz., the presentation to counsel arguing the case, while actually waiting to go on, of an elaborate reply brief, normally delivered by the hot sticky hands of the smirking junior who helped compose it. However, if filed up to three days before the hearing, reply briefs on the merits, unlike reply briefs on petition for certiorari (1967 Rule 24(4)), need not be restricted to arguments first raised

in the brief of the respondent or appellee. (But of course counsel for petitioner or appellant should always be chary of filing reply briefs even on the merits; see Section 85 of the text.)

2. Supplemental briefs, restricted to new intervening matter, may still be filed, as before, up to the time the case is called for hearing. 1967 Rule 41(5).

3. However, provided leave of court is granted, reply and supplemental briefs may still be filed after the times otherwise prescribed by the rules.

Page 279, note 10, submission of cases without argument not permitted except by leave of court.—The First Circuit now has such a provision in its Rule 27(1).

One-sided submission is similarly not favored. See *Elchuk* v. *United States,* 370 U. S. 722, where the judgment of a Court of Appeals in an *in forma pauperis* case was vacated and "remanded to that court for further proceedings in which the petitioner is to be accorded the opportunity to present oral argument on the merits of his appeal, either personally or through counsel, to the same extent as such opportunity is accorded to the United States Attorney."

Page 283, note 15, prohibition against reading long excerpts from briefs, records, and decisions in the course of oral argument. —In the December 1962 revision of the Rules of the First Circuit, the former prohibition against reading lengthy quotations from briefs, etc., was omitted.

Page 288, note 17, right of Government to recover for hospital care furnished by it in consequence of a third person's tort.— The case of *United States* v. *Standard Oil Co.,* 332 U. S. 301, has since been legislatively overruled by the Act of September 25, 1962, Pub. L. 87-693, 76 Stat. 593, now 42 U.S.C. §§ 2651-2653. The committee reports show that Congress intended to overturn the rule of the cited case. H.R. Rep. No. 1534, Sen. Rep. No. 1945, both 87th Cong., 2d sess. Consequently the United States now has the benefit at least in part of the ancient common law action, trespass *per quod servitium amisit.*

Pages 300-301, notes 30-32, present time limits for oral argument.—In the last six years, there has been a noticeable tendency in Federal appellate courts to revise sharply downwards the time allowed for oral argument. No less than seven out of the fifteen courts listed have reduced the time allowance.

District of Columbia Circuit. The normal time for oral argument is now 30 minutes (Rule 19(c)(1)), while a new provision effective in January 1967 creates a summary calendar where only 15 minutes will be allowed (Rule 4(e)).

Fourth Circuit. Reduced to 30 minutes; Rule 15(3).

Fifth Circuit. Reduced to 30 minutes; Rule 25(3).

Sixth Circuit. Reduced to 30 minutes; Rule 20(3).

Eighth Circuit. Reduced to 30 minutes; Rule 13(c).

Ninth Circuit. Here also 30 minutes is now the limit, while on some motions only 15 minutes are allowed; Rule 20(3).

Court of Customs and Patents Appeals. Rule XXIII of this court has cut the time to 30 minutes. Moreover, Rule 34 of the Rules Applicable to Appeals from the Secretary of Commerce provides that, unless otherwise directed by the court, the time for oral argument in such cases shall not exceed 20 minutes on each side.

Prior limits are left intact in the First, Second, Third, Seventh, and Tenth Circuits, and in the Court of Military Appeals. The Court of Claims' former 30-minute practice has now been codified in its Rule 65(3).

The rules of the Supreme Court in respect of time limits on oral argument were not changed by the 1967 revision. But in actual practice about half or slightly more of the cases now set down for oral argument are heard on the Summary Calendar— which means 30 minutes on a side. The Clerk's Office advises informally that, at the 1966 Term, 79 of the 150 argued cases were so heard.

The key word in the foregoing paragraph is "heard." During the 1964 and 1965 Terms, some twelve motions to remove cases from the Summary Calendar were made, of which nine were granted. In three of the successful instances, counsel were allowed an hour on a side, but in the other six, the time permitted was only 45 minutes.

During the 1966 Term, there were eight motions to remove cases from the Summary Calendar, of which only two were granted. One other case was removed from the Summary Calendar on the Court's own motion. J. Sup. Ct., Oct. T. 1966, p. 158, No. 462.

It may be ventured that the impelling factor in all the time reductions listed is the constantly increasing case load. No court today is going to return to the condition that prevailed in the

Supreme Court prior to the creation of the (then) Circuit Courts of Appeals in 1891, when it was some four years behind in hearing cases brought there as of right.

The only way courts of appeals can protect themselves, since virtually all their business is obligatory, is to cut down the time for oral argument. The Supreme Court can deflect most of the flood by denying certiorari or granting motions to dismiss or affirm; but in order to hear the maximum number of cases possible, it also must restrict the time limits for oral argument.

Page 301, note 32, time allowed for oral argument in summary calendar cases in the Supreme Court.—Supreme Court 1967 Rule 44(3) now commences, "In cases on the summary calendar, half an hour *a side,* and no more, will be allowed for argument, * * *." The italicized words are new.

Page 317, number of counsel permitted to argue orally.—(a) Supreme Court 1967 Rule 44(3) remains unchanged in respect of the passage quoted therefrom on this page.

(b) The District of Columbia Circuit's new Summary Calendar rule specifically provides that only one counsel on each side may be heard. Rule 4(e).

(c) Provisions restricting the number of counsel on each side to two remain as now stated, but revisions of the rules of two circuits require changed citations. The present references are First Circuit, Rule 27(2), and Tenth Circuit, Rule 23(d).

(d) In a recent antitrust case in which the Government received some but not all of the relief that it had sought, the Supreme Court permitted the four cross-appellants—defendants below—to be represented at the oral argument by four different counsel. *United States* v. *Grinnell Corp.,* 383 U. S. 933. While it would be wrong to rest any *post hoc propter hoc* contention upon this circumstance, it is the fact that, after argument, "substantially more drastic relief" was ordered by the Court. *United States* v. *Grinnell Corp.,* 384 U. S. 563, 596.

Page 359, note 18, American case reversing conviction where trial judge acts as prosecutor as well as judge.—The plan of this appendix has not included the addition of new authorities that were merely cumulative. But since the only citation previously available at this juncture was a Privy Council decision, it seems appropriate to add a recent Federal case on the precise issue. *Figueroa Ruiz* v. *Delgado,* 359 F. 2d 718 (C.A. 1). That opinion should be closely read and then compared with the case discussed in the text.

Page 371, last paragraph, right of retired circuit judge to participate in rehearing in banc.—Following the decision in *United States* v. *American-Foreign S.S. Corp.*, 363 U. S. 685, Congress amended the law to provide that "A circuit judge of the circuit who has retired from regular active service shall also be competent to sit as a judge of the court in banc in the rehearing of a case or controversy if he sat in the court or division at the original hearing thereof." 28 U.S.C. § 46(c) as amended by Sec. 1(b) of the Act of November 13, 1963, Pub. L. 88-176, 77 Stat. 331.

Pages 372-373, note 36, present status of abatement rule.—Rule 25(d)(1) of the Federal Rules of Civil Procedure was amended after the text was written to provide that, in the event of failure to substitute a deceased or resigned or removed public officer, "the action does not abate and his successor is automatically substituted as a party." Moreover, Rule 25(d)(2) now permits the public officer sued in his official capacity to be "described as a party by his official title rather than by name; but the court may require his name to be added."

Supreme Court Rule 48 was amended accordingly, see 366 U. S. 979, and its form was not thereafter changed in the 1967 Revision.

Pages 373-374, rehearings in the Supreme Court under its 1954 rules.—A few, a very few, additional rehearings have been granted by the Supreme Court since the listing in the text.

1. One early rehearing granted, based on a change in the disbarment provisions of the 1954 rules, should have been but was not included in the earlier enumeration. See *In re Isserman,* 345 U. S. 286, disbarment ordered by 4-4, i.e., the respondent failed to show cause in a proceeding under the old rules, rehearing granted and disbarment set aside under new Rule 8, *In re Isserman,* 348 U. S. 1. Rule 8 was left untouched in the 1967 revision of the Supreme Court's rules.

2. Three instances reflect rehearings following published opinions and orders. (a) *Williams* v. *Zuckert,* 371 U. S. 531, dismissing certiorari as improvidently granted; 372 U. S. 765, rehearing granted, judgment below vacated, and cause remanded. (b) *Shenandoah Broadcasting* v. *ASCAP,* 375 U. S. 39, certiorari granted, judgment reversed, and "cause remanded to the Court

of Appeals for consideration on its merits"; 375 U. S. 994, rehearing granted and direction amended to read, "cause remanded to the Court of Appeals for further proceedings in conformity with this opinion." (c) *Maryland* v. *United States,* 381 U. S. 41, judgment affirmed; 382 U. S. 159, rehearing and motion to remand granted.

3. In three cases in which certiorari had originally been denied, the writ was granted on rehearing. (a) *O'Connor* v. *Ohio,* 382 U. S. 19, appeal dismissed and certiorari denied; 382 U. S. 286, rehearing granted, certiorari granted, and judgment below vacated. When the court below then adhered to its original determination, certiorari was once more granted and the judgment below was reversed. 385 U. S. 92. (b) *Black* v. *United States,* 384 U. S. 927, certiorari denied; 385 U. S. 26, rehearing granted and judgment reversed. (c) *Schipani* v. *United States,* 385 U. S. 934, certiorari denied; 385 U. S. 965, time for filing petition for rehearing extended; 385 U. S. 372, "Upon the suggestion of the Solicitor General and upon an independent examination of the case," rehearing granted, order denying certiorari vacated, certiorari granted, judgment of C.A. vacated, case remanded to district court "for a new trial should the Government seek to prosecute petitioner anew."

4. In two instances where certiorari had originally been denied, it was later granted on a second petition for rehearing. (a) *Gondeck* v. *Pan American Airways,* 370 U. S. 918, certiorari denied; 371 U. S. 856, rehearing denied; 382 U. S. 25, motion for leave to file [second] petition for rehearing granted, rehearing granted, certiorari granted, and judgment reversed. (b) *United States* v. *Maryland,* 375 U. S. 954, certiorari denied; 379 U. S. 925, motion for leave to file conditional petition for rehearing denied; 382 U. S. 158, rehearing granted.

5. One litigant obtained the moral consolation of having his rehearing denied with an opinion rather than by simple order. *National Motor Freight Assn.* v. *United States,* 372 U. S. 246.

6. In a number of cases, the petitioner's hopes, buoyed when a response to his petition for rehearing was requested, later were shattered when rehearing was even then denied; first citation is to the original denial, second to the order for a response, third to the denial of rehearing. (a) *United Mine Workers* v. *White Oak Coal Co.,* 375 U. S. 966, 377 U. S. 985, 379 U. S. 871. (b) *Hill* v.

New York, 377 U. S. 998, 379 U. S. 897, 379 U. S. 951. (c) *Johnson* v. *United States,* 382 U. S. 836, 382 U. S. 923, 382 U. S. 1000. (d) *Thomas* v. *Pate,* 383 U. S. 962, 384 U. S. 924, 384 U. S. 981.

7. In the last case in which a response had been requested, the petitioner for rehearing ultimately withdrew his petition. *Wylan* v. *California,* 384 U. S. 266, appeal dismissed and certiorari denied; 384 U. S. 996, response requested; March 18, 1967, petition for rehearing withdrawn.

Pages 375-376, note 60, effect of petition for rehearing not acted on by Supreme Court during the Term.—Under former Supreme Court Rule 59(2), discussed in the text, a petition for rehearing filed with the Court during the Term automatically stayed the mandate until disposition of the petition; this meant that such a petition filed before adjournment kept the petitioner out of jail over the summer—which was of course normally the consideration motivating such last-ditch efforts.

The 1967 revision reflects a hardening of judicial attitude in this respect, and assimilates the petition for rehearing that is pending at the adjournment to the one that is first filed in vacation. The last sentence of 1967 Rule 59(2) provides, "When, however, a petition for rehearing is not acted upon prior to adjournment or is filed after the court adjourns, the judgment or mandate of the court will not be stayed unless specifically so ordered by the court or a justice thereof."

On the basis of experience—on both sides—with applications for stay of mandate made in respect of petitions for rehearing necessarily filed after adjournment, either because the decision sought to be reheard came down on the very day that the Court adjourned, or else so close thereto as to preclude the preparation and filing of a printed petition for rehearing, it may be ventured with some degree of certainty that very, very few mandates will be stayed in connection with such petitions that are still pending at the close of the Term.

Page 430, last paragraph, right of defendant to inspection of grand jury minutes containing testimony of prosecution witnesses. —The question raised in the text has been finally and fully resolved in favor of the defendant; a criminal defendant has the right to examine the grand jury minutes relating to trial testimony of prosecution witnesses, he may do so while those witnesses are available for cross-examination, and he is not required to rely on an *in camera* inspection of those minutes by the trial judge. *Dennis* v. *United States,* 384 U. S. 855. In respect of the point last mentioned, the Court said at p. 875, "In our adversary system, it is enough for judges to judge. The determination of what may be useful to the defense can properly and effectively be made only by an advocate."

Accordingly, to paraphrase only slightly the original text, "It should not therefore occasion surprise that even after more than ten years some residual bitterness still remains whenever the *Herzog* case comes to mind." For in *Herzog* the trial judge's refusal to make even an *in camera* inspection of the grand jury minutes was sustained.

Page 445, note 10, time allowed for oral argument in summary calendar cases in the Supreme Court.—The text still accurately sets forth the effect of Supreme Court 1967 Rule 44(3), which now begins—new words italicized—"In cases on the summary calendar, half an hour *a side,* and no more, will be allowed for argument, * * *."

Pp. 465-466, subparagraph (a), witness in Federal court may assert privilege against self-incrimination under State law.—In June 1964, in *Murphy* v. *Waterfront Commission,* 378 U. S. 52, the Supreme Court overruled the cases cited in the text, which had held that a Federal court could compel a witness to give testimony that might incriminate him under State law, and which similarly held that a State court could compel a witness to give testimony that might incriminate him under Federal law.

Nevertheless, I am quite certain of the soundness of the advice in the text, "Don't let yourself be diverted," and of the correctness of my refusal to be drawn into even suggesting reexamination of the earlier doctrines.

In 1952, when I argued the *Greenberg* case discussed in the text, the Court was not yet ready to overrule the earlier decisions. Indeed, it was similarly unprepared to do so even as late as the 1961 Term, as I found to my regret when I appeared in *Hutcheson* v. *United States,* 369 U. S. 599.

In that case, the petitioner asserted before a Federal body that the answers requested would tend to incriminate him under State law. In the Supreme Court I argued, with full documentation, not only that *United States* v. *Murdock,* 284 U. S. 141, was not supported by the authorities on which it relied, but also that

Chief Justice Marshall in *United States* v. *Saline Bank,* 1 Pet. 100, had specifically held that a Federal defendant *would* be permitted to assert self-incrimination under State law, and that his decision had thereafter been demonstrably misstated in *Hale* v. *Henkel,* 201 U. S. 43, 69. The latter stricture was supported by reproducing in the brief, from the original documents in the National Archives, not only the bill of complaint in the *Saline Bank* case, but also the complete text of the interrogatories against which the privilege had been successfully asserted.

To no avail; the votes that overruled *United States* v. *Murdock,* 284 U. S. 141, and *Feldman* v. *United States,* 322 U. S. 487, at the 1963 Term were simply not available at the 1961 Term; of the 6 Justices who participated in the *Hutcheson* decision, only 2 voted my way.

So, recurring to the basic admonition in the text, do not let yourself be diverted; your proposition may prevail on the wave of the future, but you are living in the present, and must argue your particular case in the light of presently accepted doctrines.

Page 467, note 61, where witness who has refused to answer questions before grand jury is ordered to answer by the judge, refusal to obey latter order is not a contempt punishable as one committed in the court's presence.—*Brown* v. *United States,* 359 U. S. 41, cited in the note, has since been specifically overruled by *Harris* v. *United States,* 382 U. S. 162. It is now the law that, where a witness who has refused to answer questions before a grand jury is then brought before the court, and the judge thereupon directs him to answer, refusal of the latter order is not a contempt committed in the presence of the court punishable summarily under Rule 42 (a), F. R. Crim. P., it is one punishable only after notice and hearing as provided in Rule 42(b).

As the Supreme Court said in the *Harris* case (382 U. S. at 165), "The appearance before the District Court was not a new and different proceeding, unrelated to the other. It was ancillary to the grand jury hearing and designed as an aid to it."

SUBJECT INDEX

A

Abbreviations
(*see also* Citations; Titles of cases)
citations, use in 134, 224
organizations, agencies, etc., names
of 225
parties, designation in brief 134
titles of cases, short forms 224
Administrative agencies
abbreviated titles of 225
amicus briefs, policy of government
agencies 271
Department of Justice 123, 383
government briefs, preparation of
123
law officers, federal, rulings as precedent 177
rulings
as precedent 175, 177
how cited 239
notice, *Federal Register* 175, 179
specialized appellate counsel 384
United States Attorneys 384
Administrative practice, proof of
251
Advocacy, appellate
appellate specialization (*see* Specialized appellate counsel)
brief (*see* Brief)
facts, marshalling of 7
duty of advocate on appeal 12, 48
importance 5, 7
lack of skill, effect of, example 9
et seq.
learning 5, 316
new counsel on appeal 387
oral argument (*see* Oral argument)
partisanship of advocate 13
purpose 280
scope of 5
teaching 6
Advocate
(*see also* Argument)

Advocate—contd.
appellate specialization (*see* Specialized appellate counsel)
appellate counsel, selection of 390
attitude toward cause 12, 332 et
seq., 359
attitude toward court 298
crusading, dangers in 357
duty on appeal 12, 48, 359
favorable presentation, duty of 48
first impression upon court 28
new counsel on appeal 387
oral argument, divided presentation 316
partisanship (*see* Partisanship of
advocate)
retention at trial level 389
skills of 7
Amicus curiae brief 269
private counsel, use by 271
Supreme Court, rules 42, 270
when appropriate 271
Analogies, use in argument 149
Annotated cases, use of collections
196
Appeal (*see* Advocacy, appellate;
Courts, appellate)
Appellate courts (*see* Courts, appellate; Supreme Court of the
United States)
Appendix in brief 120
Argument
(*see also* Brief-writing)
attitude of advocate (see Advocate;
Partisanship of advocate)
new counsel on appeal 387
on facts in brief 114
character of litigant, exposure of
52
editorializing 116
evasion of issues 104
evidence, presentation of 114
examples 398-406, 406-421
headings, argumentative 115

INDEX OF CASES*

A

AAA Case (see Butler; United States v.)

Abbate v. United States (359 U. S. 187) 186, 332

Abel v. United States (362 U. S. 217) 69

Abram; Breithaupt v. (352 U. S. 432) 332

Achilli v. United States (352 U. S. 1023) 374

Acker; Commissioner v. (361 U. S. 87) 170, 176

Acme Freight; Chicago etc. R. Co. v. (336 U. S. 465) 175

Adams v. Maryland (347 U. S. 179) 173

Adamson v. California (332 U. S. 46) 191, 200

Adan Haji Jama v. The King ([1948] A.C. 225) 359

Adkins v. Children's Hospital (261 U. S. 525) 114, 188

Adkins; Sunshine Coal Co. v. (310 U. S. 381) 328

Adler v. Board of Education (342 U. S. 485) 110

A.F. of L. v. American Sash Co. (335 U. S. 538) 192

A.F. of L. v. Swing (312 U. S. 321) 110

A.F. of L. v. Watson (327 U. S. 582, 345 U. S. 245) 225

Aiuppa v. United States (201 F.2d 287 [C.A. 6]) 443, 469

Alabama; Bailey v. (219 U. S. 219) 216

Alabama; N.A.A.C.P. v. (357 U. S. 449) 225

Alabama; Thornhill v. (310 U. S. 88) 110

Alabama Power Co. v. Ickes (302 U. S. 464) 194

Alaska v. American Can Co. (358 U. S. 224) 251

Alaska v. Troy (258 U. S. 101) 144

Alexander v. United States (181 F.2d 632 [C.A. 9], certiorari denied 340 U. S. 920) 444

Alexander v. United States ex rel. Kulick (332 U. S. 174) 56, 127

Allegheny County v. Mashuda Co. (360 U. S. 185) 91

Allegheny County; United States v. (322 U. S. 174) 109

Allen; Brown v. (344 U. S. 443) 187, 232

Allied Stevedoring Corp.; United States v. (235 F.2d 909 [C.A. 2]) 173

Alton R. Co.; Retirement Board v. (295 U. S. 330, dissent 295 U. S. 374) 66

Aluminum Co. of America; United States v. (148 F.2d 416 [C.A. 2]) 175, 209

Ambler Realty Co.; Euclid v. (272 U. S. 365) 150

American Air Transport; Civil Aeronautics Board v. (344 U. S. 4) 423

American Banana Co. v. United Fruit Co. (213 U. S. 347) 146

American Can Co.; Alaska v. (358 U. S. 224) 251

American Communications Assn. v. Douds (339 U. S. 382) 190

American-Foreign Steamship Co.; United States v. (363 U. S. 685) 371, 431

American Sash Co.; A.F. of L. v. (335 U. S. 538) 192

American Ins. Co. v. Canter (1 Pet. 511) 436

American Tobacco Co. v. United States (328 U. S. 781) 209

American Trucking Assn.; United States v. (310 U. S. 534) 170

---

* See also *Index of Appendix Cases,* p. 525.

K

Kagama; United States v. (118 U. S. 375) 99

Kahanamoku; Duncan v. (327 U. S. 304) 193

Kahn v. Anderson (225 U. S. 1) 211

Kahriger; United States v. (105 F.Supp. 322 [E.D. Pa.], reversed 345 U. S. 22) 108, 450

Kaplan; United States v. (89 F.2d 869 [C.A. 2]) 195

Katt; Testa v. (330 U. S. 386) 94, 118

Kawakita v. United States (190 F.2d 506 [C.A. 9], affirmed 343 U. S. 717) 9, 156

Kennedy, Kulick v. (157 F.2d 811 [C.A. 2]) 56

Kenniston, Levi and Laban, Trial of (14 Am. St. Tr. [Mass.]) 183

Kenny v. United States (62 C.Cls. 328) 221

Kent v. Dulles (357 U. S. 116) 174

Kiewel v. United States (204 F.2d 1 [C.A. 8]) 469

Kilpatrick v. Texas & Pacific R. Co. (337 U. S. 75) 169

King v. Mullins (171 U. S. 404) 278

King v. Waterman Steamship Corp. (272 F.2d 823 [C.A. 3]) 369

Kinsella v. Krueger (351 U. S. 470) 85, 87, 110, 112, 125, 138, 156, 164, 242, 268, 343, 375, 431-470

Kinsella v. Krueger (354 U. S. 1) 119, 268

Kinsella; Madsen v. (343 U. S. 341) 165

Kinsella v. Singleton (361 U. S. 234) 87, 140, 186, 332, 342, 441

Kinsella; United States v. (137 F.Supp. 806) 119, 226

Kinsella; United States v. (164 F.Supp. 707) 226

Kioloku, Title of, In re (25 Haw. 357, affirmed sub nom. Territory of Hawaii v. Hutchinson Sugar Co., 272 Fed. 856 [C.A. 9]) 232

Kitchens v. United States (358 U. S. 42) 104

Klaw v. Schaffer (357 U. S. 346) 373

Klein v. United States (C. Cls., Jan. 18, 1961) 368

Klesner; Federal Trade Commission v. (280 U. S. 19) 439

Knauer v. United States (328 U. S. 654) 44, 93, 112, 116, 247, 289, 329

Knight v. Bar Assn. (321 U. S. 803) 259

Knight Co.; United States v. (156 U. S. 1) 111

Korematsu v. United States (323 U. S. 214) 53

Koster v. Lumbermens Mutual Co. (330 U. S. 518) 109

Kovacs v. Cooper (336 U. S. 77) 155

Kovrak v. Ginsburg (177 F.Supp. 614 [E.D. Pa.]) 369

Kraemer; Shelley v. (334 U. S. 1) 190

Kraus Bros. & Co.; Zwack v. (237 F.2d 255) 198

Krause's Petition, In re (159 F. Supp. 687 [S.D. Ala.]) 334

Kremen v. United States (353 U. S. 346) 69

Kristensen; McGrath v. (340 U. S. 162) 367

Kroeger; Lamb v. (233 Iowa 730, 8 N.W.2d 405) 75

Kronenberg; United States v. (134 F.2d 483 [C.A. 2]) 195

Krueger; Kinsella v. (351 U. S. 470, 354 U. S. 1) (see Kinsella v. Krueger, this page)

Krug v. Santa Fe R. Co. (329 U. S. 591) 92, 127

Krulewitch; United States v. (145 F.2d 76 [C.C.A. 2]) 429

Kulick v. Kennedy (157 F.2d 811 [C.A. 2]) 56

L

Labor Board v. (see name of opposing party)

La Buy v. Howes Leather Co. (352 U. S. 249) 109

Ladner v. United States (355 U. S. 282, rehearing granted 356 U. S. 969) 374

Ladner v. United States (358 U. S. 169) 174

Lago Oil & Transport Co. v. United States (218 F.2d 631 [C.A. 2]) 371

INDEX OF APPENDIX CASES